BIOGRAPHICAL
DICTIONARY
OF
PSYCHOLOGY

BIOGRAPHICAL DICTIONARY OF PSYCHOLOGY

LEONARD ZUSNE

GREENWOOD PRESS
WESTPORT, CONNECTICUT

Library of Congress Cataloging in Publication Data

Zusne, Leonard, 1924-
  Biographical dictionary of psychology.

  Rev. ed. of: Names in the history of psychology.
1975.
  Includes index.
  1. Psychologists—Biography. 2. Psychology—
History. I. Zusne, Leonard, 1924-   . Names in
the history of psychology. II. Title.
BF109.A1Z85   1984   150′.92′2 [B]   83-18326
ISBN 0-313-24027-2 (lib. bdg.)

Library of Congress Catalog Card Number: 83-18326
ISBN 0-313-24027-2

First published in 1984

Greenwood Press
A division of Congressional Information Service, Inc.
88 Post Road West, Westport, Connecticut 06881

Printed in the United States of America

10 9 8 7 6 5 4 3 2 1

Contents

Preface

The first edition of this dictionary, published by Hemisphere Publishing Corporation in 1975, appeared under the title *Names in the History of Psychology*. Its purpose was to present short biographical statements on several hundred deceased psychologists and individuals from other fields who had made a contribution to the development of psychology from antiquity to the present.

The present edition serves the same purpose. Each biography explains the specific contributions of the subject to the development of psychology, that is, the reason for the individual's inclusion in this dictionary. In addition to standard biographical data, each biographical statement presents the main points of theoretical contributions; philosophies held; inventions and discoveries made; methodologies initiated; books and seminal articles written; research conducted; laboratories, journals, and institutions founded; and influence exercised. At the end of each statement references are given to the best, most extensive, and most readily available biographies and autobiographies that may be consulted for additional details. By bringing together in one place all of the names in the history of psychology within a wide range of significance and by gathering information from scattered sources for each biographee, this dictionary has been and continues to be the first sourcebook of its kind for the history of psychology.

The names of the individuals to be included in the first edition were selected as follows. A panel of nine prominent psychologists had rated the importance of 1,040 contributors to psychology who had lived between 1600 and 1967.[1]

1. E. L. Annin, E. G. Boring, & R. I. Watson. Important psychologists, 1600-1967. *J. Hist. Behav. Sci.*, 1968, *4*, 303-315.

The rating procedure followed was to give an individual zero points if a judge did not recognize the individual's name as belonging in the history of psychology, one point if he did so recognize the name, two points if, in addition, the judge could identify the contribution that the individual had made to psychology, and three points if he thought that the individual should be included in a list of the five hundred most prominent psychologists of all time. Thus if none of the judges had recognized an individual's name, that individual received the lowest possible score of zero; or if all nine had rated the individual most highly, the highest possible score of twenty-seven. The majority of the individuals who had received a rating of eleven or higher and whose names therefore had been published represent the majority of those included in *Names in the History of Psychology*. I added names from the period before 1600 and those of psychologists who had died after 1967 and, in my opinion, would have received at least a rating of eleven had they been rated by the panel.

The present edition contains most of the entries in the first edition, with 101 new names. About one-half of the additions are the names of important contributors to psychology who had died after the appearance of the first edition of this dictionary. The remainder come from psychology's more remote past. They were added as a result of the use of an improved method of evaluating the relative prominence of historical figures.[2] The rationale of this method is this: the more important a historical figure is judged to be by writers of histories, the more space they will give it in their histories. The importance of all of the biographees of this dictionary was evaluated by measuring the space given them by sixteen authors of histories of psychology. Their rank order or relative standing in comparison with all others is given in Appendix B. The only exceptions are eleven very recently deceased individuals who had not yet found their way into history books but are certain to do so in the future, judging from the characteristics of their careers and comparing them with those already "on the books."

In addition to the new ranking information contained in Appendix B, there is new information in Appendix C concerning the academic tenures of nineteenth- and twentieth-century psychologists and other scientists at universities and research institutions. It throws additional light on the history of psychology departments and the interactions among contributors to psychology from the historical perspective, information that is not immediately available from the perusal of individual biographies.

Other changes have been made. In contrast to the first edition, the biographees in this edition of the dictionary are arranged alphabetically rather than chronologically. Although the chronological arrangement lends historical continuity to the biographies, users of the first edition suggested that the dictionary would be easier to use if the names were placed in an alphabetical order. A chronological listing of the names according to birth date is presented in Appendix A. In

2. L. Zusne & D. P. Dailey. History of psychology texts as measuring instruments of eminence in psychology. *Revista de Historia de la Psicología*, 1982, *3*, 7-42.

addition, virtually every biography has been improved by adding information and correcting errors. The *Biographies* section of each entry in particular has been expanded. I gratefully acknowledge the comments and suggestions for improvement that were given me by Drs. Robert Epstein, Benjamin Burack, Warren Street, and Josef Brožek.

I particularly cherish the spontaneous comments concerning the usefulness of the dictionary that I have received from many quarters while the first edition was in print. I can only hope that the second will serve its users even better.

Explanatory Notes

An asterisk (*) after a name indicates that the individual is the subject of a biography in this dictionary.

Born. Died. Places of birth and death of persons who were born or died in a country other than the United States are further identified by country, *département*, or province, unless the location is a well-known city. Places of birth and death are identified by country only if the country differs from the country of the person's nationality. Large, well-known regions in Central and Eastern Europe that were partitioned after World War I and now belong to two or more countries are not further described.

Highest Degree. The individual's educational history is not recapitulated, and only the highest degree is given. All doctorates are listed. For persons without a degree, this entry reads *Education.*

Positions, Honors: This is not a complete list of all positions held. Only the most significant ones and those held for a year or more are given. Only the most significant honors are listed by name. "Editorial work" encompasses any kind of editorial position, regardless of rank.

Biographies. The biographical sources are selected sources, and the list is therefore by no means complete. Where biographical material was abundant, an attempt was made to list primarily English-language and more accessible sources. In the case of less well known individuals, fewer biographic sources are available, and such individuals may have every available source listed, including exotic ones. A complete list of all biographic sources, major and minor, is available for the 538 individuals rated eleven to twenty-seven (see Appendix B) in R. I.

Watson (Ed.), *Eminent Contributors to Psychology*, vol.2. New York: Springer, 1976. Autobiographies are listed in volume 1 of the same work, published in 1974.

Biographic sources used repeatedly have been abbreviated. The numbers following the abbreviations are volume numbers. The abbreviations are as follows:

ADB	*Allgemeine deutsche Biographie* (56 vols.). Leipzig: Duncker & Humboldt, 1875-1912. (Partially reprinted 1967.)
Biog. Lex.	I. Fischer (Ed.), *Biographisches Lexikon der hervorragenden Ärzte der letzten fünfzig Jahre (1880-1930)* (2nd & 3rd ed.) (2 vols.). Berlin: Urban & Schwarzenberg, 1962.
Biog. Mem.	*Biographical Memoirs: National Academy of Sciences.* New York: Columbia University Press, 1877-.
CE	M. J. McDonald (Ed.), *New Catholic Encyclopedia* (15 vols.). New York: McGraw-Hill, 1967.
Chalmers	A. Chalmers (Ed.), *The General Biographical Dictionary* (Rev. ed.) (32 vols.). London: Nichols, 1812-1817.
DAB	*Dictionary of American Biography* (22 vols. + Index). New York: Scribner's, 1928-1958.
DBF	Various. *Dictionnaire de biographie française* (13 vols. +). Paris: Libraire Letouzey et Ané, 1933-.
DNB	L. Stephen & S. Lee (Eds.), *Dictionary of National Biography* (21 vols. + 7 suppl.). London: Oxford University Press, 1959-.
DSB	C. C. Gillespie (Ed.), *Dictionary of Scientific Biography* (15 vols.). New York: Scribner's, 1970-.
EB	*Encyclopaedia Britannica* (24 vols.). Chicago: Encyclopaedia Britannica, 1967.
EJ	C. Roth (Ed.), *Encyclopedia Judaica* (16 vols.). New York: Macmillan, 1972.
EP	P. Edwards (Ed.), *The Encyclopedia of Philosophy* (8 vols.). New York: Macmillan, 1967.
EUI	*Enciclopedia universal ilustrada europeo-americana* (70 vols.). Madrid: Espasa-Calpe, 1907-1930.
Grande	M. M. Barthelot *et al.* (Eds.), *La grande encyclopédie* (31 vols.). Paris: Lamirault, 1886-1902.
HGP	W.K.C. Guthrie, *A History of Greek Philosophy* (6 vols.). Cambridge: Cambridge University Press, 1962-81.

Hirsch, *Biog. Lex.*   A. Hirsch *et al.* (Eds.), *Biographisches Lexikon
                                der hervorragenden Ärzte aller Zeiten und
                                Völker* (3rd ed.) (5 vols. + 1 suppl.). Munich:
                                Urban & Schwarzenberg, 1962. (1883).

HPA   C. Murchison (Ed.), *A History of Psychology in
                                Autobiography* (Vols. 1, 2, 3). Worcester,
                                Mass.: Clark University Press, 1930, 1932,
                                1936.
                                E. G. Boring *et al.* (Eds.), *A History of
                                Psychology in Autobiography* (Vol. 4).
                                Worcester, Mass.: Clark University Press, 1952.
                                E. G. Boring, & G. Lindzey (Eds.), *A History of
                                Psychology in Autobiography* (Vol. 5). New
                                York: Appleton-Century-Crofts, 1967.
                                G. Lindzey (Ed.), *A History of Psychology in
                                Autobiography* (Vol. 6). Englewood Cliffs, N.J.:
                                Prentice-Hall, 1974.

IESS   D. L. Sills (Ed.), *International Encyclopedia of the
                                Social Sciences* (18 vols.). New York:
                                Macmillan, 1968-1979.

Jewish   I. Landman (Ed.), *The Universal Jewish
                                Encyclopedia* (10 vols.). New York: Universal
                                Jewish Encyclopedia, 1939-1943.

NCAB   *The National Cyclopedia of American Biography*
                                (53 vols. + 11 suppl. vols.). New York: White,
                                1893-.

NDB   *Neue deutsche Biographie* (9 vols. so far). Berlin:
                                Duncker & Humboldt, 1953- .

Nouvelle   E. Hoefer (Ed.), *Nouvelle biographie générale* (46
                                vols.). Copenhagen: Rosenkilde & Bagger,
                                1963-1969. (1853-1866).

NYT   *New York Times.*
Obit. Not.   Royal Society of London. *Obituary Notices of
                                Fellows* (Vols. 1-8). Cambridge: The Society,
                                1932-1952.

Pagel, *Biographisches Lexikon*   J. Pagel. *Biographisches Lexikon hervorragender
                                Ärzte des neuzehnten Jahrhunderts.* Berlin:
                                Urban & Schwarzenberg, 1901.

PR   C. Murchison (Ed.), *The Psychological Register* (2
                                vols.). Worcester, Mass.: Clark University
                                Press, 1929, 1932.

Most journal and magazine titles that appear under *Biographies* have been abbreviated.
The abbreviations and the full titles follow:

Abh. preuss. Akad. Wiss.   *Abhandlungen der preussischen Akademie der
                                Wissenschaften*
Acta Otolaryng.   *Acta Otolaryngologica*

Actes XIe Cong. Int. Hist. Sci.	*Actes XIe Congrès International d'Histoire de la Science*
Ala. J. Med. Sci.	*Alabama Journal of Medical Sciences*
Allg. Z. Psychiat.	*Allgemeine Zeitschrift für Psychiatrie*
Almanach österr. Akad. Wiss.	*Almanach der österreichischen Akademie der Wissenschaften*
Amer. Ann. Deaf	*American Annals of the Deaf*
Amer. Anthropologist	*American Anthropologist*
Amer. Imago	*American Imago*
Amer. J. Ment. Defic.	*American Journal of Mental Deficiency*
Amer. J. Orthopsychiat.	*American Journal of Orthopsychiatry*
Amer. J. Psychiat.	*American Journal of Psychiatry*
Amer. J. Psychoanal.	*American Journal of Psychoanalysis*
Amer. J. Psychol.	*American Journal of Psychology*
Amer. J. Sociol.	*American Journal of Sociology*
Amer. J. Soc. Phil.	*American Journal of Social Philosophy*
Amer. Math. Mon.	*American Mathematical Monthly*
Amer. Math. Soc. Bull.	*American Mathematical Society Bulletin*
Amer. Oxon.	*American Oxonian*
Amer. Psychologist	*American Psychologist*
Amer. Rev. Sov. Med.	*American Review of Soviet Medicine*
Amer. Scholar	*American Scholar*
Amer. Sociol. Rev.	*American Sociological Review*
Amer. Speech & Hearing Ass.	*American Speech and Hearing Association*
Amer. Stat. Ass. J.	*American Statistical Association Journal*
Anat. Rec.	*Anatomical Record*
Ann. Acad. Roy. Sci. Lettr. Beaux-Arts Belg.	*Annales de l'Academie Royale des Sciences, Lettres et Beaux-Arts Belge*
Année psychol.	*Année psychologique*
Ann. Eugen.	*Annals of Eugenics*
Ann. Med. Hist.	*Annals of Medical History*
Ann. méd.-psychol.	*Annales médico-psychologiques*
Ann. Rep. Board Smithsonian Inst.	*Annual Report of the Board of Smithsonian Institution*
Ann. Sci.	*Annals of Science*
Ann. Univ. Paris	*Annales de l'Université de Paris*
Arch. Anthrop. Crim.	*Archives of Anthropology and Criminology*
Arch. Gen. Psychiat.	*Archives of General Psychiatry*
Arch. Gesch. Med.	*Archiv der Geschichte der Medizin*
Arch. Gesch. Phil.	*Archiv der Geschichte der Philosophie*
Arch. ges. Physiol.	*Archiv der gesamten Physiologie*
Arch. ges. Psychol.	*Archiv der gesamten Psychologie*
Arch. ital. biol.	*Archivio italiano di biologia*
Arch. ital. psicol.	*Archivio italiano di psicologia*
Arch. Mus. Hist. Naturwiss.	*Archiv des Museums der Historie und Naturwissenschaft*
Arch. Musikforsch.	*Archiv für Musikforschung*
Arch. neerl. physiol.	*Archives neerlandaises de physiologie*

Arch. Neurobiol.	*Archives of Neurobiology*
Arch. Neurol.	*Archives of Neurology*
Arch. Neurol. Psychiat.	*Archives of Neurology and Psychiatry*
Arch. Ophthalm.	*Archives of Ophthalmology*
Arch. psicol. neurol. psichiat.	*Archivio di psicologia, neurologia e psichiatria*
Arch. Psychiat.	*Archives of Psychiatry*
Arch. Psychiatrie	*Archiv für Psychiatrie*
Arch. Psychiat. Nervenkr.	*Archiv für Psychiatrie und Nervenkrankheiten*
Arch. psychol.	*Archives de psychologie*
Arq. brasil. psicotéc.	*Arquivos brasileiros de psicotécnica*
Austr. J. Psychol.	*Australian Journal of Psychology*
Austr. J. Psychol. Phil.	*Australian Journal of Psychology and Philosophy*
Behav. Sci.	*Behavioural Science*
Berliner klin. Wochenschr.	*Berliner klinische Wochenschrift*
Bern. Z. Gesch. Heimatk.	*Berner Zeitschrift für Geschichte und Heimatkunde*
Biog. Kulturgesch. Schweiz	*Biographie und Kulturgeschichte der Schweiz*
Biog. méd.	*Biographie médicale*
Biog. Mem. Fellows Roy. Soc.	*Biographic Memoirs of the Fellows of Royal Society of London*
Biol. Jb.	*Biologisches Jahrbuch*
Boll. bibliog. storia sci. matem.	*Bollettino bibliografico per la storia di scienza e matematica*
Boll. Ist. stor. ital. arte sanit.	*Bollettino Istituto storico italiano della arte sanitaria*
Brit. J. Anim. Behav.	*British Journal of Animal Behaviour*
Brit. J. Educ. Psychol.	*British Journal of Educational Psychology*
Brit. J. Med. Hypno.	*British Journal of Medical Hypnosis*
Brit. J. Med. Psychol.	*British Journal of Medical Psychology*
Brit. J. Phil. Sci.	*British Journal of Philosophy of Science*
Brit. J. Psychol.	*British Journal of Psychology*
Brit. J. Sociol.	*British Journal of Sociology*
Brit. J. Stat. Psychol.	*British Journal of Statistical Psychology*
Brit. Med. J.	*British Medical Journal*
Brit. Quart. Rev.	*British Quarterly Review*
Bull. Acad. méd.	*Bulletin de l'Academie de médecine*
Bull. Ass. int. psychol. appl.	*Bulletin de l'Association internationale de psychologie appliquée*
Bull. Brit. Psychol. Soc.	*Bulletin of the British Psychological Society*
Bull. Brit. Soc. Hist. Sci.	*Bulletin of the British Society of History of Science*
Bull. Canad. Psychol. Ass.	*Bulletin of the Canadian Psychological Association*
Bull. Hist. Med.	*Bulletin of the History of Medicine*
Bull. Isaac Ray Med. Library	*Bulletin of the Isaac Ray Medical Library*
Bull. Johns Hopkins Hosp.	*Bulletin of the Johns Hopkins Hospital*
Bull. Menninger Clin.	*Bulletin of the Menninger Clinic*
Bull. N.Y. Acad. Med.	*Bulletin of the New York Academy of Medicine*
Bull. psychol.	*Bulletin psychologique*
Bull. Soc. anat.	*Bulletin de la Société anatomique*
Bull. Soc. Anthrop.	*Bulletin of the Society of Anthropologists*

Bull. Soc. franç. hist. méd.	*Bulletin de la Société française de l'histoire de la médecine*
Bull. Soc. libre l'étude psychol. l'enfant	*Bulletin de la Société libre pour l'étude psychologique de l'enfant*
Bull. Soc. Med. Hist.	*Bulletin of the Society of Medical History*
Cah. int. sociol.	*Cahiers internationaux de sociologie*
Cah. psychol.	*Cahiers psychologiques*
Canad. J. Psychol.	*Canadian Journal of Psychology*
Century Mag.	*Century Magazine*
Character Pers.	*Character and Personality*
Child Devel.	*Child Development*
Child Psychol. Psychiat.	*Child Psychology and Psychiatry*
Clark Univ. Libr. Publ.	*Clark University Library Publications*
Classical Quart.	*Classical Quarterly*
Conditional Refl.	*Conditional Reflex*
Confinia psychiat.	*Confinia psychiatrica*
Contemp. Rev.	*Contemporary Review*
C. r. Acad. sci.	*Comptes rendus de l'Academie des sciences*
C. r. Acad. sci. mor. pol.	*Comptes rendus de l'Academie des sciences morales et politiques*
Deutsch. med. J.	*Deutsches medizinisches Journal*
Deutsch. med. Wochenschr.	*Deutsche medizinische Wochenschrift*
Deutsch. Rundsch.	*Deutsche Rundschau*
Deutsch. Z. Nervenheilk.	*Deutsche Zeitschrift der Nervenheilkunde*
Dis. Nerv. Syst.	*Diseases of the Nervous System*
Econ. J.	*Economic Journal*
Edinb. Med. J.	*Edinburgh Medical Journal*
Encycl. Soc. Sci.	*Encyclopedia of Social Sciences*
Ergeb. Physiol.	*Ergebnisse der Physiologie*
Eugen. Rev.	*Eugenics Review*
Évol. psychiat.	*Évolution psychiatrique*
Exp. Neurol.	*Experimental Neurology*
Extrême-Orient méd.	*Extrême-Orient médical*
Fiziol. Zh.	*Fiziologicheskiĭ Zhurnal*
Fortn. Rev.	*Fortnightly Review*
Fortschr. psychol. Anwend.	*Fortschritte psychologischer Anwendungen*
Fraser's Mag.	*Fraser's Magazine*
Grenzgeb. Med.	*Grenzgebiete der Medizin*
Heritage Indust. Psychol.	*Heritage Industrial Psychology*
Hibbert J.	*Hibbert Journal*
Hist. Biol.	*History of Biology*
Hum. Relat.	*Human Relations*
Ill. Law Rev.	*Illinois Law Review*
Int. J. Amer. Ling.	*International Journal of American Linguistics*
Int. J. Opin. Attitude Res.	*International Journal of Opinion and Attitude Research*
Int. J. Parapsychol.	*International Journal of Parapsychology*
Int. J. Psychoanal.	*International Journal of Psychoanalysis*

Int. Z. Psychoanal.	*Internationale Zeitschrift der Psychoanalyse*
J. Abn. (Soc.) Psychol.	*Journal of Abnormal (and Social) Psychology*
J. Amer. Acad. Child Psychiat.	*Journal of the American Academy of Child Psychiatry*
J. Amer. Folklore	*Journal of American Folklore*
J. Amer. Med. Ass.	*Journal of the American Medical Association*
J. Amer. Psychoanal. Ass.	*Journal of the American Psychoanalytical Association*
J. Amer. Soc. Psychical Res.	*Journal of the American Society for Psychical Research*
J. Anim. Behav.	*Journal of Animal Behaviour*
J. Appl. Psychol.	*Journal of Applied Psychology*
Jb. Bayr. königl. Akad. Wiss.	*Jahrbuch der Bayrischen königlichen Akademie der Wissenschaften*
Jb. Gesch. Mittel-Deutschlands	*Jahrbuch der Geschichte Mittel-Deutschlands*
Jb. ges. Naturkd. Württ.	*Jahrbuch der gesamten Naturkunde Württemberg*
Jb. Psychol. Neurol.	*Jahrbuch für Psychologie und Neurologie*
Jb. Psychol. Psychother.	*Jahrbuch für Psychologie und Psychotherapie*
Jb. Schopenhauer-Ges.	*Jahrbuch der Schopenhauer-Gesellschaft*
J. Chem. Educ.	*Journal of Chemical Education*
J. Child Psychol. Psychiat.	*Journal of Child Psychology and Psychiatry*
J. Comp. Neurol.	*Journal of Comparative Neurology*
J. Consult. Psychol.	*Journal of Consulting Psychology*
J. Creat. Behav.	*Journal of Creative Behavior*
J. Crim. Law Criminol.	*Journal of Criminal Law and Criminology*
J. Delinq.	*Journal of Delinquency*
J. Educ. Psychol.	*Journal of Educational Psychology*
J. Existent.	*Journal of Existentialism*
J. Existent. Psychiat.	*Journal of Existential Psychiatry*
J. Genet. Psychol.	*Journal of Genetic Psychology*
J. Gen. Physio.	*Journal of General Physiology*
J. Gen. Psychol.	*Journal of General Psychology*
J. Hist. Behav. Sci.	*Journal of History of the Behavioral Sciences*
J. Hist. Ideas	*Journal of History of Ideas*
J. Hist. Med.	*Journal of History of Medicine*
J. Hum. Psychol.	*Journal of Humanistic Psychology*
J. Ind. Psychol.	*Journal of Individual Psychology*
J. Ment. Sci.	*Journal of Mental Science*
J. Nerv. Ment. Dis.	*Journal of Nervous and Mental Disease*
J. Neurophysiol.	*Journal of Neurophysiology*
J. Opt. Soc. Amer.	*Journal of the Optical Society of America*
J. Otto Rank Ass.	*Journal of the Otto Rank Association*
J. Pers.	*Journal of Personality*
J. Pers. Assess.	*Journal of Personality Assessment*
J. Pers. Soc. Psychol.	*Journal of Personality and Social Psychology*
J. Phil.	*Journal of Philosophy*
J. Phil. Stud.	*Journal of Philosophical Studies*
J. Project. Techn.	*Journal of Projective Techniques*

J. Psychol. Med. Ment. Pathol.	*Journal of Psychological Medicine and Mental Pathology*
J. Psychol. Neurol.	*Journal of Psychology and Neurology*
J. psychol. norm. path.	*Journal de psychologie normale et pathologique*
J. Roy. Stat. Soc.	*Journal of the Royal Statistical Society*
J. Soc. Psychol.	*Journal of Social Psychology*
J. Soc. stat.	*Journal de la Societé statistique*
J. Speech Dis.	*Journal of Speech Disorders*
Kant-Stud.	*Kant-Studien*
Klin. Wochenschr.	*Klinische Wochenschrift*
Libr. Cong. Quart. J. Curr. Acq.	*Library of Congress Quarterly Journal of Current Acquisitions*
Math. Teacher	*Mathematics Teacher*
Med. Hist.	*Medical History*
Méd. int.	*Médecine interne*
Med. Klin.	*Medizinische Klinik*
Med. Life	*Medicine and Life*
Med. Woche	*Medizinische Woche*
Mém. Acad. Sci.	*Mémoirs de l'Academie des Sciences*
Mem. Accad. Sci. Torino	*Memorie della Accademia delle Scienze di Torino*
Mem. Amer. Anthrop. Ass.	*Memoirs of the American Anthropological Association*
Mem. Amer. Phil. Soc.	*Memoirs of the American Philosophical Society*
Mem. Manch. Lit. Phil. Soc.	*Memoirs of the Manchester Literary and Philosophical Society*
Mém. Soc. biol.	*Mémoirs de la Societé biologique*
Ment. Hyg.	*Mental Hygiene*
Mod. Med.	*Modern Medicine*
Monatsschr. Psychiat. Neurol.	*Monatsschrift der Psychiatrie und Neurologie*
Münch. Beit. Gesch. Lit. Naturwiss. Med.	*Münchener Beiträge zur Geschichte der Literatur, Naturwissenschaft und Medizin*
Münch. med. Wochenschr.	*Münchener medizinische Wochenschrift*
N.C. Med. J.	*North Carolina Medical Journal*
Ned. Tijdschr.	*Nederlands Tijdschrift*
Ned. Tijdschr. Psychol.	*Nederlands Tijdschrift voor Psychologie*
New England J. Med.	*New England Journal of Medicine*
Not. Rec. Roy. Soc. London	*Notes and Records of the Royal Society of London*
Occup. Psychol.	*Occupational Psychology*
Partisan Rev.	*Partisan Review*
Personnel Guid. J.	*Personnel Guidance Journal*
Personnel Psychol.	*Personnel Psychology*
Perspect. Amer. Hist.	*Perspectives of American History*
Phi Beta Phi Quart.	*Phi Beta Phi Quarterly*
Phil. Phenomenol. Res.	*Philosophical and Phenomenological Research*
Phil. Rev.	*Philosophical Review*
Phil. Sci.	*Philosophy of Science*
Phil. Stud.	*Philosophische Studien*
Phys. Bl.	*Physikalische Blätter*

Pol. Sci. Quart.	Political Science Quarterly
Pop. Sci. Mon.	Popular Science Monthly
Proc. Amer. Acad. Arts, Sci.	Proceedings of the American Academy of Arts and Sciences
Proc. Amer. Phil. Soc.	Proceedings of the American Philosophical Society
Proc. Brit. Acad.	Proceedings of the British Academy
Proc. Roy. Soc. London	Proceedings of the Royal Society of London
Proc. Roy. Soc. Med.	Proceedings of the Royal Society of Medicine
Proc. Rudolf Virchow Med. Soc.	Proceedings of the Rudolf Virchow Medical Society
Proc. Soc. Psychical Res.	Proceedings of the Society for Psychical Research
Prof. sanit. morale	Profilassi e sanità morale
Psychiat. enfant	Psychiatrie de l'enfant
Psychiat.-neurol. Wochenschr.	Psychiatrisch-neurologische Wochenschrift
Psychiat. Quart. Suppl.	Psychiatric Quarterly Supplement
Psychoanal. Quart.	Psychoanalytical Quarterly
Psychoanal. Rev.	Psychoanalytical Review
Psychoanal. Stud. Child	Psychoanalytical Study of the Child
Psychol. Anwend.	Psychologische Anwendungen
Psychol. Beit.	Psychologische Beiträge
Psychol. belg.	Psychologie belge
Psychol. Bull.	Psychological Bulletin
Psychol. clin.	Psychologie clinique
Psychol. Digest	Psychological Digest
Psychol. Forsch.	Psychologische Forschung
Psychol. franç.	Psychologie française
Psychol. Monog.	Psychological Monographs
Psychol. Rep.	Psychological Reports
Psychol. Res.	Psychological Research
Psychol. Rev.	Psychological Review
Psychol. Rundsch.	Psychologische Rundschau
Psychol. Today	Psychology Today
Psychol. Women Quart.	Psychology of Women Quarterly
Psychol. wychow.	Psychologia wychowawcza
Publ. Clark Univ. Libr.	Publications of Clark University Library
Publ. Mod. Lang. Ass.	Publications of Modern Language Association
Publ. Opin. Quart.	Public Opinion Quarterly
Quart. J. Econ.	Quarterly Journal of Economics
Quart. J. Exp. Psychol.	Quarterly Journal of Experimental Psychology
Quart. Rev.	Quarterly Review
Rass. stud. psichiat.	Rassegna di studi psichiatrici
Res. News Univ. South. Calif. Grad. Sch.	Research News of University of Southern California Graduate School
Rev. belg. psychol. pédag.	Revue belge de psychologie pédagogique
Rev. deux mondes	Revue deux mondes
Rev. int. phil.	Revue internationale de philosophie
Rev. mex. psicol.	Revista mexicana de psicología
Révol. franç.	Révolution française

Rev. Paris	*Revue de Paris*
Rev. pédag.	*Revue pédagogique*
Rev. phil.	*Revue philosophique*
Rev. psicoanál.	*Revista de psicoanálisis*
Rev. psicol. gen. aplic.	*Revista de psicología general y aplicada*
Rev. psychol. appl.	*Revue de psychologie appliquée*
Riv. int. fil. dir.	*Rivista internazionale di filosofia di diritto*
Riv. psicol.	*Rivista di psicologia*
Riv. psicol. norm. pat.	*Rivista di psicologia normale e patologica*
Scand. Sci. Rev.	*Scandinavian Scientific Review*
School & Soc.	*School and Society*
Schweiz. Arch. Neurol. Psychiat.	*Schweizer Archiv für Neurologie und Psychiatrie*
Schweiz. med. Wochenschr.	*Schweizerische medizinische Wochenschrift*
Schweiz. Z. Psychol.	*Schweizerische Zeitschrift für Psychologie*
Sci. Amer.	*Scientific American*
Sci. Mon.	*Scientific Monthly*
Sci. News	*Science News*
Sci. Prog.	*Science Progress*
Sci. Soc.	*Science and Society*
Scripta math.	*Scripta mathematica*
Scuola Ticinese, period. mens. sezione pedag.	*Scuola Ticinese, periodico mensuale, sezione pedagogica*
Sitzber. Bayer. Akad. Wiss.	*Sitzungsberichte der Bayerischen Akademie der Wissenschaften*
Skand. Arch. Physiol.	*Skandinavisches Archiv der Physiologie*
Smithsonian Inst. Ann. Rep.	*Smithsonian Institution Annual Report*
Soc. Forces	*Social Forces*
Soc. Res.	*Social Research*
Stud. Sov. Thought	*Studies of Soviet Thought*
Swiss Amer. Hist. Soc. Newsl.	*Swiss American Historical Society Newsletter*
Teach. Coll. Rec.	*Teachers College Record*
Temps mod.	*Temps modernes*
Train. Sch. Bull	*Training School Bulletin*
Trans. Roy. Soc. Edinb.	*Transactions of the Royal Society of Edinburgh*
Travail hum.	*Travail humaine*
United Presbyterian Mag.	*United Presbyterian Magazine*
Univ. Bgham. Hist. J.	*University of Birmingham Historical Journal*
Univ. Toronto Quart.	*University of Toronto Quarterly*
Verh. physikal.-med. Ges. Würzburg	*Verhandlungen der physikalisch-medizinischen Gesellschaft Würzburg*
Victorian Stud.	*Victorian Studies*
Vision Res.	*Vision Research*
Vop. Defektolog.	*Voprosy Defektologii*
Vop. Psikhol.	*Voprosy Psikhologii*
Wiener Arch. Phil. Psychol. Pädag.	*Wiener Archiv für Philosophie, Psychologie und Pädagogik*

Wiss. Z. Martin-Luther-Univ.	*Wissenschaftliche Zeitschrift der Martin-Luther Universität*
Yale J. Biol. Med.	*Yale Journal of Biology and Medicine*
Yearb. Amer. Phil. Soc.	*Yearbook of the American Philosophical Society*
Z. allg. Physiol.	*Zeitschrift für allgemeine Physiologie*
Z. angew. Psychol.	*Zeitschrift für angewandte Psychologie*
Z. Biol.	*Zeitschrift für Biologie*
Zbl. ges. Neurol. Psychiat.	*Zentralblatt für die gesamte Neurologie und Psychiatrie*
Z. diagnost. Psychol.	*Zeitschrift für diagnostische Psychologie*
Z. exp. angew. Psychol.	*Zeitschrift für experimentelle und angewandte Psychologie*
Z. f. klin. Psychol. u. Psychother.	*Zeitschrift für klinische Psychologie und Psychotherapie*
Z. ges. Neurol. Psychiat.	*Zeitschrift für gesamte Neurologie und Psychiatrie*
Zh. Vyssh. Nerv. Deyat.	*Zhurnal Vysshei Nervnoï Deyatel'nosti*
Z. Hypno.	*Zeitschrift für Hypnose*
Z. pädag. Psychol.	*Zeitschrift für pädagogische Psychologie*
Z. Phil. phil. Krit.	*Zeitschrift für Philosophie und philosophische Kritik*
Z. Psychoanal. Pädag.	*Zeitschrift für Psychoanalyse und Pädagogik*
Z. Psychol.	*Zeitschrift für Psychologie*
Z. Psychother. med. Psychol.	*Zeitschrift für Psychotherapie und medizinische Psychologie*
Z. schweiz. Stat.	*Zeitschrift für schweizerische Statistik*
Z. Sinnesphysiol.	*Zeitschrift für Sinnesphysiologie*
Z. Völkerpsychol.	*Zeitschrift für Völkerpsychologie*

BIOGRAPHICAL
DICTIONARY
OF
PSYCHOLOGY

A

ABRAHAM, KARL
German Psychoanalyst
Born: Bremen, May 3, 1877
Died: Berlin, December 25, 1925
Highest Degree: M.D., University of Freiburg, 1901
Positions: 1901-5, Berlin Municipal Mental Hospital at Dalldorf; 1905-8, Burghölzli Hospital, University of Zurich; 1908-25, private practice, Berlin

Abraham was one of Sigmund Freud's* senior collaborators. In 1910 he organized the Berlin Psychoanalytic Society, the first branch of the International Psychoanalytic Society, also founded in 1910. He elaborated Freud's views of the stages of psychosexual development, asserting that adult personality can be adequately described in terms of the results of fixation at one of the stages of psychosexual development. Abraham described the oral-passive, oral-aggressive, and anal characters. He studied and described the basic obsessive personality traits in the anal character: obstinacy, orderliness, and frugality. The explanation of the adult's personality characteristics in terms of childhood experiences was Abraham's contribution to Freud's theory and was accepted by Freud. In 1911 Abraham also offered the first psychodynamic explanation of depression. His *Selected Papers on Psychoanalysis* appeared in 1948.

Biographies: L. Eidelberg (Ed.), *Encyclopedia of Psychoanalysis*, 1968; M. Eitingen *et al.*, *Int. Z. Psychoanal.*, 1926, *12*, 195-218; S. Freud, *Int. J. Psychoanal.*, 1926, 7, 1; E. Jones *et al.*, *Int. J. Psychoanal.*, 1926, 7, 155-181; *IESS*, 1; *Jewish*, 1.

ACH, NARZISS KASPAR
German Psychologist
Born: Ermershausen, Bavaria, October 29, 1871
Died: Munich, July 25, 1946
Highest Degree: M.D., University of Würzburg, 1895; Ph.D. in psychology, University of Göttingen, 1902, under Georg Müller*
Positions: 1896-97, ship's surgeon; 1902-4, University of Göttingen; 1904-6, University of Marburg; 1906, University of Berlin; 1907-22, University of Königsberg; 1922-37, University of Göttingen, 1937-46, professor emeritus; 1910-39, editor of *Untersuchungen zur Psychologie und Philosophie* (14 vols.)

A member of the Würzburg school of "imageless thought," led by Oswald Külpe*, Ach was one of the most skilled experimental psychologists of his time. His principal object of study was the will. He was first to conduct systematic experimental research in this area. Ach published many papers and three books in it: *Über die Willenstätigkeit und das Denken* (1905), *Über den Willensakt und das Temperament* (1910), and *Analyse des Willens* (1935). Ach demonstrated experimentally that the instructions for the execution of a task sets up in the individual a predisposition to act or react in a certain way, without the individual's being necessarily aware of such a predisposition. He named it "determining tendency." To Ach, willing was a mental process in its own right, and the determining tendency was its fundamental feature. Although choice behavior is completely determined, we are convinced that we choose freely. Ach called this conviction "consciousness of freedom." He was first to study freedom of the will experimentally. The approach that he and others of the Würzburg school took in studying awareness (*Bewusstheit*, a term coined by Ach) he named "systematic experimental introspection."

Ach also made important contributions to the understanding of concept formation. He showed that concepts of objects develop through interaction with these objects. He presented his work in 1921 in *Über die Begriffsbildung*.

Ach was also an accomplished apparatus builder and inventor. He invented the *chronotyper*, a reaction time recorder for the continuous recording of closely spaced, brief reactions. He was issued more than fifty patents for various instruments, both psychological and other (such as the gyrocompass).

Beginning in the late 1920s, Ach studied applied problems, such as driver safety, applying the concept of the determining tendency to them (*Über die Determinations-psychologie und ihre Bedeutung für das Führerproblem*, 1933). Ach published forty-four articles on psychological topics.
Biographies: H. Düker, *Arch. ges. Psychol.*, 1966, *118*, 189-194; K. Marbe, *Fortschr. psychol. Anwend.*, 1914, *2*, 302-320; E. Mira y López, *Arq. brasil. psicotéc.*, 1963, *15*(2), 33-43; *CE*, 1.

ADLER, ALFRED
Austrian Physician
Born: Vienna, February 7, 1870
Died: Aberdeen, Scotland, May 28, 1937

Highest Degree: M.D., University of Vienna, 1895

Positions: 1897-1914, private practice; physician in the Austrian army during World War I; organized child guidance clinics in Vienna after war; 1920, appointed head of first individual psychology clinic in Vienna; 1926-29, lecture tours and visiting professorship, Columbia University; 1932-37, professor of medical psychology, later special lecturer and visiting professor, Long Island College of Medicine

Adler originated the school of individual psychology. He joined Sigmund Freud's* group in 1902 and was prominent among the psychoanalysts for some time. A controversy arose over Adler's emphasis on social factors in personality development and his underemphasis on the sexual factor, which led to Adler's parting ways with Freud in 1911.

Adler saw sex primarily as an attempt to obtain power over another person. Sexual abnormality is not the cause but the result of mental disturbance. Physical disease is the result of organ inferiority and external demands on the organs; the basis of neurosis is in children's reactions to their feeling inferior to and dependent upon adults. Feelings of inferiority may lead to overcompensation or to submissiveness. The individual's characteristic way of expressing individuality and reaching goals is called "style of life." A person's major goal is to strive for superiority. When inferiority is used as an excuse to give up attempts at compensation (*inferiority complex*), neurosis results. Adler emphasized ego functions and minimized the biological determinism implied in Freud's emphasis on the id. People are motivated more by goals and future expectations, even though they may be unrealizable (*fictional finalism*), than by their biology, thus creating their own personalities. He emphasized the uniqueness of each individual and the creativity of the self. Adlerian psychotherapy is much briefer than Freud's psychoanalysis and concentrates on the patient's overt difficulties.

Adler wrote numerous papers and books, among the latter *The Science of Living* (1920), *Understanding Human Nature* (1927), *The Education of Children* (1930). His work is carried on by the societies, practitioners, and journals of individual psychology.

Biographies: A. Adler, *Amer. J. Psychiat.*, 1970, *127*, 771-772; P. Bottome, *Alfred Adler: Apostle of Freedom*, 1957; H. Orgler, *Alfred Adler: The Man and His Work*, 1972; M. Sperber, *Alfred Adler: Der Mensch und seine Lehre*, 1926; *CE*, 1; *EB*, 1; *EJ*, 2; *EP*, 1; *IESS*, 1; *NDB*, 1; *NYT*, 1937, May 29, 17:1.

AGASSIZ, JEAN LOUIS RODOLPHE
Swiss-American Naturalist

Born: Motier-en-Vuly, Vaud, Switzerland, May 28, 1807

Died: Cambridge, Massachusetts, December 14, 1873

Highest Degree: Ph.D. in natural sciences, University of Erlangen, 1829: M.D., University of Munich, 1830

Positions, Honors: 1832-47, University of Neuchâtel; 1847-73, Harvard University; two honorary degrees, medals, other honors

Agassiz was already a well-known scientist when he arrived in the United States in 1846. In America Agassiz was the main opponent of Charles Darwin*. While he made a lasting contribution to the evolutionary approach to biology through his studies in paleoichthyology, he did not believe that the ancient and modern species had any genetic relationship. His contribution to psychology was through the natural sciences: his love of nature and zeal for massive data collection set an example that was emulated not only at Harvard but elsewhere. At Harvard Agassiz established the Museum of Comparative Zoology. It came to represent his idea of how graduate instruction, research, field work, and publication should be interrelated in a university setting. Agassiz's teaching and research made Harvard one of the main American centers for biology instruction and research and paved the way for its also becoming one of the leading centers in psychology. Two years after Agassiz's death, James* established the first American psychological laboratory at Harvard.

Biographies: E. C. Agassiz (Ed.), *Louis Agassiz: His Life and Correspondence*, 1900; R. Bliss, *Pop. Sci. Mon.*, 1874, *4*, 608-618; L. Cooper, *Louis Agassiz as a Teacher*, 1945; E. Favre, *Ann. Rep. Board Smithsonian Inst., 1878*, 1879, 236-261; W. James, *Science*, 1897, *5*, 285-289; E. Lurie, *Louis Agassiz: A Life in Science*, 1960; J. Marcou, *Life, Letters, and Works of Louis Agassiz*, 1896; L. J. Milne & M. J. Milne, *Famous Naturalists*, 1952; C. O. Peare, *A Scientist of Two Worlds: Louis Agassiz*, 1958; *DSB*, 1; *EB*, 1; *NCAB*, 2; *NYT*, 1873, Dec. 15, 1:3.

ALBERTUS MAGNUS, SAINT (ALBERT THE GREAT, or ALBERT OF COLOGNE)

German Scholastic Philosopher, Theologian, and Scientist
Born: Lauingen, Swabia, ca. 1200
Died: Cologne, November 15, 1280
Highest Degree: Master in theology, University of Paris, 1248
Positions, Honors: Received into the Dominican order at Padua, 1223; before 1245, taught in various places in Germany; 1248-54, University of Cologne; 1254-57, provincial of "Teutonia"; 1260-62, bishop of Regensburg; 1263-64, legate to the pope; 1270-80, lecturer at the Universities of Cologne, Strasbourg, and Würzburg; canonized and made doctor of the church in 1931

Albert the Great was one of the precursors of modern science. Teacher of Thomas Aquinas*, Albert the Great was considered the most learned scholar of his day. Embracing all knowledge of the time, he had complete mastery of Aristotle*, whom he expounded and corrected to conform with Christian teachings. One of his important contributions was to help introduce Aristotle to Western thought. Although Thomas Aquinas was more subtle and systematic than Albert the Great, he got his Aristotelean psychology from Albert. Other sciences that Albert contributed directly to were botany and zoology.

Albert's significance lies also in the attitude he took toward the acquisition of knowledge. The promise of a new age in the attitude of humans toward nature and knowledge about nature is seen in his statements that when a subject may be known only through observation, dry, scholastic arguments are of no use. Although nature is God's creation, not all of its parts may be deduced from theology. Some need to be observed, experienced, and even experimented upon. Although his own experiments were superficial and his conclusions wrong, he stressed the need for careful observation and experimentation in the realm of natural science and held that evidence obtained by experimentation was superior to that obtained by research without experimentation.

Biographies: S. M. Albert, *Albert the Great*, 1948; H. C. Scheeben, *Albertus Magnus*, 1955; M. Schwertner, *St. Albert the Great*, 1932; L. Thorndike, *A History of Magic and Experimental Science*, vol. 2, 1923; *DSB*, 1; *EB*, 1.

ALCMAEON OF CROTON
Greek Physician
Born: Croton, southern Italy, ca. 500 B.C.
Died: Place and date unknown
Education: Unknown
Positions: Unknown

Almost nothing is known of Alcmaeon's life, and only some fragments of his writings remain. Alcmaeon was an adherent of Pythagoras* and somewhat of a mystic himself, but a good observer nevertheless. He is reported to have been the first to dissect a human body. Surgical operations were the basis for his observations on sensory functioning, although the inferences he made from anatomical observations to sensory functioning are mostly incorrect. Alcmaeon was first to extirpate the human eye, as a result of which he discovered the connection between the eye and the brain. He developed theories of vision, hearing, smell, and taste; he concluded that the brain receives sensory impressions, that it is the seat of thought as well as the central or vital point of the organism. Although earlier philosophers had located the perishable aspect of the soul (*thymos*) in the lungs and the immortal aspect (*psyche*) in the head, Alcmaeon unified both and located them in the brain. To Alcmaeon, mind could exist only as long as the brain remained undamaged. Alcmaeon made a distinction between humans and animals, attributing to humans both perception and understanding, but perception only, to animals. Although he considered perception and understanding to be separate processes, he made them inherent in the one soul.

Biographies: *DSB*, 1; *EP*, 1; *HGP*, 1.

D'ALEMBERT, JEAN LE ROND
French Physicist and Mathematician
Born: Paris, November 17, 1717
Died: Paris, October 29, 1783
Education: Studied law and mathematics at Mazarin College, admitted as an advocate in 1738

Positions, Honors: Admitted to the French Academy of Sciences in 1741, received a pension from the king, but did not hold any academic positions

D'Alembert was one of the compilers and the science editor of the *Dictionnaire encyclopédique*. In the 1750s he prepared the *Discours preliminaire* of the encyclopedia, which was a review of the history and present status of the sciences. It is one of the main documents of the age of Enlightenment that changed the intellectual outlook of society. In the *Discours* d'Alembert expounded sensationalism. Elaborating on Locke* and Condillac*, d'Alembert suggested that science is to be based on physical perception, and that morality's base is the perception of inner feelings, a position shared by Hume*. D'Alembert related all knowledge to memory, imagination, and reason, with reason being the most important of the three. All ideas arise from sense perception, none being innate. *Biographies*: J. Bertrand, *D'Alembert*, 1889; R. Grimsley, *Jean d'Alembert*, 1963; J. Morley, *Diderot and the Encyclopedists*, 1886; J. Pappas, *Voltaire and d'Alembert*, 1962; *DSB*, 1; *EP*, 1.

ALEXANDER, FRANZ GABRIEL
German-American Psychoanalyst
Born: Budapest, Hungary, January 22, 1891
Died: Palm Springs, California, March 8, 1964
Highest Degree: M.D., University of Budapest, 1913
Positions: 1920-30, Berlin Psychoanalytical Institute; 1930-32, University of Chicago; 1932-56, Chicago Institute for Psychoanalysis; 1956-64, Mount Sinai Hospital, Los Angeles; 1957-64, University of Southern California

Alexander was the most prominent representative of the neo-Freudian Chicago school of psychoanalysis, which sought to apply psychoanalysis in new situations more than it sought to add to psychoanalytic theory. Alexander and the Chicago school deemphasized the origin of neuroses in the psychosexual stages of childhood and stressed, in addition to early experience, heredity and actual difficulties of the patient created by situations that are beyond his or her control. Alexander defined *neurosis* as a relationship between personality and the social setting in which the personality finds itself. The aim of psychoanalysis is "to increase the patient's ability to find gratification for his subjective needs in ways acceptable both to himself and to the world he lives in, and thus to free him to develop his capacities." Alexander's principle of surplus energy (derived from Ferenczi*) stated that sexuality is a specific discharge of unused excitation in the organism. The therapeutic emphasis is on "corrective emotional experience" to release this surplus energy, which is a form of abreaction and a process central to the therapeutic process used in the Chicago school. Planning and flexibility are two additional adaptations of the classical psychoanalytic procedure. The patient's free associations are not the main guideline in therapy. It is planned in accordance with the diagnosis and the personality of the patient and may change depending on the outcome of the therapeutic intervention, so that diverse methods may be used with different patients and with the same patient during a course of treatment. The work of the Chicago school centered around the Chicago Institute of Psychoanalysis, which Alexander founded. He is also credited with helping to establish the field of psychosomatic medicine. Already in the late 1930s he was showing that chronic emotional tension was correlated with disorders such as gastric ulcers, colitis, and asthma.

Alexander wrote some 120 articles and eighteen books. Prominent among the latter are *Psychoanalytic Therapy* (1946, with T. M. French), *Studies in Analytical Psychology* (1948), and *Fundamentals of Psychoanalysis* (1948).

Biographies: T. M. French, *Behav. Sci.*, 1964, *9*, 98-100; M. Grotjahn, *J. Nerv. Ment. Dis.*, 1965, *140*, 319-322; H. V. McLean, *Int. J. Psychoanal.*, 1965, *46*, 247-250; W. M. Mendel, *J. Exist. Psychiat.*, 1964, *4*, 287-288; G. H. Pollack, *Arch. Gen. Psychiat.*, 1964, *11*, 229-234; *EJ*, 2; *IESS*, 1; *NCAB*, H; *NYT*, 1964, Mar. 9, 29:2.

ALLPORT, FLOYD H.
American Psychologist
Born: Milwaukee, Wisconsin, August 22, 1890
Died: Syracuse, New York, October 15, 1978
Highest Degree: Ph.D. in psychology, Harvard University, 1919
Positions, Honors: 1919-22, Harvard University; 1922-24, University of North Carolina; 1924-56, Syracuse University, 1956-78, emeritus professor; editorial work, *Journal of Abnormal and Social Psychology*, 1921-25; American Psychological Distinguished Scientific Contribution Award, 1965; American Psychological Foundation Gold Medal, 1968; honorary doctorate, Syracuse University, 1974

Allport's early significant work concerned the effect of the group upon the behavior of the individual. The term *social facilitation*, which Allport introduced, describes the main finding of his experiments. Other concepts introduced by him were "conformity-producing tendency," "the J-curve hypothesis of conforming behavior," "the impression of universality," and many others. Allport's *Social Psychology* (1924), his most important work, was well received. It had the novel features of being an objective and systematic treatment of social psychology, of stressing the psychological rather than the sociological aspect of the field, and of presenting the possibility that social psychology might be an experimental field. For this, Allport is considered to be the father of experimental social psychology. After his work, group experimentation became one of the main features of social psychology. As a teacher at Syracuse University, Allport headed the first doctoral program in social psychology in the United States.

At first Allport stressed the role of the individual to the exclusion of the social factor (the "group fallacy"). His *Institutional Behavior* (1933) was a failure, but he continued to search for a principle under which both the functioning of the individual alone as well as in a group could be subsumed. This was the concept of *structure*, the notion that individual and collective behavior is to be understood in terms of the structure of events in an individual and between individuals. The theory of structure of events ("enestruence") was presented first in a journal article in 1954 and then in the last chapter of a review of perceptual theories, *Theories of Perception and the Concept of Structure* (1955). The book was much used by graduate students, but Allport's highly abstract theory of event structure failed to exercise a major influence on the thinking of social psychologists.

Biographies: *Amer. Psychologist*, 1968, *23*, 868-869; D. Katz, *Amer. Psychologist*, 1979, *34*, 351-353; *HPA*, 6.

ALLPORT, GORDON WILLARD

American Psychologist

Born: Montezuma, Indiana, November 11, 1897
Died: Cambridge, Massachusetts, October 9, 1967
Highest Degree: Ph.D. in psychology, Harvard University, 1922, under Herbert S. Langfeld*
Positions, Honors: 1924-67, Harvard University; editor, *Journal of Abnormal and Social Psychology*, 1937-49; president, American Psychological Association, 1939; APA Distinguished Scientific Contribution Award, 1964

Allport was a personality psychologist who viewed the human personality as an evolving system of habits, attitudes, and traits (*Personality: A Psychological Interpretation*, 1937). Personality involves both physiological and mental processes. Motivational systems may become autonomous (functional autonomy), causing behavior that no longer depends on the original needs. The causes of behavior are thus in the present.

Allport favored the trait approach to personality (*Trait Names: A Psycho-Lexical Study*, 1936). Traits, like habits, generalize to individuals and situations. There are traits that belong to the individual and traits that are common to some degree in most individuals. The unifying core of the personality is the proprium, or self. The self's propriate striving is directed toward the realization of its potentialities and life goals. Allport's person is motivated more by social than biological factors (*Personality and Social Encounter*, 1960), seeking new and higher goals, always trying to become something new and different, and is not satisfied with repeated reinstatements of homeostatic equilibrium (*Becoming: Basic Considerations for a Psychology of Personality*, 1955; *Pattern and Growth in Personality*, 1961).

Allport contributed also to personality-assessment methodology (*The Use of Personal Documents in Psychological Science*, 1942), originating psychological instruments such as the *A-S Reaction Study* (with Floyd Allport*) and the *Study of Values* (1931, with P. E. Vernon; rev. ed., 1951, with P. E. Vernon and G. Lindzey). The latter, based on Eduard Spranger's* classification of human types, has been widely used and researched.

Dedicated to a psychology that takes as its own the model of the human being as a person, Allport was a cofounder of the Department of Social Relations at Harvard in 1946 and was counted among the "third force," or humanistic, psychologists who reject both the behavioristic and psychoanalytic views. All-port's output of publications was large (12 books and 228 other publications), and the influence he exercised through his writings and through his personality on his students and others was great.

Biographies: *Brit. J. Psychol.*, 1968, *59*, 99-103; R. I. Evans, *Gordon Allport: the Man and His Ideas*, 1971; J. W. Mann, *Psychologia Africana*, 1968, *12*, 65-74; T. F. Pettigrew, *J. Pers. Soc. Psychol.*, 1969, *12*, 1-5; *HPA*, 5; *IESS*, 18; *NCAB*, J; *NYT*, 1967, Oct. 10, 47:1.

AMES, ADALBERT, JR.

American Ophthalmologist
Born: Lowell, Massachusetts, August 19, 1880
Died: Hanover, New Hampshire, July 3, 1955
Highest Degree: LL.B. in law, Harvard University, 1906
Positions, Honors: 1914-17, research fellow, Clark University; 1919-45, Dartmouth College; 1936-49, director of research, Dartmouth Eye Institute; 1949-55, Hanover Institute for Associated Research; LL.D., Dartmouth College, 1954; Optical Society of America Edgar D. Tillyer Medal, 1955

Dissatisfied with the practice of law, Ames turned to painting, which led him to the analysis of vision and to ophthalmology. In 1936 he established the Dartmouth Eye Clinic, where he discovered and researched the phenomenon of aniseikonia and invented the aniseikonic lenses to correct it. A study of the effects of aniseikonic lenses in persons with normal vision as well as of other unique conditions of vision led Ames to the formulation of the view of trans-actional functionalism in perception. The philosophical basis for Ames's theory came from the philosophical theory of transactions of John Dewey*. The em-pirical support came from the demonstrations that Ames devised. They were set up to show how individuals transact with their environment, that is, how they experience the consequences of their own actions. They reveal the perceptual significance of action and the observer's assumptions about the perceptual world. To the transactionalist, the demonstrations show that objects derive their meaning at least partly from their participation in a total situation and that the world we experience is the product of, not the cause of, perception.

The first demonstrations were set up in 1938. They included the distorted room, the trapezoidal window, aniseikonic lenses, and size-distance phenomena in the "thereness-thatness" apparatus. They were first set up at the Hanover Institute for Associated Research, which Ames and Hadley Cantril* organized in 1947, but were later placed in the Perception Demonstration Center at Princeton University.

Ames wrote thirty papers about vision but only seven about perception and *An Interpretative Manual for the Demonstrations in the Psychology Research Center, Princeton University* (1954). Otherwise his thinking appears in informal

memoranda bound in six volumes, now at Dartmouth College and Princeton University.
Biographies: *J. Opt. Soc. Amer.*, 1955, *45*, 333-337; *NCAB*, 44; *NYT*, 1955, July 4, 11:3.

ANAN'EV, BORIS GERASIMOVICH
Russian Psychologist
Born: Vladikavkaz (now Ordzhonikidze), Russia, August 14, 1907
Died: Leningrad, May 18, 1972
Highest Degree: Ph.D., Leningrad State Brain Research Institute, 1931; doctor of pedagogical sciences, 1940
Positions, Honors: 1931-42, Leningrad State Brain Research Institute; 1942, Psychology Division, evacuation hospital, Tblisi; 1943, Leningrad Pedagogical University; 1944-51, head, Psychology Department, Leningrad State University; 1951-60, director, Leningrad Pedagogical Research Institute; 1960-67, head of Psychology Department, Leningrad State University; 1967, dean, Psychology Faculty, Leningrad State University; editorial work, *Voprosy Psikhologii, Zeitschrift für Psychologie*; several medals, prizes

Anan'ev was one of the outstanding Soviet psychologists for several decades. He made significant contributions to several areas of psychology but especially to the area of sensation and perception. His particular interest was how perception becomes thought. He was one of the main shapers of the Soviet theory of perception. A prolific writer, Anan'ev produced more than 160 papers and books in psychology. Of the latter, the most significant are [*Psychology of Educational Evaluation*] (1935), [*Psychological Essays*] (1945), [*Theory of Inner Speech in Psychology*] (1946), [*Essays on the History of Russian Psychology in the Eighteenth and Nineteenth Centuries*] (1947), [*Materials on the Psychological Theory of Sensation*] (1948), [*Some Problems of the Theory of Perception*] (1949), [*The Problem of Concept in Soviet Psychological Science*] (1950), [*The Association of Sensations*] (1955), [*Spatial Discrimination*] (1955), [*The Sense of Touch in the Process of Perception and in Work*] (1959, coauthor), [*Man as Object of Cognition*] (1960), and [*New Developments in the Theory of Spatial Perception*] (1960).
Biographies: S. E. Drapkina & M. Y. Polyakov, *Voprosy Psikhologii*, 1982, No. 6, 138-145; V. P. Lisenkova, *Voprosy Psikhologii*, 1982, No. 6, 134-138; *Vop. Psikhol.*, 1972, *18*(3), 188; *Prominent Personalities in the USSR*, 1968.

ANAXAGORAS
Greek Philosopher
Born: Clazomenea, Asia Minor, ca. 500 B.C.
Died: Lampsacus, Mysia, ca. 428 B.C.
Education: Self-taught
Positions: 480-450 B.C., adviser to Pericles in Athens

Anaxagoras became famous for explaining the true cause of eclipses. Later, however, he was put on trial for another astronomical observation, namely, that the sun, contrary to the generally held opinion, was nothing more than a relatively small, incandescent stone.

Like other Greek philosophers, Anaxagoras speculated about the stuff that the universe was made of. He postulated that the universe was made of an infinity of ultimate substances, holding that assuming only one (as did the Ionian philosophers) or even four (as did Empedocles*) was insufficient. All objects contain all of the ultimate substances, but each in varying amounts, those that are present in the largest amount determining the appearance and nature of the object. The substances themselves are each infinitely divisible, which enables them to remain together in the different objects. This atomistic view of the world Anaxagoras shared with Democritus*.

Starting with the premise that people attribute all actions to some reason, Anaxagoras postulated a creative principle of the universe, the *nous*, which caused the primordial mixture of ultimate substances to revolve and therefore like particles to aggregate into larger masses. The *nous*, like all other substances, is material. In living organisms, *nous* enables them to extract the necessary nutrients from foodstuffs. The introduction of the *nous* as an ordering principle of the universe made Anaxagoras famous in later ages.

Anaxagoras made a number of interesting observations on matters psychological, although they are unconnected and unsystematic. He remarked on the nature and the operation of the senses, for instance. By contrast with what was being said by other philosophers, Anaxagoras insisted that perception (discrimination) occurs not by similarities but by opposites: the sensation of cold or warm arises only if objects differ in temperature from the temperature of the body, for instance.

Biographies: F. M. Cleve, *The Philosophy of Anaxagoras*, 1949; J. A. Davison, *Classical Quart.*, 1953, *3*, 33-45; L. Parmentier, *Euripide et Anaxagore*, 1892; A. E. Taylor, *Classical Quart.*, 1917, *11*, 81-87; J. Zafiropulo, *Anaxagore de Clazomène*, 1948; *DSB*, 1; *EB*, 1; *HGP*, 2.

ANGELL, FRANK
American Psychologist
Born: South Scituate, Rhode Island, July 8, 1857
Died: Palo Alto, California, November 2, 1939
Highest Degree: Ph.D. in psychology, University of Leipzig, 1891, under Wundt*
Positions: 1891, Cornell University; 1892-1922, Stanford University; editor, *American Journal of Psychology*, 1895-1925

A Wundtian laboratory psychologist, Angell did most of his research in psychophysics. His major contributions to psychology were as a teacher, especially of the introductory undergraduate course, during the thirty years he spent at Stanford, and the establishment of two early experimental psychology laboratories in America: at Cornell in 1891 and at Stanford in 1893.

Biographies: L. M. Terman, *Amer. J. Psychol.*, 1940, *53*, 138-141.

ANGELL, JAMES ROWLAND
American Psychologist
Born: Burlington, Vermont, May 8, 1869
Died: Hamden, Connecticut, March 4, 1949
Highest Degree: M.S., Harvard University, 1892; Ph.D. dissertation written, degree not completed, at University of Berlin
Positions, Honors: 1893, philosophy, University of Minnesota; 1894-1921, University of Chicago, 1894-1919, psychology, 1919-21, administration; during World War I, among psychologists who worked on the classification of army personnel; 1921-37, president, Yale University; after retirement in 1937, educational counselor to NBC, others; president, American Psychological Association, 1906; chairman, National Research Council (1919-20), Board of Trustees, Carnegie Corporation (1920-21); twenty-three honorary doctorates.

Titchener* gave functionalism its name by contrasting it with Wundt's* and his own structuralism, but Angell was the most prominent spokesman of functionalism. Although functionalism was born gradually in the work of Charles Darwin*, Cattell*, Dewey*, and others, as a school of psychology, functionalism was most closely associated with the name of Angell and the University of Chicago. Before going to Chicago Angell established a psychology laboratory at the University of Minnesota in 1893 and another one, with Dewey, at the University of Chicago in 1893-94.

In a book (*Psychology*, 1904, which saw four editions by 1908 and additional revised editions thereafter) and a paper Angell outlined the point of view of functionalism. In his book he was already accepting the observation of behavior as a valid method in psychology. His paper stated that functionalism is concerned with the how, why, and what of the psyche, that is, its function; that the mind was the mediator between the organism and its environment; and that it was psychophysical because it considered mental processes in relation to the body as they affected the body's adjustments to the environment. The useful or applied nature of mind was contrasted with the questions concerning its nature or structure.

Angell was a very talented administrator. As president of Yale University he was known as the creator of the "new Yale"—through fund raising, building programs, and expanding educational programs. He created the Yale Institute of Human Relations. As head of the Psychology Department at Chicago, Angell was also very effective, making the department the most influential one of its day.
Biographies: W. S. Hunter, *Amer. J. Psychol.*, 1949, *62*, 439-450; F. A. Kingsbury, *Psychol. Bull.*, 1946, *43*, 259-271; W. R. Miles, *Science*, 1949, *110*, 1-4; A. Ruggles, *Ment. Hyg.*, N.Y., 1949, *33*, 298-299; R. M. Yerkes, *Yearbook of American Philosophical Society*, 1949, 294-301; *Biog. Mem.*, 26; *HPA*, 3; *IESS*, 1; *NCAB*, E, 40; *NYT*, 1949, Mar. 5, 17:1.

ANOKHIN, PETR KUZ'MICH
Russian Physiologist
Born: Tsaritsyn (now Volgograd), January 26, 1898
Died: Moscow, March 6, 1974

Highest Degree: Physician, Institute of Medical Science, 1926; doctor of medical sciences

Positions, honors: 1926-30, chair of physiology, Gorkiĭ Medical Institute; 1934-45, head, Department of General Physiology of Higher Nervous Activity, All-Union Institute of Experimental Medicine; 1946-49, director, Institute of Physiology, USSR Academy of Medical Sciences; 1936-49, 1953-55, also occupied chair of physiology and pathology of higher nervous system, Postgraduate Medical Institute; 1955-74, head, Laboratory of Physiology, Vishnevskiĭ Institute of Surgery, USSR Academy of Medical Sciences; editorial work, *Fiziologicheskiĭ Zhurnal SSSR*

Anokhin first worked in Bekhterev's* laboratory and then, dissatisfied with Bekhterev's use of the reflex concept to explain all behavior, went to Pavlov*. After Pavlov's death, Anokhin became the foremost exponent of Pavlovian neurophysiology, although he did introduce considerable modifications in the Pavlovian system. While working with Pavlov, Anokhin came to the conclusion that the more complex behaviors cannot be reduced to simple reflexes, that the reflexes themselves form more complex ensembles or functional systems, and that only these functional systems make it possible to study behavior. This view was presented in [*Problems of Central and Peripheral Nervous Activity and of Its Physiology*] (1935), of which Anokhin was a coauthor. A functional system is a self-regulating system that becomes organized as a result of the interaction of *afference* (sensory input) and *reafference* (sensory feedback resulting from the organism's own actions).

Anokhin also developed a theory of amputation pains and a theory of central paralyses. Before the advent of cybernetics, he postulated the existence of feedback receptors in the nervous system. Later Anokhin developed the concept of "anticipatory reflection" that he used to explain the physiological basis of goal-directed behavior. At his death, he and his coworkers had published more than one thousand papers. His last book, *The Biology and Neurophysiology of the Conditioned Reflex* (1967; English translation, 1974), is the most psychological. Other books of psychological significance by Anokhin are [*Problems of Higher Nervous Activity*] (1940), [*Nervous Plasticity in War-Related Trauma of the Peripheral Nervous System*] (1944), [*Systemogenesis as a General Law of the Evolutionary Process*] (1948), [*Problems of Cortical Inhibition and Its Place in the Teaching on the Higher Nervous Activity*] (1948), [*General Principles of the Compensation of Functional Disturbances and Their Physiological Basis*] (1955), [*Electroencephalographic Analysis of the Conditioned Reflex*] (1958), [*A New Conception of the Architecture of the Conditioned Reflex*] (1959), and [*Contemporary Problems of General Neurophysiology and the Pathology of the Nervous System*](1965).

Biographies: M. Cole & S. Cole, *Psychol. Today*, March 1971; *Vop. Psikhol.*, 1974, No. 2, 187-188; *NYT*, 1974, Mar. 9, 32:2.

AQUINAS, SAINT THOMAS
Italian Theologian
Born: Roccasecca, near Aquino, ca. 1225
Died: Fossanova Abbey, near Priverno, Latium, March 7, 1274

Education: University of Naples, liberal arts; University of Paris, Dominican House of Studies; Cologne, theology, under Albertus Magnus (Albert the Great)*
Positions: 1252-59, teacher, University of Paris; 1259-68, teacher, various places in Italy; 1268-72, University of Paris; 1272-73, University of Naples

In psychological matters Aquinas followed Aristotle*, although he disagreed with him on a number of points. Aquinas also interpreted Aristotle to fit his ideas to the Christian theological framework. Aristotle's *nous*, the active, creative reason, was said by Aquinas to be immortal, as was the rational soul. Like Aristotle, Aquinas held the hylomorphic view of the unity of body and soul. The faculties of the soul are, from the highest to the lowest, the rational, sensitive, and vegetative faculty. The rational faculty consists of the active and the passive intellect and the will. To the five Aristotelean senses Aquinas added the interior senses. Animals are endowed with an estimative power that allows them to appreciate nonsensory relationships without the use of reason. In humans reason is involved in this function, and the corresponding interior sense is called the "cogitative power." Imagination and memory are two additional interior senses. Appetites are the sensitive appetites (the concupiscible and the irascible) and the will. Because the will is free, desire comes from the will and not from without. The possible intellect, through the power of the senses, understands, judges, and reasons about objects. It is the agent intellect, however, that makes experience intelligible by abstracting from it general, nonsensory qualities.

The Thomistic philosophy gained acceptance slowly, becoming the official philosophy of the Roman Catholic church in 1897. Thomistic psychology is also the "official" psychology of Roman Catholicism and is being taught in Catholic schools. Aquinas's psychological views are contained in the *Summa de Homine*, which is part of his *Summa Theologica* (1266-73).
Biographies: DSB, 1; EB, 2; EP, 8; IESS, 1.

ARISTOTLE
Greek Philosopher
Born: Stagira, Thrace, 384 B.C.
Died: Chalcis, Euboea, 323 B.C.
Education: Probably studied in Plato's* Academy and was Plato's student
Positions: 367-347 B.C., in Athens, but little is known about his activities there; 347-344 B.C., teacher, writer, scientific collector at Assus (Asia Minor); 344-342 B.C., collector at Mitylene (Lesbos); 342-336 B.C., tutor of Alexander the Great at Pella (Macedonia); 335-323 B.C., in Athens, established his school, the Lyceum, and completed most of his psychological writings

Regarded by many as the greatest mind that ever lived, Aristotle contributed to prescientific psychology in both quantity and quality more than any other individual. In antiquity and since the rediscovery of Aristotle in the thirteenth century and until the time of Descartes*, psychology was essentially Aristotelean psychology. Aristotle is regarded by many as the first psychologist. In his writings biology and psychology are given the amplest treatment, about one-third of the pages. Aristotle's main psychological work is *Peri Psyches*, better known under its Latin title *De Anima*. Shorter works ("On the Senses and the Sensible", "On Memory and Reminiscence," "On Sleep and Sleeplessness," and "On Dreams") are included under the common title of *Short Physical Treatises* (*Parva Naturalia*). *De Anima* was the first systematic treatise on psychology.

Although at first Aristotle was a Platonist, he gradually became convinced of the necessity of empirical observation and began to modify existing views, including those of Plato, to conform to the results of his empirical observations. In this and many other respects (such as Aristotle's rejection of the Platonic doctrine of ideal forms) the philosophies of Plato and Aristotle are antithetical. They represent a basic divergence in the way human beings and the world may be viewed, the rational and the empirical way.

Aristotle defined the *psyche* as a substance capable of receiving knowledge. Knowledge of the psyche he held to be the most valuable knowledge. Although the senses are necessary to acquire knowledge, knowledge is received only through the psyche's faculty of intelligence. Since only humans have intelligence, animals are incapable of acquiring knowledge. To Aristotle the psyche was the form aspect of existence. He held it to be the vital principle that distinguishes inorganic from organic matter. In contrast to Democritus*, who was a mechanist, Aristotle was a vitalist. Psyche to Aristotle meant life, and mental activities he held to be basically biological. Aristotle maintained, however, that body and psyche form a unity, a view that was later termed the *hylomorphic view*. He believed the main center of action of the psyche is the heart, having rejected the brain as its seat because of his observation that the brain did not seem to respond to stimulation. Although Aristotle was wrong in this respect, the explanation of mental and behavioral phenomena in biological terms characterizes all of Aristotle's psychology, so it may be said that he was laying the foundation for physiological psychology. The functions of the psyche are the nutritive, sensitive, and the rational functions, a division that Aristotle used for convenience's sake, since he believed in the unity of the psyche.

The listing of the five senses begins with Aristotle. In addition to vision, audition, smell, taste, and touch, Aristotle envisioned also a common sense or a central, coordinating sense faculty as well as one that perceives the common sensibles, such as size and number. Sensitivity is aroused by events in the environment, and memory is the persistence of sense impressions. Recall, present in humans only, is active search for memory traces and requires deliberation or thinking. Recall occurs as one idea leads to another. Similarity, contrast, and contiguity are relationships that facilitate the association of ideas. Repetition, emotion, and organization also facilitate recall. The pleasure-pain aspect of sensation causes desire, which leads to movement. An activity that is pleasurable will be repeated. Aristotle asserted that even moral virtues are not innate but that we are made perfect by habit. This beginning of a learning theory was not to be developed until the end of the nineteenth century.

Aristotle believed that thinking requires the use of images. Although some animals can imagine, only humans think. Knowing (*nous*) differs from thinking in that it is an active, creative process leading to the recognition of universals; it is akin to intuition, it does not cause movement, and it is independent of the other functions of the psyche. Since Aristotle's thinking underwent considerable changes in time, it is possible to interpret some of his statements in different ways, especially those concerning the nature of the psyche and the *nous*. A metaphysical interpretation made Aristotle acceptable to the medieval Christian world. Today's Thomistic psychology of Catholicism is based, by way of St. Thomas Aquinas*, on Aristotle. Many of Aristotle's ideas, in and out of psychology, have withstood time so well that today the thinking of both the layman and the psychologist alike shows them clearly.

Biographies: *DSB*, 1; *EB*, 2; *EP*, 1; *HGP*, 6; *IESS*, 1.

ASSAGIOLI, ROBERTO
Italian Psychiatrist
Born: Venice, February 27, 1882
Died: Capolona, Italy, August 23, 1974
Highest Degree: M.D., University of Florence, 1910
Positions: Private practice of psychiatry

Assagioli developed a conception of human psychological life and a method of therapy that he called "psychosynthesis." The Instituto di Psicosintesi, founded by Assagioli in 1926, has served as a training center and publishing house in a manner similar to the Psychoanalytic Society. Although Assagioli's ideas are closest to those of Jung*, they are based on theosophy: Assagioli's human is a septenary structure (sensation, emotion, impulse, imagination, thought, intuition, and will), centered around the self as well as a higher, transpersonal Self. The purpose of psychosynthesis is to achieve balance and harmony among these aspects of the individual. Assagioli particularly stressed the role of the will and the need for its development. His therapeutic and self-development technique is not a single or special but an eclectic technique, with emphasis on will-training exercises and creative imagery. Among Assagioli's works are [*Parapsychological Faculties and Psychological Disturbances*] (1958), *Psychosynthesis* (1971), and *The Act of Will* (1973). He was also the author of some three hundred papers.

Biographies.: *J. Hum. Psychol.*, 1975, 15(1), 5; S. Keen, *Psychol. Today,* Dec. 1974; NYT, 1974, Aug. 24, 28:3.

AUBERT, HERMANN
German Physiologist
Born: Frankfurt am Main, November, 1826
Died: Rostock, Mecklenburg, February 12, 1892
Highest Degree: M.D., University of Berlin, 1850
Positions: 1852-62, University of Breslau; 1862-92, University of Rostock; editor, *Zeitschrift für Psychologie*

Aubert was a pioneer, along with Helmholtz*, in the area of physiological optics (*Physiologie der Netzhaut*, 1865; *Grundzüge der physiologischen Optik*, 1876). In the 1850s he studied visual space perception. Aubert's phenomenon (a lighted vertical line appears to move in the dark when the observer's head is inclined, a starting point for the Werner*-Wapner sensory-tonic field theory) and the Aubert-Förster phenomenon (with the visual angle constant, small and near objects occupy more retinal area than do large and distant objects) were named after him. In the same decade he published research on cutaneous space perception and in the 1860s on psychophysics. First complete understanding of dark and light adaptation is found in Aubert (1865). He introduced both the term and the concept of *adaptation* and plotted the first curves of dark-adaptation. The first thorough experimental measurement of the retinal color zones was done by Aubert in 1865. His last contribution was to the understanding of bodily orientation (1888).

Biographies: *ADB*, 46; *EUI*, 6; Hirsch, *Biog. Lex.*, 1; Pagel, *Biographisches Lexikon*.

AUGUSTINE, SAINT, OF HIPPO (AURELIUS AUGUSTINUS)

Roman Church Father
Born: Tagaste, Numidia, November 13, 354
Died: Hippo Regius, Numidia, August 28, 430
Education: Studied rhetoric at Carthage, 370-73
Positions: 373-88, teacher of rhetoric in Carthage, Milan, and Rome; 399-430, priest, later bishop of Hippo (North Africa)

St. Augustine's contribution to psychology stems from his intense self-analysis, triggered by his sudden conversion to Christianity in 386, following a life of pleasure and dissipation and after excursions into philosophy, Manicheism, and Neoplatonism. His psychological views are passionately but unsystematically presented in his famous autobiography *Confessions* (ca. 406).

Augustine's attitude toward science was ambivalent. He was convinced, however, of the certainty of inner experience—contemplation, ecstasy, prayer, adoration, and the like. His insightful descriptions of subjective events (for example, the will, experienced freedom of the will, the self) begin the tradition of introspection and phenomenology in psychology. Augustine discussed the perception of time and concluded that time is an inner experience, that is, it is psychological. He anticipated Descartes* concerning the proof of self-existence: to doubt is to think, and to think is to exist ("For if I am deceived, I am"). We arrive at knowledge not from sense impressions but from our awareness of ourselves. The mind is a unity, but it does have several functions or faculties: reason, memory, will, and imagination. Since Augustine talked of these faculties as relatively independent entities, faculty psychology may be said to have started with Augustine. Concerning the body-soul relationship, Augustine sided with Plato* and the Neoplatonists in that he considered the soul to be immaterial and immortal and the body material and mortal. Since Aristotle* was for the time being "lost," and Augustine became a church father and a saint, his psychology was the only accepted psychology through the Dark Ages and the medieval period until the rise of scholastic Aristoteleanism.

Biographies: *DSB*, 1; *EB*, 2; *EP*, 1; *IESS*, 1.

AVENARIUS, RICHARD HEINRICH LUDWIG
German Philosopher
Born: Paris, France, November 19, 1843
Died: Zurich, Switzerland, August 18, 1896
Highest Degree: Ph.D. in philosophy, University of Leipzig, 1876
Positions: 1876, University of Leipzig; 1877-96, University of Zurich

Avenarius developed an epistemology (empiriocriticism) that influenced systematic thinking in psychology. It was essentially the same as Mach's*, but Avenarius developed it independently. It is contained in his only important work, the two-volume *Kritik der reinen Erfahrung* (1888-90). Avenarius's "System C" is a bodily system that is essential for the mind. Statements of experience (E-values) depend on System C, which in turn is affected by external stimuli or R-values. A constant process of equilibration between catabolism and anabolism occurs in system C, tending toward a state of vital balance along a course of "vital series." Two kinds of vital series are distinguished by Avenarius: independent series, or physical changes, and dependent series, which parallel the former and depend on them. They are psychological. The terms *independent* and *dependent* to signify physical and psychological facts are found later in Külpe* and Titchener*. Avenarius denied there was any difference between inner and outer experience and substituted for them pure experience as the single fact of experience. Lenin*, who opted for naive realism, criticized empiriocriticism, holding that the objective world exists independently of any experiencing entities and is the basis of all knowledge.

Biographies: F. Carstanjen, *Mind*, 1897, *6*, 449-475; J. Kodis, *Psychol. Rev.*, 1896, *3*, 603-610; *ADB*, 46; *EB*, 2; *NDB*, 1.

AVERROËS (ABU-AL-WALID MOHAMMED IBN AHMAD IBN MOHAMMED IBN RUSHD)
Arab Philosopher and Physician
Born: Córdoba, Spain, 1126
Died: Marrakesh, Morocco, 1198
Education: Studied law and medicine
Positions: 1169-71, judge in Seville, Spain; 1171-82, judge in Córdoba; 1182-84, chief physician to Abu Yaquub Yusuf; 1195-98, in exile in Lucena, Spain

Averroës, the most prominent philosopher of Arabic Spain, was an Aristotelean and Neoplatonist. Most of his work consists of commentaries on Aristotle*. These commentaries were translated into Latin in the first half of the thirteenth century and eventually gave rise to the philosophical school in Western Europe known as averroism.

Averroës's interpretation of Aristotle led the averroists to stress the superiority of reason and philosophy over faith and knowledge based on faith. They also found in Averroës justification for asserting that there was, in each person, an eternal and universal intellect, but only during the person's lifetime. Following Averroës's materialistic interpretation of Aristotle, they denied that the soul was immortal. Averroës's own position was that there is a human or material intellect and an acquired intellect, the former eternal and in no way part of the individual soul, yet one shared by all humanity. As it grasps the material to be cognized, the latter becomes acquired intellect. Although people differ in intelligence and in what they know, there is always the same amount of intellectual knowledge in the world.

Averroës's theory of the intellect influenced Latin medieval thought on the subject. His anatomical studies led him to the conclusion that it is the retina and not the lens, as was previously surmised, that was sensitive to light. This recognition was not, however, immediately accepted by others who studied optics.
Biographies: R. de Mendizábal Allende, *Averroes, un andaluz para Europa*, 1971; L. Gauthier, *Ibn Rochd (Averroès)*, 1948; E. Renan, *Averroès et l'averroïsme*, 1852 (Reprinted 1949); G. Sarton, *Introduction to the History of Science*, vol. 2, pt. 1, 1931; K. Werner, *Der Averroismus in der christlich-peripatischen Psychologie des späteren Altertums*, 1964; *DSB*, 12; *EB*, 2.

AVICENNA (ABN'-ALI AL-HASAYN IBN 'ABD ALLAH IBN SINA)
Persian Philosopher and Physician
Born: Near Bukhara, Turkistan, 980
Died: Hamadan, Persia, 1037
Education: Studied medicine
Positions: Ca. 996-1000, physician at Bukhara; ca. 1020, jurist at Korkanj, teacher of science at Gorgan, administrator at Rayy and Hamadan; 1023-37, vizier in Shamsal-Dawla, in service of ruler of Isfahan

Of the twenty-two books of Avicenna's best-known philosophical work, *Ash-Shifa* (*Sufficientia*, in Latin version), eight deal with the natural sciences, including psychology. The logic, psychology, and physics portions of the work were translated into Latin in the twelfth century. His most famous medical work, *Al-Quanun fi'l-Tibb*, became very popular in Arabic and, translated into Latin, was reprinted fifteen times before 1500. Avicenna also wrote a commentary on Aristotle's* *De Anima*.

Like other Arab philosophers of Aristotelean bent, Avicenna was also a Neoplatonist. According to Avicenna, the origin of intellect is God. There is a hierarchical order of intelligences, the tenth and last one being the "active intellect," which gives rise to the soul. The soul's essence possesses the powers of intelligence, sensation, and vegetation. Avicenna's treatment of the possible intellect, the agent intellect, and the various powers of the soul follows in essence Aristotle. He did, however, elaborate on the Aristotelean classification of the faculties of the psyche, increasing their number and systematizing them. Unlike

Aristotle, Avicenna placed the agent intellect outside the human soul, considering it a divine light that illuminates the soul and produces knowledge.

Biographies: S. M. Afnan, *Avicenna: His Life and Works*, 1958; W. F. Gohlman, *The Life of Ibn Sina*, 1974; F. Rahman, *Avicenna's Psychology*, 1952; *DSB*, 15; *EB*, 2.

B

BABINSKI, JOSEPH FRANÇOIS FELIX

French Neurologist
Born: Paris, November 17, 1857
Died: Paris, October 29, 1932
Highest Degree: M.D., University of Paris, 1885
Positions: 1890-1927, director, Hôpital de la Pitié, Paris

Babinski described various pathological reflexes occurring in disorders of the central nervous system. By far the best known among them is the Babinski reflex (the upward flexion of the big toe and the fanning of the rest when the sole of the foot is stimulated). It is found normally in young infants. If present in older individuals it signifies a lesion in the pyramidal nerve tract (upper motor neuron disorder or spastic paralysis) and is thus valuable as a diagnostic sign.

Babinski distinguished between organic and hysteric *hemiplegia* (paralysis of one-half of the body), limiting the latter to cases that could be produced or abolished by suggestion. Babinski's other work is of lesser importance to psychology. It includes the founding of the French neurological society, the Societé de Neurologie, in 1907.

Biographies: J. F. Fulton, *Arch. Neurol. Psychiat.*, 1933, *29*, 169-174; J. F. Fulton, *J. Hist. Med.*, 1958, *13*, 544-546; J. F. Fulton, *J. Nerv. Ment. Dis.*, 1933, *77*, 121-131; A. Guillain, *J. Babinski*, 1932; H. Miller, *Proc. Roy. Soc. Med.*, 1967, *60*, 399-405; J. H. Talbot, *A Biographical History of Medicine*, 1970; A. Tournay, *La vie de Joseph Babinski*, 1967; R. Wartenberg, *J. Amer. Med. Ass.*, 1967, *17*, 441-445.

BACON, FRANCIS
English Philosopher
Born: London, January 22, 1561
Died: London, April 9, 1626
Education: Admitted as outer barrister at Gray's Inn, Cambridge, England, 1582
Positions: In various capacities in the royal service, including that of lord chancellor

In science Bacon stood on the threshold between the Middle Ages and the birth of modern science in the seventeenth century. The grand purpose of Bacon's writings was to restore the knowledge of and power over nature that humanity originally had possessed. Science was to be founded again, but it was to be a new science, and the means whereby its body of knowledge would be acquired was to be new as well. Bacon analyzed the obstacles (the four idols or preconceptions) that prevented the appearance of a science that would yield tangible benefits and power over nature. He described the features of a natural philosophy that was based on the mind's capacity to remember, imagine, and reason and whose aim was to discover the forms of nature, or the permanent causes beyond observable phenomena. The Baconian method for uncovering forms of nature was to prepare exhaustive, comparative listings or tables of apparently unrelated concrete instances and, by stripping away all inessential characteristics, to arrive eventually at the one common underlying form or cause of the phenomenon studied. Basically inductive, Bacon's method differed fundamentally from the deductive method of the schoolmen, who disdained empiricism. Bacon endorsed the experimental method without qualification. Bacon's empiricism provided the basis for John Locke's* psychological theorizing. The spirit of Bacon's *Novuum organum* (1620), his major work, pervades Locke's *Essay Concerning Human Understanding*, and the postulate that the contents of the mind are sensations and reflections and nothing else is present in the first aphorism of Bacon's book. Bacon was thus a forerunner of the psychological speculations of the philosophers in the British school of empiricism and the formulator of some of the fundamental tenets of modern science, including psychology.
Biographies: E. A. Abbott, *Francis Bacon: An Account of His Life and Work*, 1885; F. H. Anderson, *Francis Bacon: His Career and His Thought*, 1962; B. Bevan, *The Real Francis Bacon*, 1960; C. D. Bowen, *Francis Bacon: The Temper of a Man*, 1963; J. G. Crowther, *Francis Bacon: The First Statesman of Science*, 1960; B. Farrington, *Francis Bacon: Philosopher of Industrial Science*, 1949; K. Fischer, *Francis Bacon of Verulam: Realistic Philosophy and Its Age*, 1957; A. W. Green, *Sir Francis Bacon: His Life and Works*, 1948; J. Spedding, *An Account of the Life and Times of Lord Bacon*, 1911; F. Steegmuller, *Sir Francis Bacon: The First Modern Mind*, 1930; *CE*, 2; *DNB*, 1; *DSB*, 1; *EB*, 2; *EP*, 1; *IESS*, 1.

BACON, ROGER
English Philosopher
Born: Either at Ilchester, Somerset, or Bisley, Gloucester, ca. 1214

Died: Oxford, ca. 1292
Education: Master of Arts, University of Paris, 1241 or later
Positions: 1241(?)-46, University of Paris; 1247-57, University of Oxford; 1257, became a Franciscan friar

Like his contemporary, Albertus Magnus*, Bacon sought his knowledge in Aristotle*, but he was also one of the first scholars to question Aristotle's authority. Bacon observed, reasoned, and also experimented. His significance lies in his attitude that experimentation is an important part in obtaining knowledge. Bacon was critical of blind reliance on authority, recommending that manuscripts be read in the original language for reliability. Not only was Bacon one of the originators of critical scholarship, but he introduced the term *experimental science* as well. He preferred knowledge based on observation and measurement. In his *Opus majus* (1268) he made a proposal for a univ. rsal encyclopedia of knowledge, intending to penetrate the secrets of nature through positive research and using the experimental method of observation.

Bacon's empiricism, however, did not preclude his believing in magic and identifying philosophy with astrology and mathematics. He declared mathematics to be the basis of all human knowledge, asserting, however, that the noblest branch of mathematics was astrology, the latter to be used in medicine, alchemy, and divination. At any rate, science and knowledge, including astrology and alchemy, were to be used to further the aims of the church. Since Bacon did not distinguish between science and pseudoscience, he could, while endorsing astrology and alchemy, also endorse scientific experimentation and fantasize about the possibility of self-propelled ships and carriages, aircraft, submarines, and other modern-sounding technical advances, all to be achieved without the use of magic. Bacon's endorsement of pseudosciences, combined with his insubordination to authorities, led to a ten-year imprisonment. He died in complete obscurity.

Biographies: A. C. Crombie, *Robert Grosseteste and the Origins of Experimental Science, 1100-1700*, 1953; T. Crowley, *Roger Bacon: The Problem of the Soul in His Philosophical Commentaries*, 1950; S. C. Easton, *Roger Bacon and His Search for Universal Science*, 1952; A. G. Little (Ed.), *Roger Bacon Essays*, 1914; L. Thorndike, *A History of Magic and Experimental Science*, vol. 2, 1929; *DSB*, 1; *EB*, 2.

BAIN, ALEXANDER
Scottish Psychologist
Born: Aberdeen, June 11, 1818
Died: Aberdeen, September 18, 1903
Highest Degree: B.A. in philosophy, Marischal College, 1840
Positions: 1840-60, freelance in London and Scotland; 1860-80, University of Aberdeen; 1880-87, lord rector, University of Aberdeen

Since Bain's life covered most of the nineteenth century, he belonged to both the outgoing school of British associationism and the new German scientific psychology. Although much of the two of his most important texts written in the 1850s were in the Scottish tradition of moral philosophy, they, for the first time, established a solid connection between psychology and actual physiological fact. Bain considered Charles Darwin* important and followed him in his own work on emotional expression in humans and animals, but he did not accept the evolutionary theory entirely. Concerning association, Bain embraced a modified form of John Stuart Mill's* "mental chemistry" and took the principle of contiguity to be the primary and similarity, the secondary principle. To the Aristotelean five senses he added the organic sense; there is an emphasis on the importance of movement, including reflexive movement. In regard to the body-mind problem, Bain was a psychophysical parallelist.

Bain wrote two texts that remained standard for the next fifty years because of their thoroughness of coverage. *The Senses and the Intellect* (1855) and *The Emotions and the Will* (1859) were his major work, two large, systematic psychological texts that saw repeated editions. Bain also wrote *On the Study of Character* (1861), *Manual of Mental and Moral Science* (1869), and *Mind and Body* (1872). In 1876 he founded the first philosophical psychology journal, *Mind*, which is still being published.

Biographies: A. Bain, *Autobiography*, 1904; *CE*, 2; *DNB*, Suppl. 2, 1; *DSB*, 1; *EP*, 1; *IESS*, 1; *NYT*, 1903, Sept. 19, 7:6.

BAIRD, JOHN WALLACE
Canadian-American Psychologist
Born: Motherwell, Ontario, May 21, 1869
Died: Baltimore, Maryland, February 2, 1919
Highest Degree: Ph.D. in psychology, Cornell University, 1902, under E. B. Titchener*
Positions, Honors: 1903, Cornell University; 1904-6, Johns Hopkins University; 1906-10, University of Illinois; 1910-19, Clark University; editorial work for several psychological journals; president, American Psychological Association, 1918

Baird achieved recognition in psychology for a number of experimental investigations, the most notable of which was a thorough study, reported in 1903, of the role of accommodation and convergence in the perception of distance. Baird concluded that convergence was the more important clue in three-dimensional space perception.

Biographies: *Amer. J. Psychol.*, 1919, *30*, 120; K. M. Dallenbach, *Publ. Clark Univ. Libr.*, 1919, *6*(2), 33-35; E. B. Titchener, *Science*, 1919, *49*, 393-394; *NCAB*, 22.

BALDWIN, JAMES MARK
American Psychologist
Born: Columbia, South Carolina, January 12, 1861
Died: Paris, France, November 8, 1934

Highest Degree: Ph.D. in philosophy, Princeton University, 1889
Positions: 1887-90, Lake Forest College; 1890-93, University of Toronto; 1893-1903, Princeton University; 1903-9, Johns Hopkins University; 1909-13, National University, Mexico City; 1931-18, École des Hautes Études Sociales, Paris; president, American Psychological Association, 1897; honorary D.Sc., Oxford University, 1900; president, International Congress of Psychology, 1909-13

Baldwin was a writer and speculative theorist. His contributions were in the areas of textbook writing, popularization of the evolutionary theory, developmental psychology, and psychological publications. His book *The Story of the Mind* (1889) appeared in many editions. He also wrote *Senses and Intellect* (1889), *Handbook of Psychology* (1890), *Feeling and Will* (1891), and *History of Psychology* (1913). Because of their happy style, the books were well received. They emphasized the importance of the evolutionary theory to the human sciences. A theory put forth by Baldwin in this connection was that the individual is constantly learning to change his heredity through his own efforts. Baldwin applied the evolutionary concept in pioneering in the study of child development in the United States. Although his developmental writings were largely theoretical, he, along with G. Stanley Hall* broke ground in this area. His developmental psychology texts include *Mental Development in the Child and the Race* (1895), *Social and Ethical Interpretations in Mental Development* (1897), and *Thought and Things or Genetic Logic* (3 vols., 1906, 1911).

With Hall, Baldwin was a cofounder of the American Psychological Association. Although he did very little experimental work himself, he did found psychological laboratories in Toronto in 1889 and Princeton in 1893, and he reestablished Hall's laboratory at Johns Hopkins. Baldwin founded the *Psychological Review* (1894), *Psychological Bulletin* (1904), *Psychological Index*, and *Psychological Monographs*. Among his editorial efforts is the publication of the four-volume *Dictionary of Philosophy and Psychology* (1901-2), to which more than sixty philosophers and psychologists contributed. Baldwin's influence on American psychology lasted only about twenty years, however, approximately between 1889 and 1909, when Baldwin left the United States.

Biographies: J. M. Baldwin, *Between Two Wars*, 1926; E. A. Chavez, *3 conferencias; la vida y la obra de 3 profesores ilustres de la Universidad nacional de México*, 1937; J. Jastrow, *Science*, 1934, *80*, 497-498; J. R. Kantor, *Psychol. Bull.*, 1935, *32*, 1-3; *Nature*, 1934, *134*, 840-841; W. M. Urban, *Psychol Rev.*, 1935, *42*, 303-306; M. R. Washburn, *Amer. J. Psychol.*, 1935, *47*, 168-169; *DAB*, 21; *HPA*, 1; *IESS*, 1; *NCAB*, 25; *NYT*, 1934, Nov. 9, 21:3.

BARTLETT, SIR FREDERICK CHARLES

English Psychologist
Born: Stow-on-the Wold, Gloucestershire, October 20, 1886
Died: Cambridge, September 30, 1969

Highest Degree: M.A. in moral sciences, University of Cambridge; mentors in psychology: W. H. R. Rivers* and C. S. Myers*
Positions, Honors: 1922-52, reader in experimental psychology, director of psychology laboratory, first professor of experimental psychology, Cambridge University; honorary doctorates from seven universities; editor, *British Journal of Psychology*, 1924-48; knighted, 1948

By heading one of the few British graduate programs in psychology for many years and by editing for twenty-four years the most significant British journal of psychology, Bartlett influenced the course of British psychology as an administrator and an educator. In his personal research Bartlett is best known for his studies of memory and social psychology. His most significant and influential work is *Remembering* (1932), which examines the influence of social factors on memory in an experimental setting. Instead of the traditional nonsense syllables, Bartlett used meaningful materials to study the effects of past experience on the assimilation of materials. He showed how individuals instead of merely reproducing the materials reworked them in the light of their past experience. The notion of schema or a conceptual model originated with Bartlett. Although the schema is constantly changing, every new experience is absorbed by way of this preexisting model. Although others found the schema idea fruitful, Bartlett seldom referred to it in his later writings. His book marked a break with the German tradition in psychology and the advent of methods to study higher thought processes without the use of introspection. Other books written by Bartlett were *Psychology and Primitive Culture* (1923, with C. S. Myers), *Textbook of Experimental Psychology* (1925), *Psychology and the Soldier* (1927), *Political Propaganda* (1941), *The Mind at Work and Play* (1951), and *Thinking: An Experimental and Social Study* (1958).
Biographies: D. E. Broadbent, *Biog. Mem. Fellows Royal Soc.* (B), 1970, 16; D. E. Broadbent, *Bull. Brit. Psychol. Soc.*, 1970, *23*, 1-3; R. B. Buzzard, *Occup. Psychol.*, 1971, *45*, 1-11; R. C. Oldfield, *Amer. J. Psychol.*, 1972, *85*, 133-140; O. L. Zangwill, *Quart. J. Exp. Psychol.*, 1970, *22*, 77-81; *HPA*, 3; *IESS*, 2.

BEAUNIS, HENRI-ÉTIENNE

French Physiologist
Born: Amboise, Indre et Loire, 1830
Died: Le Cannet, Alpes Maritimes, July 11, 1921
Highest Degree: M.D., place and date unknown
Positions: Dates unknown, University of Strasbourg; 1861-80, army surgeon; 1880-89, University of Nancy; 1889-94, Sorbonne University (University of Paris)

Beaunis was the cofounder, with Alfred Binet*, of the first French psychological laboratory, at the University of Paris, in 1889. He was also its first director. In 1895 he participated in founding, with Binet and Henri*, the French psychological journal *L'Année psychologique* and was a cofounder of the Societé

de Psychologie Physiologique. Beaunis wrote several medical books. His psychological research was mostly on hypnotism and the psychology of dreams. Concerning hypnotism, he supported the view of the Nancy school (*Le somnambulisme provoqué*, 1886). He also wrote *De l'habitude en général* (1856), *Les sensations internes* (1889), and *Travaux de laboratoire de psychologie physiologique de la Sorbonne* (1892-93). The drawing of a stack of cubes that can be seen in reversed perspective is called "Beaunis's cubes."
Biographies: F. L. Bertrand, *Alfred Binet et son oeuvre*, 1930; E. Claparède, In various, *Centenaire de Th. Ribot et Jubilé de la Psychologie Scientifique Française*, 1939; *DBF*, 5; H. Dürr, *Z. Psychol.*, 1906, *40*, 318-319; *EUI*, 7.

BEEBE-CENTER, JOHN GILBERT
American Psychologist
Born: Boston, Massachusetts, March 19, 1897
Died: Cambridge, Massachusetts, December 6, 1958
Highest Degree: Ph.D. in psychology, Harvard University, 1926
Positions: 1923-58, Harvard University

Beebe-Center began his career in psychology by writing a brilliant thesis about affective equilibrium, one of the first investigations in the area that was later known by the name of "adaptation level." He developed the topic in his 1932 book, *The Psychology of Pleasantness and Unpleasantness*, his major work. Beebe-Center spent the last years of his life in the study of taste, to which he was led by his study of the feeling value of odors. His researches on threshold determination and scaling of taste led to the development of a psychological scale of taste, with gust as the unit.
Biographies: E. G. Boring, *Amer. J. Psychol.*, 1959, *72*, 311-315.

BEERS, CLIFFORD WHITTINGHAM
American Layman
Born: New Haven, Connecticut, March 30, 1876
Died: Providence, Rhode Island, July 9, 1943
Education: Ph.B., Yale University, 1897
Honors: Cross of Chevalier, French Legion of Honor, 1932; Gold Medal of the National Institute of Social Sciences, 1933; presented with a collection of tributes, published as *Twenty-five Years After: Sidelights on the Mental Hygiene Movement and Its Founder* (1934), 1933

Beers was the founder of the mental hygiene movement. In a famous book, *A Mind That Found Itself* (1908), Beers described his mental breakdown and the poor and inhumane treatment he received in three Connecticut mental institutions during a period of three years. The book aroused interest and elicited help from the public and civic and scientific leaders, such as William James* and Adolf Meyer*. The latter suggested the term *mental hygiene* to describe the movement to educate the public in the area of mental disorders. The first Society for Mental Hygiene was organized by Beers in Connecticut in 1908 and the

National Commission for Mental Hygiene in 1909. Beers became the leader of the mental health movement, which eventually achieved worldwide proportions when the First International Congress of Mental Hygiene was convened by Beers in 1930 and the International Committee for Mental Hygiene was founded by him. The mental hygiene movement has played an important part in the development of psychiatry, children's clinics, and other measures of prevention and diagnosis of mental disorders. The widespread interest and concern that Beers's generated for it is attested by the twenty-six printings that Beers's autobiography had seen by the time of his death.

Biographies: C. W. Beers, *A Mind That Found Itself*, 1908; W. L. Cross (Ed.), *Twenty-Five Years After: Sidelights on the Mental Hygiene Movement and Its Founder*, 1934; A. Deutsch, In J. K. Hall *et al.* (Eds.), *One Hundred Years of American Psychiatry*, 1944; R. M. Frumkin, *Public Welfare in Ohio Today*, 1952, 4(2), 14-16; R. McKown, *Pioneers in Mental Health*, 1961; A. Ruggles, *Amer. J. Psychiat.*, 1944, *100*, 98-99; C. E. A. Winslow, *Ment. Hyg.*, 1944, *28*, 179-185; E. E. Winters, *Bull. Hist. Med.*, 1969, *43*, 414-443; *NCAB*, 34, E; *NYT*, 1943, July 10, 13:1.

BÉKÉSY, GEORGE VON

Hungarian-American Physicist

Born: Budapest, Hungary, June 3, 1899
Died: Honolulu, Hawaii, June 13, 1972
Highest Degree: Ph.D. in physics, University of Budapest, 1923
Positions, Honors: 1923-46, acoustics researcher, Hungarian Telephone System laboratories; 1932-46, faculty, University of Budapest; 1946, Karolinska Institute, Stockholm, Sweden; 1947-66, senior research fellow in psychophysics, Harvard University; 1966-72, professor of sensory sciences, University of Hawaii; honorary M.D., University of Berne (1959), Wilhelm University, Münster, Germany (1955), University of Padua (1962); honorary D.Sc., University of Pennsylvania, 1965; ten scientific medals; Nobel Prize in medicine and physiology, 1961

Békésy spent his life studying the physics of sensory perception, especially that of hearing. He invented the tracking method of continuous recording of a subject's hearing as the subject controls the intensity of a tone around the threshold value. By this method a complete audiogram may be obtained in less than half an hour.

Békésy's major achievement was the observation of the actual operation of the basilar membrane of the cochlea as the ear was being stimulated by sounds of different frequencies. Using a microscope and a strobe light, he saw that a sound sets up a traveling wave in the basilar membrane, whose shape varies with the frequency, intensity, and complexity of the sound. High frequencies produce maximum displacement of the basilar membrane near the oval window, and low frequencies do so near the apex of the membrane. Békésy assumed that pitch is related to maximum displacement in the basilar membrane produced by the traveling wave. He constructed a model of the cochlea and, assuming evolutionary similarity between the basilar membrane and the skin, stimulated the forearms of his subjects with this model, demonstrating very exact localization of the maximum stimulation produced by the piston-and-cylinder model in the subject's skin. Békésy's findings replaced the theory of hearing of Helmholtz*, who thought that the cells of the basilar membrane resonated to sound frequencies according to their length.

Békésy wrote a chapter about the mechanical properties of the ear for Stevens's* *Handbook of Experimental Psychology* (1951). In 1960 he presented his theory of neural quantum in the discrimination of loudness and pitch in his *Experiments in Hearing*. His second book, *Sensory Inhibition*, appeared in 1967. It reviews all of Békésy's work and describes the operation of the haptic senses, vision, audition, taste, and smell in terms of lateral inhibition, which Békésy believed to be a common feature of all sense organs. Between 1928 and 1967 he published 121 papers, most of them about hearing, specifically the cochlear mechanics, and also some on taste and skin sensations.

Biographies: E. B. Newman, *Amer. J. Psychol.*, 1973, *86*, 855-857; *NYT*, 1972, June 15, 44:4.

BEKHTEREV, VLADIMIR MIKHAILOVICH
Russian Psychiatrist and Neuropathologist
Born: Sorali, Vyatka, January 20, 1857
Died: Moscow, December 24, 1927
Highest Degree: M.D., Medical and Surgical Academy, St. Petersburg, 1881
Positions: 1885-94, University of Kazan; 1894-1913, Military Medical Academy, St. Petersburg; 1913-18, Psychoneurological Institute, St. Petersburg; 1918-27, Brain Research Institute, Petrograd (Leningrad)

Bekhterev contributed to the areas of neurophysiology, neuropathology, and the objective study of psychological phenomena. He had studied the brain since 1883, demonstrating the control of vegetative functions by the thalamic regions and the existence of nerve centers that control the sympathetic nervous system. He spent the year 1884 abroad, studying with famous individuals such as Charcot*, Flechsig*, and Wundt*. Bekhterev also studied the reticular formation, cerebellum, and skin muscle centers and demonstrated the existence of antagonistic nerve centers in the brain in 1895. Several brain structures are named in his honor.

Bekhterev published more than five hundred papers and books on neurology and psychiatry, some one hundred fifty of which are clinical publications. Significant among them are [*The Nerve Currents in Brain and Spinal Cord*] (1893), [*Fundamentals of Brain Functioning*] (1903-7), [*The Functions of the Nervous Centers*] (1909), and [*General Diagnosis of the Diseases of the Nervous System*] (1911-15).

Bekhterev founded the first psychological laboratories in Russia, one at the University of Kazan in 1886 and another at St. Petersburg in 1895. He also founded the Psychoneurological Institute in St. Petersburg in 1903 and two journals, *Neurologicheskiǐ vestnik* and *Obzor psikhiatrii, nevropatologii i eksperimental'noǐ psikhologii*. The latter was the first journal ever to have the words *experimental psychology* in its title.

Bekhterev's psychology was strictly objective and based on the concept of reflex. In contrast to Pavlov*, Bekhterev worked with both animals and humans. He used conditioned associative motor responses with humans in the belief that the salivary response was less objective than motor responses. Bekhterev first designated his view of psychology as objective psychology (*Ob'ektivnaya psikhologiya*, 1910; German and French translations, 1913) and then coined the term *reflexology* (*Obshchie osnovy refleksologii cheloveka*, 1917; English translation, *General Principles of Human Reflexology*, 1932). Bekhterev argued against the use of introspection and mentalistic terms and for an objective approach to psychological phenomena. He denied the reality of psychic processes as well as the need for psychology as an independent science, because all psychic processes were to be considered complexes of "associative reflexes," as he called the conditioned reflexes. Bekhterev also extended his conceptualization of psychology of the single individual to societal groups in [*Collective Reflexology*] (1921). *Biographies*: D. T. Azbukin, *Vop. Defektolog.*, 1928, No. 2, 3-6; N. I. Grashchenkov, [*The Role of V. M. Bekhterev in the Development of Russian Neurology*], 1959; N. I. Kasatkin, *Zh. Vyssh. Nerv. Deyat.*, 1957, *7*, 148-156; V. M. Munipov, [*V. M. Bekhterev*], 1969; V. N. Myasishchev, [*The Prominent Russian Scientist V. M. Bekhterev*], 1953; V. P. Osipov, [*Bekhterev: Life and Works*], 1947; L. Pines, *Arch. Psychiat.*, 1928, *83*, 677-687; *DSB*, 1; *EB*, 1; *Great Soviet Encyclopedia*; *IESS*, 2.

BELL, CHARLES
Scottish Anatomist
Born: Edinburgh, November, 1774
Died: Hallow Park near Worcester, Worcestershire, England, April 28, 1842
Highest Degree: Medical degree, University of Edinburgh, 1799
Positions: 1804-12, private practitioner, lecturer; 1812-36, surgeon, Middlesex Hospital; 1836-42, chair of surgery, University of Edinburgh

Bell was one of the great physiologists of the early nineteenth century. He studied the nature of hearing and the comparative anatomy of the ear, identified the role of the small bones in the middle ear as well as that of the round window (1809). He also identified the papillae of the tongue as the taste organs and mapped the tongue for taste sensitivity. Bell was also the discoverer of the polarization of neurons, which was basic to the understanding of the concept of the reflex. The third volume of Bell's *Anatomy of the Human Body* (1803) deals with the nervous system and the sense organs.

Bell's greatest discovery, one of fundamental importance to neurophysiology, was that of the existence of two kinds of nerves, sensory and motor. The significance of this discovery to psychology was that it affirmed the possibility of an experimental approach to feelings and actions. Bell described his discovery in a privately published monograph (*Idea of a New Anatomy of the Brain*) in 1811. It was not very well known nor was its significance appreciated. François Magendie* stated the distinction independently later and supported it with clearly described experiments. The principle that motor and sensory impulses are carried by separate nerves, the former leaving the spinal cord through its ventral roots and the latter entering it through its dorsal roots, became known as the "Bell-Magendie law." In the 1811 monograph Bell also suggested the existence of further specialization among the nerves, namely, that the five senses are mediated by five kinds of nerves, but he failed to name this principle, and it remained for Johannes Müller* to elaborate it and state it as the law of specific nerve energies. In 1826 Bell added to the five a sixth sense, the muscle sense.

Biographies: E. Bramwell, *Edinb. Med. J.*, 1935, *42*, 252-264; L. Carmichael, *Psychol. Rev.*, 1926, *33*, 188-217; V. Christiansen, [*Charles Bell*], 1922; G. Gordon-Taylor & E. W. Walls, *Sir Charles Bell: His Life and Times*, 1958; J. McNeill, *Trans. Roy. Soc. Edinb.*, 1844, *15*, 397-408; H. Paskind, *Bull. Soc. Med. Hist.*, 1937, *5*, 34-43; A. Pichot, *The Life and Labours of Sir Charles Bell*, 1858; A. Shaw, *A Narrative of the Discoveries of Sir Charles Bell in the Nervous System*, 1839; B. Spector, *Bull. Hist. Med.*, 1942, *12*, 314-322; *DNB*, 2; *DSB*, 1; *IESS*, 2.

BENEDICT, RUTH FULTON
American Anthropologist
Born: New York, New York, June 5, 1887
Died: New York, New York, September 17, 1948
Highest Degree: Ph.D. in anthropology, Columbia University, 1923, under Franz Boas*
Positions, Honors: 1922-48, Columbia University; president, American Anthropological Association, 1947; honorary D.Sc.

   Benedict played a significant role in the development of an interdisciplinary approach to human behavior. The part of her work that is important to psychology is her theoretical writings on the relationship between personality and cultural forms, including the phenomena of deviancy and creativity. *Patterns of Culture* (1934), her best-known work, has seen many editions and translations into other languages. Its theme, culture and personality, is treated in an analysis of three cultures, each dominated by a single motive. Here Benedict applies to groups the concepts reserved for the individual (group psychology): each culture selects a certain human characteristic and develops it to an extent impossible for a single individual. It will also tolerate the expression of certain traits and behaviors only. Deviations from them are labeled "abnormalities."

Biographies: V. Barnouw, *Univ. Toronto Quart.*, 1949, *18*, 241-253; R. Benedict, *An Anthropologist at Work: Writings of Ruth Benedict*, 1959; R. McHenry (Ed.), *Famous American Women*, 1983; M. Mead, *Amer. Anthropologist*, 1949, *51*, 456-468; A. I. Richards, *Nature*, 1948, *162*, 725; H. S. Sullivan, *Psychiatry*,

1948, *11*, 402-403; Wenner-Green Foundation for Anthropological Research, New York, *Ruth Fulton Benedict: A Memorial*, 1949; *IESS*, 2; *NCAB*, 36; *NYT*, 1948, Sept. 18, 17:1.

BENEKE, FRIEDRICH EDUARD
German Philosopher
Born: Berlin, February 17, 1798
Died: Berlin, between March (when he disappeared) and June (when he was found dead) 1854
Education: Studied theology at the University of Berlin and the University of Halle
Positions: 1824-27, University of Göttingen; 1832-54, University of Berlin

At a time when philosophical transcendentalism predominated, Beneke sought to offer an alternative view in the interpretation of psychological phenomena. He rejected the concept of innate ideas as well as that of mental faculties; neither did he accept the view that mental life is the result of associated mental experiences. In his book *Lehrbuch der Psychologie als Naturwissenschaft* (1832), Beneke offered the view that the infant possesses the capacity for many activities, or part functions, that are as yet undeveloped but that develop into the adult's complex activities with age. This view was in marked contrast to Kant's* nativism. Beneke's doctrine of traces states, although not in physiological terms, that an idea, upon its disappearance from the mind, leaves a trace. The later retrieval or revival of this trace constitutes memory. Beneke used the same analytic approach to dismantle other "faculties." This may be considered his most significant contribution to psychology.

Beneke theorized that philosophy is based on empirical knowledge and suggested that psychology should be restructured from the ground up and placed on a scientific basis. As an empirical science psychology would be propadeutic to all other sciences. In *Die neue Psychologie* (1845) and elsewhere Beneke suggested, again in a radical departure from Kant, that experimentation be used in psychology and described various experiments on memory, perception, and feeling that could be performed. In this Beneke was setting the direction that psychology was to follow shortly in its development as a scientific discipline.

Other psychological texts of Beneke's are *Erfahrungsseelenlehre als Grundlage allen Wissens* (1820), *Psychologische Skizzen* (1825-27), *Pragmatische Psychologie* (1850), and *Lehrbuch der pragmatischen Psychologie* (1853).
Biographies: F. B. Brandt, *Fr. Ed. Beneke: The Man and His Philosophy*, 1895; J. G. Dressler, *Beneke: Oder die Seelenlehre als Naturwissenschaft*, 1840-46; O. Gramzow, *Friedrich Eduard Benekes Leben und Philosophie*, 1899; *EP*, 1; *NDB*, 2.

BENTHAM, JEREMY
English Philosopher
Born: London, February 15, 1748

Died: London, June 6, 1832
Education: Law degree, Oxford University, 1763
Positions: No official positions

Although Bentham was influenced by Helvétius* and Hume*, his writings often sound like those of Hartley*. Bentham promulgated the doctrine of ethical hedonism, which in terms of his "greatest happiness principle" states that the ethical goal is the greatest happiness for the greatest numbers. This later became the underlying principle of philosophical utilitarianism. Bentham also believed that every individual acts to increase his own happiness and to minimize pain (*psychological hedonism*). Several "sanctions" or reasons were postulated by Bentham to reconcile ethical and psychological hedonism. The law acts by manipulating these sanctions—by rewarding and punishing the citizens. Bentham and his disciples' endeavors were directed toward showing that the interests of the individual and society could be made to coincide. Under the influence of Bentham reforms were instituted and legal codes drawn up and adopted by various countries. After his death his work was carried on but on a more literary level. Among the psychologically oriented philosophical utilitarians who were influenced by Bentham were James Mill*, John Stuart Mill*, Alexander Bain*, and Herbert Spencer*.

Biographies: C. M. Atkinson, *Jeremy Bentham: His Life and Work*, 2nd ed., 1909 (Reprinted 1969); G. Geis, *J. Crim. Law Criminol.*, 1955, *46*, 159-171; M. P. Mack, *Jeremy Bentham: An Odyssey of Ideas*, 1962; D. J. Manning, *The Mind of Jeremy Bentham*, 1968; P. McReynolds, *J. Hist. Behav. Sci.*, 1968, *4*, 230-244, 349-364; C. K. Ogden, *Jeremy Bentham*, 1932; L. Stephen, *The English Utilitarians*, 1950; G. Wallas, *Pol. Sci. Quart.*, 1923, *38*, 45-56; *CE*, 2; *DNB*, 2; *EB*, 3; *EP*, l; *IESS*, 2.

BENTLEY, (ISAAC) MADISON

American Psychologist
Born: Clinton, Iowa, June 18, 1870
Died: Palo Alto, California, May 29, 1955
Highest Degree: Ph.D. in psychology, Cornell University, 1899, under E. B. Titchener*
Positions, Honors: 1899-1912, Cornell University; 1912-29, University of Illinois; 1929-38, Sage professor of psychology and head of Psychology Department, Cornell University; 1938-40, consulting psychologist, Library of Congress; 1930-31, chairman, Psychology Division, National Research Council; created Committee on Psychiatric Investigation, of which he was the chairman for several years; editorial work, *Psychological Index* (1916-25), *Journal of Experimental Psychology* (1926-29), *Journal of Comparative and Physiological Psychology* (1921-35); *American Journal of Psychology* (1930-50); president, American Psychological Association, 1925; honorary LL.D., University of Nebraska

Bentley's principal contribution to psychology was as a book reviewer: he had reviewed more than 250 books in his lifetime. In addition to this and his

editorial work, he was also a writer. He wrote 2 books (*The Field of Psychology*, 1924; *The New Field of Psychology*, 1934), 11 editorials, and 157 articles and notes. Among his more notable scientific contributions are studies of the memory image, which led psychologists eventually to give up images as mental elements; a study of wetness (1900), in which Bentley synthesized wetness by combining cold with a uniform pressure, and which has hence served as a paradigm for similar experiments; a study of learning in *Paramecium* (with L. M. Day), which caused a controversy of twenty years' duration over the interpretation of its results; and additional studies in general, experimental, abnormal, and racial psychology, including a series of 17 articles about illusions in a Chicago newspaper.
Biographies: K. M. Dallenbach, *Amer. J. Psychol.*, 1956, *69*, 169-186; *NCAB*, 45; *NYT*, 1955, May 30, 13:6.

BENUSSI, VITTORIO
Italian-Austrian Psychologist
Born: Trieste, Italy, January 17, 1878
Died: Padua, Italy, 1927
Highest Degree: Ph.D. in psychology, University of Graz, 1900, under A. Meinong*
Positions: 1902-14, University of Graz; 1914-20, University of Vienna; 1920-27, University of Padua

A member of the Austrian school of act psychology, Benussi was a productive and competent researcher who produced a number of studies on optical illusions, visually and tactually perceived movement, space perception, the perception of time (*Psychologie der Zeitauffassung*, 1913), and the perception of solidity. He also invented (1914) one of the first methods of lie detection, based on the ratio of inspiration to expiration length. Although Austria's best experimentalist, Benussi was concerned with systematic issues only marginally. His theory of perception must be gathered from statements made in the various experimental articles. Benussi, following Meinong, stressed the role of the productive process (*Produktionsvorgang*) in perception, the higher mental process that combines sensory elements into unitary wholes. With Ehrenfels* and Hans Cornelius, Benussi developed the theory and thus the Austrian school of form quality. Benussi was the chief worker in this school through the first decade of the twentieth century. In the second decade the school faded away as it was being replaced by the Gestalt school, which took over and reworked some of its tenets.
Biographies: C. L. Musatti, *Arch. ital. psicol.*, 1928, *6*, 259-273; C. L. Musatti, *Riv. psicol.*, 1928, *24*, 26-42; *PR*, 3.

BERGER, HANS
German Psychiatrist
Born: Neuses, near Coburg, Bavaria, May 21, 1873
Died: Bad Blankenburg, Thuringia, June 1, 1941
Highest Degree: M.D., University of Jena, 1897

Positions: 1901-41, University of Jena

Berger obtained a recording of the electrical activity of the brain in 1903, but it was not until 1924 that he attached electrodes to his young son's scalp and, using a vacuum tube amplifier and an optical galvanometer, was able to obtain a continuous record of the rhythmic electrical activity of the brain, the electro-encephalogram (EEG). Berger published his work in a 1929 article. He named the most pronounced rhythm, the ten-cycles-per-second wave, the alpha rhythm and related it to the restful but not sleepy state of the subject.

Although Berger had always believed that mental states would reflect in the physical activity of the nervous system (*Über die körperlichen Äusserungen psychischer Zustände*, 1904; *Trauma und Psychose*, 1915), his discovery came at a time when psychiatry was under the aegis of psychoanalysis, the organic viewpoint was in eclipse, and he was met by opposition and even ridicule. It was not until Adrian in England was able to duplicate Berger's results (in 1934) that the EEG came into general use. In addition to its medical uses, the EEG has been finding ever wider application in psychological research: thinking, problem solving, states of consciousness, emotion, perception, sleep and dreaming, and other areas. The change in orientation that occurred in psychiatry and neurophysiology after 1929 was to no small extent due to Berger's discovery.
Biographies: F. A. Gibbs, *Arch. Neurol. Psychiat.*, Sept. 1941, 514-516; *New England J. Med.*, 1941, *225*, 205; *DSB*, 2; *NYT*, 1941, June 10, 23:5.

BERGSON, HENRI
French Philosopher
Born: Paris, October 18, 1859
Died: Paris, January 4, 1941
Highest Degree: Doctorate in philosophy, École Normale Supérieure, Paris, 1881
Positions, Honors: 1898-1900, École Normale Supérieure; 1900-1914, Collège de France; Nobel Prize in literature, 1928

Bergson's philosophical views, or "bergsonism" (*L'Évolution créatrice*, 1907; *Les deux sources de la morale et de la religion*, 1932), had a considerable influence on European thought before World War I. Bergson led a movement against evolutionary theory, arguing that the complexities of organic life could not have resulted from random processes and that creative evolution was necessary. In psychology Bergson opposed both associationism and Wundtian (Wundt*) structuralism to the point of denying the possibility of a scientifically based psychology. In this he was voicing a position similar to that of Dilthey* and Nietzsche* but without advocating phenomenology. Bergson opposed associationism because he believed that the associationists proceeded in a manner opposite to that dictated by the nature of mental processes. He stated that the components of inner experience cannot be treated like discrete things and the self as if it were a composite of such things. Inner experience and the outside world of facts are incommensurable, and inner experience cannot be described using the usual methods of acquisition of knowledge. Human intelligence, however, is directed toward external things. Its domain is the external world, which it seeks to manipulate and change. Intelligence can analyze it and synthesize it again, but it is inadequate to comprehend the inner world of experience. The mechanism whereby the stream of consciousness is apprehended Bergson called "intuition," which he contrasted with intelligence and stated it to be a totally different phenomenon. What in animals is called "instinct" is intuition in humans. It permits human beings to "live" their inner reality instead of just realizing, imagining, or otherwise representing it cognitively. The experience of time is made central in Bergson's philosophy. Using time as a vehicle for stating his case, Bergson presented his psychological views in, among other works, his *Essai sur les données immediates de la conscience* (1889; translated as *Time and Free Will*, 1910).

Because Bergson's notions could not be tested empirically, his influence on scientific psychology in America has been negligible. His ideas may be found, however, in the various "third force," or humanistic, psychologies.

Biographies: F. R. Challaye, *Henri Bergson*, 1929; J. Chevalier, *Henri Bergson*, 1928; A. Cresson, *Henri Bergson: Sa vie et son oeuvre*, 1941; V. Jankelevitch, *Henri Bergson*, 1931; H. M. Kallen, *William James and Henri Bergson*, 1914; H. H. Price, *Proc. Soc. Psychical Res.*, 1941, *46*, 271-276; A. Ruhe & N. M. Paul, *Henri Bergson: An Account of His Life and Philosophy*, 1914; *CE*, 2; *DSB*, 2; *EB*, 3; *EJ*, 4; *EP*, 1; *Jewish*, 2; *NYT*, 1941, Jan. 6, 15:1.

BERITASHVILI (BERITOV), IVAN SOLOMONOVICH
Georgian Physiologist
Born: Vedzhini, near Kakhati, Georgia, December 29, 1884
Died: Tblisi, Georgia, December 29, 1974
Education: Graduated from the University of St. Petersburg in physiology, 1910
Positions, Honors: 1910-15, University of St. Petersburg; 1915-19, Novorossiysk University; 1919-61, University of Tblisi; 1919-51, head, Physiological Research Laboratory (renamed Physiological Research Institute of the Georgian Academy of Sciences); editorial work, *Bol'shaya Meditsinskaya Entsiklopediya*, *Fiziologicheskiĭ Zhurnal SSSR*; several prizes, orders, medals, and awards

Sometimes called the "dean of Soviet neurophysiology," Beritashvili started publishing in 1911 and continued at a high rate, for a total of more than three hundred publications. Studies of the mammalian central nervous system occupied most of his attention. Beritashvili distinguished instinctive, conditioned, image-controlled, and conscious behaviors, the first three being common to all higher vertebrates, the fourth present only in the adult human. The image-controlled and the learned behaviors are individually acquired. The differentiation of a category of image-controlled behaviors in animals (as in delayed reaction tests) was a radical departure from Pavlov*. For this and other "idealistic" unorthodoxies, such as his admiration of foreign scientists, Beritashvili was severely criticized during the 1950 "Pavlovian sessions" of the Soviet academies of science. Beritashvili viewed conscious behavior as the product of social interaction. Such behavior involves awareness of goals and planning activity and the anticipation of results of such activity. Under certain conditions conscious behavior may become image-controlled or even conditioned behavior, although the element of consciousness is never completely lost. Among Beritashvili's books of psychological interest are [*Individually Acquired Activity of the Central Nervous System*] (1932, 1962); [*General Physiology of the Muscular and Nervous System*] (1941): [*Basic Forms of Nervous and Neuro-Psychic Activity*] (1947); [*The Morphological and Physiological Principles of Temporary Connections in the Cortex of the Cerebral Hemispheres*] (1956); [*Physiological Mechanisms of Behavior in the Higher Vertebrates*] (1957); [*The Neural Mechanisms of Spatial Orientation in the Higher Vertebrates*] (1959); *Neural Mechanisms of Higher Vertebrate Behavior* (1965, English translation of the 1961 Russian ed.); and [*Structure and Function of the Cerebral Cortex*] (1969).

Biographies: *The International Who's Who*, 38th ed.; *Prominent Personalities in the USSR*, 1968.

BERKELEY, GEORGE
English Philosopher
Born: Near Kilkenny, Ireland, March 12, 1685
Died: Oxford, January 14, 1753
Highest Degree: M.A. in philosophy, Trinity College, Dublin, 1707
Positions: No academic positions; various ecclesiastic (bishop of Cloyne) positions

Berkeley was a philosopher in the British empiricist school. His main arguments for his views were psychological. Berkeley also contributed to psychology substantive thinking concerning problems of vision. His first major publication, *An Essay Toward a New Theory of Vision* (1709), dealt with that subject. A year later *A Treatise Concerning the Principles of Human Knowledge* was published, the second of Berkeley's works of importance to psychology. Both show the influence of Locke*. Sense experience is the source of knowledge, but the only thing we can know is our experiences and ideas. Being, in fact, is perception. This view, later called mentalism, insists that although objects are real, their reality lies in the mind of God. The appearances of objects is all we can know, but the appearances are also real since God guarantees their reality through the reality of the physical world. In our minds the object and its appearance fuse.

In the mind there are the sensory ideas aroused by the passions and imagination but nothing that could be called abstract ideas. Such ideas are derived from the senses. Ideas are only perceptions and images, both of them particular, not abstract. Ideas from different sources, such as ideas arising in the different sense departments, are combined by experience into wholes. Ideas are simultaneously associated when sensations occur contiguously. Berkeley also recognized successive association and differentiated among associations by similarity, causality, and coexistence. With Locke he agreed that a person lacking previous experience would be unable to identify objects but disagreed with him concerning the nature of the primary and secondary qualities of objects. To Berkeley primary qualities were actually secondary qualities, since experience can know only itself and not something that was not derived from experience.

Berkeley's essay about vision was the first monograph in psychology. In it he argued for immateriality, using the avenue of perception. Distance, depth, and size are not seen directly "out there." Rather, we learn about spatial qualities by associating visual, tactual, and kinesthetic sensations. Depth is not a sensation but an additional property of the visual world, "suggested to the mind by the mediation of some other idea which is itself perceived in the act of seeing." Some of these ideas are what later came to be called the psychological or secondary depth cues, with the exception of motion parallax, which Berkeley did not mention. The primary cues of convergence, accommodation, and blurring receive a discussion from Berkeley but the role he assigned them is mentalistic, not materialistic: one feels the position of the eyes, not the angle between them. Berkeley's account of how sight and touch combine to produce perception of space was a landmark in the development of an empiricist theory of perception. *Biographies*: A. C. Fraser, *Berkeley*, 1894; A. C. Fraser, *Life and Letters of George Berkeley*, 1871; G. D. Hicks, *Berkeley*, 1932; A. L. Leroy, *George Berkeley*, 1959; A. Luce, *The Life of George Berkeley, Bishop of Cloyne*, 1949; G. J. Warnock, *Berkeley*, 1953; J. Wild, *George Berkeley: A Study of His Life and Philosophy*, 1936; O. Wisdom, *Brit. J. Phil. Sci.*, 1953, *4*, 78-87; *CE*, 2; *DNB*, 2; *DSB*, 2; *EB*, 3; *EP*, 1; *IESS*, 2; *NCAB*, 6.

BERLYNE, DANIEL E.

English-Canadian Psychologist

Born: Salford, Cheshire, England, April 25, 1924

Died: Toronto, Canada, November 2, 1976

Highest Degree: Ph.D. in psychology, Yale University, 1953, under C. I. Hovland*

Positions, Honors: 1952, Brooklyn College, New York City; 1953-56, University of Aberdeen; 1956, fellow, Center for Advanced Study in the Behavioral Sciences, Palo Alto, California; 1957, University of California, Berkeley; 1958, member-resident, Centre International de Epistemologie Génétique, Geneva; 1959-62, visiting scientist, National Institutes of Mental Health, Maryland; 1962-76, University of Toronto; 1968-69, NATO visiting professor, Institut d'Ésthetique et des Sciences de l'Art, University of Paris; coeditor, *Scientific Aesthetics*, 1976; president, Canadian Psychological Association, 1971-72; copresident, Eighteenth International Congress of Applied Psychology, 1974; president, International Association of Empirical Aesthetics, 1974-76; fellow of several scientific societies

Berlyne contributed both theory and experimental findings to the area of motivation, especially intrinsic motivation that results in exploratory and knowledge-seeking behavior. He began in 1947 by studying attention with a new approach and embarked on the study of exploratory behavior in 1949, the same year as did Harry Harlow*. He and Harlow were the first Western psychologists to study exploratory behavior systematically. Berlyne's work resulted in eighty-nine journal articles, forty-seven book chapters and papers, and seven books about exploratory and epistemic behavior, curiosity, response to novelty, attention, play, humor, thinking, and experimental aesthetics. His work became part of the new look at motivation of the 1960s that supplemented the previous emphasis on physiological drives and deficiency motives. Berlyne's main effort was directed toward the understanding of a variety of seemingly diverse behaviors in terms of a few motivational principles. He stressed the collative properties of stimulation—those properties that influence exploratory and related forms of behavior: novelty, surprisingness, change, ambiguity, incongruity, complexity, and uncertainty. In his collative-motivation theory Berlyne distinguished between *perceptual curiosity*, which is aroused by the collative properties of stimulation, and *epistemic curiosity*, which is related more to discomfort and relief of discomfort. In either case, behavior ensues from conflict, perceptual conflict in one case, conceptual conflict in the other. Berlyne's books in this area are *Conflict, Arousal, and Curiosity* (1960), which is his main theoretical statement and his most influential work; *Théorie du comportement et opérations* (1960, with Jean Piaget); *Structure and Direction of Thinking* (1965); and *Pleasure, Reward, Preference* (1973, editor, with K. B. Madsen).

Berlyne extended his thinking on intrinsic motivation and the experimental approach to the area of aesthetics. He wrote *Aesthetics and Psychobiology* (1971), one of the most influential books about the psychology of art, and edited *Studies in the New Experimental Aesthetics* (1974), to which he contributed seven experimental papers of his own.

Biographies: V. J. Konecni, *Amer. J. Psychol.*, 1978, *91*, 133-137.

BERNARD, CLAUDE

French Physiologist
Born: Saint-Julien, Rhône, July 12, 1813
Died: Paris, February 10, 1878
Highest Degree: M.D., Collège de France, 1843; D.Sc., 1853
Positions, Honors: 1841-54, Collège de France; 1854, Sorbonne (University of Paris) 1855-68, Collège de France; 1868-78, Museum of Natural History, Paris; numerous honors

Bernard was the most famous of the physiologists of the first half of the nineteenth century, but his contributions to psychology were not as significant. Bernard was a great experimental physiologist and founder of experimental medicine, and he helped to introduce experimentation in French psychology (*Introduction à la étude de la médecine expérimentelle*, 1865). He is known for his work on the vascular system (he demonstrated the mechanisms of vasodilation and vasoconstriction) and digestion (he demonstrated that thirst is satisfied only if water is directed into the stomach, not when it bypasses it). He also studied the effects of curare, carbon monoxide, and other poisons on the nervous system.

His discovery of and work on internal secretions paved the way to the discovery of hormones.

Bernard formulated a fundamental concept in physiology, that of a *milieu intérieur*, or internal environment (consisting of the humors, the blood, and the lymph), which remains stable despite changes within and without the organism. When this environment or balance is disturbed, the organism immediately sets to work to restore it. This concept anticipated Cannon's* concept of homeostasis. The latter, in the form of the principle of drive reduction, played an important part in psychological learning theories.

Biographies: E. B. Carmichael, *Ala. J. Med. Sci.*, 1972, *9*, 349-360; P. E. Chauffard, *Claude Bernard*, 1878; J. L. Fauré, *Claude Bernard*, 1925; M. Foster, *Claude Bernard*, 1899; F. Grande & M. B. Visscher (Eds.), *Claude Bernard and Experimental Medicine*, 1967; P. Mauriac, *Claude Bernard*, 1940; J. M. D. Olmsted, *Claude Bernard, Physiologist*, 1938; J. N. Petersen & J. Sancier, *Arch. Neurol. Psychiat.*, 1935, *34*, 179-184; E. Renan, *Éloge de Claude Bernard*, 1879; J. Schiller, *Claude Bernard et les problèmes scientifiques de son temps*, 1967; R. Virtanen, *Claude Bernard and His Place in the History of Ideas*, 1960; *CE*, 2; *DSB*, 2; *EB*, 3; *EP*, 1; *NYT*, 1878, Feb. 28, 5:1.

BERNHEIM, HIPPOLYTE
French Neurologist and Hypnotist
Born: Mulhouse, Haut Rhin, April 17, 1840
Died: Nancy, Meurthe et Moselle, 1919
Highest Degree: M.D., University of Strasbourg, 1867
Positions: 1868-72, University of Strasbourg; 1872-82, University of Nancy; 1882-1919, private practice, Nancy

Bernheim was a well-known physician at Nancy when Ambroise-Auguste Liébeault* happened to cure one of his patients of sciatica using hypnosis. Bernheim, who had failed with orthodox treatment, became a pupil of Liébeault's in 1882. Together they founded a clinic at Nancy. In this clinic treatment by hypnosis was prominent. The clinic soon became a rival of Charcot's* in Paris, both in terms of cases treated (Bernheim hypnotized some ten thousand persons during his clinical practice) and the ideas entertained concerning the nature of hypnosis. Although Charcot believed that hypnosis was the result of the hysteric makeup of a person, Bernheim, who came to represent the "Nancy school of hypnotism," thought that ordinary sleep and hypnotic sleep were similar and that most people could be hypnotized. Bernheim induced hypnotic sleep using suggestion of sleepiness and treated his patients on the assumption that medical cures could be achieved in a state of suggestibility. This was essentially a development of Braid's* view of hypnosis as suggestion.

Bernheim, along with Charcot, showed that hypnosis was a proper subject for scientific study; they also contributed to the development of clinical psychology by concentrating on neurotic cases and separating them from the more severe cases of abnormality that required hospitalization. Bernheim was first to

treat neuroses hypnotically. Among his books on the subject are *De la suggestion dans l'état hypnotique et dans l'état de veille* (1884), *De la suggestion et ses applications à la thérapeutique* (1886), *Hypnotisme, suggestion, psychothérapie, études nouvelles* (1891), and *L'Hypnotisme et la suggestion dans leurs rapports avec la médecine légale et les maladies mentales* (1897).

Biographies: H. Bernheim, *Jubilé du professeur H. Bernheim*, 1910; M. Goldsmith, *Franz Anton Mesmer: The History of an Idea*, 1934; R. Semelaigne, *Les pionniers de la psychiatrie française avant et après Pinel*, 1930, 1932; W. A. Stewart, *Psychoanalysis: The First Ten Years, 1888-1898*, 1967; *DSB*, 2; *EJ*, 4; Hirsch, *Biog. Lex.*, 1; *Jewish*, 2.

BERNOULLI, DANIEL
Swiss Mathematician, Physician, and Physicist
Born: Groningen, the Netherlands, February 8, 1700
Died: Basel, March 17, 1782
Highest Degree: Master's degree in philosophy, University of Basel, 1716; M.D., University of Basel, 1721
Positions, Honors: 1725-33, St. Petersburg Academy of Sciences; 1733-76, University of Basel; ten prizes from various academies of science

In the field of medicine Bernoulli contributed a new theory of muscular contraction (1728) that was entirely mechanical and a method for determining the shape and location of the blind spot (also in 1728).

A precursor of game and decision-making theories, he gave, in a 1738 monograph about a "new theory of the measurement of risk," a mathematical formulation of a value theory whereby the moral expectation or hope of a gain could be evaluated. He solved certain problems in risky decision making by assuming that, contrary to traditional thinking in mathematics, people act to maximize expected utility (subjective value) rather than expected value. In doing so he also assumed that utility followed a function that, in the nineteenth century Gustav Fechner* would establish for the relationship between stimulus magnitude and the strength of sensation (Fechner's law). Bernoulli made significant contributions to probability theory and introduced the calculus of probability into epidemiology and insurance.

Biographies: D. Bernoulli II, *Acta Helvetica*, 1787, *9*, 1-32; M. J. A. Condorce, *Éloges des Académiciens de l'Académie Royale des Sciences*, 1773 (Reprint, 1968); F. Huber, *Daniel Bernoulli als Physiologe und Statistiker*, 1959; R. Wo, *Biog. Kulturgesch. Schweiz*, 34th ser., 1860, pp. 151-202; *ADB*, 2; *DSB*, *IESS*, 2; *NDB*, 2.

BERNSTEIN, JULIUS
German Physiologist
Born: Berlin, December 18, 1839
Died: Halle, February 6, 1917
Highest Degree: M.D., University of Berlin, 1862

Positions: 1864-71, University of Heidelberg; 1871, University of Berlin; 1872-1917, University of Halle

In 1866 Bernstein measured the polarization of nerves and showed that the nerve impulse is a "wave of negativity." In 1902 he helped to establish the current membrane theory of nerve conduction, and the "wave of negativity" became the wave of depolarization: the nerve impulse is the small, traveling region of momentarily depolarized nerve membrane, which in a resting state is charged positively on the outside and negatively on the inside. In 1871 Bernstein stated the projection theory of nerve conduction, which postulated a point-to-point correspondence between the receptors stimulated and ganglion cells in brain centers upon which stimulation from the receptors is projected and from which stimulation irradiates along a gradient to adjacent brain cells. The theory went a long way toward explaining binocular vision, blind areas in cases of brain injury, phenomena of the cutaneous two-point threshold, the error of localization, and other perceptual phenomena. There has been little improvement upon Bernstein's ideas. Bernstein wrote several books on neurophysiology and electrobiology.

Biographies: A. Tschermak-Seysenegg, *Arch. ges. Physiol.*, 1919, *174*, 1-99; *DSB*, 15; *EJ*, 4; *Enciclopedia Italiana*, 6; *EUI*, 8; *Jewish*, 2.

BESSEL, FRIEDRICH WILHELM

German Astronomer

Born: Minden, Westphalia, July 22, 1784

Died: Königsberg, East Prussia, March 17, 1846

Education: Self-educated

Positions: 1810-46, professor of astronomy and director (since 1813) of the observatory at Königsberg

When the astronomer royal at Greenwich, Maskelyne, dismissed his assistant, Kinnebrook, for alleged gross time errors made in the observation of stellar transits, the event was described in a history of the observatory and published in 1816. Bessel read it but hypothesized that the error was in fact a matter of individual differences in reaction time between the two men. He systematically compared his own performance with those of several other astronomers over a period of years, confirming the hypothesis. He also showed that considerable variability in reaction time existed among individuals. Differences in reaction time between two astronomers were presented by Bessel in the form of an equation, $A - B = X$ sec., the "personal equation," which could be used to make observations of the two astronomers comparable. The determination of personal equations became an important aspect of astronomical observations. In the 1860s and 1870s this work was extended to include the dependence of reaction time on variables such as the brightness of the celestial object and its rate of motion. Bessel's contribution was to recognize the psychological nature of the reaction time problem and to give impetus to the study of two important phe-

nomena in the incipient experimental psychology: reaction time and the so-called complications, or mental processes involving more than one sense modality.
Biographies: F. W. Bessel, *Abhandlungen von Friedrich Wilhelm Bessel*, vol. 1, 1875-76; *Nature*, 1946, *157*, 331; *ADB*, 2; *DSB*, 2; *EUI*, 8; *NDB*, 2.

BETHE, ALBRECHT
German Physiologist
Born: Stettin, Pomerania, April 25, 1872
Died: Frankfurt am Main, October 19, 1954
Highest Degree: M.D., University of Strasbourg, 1898
Positions: 1895-96, Zoological Station, Naples; 1896-1911, University of Strasbourg; 1911-15, University of Kiel; 1915-37, 1945-52, University of Frankfurt; 1918-54, editor, *Pflügers Archiv für die gesamte Physiologie des Menschen und der Tiere*

Bethe studied the histology and physiology of the nervous system and the sense organs, especially in the invertebrates (*Allgemeine Anatomie und Physiologie des Nervensystems*, 1903). In 1899 he published a paper (with T. Beer and Jakob Uexküll*) proposing that mentalistic or psychological terms be discontinued in describing animal behavior and that objective terms like *reflex*, *reception*, and *resonance* be substituted. Earlier (1898), Bethe had written an article denying ants and bees a psyche, their complex and seemingly intelligent behavior notwithstanding. In Bethe and others, Descartes's* view of animals as machines was finding support and furnishing impetus to the behavioristic view in psychology, soon to be launched by Watson*.
Biographies: H. Schaefer, *Klin. Wochenschr.*, 1942, *21*, 511; R. Thauer, *Arch. ges. Physiol.*, 1955, *261*, 1-14; *Enciclopedia Italiana*, 6; Hirsch, *Biog. Lex.*, Suppl. 1.

BICHAT, MARIE FRANÇOIS XAVIER
French Physician
Born: Thiorette, Jura, November 11, 1771
Died: Paris, July 22, 1802
Education: Studied anatomy, University of Lyons; and surgery, University of Paris
Positions: 1800-1802, physician, Hôtel Dieu hospital

Bichat is considered the founder of histology. He was first to demonstrate that different organs have *tissues* (the term was his coinage) and membranes in common and that disease affects tissue and not the individual organ. The then-current view of anatomy as a complex of organs was changed by Bichat who stressed tissue as the fundamental building block. Bichat also emphasized the difference between conscious and unconscious life and identified two separate mechanisms in the body, the organic (vegetative) and relational (animal). In sensory physiology Bichat proposed the existence of muscular sensibility before

Charles Bell* (*Anatomie générale appliquée à la physiologie et à la médecine*, 2nd ed., 1812).

Biographies: E. H. Ackerknecht, *Medicine at the Paris Hospital, 1794-1848*, 1967; G. Canguilhem, *Actes XIe Cong. Int. Hist. Sci.*, 1965, *5*, 287-292; J. Coquerelle, *Xavier Bichat*, 1902; M. Genty, *Méd. int.*, 1934, *42*, 269, 301, 341, 381; E. Gley, *Bull. Soc. franç. hist. méd.*, 1902, *1*, 285-323; H. M. Husson, *Notice historique sur la vie et les travaux de Marie-Franç.-Xav. Bichat*, 1816; *CE*, 2; *DSB*, 2.

BINET, ALFRED

French Psychologist
Born: Nice, July 8, 1857
Died: Paris, October 18, 1911
Highest Degree: Law degree, Lycée St. Louis, Paris, 1878; Ph.D. in science, University of Paris, 1894
Positions: 1894-1911, University of Paris

Binet was the most prominent French psychologist of his time. With Henri Beaunis* he was a cofounder of the first French psychological laboratory at the Sorbonne in 1889 and, with Victor Henri*, of *L'Année psychologique* in 1895. Binet first became interested in abnormal phenomena. He wrote a book about hypnotism (*Le magnétisme animal*, 1886, with C. S. Féré*), abnormal personality (*Les altérations de la personalité*, 1892), and suggestibility (*La suggestibilité*, 1900) and was best known for his studies of suggestibility. In 1886 he wrote (with Féré) a book about thinking (*La psychologie du raisonnement*), but it was largely a theoretical work. In the 1890s he carried out a number of experiments on subjects in general psychology in the German tradition.

In 1902 his book about intelligence (*L'Étude expérimentale de l'intelligence*) already included empirical data about his two daughters and considerable discussion of the differences in intelligence between them. His interest in intelligence and individual differences in intelligence and thinking dates from around 1887. In the fall of 1904 the minister of public instruction of France appointed a committee to study the problem of and make recommendations concerning the education of retarded children in Paris. In 1905 Binet and Théodore Simon* wrote a paper in which they urged the necessity to diagnose the intelligence of children in order to implement the committee's recommendation. The first intelligence test was constructed by Binet and Simon in 1905, although the preparatory work had already been done and published in a series of papers between 1894 and 1898.

The 1905 test contained a single scale—a long series of tests of increasing difficulty. In 1908 Binet revised this instrument. The tests were arranged according to the different ages at which they were to be passed by normal children. With that revision there occurred a shift away from simple identification of retardation to the general problem of the measurement of intelligence. In 1911

Binet's last revision of the test appeared. It contained the important new idea of mental age—a score of problem-solving ability expressed as years and months.

Binet's work on intelligence led to the construction of the first intelligence scale, the precursor of the present-day Stanford-Binet Intelligence Scale, the best-known and most-researched individual intelligence test. The test introduced objective measurement of mental processes in child psychology, developmental psychology, and educational psychology and advanced the understanding of the concept of intelligence. The amount of subsequent research and practical use of intelligence tests has been such that very few psychologists may be compared to Binet in the fruitfulness of their ideas.

Biographies: F. L. Bertrand, *Alfred Binet et son oeuvre*, 1930; E. Claparède, *Arch. Psychol.*, 1911-12, *11*, 376-388; J. Delay, *Psychol. franç.*, 1958, *3*, 85-88; K. Kolle (Ed.), *Grosse Nervenärzte*, vol. 3, 1963, pp. 209-220; P. Malapert, *Bull. Soc. libre l'étude psychol. l'enfant*, 1911, No. 74, 1-5; R. Martin, *Alfred Binet*, 1924; R. H. Pollack & M. W. Brenner, In *The Experimental Psychology of Alfred Binet: Selected Papers*, 1969; H. L. Silverman & K. Krenzel, *Psychiat. Quart. Suppl.*, 1964, *38*, 323-335; T. Simon, *Année psychol.*, 1912, *18*, 1-16; T. Simon, *Bull. Soc. libre l'étude psychol. l'enfant*, 1954, No. 415, 342-360; E. B. Titchener, *Amer. J. Psychol.*, 1912, *23*, 140-141; T. H. Wolf, *Alfred Binet*, 1973; T. H. Wolf, *Amer. Psychologist*, 1961, *16*, 245-248; *DSB*, 2; *EB*, 2; *EP*, 1; *IESS*, 2.

BINGHAM, WALTER VAN DYKE

American Psychologist
Born: Swan Lake, Iowa, October 20, 1880
Died: Washington, D.C., July 8, 1952
Highest Degree: Ph.D. in psychology, University of Chicago, 1908, under J. R. Angell*
Positions: 1908-10, Teachers College, Columbia University; 1910-15, Dartmouth College, established psychological laboratory there; 1915-24, Carnegie Institute of Technology, 1916, organized and directed Division of Applied Psychology and Bureau of Salesmanship Research; 1924-34, director, Personnel Research Federation, Inc.; 1924-40, independent research and private practice in industrial psychology, summer teaching at Harvard and University of Minnesota, consultant to government agencies on personnel classification matters; 1940-47, chief psychologist, Adjutant General's office; editorial work, *Personnel Journal* (1923-37), *Journal of Consulting Psychology*, *Journal of Applied Psychology*, *Character and Personality*, and *Personnel Psychology*; president, American Association of Applied Psychologists, 1941

Bingham pioneered in the practice of industrial psychology, occupational guidance, personnel selection and classification, accident reduction, and psychological testing. Throughout his career he worked for the establishment of an industrial psychology based on experimental psychology and thereby left an impression on the development of applied psychology in the United States.

Bingham exercised his influence through the study of many problems in applied psychology (he wrote more than two hundred papers and books) and through participation in numerous governmental and civic bodies concerned with personnel problems, manpower, accident prevention, and applied psychology in general. Bingham was a cofounder of the Psychological Corporation in 1921 and one of its directors for the rest of his life. During World War I he was one of the seven psychologists who developed intelligence testing in the U.S. Army, and he worked with W. D. Scott* on the classification of army personnel. In World War II he also did personnel work for the armed forces. Two of his books of enduring value are *Aptitude and Aptitude Testing* (1937) and *How to Interview* (1931, with B. V. Moore).

Biographies: H. E. Burtt, *Psychol. Rev.*, 1952, *59*, 403-404; L. W. Ferguson, *Heritage Indust. Psychol.*, 1963, No. 2, pp. 13-23; *Personnel Guid. J.*, 1953, *31*, 253-254; L. L. Thurstone, *Personnel Psychol.*, 1952, *5*, 155-156; *HPA*, 4; *IESS*, 2; *NCAB*, 39; *NYT*, 1952, July 9, 27:5.

BINSWANGER, LUDWIG
Swiss Psychiatrist
Born: Kreuzlingen, Thurgau, April 13, 1881
Died: Kreuzlingen, February 5, 1966
Highest Degree: M.D., University of Zurich, 1907
Positions: 1910-56, psychiatrist and chief medical director, Sanitorium Bellevue, Kreuzlingen

Under the influence of Dilthey*, Heidegger, and Husserl*, Binswanger developed *Daseinsanalyse*, or existential analysis, a combination of phenomenology, existentialism, and psychoanalysis. It was a reaction to the view that human beings are only organisms. Without denying the value of the natural sciences approach, Binswanger stressed the necessity to understand the present meaning-context of the patient, because the past and the entire "world design" exist in the patient in the present; they *are* the patient. Psychological knowledge is possible only if one human being communes with another lovingly.

Besides writing several books about psychiatry, Binswanger wrote psychological works such as *Einführung in die Probleme der allgemeinen Psychologie* (1922) and *Wandlungen in der Auffassung und Deutung des Traumes* (1928).

Biographies: H. Holt, *J. Existent.*, 1966, *7* (25), 93-96; R. Kuhn, *Schweiz. Arch. Neurol. Psychiat.*, 1967, *99*, 113-117; D. Larese, *Ludwig Binswanger: Versuch einer kleinen Lebensskizze*, 1965; *EP*, 1.

BLEULER, (PAUL) EUGEN
Swiss Psychiatrist
Born: Zollikon, near Zurich, April 30, 1857
Died: Zollikon, July 15, 1939
Highest Degree: M.D., University of Zurich, 1883
Positions: 1886-98, Psychiatric Hospital, Rheinau; 1898-1927, professor of psy-

chiatry and director of psychiatric clinic and university hospital (Burghölzli), University of Zurich

Before Jung's* time Bleuler was the best-known psychiatrist in Switzerland. He was influenced by both Wundt* and Freud* and tried to reconcile the two in relation to psychopathology. In doing so Bleuler pioneered in introducing Freudian thinking in psychiatry. He was particularly interested in *dementia precox*. In his monumental work *Dementia precox, oder Gruppe der Schizophrenien* (1911), Bleuler coined the term *schizophrenia* and substituted it for *dementia precox*. He also invented the term *autistic thinking*. In general, he described schizophrenia, arguing that it was a heterogeneous collection of disorders, not incurable, that mental deterioration in schizophrenia was not inevitable, and that individuals suffering from it did not lack emotionality. Bleuler emphasized the regressive behavior in schizophrenics and thought that the etiology of delusions was to be sought in any discrepancy between aspiration and ability. He stressed conscious and unconscious motivational factors, adding the dynamic dimension to the etiology of schizophrenia. Bleuler published more than 150 psychiatric papers and books.

Biographies: A. A. Brill, *Amer. J. Psychiat.*, 1939, *96*, 513-516; H. Devine, *Psychiat.-neurol. Wochenschr.*, 1927, *29*, 216-218; R. Gaupp, *Z. ges. Neurol. Psychiat.*, 1940, *168*, 1-35; E. Jones, *Int. J. Psychoanal.*, 1940, *21*, 111-112; J. Klaesi, *Monatsschr. Psychiat. Neurol.*, 1957, *134*, 353-361; E. Minkowski, *Ann. méd.-psychol.*, 1939, *97*, 420-423; J. E. Staehelin, *Schweiz. med. Wochenschr.*, 1939, *69*, 931-935; various, *Zbl. ges. Neurol. Psychiat.*, 1923, *82*, 1-420; various, *Schweiz. Arch. Neurol. Psychiat.*, 1941, *46*, 1-32; G. Zilboorg, *Psychoanal. Quart.*, 1939, *8*, 383-384; *IESS*, 2; *NDB*, 2.

BLIX, MAGNUS (GUSTAV)
Swedish Physiologist
Born: Säbrå, Västernorrland, December 25, 1849
Died: Lund, February 14, 1904
Highest Degree: M.D., University of Uppsala, 1879
Positions: 1879-99, assistant, Physiological Institute, University of Uppsala; 1899-1904, University of Lund

Blix did his most important work on muscular warmth ([*Studies on Muscular Warmth*], 3 vols., 1899-1900), and muscle mechanics ([*On the Problem of Human Work Capacity*], 1901). In 1880 (*Ophthalmometric Studies*, 1880) he invented a new ophthalmoscope that made it possible to measure the thickness of the cornea in the living human eye. More specifically psychological was his monograph on the Poggendorff illusion (1900). His most important contribution to psychology, however, was his discovery, in 1882, of sensory sites on the skin that mediated the sensations of warm, cold, and pressure.

Biographies: Anon. (Biographical paper given at the Royal Academy of Science, 31st March, 1928) *Levnadsteckningar Svenska Vetenskapsakad: Ledamöter*, 1921-1928, *6*, 251-280; *Biog. Lex.*

BLONSKIĬ, PAVEL PETROVICH

Russian Psychologist, Educator, and Philosopher

Born: Kiev, May 26, 1884

Died: Moscow, February 15, 1941

Education: Degree from the School of History and Philology, University of Kiev, 1907

Positions: 1907-13, secondary schoolteacher, Moscow; 1913-41, Moscow State University; 1917-33, Second Moscow State University; 1917-41, Institute of Psychology

Blonskiĭ's *Ocherk nauchnoĭ psikhologii* (1921) was a first attempt in the history of Soviet psychology to build a system of materialistic psychology, based on dialectic materialism, the evolutionary doctrine, and materialistic monism. In a collection of essays, *Psikhologicheskie ocherki* (1927), Blonskiĭ wrote about the evolution of consciousness, the nature of sleep, and his own research on the content of a base radical in the human saliva as a function of the type of mental activity engaged in by the subject. This paper led to additional research of the phenomenon in the West. Blonskiĭ's most important psychological work was *Pamyat' i myshlenie* (1935), a treatise about memory and thinking that was complemented by a monograph about the development of thinking in schoolchildren, *Razvitie myshleniya shkol'nika* (1935). These works included Blonskiĭ's own research on thinking in which he used a word-association technique. His *Ocherki detskoĭ seksual'nosti* (1935) was a unique monograph in that, with the exception of some published lectures and the *Book for Parents* of the educator A. S. Makarenko, it was the only work in Soviet education or psychology on sexual development and sex education ever published. It continues to occupy that position. Blonskiĭ wrote only twenty-seven articles, monographs, and books in psychology, some of them in German, but his educational writings contain much psychological material.

Biographies: *Great Soviet Encyclopedia*, 3; *Who Was Who in the USSR*, 1972.

BOAS, FRANZ

German-American Anthropologist

Born: Minden, Westphalia, Germany, July 9, 1858

Died: New York, New York, December 21, 1942

Highest Degree: Ph.D. in physics, University of Kiel, 1881

Positions: 1888-92, Clark University; 1896-1937, Columbia University; many other nonteaching positions in anthropology; editorial work for anthropological journals; four honorary degrees; president, American Association for the Advancement of Science, 1931

In anthropology Boas was an outstanding figure: he restructured anthropology by separating it into physical anthropology, linguistics, and ethnology; demonstrated the diffusion of cultural traits (rather than cultural evolution); wrote more than six hundred papers and several books, among them a monumental study of the Kwakiutl Indians; was one of the founders of the American Anthropological Society; and developed the Columbia University Anthropology Department into one of the foremost in the country.

Boas was influenced by German psychology, especially by Wundt* and his ethnopsychology. He performed some psychophysical experiments, finding that the previous experiences of his subjects made a difference in the results. At Clark University, under the influence of G. Stanley Hall*, Boas initiated the first American longitudinal growth study in 1891. His studies of the plasticity of the human organism (for example, the demonstration of changes in skull shape in European emigrants brought about by environmental influence) also show Hall's influence. Toward the end of his life Boas shifted his emphasis on psychological explanations of cultural phenomena and the psychological description of environmental conditions that modify a person's behavior. He argued conclusively against the concept of pure races, asserting that race was largely a matter of environment. He investigated motor behavior, posture, walking, and gestures. Boas reversed Tylor's* rationalistic position by asserting that behavior is influenced by and occurs within a culture, that culture is not just the product of a person's mind. Thinking and acting follow paths etched by the individual's culture from birth. Yet although culture affects the individual, the individual also affects culture. To psychology his most significant book is *The Mind of Primitive Man* (1911, 1938).

Biographies: R. Benedict, *Science*, 1943, *97*, 60-62; F. C. Cole, *Amer. J. Sociol.*, 1943, *48*, 603; J. P. Foley, Jr., *Science*, 1943, *97*, 330; M. J. Herskovits, *Franz Boas: The Science of Man in the Making*, 1953; R. Jakobson, *Int. J. Amer. Ling.*, 1944, *10*, 188-195; A. L. Kroeber, *Mem. Amer. Anthrop. Ass.*, 1943, No. 61, 5-26; R. H. Lowie, *Sci. Mon.*, 1943, *56*, 183-184; B. J. Stern, *Sci. Soc.*, 1943, *7*, 289-320; G. W. Stocking, Jr., *Amer. Anthropologist*, 1960, *62*, 1-17; *DSB*, 2; *EB*, 3; *IESS*, 2; *NCAB*, 12; *NYT*, 1942, Dec. 22, 25:1.

BONNET, CHARLES
Swiss Biologist and Philosopher
Born: Geneva, March 3, 1720
Died: Genthod, near Geneva, May 20, 1793
Highest Degree: Doctorate in law, 1743
Positions: Practice of law

From law Bonnet turned to biology, where he made well-known contributions to the study of insects. Failing eyesight made him turn to philosophy. In his philosophy Bonnet repeated Condillac*, including Condillac's parable of the sentient statue that develops memory, thinking, discrimination, judgment, desire, and aversion by being endowed originally with a single sense. Bonnet considered Condillac incomplete in that he believed that mere sequences of sensory impressions were insufficient to render a sentient being. He therefore gave an organizing and creative role to an active soul. Bonnet also differed from Condillac by giving the statue nerves. Bonnet's neurophysiology was largely speculative, although in his speculations he anticipated discoveries such as the specificity of nerve energies. His neurophysiologically based empiricism makes him a precursor of the physiological psychology that was to develop in the nineteenth century. His works of psychological importance are *Essai de psychologie* (1754) and *Essai analytique sur les facultés de l'âme* (1760). Through his other philosophical writings that involved biological themes, such as epigenesis, the principle of continuity in nature (he was first to use the term *evolution*), and the indestructibility of organisms, Bonnet considerably influenced philosophical thought of his day. His *Essai de psychologie* was significant in that it introduced the term *psychology* in the French language.

Biographies: G. Bonnet, *Charles Bonnet*, 1929; C. Bonnet, *Mémoires autobiographiques*, 1948; J. Rostand, *Un grande biologiste: Charles Bonnet, expérimentateur et théoricien*, 1966; *DSB*, 2; *EP*, 1; Hirsch, *Biog. Lex.*, 1.

BOOLE, GEORGE
English Mathematician
Born: Lincoln, Lincolnshire, November 2, 1815
Died: Cork, Ireland, December 8, 1864
Education: Mostly self-educated
Positions, Honors: 1849-64, Queen's College, Cork; honorary LL.D., University of Dublin; prizes

In an 1847 book, *Mathematical Analysis of Logic*, Boole demonstrated that logic belongs with mathematics rather than metaphysics. Then in *An Investigation of the Laws of Thought on Which Are Founded the Mathematical Theories of Logic and Probabilities* (1854), his principal work, Boole established a new branch of mathematics, symbolic logic, in which symbols are used to represent logical operations. In his book Boole proposed "to investigate the fundamental laws of those operations of the mind by which reasoning is performed; to give expression to them in the symbolic language of calculus ... to collect from ... these inquiries, some probable intimations concerning the nature and constitution of the human mind." The calculus (Boolean algebra) is derived not from mathematics but from the nature of logical thinking, and the mathematical symbols used represent not numbers but objects of thought. Thus at a time when Gustav Fechner* was giving mathematical expression to sensations, Boole was translating thought into mathematical symbols. Boole also showed that the symbols of his calculus could be made to take on only two values, 0 and 1, to perform all of the necessary operations. Boole's two-valued algebra is used today in the field of electronic computers that employ the binary system to represent, in effect, the operations of human logical thought.

Biographies: R. R. H. Harley, *Brit. Quart. Rev.*, 1866, July; W. Kneale, *Mind*, 1948, *57*, 149-175; A. Macfarlane, *Lectures on Ten British Mathematicians of the Nineteenth Century*, 1916; G. Taylor, *Not. Rec. Roy. Soc. London*, 1956, *12*, 44-52; *CE*, 2; *DNB*, 2; *DSB*, 2; *EP*, 1.

BORING, EDWIN GARRIGUES
American Psychologist
Born: Philadelphia, Pennsylvania, October 23, 1886
Died: Cambridge, Massachusetts, July 1, 1968
Highest Degree: Ph.D. in psychology, Cornell University, 1914, under E. B. Titchener*
Positions, Honors: 1919-22, Clark University; 1922-68, Harvard University, 1956-68, Edgar Pierce Professor Emeritus; president, American Psychological Association, 1928; editor, *American Journal of Psychology*, 1920-68; founder and editor, *Contemporary Psychology*, 1956-61; president, Seventeenth International Congress of Psychology, 1963; American Psychological Foundation Gold Medal, 1959; two honorary Sc.D. degrees

Boring was a general-experimental psychologist who did research on a wide spectrum of phenomena. Some of the papers stemming from this work are classics, such as the ones about visceral sensitivity (1915), the moon illusion (1940), and visual size (1941). Boring wrote 176 papers, 202 editorials, and 45 book reviews. Only relatively few of the papers are on his own research. Most of them are theoretical, as is his book *The Physical Dimensions of Consciousness* (1933), in which Boring discussed basic terms in psychology, such as *consciousness* and *sensation*, and showed how psychology could operate without reference to the body-mind dualism. The book marked his veering away from Titchenerian dualism toward a monism. Boring is best known for his work as a historian of psychology, however. He first published his *History of Experimental Psychology* in 1929. The theme of this book was the interaction between the spirit of the times and the individual scientist that spells out scientific development. The book soon became a classic. In 1950 the second edition of the text appeared, which is still the outstanding volume about the history of psychology. Boring's influence on generations of psychologists has been largely by way of his history book and his teaching of psychology at Harvard, especially of Psychology One, the introductory course. Boring's other historical text, *Sensation and Perception in the History of Experimental Psychology* (1942), although it brings together a prodigious amount of information, has had a much lesser impact. Because of his long association with general psychology and Harvard University, Boring also became well known outside of psychology and was often referred to as "Mr. Psychology" in the popular press.
Biographies: E. G. Boring, *Psychologist at Large*, 1961; H. Helson, *Amer. Psychologist*, 1970, *25*, 625-629; J. Jaynes, *J. Hist. Behav. Sci.*, 1969, *5*, 99-112; A. Mace, *Bull. Brit. Psychol. Soc.*, 1969, 22(75), 99-100; S. S Stevens, *Amer. J Psychol.*, 1968, *81*, 589-606; *HPA*, 4; *IESS*, 2; *NYT*, 1968, July 2, 26:2.

BOURDON, BENJAMIN BIENAIMÉ
French Psychologist
Born: Montmartin-sur-mer, Manche, August 5, 1860

Died: Rennes, Ille-et-Vilaine, July 11, 1943
Highest Degree: *Agrégé* in philosophy, University of Paris, 1885; doctor of letters, 1892
Positions: 1889-90, University of Lille: 1890-1930, University of Rennes

A few years after beginning his career at Rennes, Bourdon established one of the earliest psychological laboratories in France in 1896. He was an experimentalist and did a large number of experimental studies, most of them on sensation (hearing, equilibrium) and perception (visual space, form, illusions, movement), but also on intelligence, memory, and language. He wrote chapters about sensation and perception for the first and second editions of G. Dumas's* treatise on psychology and books such as *L'Expression des émotions et des tendences dans la langage* (1892), *La perception visuelle de l'espace* (1902), and *L'Intelligence* (1926), the latter dealing with types of memory and association.
Biographies: J. Beuchet, *Bull. psychol.*, 1962, *16*, 176-224; H. Piéron, *Psychol. franç.*, 1961, *6*, 163-172; *HPA*, 2; *PR*, 3.

BOWDITCH, HENRY PICKERING
American Physiologist
Born: Boston, Massachusetts, April 4, 1840
Died: Boston, Massachusetts, March 13, 1911
Highest Degree: M.D., Harvard University, 1866
Positions, Honors: 1871-93, Harvard University; editorial work, *Journal of Physiology*, 1877-98; five honorary degrees

Bowditch opened the first American physiological laboratory at Harvard in 1871. He was an eclectic physiologist who collaborated with psychologists such as James* and G. Stanley Hall*. Hall, who received his degree from James, did his dissertation on the muscular sense in Bowditch's laboratory. Later (1882) Bowditch and Hall published a paper about apparent motion in which the waterfall illusion machine was described and used in psychology for the first time. Bowditch was first to demonstrate the all-or-none law of nerve-impulse transmission in heart muscle fibers (1871). The principle that nerves cannot be fatigued is referred to as Bowditch's law.
Biographies: W. B. Cannon, *Science*, 1938, *87*, 471-474; F. W. Ellis, *New England J. Med.*, 1938, *219*, 819-828; G. S. Minot, *Science*, 1911, *33*, 598-601; G. Roser, *Bull. Hist. Med.*, 1936, *4*, 609-650; *Biog. Mem.*, 10; *DSB*, 2; *NCAB*, 12; *NYT*, 1911, Mar. 14, 11:4.

BRAID, JAMES
Scottish Physician
Born: Rylaw House, Fife, ca. 1795
Died: Manchester, England, March 25, 1860
Highest Degree: Degree in medicine, University of Edinburgh
Positions: Private practice of medicine, Manchester

Within five weeks after a mesmerist had given a stage demonstration at Manchester, Braid had his own theory of the nature of mesmerism. He presented his theory, along with a demonstration, on that same stage. Then and in his subsequent work, Braid was a moderate, seeking the middle ground between the mesmerists and the medical profession. Braid continued experimenting and writing, providing a scientific foundation for the phenomenon that he named "hypnotism" (developed from the term *neurypnology*, which was a contraction of neurohypnology). He published several books and many articles about hypnotism: *Neurypnology; or, The Rationale of Nervous Sleep, Considered in Relation with Animal Magnetism* (1843), *The Power of the Mind over the Body* (1846), *Observations on Trance* (1850), *Magic, Witchcraft, Animal Magnetism, and Electro-Biology* (1852), *Hypnotic Therapeutics, with an Appendix on Table-Moving and Spirit-Rapping* (1843), *Observations on the Nature and Treatment of Certain Forms of Paralysis*, (1855). These works eventually resulted in the acceptance of hypnotism as a valid phenomenon by the scientific world, as well as of Braid's explanation of the phenomenon. Braid's first theory stressed sensory fixation, later eyelid fatigue, then attentional fixation (monoideism), and, finally, suggestion as the crucial factor in hypnotism. The scientific understanding of hypnotism that began with Braid was psychological from the outset. The study and use of hypnotism in clinical settings spread first to France, where for some time (1860-1875) it was known as "Braidism."

Biographies: J. M. Bramwell, *Brain*, 1896, *73*, 90-116; J. M. Bramwell, *Proc. Soc. Psychical Res.*, 1896-1897, *12*, 127-166; M. Goldsmith, *Franz Anton Mesmer: The History of an Idea*, 1934; G. Newbold, *Brit. J. Med. Hypno.*, 1950, *1*, 3-7; *DNB*, 2, Suppl. 5.

BRENTANO, FRANZ

German Philosopher and Psychologist
Born: Marienburg-am-Rhein, near Cologne, June 16, 1838
Died: Zurich, Switzerland, March 17, 1917
Highest Degree: Ph.D. in philosophy, University of Tübingen, 1864
Positions: 1866-74, University of Würzburg; 1874-94, University of Vienna

The history of Brentano as a psychologist begins with the publication, in 1874, of a book by which he is best known, *Psychologie vom empirischen Standpunkt*. It was a psychology intended to replace all existing psychologies. It was philosophical psychology (because Brentano saw no essential difference between philosophy and psychology) but with an empirical emphasis. To Brentano "empirical" meant pure psychic activity or experience and only indirectly referred to the Lockean notion of sense-derived knowledge. Brentano's reaction to Wundt's* *Physiologische Psychologie*, published a year earlier, was to say that scientific psychology was not physiological psychology, although it might use the physiological approach as a method. Brentano argued but did not experiment. He argued that psychological phenomena possess immanent objectivity. Psychological phenomena are acts, mental acts. The act of seeing is mental. What is seen "inexists" in the act of seeing by intention. The quality of what is seen, the structure of experience (the content), belongs to the physical world.

Brentano's philosophy was basically that of Aristotle*, which he brought to bear upon contemporary psychological thinking. Brentano wrote only seven other papers and books of importance to psychology: *Sinnespsychologie* (1907), *Von der Klassifikation der psychischen Phänomene* (1911), two articles about sensation, and three about optical illusions. In the papers about optical illusions Brentano advanced the theory that the Müller-Lyer* illusion is owing to the overestimation of acute angles and the underestimation of obtuse ones.

Brentano exercised great influence on psychological thinking in Germany and abroad because of the effectiveness of his writings and his personality. "Act" psychology (also known as the Austrian school of psychology) became an alternative to Wundt's "content" psychology to those who favored phenomenological argument over experimentation. Brentano's idea, that the basis of experience is subjective perception, was basic to the imageless thought school of Würzburg and the development of the phenomenological branch of psychology.

Biographies: H. Bergman, *Rev. int. phil.*, 1966, *20*, 349-372; M. D. Hernández, *Francisco Brentano*, 1953; O. Kraus, *Franz Brentano: Zur Kenntniss seines Lebens und seiner Lehre*, 1919; M. Puglisi, *Amer. J. Psychol.*, 1924, *35*, 414-419; M. Puglisi, *Bilychnis*, 1921, *17*, 1-12; A. C. Rancurello, *A Study of Franz Brentano*, 1968; E. Sussman, *Amer. Psychologist*, 1962, *17*, 504-506; *CE*, 2; *EB*, 4; *EP*, 1; *NDB*, 2.

BRETT, GEORGE SIDNEY
English-Canadian Psychologist
Born: Briton Ferry, Wales, August 5, 1879
Died: Toronto, Canada, October 27, 1944
Highest Degree: M.A., Oxford University, 1902
Positions: 1908-44, University of Toronto, 1926-32, head of Psychology Department, 1932-44, dean of Graduate School

Brett's main contribution to psychology was his *History of Psychology*. Its three volumes (vol. 1, 1911; vols. 2 and 3, 1921) contained more than 1,100 pages, and it was the first history of psychology written in the English language. Before the appearance of Boring's* *History of Experimental Psychology* in 1929, Brett's was the principal history text used in English-speaking countries. Brett also wrote the article about the history of psychology for the fourteenth edition of the *Encyclopaedia Britannica* (1929). He left behind more than one hundred thirty publications, most of them in areas other than psychology.

Biographies: H. Brown, *Isis*, 1945-46, *36*, 110-114; *Bull. Canad. Psychol. Ass.*, 1944, *4*, 7; J. A. Irving, *Psychol. Rev.*, 1947, *54*, 52-58; *NYT*, 1944, Oct. 28, 15:3.

BREUER, JOSEF
Austrian Psychoanalyst
Born: Vienna, January 15, 1842

Died: Vienna, June 20, 1925
Highest Degree: M.D., University of Vienna, 1867
Positions: 1867-71, University of Vienna; after 1871, private practice, Vienna

Breuer is known both as the discoverer (independently of Ernest Mach*) of the function of the semicircular canals (described in three papers dated 1873, 1874, and 1875) and as Sigmund Freud's* intimate friend and father figure—more as the latter. Breuer reinforced Freud's biological orientation in interpreting psychic events in terms of related nervous and psychic excitation and organismic energy balance and surplus. Together they wrote papers about aphasia and hysteria. It was Breuer's famous patient, Anna O., who set Freud's thinking along lines that later became the foundation of psychoanalysis. Breuer had treated Anna O., a hysteric patient, using hypnosis and allowing her to talk freely of her problems under hypnosis. As a result, the symptoms decreased or disappeared. Breuer and Freud called the phenomenon "catharsis." During the course of Anna O.'s treatment, begun in 1880, she developed a *transference* (displacement of affect from the parent to the analyst) to Breuer, and Breuer discovered countertransference in himself. He stopped treating Anna O., and Freud took over. The book by Breuer and Freud, *Studien über Hysterie* (1895), is held to mark the beginning of psychoanalysis. Within the next two years the relationship between Breuer and Freud cooled, however, and they went their separate ways.
Biographies: S. Bernfeld, *Psychoanal. Quart.*, 1944, *13*, 341-362; A. Kleyn, *Acta Otolaryng.*, 1926, *10*, 167-171; M. Schlessinger *et al.*, *J. Amer. Psychoanal. Ass.*, 1967, *15*, 404-422; W. A. Stewart, *Psychoanalysis: The First Ten Years, 1888-1898*, 1967; *DSB*, 2; *EJ*, 4; *Jewish*, 2; *NDB*, 2.

BRIDGMAN, PERCY WILLIAMS
American Physicist
Born: Cambridge, Massachusetts, April 21, 1882
Died: Randolph, New Hampshire, August 20, 1961
Highest Degree: Ph.D. in physics, Harvard University, 1908
Positions, Honors: 1908-54, Harvard University; Nobel Prize in physics, 1946; numerous other awards, honors, and honorary degrees

In his 1927 book, *The Logic of Modern Physics*, Bridgman argued that any concept is equivalent to the set of operations by which it is obtained. A physical phenomenon is equivalent to the set of operations by which it is observed or measured. Concepts that cannot be tested by observation are meaningless. That which cannot be observed has no place in science. Thus the question of whether or not one person's red is the same as another's cannot be answered because sensory (subjective) qualities cannot be specified absolutely. Operationism, a form of logical positivism, was born at Harvard and popularized by Harvard psychologists, notably S. S. Stevens*. Psychologists, then under the aegis of behaviorism, were ready to accept operational definitions and reject nonobservable concepts, and thus operationism (which Bridgman did not name) was born. It did not become a school, and moderation having set in its use after World

War II, operational definitions are now being used as a technique and a means of clarifying one's thinking.

Biographies: P. W. Bridgman, *Reflections of a Physicist*, 1950; *Nature*, 1946, *158*, 825-826; *Nature*, 1949, *163*, 793; Royal Society, *Biog. Mem. Fellows Roy. Soc.*, 1962, *8*, 27-40; *Biog. Mem.*, 51; *DSB*, 2; *EP*, 1; *NCAB*, 48.

BRILL, ABRAHAM ARDEN

American Psychoanalyst

Born: Kanczuga, Galicia, Austria-Hungary, October 12, 1874

Died: New York, New York, March 2, 1948

Highest Degree: M.D., Columbia University, 1903

Positions: 1907-12, studied in Paris, Zurich, and Vienna (under Sigmund Freud*); 1912, practice of psychoanalysis in New York, teaching at Columbia University and New York University

Although the 1909 Clark University conference exposed Freud and other European psychoanalysts to Americans physically, Brill was instrumental in presenting their ideas in printed form. The first translation of a book by Freud was done by Brill (*Selected Papers on Hysteria*, 1909). He translated nine more works by Freud and wrote several in which he expounded psychoanalysis: *Psychoanalysis—Its Theories and Practical Applications* (1921), *Fundamental Conceptions of Psychoanalysis* (1922), and *Freud's Contribution to Psychiatry* (1944). Brill was also responsible for founding the New York Psychoanalytic Society in 1911.

Biographies: A. A. Brill, *J. Nerv. Ment. Dis.*, 1942, *95*, 537-549; E. Jones, *Free Associations: Memories of a Psychoanalyst*, 1959; P. R. Lehrmann, *Psychoanal. Quart.*, 1948, *17*, 155-160; S. Lorand, *Int. J. Psychoanal.*, 1948, *29*, 103; G. Mora, *Bull. N.Y. Acad. Med.*, 1971, *47*, 550-566; C. P. Oberndorf, *Psychoanal. Rev.*, 1948, *35*, 389-393; *Psychoanal. Quart.*, 1948, *17*, 161-163; Various, *Psychoanal. Rev.*, 1941, *28*, 1-11; F. Wittels, *Psychoanal. Rev.*, 1948, *35*, 394-398; *EJ*, 4; *Jewish*, 2; *NCAB*, E; *NYT*, 1948, Mar. 3, 23:1.

BROCA, PAUL

French Surgeon and Anthropologist

Born: Sainte-Foy-la-Grande, Gironde, June 28, 1824

Died: Paris, July 9, 1880

Highest Degree: M.D., University of Paris, 1849

Positions: 1853-80, University of Paris; hospital appointments

On the basis of his theory of the cerebral localization of functions, Broca predicted that a certain patient with a disorder in speech articulation that had come to his attention would have a lesion in the third left frontal convolution of the brain. When the patient died, a postmortem confirmed Broca's prediction, and Broca took the brain to the Société de Anthropologie for a demonstration. (He published a paper on the case in 1861). The demonstration impressed scientists greatly, made a case for the exact localization of brain functions, and made Broca himself famous. The area of the brain involved was later named in his honor. Broca continued to argue that the convolutions of the cerebral cortex were the guides for localizing brain functions.

Broca made it a general practice to trephine the skull for brain tumor operations on the basis of predictions made from symptoms and his theory of brain functions. He is considered to be the founder of modern brain surgery in France. Broca is even better known for his work in physical anthropology, which occupied him during the latter part of his life.

Biographies: E. Dally, *Bull. Soc. Anthrop.*, 1884, *7*, 921-956; M. Genty, *Biog. méd.*, 1935, *9*, 209-224; B. Hollander, *In Search of the Soul and the Mechanisms of Thought, Emotion, and Conduct*, ca. 1920; *Biog. Lex.*, 1, Suppl.; *DSB*, 2; *IESS*, 2; *NYT*, 1880, July 11, 7:2.

BROWN, THOMAS
Scottish Philosopher
Born: Kirkmabreck, Kirkcudbright, January 9, 1778
Died: London, England, April 2, 1820
Highest Degree: M.D., University of Edinburgh, 1803
Positions: 1810-20, professor of moral philosophy, University of Edinburgh

Although Brown was trained in medicine, he soon turned to philosophy and became Dugald Stewart's* disciple. He prepared Stewart's lectures, which after Brown's death were published as *Lectures on the Philosophy of the Human Mind* (1920). Although Brown may be counted with the Scottish school that opposed associationism, he resorted to associationistic principles anyway but, following Berkeley*, used the term *suggestion*. Also, although Reid*, in denying the association of ideas, had to resort to God to make human sensations into perceptions, Brown solved the problem of objective reference by saying that it is the felt resistance in muscular exertion that supplies us with the idea of an external world. Brown's theory of space perception links Berkeley with Lotze* and Wundt* through its appeal to muscular sensations. Brown furthered associationism by postulating for the first time the secondary laws of association (or, as he called them, laws of suggestion): relative duration of the sensations; their relative liveliness, frequency, and recency; the reinforcement of one idea by many others; and individual differences in experience, makeup, health, bodily efficiency, and the attending circumstances. His primary laws were similarity, contrast, and spatial and temporal contiguity. From these simpler instances of "suggestion" Brown distinguished relative "suggestions," such as resemblance, difference, and proportion, which anticipated the recognition by future psychologists that mere association does not account for all cognitions. Relative suggestions supplemented the modulating effect of the secondary laws on the primary ones. Modern learning experiments study the effects on learning of the very factors postulated by Brown. Of Brown's secondary laws of association, a major contribution to the associationistic doctrine, only frequency had been suggested earlier (for instance, by Aristotle*). It became the number-of-trials variable in Ebbinghaus's* studies of memory and, later, in learning experiments. The recognition of the complexity of the associative process was given further recognition by Brown when, in anticipation of John Stuart Mill's* contribution to the doctrine of association, he spoke of "mental chemistry" as the process of blending of ideas that results in a new and different idea.

Biographies: D. Welsh, *Account of the Life and Writings of Thomas Brown*, 1825 (Reprinted since 1934 in all editions of Brown's *Lectures*); *DNB*, 7; *EP*, 1.

BROWN, WILLIAM
English Psychologist
Born: Slinfold, Sussex, December 5, 1881
Died: Oxford, May 17, 1952
Highest Degree: D.Sc. in mathematics, University of London, 1910; D.M., Oxford University, 1918
Positions: 1914-21, reader in psychology, University of London; 1921-47, Wilde readership in mental philosophy, Oxford University; 1925-31, psychotherapist, King's College Hospital; 1936-45, director of Institute of Experimental Psychology, Oxford University; president, British Psychological Society, 1951

In his most important work, *Essentials of Mental Measurement* (1911; rev. ed., 1921, 1925, with Godfrey H. Thomson*), Brown attempted to give a joint treatment to psychophysical methods and psychological statistics. He took issue with Spearman* on the question of interpretation of factor-analytical results related to intelligence measurement. Brown argued that the hierarchical order in matrices of intercorrelations could be produced by random overlapping of group factors, with no general factor in evidence. Later in his career Brown devoted increasingly more time to abnormal psychology and psychiatry, emphasizing the importance of suggestion (*Suggestion and Mental Analysis*, 3rd ed., 1923; *Mind and Personality*, 1926; *Mind, Medicine, and Metaphysics*, 1936; *Psychological Methods of Healing*, 1938; *Psychology and Psychotherapy*, 5th ed., 1944; *Personality and Religion*, 1946). Even so, he is credited with establishing the first psychological laboratory (Institute of Experimental Psychology) at Oxford in 1936.

Biographies: *Nature*, 1946, *158*, 938; *Nature*, 1952, *170*, 911; J. D. Sutherland, *Brit. J. Med. Psychol.*, 1953, *26*, 1; *PR*, 3.

BROWN-SÉQUARD, CHARLES-EDOUARD
French Physiologist
Born: Port-Louis, Mauritius, April 8, 1817
Died: Sceaux, near Paris, April 2, 1894
Highest Degree: M.D., University of Paris, 1846
Positions: 1859-63, head of a hospital in London; 1864-67, Harvard University; for some years did research, lectured, and practiced medicine in France, United States, England, and other countries; 1878-94, Collège de France

Brown-Séquard's reputation as neurophysiologist started with his M.D. thesis on the spinal cord. His major contribution to physiology was the demonstration of the crossing over of sensory fibers in the spinal cord and the study of the consequences of experimental lesions in the nervous system, especially the spinal cord. The Brown-Séquard syndrome is a set of symptoms resulting from lateral hemisection of the spinal cord, such as the paralysis of one side of the body and contralateral anesthesia. Brown-Séquard also did research on the sympathetic nervous system, epilepsy, paralysis, and the brain in general. He founded and edited the *Journal de physiologie de l'homme et des animaux.*
Biographies: M. P. Berthelot, *Mém. Acad. Sci.*, 1904, *47*; ccxxi-cclviii; E. B. Carmichael, *Ala. J. Med. Sci.*, 1972, *9*, 224-237; L. Delhoume, *De Claude Bernard à d'Arsonval*, 1939; E. Dupuy, *Mém. Soc. biol.*, 1894, *46*, 759-770; W. Goddy, *Proc. Roy. Soc. Med.*, 1964, *57*, 189-192; R. H. Major, In *Essays in Biology in Honor of Herbert M. Evans*, 1943, pp. 369-377; J. M. Olmsted, *Charles-Edouard Brown-Séquard: A Nineteenth Century Neurologist and Endocrinologist*, 1946; T. C. Ruch, *Yale J. Biol. Med.*, 1946, *18*, 227-238; J. Schiller, *J. Hist. Med.*, 1966, *21*, 260-270; *DSB*, 2; *NYT*, 1894, Apr. 3, 5:5.

BRÜCKE, ERNST WILHELM VON
German-Austrian Physiologist
Born: Berlin, Germany, June 6, 1819
Died: Vienna, Austria, January 7, 1892
Highest Degree: M.D., University of Berlin, 1842
Positions: 1848-49, University of Königsberg; 1849-91, University of Vienna

Brücke was one of Sigmund Freud's* teachers. In Brücke's Physiological Institute Freud acquired the view that the human being is an interacting energy system. Brücke had developed the idea as a student. In his twenties he, Ludwig*, Du Bois-Reymond*, and Helmholtz* had formed a pact to fight vitalism. Du Bois-Reymond and Brücke pledged between them the additional oath that they would prove and make it an accepted truth that "no other forces than common physical-chemical ones are active within the organism." This strict physicalistic physiology Brücke passed on to his students, including Freud. Brücke also did work in psychophysics. Of enduring value was his thorough study (1878) of change in hue as a function of change in light intensity. Since Wilhelm von Bezold had briefly described the phenomenon earlier (1873), it was named the Bezold-Brücke phenomenon. It refers to the shift toward either yellow or blue of spectral colors when their intensity is increased.
Biographies: E. T. v. Brücke, *Ernst Brücke*, 1928; W. A. Stewart, *Psychoanalysis: The First Ten Years*, 1962; *ADB*, 47; *DSB*, 2; Hirsch, *Biog. Lex.*, 1.

BRUNSWIK, EGON
Austrian-American Psychologist
Born: Budapest, Hungary, March 18, 1903
Died: Berkeley, California, July 7, 1955

Highest Degree: Ph.D. in psychology, University of Vienna, 1927, under Karl Bühler*

Positions: 1927-35, University of Vienna; 1935-36, visiting professor, established first psychological laboratory (School of Education), University of Ankara; 1936-55, University of California at Berkeley

Brunswik's theoretical approach to psychology, probabilistic functionalism, is based on his belief that the method of psychology should rest on that of the physical sciences and that the matter of concern of psychology should be an analysis of how organisms adjust to the environment. To Brunswik common methodology does not mean common laws, however. The aim of experimentation in psychology is the analysis of the organism's ability to estimate or "attain" the value of the *distal stimulus* (energy configuration at the source) even though the *proximal stimulus* (energy configuration at the receptor) varies. Adjustment to the environment thus occurs under probabilistic, that is, partly unpredictable, conditions. In the use of environmental cues the perceiver therefore engages in a process resembling statistical reasoning, for instance, the weighting of probabilities. An organism attains increasingly more veridical perception by incorporating, through contiguity, new cues to an existing cue-family hierarchy. Much of this acquisition is unconscious. The degree to which a distal property and a proximal cue vary together determines the degree of the "ecological validity" of the cue with respect to that property.

Since the concern of psychology is the functional adaptation of organisms to the natural environment, the design of experiments should be not systematic, as in the physical sciences, but representative; that is, their results should have validity in predicting, by statistical generalizations, behavior in the organism's natural habitat. Many of Brunswik's experiments were thus directed at the phenomenon of perceptual constancy and its achievement, which he conducted in natural settings. The Brunswik ratio, which predicts the matching of colors when stimulus and matching samples are under two different illuminations, was one outcome of his constancy research.

Brunswik and his probabilistic functionalism theory created no following, and his output of scientific papers was small, about twenty. His thinking, however, has exercised considerable attraction to psychologists, and Brunswik's ideas may be found in writings of a considerable number of contemporary psychologists. Brunswik was the author of the following books: *Wahrnehmung und Gegenstandswelt* (1934), *Experimentelle Psychologie in Demonstrationen* (1935), and *Perception and the Representative Design of Psychological Experiments* (1956). *Biographies*: E. C. Tolman, *Amer. J. Psychol.*, 1956, *69*, 315-324 (Reprinted in K. R. Hammond [Ed.], *The Psychology of Egon Brunswik*, 1966, pp. 1-12); A. Wellek, *Psychol. Rundsch.*, 1946, *7*, 155-156; *IESS*, 2; *PR*, 3.

BRYAN, WILLIAM LOWE
American Psychologist
Born: Bloomington, Indiana, November 1, 1860

Died: Bloomington, Indiana, November 21, 1955
Highest Degree: Ph.D. in psychology, Clark University, 1892, under G. S. Hall*
Positions: With the exception of two years abroad (University of Berlin, 1886-87; University of Paris, University of Würzburg, 1900-1902), Bryan held positions at Indiana University, at first in fields other than psychology (1884-92), then in psychology (1892-1902), and finally as president (1902-37); president, American Psychological Association, 1903

In psychology Bryan is known for having established a psychological laboratory at Indiana University in 1888 and for a study (published in two papers in 1897 and 1899), performed with N. Harter, of the acquisition of telegraphic skill. It showed an early example of a learning curve, including a learning plateau in the consolidation phase of two separate skills. Also, in the summer of 1902 Bryan performed experiments on abstraction with Oswald Külpe* at Würzburg. They cast in doubt the proposition that all attributes of a sense impression can exist simultaneously in the mind. Bryan produced only a moderate amount of research in psychology, since he became an administrator early in his career. After 1902 he supported psychology financially and by personal encouragement.
Biographies: D. G. Ellson, *Amer. J. Psychol.*, 1956, *69*, 325-327; J. R. Kantor, *Science*, 1956, *123*, 214; *NCAB*, 13; *NYT*, Nov. 22, 1955, 35:3; *Who Was Who in America*, 3.

BUFFON, GEORGE LOUIS LECLERC DE
French Naturalist
Born: Montbard, Côte d'Or, September 7, 1707
Died: Paris, April 16, 1788
Education: Studied law at the University of Dijon, 1723-26; possibly medicine and botany at Collège de l'Oratoire, Angers, 1728-30
Positions: 1742-88, keeper of Jardin du Roi

Buffon created original ideas in many areas of the natural sciences. He anticipated, for instance, Lamarck's* idea of the inheritance of acquired characteristics. In his *Histoire naturelle de l'homme* (1749), Buffon approached humans in the same way he approached animals, including human social and intelligent behavior. Although recognizing that humans are superior to animals by virtue of reason, he showed that it was the evolution of the biological organism that made reason possible. Reason developed from language, and language developed because humans lived in a society. Society, in turn, was necessary because of the slow physical development and long period of dependency of humans. Buffon applied the same reasoning to animals, demonstrating how the nature of their social life determined their level of intelligence. More generally, Buffon presented a speculative but bold theory of organic evolution that, while postulating the original creation of species, assumed that they undergo chance variation, improvement, and deterioration from generation to generation. Buffon thus contributed to the several streams of evolutionary thinking that came together in Charles Darwin's* evolutionary theory.

In a 1743 paper Buffon used the phrase *accidental colors* to denote afterimages, flight of colors, color contrast, and other events in which color is seen without an adequate color stimulus. He was first to describe in detail the formation of successive color contrast.

Biographies: L. F. B. Bertin *et al.*, *Buffon*, 1952; A. de Chesnel, *Vie de Buffon*, 1843; O. Fellows & S. Milliken, *Buffon*, 1972; L. Hanks, *Buffon avant l' "Histoire naturelle,"* 1966; P. Sagnac, *Révol. franç.*, 1925, *78*, 3-15; *CE*, 2; *DSB*, 2; *EB*, 4; *EP*, 1.

BÜHLER, CHARLOTTE B.
Austrian-American Psychologist
Born: Berlin, Germany, December 20, 1893
Died: Los Angeles, California, February 3, 1974
Highest Degree: Ph.D., University of Munich, 1918
Positions: 1920-23, Technische Hochschule, Dresden; 1923-38, University of Vienna; 1938-40, University of Oslo; 1940-43, St. Catherine's College, St. Paul; 1943, Clark University; 1943, Minnesota General Hospital; 1945-53, Los Angeles County General Hospital; 1950-58, University of Southern California and private practice

Charlotte Bühler collaborated with Karl Bühler* (they were later married) and shared his ideas during the latter's early phase of work, as may be seen in Karl Bühler's 1918 book *Die geistige Entwicklung des Kindes*. They both directed the Psychological Institute in Vienna between 1926 and 1938, an important child-study center before World War I. Charlotte Bühler developed Karl Bühler's concepts in child psychology but eventually departed from his static conceptions toward a more dynamic formulation. Her views of childhood were positive and competed with the negative views presented by psychoanalysis. She brought the same positive outlook to the analysis of adulthood and old age. She saw the adult as being shaped by strivings for self-realization and the older person by an evaluation of past life. With Erik Erikson, whose views are similar, Bühler pioneered in the area of adult developmental psychology by providing a first major theoretical formulation. The nature of her views of personality development fitted her with psychologists of the "third force in psychology," with which she became identified. She helped found the Association for Humanistic Psychology in the early 1960s and was later president of that organization. Bühler's major books are *Soziologische und psychologische Studien über das erste Lebensjahr* (1927); *Kindheit und Jugend* (1928); *The First Year of Life* (1930); *Der menschliche Lebenslauf als ein psychologisches Problem* (1933); *Vom Geburt zum Reifealter* (1935); *Kind und Familie* (1937); *Childhood Problems and the Teacher* (1952); *Values in Psychotherapy* (1962); *Psychology for Contemporary Living* (1968, English translation of 1962 German edition); *The Course of Human Life: Studies of Goals in the Humanistic Perspective* (1970);

Humanistic Psychology and Education (1970, with F. Massarik); and *Introduction into Humanistic Psychology* (1972).
Biographies: C. Bühler, In L. J. Pongratz, W. Traxel, & E. G. Wehner (Eds.), *Psychologie in Selbstdarstellungen*, 1972, pp. 9-42; F. Massarik, *J. Hum. Psychol.*, 1974, *14*(3), 4-6; *EJ*, 4; *Who's Who of American Women*, 8th ed.

BÜHLER, KARL
German-Austrian Psychologist
Born: Meckesheim near Heidelberg, West Germany, May 27, 1879
Died: Los Angeles, California, October 24, 1963
Highest Degree: M.D., University of Freiburg, 1903; Ph.D. in philosophy, University of Strasbourg, 1904.
Positions, Honors: 1906-7, University of Berlin; 1907-9, University of Würzburg; 1909-13, University of Bonn; 1913-14, University of Munich; 1918-22, Technische Hochschule Dresden; 1922-38, University of Vienna; 1939, Scholastica College, Duluth, Minnesota; 1940-45, St. Thomas College, St. Paul, Minnesota; 1945-55, Cedars of Lebanon Hospital and University of Southern California; editorial work, *Journal of General Psychology*, 1928-64; honorary president, Sixteenth International Congress of Psychology, 1960; Wilhelm Wundt Medal

Member of the Würzburg school of imageless thought at one time, Bühler published important papers on the subject between 1907 and 1909. His method for studying thought processes was not approved of entirely even by members of the Würzburg school. The method, the *Ausfragemethode*, consisted of the experimenter posing complex mental problems to solve and the observer freely describing what was on his or her mind as the problem was being solved. Bühler proposed that a new element, thought, had to be accepted if all attributes of thinking were to be fully explained. Thought was believed by Bühler to be of three kinds: consciousness of rule, consciousness of relation, and intention, each corresponding to a different type of mental process.

In the 1920s, at the Psychological Institute in Vienna that they had founded, Bühler and his wife, Charlotte Bühler*, were the center of child study in Austria. Bühler wrote *Die geistige Entwicklung des Kindes* (1918) and *Umriss der seelischen Entwicklung des Kindes* (1930), suggesting three stages of development—instinct, habit, and intellect—and emphasizing biological factors at the expense of social determinants of behavior. Instead of the IQ, the Bühlers suggested the concepts of developmental age and the developmental quotient. Bühler's 1918 book was the first systematic treatment of the developmental psychology of the child.

Bühler recognized that psychological research is not exhausted through the study of the inner subjective processes. He ventured into a semantic analysis of social relations, distinguishing information production (*Kundgabe*) from information reception (*Kundnahme*) in both humans and animals. Human speech belongs to the group of semantic institutions that serve to guide humans in their relationships. Additional books by Bühler were *Die Gestaltwahrnehmung* (1913), *Wahrnehmungstheorie* (1922), *Die Krise der Psychologie* (1926-27), *Ausdruckstheorie* (1934), and *Das Gestaltprinzip im Leben der Menschen und Tiere* (1958). *Biographies*: H. Bolgar, *Amer. J. Psychol.*, 1964, *77*, 674-678; J. F. T. Bugenthal *et al.*, *J. Gen. Psychol.*, 1966, *75*, 181-218; P. L. Garvin, *Language*, 1964, *40*, 663-664; A. Janik & S. Toulmin, *Wittgenstein's Vienna*, 1973; G. Lebzeltern, in *Die Uhren der Lebewesen und Fragmente aus dem Nachlass*, 1969, pp. 7-64; H. Roracher, *Almanach österr. Akad. Wiss.*, 1964, *114*, 321-330; H. Roracher, *Psychol. Rundsch.*, 1964, *15*, 228; A. Wellek, *Arch. ges. Psychol.*, 1964, *116*, 3-8; A. Wellek, *Z. exp. angew. Psychol.*, 1959, *6*, iii-iv; *IESS*, 2.

BURNHAM, WILLIAM HENRY
American Psychologist
Born: Dumbarton, New Hampshire, December 3, 1855
Died: Dumbarton, New Hampshire, June 25, 1941
Highest Degree: Ph.D. in psychology, Johns Hopkins University, 1888, under G. S. Hall*
Positions, Honors: 1888-89, Wittenberg College, Potsdam State Normal School, Johns Hopkins University; 1890-1926, Clark University, 1926, professor emeritus; editorial work, *Pedagogical Seminary*; honorary LL.D., Clark University

G. S. Hall brought Burnham from Johns Hopkins to Clark to head the new Department of Pedagogics (educational psychology and mental hygiene). Initially, Burnham did some work on memory and then in educational psychology and mental hygiene. He always interrelated educational psychology and mental hygiene, holding that both dealt with adjustment. Burnham is considered one of the founders of the mental hygiene field. He was a member of the National Committee for Mental Hygiene from 1917 to 1941. Borrowing freely from the theories of other psychologists, Burnham outlined the development and constitution of the "normal" mind and the wholesome personality. To him the wholesome personality was well integrated and therefore able to strive for excellence and accomplish a great deal. The influence of the psychoanalytic writers, especially that of Adler*, is obvious in him but minus the sex aspect. Burnham's ideas on education and mental hygiene were advanced, and he was very well known and influential during his lifetime. Working in the shadow of Hall and having a modest personality prevented him from becoming a better known figure in the history of psychology. Burnham's most cited book is *The Normal Mind* (1924). He also wrote *Great Teachers and Mental Health* (1926), *The Wholesome Personality* (1932), about seventeen papers, and some thirty-five signed articles for P. Monroe's *Cyclopedia of Education* (1911-13).
Biographies: L. A. Averill, *Ment. Hyg.*, 1941, *25*, 647-649; E. S. Conklin, *Amer. J. Psychol.*, 1941, *54*, 611-612; H. D. Sheldon, *J. Soc. Psychol.*, 1946, *24*, 227-247; W. Story & L. N. Wilson (Eds.), *Clark University, 1889-1899*, 1899; *NYT*, 1941, June 26, 23:6.

BUROS, OSKAR K.
American Psychologist
Born: Lake Nebagamon, Wisconsin, June 14, 1905
Died: New Brunswick, New Jersey, March 19, 1978
Highest Degree: M.A. in psychology, Columbia University, 1928
Positions, Honors: 1929-30, Teachers College, Columbia University; 1932-65, Rutgers University; 1946-65, director, Institute of Mental Measurements; 1965-78, professor emeritus of educational measurement and statistics, emeritus director, Institute of Mental Measurements, Rutgers University; president, Gryphon Press, 1940-78; Educational Testing Service Award for Distinguished Service to Measurement, 1973; honorary D.Sc., Upsala University, 1973; other awards and honors

Buros was the originator and publisher of the most authoritative source of information about English-language psychological tests, the *Mental Measurements Yearbook*, which he edited periodically since 1938. He also edited *Reading Tests and Reviews* (1968) and *Personality Tests and Reviews* (1969) and wrote *Tests in Print* (1961). These works contained the descriptions, evaluations, and research bibliographies of commercially available psychological tests. With these guides for the consumer of psychological tests Buros provided an invaluable service that benefited both psychologists and the public in general.
Biographies: H. G. Gough, *Amer. Psychologist*, 1980, *35*, 296-297; *J. Pers. Assess.*, 1978, *42*, 450-451; *American Men and Women of Science*, 12th ed.; *NYT*, 1978, Mar. 21, 38:3.

BURT, SIR CYRIL LODOWIC
English Psychologist
Born: London, March 3, 1883
Died: London, October 10, 1971
Highest Degree: D.Sc., Oxford University, 1906
Positions, Honors: 1908-13, University of Liverpool; 1913-15, Cambridge University; 1913-30, psychologist, Education Department, London County Council; 1924-31, professor of education, University of London; 1931-50, professor and chair of psychology, University College, London; during World War I employed by the National Institute of Industrial Psychology, Industrial Health Research Board, London School of Hygiene, and other bodies; editor, *British Journal of Statistical Psychology*; president, British Psychological Society, 1942; two honorary LL.D. degrees; Thorndike Prize, American Psychological Association, 1971; knighted, 1946

Although Burt's primary contributions were to the areas of mental tests and statistical procedures during a period of about twenty years, during which time he was the most influential individual in the area of mental measurement, his scientific activity spanned sixty-three years, during which time he wrote a dozen books and more than three hundred papers. He was one of the psychologists who in the 1930s developed the statistical technique of factor analysis. He held the position, common to factor analysts at the present time, that the various factor-analytical methods are basically reconcilable. His best-known work in this area is *The Factors of the Mind* (1941), in which his hierarchical model of mental abilities is presented.

Burt is considered the father of British educational psychology. In 1903 he helped to set up the first child-guidance clinic in England and in 1913 was employed by the London County Council as a psychologist, the first appointment of a psychologist to an educational authority in the world. He revised and standardized the Binet intelligence test and others (*Distribution of Educational Abilities*, 1917; *Mental and Scholastic Tests*, 1921; *Handbook of Tests for Use in Schools*, 1923; *Study in Vocational Guidance*, 1926; *The Measurement of Mental Capacities*, 1927). In 1940, in his capacity of government advisor, Burt played an important role in establishing the British educational practice, now abolished, of guiding a student's educational career on the basis of an IQ test given at age eleven. His work with disadvantaged children led to the publication of *The Young Delinquent* (1925), *The Backward Child* (1937), *The Subnormal Mind* (1935), and *The Causes and Treatment of Backwardness* (1952).

Burt pioneered in research on the components of mental ability. He introduced here the statistical methods developed by Fisher*, analyzing mental abilities into the hereditary and environmental components and their interaction. Burt contended that 85 percent of intelligence, as measured by an intelligence test, was attributable to hereditary factors. These conclusions were based on Burt's own extensive studies of the intelligence of identical twins reared apart.

In his last book, *The Psychological Study of Typography* (1959), Burt presented the results of his studies of the effects of typographic factors on the readability and aesthetic quality of type faces in use in children's books and scientific journals.

Biographies: *Amer. J. Ment. Defic.*, 1972, *76*, 389-390; L. S. Hearnshaw, *Cyril Burt, Psychologist*, 1979; *J. Child Psychol. Psychiat.*, 1972, *13*, 73-75; A. R. Jensen, *Psychometrika*, 1972, *37*, 115-117; *HPA*, 4; *IESS*, 18.

BYKOV, KONSTANTIN MIKHAÏLOVICH

Russian Physiologist

Born: Chukhlom, Kostroma province, January 21, 1886
Died: Leningrad, May 13, 1959
Highest Degree: Doctor of medicine, University of Kazan, 1915
Positions, Honors: 1911-15, University of Kazan; 1915-17, military physician; 1921-32, Leningrad Institute of Experimental Medicine and State Teachers Training Institute; 1923-28, Red Army physiological laboratories; 1927-50, University of Leningrad, 1928-40, physiology chair; 1932-51, head of physiology departments of four medical and physiological research institutes; 1950-59, director, Pavlov Institute of Physiology, Leningrad; editor of numerous scientific publications, president of scientific societies; numerous orders, medals, and prizes

In 1926 Bykov and I. A. Alekseev-Berkman reported the first data on the formation of conditioned urinary reflexes. In 1928 Bykov demonstrated that an interoceptive conditioned stimulus could cause a conditioned contraction of the striped muscles in dogs. He did a great deal of work on conditioning, especially interoceptive conditioning, afterwards. Bykov worked under Pavlov* between 1921 and 1932, publishing his main monographs in the 1940s: *The Cerebral Cortex and the Internal Organs* (2nd ed., 1944; English translation, 1957) and *The Corticovisceral Theory of the Pathogenesis of Peptic Ulcers* (1949, with I. T. Kurtsin; English translation, 1966). He published a total of some six hundred papers, directing fifty-five candidate (Ph.D.) and thirty-five doctoral theses.

In 1950 Bykov was instrumental in the "pavlovization" of Soviet science. Between June 28 and July 4, 1950, he served as the chairman of the Scientific Council on Pavlov's Physiological Theory of the USSR Academy of Sciences and was one of the main speakers at the joint session of the USSR Academy of Sciences and the USSR Academy of Medical Sciences, at which the development and application of Pavlov's doctrine was urged on both physiologists and psychologists, and where the school of physiology represented by L. A. Orbeli and I. S. Beritashvili* was denounced.

Biographies: I. T. Kurtsin, *Zh. vyssh. Nerv. Deyat.*, 1956, *6*, 346-351; A. V. Solov'ev, *Zh. vyssh. Nerv. Deyat.*, 1959, *9*, 637-640; *Who Was Who in the USSR*, 1972.

C

CABANIS, PIERRE JEAN GEORGES
French Physician and Philosopher
Born: Departament of Corrèze, June 5, 1757
Died: Rueil, Hauts de Seine, May 5, 1808
Education: Studied medicine at the University of Paris, 1777-83
Positions: Before 1789, professor, Academie at Warsaw; 1789-95, administrator of Paris hospitals; 1795-99, professor of hygiene, University of Paris, 1799, professor of legal medicine and the history of medicine

With Destutt de Tracy*, Condorcet*, Lavoisier*, and Laplace*, Cabanis was one of the leaders of the *Idéologues*, who held that the mind, like chemical composition, could be analyzed, reducing ideas to the original sensations; that the study of human nature could be reduced to the study of physics and physiology; and that the pursuit of pleasure, happiness, and self-preservation were the only motives. Cabanis is also sometimes called the father of physiological psychology (as an alternate to Descartes*), although his physiological psychology was not a systematic affair but an attempt to explain mental events in terms of physiological and anatomical knowledge.

Cabanis began to formulate ideas of importance to psychology when in 1795 he was asked to find out if a person was still conscious after having been guillotined. Cabanis decided that it is the brain that secretes thought; hence a decapitated body is not conscious. Cabanis organized his ideas on this and related matters in his *Rapports du physique et du moral de l'homme* (1802), his most important work. Cabanis was more materialistic than Descartes, whose dualism he rejected, but not as materialistic as La Mettrie*. To Condillac's* analysis of the origin of mental states (the figure of the sentient statue that develops all of the mental functions beginning with the sense of smell alone), Cabanis added the idea that mental states show developmental levels as a function of the individual's age. At any time the mind also shows levels of awareness: unconscious instincts, semiconscious states, and the conscious state that exists by virtue of the brain's activity. Cabanis taught that bodily sensations were essential to the development of awareness and that senses such as smell alone would not be enough to develop a fully sentient being.

Biographies: H. Baruk, *La psychiatrie française de Pinel à nos jours*, 1967; G. Canguilhem, *Études d'histoire et de philosophie des sciences*, 1968; A. Guillois, *Le salon de Mme Helvétius: Cabanis et les idéologues*, 1894; R. La Roche, In P. J. G. Cabanis, *An Essay on the Certainty of Medicine*, 1823, pp. 5-21; C. Lehec, In P. J. G. Cabanis, *Oeuvres philosophiques*, vol. 1, 1956, pp. v-xxi; L. Peisse, *Notice historique et philosophique sur la vie, les travaux et les doctrines de P. J. G. Cabanis*, 1844; F. Picavet, *Les idéologues...*, 1891; C. A. Pierson, *Georges Cabanis: Psychophysiologiste et sénateur...*, 1946; C. de Remusat, *Rev. deux Mondes*, 1844, Oct. 15, 316-349; E. Schiff, *Pierre Jean Georges Cabanis: Der Arzt und Philosoph*, 1886; *DSB*, 3; *EP*, 2.

CALKINS, MARY WHITON

American Psychologist

Born: Hartford, Connecticut, March 30, 1863

Died: Newton, Massachusetts, February 27, 1930

Highest Degree: Ph.D. in psychology, Harvard University, 1895, under William James*

Positions, Honors: 1891-1930, Wellesley College; president, American Psychological Association, 1905

At Wellesley Calkins set up its first psychological laboratory and in 1896 published a paper in which the methodology for paired-associates learning was first presented. The method was reinvented by Georg Müller* a few years later and has been used widely ever since. Her chief interest was psychology as a science of the self, which she contrasted with the view of psychology as a succession of experiences. A paper expressing this view, "Psychology as a Science of Selves," published in 1900, raised criticism and objections by others. She answered the criticisms in her 1905 presidential address at the American Psychological Association meeting and in subsequent papers. Her views were gathered in a systematic treatise in 1910 when *A First Book in Psychology* (2nd ed., 1914) appeared. Its main theme was the blending of conceptions of psychology of the self and psychology of succeeding mental events into a single conceptual framework. Calkins's concept of the psychic element and the doctrine of rational elements of experience also appear in her other books: *Introduction to Psychology* (1901) and *Der doppelte Standpunkt in Psychologie* (1905).

Biographies: R. Calkins, *In Memoriam: Mary Whiton Calkins, 1863-1930*, 1931; F. Converse, *Wellesley College: A Chronicle of the Years 1878-1938*, 1939; B.

Edgell, *Brit. J. Psychol.*, 1930-1931, *21*, 95; L. Furumoto, *Psychol. Women Quart.*, 1980, *5*(1), 55-68; E. Harms, *Arch. ges. Psychol.*, 1931, *80*, 555; J. Loewenberg & H. D. Roelofs, *Phil. Rev.*, 1930, *39*, 323; P. Magg, *Personalist*, 1947, *28*, 44-53; R. McHenry (Ed.), *Famous American Women*, 1983; *DAB*, 21; *HPA*, 1; *NCAB*, 13.

CANNON, WALTER BRADFORD
American Physiologist
Born: Prairie du Chien, Wisconsin, October 19, 1871
Died: Franklin, New Hampshire, October 1, 1945
Highest Degree: M.D., Harvard University, 1900
Positions: 1900-1942, Harvard University; many lectureships, consulting and research posts, trusteeships

Cannon first studied the physiology of thirst and hunger. With A. L. Washburn he performed the classic experiment (1912) demonstrating the simultaneity of felt hunger pangs and stomach contractions. With both thirst and hunger Cannon stressed the importance of local stimulation. Local stimuli were the result of drive-related imbalance in the organism. Its subjective experience initiated action to restore the balance. Study of digestive activities led Cannon to the discovery of the effects of strong emotions on digestion. Further research led him to a broadened concept that included diverse adaptive changes in the physiology of the body under emotion, stress, and tissue need. It was presented in a well-known book, *Bodily Changes in Pain, Hunger, Fear, and Rage* (1915; rev. eds., 1929, 1946). The book presented an influential critique of James's* theory of emotion, which had been the dominant one until then, and offered a substitute theory, now known as the Cannon-Bard theory of emotion. Cannon viewed emotion as an emergency reaction (emergency theory of emotion) that makes the body marshall available resources to cope with an emergency. Cannon's research on the hypothalamus led him to identify it as the control center in emotional behavior.

During World War I Cannon began the study of the effects of traumatic shock. He published his findings in *Traumatic Shock* (1923). Cannon also studied the effects of endocrine secretion on the functioning of the nervous system, particularly of the adrenal gland and its role in mobilizing the energy resources of the body under stress. He discovered and named the hormone *sympathin*, which stimulates heart activity. Other discoveries of the action of the autonomic nervous system followed, resulting in Cannon's formulating the concept of homeostasis (in *The Wisdom of the Body*, 1932; rev. ed., 1939), or the tendency of the body to maintain a steady internal environment. This concept has strongly influenced psychological thinking concerning motivation and learning, for example, Clark Hull's* concept of drive reduction as the basis of learning.

Biographies: W. B. Cannon, *The Way of an Investigator*, 1945; C. K. Drinker, *Science*, 1945, *102*, 470-472; J. H. T., *J. Amer. Med. Ass.*, 1968, *203*, 1063-

1065; L. G. Leibson, *Amer. Rev. Sov. Med.*, 1946, *4*, 155-162; M. G. Ya-roshevskii & S. A. Chesnokova, *Fiziol. Zh.*, 1971, *57*, 1559-1562; R. M. Yerkes, *Psychol. Rev.*, 1946, *53*, 137-146; *DSB*, 15; *IESS*, 2; *NCAB*, 34; *NYT*, 1945, Oct. 2, 23:1.

CANTRIL, (ALBERT) HADLEY, JR.
American Psychologist
Born: Hyrum, Utah, June 16, 1906
Died: Princeton, New Jersey, May 29, 1969
Highest Degree: Ph.D. in psychology, Harvard University, 1931
Positions: 1931-32, Dartmouth College; 1932-35, Harvard University; 1935-36, Columbia University; 1936-55, Princeton University; 1955-69, board chairman and senior counselor, Institute for International Social Research; 1939-57, head, Office of Public Opinion Research

Cantril's work focused on public opinion and its measurement. He established the office of Public Opinion Research at Princeton. Based on the polls of this office and those of others, he advised President Roosevelt on American attitudes toward the war and Presidents Eisenhower and Kennedy on the psychological aspects of foreign policy. During World War II he advised the secretary of war and the Office of War Information.

Cantril was also one of the main contributors to the transactionalist view of perception that originated with Adalbert Ames*. He used public-opinion-polling techniques to obtain data on the perception of social events, people, and other countries that were relevant to the transactionalist view. Since such perception is a function of assumptions, sets, and motives, "the exact nature of what really is happening cannot be determined and actually presents misleading information." With the transactionalists Ittelson and Ames, Cantril wrote papers such as "Psychology and Scientific Research" (1949) and the oft cited "They Saw a Game: A Case Study" (1954, with A. H. Hastorf) as well as the book *The Invasion from Mars* (1940), which was a study of the psychological effects of the famous radio broadcast of H. G. Wells's *War of the Worlds* by Orson Welles. Some of his other seventeen books are *Understanding Man's Social Behavior* (1947), *The "Why" of Man's Experience* (1950), *How Nations See Each Other* (1953, with W. Buchanan), *Perception: A Transactional Approach* (1954, with W. H. Ittelson), and *The Politics of Despair* (1958). Cantril wrote more than one hundred papers and articles.

Biographies: G. Gallup, *Publ. Opin. Quart.*, 1969, *33*, 506; F. P. Kilpatrick, *J. Ind. Psychol.*, 1969, *25*, 219-225; *IESS*, 18; *NYT*, 1969, May 30, 27:2.

CARMICHAEL, LEONARD
American Psychologist
Born: Philadelphia, Pennsylvania, November 9, 1898
Died: Washington, D.C., September 16, 1973

Highest Degree: Ph.D. in psychology, Harvard University, 1924, under W. F. Dearborn*

Positions, Honors: 1925-27, Princeton University; 1927-38, Brown University; 1938-52, Tufts College; secretary, Smithsonian Institution, 1953; chairman, Committee for Research and Exploration, National Geographic Society, 1964; president, American Psychological Association (1940), American Philosophical Society (1970-73); twenty-three honorary degrees; two presidential citations

Carmichael's early interest was the psychobiology of development, in which area he published several important monographs and papers. In the 1920s and 1930s there appeared the oft-cited papers on the development of amblystoma and frog tadpoles in an anesthetic, the righting reflex in cats, behavioral development in guinea pigs as a function of fetal stimulation, and others. The main finding in these papers was that genetic determinants were more important in development than environmental ones. Carmichael also wrote chapters about prenatal behavior for several edited works, including a widely used *Manual of Child Psychology* (1946; 2nd ed., 1954), of which he was the editor. In 1935 he reported (with H. H. Jasper) the development of the electroencephalograph and the first recording of the EEG in America. Although Carmichael was mainly an administrator during his Tufts period, he did research on reading and eye movements that resulted in the publication (with W. F. Dearborn) of the well-known volume *Reading and Visual Fatigue* (1947). During World War II Carmichael recruited psychologists for the war effort. As director of the National Roster of Scientific and Specialized Personnel he eventually presided over a staff of more than four hundred people. He became involved in numerous committees, boards, and so on of the armed forces, the national government, and scientific organizations that were engaged in the management of scientific manpower resources, as well as in a very large number of civic organizations. His positions on various boards, as the chief executive of the Smithsonian Institution, and as government consultant allowed Carmichael to present psychology to the public and to speak for it very effectively.

Biographies: L. C. Mead, *Amer. J. Psychol.*, 1974, *87*, 517-525; *Sci. News*, 1973, *104*, 182; *HPA*, 5; *IESS*, 18; *NCAB*, F; *NYT*, 1973, Sept. 17, 36:1.

CARPENTER, WILLIAM BENJAMIN
English Physiologist

Born: Exeter, Devon, October 29, 1813

Died: London, November 19, 1885

Highest Degree: M.D., University of Edinburgh, 1839

Positions, Honors: 1844, Royal Institute, London; 1845-56, University College, London; 1856-79, University of London; LL.D., University of Edinburgh, 1871

Of Carpenter's numerous publications, his *Principles of Mental Physiology* (1874) is the most important to psychology. In this work he coined the term *unconscious cerebration*, of which he said "thought and feeling could be regarded as an expression of brain-change," the latter being sensations created by the brain itself and no less real than the external sensations that it interprets. The concept led to a fruitful controversy with Thomas Laycock who, although holding a view of the reflex function of the brain similar to that of Carpenter's, asserted that the stimulus for the reflexes arose in the brain itself; Carpenter maintained that a physiological stimulus external to the brain was responsible. Another coinage of Carpenter's was ideomotor action: "Ideas may become the sources of muscular movements, independently either of volitions or of emotions." Carpenter was referring to ideas that are the result of attentive expectations and lead to the behaviors observed in the use of the ouija board and the divining rod.

Biographies: J. E. Carpenter, In W. B. Carpenter, *Nature and Man: Essays, Scientific and Philosophical*, 1888, pp. 3-152 (Reprinted 1970); E. R. Lankester, *Nature*, 1885, *33*, 83-85; *DNB*, 3; *DSB*, 3.

CARR, HARVEY A.
American Psychologist
Born: Indiana, April 30, 1873
Died: Culver, Indiana, June 21, 1954
Highest Degree: Ph.D. in psychology, University of Chicago, 1905, under J. R. Angell*
Positions: 1906-8, Pratt Institute, Brooklyn; 1908-38, instructor to chairman of Psychology Department, University of Chicago; president, American Psychological Association, 1926

Carr was an experimental psychologist and a leading exponent of the functional point of view in psychology, associated with the University of Chicago. In 1926 he succeeded James Rowland Angell, the first psychologist-functionalist, as chairman of the Department of Psychology at Chicago. Under his leadership the Chicago Psychology Department was the best in the United States. During Carr's time at Chicago, one hundred fifty Ph.D. degrees in psychology were granted, and fifty-three of these doctorates were directed by Carr.

Carr's views on functionalism are presented in his book *Psychology: A Study of Mental Activity* (1925). By the time Carr wrote his book the period of controversy concerning functionalism was over, and the book served mainly to clarify further the meaning of function and functionalism. The meanings of function as utility and as activity were said by Carr to be combined in psychology in that both implied what is meant in mathematics by $y = f(x)$, that is, a functional or contingent relationship between psychological antecedents and their consequents. Functionalism was also amplified by Carr in his book in that to the antecedent-consequent relationship he added motivation as the guiding factor. Carr's viewpoint was representative of so many American psychologists even while he was at Chicago that he was able to maintain that functional psychology was American psychology. Carr did research in comparative psychology, systematic learning, and visual space perception. His work in the latter area is presented in his *Introduction to Space Perception* (1935).

Biographies: F. A. Kingsbury, *Psychol. Bull*, 1946, *43*, 259-271; H. L. Koch, *Psychol. Rev.*, 1955, *62*, 81-82; W. B. Pillsbury, *Amer. J. Psychol.*, 1955, *68*, 149-151; *HPA*, 3; *PR*, 3; *Who Was Who in America*, 3.

CATTELL, JAMES McKEEN

American Psychologist

Born: Easton, Pennsylvania, May 25, 1860

Died: Lancaster, Pennsylvania, January 20, 1944

Highest Degree: Ph.D. in psychology, University of Leipzig, 1886, under Wilhelm Wundt*

Positions: 1887-91, University of Pennsylvania; 1891-1917, Columbia University; founder and president, Psychological Corporation, 1917; president, American Psychological Association (1895), Ninth International Congress of Psychology (1929); *Psychological Review* (1894-1903), *Popular Science Monthly* (1900-1915), editor, *Science* (1904-44), *American Naturalist* (1907-44), *School and Society* (1915-39), and *Scientific Monthly* (1915-43)

Cattell never wrote a text and was author of relatively few papers. His influence on psychology was very strong, nevertheless, mainly because of his personality and because he happened to represent the functionalist point of view in the form of mental tests when Americans were most ready to accept both. His ability and willingness to speak out fearlessly on issues, psychological and social, and to be involved in public affairs made him prominent.

Cattell was the first American to receive a doctorate from Wundt. While at Leipzig Cattell, like Wundt, studied reaction time but, unlike Wundt, related it to individual differences. Individual differences became the leitmotif of all of Cattell's subsequent work. He studied the tachistoscopic perception of objects, which introduced reaction time as a measure of sensory differences; reading time in different languages; and the latency of associations, which laid the foundation for future work on association. In this connection Cattell invented the lip key and the voice key. His work on reaction time was as important as Wundt's.

At the University of Pennsylvania Cattell came to occupy the world's first chair in psychology. He also established there a psychological laboratory in 1887, which was the first formally recognized psychological laboratory in the United States. At Pennsylvania Cattell studied the difference threshold, with emphasis less on the size of the threshold and more on the size of the observer error. This work resulted in a well-known monograph that Cattell wrote with G. S. Fullerton* in 1892 (*On the Perception of Small Differences*). Cattell also proposed a substitute for Fechner's law in the form of $S = k\sqrt{R}$, where S was errors of judgment.

On his arrival at Columbia University, Cattell established a psychological laboratory in 1891. He started promoting the idea of mental tests in the 1890s, and his time at Columbia is associated with the mental-test movement. The term *mental test* was coined by Cattell in an 1890 article published in *Mind*. In the 1890s Cattell published the results of tests given to a large number of Columbia University students in the manner of Galton*. Cattell measured variables such as reaction time and visual acuity, but they failed to correlate with the "higher mental processes" or even with grades. Cattell's "anthropometric test movement" died as other psychologists began to pay attention to Binet* who was developing direct measures of the "higher mental processes." The Psychological Corporation, founded by Cattell in 1921 for the promotion of applied psychology and still in existence, has played an important role in the development of psychometric instruments and professional psychology in general.

Around 1903 Cattell started working on the scientific eminence of psychologists and then on the eminence of scientists in general. The rankings he obtained were published in the form of stars after the names of scientists described in *American Men of Science*, a publication Cattell edited between 1906 and 1938. In connection with this undertaking, Cattell invented the method of order of merit, a psychological scaling method now in general use.

Biographies: P. S. Achilles, *J. Appl. Psychol.*, 1941, *25*, 609-618; E. G. Conklin *et al.*, *Science*, 1944, *99*, 151-165, 232-233; M. M. Sokal, *Amer. Psychologist*, 1971, *26*, 626-635; F. L. Wells, *Amer. J. Psychol.*, 1944, *57*, 270-275; R. S. Woodworth, *Psychol. Rev.*, 1944, *51*, 201-209; *DAB*, 23; *DSB*, 3; *IESS*, 2; *NCAB*, 34; *NYT*, 1944, Jan. 21, 16:3.

CHARCOT, JEAN-MARTIN
French Neurologist
Born: Paris, November 29, 1825
Died: Paris, August 16, 1893
Highest Degree: M.D., University of Paris, 1853
Positions, Honors: 1856-60, physician at Central Hospital bureau; 1860-62, University of Paris; 1862-93, senior physician, La Salpêtrière hospital, Paris; president (honorary), First International Congress of Psychology, 1889

Charcot is often called the father of neurology because of his skill in relating patients' symptoms to the anatomy of the nervous system (*Leçons sur les maladies du système nerveux*, 5 vols., 1872-93). He was famous both as a physician and as a teacher. The neurological clinic that he established at La Salpêtrière hospital in Paris was the best in the nineteenth century. Pierre Janet* was his pupil. Sigmund Freud* worked under Charcot for a year and would later refer to him as "my master." Freud learned hypnosis from Charcot and later used it in his own practice. It was Charcot who had planted in him the idea that sexual problems could underlie behavior disorders.

When the phenomenon of hypnotism was declared to be genuine, Charcot began an intensive study of it. His demonstrations of hypnosis began in 1878. On observing that both in hysteria and in hypnosis a great variety of bodily symptoms were simulated, that the symptoms of hysteric patients could be modified by hypnosis, and that it was mostly hysteric patients who could be deeply hypnotized, Charcot concluded that hypnotic phenomena were caused by hysteria and that therefore only hysterics could be hypnotized. Charcot presented his view to the French Academy of Sciences in 1882, and it was completely accepted. A rivalry developed between Charcot and the Nancy school of hypnotism, represented by Liébeault* and Bernheim*, who thought that there was no essential difference between hypnosis and sleep and considered the former a type of suggestibility and therefore a normal rather than a pathological phenomenon. Although later research supported the Nancy school, it was the contribution of Charcot that the neuroses were identified as a separate clinical entity that could be dealt with outside the walls of a mental hospital.

Biographies: C. Féré, *Rev. deux Mondes*, 1894, *122*, 410-424; S. Ferenczi, *Int. Z. Psychoanal.*, 1925, *11*, 257-260; G. Guillain, *J. M. Charcot, 1825-1893: His Life—His Work*, 1959; P. Janet, *Rev. phil.*, 1895, *39*, 569-604; J.-L. Langlois, *Bull. Isaac Ray Med. Library*, 1954, *2*, 1-14; A. Lubimoff, *Le Professeur Charcot*, 1895; F. H. Mackay & E. LeGrand, *Arch. Neurol. Psychiat.*, 1935, *34*, 390-400; L. R. Sanguinetti, *Rass. stud. psichiat.*, 1926, *15*, 201-242; J. C. Tomlinson & W. Haymaker, *Arch. Neurol. Psychiat.*, 1957, *77*, 44-48; *DSB*, 3; *EB*, 5; *IESS*, 2.

CLAPARÈDE, EDOUARD

Swiss Psychologist
Born: Geneva, March 24, 1873
Died: Geneva, September 29, 1940
Highest Degree: M.D., University of Geneva, 1897
Positions: 1897-98, La Salpêtrière hospital, Paris; 1904-40, University of Geneva

Claparède's interests covered a wide variety of subjects. He did some early studies on sleep and animal psychology, wrote sixty-two major articles, and, in 1901, founded the *Archives de psychologie* (with Théodore Flournoy*), which he edited until his death. Claparède's view of behavior was at first biological and then functional and purposive, stressing the adaptive response of the organism to the momentary situation ("law of momentary interest"). He shunned broad, theoretical speculations. Later, he became interested in child study. Claparède saw the study of the child as playing the same role in psychological research as the clinical patient is playing in medical research. He became a leader in establishing the scientific study of child psychology. His best-known book is *Psychologie de l'enfant et pédagogie expérimentale* (1909), which has been translated into many languages. In 1912 Claparède established the Jean Jacques Rousseau Institute, a teachers' training institute specializing in preschool and lower grade schoolchildren, as well as a child-research center. Claparède's work has had a direct influence on Jean Piaget*.

Biographies: *Acta Psychologica*, 1940, *5*(4), 1-6; P. Bovet, *Arch. psychol.*, 1941, *28*, 183-191; P. Gasca Diez, *Riv. psicol. norm. pat.*, 1941, *37*, 106-117; E. Lerner, *Amer. J. Psychol.*, 1941, *54*, 296-299; H. T. Lovell, *Austr. J. Psychol. Phil.*, 1942, *20*, 81-85; W. B. Pillsbury, *Psychol. Rev.*, 1941, *48*, 271-278; A. Szeminska, *Psychol. wychow*, 1946, *12*, 4-14; various, *Scuola Ticinese, period. mens. sezione pedag.*, 3rd ser., 1973, *2*, 1-18; *HPA*, 1; *IESS*, 2.

COGHILL, GEORGE ELLETT

American Anatomist
Born: Beaucoup, Illinois, March 17, 1872
Died: Gainesville, Florida, July 23, 1941
Highest Degree: Ph.D. in zoology, Brown University, 1902
Positions, Honors: 1902-6, Pacific University; 1906-7, Willamette University; 1907-13, Denison University; 1913-25, Kansas State University; 1925-35, Wistar Institute of Anatomy and Biology, Philadelphia; president, American Association of Anatomists, 1933; editor, manager, *Journal of Comparative Neurology*, 1904-41; three honorary degrees

Coghill was a developmental psychobiologist whose work on the behavioral development in embryos of the salamander Amblystoma became well known. Coghill observed the embryos from the time they began to respond to stimulation to the point of fully developed behavior. His conclusion was that reflexes, rather than being elementary phenomena, arise by differentiation from a preexisting behavior pattern. Coghill published his work in twelve parts as ''Correlated Anatomical and Physiological Studies of the Growth of the Nervous System in Amphibia'' between 1914 and 1936. A psychologically relevant book written by Coghill was *Anatomy and the Problem of Behavior* (1929). Coghill applied his conclusions also to the human fetus, which stirred a controversy concerning the universality of the principle of differentiation of reflexes.
Biographies: C. J. Herrick, *George Ellett Coghill: Naturalist and Philosopher*, 1949; C. J. Herrick, *Science*, 1941, *94*, 202-204; *J. Comp. Neurol.*, 1941, *75*, 190-198; *Biog. Mem.*, 22; *DSB*, 2; *NYT*, 1941, July 24, 17:4.

COLERIDGE, SAMUEL TAYLOR

English Poet, Critic, Philosopher
Born: Ottery St. Mary, Devon, October 21, 1772
Died: Highgate, London, July 25, 1834
Education: Attended Jesus College, Cambridge, left without degree in 1794
Positions: No academic or research positions

While at first accepting Hartley's* associationism enthusiastically (as well as his theology, including the ascending scale of affections), Coleridge became a student and interpreter of Kant* (because he could not describe poetic creativity in Hartley's mechanistic terms) and attacked the utilitarians (Bentham*, James Mill*). After a visit to Germany in 1798 and 1799, Coleridge came back enthused about *Naturphilosophie*, rejecting materialism and stressing the presence of spirit in nature (Schelling's* influence). His new view was that mind and nature are not opposed to each other but are only apparently different qualitatively: nature is mind that is not yet aware of itself. Nature is bounded by space, time, and cause-effect but mind is free. The first cause of both is an unconditioned synthesis of both object and subject, nature and mind, namely, God. From this basis of dialectic metaphysics Coleridge developed a theory of artistic creation. Art and artist are also part of the universal contradiction, and art evolves from a struggle between opposites. Artistic fusion is achieved through the use of the faculty of imagination. Coleridge's speculative psychology distinguishes three types of imagination: primary, secondary, and fancy. Secondary imagination is the synthesizing ability of the poet to fuse mind and nature.

Coleridge's influence on contemporary thinkers was considerable. More specifically, he popularized the use of the term *psychology* in English (after it had already gained currency in German and French) as a substitute for *mental philosophy* and similar terms.

Biographies: W. J. Bate, *Coleridge*, 1968; J. D. Campbell, *Samuel Taylor Coleridge: A Narrative of the Events of His Life*, 1896; N. Freeman, *Coleridge: The Damaged Archangel*, 1971; J. L. Lowes, *The Road to Xanadu: A Study in the Ways of Imagination*, 1927; *DNB*, 4, Corr., 49; *EP*, 2.

COMENIUS, JOANN AMOS (JAN AMOS KOMENSKY)
Moravian Educator
Born: Nivnice, Moravia, March 28, 1592
Died: Amsterdam, the Netherlands, November 15, 1670
Education: Graduated from the University of Heidelberg in 1614
Positions: No academic appointments

His intense interest in practical education and the religious persecution of the times combined to send Comenius on educational missions to various European countries, where he spent some forty years of his life. He wrote widely about his theories of practical education. Their philosophical basis was materialistic sensationalism. Comenius stressed learning through experience and teaching by means of demonstrations and illustrations. He made up the first picture book for children in 1658. In his most famous work, *The Great Didactic* (1657), Comenius presented educational principles such as learning with understanding, the use of concrete examples to demonstrate abstract principles, gradualness and sequentiality in the presentation of materials: "from the concrete to the abstract," "from the specific to the general," "from the easy to the difficult," "from the better known to the less known," "from that which is close to that which is away," and others. Comenius also stressed the presentation of materials in accordance with the child's developmental level, the avoidance of physical punishment in school, and teaching in the child's native language. Many of the main features of the contemporary system of teaching children, such as group instruction in classrooms, classes, exercises and tests in the classroom, and the planned school year, were introduced by Comenius.

Biographies: M. Blekestad, *Comenius: Versuch eines Umrisses vom Leben, Werk und Schicksal des Jan Amos Komensky*, 1969; A. Gindley, *Über des Johann Amos Comenius Leben und Wirksamkeit in der Fremde*, 1892; A. Heyberger, *Jean Amos Comenius (Komensky): Sa vie et son oeuvre d'éducateur*, 1928; J. Kvacala, *J. A. Comenius*, 1914; S. S. Laurie, *J. A. Comenius, Bishop of the Moravians: His Life and Educational Work*, 1893; J. Needham (Ed.), *Teacher of Nations*, 1943; M. Spinka, *John Amos Comenius: That Incomparable Moravian*, 1943; *ADB*, 4; *DSB*, 3; *EP*, 2; *NDB*, 3.

COMTE, (ISADORE) AUGUSTE (MARIE FRANÇOIS)
French Philosopher
Born: Montpellier, January 19, 1798
Died: Paris, September 5, 1857
Education: Studied science at École Polytechnique in Paris, 1814-16
Positions: 1816-18, teacher of mathematics in Paris; 1826-32, lecturer in Paris; 1832-42, tutor, examiner, École Polytechnique

In 1838 Comte coined the term *sociology* and attempted to systematize a new science under that name. He believed that individual behavior is largely the product of the society and not of the individual's experience or personality. He also believed that data in science are social and that the study of one's own inner self is impossible. Humans can be understood only in relation to each other; hence data in science are those that are arrived at by observation and concerning whose existence agreement exists. Data are therefore not inferred. Positive data are basic, observational, and preinferential. Comtian positivism thus doubted the validity of a science based on introspection.

In his *Système de politique positive* (one of the six volumes of his main work *Cours de philosophie positive*, published between 1830 and 1842), Comte presented a *Tableau cerebral*, which relates cerebral areas and functions or faculties. Comte accepted Gall's* anatomy and, in a sense, may be seen as holding the views of a physiological psychologist. He denied that there could be function without organs and stated that the brain and the nervous system were the site of intellectual and emotional functions.

Comte represented the evolutionary viewpoint in the social sciences. He postulated three stages in human evolution: theological, metaphysical, and positive (or scientific). John Stuart Mill* was instrumental in making Comte's views known. As the evolutionary viewpoint was gathering momentum in Comte's time, Comte exercised a tremendous influence on the development of thinking in the social sciences.

Biographies: P. Arbausse-Bastide, *Auguste Comte*, 1968; A. Cresson, *Auguste Comte*, 1950; G. Deherme, *Auguste Comte et son oeuvre*, 1909; H. G. Gouhier, *La vie d'Auguste Comte*, 1931; G. H. Lewes, *Fortn. Rev.*, 1866, *3*, 385-410; J.-V. Lonchampt, *Notice sur la vie et l'oeuvre d'Auguste Comte*, 1900; F. S. Marvin, *Comte: The Founder of Sociology*, 1937; A. Robinet, *Notice sur l'oeuvre et la vie d'Auguste Comte*, 1891; E. Seillière, *Auguste Comte*, 1924; *DSB*, 3; *EP*, 2; *IESS*, 3.

CONDILLAC, ÉTIENNE BONNOT DE
French Philosopher
Born: Grenoble, Isère, September 30, 1715
Died: Beaugency, Loiret, August 3, 1780
Education: Studied theology at Saint Suplice, Sorbonne; ordained, 1740
Positions: Various appointments as priest, tutor; no academic or research positions

As a philosophical empiricist and sensationalist, Condillac established Locke's* philosophy in France. His *Essai sur l'origine des connaissances humaines* (1746) presented Locke's ideas but with the qualification that although Locke was right in saying that ideas arise from sensations, he probably was not correct when he said that ideas also arise from reflection. In his *Traité des systèmes* (1749) Condillac spoke out against the innate ideas, faculties, and monads of his predecessors in philosophy. The *Traitè des sensations* (1754) is Condillac's best-known work. It includes the famous analogy of the statue, organized like a human being but with no previous experience, that, by starting out with a single sense, develops attention, memory, judgment, desire, aversion, imagination, and other mental processes. Condillac's style of writing, coupled with the susceptibility of the French to cold, analytic examination of human affairs at that time, were responsible for his success as a philosopher.

Biographies: G. Baguenault de Puchesse, *Condillac: Sa vie, sa philosophie, son influence*, 1910; R. Lenoir, *Condillac*, 1924; M. d. Pra, *Condillac*, 1942; *DSB*, 3; *EP*, 2; *IESS*, 3.

CONDORCET, MARIE JEAN ANTOINE (MARQUIS DE)

French Philosopher and Mathematician
Born: Ribemont, Aisne, September 17, 1743
Died: Bourg-la-Reine (Paris), April 8, 1794
Education: Degree in philosophy, Collège de Navarre, Paris, 1759
Positions: Various political appointments

Condorcet was a precursor of the social sciences. His chief endeavor was to use the approach of the natural sciences and of mathematics in the study of social problems. His thesis was that experience is probabilistic, and that the relationship between the physical sciences and the human sciences lies in probability calculus. In his *Essai sur l'application de l'analyse à la probabilité des décisions rendues à la pluralité des voix* (1785; 2d rev. ed., 1805, under the title *Eléments du calcul des probabilités et son application aux jeux de hasard, à la lotterie, et aux jugements des hommes*), Condorcet offered a probabilistic model of collective decision making. He believed that social mathematics and an exact analysis of ideas would work toward liberation from passion and into reason in mutual interactions. He demonstrated the power of reason in human affairs in his *Esquisse d'un tableau historique des progrès de l'esprit humain* (1795). A similar effort, "Tableau général de la science, qui a pour objet l'application du calcul aux sciences morales et politiques," published in a journal in 1793, remained unfinished.

Biographies: F. Alengry, *Condorcet*, 1904; D. F. J. Arago, In *Smithsonian Inst., Ann. Rep., 1878*, 1879, pp. 180-235; K. M. Baker, *Condorcet*, 1974; A. Burlingame, *Condorcet: The Torchbearer of the French Revolution*, 1930; A. Diannyère, *Notice sur la vie et les ouvrages de Condorcet*, 1799; C. Henry, *Boll. bibliog. storia sci. matem.*, 1883, *16*, 271-297; F. L. Hincker, In M. J. A. N. Condorcet, *Esquisse d'un tableau historique des progrès de l'esprit humain*,

1966, pp. 7-59; A. Koyré, *J. Hist. Ideas*, 1948, *9*, 131, 152; F. E. Manuel, *Prophets of Paris*, 1962; J. F. E. Robinet, *Condorcet: Sa vie, son oeuvre*, 1890-1895; J. S. Schapiro, *Condorcet and the Rise of Liberalism*, 1934; *DSB*, 3; *EP*, 2; *IESS*, 3.

COOLEY, CHARLES HORTON
American Sociologist
Born: Ann Arbor, Michigan, August 17, 1864
Died: Ann Arbor, Michigan, May 8, 1929
Highest Degree: Ph.D. in political economy, University of Michigan, 1894
Positions: 1894-1929, University of Michigan; president, American Sociological Society, 1918

Cooley's important psychological contributions were in the field of social psychology. He considered the self and the society inseparable, each contributing to the identity of the other. Like James* and Baldwin*, Cooley considered communication between individuals the essential characteristic of social relations. People respond to what they think the other person is, not what he actually is. The society exists therefore in an individual's mind. Likewise, the abstract individual, without reference to society, is inconceivable. Individuality is shaped by the primary groups: the family, peer group, neighborhood. Personality traits and attitudes arise in the course of interaction in such face-to-face relationships. The child sees himself as others see him (the "looking-glass self"). Society and the individual are "collective and distributive aspects of the same thing." Cooley's best-known works are *Human Nature and the Social Order* (1902), *Social Organization* (1909), and *Social Process* (1918).
Biographies: R. Dewey, In H. E. Barnes (Ed.), *An Introduction to the History of Sociology*, 1948, pp. 611-623; E. C. Jandy, *Charles Horton Cooley: His Life and Social Theory*, 1942; A. E. Wood, *Amer. J. Sociol.*, 1930, *35*, 707-717; *IESS*, 3.

COPERNICUS, NICOLAUS
Polish Astronomer
Born: Torun, Bydgoszcz, February 19, 1473
Died: Frauenburg (now Frombork), near Elbing (Elblag), Gdansk, May 24, 1543
Highest Degree: Doctor of canon law, University of Ferrara, 1503
Positions: 1497-1543, canon of cathedral chapter of Frombork; 1497-1501, 1501-3, on study leave; 1503-12, advisor to bishop of Warmia

Copernicus's one great book, *De revolutionibus orbium coelestium libri VI*, appeared in the year of his death. In this book Copernicus explained how the Earth, instead of being the center of the universe, is just one of several planets, all rotating around the Sun. The heliocentric view of the world, made public in the same year as Vesalius's* anatomical treatise, marks the beginning of modern astronomy. The works of Copernicus and Vesalius also mark the beginning of modern science.

Copernicus believed in a perfect natural order that allows its laws to be discovered and in the empirical testing of theory through observation: he rejected the Ptolemaic geocentric universe because it did not agree with astronomical observations and substituted the scientifically more plausible heliocentric theory. Although the geocentric theory pictured humanity at the center of the universe, the heliocentric theory relegated it to a peripheral position, suggesting the possibility that other souls might exist elsewhere besides Earth. The loss of human importance implied in the heliocentric view, while furthering objectivity in science, is also seen by some as having caused, at least partly, human unhappiness, even neuroticism. The significance of Copernicus for psychology lies in the changed view of the position of humanity in the universe that he brought about, a change that eventually permitted the scientific study of human consciousness and behavior.

Biographies: A. Armitage, *Copernicus: Founder of Modern Astronomy*, 1939; A. Armitage, *The World of Copernicus*, 1947; S. P. Mizwa, *Nicholas Copernicus*, 1943; *DSB*, 3; *EB*, 6; *The McGraw-Hill Encyclopedia of World Biography*, vol. 3.

COUÉ, EMILE
French Hypnotist
Born: Troyes, Aube, February 26, 1857
Died: Nancy, July 2, 1926
Education: Graduated in pharmacy
Positions: 1882-91, druggist; 1910-26, operated a hypnotic clinic

Coué followed the apothecary trade for twenty-eight years and then became interested in suggestion and hypnotism (in 1901) and took up their study with Liébeault* and Bernheim* at Nancy. In 1910 he opened his own clinic at Nancy. Unlike other hypnotists, Coué taught his clients self-help. Self-help was accomplished through self-suggestion (he is thought to have coined the term *autosuggestion*), as when a client was told to repeat formulas expressing faith in self-improvement, such as "Every day in every way I am getting better and better." Coué presumed to cure even organic disorders by the power of imagination. He became famous and went on lecture tours in England and the United States. He published a number of books, among them *Self-mastery Through Conscious Autosuggestion* (1922) and *My System* (1923).

Biographies: C. Baudouin, *Action Pensée*, 1946, 22, 97-105; C. Baudouin *et al.*, *Emile Coué and His Life-Work*, 1923; E. B. Kirk, *My Pilgrimage to Coué*, 1922; H. Macnaghten, *Emile Coué: The Man and His Work*, 1922; *EB*, 6; *NYT*, 1926, July 3, 13:3.

COUSIN, VICTOR
French Philosopher
Born: Paris, November 28, 1792
Died: Cannes, January 13, 1867

Education: Graduated from École Normale Supérieure, Paris, 1812
Positions: 1815-21, 1828-30, Sorbonne; 1835-40, École Normale Supérieure, Paris; from 1840, in political life

Cousin adopted the psychological approach to philosophy in the manner of Marie Maine de Biran* and Thomas Reid*, but in his later life he was influenced by Friedrich Schelling*. Cousin opposed the extreme sensationism of Etienne Condillac* and the materialism and atheism that he thought resulted from it but accepted the view that sensations inform us about the external world, as did philosophers in the Scottish school of common sense. From this psychological premise Cousin arrived at an ontology and the recognition of God as the ultimate causal substance.

Biographies: E. Bersot, *Victor Cousin et la philosophie de notre temps patrie*, 1879; J. Berthélemy-Sain Hilaire, *M. Victor Cousin: Sa vie et sa correspondence*, 1895; P. A. R. Janet, *Victor Cousin et son oeuvre*, 1885; F. A. A. Mignet, *Notice historique sur la vie et les travaux de M. Victor Cousin*, 1860; J. Simon, *Victor Cousin*, 1888; *EP*, 2; *NYT*, 1867, Jan. 27, 5:1.

CROCE, BENEDETTO

Italian Philosopher, Historian
Born: Pescasseroli, L'Aquila, February 25, 1866
Died: Naples, November 20, 1952
Education: Studied law at the University of Rome
Positions: 1910; appointed senator for life; did not hold any remunerated positions; founder and editor, *La critica*; three honorary degrees; medal from Columbia University

Croce was the best-known Italian philosopher of the twentieth century and the foremost exponent of Italian neoidealism (historical idealism), which asserts the self-creative and self-creating mind to be the only reality. Croce's writings have been collected in more than sixty volumes. For psychology his most significant book is *Aesthetic as Science of Expression and General Linguistics* (1909 translation of the 1902 Italian edition). Croce viewed aesthetic experience as a type of cognition of a primitive kind. He stressed intuition and the nonconceptual communication that takes place through the language of poetry. Art to him was the expression of emotion that was a particular kind of cognition—nonconceptual cognition. The expression of emotion through art partakes of a universal character since emotion is the common denominator. Intuitions as images yield an experience of the universal human spirit. Aesthetic thus becomes the science of intuitive cognitions. Croce is significant to the social sciences as a philosopher of history. He considered history a form of art, made philosophy the methodology of history, and asserted that historic truth constitutes the work of the historian as he reconstructs the past in his mind.

Biographies.: G. Castellano, *Benedetto Croce: Il filosofo, e lo storico*, 1936; B.

Croce, *An Autobiography*, 1945; F. Flora (Ed.), *Benedetto Croce*, 1953; F. Nicolini, *Benedetto Croce: Vita intellectuale*, 1962; G. Prezzolini, *Benedetto Croce*, 1909; C. J. S. Spriggs, *Benedetto Croce: Man and Thinker*, 1952; *EB*, 6; *EP*, 2; *IESS*, 3; *NYT*, 1952, Nov. 21, 25:1.

CROZIER, WILLIAM JOHN
American Physiologist
Born: New York, New York, May 24, 1892
Died: Belmont, Massachusetts, November 2, 1955
Highest Degree: Ph.D. in zoology, Harvard University, 1915
Positions: 1915-18, Bermuda Biological Station; 1918-19, University of Illinois; 1919-20, University of Chicago; 1920-25, Rutgers University; 1925-55, Harvard University; editorial work, *Journal of General Physiology*, 1924-55

Crozier influenced psychology through his theory and experimentation on animal behavior and the sensory processes. He studied the different types of tropisms and the factors that influence tropistic behavior. He thought that his major contribution was the "parametric analysis" of behavior, by which he meant the identification and study of meaningful parameters in equations describing aspects of behavior so as to test hypotheses about the underlying mechanisms. In the area of sensory processes Crozier wrote a chapter about chemoreception for the *Handbook of General Experimental Psychology* (1934) and did a large number of experiments on critical flicker fusion. He wrote a total of about three hundred scientific papers.
Biographies: H. Hoagland, *Amer. J. Psychol.*, 1956, *69*, 135-138; *NYT*, 1955, Nov. 3, 31:2; *PR*, 3; *Who Was Who in America*, 3.

CUVIER, GEORGES LEOPOLD CHRETIEN FREDERIC DAGOBERT, BARON
French Biologist
Born: Montbéliard, Doubs, August 23, 1769
Died: Paris, May 13, 1832
Education: Studied natural science at the Stuttgart Academy for four years
Positions: 1795-99, Museum of Natural History, Paris; 1799-1832, Collège de France

Cuvier played a leading role in the development of paleontology and comparative anatomy. His doctrine of the correlation of parts claimed that since the parts of an animal are functionally and structurally appropriately related (at creation, not through adaptation), the entire animal could be reconstructed from a single bone. He believed, however, in spontaneous generation, the fixity of species, and the preformation of the embryo. His opposition to the idea of evolution was such that, when faced with the evidence of paleontology, he opted for the theory of catastrophism promulgated by Bonnet*. Cuvier's influence in France was so great that it was an obstacle to the acceptance of the point of view of evolutionists, such as Lamarck's*. Cuvier also appears to have been persuaded by Napoleon to reject (in 1808) the application of the phrenologist Gall* for membership in the Institut de France (later Académie de Science).

Biographies: W. Coleman, *Georges Cuvier, Zoologist*, 1964; R. Dujarric de la Rivière (Ed.), *Cuvier: Sa vie, son oeuvre, pages choisies*, 1969; P. Flourens, *Ann. Rep. Board Smithsonian Inst.*, 1868, 121-140; P. Huard & M. Montagne, *Extrême-Orient méd.*, 1949, *1*, 170-259; E. Kuhn-Schnyder, *Jb. ges. Naturkd. Württ.*, 1969, *124*, 65-105; S. B. Lee, *Memoirs of Baron Cuvier*, 1833; G. Legée, *Hist. Biol.*, 1969, *2*, 10-34; J. Pirier, *Rev. Paris*, 1832, *39*, 85-115; various, *Arch. Mus. Hist. Naturwiss.*, 1932, *9*, 1-134; *DSB*, 3.

D

DALLENBACH, KARL M.
American Psychologist
Born: Champaign, Illinois, October 20, 1887
Died: Austin, Texas, December 24, 1971
Highest Degree: Ph.D. in psychology, Cornell University, 1913, under E. B. Titchener*
Positions: 1913-15, University of Oregon; 1915-16, Ohio State University; 1916-48, Cornell University; 1948-58, professor, later chairman of Psychology Department, University of Texas

Of those students of Wundt's* who remained most faithful to him, Titchener was the most prominent. Dallenbach held the same relationship to Titchener. Dallenbach believed that psychology's first business was experimentation, although he did not necessarily use introspection as his main tool. Like Titchener, his main interest lay in sensation and perception. Dallenbach did not develop any major theories and he never wrote a book. He did contribute, however, almost two hundred fifty papers. Of them, almost one hundred were contributions to scientific thought or new experimental data, most of them about sensation and perception but also about attention, memory, and cognitive processes. His studies on facial vision and retention during sleep belong to the classical psychological literature. A physical monument to Dallenbach the experimentalist is the psychological laboratory at the University of Texas, Mezes Hall, designed by Dallenbach and the building of which he supervised.

A contribution that is considered by some to have been an even greater one was Dallenbach's purchase, from G. Stanley Hall*, and consequent rescue of the first American psychological journal, the *American Journal of Psychology*, in 1920. Dallenbach was the owner of this journal for the next forty-eight years and editor for forty-two. His involvement with the journal was such that he referred to its volumes as his "books."

Biographies: E. G. Boring, *Amer. J. Psychol.*, 1958, *71*, 1-40; R. B. Evans, *Amer. J. Psychol.*, 1972, *85*, 463-476; *HPA*, 5; *NYT*, 1971, Dec. 25, 20:5.

DALTON, JOHN
English Chemist
Born: Eaglesfield, Cumberland, September 6, 1766
Died: Manchester, Lancashire, July 27, 1844
Education: Largely self-taught; two honorary degrees
Positions: 1793-99, professor of mathematics and philosophy, New College, Manchester; from 1799, private tutor

Dalton's scientific fame rests principally on his advocacy of the atomic theory in chemistry and his investigations of gases, vapor, and steam. In psychology he is known for his study and description of color blindness. In a 1794 presentation to the Manchester Literary and Philosophical Society, Dalton described his own inability to see reds and greens. He theorized that it might be due to the absorption of these colors by the ocular media. A postmortem examination of his eyes, for which he himself had provided, disproved his theory. The study and understanding of the nature of color blindness dates from 1794. For a time (since 1827) color blindness was called Daltonism. It is still called that in some languages.

Biographies: E. M. Brockbank, *John Dalton: Experimental Physiologist and Would-Be Physician*, 1929; F. Greenaway, *John Dalton and the Atom*, 1966; F. Greenaway, *Mem. Manch. Lit. Phil. Soc.*, 1958-1959, *100*, 1-98; W. C. Henry, In *Works of the Cavendish Society*, vol. 29, 1854; E. C. Patterson, *John Dalton and the Atomic Theory: The Biography of a Natural Philosopher*, 1970; A. Thackray, *John Dalton: Critical Assessment of His Life and Science*, 1972; *DNB*, 5; *DSB*, 3, 15.

DARWIN, CHARLES
English Naturalist
Born: Shrewbury, Shropshire, February 12, 1809
Died: Down, Kent, April 19, 1882
Education: Studied medicine at the University of Edinburgh, 1825-28; studied for ministry at Cambridge University, graduated in 1831
Positions: 1831-36, naturalist, H.M.S. *Beagle*

Darwin's world fame is based on his theory of evolution. Although he did not originate the idea that species of plants and animals undergo changes (it was held by men such as George Buffon*, Jean Lamarck*, and his own grandfather, Erasmus Darwin*), he contributed to the idea a large amount of systematic, comparative observations and a theory of how evolution takes place. Darwin, having garnered his observations during the five-year voyage of the *Beagle*, read Malthus's* *Essay on the Principle of Population* soon after his return, which furnished him with the idea that the struggle for existence would favor the survival of the favorable variations of plants and animals while unfavorable ones would perish. Darwin marshaled the evidence for evolution as no one had done before and provided a theory of how it happens in his great work *Origin of Species*, published in 1859. He spent the rest of his life developing and defending his ideas.

To psychology Darwin's books that are of particular importance, aside from *Origin*, are *The Descent of Man* (1871) and *The Expression of Emotions in Man and Animals* (1872). They spell out the basic assumption underlying psychology, namely, that humans are on a continuum with the rest of the animal world, and that since animals can be studied by the scientific method, so can humans. Evolutionary biology, founded by Darwin, gave impetus to phylogenetic, or comparative, psychology. The evolutionary viewpoint concerning the development of both structure and function, at first represented by the functionalist school of psychology (John Dewey*, James Rowland Angell*, Harvey Carr*), is now a widely accepted point of view in psychology. Ontogenetic psychology, which had its beginnings around 1880, was greatly influenced by Darwin's theory. G. Stanley Hall*, who pioneered in child study in the United States, did so along the lines of evolutionary theory, as did another pioneer, James Mark Baldwin*. The child's developmental history was seen by many as a key to the developmental history of humanity. Darwin himself contributed to the developmental literature by writing a biography of his first-born son (1877).

Biographies: P. Appleman (Ed.), *Darwin*, 1970; M. F. Ashley-Montagu, *Darwin: Competition and Cooperation*, 1952; N. Barlow (Ed.), *The Autobiography of Charles Darwin*, 1958; F. E. Darwin, *Charles Darwin*, 1902; G. De Beer, *Charles Darwin: A Scientific Biography*, 1965; F. Huxley, *Amer. Scholar*, 1958-1959, *28*, 489-499; 1959-1960, *29*, 85-93; W. Irvine, *Apes, Angels, and Victorians: The Story of Darwin, Huxley, and Evolution*, 1955; R. Olby, *Charles Darwin*, 1967; A. Weismann, *Ann. Rep. Board Smithsonian Inst.*, 1909, 431-452; G. West, *Charles Darwin: A Portrait*, 1938; W. Wichler, *Charles Darwin: The Founder of the Theory of Evolution and Natural Selection*, 1961; *DNB*, 5; *DSB*, 3; *IESS*, 4; *NYT*, 1882, Apr. 21, 5:1.

DARWIN, ERASMUS
English Physician and Biologist
Born: Elston Hall, Nottinghamshire, December 12, 1731
Died: Breadsall Priory near Derby, Derbyshire, April 18, 1802
Highest Degree: M.D., University of Edinburgh, 1754
Positions: Since 1756, private practice of medicine

Darwin intimated the evolutionary theory, although he attributed the main role in evolution to purposeful adaptation, in anticipation of Lamarck's* theory. Fearing for his reputation, Darwin did not present his views until late in life.

Since at least the initial works in which the idea was presented were written in verse, it was that much less effective. Darwin is also counted as one of the lesser British associationists. The doctrine of association of ideas is presented in his *Zoonomia* (1794). This work also presents one of the earliest accounts of vertigo and the apparent negative after-rotation. The 1801 edition of the work also introduces the (incorrect) theory that hunger is the quiescent state of the stomach when it has nothing to do.

Biographies: N. Barlow, *Not. Rec. Roy. Soc. London*, 1959, *14*(1), 85-98; H. Cohen, *Univ. Bgham. Hist. J.*, 1967, *11*, 17-40; J. Dowson, *Erasmus Darwin: Philosopher, Poet, and Physician*, 1861; D. King-Hele, *Erasmus Darwin*, 1963; E. Krause, *The Scientific Works of Erasmus Darwin*, 1887, pp. 1-107, 129-216; H. Pearson, *Doctor Darwin: A Biography*, 1943; A. Seward, *Memoirs of the Life of Dr. Darwin* ..., 1804; *DNB*, 5; *DSB*, 3; *EP*, 2.

DASHIELL, JOHN FREDERICK

American Psychologist
Born: Indianapolis, Indiana, April 30, 1888
Died: Alexandria, Virginia, May 3, 1975
Highest Degree: Ph.D. in psychology, Columbia University, 1913
Positions, Honors: 1913-14, Waynesburg College; 1914-15, Princeton University; 1915-17, University of Minnesota; 1917-19, Oberlin College; 1919-58, University of North Carolina, 1920-49, chairman, Psychology Department; 1958-75, Kenan Professor Emeritus; 1958-74, Wake Forest College and University of Florida; editorial work, McGraw-Hill (Publications in Psychology, 1931-50) and *Psychological Monographs* (1935-47); president, American Psychological Association and Society of Experimental Psychologists, 1938; American Psychological Foundation Gold Medal, 1960

Dashiell organized the Psychology Department at the University of North Carolina. From the outset psychology was taught as a natural science, with full laboratory, which was the first such undergraduate program in the United States. After his retirement, Dashiell reorganized psychology at Wake Forest College in a similar manner. He was an experimental psychologist who worked in a wide variety of areas such as spatial orientation, monocular diplopia, fatigue and efficiency, and animal learning. The common denominator of what he did was eclecticism, synthesis, coordination, and reconciliation of differing viewpoints. He stressed this theme explicitly in several articles. Dashiell wrote a textbook, *Fundamentals of Objective Psychology* (1928), that was revised under the title of *Fundamentals of General Psychology* (1937), *Direction Orientation in Maze Running by the White Rat* (1930), and *An Experimental Manual of Psychology* (1931)

Biographies: *Amer. Psychologist*, 1960, *15*, 798-799; *HPA*, 5; *NCAB*, F; *NYT*, 1975, May 4, 61:2.

DEARBORN, WALTER FENNO
American Psychologist
Born: Marblehead, Massachusetts, July 19, 1878
Died: St. Petersburg, Florida, June 21, 1955
Highest Degree: Ph.D. in psychology, Columbia University, 1905, under J. McK. Cattell*; M.D., University of Munich, 1913
Positions: 1905-9, University of Wisconsin; 1909-12, University of Chicago; 1912-47, Harvard University, since 1917, professor and director, Psychological Clinic of Harvard Graduate School of Education; 1947-53, director, Psycho-Educational Clinic, Lesley College

Dearborn was an educational psychologist who did research on reading problems, the relationship between physical growth and intelligence, and intelligence testing. He and his students produced many papers in these areas. In the area of testing Dearborn produced *The Dearborn Group Tests of Intelligence* (1920). With J. W. M. Rothney he wrote *Predicting the Child's Development* (1941), which dealt with the correlation between mental and physical growth. Dearborn's studies showed that the correlation was a matter of individual differences and, on the average, so low as to be practically zero. With L. Carmichael*, Dearborn wrote the well-known book *Reading and Visual Fatigue* (1947). In *The Psychology of Teaching Reading* (1952), Dearborn stressed the role of motivation, emotion, and cognitive factors in learning to read.
Biographies: H. S. Langfeld, *Amer. J. Psychol.*, 1955, *68*, 679-681; *NYT*, 1955, June 22, 29:4; *PR*, 3; *Who Was Who in America*, 3.

DECROLY, OVIDE JEAN
Belgian Psychologist
Born: Ronse (Renaix), Belgium, July 23, 1871
Died: Brussels, September 12, 1932
Highest Degree: Dr. en médecine, University of Ghent, 1896
Positions, Honors: 1901-6, private institution for exceptional children; 1906-8, Office for Vocational Guidance, Brussels; 1908-14, private experimental school for mentally retarded children; 1914-16, classes for mentally retarded children, Brussels; 1916-19, League for Orphans' Homes; 1919-32, University of Brussels; several medals, various honors

In a 1910 paper, published with J. Degand, Decroly reported on a study of the intelligence of Belgian children in which it was found that these children were a year and a half ahead of the Parisian children studied by Binet*. It was soon realized that the difference was the result of the higher social class standing of the Belgian children, which, in turn, opened up the problem field of the relationship between social class and intelligence. Decroly continued working in the area of child psychology in which he published eight books between 1912 and 1930. These books reflect Decroly's research and thinking about the child. They eventually found a concrete expression in what became known as the "Decroly method" in education, a set of educational principles based on psychological insights that deviated considerably from the traditional pedagogical prescription. Decroly published some 130 titles, most of them on child psychology, intelligence, educational psychology, and the exceptional child.

Biographies: Decordes (No init.), In H. Wallon, *L'Oeuvre du Dr. O. Decroly: Journée Internationale, Paris, 16 mars, 1953*, 1955, pp. 15-17; M. Flayol, *Le Dr. O. Decroly, éducateur*, 1934; J. Nuttin, *Psychology in Belgium*, 1961; R. Pasquasy *Psychol. belg.*, 1971, *11*, 249-262; M. Peers, *Ovide Decroly*, 1942; *CE*, 4; *PR*, 3.

DELABARRE, EDMUND BURKE
American Psychologist
Born: Dover, Maine, September 25, 1863
Died: Providence, Rhode Island, March 16, 1945
Highest Degree: Ph.D. in psychology, University of Freiburg, 1891, under H. Münsterberg*
Positions: 1892-96, Brown University; 1896, Harvard University; 1897-32, Brown University

A year after obtaining his doctorate, Delabarre established a psychological laboratory at Brown University and became one of the twenty-six individuals who founded the American Psychological Association. From 1896 to 1897 he ran William James's* laboratory at Harvard. Delabarre published both experimental and theoretical papers about philosophical psychology, consciousness, visual perception, social psychology, and muscular sensations. He had formulated a motor theory of consciousness and planned to write a systematic treatise on it, but never did. He likewise failed to publish many of his experiments, involving hundreds of hours of work that he had spent observing muscular movements. For this purpose Delabarre invented the first long-tape *kymograph* to record lengthy observations of muscular movements. In 1898 he also made the first eye-movement recordings using a mechanical device—a cup on the eye traced paths on a kymograph tape. Because of his failure to publish much of his work, Delabarre's influence of psychology was slight.

Biographies: L. Carmichael, *Amer. J. Psychol.*, 1945, *58*, 406-409; H. Schlosberg, *Psychol. Rev.*, 1945, *52*, 183-186; R. S. Woodworth, *Science*, 1945, *102*, 369; *NYT*, 1945, Mar. 17, 13:4; *Who Was Who in America*, 2.

DELACROIX, HENRI
French Psychologist
Born: Paris, December 2, 1873
Died: Paris, December 3, 1937
Highest Degree: *Agrégé* in philosophy, Sorbonne, 1894; Doctorate in letters, Sorbonne, 1899
Positions: 1899-1903, University of Montpelier; 1903-9, University of Caen; 1909-37, Sorbonne (University of Paris)

Delacroix, a philosophical psychologist, had interest in and published papers and books in a number of areas, especially the psychology of mysticism. On this subject he published several papers and the book *Étude d'histoire et de psychologie de mysticisme* (1908; 2nd ed., 1938). He attributed mysticism to unconscious activity but analyzed it both sympathetically and exactly. Delacroix was interested more in the historical than the experimental approach to psychological topics. This preference characterizes the books he published in the areas of child development, the psychology of language, and the psychology of art: *La psychologie de Stendhal* (1918); *Le langage et la pensée* (1924); *L'Analyse psychologique de la fonction linguistique* (1926); *Psychologie de l'art* (1927); *L'Enfant et le langage* (1934); and *Les grandes formes de la vie mentale* (1934). *Biographies*: P. Guillaume, *J. psychol. norm. path.*, 1937, *34*, 593-605; *DBF*; *EUI*, 17; *PR*, 3.

DELBOEUF, JOSEPH REMI LEOPOLD
Belgian Psychologist
Born: Liège, Belgium, September 30, 1831
Died: Bonn, Germany, August 14, 1896
Highest Degree: Ph.D.
Positions: 1863-66, University of Ghent; 1866-96, University of Liège

Delboeuf began psychophysical experimentation on brightness in 1865 under the influence of Fechner*. In psychophysics Delboeuf's contributions rank right after those of Fechner and G. E. Müller*. The most important idea that Delboeuf introduced was that of the sense distance (*contraste sensible*). Fechner had thought that sensations, like distances, were magnitudes, and that, like distances, they could have zero value. Objections were made to this notion, especially since, introspectively, sensations do not appear to have magnitude. Delboeuf modified Fechner's notion by asserting that although sensations are not magnitudes, they can be ranked on a continuum, so that differences or distances between them may be established. This idea came to underlie the measurement of sensations in the twentieth century.

Delboeuf published several critical monographs about psychophysics during a period of ten years: *Étude psychophysique* (1873) and *Théorie générale de la sensibilité* (1876), reprinted together as *Eléments de psychophysique* (1883); *Examen critique de la loi psychophysique* (1883); and others. Delboeuf's name is also attached to the illusion of contrasting circles, which he first described in 1893. Many experiments have been performed on this illusion since that time. Finally, as a pioneer of psychology in Belgium, Delboeuf established a psychological laboratory at Liège. During the last years of his life he turned his attention to hypnotism, siding with the Nancy school in the interpretation of its nature. He wrote a volume in this area, *De l'origin des effets curatifs de l'hypnotisme* (1887).
Biographies: A. Forel, *Z. Hypno.*, 1897, *5*, 1-6; G. S. Hall, *Amer. J. Psychol.*, 1896, *8*, 312; J. Nuttin, *Psychology in Belgium*, 1961; *EUI*, 17.

DEMOCRITUS
Greek Philosopher
Born: Abdera, Thrace, ca. 470 B.C.
Died: Ca. 370 B.C., place unknown
Education: Student of Leucippus; traveled widely to study
Positions: Teacher of philosophy

Democritus, one of the most eminent of the ancient Greek philosophers, was a materialist, determinist, and atomist. He is particularly celebrated for his atomic view of the world. Although his atoms were not those of modern physics, they were tiny, in ceaseless motion, and constituted all matter, including the mind. The atoms of the mind were round, fiery, slippery, moved very fast, and showed "subtlety of action." Following Empedocles*, Democritus held that sensation and perception occur as atoms outside the body come in contact with atoms of the body, including those of the mind. The notion of sensory thresholds was adumbrated by Democritus when he stated that the nonbodily atoms had to possess certain strength before they could make an impression on the body. Democritus held that the shape of the atoms impinging upon the sense organs determined the quality of the sensations produced by them, but that all senses were basically touch because the essence of sensation was the contact between external and bodily atoms. This included vision: visual objects, said Democritus, continuously emit images of themselves that mold the atoms of the air accordingly. The aerial copy of the object creates visual impression upon contact with the eye. This original statement of the representative theory of perception persisted in scientific circles through the nineteenth century and still lingers in the conception of vision of the "man in the street." Since the atoms that emanate from the sensible objects may mix with others before reaching the perceiver, the senses may distort reality. In addition, since sensation is only the movement of atoms, sensations are only subjective experiences to which nothing real corresponds outside the perceiver. They are what was from the seventeenth century onward called the "secondary qualities" of real objects, important to Locke*, Descartes*, and others.
Biographies: *DSB*, 4; *EB*, 7; *HGP*, 2.

DENNIS, WAYNE
American psychologist
Born: Washington County, Ohio, September 1, 1905
Died: Richmond, Virginia, July 21, 1976
Highest Degree: Ph.D. in psychology, Clark University, 1930
Positions: 1929-42, University of Virginia; 1942-43, professor and head of Psychology Department, Louisiana State University; 1945-51, professor and head of Psychology Department, University of Pittsburgh; 1951-70, Brooklyn College, 1951-62, head of Psychology Department; 1962-64, executive officer, graduate program in general psychology, City University of New York; 1955-56, 1958-59, 1964-65, 1974-75, visiting professor, American University of Beirut; 1943-

45, head, Human Engineering Section, Special Services Division, Office of Naval Research; editor, *Psychological Bulletin*, 1953-58

Dennis's main contribution to psychology was several classic studies of the effects of early experience on maturation that have been widely cited in the literature and textbooks. His early work showed the dominance of hereditary factors in development, such as his paper about the effects of restricted practice upon reaching, sitting, and standing of two infants (1935) and the effect of cradling practices upon the onset of walking in Hopi Indian children (1940). Even in these early studies Dennis observed the effects of the environment. He became particularly aware of them during his stays in Beirut and the associated side trips to Iran. His monograph about infant development under environmental handicap (1957) and papers such as those about the causes of retardation among institutionalized children in Iran (1960) and the effect of supplementary experiences upon the development of institutionalized children (1965) belong to his period of cross-cultural studies and show the deleterious effects of restricted stimulation in early life. Here belong also his cross-cultural studies of intelligence by means of the Draw-a-Man Test and of the acquisition of values by children (*Group Values Through Children's Drawings*, 1966). Other books by Dennis include *The Hopi Children* (1940) and *Children of the Creche* (1973). He edited a series of books about current trends in psychology (1947, 1948, 1949, 1950, 1951), four books of readings (1948, 1949, 1951, 1972), and one entitled *Cross-Cultural Studies of Behavior* (1970). His publications total one hundred thirty. *Biographies*: J. McV. Hunt, *Child Development*, 1977, 48, 330-332; *Contemporary Authors*, vol. 17-20, 1st rev.; *NYT*, 1976, July 24, 26:6; *Who's Who in America*, 1976-77.

DESCARTES, RENÉ
French Philosopher
Born: La Haye, Touraine, March 31, 1596
Died: Stockholm, Sweden, February 11, 1650
Highest Degree: Law degree from University of Poitiers, 1616
Positions: No academic appointments

Descartes was the first great thinker of the modern age. He represents a break from the scholasticism that had dominated philosophy in the Middle Ages. Since much of Descartes's thinking was psychological, he may also be called the first great psychologist of the modern age. Descartes arrived at epistemological certainty by, first, doubting everything and then realizing that one certainty did remain, namely, that of his own existence, because he could not doubt that he was thinking, and that meant that he existed. From the fact of his own existence Descartes arrived at the conclusion that God exists and, since God is perfect and therefore would not deceive humans, that the world was real and could be studied confidently. Descartes believed that mind and body were two separate things. Mind is unextended substance whose nature is thought; it can exist independently of the extended substance of the body. Descartes was thus a dualist; he believed, however, that mind and body interact and that this interaction takes place in a particular site in the body, the pineal gland.

The mind has faculties, or powers, volition, and understanding. Thinking leads to ideas, which are either derived or innate. One innate idea is that of the freedom of will. Volition is thus unlimited, but understanding is limited. Other innate ideas include those of God, infinity, unity, and the geometric axioms. Understanding is the fundamental aspect of thought. It alone can perceive truth. Memory, imagination, and the senses are aids to understanding, but they are subject to error. Even though sense impressions are not as reliable as understanding, they are convenient guides to reality and not mere copies or pictures of objects. Descartes thus dismissed the representative theory of perception as false.

Descartes failed to endow animals with a mind. Animals were to be considered mere machines, with no thought and no freedom of will. The human body is likewise to be explained in mechanistic terms. Much of our motor behavior is reflexive and not dependent on mind. In Descartes may be found one of the first statements of the reflex theory of action. Descartes also did some actual physiological work, such as demonstrating the inversion, by the lens, of the visual image in the retina of a bull's eye. A portion of Descarte's *Treatise on the World* called *L'Homme* (1661) may be considered the first systematic attempt at presenting a physiological psychology. Additional statements concerning physiological psychology were made by Descartes in his *Dioptric* (1637), a treatise about optics and the eye (including the theory that distance is estimated by feeling the angle between converging eyes, accommodation, from aerial perspective and size constancy, as well as the correct hypothesis that retinal images are focused as the curvature of the lens changes), and *Passions of the Soul* (1649). The latter volume deals with emotions and motives. Motion of vital spirits of the body affect the mind, but the mind also directs the flow of vital spirits to the various parts of the body to produce action. The function of the passions is to excite the will to action, although the will must control the passions. The conflict between the will and the activity of vital spirits in the body gives rise to passions.

Descartes's influence on later psychological thinking lies in his interactional dualism (developed into a parallelism by Wundt* and Titchener*) and his emphasis on the cognitive and intellectual (and therefore existential and phenomenological) aspects of mental life in contrast to its conative aspects. This influence, including the notion of innate ideas, persisted to the end of the nineteenth century. His physiological work and views of the functioning of the brain, the nervous system, and the body established him as a precursor of physiological psychology and, in spite of himself, as the father of the mechanistic and materialistic view of human beings that developed in eighteenth-century France.

Biographies: C. Adam, *Vie et oeuvre de Descartes*, 1910 (Reprinted 1937); F. Alquié, *Descartes: L'Homme et l'oeuvre*, 1956; L. Brunschvicg, *René Descartes*, 1937; E. Cassirer, *Descartes: Lehre, Persönlichkeit, Wirkung*, 1939; M.

Deutscher, In R. Harré (Ed.), *Early Seventeenth Century Scientists*, 1965, pp. 159-181; E. Haldane, *Descartes: His Life and Times*, 1966; G. Lewis, *René Descartes, Français, philosophe* 1953; G. Milhaud, *Descartes savant*, 1921; C. Serrurier, *Descartes: L'Homme et le penseur*, 1951; J. R. Vrooman, *René Descartes: A Biography*, 1970; *DSB*, 4; *EB*, 7; *EP*, 2; *IESS*, 4.

DESSOIR, MAX
German Psychologist
Born: Berlin, February 8, 1867
Died: Königstein-im-Taunus, Hesse, July 19, 1947
Highest Degree: Ph.D. in philosophy, University of Berlin, 1889, under W. Dilthey*; M.D., University of Würzburg, 1892
Positions: 1889-1933, University of Berlin

Dessoir's main interest was in aesthetics, in which area he published several books and articles; founded a journal in 1906, which he edited throughout his career; and exercised some influence, especially in the United States. In connection with his medical studies, Dessoir did research on cutaneous aftersensations, making a distinction (1892) between *continuous aftersensations* (primary aftersensations) and *intermittent aftersensations* (secondary aftersensations). Many of his writings are in the area between medicine and psychology, such as *Bibliographie des modernen Hypnotismus* (1888), *Das Doppel-Ich* (1890; 2nd ed., 1896), and *Das Ich, der Traum, der Tod* (1947). One other area of interest to Dessoir was parapsychology, which he endeavored to clear of quackery, trickery, and superstition. In this area he wrote *Vom Jenseits der Seele* (1917) and a number of papers. In 1911 Dessoir published a history of psychology, *Abriss einer Geschichte der Psychologie*, which was immediately translated into English (*Outlines of the History of Psychology*, 1912) and became, to English-speaking psychologists, his best-known book.

Biographies: M. Dessoir, *Buch der Erinnerung*, 1946; J. Günther, *Deutsch. Rundsch.*, 1947, *9*, 223; C. Herrmann, *Max Dessoir: Mensch und Werk*, 1929; F. Romero, *Nosotros*, 1926, *52*, 277-279; R. Schantz, *Grenzgeb. Med.*, 1948, *1*, 24-26; A. Werner, *Philosophia*, 1937, *2*, 299-307; *EJ*, 5; *EP*, 2; *Jewish*, 3; *NDB*, 3; *NYT*, 1947, July 23, 23:6.

DESTUTT DE TRACY, ANTOINE LOUIS CLAUDE
French Philosopher
Born: Province of Bourbonnais, July 20, 1754
Died: Paris, March 9, 1836
Education: University of Strasbourg
Positions: Career in the French army

One of the principal *idéologues*, Destutt de Tracy called his philosophy "idealogy." Under the influence of Cabanis*, another *idéologue*, Destutt de Tracy stressed the physiological aspect of sensation and included idealogy under zoology. Perception, memory, judgment, and will are nothing, according to him, but aspects of sensation. The brain "secretes" thought, just as other organs of the body secrete liquids. Thinking is all conscious processes, whereas immediate impressions, be they sensory, emotional, or intellectual, are feelings. Feelings are imageless; they are only awareness of content. The content is ideas: sensations, memories, judgment, and desires. The idea of touch assures us of the existence of an external world. Destutt de Tracy's main work was *Eléments d'idéologie* in four volumes (1801-15). Together with other *idéologues*, such as Cabanis, Condorcet*, Laplace*, and Lavoisier*, Destutt de Tracy contributed to the establishment of the line of psychological thought that eventually led to scientific psychology.

Biographies: M. Mignet, *Rev. deux Mondes*, 1842, 684-711; F. Picavet, *Les idéologues*, 1891; M.-S. Newton de Tracy, In J. M. Dorsey, *Psychology of Political Science*, 1973, pp. 156-19l; *EP*, 2.

DE VRIES, HUGO MARIE
Dutch Botanist and Geneticist
Born: Haarlem, near Amsterdam, February 16, 1848
Died: Lunteren, near Amsterdam, May 21, 1935
Highest Degree: Ph.D., University of Leiden, 1870
Positions, Honors: 1871-75, University of Amsterdam; 1876-77, Prussian Ministry of Agriculture, Würzburg; 1877, University of Halle, 1878-1918, University of Amsterdam; Darwin Medal, 1906; Linnean Gold Medal, 1928; many honorary doctorates

De Vries was one of three investigators who independently rediscovered Mendel's* laws of heredity in 1900. Later, in *The Mutation Theory* (1910-11, English version of the 1900-1903 German edition), De Vries presented the modern version of the Darwinian theory of evolution—the mutation theory of organic evolution. According to this theory, a new species appears suddenly as the result of mutation and not as the result of gradual changes. It is natural selection that determines which mutation will become extinct and which will evolve further. Another contribution of De Vries was his pangenesis theory, which states that the nucleus of a cell carries every hereditary characteristic, whether manifest or latent. De Vries thus contributed to psychology by furthering our understanding of the mechanics of heredity and therefore of behavioral genetics.

Biographies: Various, *Hugo de Vries: Sechs Vorträge zur Feier seines achtzigsten Geburtstages*, 1929; C. Zirkle, *Journal of History of Biology*, 1968, *1*, 205-218; DSB, 14; *EB*, 7; *Obit. Not.*, 1.

DEWEY, JOHN
American Philosopher
Born: Burlington, Vermont, October 20, 1859
Died: New York, New York, June 1, 1952
Highest Degree: Ph.D. in philosophy, Johns Hopkins University, 1884
Positions: 1884-94, University of Michigan; 1894-1904, University of Chicago;

1904-29, Columbia University; president, American Psychological Association, 1899

Although Dewey's doctorate was in philosophy, he wrote his dissertation on Kant's* psychology. During his stay at Michigan Dewey taught psychology as well as philosophy and wrote a text for the "new" (experimental and evolutionary) psychology (*Psychology*, 1886). It was a philosophically sophisticated text, second in the English language (after Sully's* 1884 text), but was soon replaced by texts that stressed psychology more than philosophy.

The period of Dewey's impact on psychology coincided with his ten years' stay at Chicago. Dewey accepted the evolutionary point of view and stood for social change, the use of philosophy to deal with human problems, and the value of science and experimentation. He held that ideas are plans for action, that they arise when an individual faces a problem and accomplish their function by solving the problem. He laid the foundation of what was to become the functionalist school of psychology, influential during the 1920s and 1930s. Dewey's pragmatic philosophy and his personal brilliance influenced James Rowland Angell* who was at Chicago at that time. It was under the leadership of Angell that functionalism developed as a formal school.

Dewey's first important publication in the Chicago school was his 1896 paper "The Reflex Arc Concept in Psychology." In it he argued against elementism's abstraction of the sensory and motor aspects of the reflex and against treating it as an open arc. Dewey insisted that the stimulus in a reflex is inseparable from the response, in that the response serves to modify the way the stimulus is perceived the next time, so the reflex is actually a circular arrangement and serves to adapt the organism to the environment. Dewey pleaded for a psychology of acts and functions of the whole organism. After the Chicago period, Dewey's contributions to psychology declined, although he kept using psychology in his educational and philosophical writings. His greatest achievement was educational reform, for which he is called the father of progressive education and of learning by doing.

Biographies: R. J. Bernstein, *John Dewey*, 1966; J. Blewett (Ed.), *John Dewey: His Thought and Influence*, 1960; E. G. Boring, *Amer. J. Psychol.*, 1953, *66*, 145-147; G. Dykhuisen, *The Life and Mind of John Dewey*, 1973; E. Edman (Ed.), *John Dewey: His Contribution to the American Tradition*, 1955; S. Hook, *John Dewey: An Intellectual Portrait*, 1939; S. Hook (Ed.), *John Dewey: Philosopher of Science and Freedom*, 1950; F. A. Kingsbury, *Psychol. Bull.*, 1946, *43*, 259-271; J. H. Randall, *J. Phil.*, 1953, *50*, 5-13; A. G. Wirth, *John Dewey as Educator*, 1966; *Biog. Mem.*, 30; *EB*, 7; *EP*, 2; *IESS*, 4; *NCAB*, 40, A; *NYT*, 1952, June 2, 1:2.

DIDEROT, DENIS
French Philosopher
Born: Langres, Haute-Marne, October 5, 1713
Died: Paris, July 30, 1784

Highest Degree: Master of Arts, University of Paris, 1732
Positions: Writer and encyclopedist

Diderot, the encyclopedist of the Enlightenment, was philosophically a sensationalist, empiricist, materialist, and a believer in the scientific method. In concert with Condillac*, Diderot considered thought to be the property of the brain. He believed memory was a material phenomenon and sought to provide a physiological basis for both memory and the Lockean association of ideas. In general, Diderot endeavored to provide psychology with a scientific basis. His thoughts on these matters may be found in his *Rêve de d'Alembert* (1769) and *Eléments de physiologie* (not published until 1875). In his *Lettre sur les aveugles* (1749) and *Lettre sur les sourdes et muets* (1751), Diderot discussed communication on the basis of actual case histories of blind and deaf people. The former work may be considered the first scientific study of blindness. There Diderot tackled the Lockean question of what the world would look like to a newly sighted person and cast doubt on the associationist and empiricist answer that visual identification would be impossible without touch. Diderot held it meaningless to consider each sense in isolation and thought that since vision and touch were coordinated, perhaps the newly sighted person could make visual identifications after all.

Of particular importance to psychology was the article "Psychology" that Diderot wrote for the great French *Encyclopédie*, of which he was the editor-in-chief, because as one of the great works of the Enlightenment, the volumes of the encyclopedia spread knowledge among both specialists and laymen. The article was instrumental in making the term *psychology* familiar in the French language.

Biographies: L. G. Crocker, *The Embattled Philosopher: A Biography of Denis Diderot*, 1954; L. Ducros, *Les encyclopédistes*, 1967; H. Lefèbvre, *Diderot*, 1949; J. L. Leutrat, *Diderot*, 1968; L. K. Luxembourg, *Francis Bacon and Denis Diderot: Philosophers of Science*, 1967; J. Mayer, *Diderot: Homme de science*, 1959; D. Mornet, *Diderot: L'Homme et l'oeuvre*, 1941; R. Pomeau, *Diderot: Sa vie, son oeuvre, avec un exposé de la philosophie*, 1967; A. M. Wilson, *Diderot*, 1972; *DSB*, 4; *EB*, 7; *EP*, 2.

DILTHEY, WILHELM
German Philosopher

Born: Biebrich-am-Rhein, near Wiesbaden, November 19, 1833
Died: Seis, Austria, October 3, 1911
Highest Degree: Ph.D. in philosophy, University of Berlin, 1864
Positions: 1865-66, University of Berlin; 1867, University of Basel; 1868-70, University of Kiel; 1870-82, University of Breslau; 1882-1911, University of Berlin

Dilthey's domain was the philosophical understanding of history. He analyzed the process by which the historian apprehends history. The apprehension (*Verstehen*) enables the historian to grasp all cultural manifestations as expressions of an underlying philosophy of life of the particular culture. The historian's comprehension is thus determined by the ''mind'' of the cultural group to which the historian belongs. Dilthey's emphasis was on the importance of the whole cultural fabric in thinking, the total structure of mind rather than its elements, and on *Verstehen* rather than reasoning.

Dilthey made a distinction between the natural sciences and the cultural sciences (*Geisteswissenschaften*) and classified psychology with the latter. In an 1894 paper (''Ideen über eine beschreibende und zergliedernde Psychologie'') Dilthey made the programmatic statement that human nature is qualitatively the same in all, individual differences being merely quantitative, and that therefore a descriptive and classificatory psychology of personality is both possible and desirable. In this paper Dilthey mentioned five great areas of human activity— religion, art, economy, politics, and science—to which Eduard Spranger*, a student of Dilthey's, added a sixth, the social sphere, and presented a sixfold classification of human types. This later became the basis of a personality profile, *Study of Values*, of which Gordon Allport* was the first author.

Dilthey was opposed to the ''new'' Wundtian (Wundt*) psychology and held that laboratory psychology was inadequate to understand human nature, because such an understanding could come only from the study of the total mental life. Although natural science analyzes and refers to elements to explain, cultural science begins with wholes and, by describing them, understands. Dilthey and Spranger were the godfathers of that current in psychology that prefers synthesis to analysis, wholes to parts, insight to rational analysis, and emphasizes existence rather than essence.

Biographies: H. Holborn, *J. Hist. Ideas*, 1950, *11*, 93-118; E. Spranger, *Wilhelm Dilthey*, 1912; *CE*, 4; *EP*, 2; *IESS*, 4; *NDB*, 3.

DIX, DOROTHEA LYNDE
American Humanitarian
Born: Hampden, Maine, April 4, 1802
Died: Trenton, New Jersey, July 17, 1887
Education: Privately educated
Positions: Teacher, tutor, school director

In 1841 Dix became interested in the conditions prevailing at insane asylums as well as prisons and alms houses. The rest of her life was devoted to the betterment of the life of the inmates of these institutions. Dix started in Massachusetts, and through her efforts legislation was passed to alleviate the conditions of the mentally ill, including the separate institutionalization of the mentally ill and criminals. Her work eventually extended to other states and countries. For forty years she campaigned ceaselessly and energetically but in a subdued and dignified manner to achieve more humane conditions in asylums and other institutions. Through presentations to the Congress, journalism, and carefully chosen spokesmen, she was able to raise many millions of dollars for new and modern mental hospitals and to remove chains, ropes, and other indignities from mental patients. Because of her singular effort twenty states had established separate institutions for the insane within thirty years of the beginning of her work. She then performed the same service in Scotland and thirteen other European countries.

Biographies: W. J. Browne, *Amer. J. Psychiat.*, 1969, *126*, 335-341; H. E. Marshall, *Dorothea Dix: Forgotten Samaritan*, 1937; R. McHenry (Ed.), *Famous American Women*, 1983; S. Rypins, *Psychiat. Quart. Suppl.*, 1948, *22*, 277-289; F. R. Taylor, *N.C. Med. J.*, 1949, *10*, 317-320; F. Tiffany, *Life of Dorothea Lynde Dix*, 1890; *DAB*, 5; *NCAB*, 3, 6, 8, 10.

DODGE, RAYMOND
American Psychologist
Born: Woburn, Massachusetts, February 20, 1871
Died: Tryon, North Carolina, April 8, 1942
Highest Degree: Ph.D. in psychology, University of Halle, 1896, under Benno Erdmann*
Positions, Honors: 1898-1924, Wesleyan University; 1924-36, Yale University; editorial work, *Psychological Bulletin* (1904-10), *Psychological Review* (1910-15), *Psychological Monographs* (1927-37), and others; president, American Psychological Association, 1916

Dodge was a productive and versatile general experimental psychologist. His main areas of research were motor performance (effects of alcohol), physiological psychology (vestibular reactions), and military research during World War I (selection and training of Navy gunners) and many areas in vision and visual perception, in particular eye movements. He invented the Erdmann-Dodge tachistoscope, the Dodge mirror tachistoscope (1907), and the apparatus for recording horizontal and vertical eye movements (1901) that used the photographic technique. He was first to measure and classify eye movements, and he observed eye movements in his studies of reading and other visual tasks. Dodge discovered that in reading the eyes do not glide smoothly along the lines of letters but proceed in jumps, with brief stops between jumps. This discovery found practical application in education.

Dodge wrote *Psychological Effects of Alcohol* (1915, with F. G. Benedict), *Elementary Conditions of Human Variability* (1927), and *The Craving for Superiority* (1931).

Biographies: M. A. May, *Psychol. Monog.*, 1936, *47*(212), xvii-xviii; C. E. Seashore, *Science*, 1942, *95*, 472-473; P. W. Stansbury, *Psychol. Monog.*, 1936, *47*(212), xxv-xxviii; R. S. Woodworth, *Psychol. Rev.*, 1942, *49*, 395-402; R. M. Yerkes, *Amer. J. Psychol.*, 1942, *55*, 584-600; *HPA*, 1; *NCAB*, 32, E; *NYT*, 1942, Apr. 9, 19:1.

DOLL, EDGAR ARNOLD
American Psychologist
Born: Cleveland, Ohio, May 2, 1889
Died: Bellingham, Washington, October 22, 1968

Highest Degree: Ph.D. in psychology, Princeton University, 1920
Positions, Honors: 1912-13, University of Wisconsin; 1913-19, assistant psychologist, Vineland Training School; 1919-23, director, Division of Education and Classification, New Jersey State Department of Institutions and Agencies; 1923-25, Ohio State University; 1925-49, director of research, Vineland Training School; 1949-53, coordinator of research, Devereux Foundation; 1953, consulting psychologist, Bellingham, Washington, public schools; 1954, consultant, Washington State Cerebral Palsy Center; president, American Association of Mental Deficiency (1936), American Orthopsychiatric Association (1937); American Association of Applied Psychology (1941); honorary citations from American Psychological Association, American Association for Mental Deficiency

Doll was an important worker in the field of mental deficiency: *Clinical Studies in Feeblemindedness* (1917, with W. M. Phelps and R. M. Patterson) and *Mental Deficiency Due to Birth Injury* (1932). While working for the state of New Jersey, Doll developed a classification system for use in state prisons that had a lasting influence on penology. To distinguish mental deficiency from intellectual subnormality, Doll developed six criteria, one of which was that mental deficiency, unlike intellectual subnormality, was incurable. With this differentiation in mind, Doll constructed the Vineland Social Maturity Scale (1935) during his second stay at the Training School. This scale and the associated concept of Social Quotient (SQ), computed in a manner analogous to the IQ, is still one of the most widely used scales for the assessment of social development. While at the Devereux Foundation, Doll developed the concept of neurophrenia, a central nervous system disorder. In 1953 he published a statistical and theoretical manual, *The Measurement of Social Competence*; and in 1966, another scale, the Preschool Attainment Record.
Biographies: E. E. Doll, *Amer. J. Ment. Defic.*, 1969, *73*, 681-682; *Train. Sch. Bull.*, 1969, *65*, 115; *NYT*, 1968, Nov. 2, 37:5.

DONALDSON, HENRY HERBERT

American Neurologist and Psychologist
Born: Yonkers, New York, May 12, 1857
Died: Philadelphia, Pennsylvania, January 23, 1938
Highest Degree: Three years of neurological studies in the United States and Europe; Ph.D. in psychology, Johns Hopkins University, 1895, under G. S. Hall*
Positions, Honors: 1883-89, biology; Johns Hopkins University; 1889-92, neurology, Clark University; 1892-1906, neurology, University of Chicago; 1906-30, neurology, Wistar Institute; two honorary degrees

Donaldson was internationally known as a neurologist. Between 1890 and 1891 he conducted one of the most thorough studies of a single human brain, that of the deaf-mute Laura Bridgman, and later published a volume on *The Growth of the Brain* (1895). He was one of the independent discoverers (in 1885) of differences in thermal sensitivity in the skin and of the punctiform nature of temperature sensitivity. He could not find any specialized nerve endings in the skin, however, which finding still stands. At the Wistar Institute Donaldson was instrumental in introducing the albino rat as an experimental subject, developed the Wistar stock of rats, published a volume on *The Rat* (1924), and was one of Karl Lashley's* teachers.

Biographies: American Physiological Society, *History of the American Physiological Society, Semi-Centennial, 1887-1938*, 1938; K. M. Dallenbach, *Amer. J. Psychol.*, 1938, *51*, 434-435; J. P. McMurrich & C. M. Jackson, *J. Comp. Neurol.*, 1938, *69*, 172-179; A. Meyer, In *The Collected Papers of Adolf Meyer*, vol. 3, 1951, pp. 542-544; *Biog. Mem.*, 20; *DAB*, 22; *DSB*, 4; *NCAB*, 28; *NYT*, 1938, Jan. 24, 23:3.

DONDERS, FRANCISCUS CORNELIS
Dutch Ophthalmologist
Born: Tilburg, Holland, May 27, 1818
Died: Utrecht, March 24, 1889
Highest Degree: M.D., University of Utrecht, 1842
Positions: 1842-52, military school, Utrecht; 1852-89, University of Utrecht

Donders's initial work of interest to psychology was in the areas of eye movements, accommodation, and vowel sounds. In 1846 he stated the principle that for any direction of regard the eye always assumes the same position. This was later (1886) named Donders's law by Helmholtz*. In 1854 Donders was the cofounder, with A. von Gräfe, of *Archiv für Ophthalmologie*, and in 1864 he published a book dealing with anomalies of refraction and accommodation. In an 1857 paper Donders listed the resonance values of the mouth cavity for the vowels that he had determined. Not long before his death (1881), he proposed a color-vision theory.

In the 1860s Donders became interested in the measurement of reaction time. He published his first report on it in 1865. Although he had been working on it before that date, Donders's reaction-time work is usually dated from 1868 when his original Dutch article was published in German. After some work on simple reaction time, it occurred to Donders that if the simple task of giving a prescribed response to a single stimulus were complicated by adding, for instance, discrimination, and the reaction time were prolonged, this prolongation would be the measure of additional mental process required to perform the more complicated task. The subtraction of simple reaction time from the total reaction time in a compound reaction task gave Donders the duration of the mental process required to perform the task. The last three decades of the nineteenth century are sometimes called the age of mental chronometry. Initiated by Donders, mental chronometry was expanded by Wundt*. Although complicating the reaction time task does increase the time needed for its execution, the increase is not constant, and the subtraction method was later abandoned. Psychologists kept studying and using reaction time to an ever-increasing extent, however, and today reaction time is a standard response measure in the study of a great variety of psychological phenomena.

Biographies: W. Bowman, *Acta Psychologica*, 1969, *30*, 389-408; F. P. Fischer & G. T. Doesschate, *Franciscus Cornelis Donders*, 1958; E. C. v. Leersum (Ed.), [*The Life Work of Franciscus Cornelis Donders*], 1932; J. Moleschott, *Franciscus Cornelis Donders: Festgruss zum 27. Mai 1888*, 1888; C. A. Pekelharing, *Janus* 1919, *24*, 57-76; R. L. Pfeiffer, *Bull. N.Y. Acad. Med.*, 1936, *12*, 566-581; H. W. Williams, *Proc. Amer. Acad. Arts, Sci.*, 1889, *24*, 465-470; *DSB*, 4.

DOWNEY, JUNE ETTA
American Psychologist
Born: Laramie, Wyoming, July 13, 1875
Died: Trenton, New Jersey, October 11, 1932
Highest Degree: Ph.D. in psychology, University of Chicago, 1907, under J. R. Angell*
Positions: 1905-32, University of Wyoming

Downey's book *The Will Temperament and Its Testing* (1924) and the will temperament test it described attracted much attention at the time and stimulated research in personality, although the test itself was found to have considerable limitations. Downey was also interested in motor behavior, especially the different aspects of writing, including graphology. She published many papers in this area and the book *Graphology and Psychology of Handwriting* (1919). In a third area of interest, aesthetics, she was a coauthor (with E. E. Slosson) of *Plots and Personalities* (1922) and *Creative Imagination* (1929). Downey left a total of seventy-six publications.

Biographies: J. E. Anderson, *Amer. J. Psychol.*, 1933, *45*, 363-364; Faculty of the University of Wyoming, *In Memoriam: June Etta Downey, 1875-1932*, 1934; R. McHenry (Ed.), *Famous American Women*, 1983; R. S. Uhrbrock, *J. Gen. Psychol.*, 1933, *9*, 351-364; *DAB*, 21; *PR*, 3; *Who Was Who in America*, 1.

DREVER, JAMES, SR.
Scottish Psychologist
Born: Orkney Islands, April 8, 1873
Died: Edinburgh, August 11, 1950
Highest Degree: D.Phil. in psychology, Edinburgh University, 1917
Positions: 1919-44, University of Edinburgh; during World War II, War Office personnel selection position; president, British Psychological Society (1935-38); Twelfth International Congress of Psychology (1948); editorial work, *British Journal of Psychology Monographs*

Drever's output of publications was modest. He worked in the areas of educational psychology (*Introduction to the Psychology of Education*, 1922), general psychology (*Instinct in Man*, 1917; *Psychology of Everyday Life*, 1921; 11th ed., 1940; *An Introduction to Experimental Psychology*, 1926), juvenile delinquency, and the psychology of the deaf. He also wrote *The Psychology of Industry* (1921) and a *Dictionary of Psychology* (1952; rev. ed., 1964). Drever's main contribution was through teaching and the directing of the George Combe Psychological Laboratory at the University of Edinburgh. Between 1931 and 1944 he occupied the first chair in psychology at a Scottish university. The finest training in psychology in Great Britain in the 1920s and 1930s was to be had at Edinburgh, where Drever was placing a strong emphasis on experimentation in training psychologists.

Biographies: M. Collins, *Brit. J. Psychol.*, 1951, *42*, 311-314; M. Collins, *Psychol. Rev.*, 1951, *58*, 1-4; J. Drever, *Occup. Psychol.*, 1948, *22*, 20-30; J. Drever, Jr., *Brit. J. Educ. Psychol.*, 1951, *21*, 1-2; B. Semeonoff, *Amer. J. Psychol.*, 1951, *64*, 283-284; *HPA*, 2; *PR*, 3.

DRIESCH, HANS ADOLF EDUARD

German Biologist and Philosopher

Born: Bad Kreuznach, Rhineland-Palatinate, October 28, 1867
Died: Leipzig, April 17, 1941
Highest Degree: Ph.D. in natural science, University of Jena, 1889
Positions, Honors: 1891-1900, Naples Zoological Station; 1906-9, University of Aberdeen; 1909-20, University of Heidelberg; 1920-21, University of Cologne; 1921-41, University of Leipzig; several honorary degrees

Driesch was a developmental physiologist and an exponent of vitalism. In a well-publicized experiment, he cut up the blastula of a sea urchin and observed every part of the blastula develop into a complete organism. He therefore decided that life cannot be explained merely in physical, chemical, or mechanistic terms and proposed a theory of organic development (*Analytische Theorie der organischen Entwicklung*, 1894) according to which an immaterial principle, *entelechy*, was responsible for the development of the egg. In *Die Lokalisation morphogenetischer Vorgänge: Ein Beweiss vitalistischen Geschehens* (1899) and *Die Seele als elementarer Naturfaktor* (1903), Driesch elaborated his theory further. In the 1920s he turned to psychology, publishing a successful *Grundprobleme der Psychologie* (1925), *Parapsychologie* (1932), and *Alltagsrätsel des Seelenlebens* (1939), but also continued to publish a large number of papers and books on the science and philosophy of the organism.

Biographies: H. A. E. Driesch, *Lebenserinnerungen*, 1951; H. A. E. Driesch, In R. Schmidt (Ed.), *Die Philosophie der Gegenwart in Selbstdarstellungen*, vol. 1, 1923, pp. 49-78; E. Ungerer, *Naturwissenschaften*, 1941, *29*, 457-462; A. Wenzl (Ed.), *Hans Driesch: Persönlichkeit und Bedeutung für Biologie und Philosophie von heute*, 1951; *Biog. Lex.*; *DSB*, 4; *EB*, 7; *NDB*, 4; *NYT*, 1941, Apr. 18, 21:1.

DU BOIS-REYMOND, EMIL
German Physiologist
Born: Berlin, November 7, 1818
Died: Berlin, December 26, 1896
Highest Degree: Ph.D. in physiology, University of Berlin, 1843
Positions: 1848-54, Berlin Academy of Arts (Kunstakademie); 1854-96, University of Berlin

Du Bois-Reymond played a prominent role in the development of neurophysiology in the nineteenth century. He became interested in the question of animal electricity and studied it using the newly invented galvanometer. His first paper about animal electricity appeared in 1843, followed by the two volumes of *Untersuchungen über thierische Elektricität* (1848, 1849). This work marks the beginning of modern electrophysiology. Du Bois-Reymond's theory of the polarization of animal tissue eventually turned out to be wrong, but his work stimulated further research on the conduction of nerve impulses. He showed that explanations of nerve conduction in terms of animal spirits or activity of the soul was unnecessary since it was demonstrably a material phenomenon. He thus fulfilled the pledge that he and three other students of Johannes Müller* had made, namely, to fight vitalism and to establish and compel acceptance of the truth that no forces other than physical and chemical ones are active within the organism. To Helmholtz*, Du Bois-Reymond's work suggested that the velocity of the nerve impulse was finite and measurable. When he succeeded in measuring it, he sent his paper to Du Bois-Reymond to be read before the Physikalische Gesellschaft in Berlin. Several famous psychologists were Du Bois-Reymond's students: Wilhelm Wundt*, James Sully*, G. Stanley Hall*, Vladimir Bekhterev*, and Ivan Sechenov*, among others.

Biographies: H. Boruttau, *Emil Du Bois-Reymond*, 1922; E. Metze, *Emil du Bois-Reymond*, 1918; K. E. Rothschuh, In *Von Boerhaave bis Berger*, 1964, pp. 85-105; P. W. Ruff, *Emil du Bois Reymond*, 1980; A. D. Waller, *Proc. Roy. Soc. London*, 1905, *75*B, 124-127; *ADB*, 48; *DSB*, 4; *EP*, 2; Hirsch, *Biog. Lex.*, 1; *NDB*, 4.

DUMAS, GEORGE
French Psychologist
Born: Lédignan, Provence, March 6, 1866
Died: Lédignan, Provence, February 13, 1946
Highest Degree: *Agrégé* in philosophy, 1889, under T. A. Ribot*; *docteur en médecine*, 1890; *docteur en lettres*, 1900; all from École Normale Supérieure, Paris
Positions: 1894-1902, Collège Chapatal; 1897-1939, director of Psychological Laboratory, Clinic of Mental Disorders, Medical School, Sorbonne (University of Paris)

Like those of his teacher Ribot, Dumas's interests tended in the direction of abnormal psychology, in which area he wrote *Les états intellectuels dans la* *mélancolie* (1894), *Névroses et psychoses de guerre chez les Austro-Allemands* (1918), and *Troubles mentaux et troubles nerveux de guerre* (1920). His other books dealt with emotion: *Tolstoi et la philosophie de l'amour* (1893), *La tristesse et la joie* (1900), *Psychologie de deux messies positivistes: Saint-Simon et Auguste Comte* (1905), and *La sourire: Psychologie et physiologie* (1906). With Pierre Janet*, Dumas founded the *Journal de psychologie normale et pathologique* in 1903, but he is best known as the author of a two-volume treatise on psychology, the *Traité de psychologie* (1923-24), which was later revised and expanded into a multivolume *Nouveau traité de psychologie*. Its publication began in 1930, and Dumas served as editor and coauthor.

Biographies: L. Litwinski, *Brit. J. Psychol.*, 1946, *37*, 6-7; I. Meyerson, *J. psychol. norm. path.*, 1946, *39*, 7-10; M. Reuchlin, *Histoire de la psychologie*, 1957; *Rev. psicol. gen. aplic.*, 1948, *3*, 417-423; *EUI*, 18(2).

DUNCKER, KARL
German Psychologist
Born: Leipzig, February 2, 1903
Died: Swarthmore, Pennsylvania, February 23, 1940
Highest Degree: Ph.D. in psychology, University of Berlin, 1929
Positions: 1929-37, University of Berlin: 1938-40, Swarthmore College

Duncker was a Gestalt psychologist who contributed to the understanding of the wholistic experience through his work on apparent movement and the psychology of creativity and problem solving. A classic work of Duncker's was his 1929 monograph about apparent movement (*Über induzierte Bewegung*). Around 1930 he first proposed the concept of *functional fixity* (inability to find the solution to a new problem because it is attempted using old methods that are not suitable in the new situation) as related to problem solving. In a 1935 monograph (*Zur Psychologie des produktiven Denkens*) that now belongs to the classic psychological literature, Duncker gave a detailed description of the organization of problem solving, the establishment of the general range of the problem and its possible solutions, the stage of functional solutions, and the stage of specific solutions.

Biographies: PR, 3.

DUNLAP, KNIGHT
American Psychologist
Born: Diamond Springs, California, November 21, 1875
Died: Columbia, South Carolina, August 14, 1949
Highest Degree: Ph.D. in psychology, Harvard University, 1903, under H. Münsterberg*
Positions, Honors: 1902-6, University of California at Berkeley; 1906-36, Johns Hopkins University; 1936-47, University of California at Los Angeles; president, American Psychological Association, 1922

Dunlap was a versatile general-experimental psychologist. In a paper about color vision (1915) he demonstrated the difference between actual and potential stimuli; he showed that both kinds must be regarded as actually existing. In 1918 he and Madison Bentley* demonstrated that the nystagmic eye movements produced by head rotation could be modified or abolished. In 1921 Dunlap demonstrated the binocular transfer of momentary local blindness, which necessitated the revision of theories of nervous interaction. In these and other research studies Dunlap's interest was focused on the body-mind relationship. Assuming that one motor act or glandular discharge could serve as a stimulus to another, he theorized that the same set of principles could explain the formation of both habits of thought and habits of action.

Later Dunlap's interests shifted to abnormal and social psychology and the psychology of religion (*Social Psychology*, 1925; *The Dramatic Personality of Jesus*, 1933). Dunlap wrote additional books on a variety of subjects: A *System of Psychology* (1912), *Psychobiology* (1914), *Habits: Their Making and Unmaking* (1932), *Religion: Its Functions in Human Life* (1946), and several others. Dunlap was also the inventor of several pieces of apparatus: Dunlap chronoscope, Dunlap chair for vestibular investigation, Dunlap steadiness plate, and others. According to Dunlap himself, his contributions to psychology were (1) attack on introspection; (2) insistence on response as the basis of mental processes; (3) attack on images and insistence that objects of perception are real objects rather than "psychic"; (4) emphasis on periphery, rather than the brain, as the fundamental determiner of psychological qualities; (5) elimination of the "instinct" concept; (6) view of consciousness as an inference from response; and (7) changes in the view of heredity.

Biographies: R. M. Dorcus, *Amer. J. Psychol.*, 1950, *63*, 114-119; K. G. Moore, *Psychol. Rev.*, 1949, *56*, 309-310; *HPA*, 2; *NCAB*, 39; *Who Was Who in America*, 2.

DURKHEIM, EMILE
French Sociologist
Born: Epinal, Vosges, April 15, 1858
Died: Paris, November 15, 1917
Highest Degree: École Normale Supérieure, Paris, *agrégé* in 1882
Positions: 1887-1902, University of Bordeaux; 1902-17, University of Paris

A leader in French sociology at the turn of the century, Durkheim stressed the differences between sociology and psychology. Collective consciousness differs from individual consciousness. Collective representations, which constrain the individual, are outside the individual and give members of a society the same view of the world. The society, however, plays no role in creating a person's individual representations. There are, as it were, two separate and almost opposite beings within each individual, the personal and the collective.

Durkheim presented an influential and enduring analysis of suicide. The causes of suicide are entirely social, be they egoistic, altruistic, or anomic (normless). The source of religion is society itself, and God is society personified. Religion, in turn, gives rise to categories of thought, such as class, force, space, and time. Psychologically relevant books written by Durkheim are *De la division du travail social* (1893), *Règles de la méthode sociologique* (1894), *Suicide* (1897), and *Les formes élémentaires de la vie religieuse* (1912).

Biographies: H. Alpert, *Emile Durkheim and His Sociology*, 1961; R. Bierstedt, *Emile Durkheim*, 1966; G. Davy, *Émile Durkheim*, 1927; J. Duvignaud, *Durkheim: Sa vie, son oeuvre, avec un exposé de sa philosophie*, 1965; S. Lukes, *Emile Durkheim: His Life and Work*, 1973; R. A. Nisbet, *Emile Durkheim*, 1965; F. Pécaut, *Rev. pédag.*, 1918, 27, 1-20; E. Wallwork, *Durkheim: Morality and Milieu*, 1972; *EB*, 7; *EJ*, 6; *EP*, 2; *IESS*, 4; *Jewish*, 3.

E

EBBINGHAUS, HERMANN
German Psychologist
Born: Barmen (now part of Wuppertal), North Rhine-Westphalia, January 24, 1850
Died: Halle (Saale), Saxony-Anhalt, February 26, 1909
Highest Degree: Ph.D. in philosophy, University of Bonn, 1873
Positions: 1880-93, University of Berlin; 1894-1905, University of Breslau; 1905-8, University of Halle

After obtaining his Ph.D., Ebbinghaus studied independently for seven years. It was during this time that he came across a copy of Fechner's* *Elements of Psychophysics* and decided to apply the scientific method to the study of processes "higher" than sensation. The idea that the higher process should be memory Ebbinghaus got from the British associationists, as well as the idea that repetition, or frequency of association, should be the measure of memory. The method that Ebbinghaus used to study memory was his own invention. To avoid preestablished associations of ordinary verbal materials, Ebbinghaus devised some twenty-three hundred consonant-vowel-consonant combinations, or nonsense syllables. Using himself as the sole subject, Ebbinghaus learned lists of nonsense syllables (as well as poetry) to mastery and recorded the amounts retained, or the trials necessary for relearning, after a passage of time. The nonsense syllables, the mastery method, and the savings method are still standard methodology in human learning laboratories today.

In 1885 Ebbinghaus published the classic monograph *Über das Gedächtnis* (English translation, *Memory*, 1913), which included, among other things, the famous forgetting curve. Ebbinghaus had launched the scientific study of learning and memory entirely on his own and with a high degree of originality. He had done it even before opening the psychological laboratory at the University of Berlin in 1886. Ebbinghaus's ability to control sources of error and to quantify his results precisely was such that his work is still quoted today as valid research rather than just because of its historical interest. To publish work emanating from places other than Wundt's* Leipzig laboratory, Ebbinghaus and König* founded the *Zeitschrift für Psychologie und Physiologie der Sinnersorgane* in 1890. After this Ebbinghaus began to study vision (he published a color-vision theory in 1893), content to let others, notably Georg Müller*, develop the breakthrough of experimental psychology into the area of the higher mental processes.

At Breslau Ebbinghaus established another laboratory (1894) and published (1897) a new method for testing the mental ability of schoolchildren, the "Ebbinghaus completion test," which is still used. He thus made an original contribution to the study of another higher mental process. In 1897 he published the first volume of a highly successful textbook of psychology, *Grundzüge der Psychologie*, which saw three editions by 1911. In it (1902 ed.) appear Ebbinghaus's further contributions to psychology, such as the first modern version of the phenomenology of color perception. Ebbinghaus influenced his contemporaries by his personality and style, however, not by his systematic views or publications. Of lasting importance to psychology, therefore, is solely his work on human memory.

Biographies: E. R. Jaensch, *Z. Psychol.*, 1909, *51*, iii-viii; L. Postman, *Amer. Psychologist*, 1968, *23*, 149-157; D. Shakow, *Amer. J. Psychol.*, 1930, *42*, 505-518; R. S. Woodworth, *J. Phil.*, 1909, *6*, 253-256; *IESS*, 4; *NDB*, 4.

EDWARDS, JONATHAN

American Philosopher and Theologian
Born: East Windsor, Connecticut, October 5, 1703
Died: Princeton, New Jersey, March 22, 1758
Highest degree: M.A., Yale College, 1722
Positions: 1722-23, minister, New York State; 1724-25, instructor, Yale College; 1726-50, pastor, Northampton, Massachusetts; 1751-56, missionary, Stockbridge, Massachusetts; 1757-58 (6 months), president, College of New Jersey

Edwards is considered by some to have been the most influential pre-Revolutionary American thinker. He wrote about psychological questions in relation to religion, the emotions (*A Treatise Concerning Religious Affections*, 1746), and the freedom of the will (*Inquiry into the Freedom of the Will*, 1757) and occasionally treated his parishioners' emotional problems with psychological techniques. His *Treatise* and *Inquiry* may be considered the first psychological works written by an American.

Edwards was influenced by Locke*, but he also showed some originality of ideas. This originality is all the more remarkable because Edwards worked in relative isolation, never meeting a great thinker or scientist and never going abroad. Edwards's psychological thinking focused on the question of salvation, especially the validity of conversion, which led him to consider how the mind functions in conversion. He came to the conclusion that one cannot know with certainty whether one's own or anyone else's mind has been altered by God: because mind is an inseparable mixture of reason and emotions, reason is always fallible; hence one's rational judgments can never be relied on. In his *Inquiry* Edwards, like Hume* and Spinoza*, argued not only that there is no free will but that all human choices are actually those of God. In his sermon "Men Naturally God's Enemies" he adumbrated Sigmund Freud's* idea of the hate of the father as a symbol of authority and the unconscious desire of those led to kill their leader.

Biographies: A. O. Aldridge, *Jonathan Edwards*, 1964; A. V. G. Allen, *Jonathan Edwards*, 1889; J. G. Blight, In J. Brozek (Ed.), *Explorations in the History of American Psychology*, 1983; E. H. Davidson, *Jonathan Edwards*, 1966; F. Davidson, *American Association of University Professors Bulletin*, 1948, *34*, 364-374; S. E. Dwight, In *The Works of President Edwards*, vol. 1, 1830, pp. 1-625; S. Hopkins, *The Life and Character of the Late Reverend Mr. Jonathan Edwards*, 1765 (Reprinted in D. Levin [Ed.], *Jonathan Edwards: A Profile*, 1969, pp. 1-86); A. C. McGiffert, *Jonathan Edwards*, 1932; P. Miller, *Errand Into Wilderness*, 1956; P. Miller, *Jonathan Edwards*, 1949; O. E. Winslow, *Jonathan Edwards*, 1961; *DAB*, 6; *EB*, 8; *EP*, 2; *NCAB*, 5.

EHRENFELS, CHRISTIAN VON

Austrian Philosopher
Born: Rodaun, near Vienna, June 20, 1859
Died: Lichtenau, Bavaria, September 8, 1932
Highest Degree: Ph.D. in philosophy, University of Vienna, 1885, under F. Brentano*
Positions: 1885-88, University of Graz; 1889-96, University of Vienna; 1896-1929, University of Prague

Ehrenfels was one of the important names in the Austrian school of act psychology, although only incidentally, because he was mainly a philosopher. Ehrenfels developed Mach's* idea that there are sensations of form. He decided that form is not a combination of other qualities but a new one, form quality (*Gestaltqualität*). The idea was presented in a paper in 1890. In the perception of a square, the four lines are the sensations or the foundation (*Fundamente*) of the perception of the square. This perception is not caused by any one of the lines alone but is experienced when all are brought together (*Grundlage*) and are perceived jointly. Form-quality may persist even when the elements change; hence all squares are perceived essentially the same, melodies are heard as the same when transposed to a different key, and the like. Form-qualities are temporal or spatial, and each may form the *Grundlage* for the experience of higher levels of form-quality.

Ehrenfels, by realizing that Wundt's* elementism failed to explain many aspects of perception, took a step toward what was later called Gestalt psychology. At the same time, unlike Max Wertheimer*, who held that the original elements disappear in the perception of the whole, Ehrenfels still thought of form-quality as a derivative of the *Fundamente* and not as independently given. With Alexius von Meinong* and Hans Cornelius, Ehrenfels originated the form-quality school, the immediate precursor of Gestalt psychology.

Biographies: F. Weinhandl (Ed.), *Gestalthaftes Sehen: Ergebnisse und Aufgaben der Morphologie: Zum hundertjährigen Geburtstage von Chr. v. Ehrenfels*, 1960; *CE*, 5; *EP*, 2; *EUI*, 19; *NDB*, 4.

ELLIOTSON, JOHN

English Physician
Born: London, October 29, 1791
Died: London, July 29, 1868
Highest Degree: M.D., Cambridge University, 1821
Positions: 1817-37, professor of practice of medicine and senior physician, University College and University College Hospital, London

Before 1837, when Elliotson saw a demonstration of mesmerism and became immediately enthused about its medical uses, he had introduced several innovations in medical practice in spite of the initial skepticism and even ridicule of other physicians. Elliotson's troubles with the medical profession continued to increase from there on. He began to apply mesmerism in treating his patients at the University College Hospital. Elliotson would "magnetize" an object, apply it to the affected spot, and a cure would be achieved. Demonstrations that belief on the part of the patient, that is, suggestion, was necessary did not change Elliotson's attitude toward mesmerism. Mesmerism was in disrepute at the time, and the Council of the University College forbade its use at the college. Elliotson resigned and proceeded to study and use mesmerism on his own, in opposition to the medical establishment. In 1843 he began publishing a journal, the *Zoist*, to print papers about "cerebral physiology and mesmerism" that other journals would not accept. Elliotson not only had become interested in phrenology but believed that "magnetic" hands, as they touched parts of a person's head, would stimulate the underlying (according to the phrenologists) functionally specific area and faculty. *Zoist*, however, ceased publication in 1856. Some time during this period Elliotson also became interested in the anesthetic use of mesmerism as reports on James Esdaile's* operations performed on patients in mesmeric trance began to reach England. He founded a mesmeric hospital in 1849. The discovery of the anesthetic uses of ether, nitrous oxide, and chloroform in the mid-1840s, however, prevented the development of this application of mesmerism.

Biographies: J. M. Bramwell, *Hypnotism: Its History, Practice and Theory*, 1903; M. Goldsmith, *Franz Anton Mesmer: The History of an Idea*, 1934; B.

Hollander, *In Search of the Soul and the Mechanisms of Thought, Emotion and Conduct*, ca. 1920; G. Newbold, *Brit. J. Med. Hypno.*, 1950, *1*, 2-7; G. Rosen, *Bull. Hist. Med.*, 1936, *4*, 600-603; G. Rosen, *J. Hist. Med.*, 1946, *1*, 526-550; J. H. H. Williams, *Doctors Differ*, 1952; *DNB*, 6.

ELLIOTT, RICHARD M.

American Psychologist
Born: Lowell, Massachusetts, end of 1887
Died: Minneapolis, Minnesota, May 1969
Highest Degree: Ph.D. in psychology, Harvard University, 1913, under Hugo Münsterberg*
Positions: 1914-15, Harvard University; 1915-18, Yale University; 1918, U.S. Army Sanitary Corps; 1919-56, University of Minnesota, 1919-51, head, Psychology Department

An administrator, teacher, and editor, Elliott did not produce any research or empirical publications. In 1924 he founded the Century Psychology Series, begun with E. G. Boring's* *History of Experimental Psychology*, and remained its editor until his death. Elliott's main contribution to psychology was as the head of the Psychology Department at the University of Minnesota. A short time after his arrival at Minnesota, Elliott had made the department into one of the top departments in the country. From the very beginning of his tenure, psychology at Minnesota was a natural science. Elliott favored behaviorism and applied psychology. Hired by Elliott, the Minnesota psychology faculty at one time or another included names such as Robert Yerkes*, Karl Lashley*, Herbert Woodrow, Florence Goodenough*, Edna Heidbreder, Donald Paterson*, and B. F. Skinner. He developed the introductory psychology course to the point where students in several other colleges were required to take it, and course enrollment reached thousands. A few years after his arrival at Minnesota, Elliott was able to acquire a building for psychology. It was replaced by a new one in 1969 and named Elliott Hall in his honor.
Biographies: K. McCorquedale, *Amer. J. Psychol.*, 1975, *88*, 503-504; *HPA*, 4.

ELLIS, (HENRY) HAVELOCK

English Psychologist
Born: Croydon, Surrey, February 2, 1859
Died: Washbrook, Suffolk, July 8, 1939
Highest Degree: Physician's license, St. Thomas Hospital, London, 1889
Positions: No official or academic positions

Ellis was principally a writer, his main topic, the psychology of sex. Ellis never held any academic or official positions and never delivered a lecture or address. His literary style won prominence for his books. They broke the silence that had long surrounded the topic of sex and promoted its scientific study. Ellis brought data to an area of speculation—numerous case histories from all over the world. Through his writings Ellis promoted a more natural, healthy, and liberal attitude toward sex and marriage. His most important work is the seven volumes of *Studies in the Psychology of Sex*, published between 1898 and 1928. Other books that Ellis wrote on the same subject are *Man and Woman* (1894), *Sexual Inversion* (1897), *Sex in Relation to Society* (1910), *The Erotic Rights of Women* (1918), *The Play-Function of Sex* (1921), *The Dance of Life* (1923), *Marriage Today and Tomorrow* (1929), and *More Essays on Love and Virtue* (1931). Although Ellis was one of the first physicians to comment favorably upon Freud's* theories, he did criticize Freud's emphasis on sex in the interpretation of dreams (*The World of Dreams*, 1911). He introduced the terms *autoeroticism* and *narcissistic* (love of or affection for oneself). These words eventually found their way into psychoanalytical terminology.

Biographies: E. M. Brecher, *The Sex Researchers*, 1969; A. Calder-Marshall, *The Sage of Sex: A Life of Havelock Ellis*, 1960; J. S. Collis, *Havelock Ellis: Artist of Life*, 1959; F. Delisle, *Friendship's Odyssey; or, In Love With Life*, 1964; H. Ellis, *My Life*, 1939; J. C. Flugel, *Brit. J. Educ. Psychol.*, 1941, *11*, 1-7; T. Goldberg, *Havelock Ellis*, 1926; H. Peterson, *Havelock Ellis: Philosopher of Love*, 1928; H. Read, *A Coat of Many Colours*, 1956; *DNB*, Suppl. 4; *IESS*, 5; *NYT*, 1939, July 11, 19:1.

EMMERT, EMIL
Swiss Ophthalmologist
Born: Bern, December 1, 1844
Died: Bern, October 10, 1911
Highest Degree: M.D., University of Bern, 1868
Positions: 1870-1911, University of Bern

In an 1881 article Emmert formulated the following law: if l is the linear size of an object, d its distance from the observer, L the linear size of the object's afterimage, and D the distance between the observer and the surface on which the afterimage is seen, then $l/L = d/D$. This formulation was later named Emmert's law. Although Emmert wrote several books about vision (*Die Organe des Sehens der verschiedenen Thierkreisen*, 1872; *Gesichtswahrnehmungen und Sinnestäuschungen*, 1872; *Ueber funktionelle Störungen des menschlichen Auges*, 1876; *Ueber Refraktions- und Accomodationsverhältnisse des menschlichen Auges*, 1876; *Auge und Schädel*, 1880), the law of afterimage size is his one lasting contribution to psychology.

Biographies: *Biog. Lex.*; Pagel, *Biographisches Lexikon*.

EMPEDOCLES OF AKRAGAS
Greek Philosopher
Born: Akragas, Sicily, ca. 490 B.C.
Died: Peloponnesus, ca. 430 B.C.
Education: Pupil of Parmenides
Positions: Aristocrat, in political life

Empedocles, a pre-Socratic philosopher, argued for the existence of four elements of which everything is composed: earth, fire, air, and water. Upon decomposition of objects, the elements return to their original state, unchanged. Empedocles endowed all things with life and the power of thought, humans differing from other things by their greater power of thought. He believed thinking occurred in the blood and equated the soul with thinking. He considered the body to be mortal, the soul immortal. According to Empedocles the soul lives on to inhabit other bodies (*metampsychosis*). Perception was explained by Empedocles in terms of objects giving off emanations that affect the sense organs of perceivers. In various forms this view came to be held by other Greek philosophers as well as philosophers of later centuries. One positive discovery that is attributed to Empedocles is that of the inner ear.

Biographies: *DSB*, 4; *EB*, 8; *EP*, 2; *HGP*, 2.

ENGLISH, HORACE BIDWELL

American Psychologist

Born: Eagle, Nebraska, October 1, 1892

Died: Columbus, Ohio, July 20, 1961

Highest Degree: Ph.D. in psychology, Yale University, 1916

Positions, Honors: 1916-27, Wellesley College; 1927-30, Antioch College; 1930-61, Ohio State University; president, American Association for Applied Psychology, 1937-40

English was an educational psychologist, author of important studies on learning and memory. Although he wrote a number of papers and books in these areas (*Studying the Individual Child*, 1941, with V. C. Raimy; *Child Psychology*, 1952; *The Dynamics of Child Development*, 1961), he is best known for having written, with his wife, A. C. English, *A Comprehensive Dictionary of Psychological and Psychoanalytic Terms* (1958).

Biographies: *J. Consult. Psychol.*, 1940, *4*, 1; *PR*, 3; *Who Was Who in America*, 4.

EPICURUS

Greek Philosopher

Born: Island of Samos, 341 B.C.

Died: Athens, 270 B.C.

Education: Pupil of Nausiphanes of Teos(?)

Positions: 309-306 B.C., teacher in Mytilene and Lampsacus; 306-270 B.C., teacher in own school in Athens

Concerning the soul, Epicurus denied immaterial reality, immortality of the soul, universal ideas, universal reason, and spoke of the soul and reason only as they pertain to a particular individual. Having accepted the atomistic theory, Epicurus was led to the conclusion that the soul is material and inheres in all parts of the body as minute soul-atoms. However, upon the dissolution of the body at death the soul also dissolves. Sensing is likewise a material process.

Sensations occur as objects emit faint replicas of themselves and they enter the sense organs and, through them, contact the soul. In restating the representational theory of perception, Epicurus was restating the view of Empedocles*, Democritus*, and other Greek philosophers who had preceded him. Anticipating the English empiricists, Epicurus asserted that sensations are the only source of knowledge. Sensory impressions are true, and error arises only from opinions that go beyond that which is given by sensations. Concepts are formed through repeated sense perceptions; they also form the basis for generalizations.

Philosophically, Epicurus was principally concerned with ethics. The Epicurean ethics of pleasure is based on sensation: the criterion for good and evil is the quality of the sensations involved. Happiness, however, does not lie in the active seeking of pleasure but in achieving a quiet mind that is troubled neither by striving nor fear.

Biographies: C. Bailey, *Epicurus*, 1926 (Reprinted 1970); N. W. DeWitt, *Epicurus and His Philosophy*, 1954; R. D. Hicks (Ed.), *Lives of Eminent Philosophers*, by Diogenes Laërtius, 1925; *DSB*, 4; *EB*, 8.

ERASISTRATUS

Greek Physician and Anatomist
Born: Iulus, island of Chios, ca. 304 B.C.
Died: Samoa, ca. 250 B.C.
Education: Studied in Athens under Metrodotus and Theophrastus*
Positions: Court physician for Seleucus Nicator, king of Syria, at Antioch; physician and anatomist at Alexandria, where he and Herophilus* established a school of anatomy

Erasistratus is considered the father of physiology. Among Erasistratus's many discoveries and speculations concerning anatomy and physiology, those important to psychology are the following: Air from the lungs passes to the heart, where it becomes vital spirits. Through the blood stream, vital spirits are distributed as the "breath of life." In the brain, vital spirits are transformed into animal spirits and stored in the ventricles of the brain. The nerves, which Erasistratus distinguished from the blood vessels, carry the animal spirits (*pneuma*) involved in sensation and motion. Muscular contraction is caused by the expansion of the *pneuma*. Descartes*, among others, accepted this teaching. Erasistratus distinguished between motor and sensory nerves, a distinction that had to be rediscovered by Bell* and Magendie* in the nineteenth century. He also traced both kinds of nerves to the brain. He thought the brain to be the seat of intellect and that functions were localized in the brain. Erasistratus compared the convolutions of the brain in humans and animals and concluded that the convolutions were related to intelligence. After Herophilus died, Erasistratus continued his work, but his own death brought about a decline of the Alexandrian school.

Biographies: *DSB*, 4.

ERDMANN, BENNO
German Philosopher and Psychologist
Born: Guhren near Glogau, Silesia, May 30, 1851
Died: Berlin, June 7, 1921
Highest Degree: Ph.D. in philosophy, University of Berlin, 1873
Positions: 1876-78, University of Berlin; 1878-84, University of Kiel; 1884-90, University of Breslau; 1890-98, University of Halle; 1898-1909, University of Bonn; 1909-21, University of Berlin

As a psychologist Erdmann was interested in thinking. He distinguished between thinking (hypological thinking), imagination (discursive thinking), and fantasy (intuitive thinking). Logic he held to be the norms of thinking. For this reason its problems cannot be resolved through experimental psychology. Experimental psychology cannot be ignored, however, and logic must maintain close contact with it. On the subject of thinking Erdmann wrote three books: *Umriss zur Psychologie des Denkens* (1900), *Die Funktionen der Phantasie im wissenschaftlichen Denken* (1913), and *Grundzüge der Reproduktionspsychologie* (1920).
Biographies: E. Becher, *Arch. ges. Psychol.*, 1922, *42*, 150-182; R. Dodge, *Amer. J. Psychol.*, 1922, *33*, 155-156; *NDB*, 4.

ESDAILE, JAMES
English Surgeon
Born: Montrose, Angus, Scotland, February 6, 1808
Died: Sydenham (London), January 10, 1859
Highest Degree: M.D., University of Edinburgh, 1830
Positions: 1831-51, various appointments as surgeon in India

In 1845, after reading of Elliotson's* work with mesmerism, Esdaile tried it on a patient suffering from great pain. Finding that he was successful in eliminating pain by this method, Esdaile began to use mesmerism for anesthetic purposes in performing his operations. Although the medical profession remained in opposition, he received some support from the government. Working in several hospitals in India, Esdaile performed 291 operations on patients in a mesmeric trance before he left India. His reports lay buried in government files, since the medical journals in both India and England refused to publish them. Esdaile published a book in 1846 (*Mesmerism in India and Its Practical Application in Surgery and Medicine*) and still another in 1851 (*The Introduction of Mesmerism, as an Anesthetic and Curative Agent, into the Hospitals of India*), both dealing with his work with mesmerism. It remained for Braid*, however, to attach a different label to mesmerism—''hypnotism''—and to give it scientific respectability.
Biographies: J. M. Bramwell, *Hypnotism: Its History, Practice and Theory*, 1903; G. Rosen, *J. Hist. Med.*, 1946, *1*, 527-550; *DNB*, 19; *EUI*, 20.

ESQUIROL, JEAN ÉTIENNE DOMINIQUE

French Psychiatrist
Born: Toulouse, February 3, 1772
Died: Paris, December 13, 1840
Highest Degree: Docteur en médecine, La Salpêtrière, Paris
Positions: 1811-23, physician, La Salpêtrière; 1823-26, chief inspector, University of Paris; 1826-38, chief physician, asylum at Charenton

Esquirol continued Pinel's* efforts at bettering the life of the inmates of insane asylums. In 1817 Esquirol began lecturing on the treatment of the insane, which resulted in the appointment of a commission to investigate such treatment. Esquirol was responsible for planning the asylums at Rouen, Nantes, and Montpellier. He also wrote a cardinal work about mental disorder, *Des maladies mentales* (1838). It constituted an advance away from speculation and superstition toward a more rational and objective view of mental disorders. It was a first work of this kind. Esquirol differentiated between hallucinations and illusions, emphasized environmental and age factors as precipitants of mental disorders, and the role of emotions in such disorders. He continued to develop Pinel's statistical classification of inmates by age, disorder, and other characteristics. It later became the established practice to keep ample records on patients as one approach to the understanding of the origin of mental disorders.
Biographies: M. K. Amdur & E. Messinger, *Amer. J. Psychiat.*, 1939, *96*, 129-135; M. Dumas, *Étienne Esquirol: Sa famille, ses origines, ses années de formation*, 1971; G. Ferrus, *Des aliénés*, 1834; K. Kolle (Ed.), *Grosse Nervenärzte*, vol. 2, 1959, pp. 87-97; G. Mora, *Amer. J. Psychiat.*, 1972, *129*, 562-567; R. Semelaigne, *Les pionniers de la psychiatrie française avant et aprés Pinel*, 2 vols., 1930, 1932.

EULER, LEONHARD

Swiss Mathematician
Born: Basel, April 15, 1707
Died: St. Petersburg, Russia, September 7, 1783
Highest Degree: Master's in philosophy, University of Basel, 1723
Positions, Honors: 1727-41, Academy at St. Petersburg; 1741-66, Academy of Sciences, Berlin; 1766-83, Academy at St. Petersburg; numerous prizes

In philosophy Euler opposed both Leibniz* (specifically, his theory of monads) and von Wolff*. In physics he advocated the wave theory of light and held that color was due to the different frequencies of light waves. Otherwise, Euler's contributions lie almost entirely in the area of mathematics. He was the most prolific mathematician of all times, producing numerous books and some eight hundred treatises in mathematics. Gustav Fechner* acknowledged his debt to Euler, among others, for demonstrating that the pitch of tones follows Weber's* law and thus contributing to the formulation of the logarithmic law of psychophysics.
Biographies: D. Brewster, In L. Euler, *Letter of Euler to a German Princess*

on *Different Subjects in Physics and Philosophy*, 1872, pp. 15-28; L. G. Du Pasquier, *Léonard Euler et ses amis*, 1927; B. F. Finkel, *Amer. Math. Mon.*, 1897, *4*, 297-302; R. Fueter, *Léonard Euler*, 1948; F. Horner, In L. Euler, *Elements of Algebra*, 1840, pp. viii-xxii; A. Speiser, *Leonhard Euler und die deutsche Philosophie*, 1934; O. Spiess, *Leonhard Euler*, 1929; H. W. Turnbull, In J. R. Newman (Ed.), *The World of Mathematics*, vol. 1, 1956, pp. 75-168; *ADB*, 6; *DSB*, 4; *NDB*, 4.

EWALD, ERNST JULIUS RICHARD

German Physiologist
Born: Berlin, February 14, 1855
Died: Konstanz, Baden-Württemberg, July 22, 1921
Education: Studied mathematics, physics, medicine, and physiology at the University of Strasbourg; graduated in 1884
Positions: 1880-1921, University of Strasbourg; editorial work, *Zeitschrift für Psychologie und Physiologie der Sinnesorgane*

Ewald specialized in the physiology of the end organs and thus contributed to the understanding of sensations. He formulated (in 1899 and 1903) the pressure-pattern theory of hearing. He could make a demonstration of it because it was based on the observation that different tones produce different patterns in sand on plaques and membranes. Ewald postulated that for each combination of intensity and frequency there was a unique "acoustic image" that acted upon the basilar membrane, producing perception of the sound. Since the theory was less parsimonious than Helmholtz's*, which assumed only that nerve fibers in the inner ear each resonate to a sound wave of the appropriate length, it did not prevail. Ewald also invented a *pneumatic hammer*, a tiny cylinder and piston that could be used to stimulate directly the semicircular canals in experimental animals.

Biographies: A. Bethe, *Arch. ges. Physiol.*, 1922, *193*, 109-127; M. Gildmeister, *Z. Sinnesphysiol.*, 1921, *53*, 123-128; *Biog. Lex.*; *NDB*, 4; *World Who's Who in Science*, 1968.

EXNER, SIGMUND

Austrian Physiologist
Born: Vienna, April 5, 1846
Died: Vienna, February 5, 1926
Highest Degree: M.D., University of Vienna, 1870
Positions, Honors: 1870-1926, University of Vienna; editorial work, *Zeitschrift für Psychologie*; three honorary doctorates

Besides physiological work that had no direct implications for psychology, Exner did notable work on adaptation to hue (which supported the Young*-Helmholtz* theory of color vision), rate-threshold for pitch (or the continuum of noises and tones), and apparent movement. In 1873 Exner began using the term "reaction-time experiment." He knew that reaction time was affected by the subject's motivation. He also worked on the physiology of the senses, brain localization, illusions, color contrast, and the orientation of birds in flight.

Exner wrote numerous papers. Of his books the following are relevant to psychology: *Untersuchungen über die Localisation der Funktionen in der Grosshirnrinde des Menschen* (1881), *Die Physiologie der facettierten Augen von Krebsen und Insecten* (1891), and *Entwurf zu einer physiologischen Erklärung der psychischen Erscheinungen* (1894).

Biographies: Hirsch, *Biog. Lex.*, 2, Suppl.; *NDB*, 4; *World Who's Who in Science*, 1968.

F

FABRE, JEAN HENRI
French Biologist
Born: Saint-Léons, Aveyron, December 21, 1823
Died: Serignac, Provence, October 11, 1915
Highest Degree: Ph.D. in natural sciences, University of Paris, 1854
Positions: High school teacher, independent researcher, textbook writer

Although Fabre taught school most of his life, his one real interest had always been insects. He began to devote all of his time to insects in 1879, the year of his retirement, and continued collecting insects and describing their behavior for the next twenty-five years. He published his observations in the ten-volume *Souvenirs entomologiques* (1878-1907). Parts of this work were translated into English under the titles of *The Life and Love of the Insect* (1911), *Social Life in the Insect World* (1912), *The Life of the Fly* (1913), and others. Fabre thus contributed to the development of animal psychology during its preexperimental period.

Biographies: P. F. Bicknell, *The Human Side of Fabre*, 1923; M. Coulon, *La génie de J. H. Fabre*, 1924; H. Cuny, *Jean-Henri Fabre et le problème de l'instinct*, 1967; A. Fabre, *The Life of Jean-Henri Fabre*, 1921; J. H. Fabre, *The Life of the Fly*, 1913; G. V. Legros, *Fabre: Poet of Science*, 1913; E. Rabaud, *Fabre et la science*, 1925; E. W. Teale, In *The Insect World of J. Henri Fabre*, 1949, pp. ix-xvi; W. M. Wheeler, *J. Anim. Behav.*, 1916, *6*, 74-80; *DSB*, 4; *NYT*, 1915, Oct. 12, 11:4.

FARADAY, MICHAEL
English Chemist and Physicist
Born: Newington, Surrey, September 22, 1791
Died: Hampton Court, Middlesex, August 25, 1867
Education: Mostly self-taught
Positions: 1813-1862, Royal Institute
   Author of numerous discoveries in chemistry and electricity, Faraday also wrote an early paper about geometric illusions (1831). He contributed to psychology indirectly when in the 1850s he laid the foundation of the field theory, based on his work with electricity and magnetism. The idea of fields of force was developed further by James Clark Maxwell*, Faraday's disciple. Field theory was introduced in psychology by the Gestalt psychologists, such as Köhler* and Lewin*. Since then the concept has been used in psychology in a variety of theoretical contexts.
Biographies: J. Agassi, *Faraday as a Natural Philosopher*, 1971; H. Bence-Jones, *The Life and Letters of Faraday*, 1870; H. Kondo, *Sci. Amer.*, 1953, *189*(4), 90-99; D. K. C. MacDonald, *Faraday, Maxwell, and Kelvin*, 1964; W. Ostwald, *Michael Faraday*, 1924; W. L. Randall, *Michael Faraday*, 1925; A. A. de la Rive, *Ann. Rep. Board Smithsonian Inst.*, 1867, 227-245 (Reprinted in B. Z. Jones [Ed.], *The Golden Age of Science*, 1966, pp. 217-245); S. P. Thompson, *Michael Faraday: His Life and Work*, 1898; J. Tyndall, *Faraday as a Discoverer*, 1961; L. P. Williams, *Michael Faraday: A Biography*, 1965; *DNB*, 6; *DSB*, 4; *EB*, 9; *EP*, 3; *NYT*, 1867, Aug. 28, 4:7.

FARRAND, LIVINGSTON
American Anthropologist
Born: Newark, New Jersey, June 14, 1867
Died: New York, New York, November 8, 1939
Highest Degree: M.D., Columbia University, 1891; two years of postdoctoral studies in physiological psychology at Cambridge University and University of Berlin
Positions, Honors: 1893-1914, Columbia University, 1893-1901, teaching psychology, 1901-14, teaching anthropology; 1914-19, president, University of Colorado; 1921-37, president, Cornell University; thirteen honorary degrees; numerous medals and citations for public health and Red Cross-related work
   In psychology Farrand was a coauthor, with Cattell*, of a classic study, begun in 1894, of the physical and mental measurements of Columbia University students, along the lines of Galton's* research. The purpose of the tests (known as the "freshman tests") was to study the development of abilities and personality and their correlation. The project continued for several years and represented one of the earliest correlational studies.
Biographies: T. Parran, *Science*, 1939, *90*, 583-584; P. Van Inge, *Bull. N.Y. Acad. Med.*, 2nd ser., 1940, *16*, 124-126; R. S. Woodworth, *Amer. J. Psychol.*, 1940, *53*, 302; *DAB*, 22; *NCAB*, 40, A; *NYT*, 1939, Nov. 9, 23:1; *PR*, 3; *Who Was Who in America*, 1.

FEARING, FRANKLIN
American Psychologist
Born: Durango, Colorado, November 24, 1892
Died: Santa Monica, California, March 26, 1962
Highest Degree: Ph.D. in psychology, Stanford University, 1926
Positions: 1926-28, Ohio Wesleyan University; 1928-35, Northwestern University; 1935-60, University of California in Los Angeles; editorial work, *Journal of Psychology*, 1937-62

Fearing worked at first in the area of physiological psychology. At Northwestern University he established a laboratory for the study of the inner ear in relation to the maintenance of balance and posture. He is best known for his volume *Reflex Action* (1930). After moving to the University of California, Los Angeles, Fearing began work in social psychology, specializing in mass communication.

Biographies: *American Men of Science*. vol. 3, 9th ed., 1956; *NCAB*, 48; *PR*, 3.

FECHNER, GUSTAV THEODOR
German Philosopher, Physicist, and Psychologist
Born: Gross-Särchen, Lower Lusatia, April 19, 1801
Died: Leipzig, November 18, 1887
Highest Degree: M.D., University of Leipzig, 1822
Positions: 1824-87, University of Leipzig; until 1840, teaching physics; pensioned in 1844 because of poor eyesight, engaged in philosophy

Scientific psychology begins with Fechner. He first made a name for himself as a physicist (an interest acquired after obtaining the medical degree) and then became even more prominent by relating his interest in physics to his basic interest in philosophy and metaphysics. The field of psychophysics that developed therefrom was entirely a by-product of his philosophical interests. He is celebrated, nevertheless, as a psychophysicist and not as a philosopher.

Stimulated by his desire to prove that mind and body are aspects of the same unity (the identity hypothesis), Fechner, on October 22, 1850, conceived of the idea of how to measure sensation. He reasoned that if the exact relationship between stimulus energy and the sensation it produced were known, then by measuring physical energy, which is easy, one could measure sensation. The physiologist Ernst Heinrich Weber* had just formulated the law that now bears his name, namely, that the ratio of a just noticeable difference in a stimulus and the original stimulus is a constant. Fechner integrated Weber's fraction and arrived at the equation that shows that sensation is directly proportional to the logarithm of the stimulus: $R = k \log S$ (Fechner's law).

The program for the development of psychophysics Fechner described in 1851 in a philosophical treatise entitled *Zend-Avesta*. Fechner then proceeded to work out the three basic psychophysical methods for establishing the lower (absolute) and upper (terminal) thresholds of sensation as well as the difference thresholds for deep pressure, visual brightness, and tactual and visual distance. The methods of limits, average error, and the constant method are still basic in psychophysics today. They were the first methods of mental measurement and therefore initiated the era of quantitative experimental psychology.

In 1860 Fechner published his theory and experimental findings in *Elemente der Psychophysik*, which treated the "exact science of the functional relations of dependency between body and mind." Fechner then turned to experimental aesthetics and spent the next ten years developing still another field of inquiry. He contributed a dozen papers on the subject, including one about the golden section and several about the authenticity of paintings. This work culminated in a book, *Vorschule der Aesthetik* (1876), which laid the foundation for experimental aesthetics. By this time psychophysics was beginning to be incorporated in the "new" psychology, and Fechner published two more books and several articles on the subject. The *Elements*, however, remained his main psychological work and a cornerstone of the new scientific psychology that experimented and measured, not merely speculated.

In addition to Fechner's law, Fechner's name is associated with the following phenomena: *Fechner's colors* (subjective colors seen in relatively slowly rotating discs with black-and-white patterns) and *Fechner's paradox* (that a visual target viewed with two eyes will appear brighter if one eye is suddenly covered up).
Biographies: T. Achelis, *Z. Völkerpsychol.*, 1889, *19*, 164-192; F. Angell, *Pop. Sci. Mon.*, 1913, *83*, 40-49; J. M. Baldwin, *Psychol. Rev.*, 1906, *13*, 141; W. Bölsche, *Deutsch. Rundsch.*, 1897, *92*, 344-369; M. Brasch, *Leipziger Philosophen*, 1894; G. Elsas, *Grenzboten*, 1888, *47*(2), 73-80; I. Hermann, *Gustav Theodor Fechner*, 1926; J. E. Kuntze, *Gustav Theodor Fechner*, 1892; K. Lasswitz, *Gustav Theodor Fechner*, 1910; M. Wentscher, *Fechner und Lotze*, 1925; W. Wirth, In *Sächsische Lebensbilder*, vol. 2, 1938, pp. 97-113; W. Wundt, *Gustav Theodor Fechner*, 1901; W. Wundt, *Phil. Stud.*, 1887-1888, *4*, 471-478; *ADB*, 55; *DSB*, 4; *EB*, 9; Hirsch, *Biog. Lex.*; *IESS*, 5; *NDB*, 5.

FENICHEL, OTTO
Austrian Psychoanalyst
Born: Vienna, December 2, 1897
Died: Los Angeles, California, January 22, 1946
Highest Degree: M.D., University of Vienna, 1922
Positions: 1924-33, Berlin Psychoanalytical Institute; 1933-35, private practice and training of psychoanalysts, Oslo, Norway; 1935-37, private practice and training of psychoanalysts, Prague, Czechoslovakia; 1938-46, private practice of psychoanalysis, California

Fenichel was an orthodox Freudian psychoanalyst and a prolific contributor to the psychoanalytic literature. He published seventy-two papers and made more than two hundred oral presentations. His most notable book is *The Psychoanalytic Theory of the Neuroses* (1945), which is a systematic treatment of all types of neuroses from the psychoanalytic point of view. His ability to synthesize and consolidate psychoanalytic knowledge caused this book as well as his other writings to be widely read and therefore influential. Other books by Fenichel are *Outline of Clinical Psychoanalysis* (1931) and *Problems of Psychoanalytic Technique* (1939). The collected papers of Fenichel were published in 1953 and 1954.

Biographies: R. R. Greenson, In F. Alexander, S. Eisenstein & M. Grotjahn (Eds.), *Psychoanalytic Pioneers*, 1966, pp. 439-449; A. Koch, *Rev. psicoanál.*, Buenos Aires, 1946, *4*, 157-158; R. M. Loewenstein, *Psychoanal. Quart.*, 1946, *15*, 139-140; E. Simmel, *Int. J. Psychoanal.*, 1946, *27*, 67-71; *EJ*, 6.

FÉRÉ, CHARLES SAMSON

French Psychiatrist
Born: Auffay, Seine Maritime, June 13, 1852
Died: Paris, April 22, 1907
Highest Degree: Dr. en médecine, University of Paris, 1882
Positions: 1882-1907, Bicêtre Hospital, Paris

Féré was an early collaborator of Binet's*. With Binet he wrote two books, *Le magnétisme animal* (1886), which stressed the increased sensitivity to touch in hypnotized animals, and one about reasoning, *La psychologie du raisonnement* (1886). In 1885 Féré discovered the changes that take place in the conductance of the skin during emotional arousal. It was named the "psychogalvanic reflex" and renamed the "galvanic skin response" (GSR) later. It has been measured in innumerable psychological studies and is the central measure taken in the polygraph technique.

In connection with his studies of fatigue, Féré built the first ergograph. These studies were conducted by Féré in relation to his doctrine of dynamogenesis, presented in his 1887 book *Sensation et mouvement*. The theory originated in Féré's observation that the strength of muscular contractions is increased by external stimuli, even apparently irrelevant stimuli, so they seem to release energy within the organism.

Féré wrote many books about psychopathology, psychiatry, and heredity, degeneracy, and criminality. His *La pathologie des émotions* (1892) was translated into English in 1899.

Biographies: *Biog. Lex.*; *EUI*, 23.

FERENCZI, SANDOR

Hungarian Psychoanalyst
Born: Miskolc, Hungary, July 16, 1873
Died: Budapest, May 22, 1933
Highest Degree: M.D., University of Vienna, 1894
Positions: 1895-1900, City Hospital, Budapest; 1900-1919, private practice, hospital appointments in Budapest; 1919-33, University of Budapest

Ferenczi was one of the members of Sigmund Freud's* inner circle. He was the founder and coeditor of the *Internationale Zeitschrift für Psychoanalyse*, the founder of the Hungarian Psychoanalytic Society (in 1913), and the holder of the first professorship in psychoanalysis.

Ferenczi introduced two new methods of therapy. One, the active therapy method, was based on Freud's theory of privation. When patients resisted free association, Ferenczi ordered abstinence from eating, defecation, or sex, expecting the dammed-up libido to provide the energy needed for therapy and to clarify the patient's defenses. Ferenczi abandoned this therapy in 1927 because it did not work and switched to permissive therapy, which was based on the idea that a loving environment would provide the necessary therapeutic action by compensating for the lack of love and attention experienced by the patient during childhood. Ferenczi's most important books are *Actual- und Psychoneurosen* (1908), *Introjektion und Transferenz* (1909), *Die Entwicklung der Psychoanalyse* (1924), and *Thalasso: Versuch einer Genitaltheorie* (1924).

Biographies: M. Balint, *Int. J. Psychoanal.*, 1949, *30*, 215-219; I. Barande, *Sándor Ferenczi*, 1972; B. R. Berkey & L. M. Roberts, *Dis. Nerv. Syst.*, 1968, *29*, 457-461; L. Eidelberg (Ed.), *Encyclopedia of Psychoanalysis*, 1968; P. Federn, *Int. J. Psychoanal.*, 1933, *14*, 467-485; N. G. Hale, Jr. (Ed.), *James Jackson Putnam and Psychoanalysis*, 1971; E. Jones, *Int. J. Psychoanal.*, 1933, *14*, 463-466; S. Lorand, In F. Alexander, S. Eisenstein, & M. Grotjahn (Eds.), *Psychoanalytic Pioneers*, 1966, pp. 14-35; S. Radó, *Psychoanal. Quart.*, 1933, *2*, 356-358; E. Simmel, *Imago*, 1933, *19*, 296-311; *IESS*, 5.

FERNBERGER, SAMUEL WEILLER
American Psychologist
Born: Philadelphia, Pennsylvania, June 4, 1887
Died: Philadelphia, Pennsylvania, May 2, 1956
Highest Degree: Ph.D. in psychology, University of Pennsylvania, 1912, under F. M. Urban*
Positions: 1912-20, Clark University; 1920-56, University of Pennsylvania; editorial work, *Psychological Bulletin* (1918-30), *Journal of Experimental Psychology* (1930-46), and *American Journal of Psychology* (1925-56)

Fernberger was a psychophysicist, but he contributed to many different fields in psychology. In psychophysics several of his papers are classics. In 1914 he showed, for instance, that by changing the observer's attitude toward perceiving difference, the category of "equal" in the constant stimulus method may be eliminated. Most of his work in psychophysics was on lifted weights using the constant stimulus method. Fernberger wrote several oft-cited papers about facial expression in emotion, memory span, and the range of visual apprehension. He also did several statistical studies in the history of psychology and of the professional activities of psychologists. Fernberger wrote one book, *Elementary General Psychology* (1936).

Biographies: F. W. Irwin, *Amer. J. Psychol.*, 1956, *69*, 676-680; *NYT*, 1956, May 4, 25:2; *PR*, 3; *Who Was Who in America*, 3.

FEUERBACH, PAUL JOHANN ANSELM VON
German Jurist
Born: Hainichen, near Jena, November 14, 1775
Died: Frankfurt am Main, May 29, 1833
Highest Degree: Ph.D. in philosophy, University of Jena, 1795; J.D., 1799
Positions: 1795-1802, University of Jena; 1802-4, University of Kiel; 1804-5,
University of Landshut

Feuerbach advocated the Kantian (Kant*) doctrine that punishment should be given for its own sake to enforce the law and to act as a deterrent rather than to prevent wrongdoing individually (*Anti-Hobbs*, 1798; *Über Philosophie und Empirie in ihrem Verhältnisse zur positiven Rechtswissenschaft*, 1804). This became known as the "psychological-coercive," or intimidation, theory of punishment. Feuerbach is even better remembered for having contributed one of the first documented cases to the social-deprivation literature, the account of Caspar Hauser, who, Feuerbach believed, "was kept in a dungeon from early childhood to the age of seventeen, separated from all communication with the world" and then mysteriously turned up in Nuremberg, letter of recommendation in hand. Influenced by Rousseau's* thesis of the "noble savage," Feuerbach, in an 1832 work, proposed, and the public readily accepted, the notion that Caspar Hauser was a "child of nature," noble and unspoiled. The accumulating evidence that Hauser was probably a fraud and a pathological liar did not change Feuerbach's or the public's minds, and the Caspar Hauser story continued to be accepted as genuine. It created a literature of more than one thousand items.

Biographies: H. Blohm, *Feuerbach und das Reichsstrafgesetzbuch von 1871*, 1935; L. Feuerbach, *Anselm Ritter v. Feuerbachs Leben und Werke*, 1852; G. Radbruch, *Paul Johann Anselm von Feuerbach: Ein Juristenleben*, 1934; T. Spoerri, *Genie und Krankheit: Eine psychopathologische untersuchung der Familie Feuerbach*, 1952; *ADB*, 6; *EUI*, 23; *NDB*, 5.

FICHTE, JOHANN GOTTLIEB
German Philosopher
Born: Rammenau, Upper Lusatia, May 19, 1762
Died: Berlin, January 27, 1814
Education: Studied theology and philosophy at Jena and Leipzig
Positions: 1794-99, University of Jena; 1805-8, University of Erlangen; 1809-12, University of Berlin

Fichte was a philosophical successor of Kant*. His philosophy focused on the a priori characteristics of the notions of time and space. He was strongly interested in the practical or moral aspects of Kant's teachings, which led him to state that knowledge depends on moral convictions and acts. The world of nonself is a scene where people act out their duties and which acquires its significance from the self. Individual differences determine the philosophy a person chooses as well as the kinds of other interests one may develop: "The kind of philosophy one chooses depends upon the kind of person one is'' (*Die Bestimmung des Menschen*, 1800).

Biographies: R. Adamson, *Fichte*, 1908; K. Fischer, *Fichtes Leben, Werke und Lehre*, 1900; X. León, *Fichte et son temps*, 1922-1927; A. Messer, *Fichte: seine Persönlichkeit und seine Philosophie*, 1920; M. Wundt, *J. G. Fichtes Leben und seine Lehre*, 1927; *ADB*, 6; *EJ*, 6; *EP*, 3; *NDB*, 5.

FISHER, SIR RONALD AYLMER

English Statistician

Born: London, February 17, 1890

Died: Adelaide, Australia, July 29, 1962

Education: Studied mathematics and physics at Cambridge University; graduated in 1912

Positions, Honors: 1918-33, Rothamsted Experimental Agriculture Station; 1933-43, University College, London, Galton Professor of Eugenics; 1943-57, Cambridge University; 1957-62, University of Adelaide; knighted, 1952; numerous medals, honors

Although tests of the statistical significance of differences were performed before Fisher, his contributions were such that the era of contemporary analytical statistics begins with him. He was first to make a clear distinction between *population parameters* and *sample statistics* (his terms). He contributed heavily to the theory of experimentation. His two books most important to psychology (*Statistical Methods for Research Workers*, 1925; *The Design of Experiments*, 1935) contain largely his own findings. They are addressed primarily not to the statisticians but to research workers in different areas and place powerful tools in their hands. Fisher developed the technique of analysis of variance. The *F* in the *F* statistic stands for Fisher. He also developed small sample and nonparametric techniques. Terms like *null hypothesis, degrees of freedom, randomized block design*, and *treatment* were coined by Fisher. Fisher himself was instrumental in publicizing his work and in having it accepted, although in the course of these activities he developed vigorous controversies and polemic exchanges. Although he wrote *Statistical Methods* in 1925, these methods did not begin to be applied by American psychologists until his visit to the United States in 1931. Since then he has influenced psychologists' approach to experimentation more than any other person.

Biographies: *Brit. J. Stat. Psychol.*, 1962, *15*, 197-198; M. G. Kendall, *Biometrika*, 1963, *50*, 1-15; P. C. Mahalanobis, *Biometrics*, 1964, *20*, 238-251; P. C. Mahalanobis, *Sankhya*, 1938, *4*, 265-272; G. A. Miller, *Amer. J. Psychol.*, 1963, *76*, 157-158; J. Neyman, *Science*, 1968, *156*, 1456-1460; Royal Society, *Biog. Mem. Fellows Roy. Soc.*, vol. 9, 1963, pp. 91-130; F. Yates, *Nature*, 1962, *195*, 1151-1152; *DSB*, 5; *IESS*, 5.

FITTS, PAUL MORRIS
American Psychologist
Born: Martin, Tennessee, May 5, 1912
Died: Ann Arbor, Michigan, May 2, 1965
Highest Degree: Ph.D. in psychology, University of Rochester, 1938, under L. Carmichael*
Positions: 1938-41, University of Tennessee; 1942-44, assistant chief, Psychology Branch, Air Surgeon HQ, U.S. Army Air Forces; 1945-49, chief, Psychology Branch, Aeromedical Laboratory, U.S. Air Force Air Matériel Command; 1949-58, Ohio State University; 1958-65, University of Michigan, since 1962, director of Human Performance Center; member of numerous panels and consultant to many firms and government units

Fitts's work was in human engineering, particularly in equipment design (he edited *Psychological Research on Equipment Design*, 1947). His work helped to define a new field in psychology, engineering psychology. Fitts's experience with the U.S. Air Force oriented him particularly to problems encountered in the work of aircraft pilots. Both in the air force and later at the Ohio State University Laboratory of Aviation Psychology (which he directed), Fitts contributed to the solution of problems related to cockpit design, radar operator training, and related areas. His monograph (with J. A. Leonard) about visual pattern recognition (*Stimulus Correlates of Visual Pattern Recognition*, 1957) summarizes some basic work done by a group of investigators under his direction in the area of visual form perception but addresses the solution of practical problems in visual information processing by aviation personnel. One result of this work was the construction of a type of easily quantifiable and generalizable visual stimulus, the Ohio metric histoform. Another result was one of the first instances of the use of information-theoretical measures in psychology, here applied to visual stimuli, specifically in the form of redundancy measures.

Fitts wrote several chapters about engineering psychology and equipment design for S. S. Stevens's* *Handbook of Experimental Psychology* (1951), edited *Human Engineering for an Effective Air Navigation and Traffic Control System* (1951) and *Human Engineering Concepts and Theory* (1959), and wrote the volume *Human Performance* (1967).
Biographies: *American Men of Science*, 10th ed., vol. 2, *The Physical and Biological Sciences*.

FLECHSIG, PAUL EMIL
German Neuranatomist and Neurologist
Born: Zwickau, Saxony, June 29, 1847
Died: Leipzig, July 22, 1929
Highest Degree: M.D., University of Leipzig, 1870
Positions, Honors: 1872-1921, University of Leipzig; two honorary doctorates

Flechsig originated the ontogenetic method of studying the structure of the central nervous system. By following the myelinization process in axons, he was able to isolate and identify functions of nerve tracts and cortical projection areas. Based on this technique Flechsig prepared a map of cortical localization. He distinguished between sensory projection areas and association areas of the cortex on the basis of their rates of maturation (*myelinization*). Although the sensory projection system matures prenatally, the association system matures after birth and underlies the higher intellectual functions.

Flechsig published about fifty titles. Those works of importance to psychology are *Die körperlichen Grundlagen der Geistesstörungen* (1882), *Plan des menschlichen Gehirns* (1883), *Die Lokalisation der geistigen Vorgänge* (1896), and *Gehirn und Seele* (1894).

Biographies: P. M. Flechsig, *Meine myelogenetische Hirnlehre: Mit biographischer Einleitung*, 1927; G. Pfeifer, *Schweiz. Arch. Neurol. Psychiat.*, 1930, *26*, 258-264; P. Schröder, *Arch. Psychiat.*, Berlin, 1930, *91*, 1-8; *DSB*, 5; Hirsch, *Biog. Lex.*, 2, Suppl.; *NDB*, 5.

FLOURENS, PIERRE JEAN MARIE

French Physiologist
Born: Maureilhan, Hérault, April 1, 1794
Died: Montgeron, near Paris, December 6, 1867
Highest Degree: M.D., University of Montpellier, 1813
Positions, Honors: 1828-30, Collège de France; 1830-55, Museum of Jardin du Roi; 1855-67, Collège de France; elected permanent secretary of the Academy of Sciences, 1833; elected to the French Academy, 1840

Flourens's main contribution was to physiological psychology, which he made through his work on the localization of brain functions. Using the method of extirpation, which he introduced, he concentrated on the cerebral hemispheres, the cerebellum, the corpora quadrigemina, the medulla oblongata, the spinal cord, and the nerves to isolate each from the other and to remove each cleanly and so determine its function. Flourens correctly established the functions of the six main divisions of the nervous system of animals: although each has a specific and unitary role (*action propre*), the brain also acts as a whole (*action commune*). In this Flourens anticipated the much later work of Lashley* and Franz*. In moving away from the speculations of the philosophers concerning brain function and at the same time rejecting the extreme specificity of the phrenologists (whom he severely criticized), Flourens, through the precision of his technique and his clear and forceful presentations materially advanced knowledge concerning the anatomical substrate of behavior. His main work is *Recherches expérimentales sur les propriétés et les fonctions du système nerveux dans les animaux vertébrés* (1824).

Biographies: B. Hollander, *In Search of the Soul and the Mechanisms of Thought, Emotion, and Conduct*, ca. 1920; G. Legée, *Hist. Biol.*, 1969, *2*, 10-34; J. M. Olmsted, In E. A. Underwood (Ed.), *Science, Medicine, and History: Essays in Honor of Charles Singer*, vol. 2, 1953, pp. 290-302; *DSB*, 5; *EB*, 9; Hirsch, *Biog. Lex.*, 2, Suppl.; *IESS*, 5.

FLOURNOY, THÉODORE
Swiss Psychologist
Born: Geneva, August 15, 1854
Died: Geneva, November 5, 1920
Highest Degree: M.D., University of Strasbourg, 1878
Positions, Honors: 1908-20, University of Geneva; president, Sixth International Congress of Psychology, 1909

Flournoy initiated scientific psychology in French-speaking Switzerland. With E. Claparède* he founded *Archives de Psychologie* in 1901. In this journal he published many studies on different subjects. Flournoy also wrote several books about psychology, parapsychology, metaphysics, spiritualism, and religion: *Métaphysique et psychologie* (1890), *Des phénomènes de synopsie* (1893), *Les principes de la psychologie religieuse* (1903), and *Esprits et mediums* (1911). The book that made him known was *Des Indes à la planète Mars: Étude sur un cas de somnambulisme avec glossolalie* (1900), which was translated into English (*From India to the Planet Mars*) the year it was published and reprinted in 1963. It was a study of a bizarre case of dissociation, suggestion, and glossolalia, all related to the belief in spirits and similar to that described by the Swiss psychiatrist C. G. Jung* in his doctoral dissertation in 1902. Because Flournoy used psychological explanations to account for the extraordinary phenomena he observed, his may be considered one of the early works in the area of anomalistic psychology.

Biographies: E. Claparède, *Arch. psychol.*, Geneva, 1921, *18*, 1-125; J. H. Leuba, *Psychol. Bull.*, 1921, *18*, 232-233; E. B. Titchener, *Amer. J. Psychol.*, 1921, *32*, 154; *EUI*, 24.

FLUGEL, JOHN CARL
English Psychologist
Born: London, June 13, 1884
Died: London, August 7, 1955
Highest Degree: D.Sc., University of London, 1908
Positions: 1909-55, University College, London; president, British Psychological Society, 1932-35; secretary, International Psychoanalytical Association, 1919-24

Flugel combined the academic psychologist with the psychoanalyst, believing that the two approaches, rather than being contradictory, had a common goal, a better understanding of human relations. He directed the work of the psychological laboratory of the University of London for more than twenty years but was as much interested in human and especially international relations. This attitude and his wide educational background enabled him to present psychoanalysis in a more objective and acceptable way than could many other adherents of Sigmund Freud*. Flugel's first book, *The Psychoanalytic Study of the Family*, attracted much attention and introduced the concept of the Oedipus conflict to the general public. This was followed by a number of others: *Practice, Fatigue,* *and Oscillation* (1928), *The Psychology of Clothes* (1930), *An Introduction to Psychoanalysis* (1932), *Men and Their Motives* (1936), *Man, Morals, and Society* (1945), *Population, Psychology, and Peace* (1947), a total of about eighty publications. He is best known for a classic volume in the history of psychology, *A Hundred Years of Psychology: 1833-1933* (1933).

Biographies: E. Jones, *Int. J. Psychoanal.*, 1956, *37*, 193-197; T. H. Pear, *Brit. J. Psychol.*, 1956, *47*, 1-4; R. W. Russell, *Amer. J. Psychol.*, 1956, *69*, 328-329; J. D. Sutherland, *Brit. J. Med. Psychol.*, 1956, *29*, 1.

FOREL, AUGUSTE HENRI
Swiss Psychiatrist and Entomologist
Born: Near Morges, Vaud, September 1, 1848
Died: Yvorne, Vaud, July 27, 1931
Highest Degree: M.D., University of Zurich, 1871
Positions, Honors: 1873-79, University of Munich; 1879-98, director, Burghölzli hospital, Zurich, professor of psychiatry, University of Zurich; 1898-1931, private practice of medicine, work for the Order of Good Templars and Swiss and international peace organizations; honorary Dr. phil., 1896

Forel worked as a psychiatrist (he succeeded in curing alcoholics by having them join a society of teetotalers), wrote books and papers about legal psychiatry (*Crime et anomalies mentales constitutionelles*, 1902) and brain anatomy (he discovered the origin of the auditory nerve in the rabbit), and founded the Society for Psychotherapy and Medical Psychology. He also wrote books about psychology (*L'Âme et le système nerveux*, 1906; *L'Activité psychique*, 1919; *Notre vie mentale*, 1929) and a variety of psychological topics: memory (*Das Gedächtnis und seine Abnormitäten*, 1885), hypnotism and suggestion (he founded the Zeitschrift für Hypnotismus in 1892 and wrote *Der Hypnotismus* in 1889, which was to appear in many editions), mental hygiene (*Hygiene der Nerven und des Geistes im gesunden und kranken Zustand*, 1903), and sex (*The Sexual Question: A Scientific, Psychological, Hygienic, and Sociological Study*, which was published first in German in 1905, translated into English in 1922 and in many other languages, and saw numerous editions). He is known principally as an entomologist who studied ants and their behavior very thoroughly for almost fifty years. His greatest work, *The Social World of the Ants Compared with That of Man* (1910; English translation, 1930), was a major contribution to comparative psychology. Forel wrote his first work about ants in 1874. It was followed by a number of others, some of which also made a contribution to that field, such as *The Sense of Insects* (1887; English translation, 1908) and a number of shorter monographs.

Biographies: A. Forel, In L. R. Grote (Ed.), *Die Medizin der Gegenwart in Selbstdarstellungen*, vol. 6, 1927, pp. 53-87; A. Forel, *Out of My Life and Work*, 1937; A. Meyer, *Arch. Neurol. Psychiat.*, Chicago, 1931, *26*, 1303-1305; A. V.

Muralt, *August Forel*, 1928; O. Volkart, *August Forel*, 1918; J. Wagner, *August Forel; La vie, l'oeuvre, l'homme*, 1918; A. Wettley, *August Forel: Ein Arztleben im Zwiespalt seiner Zeit*, 1953; W. H. v. Wyss, *50 Jahre Psychophysiologie in Zürich*, 1948; *DSB*, 5.

FOURIER, FRANÇOIS CHARLES MARIE
French Social Reformer
Born: Besançon, Doubs, April 7, 1772
Died: Paris, October 10, 1837
Education: Largely self-taught
Positions: Commercial salesman, Marseille; 1799-1816, civil servant, Lyons; after 1816, on inherited income

Fourier published his social-philosophical views first in 1808 in a book entitled *Théorie des quatre mouvements et des destinées générales*. All social ills Fourier attributed to individualistic competition and hence proposed that society be reorganized on the basis of cooperation. Fourier held that repression of passions is responsible for human discontent, crime, and immorality, and that by allowing them free rein, behavior would naturally follow the happy medium between extremes. Fourier's plan for reorganizing society involved groups of sixteen hundred persons, called *phalanges*, that would reside in the same building. Actual attempts at cooperative communal living were made in France and in America, but they failed. What ties Fourier into the fabric of the development of psychology was a theory of human destiny that played its part in eventually producing the mainstream of evolutionary thinking in the nineteenth century. Fourier saw humanity as progressively improving itself and its lot throughout its evolutionary history, in which each stage of development covers thousands of years.
Biographies: A. Bebel, *Charles Fourier: Sein Leben und seine Theorien*, 1890; O. S. Debout, In *Oeuvres complètes de Charles Fourier*, vol. 1, 1966, i-xxvii; C. Gide, *Fourier: Prècurseur de la co-opération*, 1924; M.-A. Gromier, *La vie, les oeuvres, les disciples de Charles Fourier*, 1906; F. Manuel, *Prophets of Paris*, 1962; C. Pellarin, *C. Fourier: Sa vie et sa théorie*, 1871; N. V. Riasanovsky, *The Teaching of Charles Fourier*, 1969; *EP*, 3; *IESS*, 5.

FRANKLIN, BENJAMIN
American Philosopher, Printer, and Diplomat
Born: Boston, Massachusetts, January 6, 1706
Died: Philadelphia, Pennsylvania, April 17, 1790
Education: Self-educated
Honors: Several honorary degrees from American and English universities; membership in many scientific societies; Copley Medal, Royal Society, 1753

Franklin's name enters the history of psychology in two contexts. In 1765 he showed that an afterimage may be positive when seen with closed eyes but negative when seen on a light field with the eyes open. The demonstration came to be known as the "Franklin experiment" and was much discussed by scientists.

During his stay in France as the American ambassador, Franklin was appointed (in 1784) by the French government to head a commission created to investigate Franz Anton Mesmer*, who was active in Paris at that time. The commission's findings (based, among other things, on several experiments on hypnosis performed by Franklin) was that imagination was responsible for Mesmer's alleged cures. When a follower of Mesmer, Marquis de Puységur*, claimed to have achieved cures by having afflicted persons stand under trees that he had "magnetized," Franklin performed the experiment of telling some peasants that certain trees had been "magnetized." Those who stood under these trees were cured as effectively as Puységur's patients, which confirmed to Franklin the commission's earlier conclusion that "imagination" or suggestion was at work. Franklin's experiments were thus the first instance of the empirical study of the factors involved in hypnosis.

Biographies: A. O. Aldridge, *Franklin and His French Contemporaries*, 1957; C. L. Becker, *Benjamin Franklin*, 1946; P. L. Ford, *The Many-Sided Franklin*, 1899; B. Franklin, *Benjamin Franklin: A Biography in His Own Words*, 1972; B. Hindle, *The Pursuit of Science in Revolutionary America*, 1956; R. L. Ketcham, *Benjamin Franklin*, 1965; J. Parton, *Benjamin Franklin*, 1914; *DAB*, 6; *DSB*, 5; *EB*, 9; *EP*, 3; *NCAB*, 1.

FRANZ, SHEPHERD IVORY
American Psychologist
Born: Jersey City, New Jersey, May 27, 1874
Died: Los Angeles, California, October 14, 1933
Highest Degree: Ph.D. in psychology, Columbia University, 1899, under J. McK. Cattell*
Positions, Honors: 1899-1900, instructor in physiology, Harvard University; 1901-4, instructor in physiology and medical physics, Dartmouth College; 1904-6, pathological physiologist and psychologist, McLean Hospital for the Insane, Waverly, Massachusetts; 1907-24, professor of psychology, George Washington University (St. Elizabeth's Hospital); 1924-33, professor of psychology, University of California at Los Angeles; editorial work, *Psychological Monographs* and *Psychological Bulletin*, 1914-24; honorary LL.D. and M.D.; president, American Psychological Association, 1920

Franz pioneered in relating psychology to the physiology of the brain. He did this by using both the physiologist's method of extirpation of brain tissue and the psychologist's method of studying animal learning. The relationships studied by Franz were those between learned behaviors and their cortical localization. He found that a habit lost through extirpation could be relearned, lost again, and so on several times. It suggested that neither the site nor the extent of brain damage in mental patients was directly related to the severity of behavioral impairment. Franz showed that complete frontal lobectomy in cats and monkeys led to loss of recent habits but not of old habits, that the lost habits could be relearned, and that the loss of one lobe only led to a decrease in the efficiency of the behavior involved but not to its complete loss. Such findings, in addition to his demonstration that even the motor functions were not very precisely localized in the brain, were surprising at the time. Franz jokingly began to refer to attempts to localize brain functions exactly as the "new phrenology." Karl Lashley*, who worked with Franz at St. Elizabeth's Hospital, eventually took over from him and developed further this line of research, helping to swing the localization pendulum even further toward Flourens*. Books by Franz include *Handbook of Mental Examination Methods* (1912), *Nervous and Mental Reeducation* (1924), and *Persons, One and Three: A Study in Multiple Personalities* (1933).

Biographies: K. Dunlap, *J. Gen. Psychol.*, 1934, *10*, 3; S. Fernberger, *Psychol. Bull.*, 1933, *30*, 741-742; R. S. Woodworth, *Amer. J. Psychol.*, 1934, *46*, 151-152; *DAB*, 21; *HPA*, 2; *NCAB*, A.

FRENKEL-BRUNSWIK, ELSE
Austrian-American Psychologist
Born: Lemberg, Austria, August 18, 1908
Died: Berkeley, California, March 31, 1958
Highest Degree: Ph.D. in psychology, University of Vienna, 1930, under K. Bühler*
Positions: 1931-38, University of Vienna; 1938-58, University of California, Berkeley

Else Frenkel-Brunswik's major contribution to the field of psychology was in connection with the development of scales of ethnocentrism and of authoritarianism (the F scale) and the study of prejudice, using new methods and testing new hypotheses concerning prejudice. The work was published in collaboration with others (T. W. Adorno, E. Frenkel-Brunswik, D. L. Levinson, and R. N. Sanford, *The Authoritarian Personality*, 1950). Frenkel-Brunswik's own specific contributions were the construction and analysis of the semistructured interviews with the subjects of the study. A concept developed by her in connection with the study of the authoritarian personality was intolerance of ambiguity. Her total output was only sixteen papers and a book written with E. Weisskopf, *Wunsch und Pflicht im Aufbau des menschlichen Lebens* (1937).

Biographies: T. Adorno, *Perspect. Amer. Hist.*, 1968, *2*, 338-370; L. Lowenthal, *Amer. Sociol. Rev.*, 1958, *23*, 585-586; *IESS*, 5.

FREUD, ANNA
Austrian-English Psychoanalyst
Born: Vienna, Austria, December 3, 1895
Died: London, England, October 8, 1982
Education: Cottage Lyceum, Vienna; no academic degrees
Positions, Honors: 1923-38, practicing psychoanalyst, Vienna; 1939-45, child therapist, Hampstead War Nursery, London; founder (1947) and director (since 1952), Hampstead Child Therapy Course and Clinic; honorary LL.D., Clark

University (1950), University of Sheffield (1966); honorary Sc.D., Jefferson Medical College, 1964; honorary degrees, University of Chicago (1966), Yale (1968), Columbia (1978), Harvard (1980); honorary M.D., University of Vienna, 1975; Grand Decoration of Honor in Gold, Austria, 1975; editor, *The Psychoanalytic Study of the Child* (1947-82), *The Standard Edition of the Complete Psychological Works of Sigmund Freud* (24 vols., 1953-56)

Until Sigmund Freud's* death, his youngest child, daughter Anna, had been his steady companion, assistant, and executive secretary in the business of the Vienna Psychoanalytic Society and the International Psychoanalytic Association. She learned psychoanalysis from her father, specializing in child and adolescent psychology. In 1970 her colleagues named her the most outstanding living child psychoanalyst. She kept up a steady output of publications after her first publication in 1922, and her bibliography lists more than one hundred articles and several books.

Anna Freud and Melanie Klein* initiated child psychoanalysis and systematized the direct treatment of children (*Introduction to the Technique of Child Analysis*, 1928; *Psychoanalytic Treatment of Children*, 1946). Anna Freud produced more research and collected more data on children than any other psychoanalyst (*Psychoanalysis for Teacher and Parents*, 1931; *Young Children in Wartime*, 1942; *War and Children*, 1943, with D. T. Burlingham; *Infants Without Families*, 1944). Her most important contribution was the editorship of *The Psychoanalytic Study of the Child*. She and her colleagues at Hampstead also developed a diagnostic developmental profile to be used in assessing possible relationships between childhood development and psychopathology. Her theoretical contributions involved the development of an ego psychology and the role of ego defense mechanisms, especially those of displacement and identification (*The Ego and the Mechanisms of Defense*, 1936). Her position that in child-custody cases the psychological parent should be given the custody of the child (*Beyond the Best Interests of the Child*, 1973, with J. Goldstein and A. Solnit) has influenced decisions in child-custody cases in the United States. Her other works are *The Enrichment of Childhood* (1966, with W. D. Well), *Children in Hospital* (1966, with T. Bergmann), *Normality and Pathology in Childhood* (1966), *Problems of Psychoanalytic Technique and Therapy* (1973), and *Before the Best Interests of the Child* (1979).

Biographies: D. J. Jackson, *Psychol. Rep.*, 1982, *50*, 1191-1198; R. S. Stewart, *New York Times Book Review*, 1977, *41*(41,637), sec. 7, Jan. 23, 1, 12; *IESS*, 18; *International Encyclopaedia of Psychiatry, Psychology, Psychoanalysis. and Neurology*, 5; *Who's Who*, 1978-79; *NYT*, 1982, Oct. 10, 46:1-5.

FREUD, SIGMUND
Austrian Psychoanalyst
Born: Freiberg, Moravia, Austria-Hungary, May 6, 1856
Died: London, England, September 23, 1939
Highest Degree: M.D., University of Vienna, 1881

Positions: 1882-86, physician, General Hospital, Vienna; 1886-1938, private practice, Vienna

As the founder of psychoanalysis, Freud contributed to psychological thought more than any other single individual in the twentieth century. He began as a successful neurologist (he coined the term *agnosia*); associated himself with Joseph Breuer*, who had been using hypnosis with hysteric patients; and began to use hypnosis himself. He found that it did not always work, however. A year spent studying with Charcot* gave him the idea that sexual problems may underlie hysteria. The study of one of Breuer's patients, Anna O., convinced him of this possibility, and in 1895 Freud and Breuer published *Studies in Hysteria*. The book contained many of the now classical concepts of psychoanalysis, such as defense, resistance, repression, and abreaction, and the psychoanalytical school of thought is often dated from it.

About the same time Freud chanced upon the method of free association and began to interpret his patients' dreams. His greatest work was *Interpretation of Dreams*, published in 1900. The object of these techniques was to uncover the patient's unconscious motives as they manifested themselves in speech, recovered memories, and dreams (*The Psychopathology of Everyday Life*, 1904). The role that Freud assigned the unconscious and unconscious motivation counts as his greatest contribution to psychology. His fame began to spread in the 1900s, when disciples also began to gather around him. In 1905 Freud published *Three Essays on the Theory of Sexuality*, which introduced the novel and startling idea that all children are born with a sexual drive. International recognition of Freud began when G. Stanley Hall* invited Freud and other psychoanalysts to the United States in 1909.

Although his most important disciples broke off their relationship with Freud a few years later, Freud's fame grew from here on as he elaborated his theory and kept publishing additional volumes about his theory of personality and psychosexual development. Like many of Freud's other notions, the idea that conscience is not implanted by God but develops through identification with a parent was iconoclastic, but it became accepted. Similarly, his view of infant sexuality destroyed the benevolent view of the child held since the time of Rousseau*, but it did give parents finally a key to the understanding of the irrational behaviors of their offspring. The tripartite division of the psychological person (id, ego, superego); the oral, anal, and phallic stages of development and personality types; the Oedipus complex; libido; castration anxiety; and ego defense mechanisms are some of the ideas that are part of the vocabulary of not only the psychiatrist and the psychologist but the layman as well. In later years Freud's outlook widened, and psychoanalysis was applied to broad cultural phenomena, such as literature, religion, and civilization as such. *Beyond the Pleasure Principle* (1920), *The Future of an Illusion* (1927), *Civilization and Its Discontents* (1930), and *Moses and Monotheism* (1939) belong to this period of Freud's life. The standard edition of his collected works fills twenty-four volumes. What is in them has become part not only of psychology's heritage, creating thousands of titles of research, observation, and theory, but of the heritage of Western culture.

Biographies: S. Freud, *Amer. J. Psychol.*, 1910, *21*, 181-218; S. Freud, *An Autobiographical Study*, 1935; S. Bernfeld, *Int. J. Psychoanal.*, 1951, *32*, 204-217; A. A. Brill, In *The Basic Writings of Sigmund Freud*, 1938, pp. 3-32; G. Costigan, *Sigmund Freud: A Short Biography*, 1965; J. C. Flugel, *Brit. J. Psychol.*, 1940, *30*, 173-182; M. Freud, *Glory Reflected: Sigmund Freud, Man and Father*, 1957; E. Freud *et al.* (Eds.), *Sigmund Freud: Sein Leben in Bildern und Texten*, 1977; E. Jones, *The Life and Work of Sigmund Freud*, 1953-1957; R. M. Loewenstein, *Bull. N.Y. Acad. Med.*, 1951, *27*, 623-637; A. Mette, *Sigmund Freud*, 1956; H. A. Murray, *Amer. J. Psychol.*, 1940, *53*, 134-138; P. Roazen (Ed.), *Sigmund Freud*, 1973; M. Robert, *The Psychoanalytic Revolution: Sigmund Freud's Life and Achievements*, 1966; H. Sachs, *Freud, Master and Friend*, 1944; R. L. Schoenwald, *Freud: The Man and His Mind*, 1956; M. Schur, *Freud: Living and Dying*, 1971; F. Wittels, *Freud and His Time*, 1931; R. Wollheim, *Sigmund Freud*, 1971; G. Zilboorg, *Sigmund Freud: His Exploration of the Mind*, 1962; *Biog. Lex.*; *CE*, 6; *DSB*, 5; *EB*, 18; *EJ*, 7; *EP*, 3; *IESS*, 6; *Jewish*, 4; *NDB*, 5; *NYT*, 1939, Sept. 24, 1:2.

FREY, MAXIMILIAN RUPPERT FRANZ VON
German Physiologist
Born: Salzburg, Austria, November 16, 1852
Died: Würzburg, Germany, January 25, 1932
Highest Degree: M.D., University of Leipzig, 1877
Positions: 1882-98, University of Leipzig; 1898-99, University of Zurich; 1899-1932, University of Würzburg

Frey is known for his authoritative work on haptic sensations. Although practically nothing was known previously about the sensory physiology of the skin, Frey's papers, written between 1894 and 1897, provided textbook writers with the basic information. Frey confirmed the existence of sensory spots for warm, cold, and pressure; he established pain as an additional (fourth) haptic sense modality and conducted quantitative studies relating stimulus characteristics and sensations. He discovered paradoxical cold (a hot stimulus yielding the sensation of cold) and the fact that the stimulus for pressure is not simply force but tension of the area of the skin that is depressed. Frey found for each of the four haptic senses a specific end organ in the skin and invented two classical instruments for studying cutaneous sensitivity: the limen gauge and the stimulus hair or hair aesthesiometer. Frey wrote some fifty-two papers about the haptic system. Much of the information was collected in his *Vorlesungen über Physiologie* (1904), which was issued in three editions.

Biographies: E. G. Boring, *Amer. J. Psychol.*, 1932, *44*, 584-586; P. Hoffmann, *Verh. physikal.-med. Ges. Würzburg*, 1932, *57*, 56-66; P. Hoffmann, *Z. Biol.*, 1932, *92*, i-v; H. Rein, *Ergeb. Physiol.*, 1933, *35*, 1-12; *Biog. Lex.*; *NDB*, 5; Pagel, *Biographisches Lexikon*.

FRITSCH, GUSTAV THEODOR
German Anatomist and Anthropologist
Born: Cottbus, Saxony, March 5, 1838
Died: Berlin, June 12, 1927
Highest Degree: M.D., University of Berlin, 1862
Positions: 1876-1921, University of Berlin, since 1899, honorary professor

Fritsch's contribution to psychology was the set of famous experiments, performed with E. Hitzig* (Über die elektrische Erregbarkeit des Grosshirns, 1870), that established the electrical excitability of brain tissue. The dogma held by most authorities was that the brain was insensitive and inexcitable. Applying electric current, rather than mechanical or chemical stimulation, to various portions of the brain of the dog, Fritsch and Hitzig established not only that motor responses could be elicited in this way but that muscular contractions were controlled by certain areas of the brain only, as well as the exact location of some of the more specific motor centers.

Biographies: C. Benda, *Deutsch. med. Wochenschr.*, 1927, *53*, 1273; R. Du Bois-Reymond, *Med. Klin.*, 1927, *23*, 1047-1048; H. Grundfest, *J. Hist. Med.*, 1963, *18*, 125-129; C. L. Herrick, *J. Comp. Neurol.*, 1892, *2*, 84-88; *DSB*, 5; Hirsch, *Biog. Lex.*, 2, Suppl.; *NDB*, 5.

FRÖBEL, FRIEDRICH WILHELM AUGUST
German Educator
Born: Oberweissbach, Thuringia, April 21, 1782
Died: Marienthal, Brunswick, June 21, 1852
Education: A few university courses at the University of Jena and the University of Göttingen
Positions: No academic appointments

It was not until Fröbel was thirty-four years old that, having pursued a variety of occupations, he entered the field of education, establishing schools and training others in his method of education. He was influenced by Rousseau* and Comenius* and followed Pestalozzi*. Fröbel developed the idea of the kindergarten in 1836. In kindergartens young children were to be educated to develop all of their potentialities, mainly through activities. Fröbel established the first kindergarten in Blankenburg in 1837 and spent the rest of his life as an educator of both children and teachers who were to educate them in his kindergartens.

Fröbel's educational philosophy was determined by his belief that life, nature, and spirit each have an inner unity. The development of nature shows itself in the development of the individual mind, and the educational process should reflect the natural inner development of the pupil. Education should unfold the whole person: religion unfolds the individual's emotions, natural science reveals God, and mathematics shows the order that reigns in the universe. Self-activity and instructive play were to be the basic features of the kindergarten Fröbel introduced toys and devices (''gifts'') to stimulate learning through play. *The Education of Man* (1826) is Fröbel's most important book.

Biographies: R. Boldt & W. Eichler, *Friedrich Wilhelm August Fröbel*, 1982; F. Fröbel, *Autobiography of Friedrich Fröbel*, 1889 (Reprinted 1971); M. H. Kriege, *Friedrich Fröbel: A Biographical Sketch*, 1876; M. A. Kuntze, *Friedrich Fröbel: Sein Weg und sein Werk*, 1930; I. M. Lilley, In *Friedrich Fröbel: A Selection from His Writings*, 1967, pp. 1-30; G. Palm, *Friedrich Fröbel: Der Mensch, Denker, und Erzieher*, 1940; E. A. Shirreff, *A Short Sketch of the Life of Friedrich Fröbel*, 1887; *ADB*, 8; *EB*, 9; *EP*, 3; *NDB*, 5.

FRÖBES, JOSEPH

German-Dutch Psychologist
Born: Betzdorf, Rhineland-Palatinate, Germany, August 26, 1866
Died: Cologne, Germany, March 24, 1947
Education: Jesuit training in philosophy, 1886-89; theological training, 1894-99, ordained priest, 1900; University of Göttingen, 1902-4
Positions: 1904-25, Ignatiuskolleg, Valkenburg (Limburg), Holland

Fröbes was a Neothomist who kept philosophical psychology separate from experimental psychology, holding that philosophical beliefs are irrelevant to the validity of experimental work. Even so, he made it his life's work to integrate philosophical and empirical psychology, believing that each would profit from a consideration of the other. Fröbes achieved this integration in his textbooks, especially those dealing with philosophical psychology. He was the first Catholic writer of psychological texts. His *Lehrbuch der experimentellen Psychologie* (vol. 1, 1915; rev. ed. 1923; vol. 2, 1920; rev. ed. 1929) was much used and may be considered his major accomplishment. His major texts of philosophical psychology were *Psychologia sensitiva* (1908), *Psychologia rationalis* (1911), and *Psychologia speculativa* (1927). Fröbes also wrote many papers about diverse psychological subjects.
Biographies: *CE*, 6; *EUI*, 24; *HPA*, 3; *NDB*, 5; *PR*, 3.

FROMM, ERICH

German-American Psychoanalyst and Social Philosopher
Born: Frankfurt am Main, Germany, March 23, 1900
Died: Muralto, Ticino, Switzerland, March 18, 1980
Highest Degree: Ph.D., University of Heidelberg, 1922; graduated from Berlin Psychoanalytical Institute, 1931
Positions: 1929-32, lecturer, Psychoanalytical Institute, Frankfurt, also at Institute for Social Research, Frankfurt; 1933-34, Chicago Institute for Psychoanalysis; 1934-39, International Institute for Social Research, New York City; 1934-49, private practice, New York City; 1940-41, guest lecturer, Columbia University; 1941-42, lecturer, American Institute of Psychoanalysis, New York; 1949, Terry lecturer, Yale University; 1941-50, Bennington College, also fellow, faculty of William Allanson White Institute of Psychiatry, Psychoanalysis and Psychology, New York City; 1951-61, professor, National University of Mexico,

Mexico City; 1957-61, Michigan State University; 1962-65, adjunct professor, New York University

Influenced by the theories of Karl Marx*, Fromm extended Sigmund Freud's* psychoanalytical teachings to consider the shaping of human character by the society, as a result of which the needs and personality characteristics of the members of a society are in accord with societal needs. In numerous books that enjoyed wide popularity among the general public, Fromm spoke of freedom in society, human destructiveness, and the concept of love. Most of his works analyze the human condition in modern industrial society psychoanalytically, sociologically, and philosophically. His two most influential works are *Escape from Freedom* (1941) and *The Art of Loving* (1956).

Fromm described the paradoxical nature of the human condition that makes humans part of both the animal kingdom and the realm of humans with its unique property of self-awareness, both circumstances leading to alienation and loneliness. All societies attempt to resolve this problem. The conditions of human existence give rise to certain needs: for relatedness, transcendence, rootedness, identity, and a frame of orientation. These needs are met in accordance with the particular structure of the society of which the individual is a member. The result is social-character, or modal-character, structure that describes most members of the society. Fromm described the receptive, exploitative, hoarding, marketing, productive, necrophilous, and biophilous characters. Although they parallel to some extent Freud's characters, the roots of the Frommian characters lie not so much in the family as in society at large.

Fromm also wrote *Man for Himself* (1947), *Psychoanalysis and Religion* (1950), *The Forgotten Language* (1951), *The Sane Society* (1955), *Sigmund Freud's Mission* (1958), *May Man Prevail?* (1961), *The Dogma of Christ* (1962), *The Chain of Illusion* (1963), *The Heart of Man* (1964, with M. Maccoby), *The Revolution of Hope* (1968), *Social Character in a Mexican Village* (1970), *The Anatomy of Human Destructiveness* (1973), and *To Have or to Be?* (1976).

Biographies: D. Elkind, *Amer. Psychologist*, 1981, *36*, 521-522; R. I. Evans, *The Making of Psychology*, 1976; V. J. Nordby & C. S. Hall, *A Guide to Psychologists and Their Concepts*, 1974; *Contemporary Authors*, vols. 73-76; *Current Biography*, 1967; *IESS*, 18; *NYT*, 1980, Mar. 19; *Who's Who in America*.

FULLERTON, GEORGE STUART

American Philosopher

Born: Fatehgarh, India, August 18, 1859

Died: Poughkeepsie, New York, March 23, 1925

Highest Degree: A.M., University of Pennsylvania, 1882

Positions, Honors: 1883-1904, University of Pennsylvania; 1904-17, Columbia University; president, American Psychological Association, 1896; honorary Ph.D., LL.D., Muhlenberg College, 1900

With J. McK. Cattell*, Fullerton published an important monograph, *On the Perception of Small Differences*, in 1892. Using the functionalist approach to a classical problem in psychophysics, Fullerton and Cattell concluded that sensory variability is an error in the perceiving organism as it strives to discriminate perfectly. They recommended the use of the probable error as a measure of discrimination rather than the usual measure of difference threshold, and that the critical point of discrimination be the 75 percent and not the 50 percent judgment level. The Fullerton-Cattell law reads that the errors of observation and just noticeable differences are proportional to the square root of the magnitude of the stimulus. It is also known as the square root law and was proposed as a substitute for Weber's law.

Biographies: *American Men of Science*, 3rd ed.; *NCAB*, 12; *Who Was Who in America*, 1.

FULTON, JOHN FARQUHAR

American Physiologist

Born: St. Paul, Minnesota, November 1, 1899

Died: New Haven, Connecticut, May 29, 1960

Highest Degree: Ph.D. in physiology, Oxford University, 1925; M.D., Harvard University, 1927

Positions, Honors: 1923-25, demonstrator in physiology, Oxford University; 1929-60, Yale University, 1929-51, professor of physiology, 1951-60, head, Department of History of Medicine; nine honorary degrees, recipient of several medals and other honors

In 1926 Fulton published a book dealing with *Muscular Contraction and the Reflex Control of Movement*. Pursuing this topic further, Fulton discovered, in 1928, that the nervous structures called muscle spindles are triggered by stretching the muscle. In 1929 Fulton established the first primate laboratory for experimental physiology in America and later founded, with Dusser de Barenne, the *Journal of Neurophysiology*. Fulton wrote additional books in physiology, including the revision of the fifteenth edition of *Howell's Textbook of Physiology* (1946). Of interest to psychology is his text on *Frontal Lobotomy and Affective Behavior* (1951) and his many publications in the history of medicine.

Biographies: *Brit. Med. J.*, 1960, *1*, 1815-1816; K. J. Franklin, *Nature*, 1960, *187*, 110-111; H. E. Hoff, *Amer. Oxon.*, 1961, *26*, 33-38; *Lancet*, 1960, *1*, 1301-1302; C. D. Leake, *Isis*, 1960, *51*, 560-562; A. Muirhead, J. *Hist. Med.*, 1962, *17*, 2-15; *DSB*, 5; *NCAB*, 25; *NYT*, 1960, May 30, 17:1; *PR*, 3; *Who Was Who in America*, 4.

G

GALEN

Greek-Roman Physician

Born: Pergamum, Asia Minor, 130 A.D.

Died: Possibly in Sicily, ca. 200 A.D.

Education: Studied philosophy and medicine at Pergamum between 145 and 150 A.D.

Positions: 150-58 A.D., travel and study; 158-61 A.D., surgeon to gladiators at Pergamum; 161 A.D., physician to emperors of Rome

Galen was the first experimental physiologist. He had wide and good knowledge of anatomy, and his medical work was so impressive that it was being held as valid for thirteen centuries. Concerning the soul, Galen adhered to Plato*, holding that the brain and the nervous system are the seat of intelligence. Galen also accepted the pneumatistic (animal spirits) doctrine of Erasistratus*. To the four ventricles of the brain Galen assigned the function of producing and directing, through the nerves, animal spirits of the soul. The flow of animal spirits caused movement of the muscles, he thought.

Galen knew the effects of cutting the spinal cord, such as loss of sensation and motor disturbances, and that some nerves mediated motion while others were involved in sensation. He described the cerebral aqueduct and attributed the correct function to the optic chiasma, the production of singleness in binocular vision. Galen took from Hippocrates* the association established by the latter between the four elements of Empedocles* and the four bodily humors—blood, black bile, yellow bile, phlegm—and developed it into the fourfold typology of the sanguine, melancholic, choleric, and phlegmatic temperaments. The fourfold division was used by Galen primarily to explain pathology and only secondarily behavior, but in the hands of his epigones it became the first personality theory, surviving until the nineteenth century. Pavlov's* identification of four types of the nervous system, albeit on a very different basis, and his reference to sanguine and phlegmatic dogs gave the Galenic temperaments a new lease on life. *Biographies*: *DSB*, 5; *EP*, 3.

GALILEI, GALILEO
Italian Mathematician, Astronomer, and Physicist
Born: Pisa, February 15, 1564
Died: Arcetri, near Florence, Tuscany, January 8, 1642
Education: Studied medicine, mathematics, and science at the University of Pisa, 1581-85
Positions: 1589-92, University of Pisa; 1592-1610, University of Padua; 1610-16, first philosopher and mathematician of the grand duke of Tuscany

Of Galileo's three major contributions to the development of modern science—the demonstration of heliocentrism, the introduction of experimental mechanics and physics, and the founding of the modern experimental method in science—the third is of significance to psychology. By asserting that the "book of nature is written in mathematical characters" and that only those versed in mathematics could read it, Galileo pitted mathematical rationalism against Aristotle's* logical and verbal rationalism. The mathematical approach to nature was the foundation of the scientific method, which Galileo himself consistently used. By way of the natural sciences the scientific method found its way into psychology, since the early practitioners of scientific psychology were natural scientists themselves.

Galileo's first full discussion of the scientific method is found in a polemic reply entitled *Saggiatore...*, published in 1623. In this work may also be found Galileo's discussion of *primary* and *secondary qualities*, although the terms themselves were coined by John Locke*. Galileo took Democritus's* view that sensations are nothing but subjective experiences to which nothing real corresponds in the outside world and developed it further, separating the psychological from the physical and asserting that since sensations are a subjective phenomenon, they are not a proper object of study for the natural scientist. Galileo overlooked the fact that, for instance, his own telescopic observations were based entirely on his own visual sensations, but the attitude that subjective experience is somehow not as real as the reality "out there" persists even today. A specific contribution of Galileo's to the psychology of acoustics was his discovery and demonstration that pitch depends on the frequency of vibrations of the sound-producing body.

Biographies: A. Banfi, *Galileo Galilei*, 1949; J. Brodrick, *Galileo: The Man, His Work, His Misfortunes*, 1964; Centre International de Synthèse, *Galileo: Aspects de sa vie et de son oeuvre*, 1968; J. Fahie, *Galileo: His Life and Works*, 1903; L. Geymonat, *Galileo Galilei: A Biography and Inquiry into His Philosophy of Science*, 1965; D. Knight, In R. Harré (Ed.), *Early Seventeenth Century*

Scientists, 1965, pp. 49-80; E. McMullin (Ed.), *Galileo: Man of Science*,1968; L. Olschki, *Galilei und seine Zeit*, 1927 (Reprinted 1965); P. Paschini,*Vita e opere di Galileo Galilei*, 1965; G. de Santillana, *The Crime of Galileo*,1955; F. S. Taylor, *Galileo and the Freedom of Thought*, 1938; *DSB*, 5; *EB*, 9; *EP*, 3.

GALL, FRANZ JOSEPH
German Physician and Anatomist
Born: Tiefenbrunn, Baden, March 9, 1758
Died: Paris, France, August 22, 1828
Highest Degree: M.D., University of Vienna, 1785
Positions: 1785-1807, private practice of medicine, Vienna; from 1796, lecturer in phrenology; 1807-28, practice of medicine, Paris

Attracted since boyhood to the relationship between head shape and personality, Gall established phrenology soon after receiving medical training, although the name was given to it later by his collaborator Spurzheim*. Forbidden to lecture on phrenology in Vienna, Gall and Spurzheim went on a lecture tour in Germany and then settled in Paris, where Gall achieved fame.

Between 1810 and 1819 Gall published *Anatomie et physiologie du système nerveux en général* in four volumes (the first two written with Spurzheim), of which the last three presented the phrenological doctrine. The first volume dealt with the nervous system in general and made several important contributions to science. Gall believed that mind could be divided into separate faculties. These faculties he obtained from the Scottish philosophers Thomas Reid* and Dugald Stewart*. After Spurzheim's subsequent elaboration, a list of thirty-seven such faculties was eventually used in phrenology. Gall also believed that the faculties were discretely localized in the brain, and that the exercise of or innate prominence of a faculty would enlarge the appropriate brain area that, in turn, would show up as a cranial prominence. The correlations between ''bumps'' on the skull and personality characteristics were obtained from persons with well-known and pronounced mental traits. Between 1823 and 1825 Gall published his definitive statement on phrenology (which he called organology), a six-volume work entitled *Sur les fonctions du cerveau*.

Aided by Spurzheim's propaganda efforts, phrenology flourished for a century, with numerous societies and journals to further its work, although it was never accepted by orthodox science. The followers of Gall made phrenology into a folly, and the stigma of a quack became attached to him. The notion of faculties and the exact cortical localization of such faculties became immediately, and correctly, suspect among scientists.

The significance of phrenology and of Gall lies not so much in the doctrine as in the impetus they gave to scientific thought. Gall was correct in assigning the brain the role of the seat of mental activities, and he established the brain as such in the mind of the ordinary person. Gall was wrong in detail because of faulty methodology, but the possibility of the localization of brain functions could not be denied. Flourens's* work on the correct localization of brain functions stands out largely by contrast with phrenology. In opposing it Flourens's own views seemed less radical than they actually were.

Biographies: N. Capen, In F. J. Gall, *Works*, vol. 1, 1835, pp. 2-52; J. D. Davies, *Phrenology: Fad and Science*, 1955; T. Kirchhoff, In *Deutsche Irrenärzte*, vol. 1, 1921, pp. 22-24; J. Létang, *Gall et son oeuvre*, 1906; P. J. Möbius, *Franz Joseph Gall*, 1905; *ADB*, 8; *DSB*, 5; *EB*, 9; Hirsch, *Biog. Lex.*, 2, Suppl.; *IESS*, 6; *NDB*, 6.

GALTON, SIR FRANCIS
English Scientist
Born: Birmingham, February 16, 1822
Died: Haslemere, Surrey, January 17, 1911
Highest Degree: B.A., Cambridge University, 1844
Positions, Honors: No academic or official positions; knighted, 1909

Although primarily a scientist at large, Galton's contributions to scientific psychology were such that he may be called one of its founding fathers. Specifically, he founded the study and measurement of individual differences, a field that saw its next major expansion in the hands of J. McK. Cattell*. The reading of Charles Darwin's* *Origin of Species* led Galton to study anthropology and heredity. In 1869 he published *Hereditary Genius*, a study of the variability of human intellect through the biographies of eminent individuals. Galton's thesis was that eminence runs in families, that there are specific forms of eminence in the various fields of human endeavor, and that mental traits are inherited in the same way as physical traits are. The problems of heredity and the improvement of the human race were always Galton's first concern. In 1876 he also conducted the first behavioral study of twins in an effort to separate environmental from genetic influences. The juxtaposition of the terms *nature* and *nurture* first occurs in Galton's paper, and the problem of the inheritance of intelligence that still occupies psychology was set up by Galton's work.

Quételet* had applied the normal law of error of Laplace* and Gauss* to biological measures. Galton extended Quételet's work to behavioral measurements and found it applicable. Galton concluded that statistical treatment of psychological measures in general was appropriate. His most important contribution here was the development of the statistical measure of correlation (in 1877) that was later elaborated by his student and biographer Karl Pearson*. The principle of the regression toward the mean is a formulation of Galton's. Galton then proceeded to collect a variety of psychological measurements on many individuals and to treat the data statistically. In 1882 he established a laboratory in London where physical measurements, sensory acuity measurements, and reaction-time measurements were taken on those who applied, for a fee. It was the first mental test center in the world, and his activities there made Galton the first psychological practitioner. Several pieces of apparatus of Galton's invention were used there, among them the Galton whistle that produced tones between 6,500 and 84,000 cycles and the Galton bar for distance estimation. In 1901 Galton, Pearson, and W. F. R. Weldon founded the journal, *Biometrika*.

Galton's psychological contributions were published in 1883 in a volume entitled *Inquiries into Human Faculty and Its Development*. Prominent among them, in addition to those already mentioned, are his study of imagery, the description of specific imagery types, and the discovery of synesthesia; work on reaction time in word association, which also demonstrated, for the first time, the importance of the effect of childhood experiences upon adult thinking; and the development of specifically mental tests. The methodology used by Galton included introspection, his own and that of others, and experimentation and measurement, but not of the elaborate type employed by continental psychologists. Instead, he used tests, including mental tests. He was the first to use extensively the questionnaire method for gathering data in psychology. In sum, Galton's work in psychology spelled out the emergence of a fundamental assumption in psychological science, namely, that all individuals differ among themselves, that they differ consistently, and that therefore these differences can be measured.

Biographies: F. Galton, *Memories of My Life*, 1908; C. Burt, *Brit. J. Stat. Psychol.*, 1962, *15*, 1-49; J. McK. Cattell, *Pop. Sci. Mon.*, 1911, *78*, 309-312; F. Darwin, *Eugen. Rev.*, 1968, *60*, 3-11; D. Forrest, *Francis Galton*, 1973; K. Pearson, *The Life, Letters, and Labours of Francis Galton*, 1914-1930; *DNB*, Suppl. 1; *DSB*, 5; *EB*, 9; *IESS*, 6; *NYT*, 1911, Jan. 19, 9:3.

GALVANI, LUIGI

Italian Physiologist
Born: Bologna, September 9, 1737
Died: Bologna, December 4, 1798
Education: Degree in medicine and philosophy, University of Bologna, 1759
Positions: 1762-91, University of Bologna

Galvani discovered that a frog's leg would twitch if a nerve at its cut end was connected to its outside by two pieces of different metals. Although Galvani believed that it was animal tissue that generated electricity, he had actually built the first wet battery. He described his experiment in 1791 ("De viribus electricitatis in motu musculari"). The belief in and investigation of animal electricity, started by Galvani, spread and eventually led to the correct view concerning the nature of the nerve impulse through the work of the great nineteenth-century physiologists. Volta, on the other hand, showed that animal tissue was not necessary to generate electricity. The inorganic voltaic battery, in turn, played an important role in the work of the neuranatomists and neurophysiologists as they studied the structure and functioning of the nervous system. The significance of Galvani's discovery was twofold: by showing how nerves affect muscles, he placed on a physical basis that which even to Descartes* had been a mystery;

and it was the most important eighteenth-century discovery among the ones that would pave the way to psychological materialism.

Biographies: G. C. Pupilli, In L. Galvani, *Commentary on the Effect of Electricity on Muscular Motion*, 1953, pp. ix-xx; M. Sirol, *Galvani et le Galvanisme*, ca. 1939; *CE*, 6; *DSB*, 5; *EB*, 9; *EIU*, 25; Hirsch, *Biog. Lex.*, 2, Suppl.

GANTT, W. HORSLEY

American Psychiatrist

Born: Winginia, Virginia, October 24, 1892

Died: Baltimore, Maryland, February 26, 1980

Highest Degree: M.D., University of Virginia, 1920

Positions, Honors: 1929-67, Johns Hopkins University, 1967-80, professor emeritus; 1950-74, director, Pavlovian conditioning laboratory, Veterans Administration Hospital, Perry Point, Maryland; 1974-80, University of Louisville; eight awards; honorary doctorate, University of Louisville, 1979; founder, *Pavlovian Journal of Biological Science* and Pavlovian Society

As a member of the American Relief Mission to USSR, Gantt spent the years 1920-23 with Pavlov*. Very impressed with Pavlov, he remained his true disciple throughout his life. Gantt is best known for his translation of the two volumes of Pavlov's *Lectures on Conditioned Reflexes* (1928, 1941) into English. He also picked up on Pavlov's discovery of maladaptive behavior in dogs under conditions of impossible discriminations and induced asthma, manic activity, and nervous breakdown in animals by the same technique, thus demonstrating that environmental stress and not sex or childhood experiences (as taught by Sigmund Freud*) was responsible for neuroses. Gantt himself thought that his theories of *schizokinesis* (cardiac reactions to stress have a faster onset than other body reactions) and *autokinesis* (a conditional disturbance of the body can repeat itself without repetition of the original experience that caused it) were his most important contributions. Gantt produced more than seven hundred scientific publications.

Biographies: F. J. McGuigan, *Amer. Psychologist*, 1981, *36*, 417-419; *NYT*, 1980, Feb. 28, D 19:4.

GASSENDI, PIERRE

French Philosopher and Scientist

Born: Champtercier, Provence, January 22, 1592

Died: Paris, October 24, 1655

Highest Degree: Doctorate in philosophy, University of Avignon, 1616

Positions: 1617-44, University of Aix; 1645-48, taught mathematics, Royal College of France

Although Descartes* tried to ignore the ancient philosophers, including Aristotle*, Gassendi, a contemporary of Descartes, wrote a book opposing Aristotle. He also opposed Descartes, though, on the most fundamental issue, that of the origin of knowledge, Gassendi believed that sensory perception was more fundamental than intuition. In this he anticipated Locke* and Berkeley*, although not the latter's radical mentalism. In an argument that modern philosophy has little to add to, Gassendi argued against Descartes's dualism and advanced natural monism. His thought was part of the emerging French materialism that bloomed in the eighteenth century, furthering the emergence of scientific psychology. Gassendi also made a contribution to sensory psychology by being first to measure the velocity of sound (in 1624) and by showing that, contrary to Aristotle's opinion, sound travels at the same rate regardless of pitch.

Biographies: J. Bougerel, *Vie de Pierre Gassendi...*, 1737; G. S. Brett, *The Philosophy of Gassendi*, 1908; Centre International de Synthèse, *Pierre Gassendi, 1592-1655: Sa vie et son oeuvre*, 1955; B. Rochot *et al.*, *Pierre Gassendi: Sa vie et son oeuvre*, 1955; *CE*, 6; *DSB*, 5; *EB*, 10; *EP*, 3; *EUI*, 25.

GAUSS, KARL FRIEDRICH
German Mathematician
Born: Braunschweig, Lower Saxony, April 30, 1775
Died: Göttingen, Lower Saxony, February 23, 1855
Highest Degree: Ph.D. in mathematics, University of Göttingen, 1799
Positions: 1807-55, director of the Göttingen observatory

Although it was Laplace* and de Moivre who pioneered in the mathematical theory of errors, Gauss's developments of it were so important that the law of errors and the curve that goes with it are often called Gaussian. Errors, such as those made in target practice, as well as many natural and biological phenomena follow, when plotted, the Gaussian or normal curve of distribution: the majority of the observations center about the mean value, the frequency of higher and lower values falling off so that the resulting distribution assumes the shape of a bell. Gauss expanded the theory of errors in *Theoria motus corporum coelestium* (1809).

The role of the normal curve in statistics, especially inferential statistics (statistical decision making) is crucial. Psychologists have been very heavy users of statistics, and psychologists doing research (and therefore constantly making statistical decisions) and those who deal with individual differences (and are called upon to interpret the IQ or any other test scores) use the normal curve daily.

Biographies: E. T. Bell, In J. R. Newman (Ed.), *The World of Mathematics*, vol. 1, 1956, pp. 295-339; G. W. Dunnington, *Carl Friedrich Gauss, Titan of Science: A Study of His Life and Work*, 1955; T. Hall, *Carl Friedrich Gauss: A Biography*, 1970; *ADB*, 8; *DSB*, 5; *EUI*, 25; *IESS*, 6; *NDB*, 6.

GELB, ADHEMAR MAXIMILIAN MAURICE
German Psychologist
Born: Moscow, Russia, November 18, 1887
Died: Schömberg, Baden-Württemberg, August 7, 1936

Highest Degree: Ph.D. in psychology, University of Berlin, 1910, under C. Stumpf*

Positions: 1909-12, University of Berlin; 1912-15, Akademie der Sozialwissenschaften (Academy of Social Sciences), Frankfurt am Main; 1915-19, Frankfurt Hospital for Brain Damaged; 1919-31, University of Frankfurt; 1931-33, University of Halle

Gelb was a Gestalt-oriented psychologist whose work with Kurt Goldstein* on soldiers with brain lesions resulted in numerous papers about the effect of brain damage on perception, speech, and color vision, as well as the book, written with Goldstein, *Psychologische Analysen hirnpathologischer Fälle* (1920). Gelb also did research on figure-ground. He is the discoverer of the Gelb phenomenon: a spot of colored light has a higher threshold when projected inside a figure than when projected upon adjacent ground.

Biographies: R. Bergius, *Psychol. Beit.*, 1963, *7*, 360-369; *NDB*, 6; *PR*, 3.

GEMELLI, AGOSTINO (EDOARDO)

Italian Psychologist

Born: Milan, January 18, 1878

Died: Milan, July 15, 1959

Highest Degree: M.D., University of Pavia, 1902; Ph.D. in philosophy, University of Louvain, 1911; studied psychology under O. Külpe* at Bonn and Munich and under F. Kiesow* in Turin

Positions: 1914-22, University of Turin; 1922-59, Catholic University, Milan

Gemelli was a very productive psychologist (a bibliography of more than four hundred items, dozens of books) who worked in several areas of psychology: perception, language (electroacoustical analysis of speech), youth and developmental psychology, and applied psychology. He was the founder (in 1921) and perpetual rector of the Università Cattolica del Sacro Cuore in Milan and contributed to the development of psychology in Italy through research and teaching at that university. In 1920 he founded, with Kiesow, the *Archivio italiano di psicologia*, established a psychological laboratory at the Catholic University soon after its founding, and began to issue a series of publications from it, the *Contributi del Laboratorio di Psicologia della Università Cattolica del Sacro Cuore*. Later, in 1940, he also founded the *Archivio di psicologia, neurologia e psichiatria*.

Gemelli's most important contributions were in the area of applied psychology: criminal, military, industrial, and clinical. He acquired a name during World War I in connection with his work on pilot selection for the Italian armed forces. In 1952 he organized the first Italian symposium on clinical psychology, which gave a strong impetus to the development of clinical psychology in Italy, theretofore largely a province of the physician.

In his experimental work on the physiology of emotions in animals (using visceral deafferentation), Gemelli concluded that emotion is both a physiological and a psychological phenomenon, inseparably so, and that it involves the whole organism. This conclusion developed into Gemelli's own way of thinking, the "personalistic orientation," or *soggettività*, according to which a human being is a biological entity in the first place. In addition, humans are also entities of personal, subjective experience, which is not merely a function of the biological structure but an independent, innate characteristic. Both the biological and subjective aspects must be considered to understand the nature of human beings. This view led Gemelli to reject the behavioristic, the Gestalt, and the psychoanalytical schools of thought.

Biographies: L. Ancona, *Amer. J. Psychol.*, 1960, *73*, 156-159; L. Ancona, *Arch. psicol. neurol. psychiat.*, 1959, *20* 397-405; P. Bandilli, *Padre Agostino Gemelli's profilo*, 1926; A. Gemelli, In R. Schmidt (Ed.), *Die Philosophie der Gegenwart in Selbstdarstellungen*, vol. 7, 1929, pp. 43-67; H. Misiak & V. M. Staudt, *Catholics in Psychology*, 1954, pp. 126-152; H. Piéron, *Bull. Ass. int. psychol. appl.*, 1959, 8(2), 44-47; various, *Vita Pensiero*, 1959, *42*, 507-716; *CE*, 6; *HPA*, 4; *NYT*, 1959, July 16, 27:5.

GESELL, ARNOLD LUCIUS
American Psychologist
Born: Alma, Wisconsin, June 21, 1880
Died: New Haven, Connecticut, May 29, 1961
Highest Degree: Ph.D. in psychology, Clark University, 1906, under E. C. Sanford*; M.D., Yale University, 1915
Positions, Honors: 1907, State Normal School, Platteville, Wisconsin, 1908-11, Los Angeles State Normal School; 1911-61, Yale University; honorary D.Sc., Clark University (1940), University of Wisconsin (1953)

After receiving his doctorate in psychology, Gesell became interested in the growth and development of children. He obtained a medical degree to understand better the physical basis of development. During his medical training he established the Clinic of Child Development at Yale University. He devoted the rest of his life to the study of the development of the child. In his work he published some thirty books on the subject. The three-volume *Atlas of Infant Behavior* (1934) contains a vast amount of data and is representative of Gesell's work. The data are largely descriptive observations of children's behavior summarized in the form of developmental schedules. In his observations Gesell often used the film camera, which was one of the first instances of such use of the camera for scientific research. In the end Gesell had filmed some twelve thousand children.

From G. Stanley Hall*, Gesell inherited an evolutionary outlook on development. He was a maturationist who assigned environment the role of the setting for growth but did not believe that environment played a major role in the child's development. Gesell felt that the tendency to grow was the strongest force in life and that it could not therefore be much affected by environmental influences. Gesell considered as his main task the description of the developmental stages that children passed through as they matured. Personality differences were explained by Gesell in terms of constitutional differences. In general, mental development in his view followed closely the development of the nervous system. This easy-to-understand approach to development appealed to parents, and Gesell soon became a popular authority on child development among parents, who eagerly used his developmental norms to check on the development of their own offspring.

Gesell received continued recognition for his work, notably in terms of some 195 research grants. Although behaviorism and psychoanalysis made their impact on developmental thought and childrearing practices during the decades of Gesell's work, he was little influenced by them, persisting in his original viewpoint. In 1950 the Gesell Institute of Child Development was incorporated. It continues Gesell's developmental research work today. A well-known observational tool that has resulted from Gesell's and the institute's work is the Gesell Developmental Scales. These scales are developmental inventories for infants and preschoolers measuring motor, language, cognitive, and social behaviors. The Gesell Institute's *Child Behavior* (1951, by Ilg and Ames), a popular presentation of the Gesellian view of development, has sold more than a million copies.

Biographies: L. B. Ames, *Science*, 1961, *134*, 266-267; *DSB*, 5; *HPA*, 4; *IESS*, 6; *NCAB*, 49; *NYT*, 1961, May 30, 17:1; *PR*, 3; *Who Was Who in America*, 4.

GEULINCX, ARNOLD
Flemish Philosopher
Born: Antwerp, Flanders, 1624 (baptized January 31)
Died: Leiden, the Netherlands, November 1669
Highest Degree: Doctor of medicine, University of Leiden, 1658
Positions: 1646-58, University of Louvain; 1662-69, University of Leiden

The problem of how the body, an extended substance, and mind, an unextended substance, interact was never solved by Descartes*, the originator of modern philosophical dualism. The Cartesian philosopher Geulincx tried to solve the problem by asserting that there was no contact between body and mind: God, who was neither body nor mind but comprised both, was the cause of all action. Body and mind are like two clocks that keep perfect time. Although they do not affect each other, they give the appearance of interaction. Two events, A and B, which seem to be causally connected, are only an occasion for God, when event A occurs, to cause event B, as in the case of a seeming body-mind interaction. Geulincx's view came to be called "occasionalism," a form of dualistic parallelism.

Biographies: P. Damiron, *C. r. Acad. sci. mor. pol.*, 1844, *6*, 96-114;V. v. d. Haeghen, *Geulincx: Étude sur sa vie, sa philosophie et ses ouvrages*, 1886; J. P. N. Land (Ed.), *Arnold Geulincx und seine Philosophie*, 1895; B. Samtleben, *Geulincx: Ein Vorgänger Spinozas*, 1885; *CE*, 6; *EP*, 3; *EUI*, 25.

GIBSON, JAMES J(EROME)
American Psychologist
Born: McConnelsville, Ohio, January 27, 1904
Died: Ithaca, New York, December 11, 1979

Highest Degree: Ph.D. in psychology, Princeton University, 1928, from E. B. Holt*

Positions, Honors: 1928-49, Smith College; 1941-46, U.S. Army Air Forces; 1949-72, Cornell University, 1961-72, chairman, Psychology Department, 1972-79, professor emeritus; 1954-55, visiting professor, University of California at Berkeley; 1955-56, senior research Fulbright scholar, Oxford University; 1958-59, member, Institute of Advanced Studies in Behavioral Sciences, 1963-64, fellow; Warren Medal, 1952; American Psychological Association Distinguished Scientific Contribution Award, 1961; National Institutes of Health Award, 1964; honorary D.Sc., University of Edinburgh, 1974, D.Phil., University of Uppsala, 1976

In the citation that accompanied Gibson's award from the American Psychological Association, his experimental and theoretical contributions to the psychology of perception were described as being "among the most distinguished of our time." Gibson offered a view of how we perceive the world that differed radically from the traditional view in which perception was held to be the result of mental activity that organized sensations and sensations, in turn, being the result of various energies stimulating our sense organs. In his first and most influential book, *The Perception of the Visual World* (1950), Gibson showed that the most significant aspect of the perception of the real, three-dimensional world (as contrasted with the visual field, or a two-dimensional, pictorial representation of the world) is the variety of optical gradients present in the textured optical array projected by the lens on the retina. These gradients (of shadows, texture, transformations generated by the movement of the observer or object, and so on) contain all of the information about the three-dimensional world. The essence of this information is perceptual invariants, or higher order variables of stimulation, that completely specify the perception of edges, surfaces, and depth and account for the perceptual constancies. This obviates the need to theorize about how elementary sensations become complex perceptions. There is a psychophysical correspondence between stimulation and perception. Perception does not depend on sensory impressions but on the pickup of information from the environment.

Gibson extended this approach to vision to other sense modalities. In *The Senses Considered as Perceptual Systems* (1966) he argued that there are not so many sense modalities producing so many kinds of sensory impressions but five perceptual systems that are characterized by the manner in which they extract information about objects and events. In his last book, *The Ecological Approach to Visual Perception* (1979), Gibson once again emphasized the need to study vision in terms of people behaving in the real world performing meaningful tasks rather than subjects responding under the artificial and information-poor conditions of the laboratory. He produced support for his view in his own experiments, and it was provided also by the experiments of his wife and collaborator, Eleanor Gibson, his students, and his colleagues. The ecological approach to the perception of space is one that has become generally accepted in psychology.

Biographies: American Psychological Association, *Amer. Psychologist*, 1961, *16*, 799-802; J. Fox, *Perception*, 1980, *9*, 117; V. J. Nordby & C. S. Hall, *A Guide to Psychologists and Their Concepts*, 1974; A. D. Pick *et al.*, *Amer. J. Psychol.*, 1982, *95*, 693-700; *American Men and Women of Science*, 14th ed., Physical and Biological Sciences; *Contemporary Authors*, vols. 85-88; *HPA*, 5; *NYT*, 1979, Dec. 13, II, 23:5.

GODDARD, HENRY HERBERT
American Psychologist
Born: Vassalboro, Maine, August 14, 1866
Died: Santa Barbara, California, June 18, 1957
Highest Degree: Ph.D. in psychology, Clark University, 1899, under G. S. Hall*
Positions: 1899-1906, Pennsylvania State Teachers College at Westchester; 1906-17, Vineland (New Jersey) Training School for the Feeble-Minded; 1918-21, Ohio State Bureau of Juvenile Research; 1922-38, Ohio State University

Goddard established the first laboratory for the psychological study of the feebleminded (at Vineland, New Jersey) and is known principally for his study of feeblemindedness. At Vineland the concept of feeblemindedness was extended to include borderline cases, since owing to their number they were seen as constituting a socioeconomic and educational problem. Goddard coined and applied the term *moron* to such cases.

Goddard wrote several books, most of them on feeblemindedness and intelligence (*Feeblemindedness: Its Cause and Consequences*, 1914; *School Training of Defective Children*, 1915; *Human Efficiency and Levels of Intelligence*, 1920; *School Training of Gifted Children*, 1928). The one for which he is best known is *The Kallikak Family* (1913), in which Goddard attempted to show that feeblemindedness is inherited and runs through successive generations. The book aroused considerable controversy. To study feeblemindedness Goddard, in 1910, prepared his own revision of the Simon*-Binet* Scale of intelligence, which thus became the first English-language version of an intelligence test. Through his books, activities, and fervent presentations, Goddard, during his time, was influential in psychological and sociological circles and was well known in the general public. Although he did believe that feeblemindedness was caused mainly by faulty heredity, his major contribution was to show that mentally defective individuals can be trained for useful occupations.
Biographies: H. E. Burtt & S. L. Pressey, *Amer. J. Psychol.*, 1957, *70*, 656-657; *EUI*, 26; *NCAB*, 15; *PR*, 3; *Who Was Who in America*, 4.

GOETHE, JOHANN WOLFGANG VON
German Poet, Author, and Philosopher
Born: Frankfurt am Main, August 28, 1749
Died: Weimar, Thuringia, March 22, 1832
Education: Studied law at Leipzig and Strasbourg, graduated in 1771

Positions: Adviser to Duke Karl August of Weimar

Goethe's contributions to science date from the period 1775-86. Among them may be counted his principle of metamorphosis of homologous parts in animals and plants, which was a contribution to the theory of evolution, and his theory of color. Goethe attacked Newton's* theory that white light is composed of different chromatic lights, but his attacks were not accepted by scientists. Frustrated, Goethe produced in 1810 his own 1,411-page work on the phenomenology of color vision (*Zur Farbenlehre*). Although the theory itself played no major role in the history of color vision study, Goethe's book did stimulate color research. Purkinje* dedicated one of his volumes about vision to Goethe; it stimulated even Schopenhauer* to produce his own color-vision theory. Goethe's work on color contains many valid and original observations about the perception of color, such as irradiation, dark and light adaptation, positive and negative afterimages, color contrast, colored shadows, color blindness, and others. His color theory was based on the observation that all colors are darker than white. He took blue and yellow as the two primary colors and related the rest to them. Even though the theory was sterile, Goethe was a famous figure, and his theory continued to be cited through the first half of the nineteenth century while that of Thomas Young* was ignored.

Although Goethe's color theory was bad, his phenomenological observations were good. Goethe strongly believed that the method of science was intuitive observation and not experimentation. He may be said to have started the phenomenological tradition in modern psychology. Goethe also exercised some degree of influence on Sigmund Freud*. Freud acknowledged that an essay about nature by Goethe had been one of the factors that influenced him to take up the medical profession. In Goethe's writings certain aspects of Freud's libido theory also may be found.

Biographies: A. Bielschowsky, *The Life of Goethe*, 3 vols., 1905-8; H. Duentzer, *Abhandlungen zu Goethes Leben und Werken*, 2 vols., 1885; B. Gajek & F. Götting, *Goethes Leben und Werk in Daten und Bildern*, 1966; J. W. v. Goethe, *Poetry and Truth from My Own Life*, 2 vols., 1913; R. Kühn, *Goethe: Eine medizinische Biographie*, 1949; G. H. Lewes, *The Life and Works of Goethe*, 1908; H. Viehoff, *Goethes Leben*, 5th ed., 1887; *ADB*, 9; *DSB*, 5; *EB*, 10; *EP*, 3.

GOLDSCHEIDER, ALFRED
German Physiologist
Born: Sommerfeld, Saxony, August 4, 1858
Died: Berlin, April 10, 1935
Highest Degree: M.D., Friedrich-Wilhelm Institut, Berlin, 1881
Positions: 1894-1906, Moabit Hospital, Berlin; 1906-10, Virchow Hospital (Wirchow-Institut), Berlin; 1910-33, Berliner Polyklinik (Berlin Polyclinic)

In 1884 and independently of Blix*, Goldscheider discovered separate sensory spots in the skin that mediated the perception of warmth, cold, and pressure.

Goldscheider believed pain was not a separate sense modality but resulted from increased pressure (the intensive or summation theory of pain). In this view he was opposed by Frey*, who believed that pain was a separate sense modality. Frey's view eventually won out. Goldscheider also discovered, independently of Rubin*, *paradoxical warmth* (a cold stimulus causing the sensation of warmth). In a series of papers about kinesthesis, published between 1887 and 1893, Goldscheider established, among other things, the present tripartite components of kinesthesis: muscles, tendons, and joints. He wrote many papers about haptic sensations, aftersensations, and thresholds, as well as more than a dozen books about physiology and medicine.
Biographies: *EUI*, 26.

GOLDSTEIN, KURT
German-American Neurologist
Born: Kattowitz, Upper Silesia, Germany, November 6, 1878
Died: New York, New York, September 19, 1965
Highest Degree: M.D., University of Breslau, 1903
Positions: 1907-15, University of Königsberg; 1916-29, University of Frankfurt; 1929-33, Moabit Hospital, Berlin; 1933-35, University of Amsterdam; 1936-40, Columbia University, New York State Psychiatric Institute and Hospital, Montefiore Hospital; 1938-40, William James lecturer, Harvard University; 1940-45, Tufts Medical School; since 1946, visiting professor of psychology, City College of New York, New School for Social Research, and later Brandeis University

At both Frankfurt and Berlin, Goldstein engaged in considerable clinical and organizational activity. He organized the University of Frankfurt Institute for Research into the Aftereffects of Brain Injuries; he was a cofounder of the International Society for Psychotherapy and the journal *Allegemeine ärztliche Zeitschrift für Psychotherapie*. He became affiliated with Gestalt psychology and was, with Wertheimer*, Köhler*, Koffka*, and Gruhle*, one of the cofounders of the Gestalt-psychological journal *Psychologische Forschung* (1921). Influenced both by Gestalt thinking and the holistic tradition of German science, Goldstein began to use Gestalt concepts in his clinical neurology work. His experiences with cases of brain injury (*Die Behandlung, Fürsorge und Begutachtung hirnverletzter Soldaten*, 1919) led him to postulate that an organism must be considered as a whole whenever a particular aspect of its functioning is evaluated. The holistic-organismic theory was presented by Goldstein in his major work *Der Aufbau des Organismus* (1934; English translation, *The Organism*, 1938). Goldstein asserted there was no localization of behavior in specific regions of the cortex; rather, behavior resides in the network of the central nervous system. The smooth functioning of each portion of the brain is guaranteed by the whole brain. Even when injured, the organism seeks to function adequately. There is only one drive in any organism, that of self-actualization. The organism realizes its particular nature when it reaches adequacy in the relationship between what it does and the environmental conditions (*Remarks on Localization*, 1946).

The Goldstein signs of brain injury include a rise in the threshold of excitation (slowing down of reactions), perseveration, disturbance of attention, blurring of figure and ground, and loss of the ability to abstract. Goldstein divided human acts into the abstract and the concrete. Impairment in abstract thinking (attention, planning, discrimination, hypothesizing) leaves concrete operations (those guided by external stimulus properties) unaffected and vice versa. The Goldstein-Gelb* and Goldstein-Scheerer* tests are test batteries that measure the ability to form concepts and are used to diagnose brain lesion. Goldstein wrote some 250 papers, chapters in handbooks, and books. Several of his books have been translated into other languages.

Biographies: W. Eliasberg, *Proc. Rudolf Virchow Med. Soc.*, N.Y., 1965, *24*, 185-194; H. Jonas, *Soc. Res.*, 1965, *32*, 351-356; J. Meiers, *J. Ind. Psychol.*, 1966, *22*, 116-125; D. Shakow, *Amer. J. Psychol.*, 1966, *79*, 150-154; M. L. Simmel, *J. Hist. Behav. Sci.*, 1966, *2*, 185-191; various, In M. L. Simmel (Ed.), *The Reach of Mind: Essays in Memory of Kurt Goldstein*, 1968; *EJ*, 7; *IESS*, 6; *Jewish*, 5.

GOLGI, CAMILLO
Italian Histologist, Neurologist, and Pathologist
Born: Cortona, Tuscany, July 7, 1843
Died: Pavia, Lombardy, January 21, 1926
Highest Degree: M.D., University of Pavia, 1865
Positions, Honors: 1875-1926, University of Pavia; Nobel Prize in physiology and medicine, 1906

In 1873 Golgi used silver nitrate to stain nerve cells, which was a cornerstone in the study of the nervous system. He eventually developed a theory of the nervous system as a network formed by the axons and dendrites. His studies of the nervous system were important enough to have several of its structures named after him, such as the Golgi apparatus. Golgi gave the first complete description (in 1880) and his name to the nerve endings in tendons, near the points of attachment for muscles (Golgi tendon organ, or Golgi spindle), whose stimulation informs the organism concerning the position of its limbs. The Golgi-Mazzoni corpuscle is assumed to mediate pressure sensations. Golgi's work of importance to sensory psychology is described in his *Untersuchungen über den feineren Bau des centralen und peripherischen Nervensystems* (1894; published in Italian, 1885).

Biographies: E. Bertarelli, *Camillo Golgi ed il suo tempo*, 1950; G. Pilleri, In K. Kolle (Ed.), *Grosse Nervenärzte*, vol. 2, 1959, pp. 3-12; C. Sacerdotti, *Arch. ital. biol.*, 1926, *76*, 140-148; T. Stevenson, *Nobel Prize Winners in Medicine and Physiology, 1901-1950*, 1953, pp. 32-40; *DSB*, 5; *EUI*, 26; Hirsch, *Biog. Lex.*, 2, Suppl.

GOLTZ, FRIEDRICH LEOPOLD

German Physiologist

Born: Poznan, Poland, August 14, 1834

Died: Strasbourg, May 4, 1902

Education: Mainly self-taught

Positions: 1870-72, University of Halle; 1872-1902, University of Strasbourg

An adherent of Flourens*, Goltz worked (1869-99) on the localization of cerebral functions, especially in dogs, and on labyrinthine sensitivity. In 1870 he showed that cold and hot water, applied externally to the ear, caused vertigo, nausea, and ocular nystagmus. He theorized, correctly, that the semicircular canals were not involved in hearing but in equilibrium.

Biographies: J. R. Ewald, *Arch. ges. Physiol.*, 1903, *94*, 1-64; H. Kraft, *Münch. med. Wochenschr.*, 1902, *49*, 965-970; *DSB*, 5; *EUI*, 26; Hirsch, *Biog. Lex.*, 2, Suppl.; *NDB*, 6.

GOODENOUGH, FLORENCE LAURA

American Psychologist

Born: Honesdale, Pennsylvania, August 6, 1886

Died: Saint Paul, Minnesota, April 4, 1959

Highest Degree: Ph.D. in psychology, Stanford University, 1924, under L. Terman*

Positions: 1924-25, Minneapolis Child Guidance Clinic; 1925-59, Institute of Welfare, University of Minnesota

Goodenough was a prominent worker in the areas of child psychology and child development. She is best known for her study of intelligence and children's drawings. In *Measurement of Intelligence by Drawings* (1926), Goodenough presented her Draw-a-Man Test, a nonlanguage intelligence test for children in which the subject is instructed to make a picture of a person and intelligence is evaluated in terms of the completeness of the drawing. In the 1940s it was the third most widely used psychometric instrument and is still in use today. Goodenough wrote a number of papers on the subject of intelligence testing and related matters, as well as *Minnesota Preschool Scales* (1940, with K. M. Maurer and J. J. Van Wagenen), *The Mental Growth of Children from Two to Fourteen Years* (1942, with K. M. Maurer), *and Mental Testing* (1949).

Biographies: D. B. Harris, *Child Development*, 1959, *30*, 305-306; *PR*, 3.

GOSSET, WILLIAM SEALY

English Statistician

Born: Canterbury, Kent, June 13, 1876

Died: London, October 16, 1937

Education: Studied chemistry and mathematics at Oxford University

Positions: 1899-1935, Guinness, Son & Co., Dublin; 1935-37, Guinness, Son & Co., London

Gosset produced his statistical work while working as a brewer and later as

statistician for the famed Guinness brewing company, but was prohibited by the company's rules from publishing his research on the variability in the brewing process. The rules were relaxed to allow Gosset to publish under a pseudonym. Under the pseudonym of "Student," Gosset published a paper in 1908 ("The probable error of a mean") in which he pointed out that the distribution of the ratio of the mean to its standard error does not follow a normal curve if the sample is small. The statistic t (Student's t), now widely used in tests of differences between means of small samples, was contributed by Gosset.
Biographies: R. A. Fisher, *Ann. Eugen.*, 1939, *9*, 1-9; L. McMullen, *Biometrika*, 1939, *30*, 205-210; E. S. Pearson, *Biometrika*, 1939, *30*, 210-250; *DNB*, Suppl. 4; *DSB*, 5; *IESS*, 6.

GRAHAM, CLARENCE HENRY
American Psychologist
Born: Worcester, Massachusetts, January 6, 1906
Died: New York, New York, July 25, 1971
Highest Degree: Ph.D. in psychology, Clark University, 1930, under J. P. Nafe
Positions, Honors: 1930-31, Temple University, Johnson Foundation; 1931-32, University of Pennsylvania; 1932-36, Clark University; 1936-45, Brown University; 1945-71, Columbia University; honorary D.Sc., Brown University, 1958; medals, awards, merit certificates from the Society of Experimental Psychologists, American Psychological Association, Optical Society of America, National Academy of Sciences, American Academy of Arts and Sciences, president of the United States

Although Graham worked on a variety of problems, most of his work was in the areas of vision and visual perception. He worked first on achromatic vision (critical flicker frequency, luminosity curves, and area-intensity problem experiments, some of them in collaboration with Ragnar Granit and Keffer Hartline, whose work in vision was later rewarded with the Nobel Prize), then color vision, and during his last years, space and movement perception. His best-known studies are those of color vision, which he, in collaboration with Yun Hsia, contributed during a period of some twenty years while at Columbia University. These studies produced many new facts about color vision. Graham left behind about ninety publications, many of which are classics in the literature on vision. He wrote one important book, *Vision and Visual Perception* (1965, in collaboration with J. L. Brown, N. R. Bartlett, Y. Hsia, C. G. Mueller, and L. A. Riggs).
Biographies: *Amer. Psychologist*, 1966, *21*, 1194-1198; F. A. Geldard, *Amer. J. Psychol.*, 1972, *85*, 291-294; *J. Opt. Soc. Amer.*, 1963, *53*, 1015-1018; *HPA*, 6; *NYT*, 1971, July 26, 28:1.

GROOS, KARL THEODOR
German Psychologist and Philosopher
Born: Heidelberg, Baden-Württemberg, December 10, 1861
Died: Tübingen, Baden-Württemberg, March 27, 1946

Highest Degree: Ph.D. in philosophy, University of Heidelberg, 1884
Positions: 1892-98, University of Giessen; 1898-1901, University of Basel; 1901-11, University of Giessen; 1911-29, University of Tübingen

Groos concentrated on studying play and development in children, suggesting that play serves as training for serious activities in the future (*Die Spiele der Thiere*, 1896; *Die Spiele der Menschen*, 1899; *Das Seelenleben des Kindes*, 1903, six editions by 1923). Groos's work was mainly a philosopher's attempt to synthesize psychology, philosophy, and biology. He also produced works about aesthetics and the psychological analysis of documents.

Biographies: *EUI*, 26; *HPA*, 2; *NDB*, 7; *PR*, 3.

GROSSETESTE, ROBERT
English Scholar
Born: Suffolk, ca. 1168
Died: Buckden, Buckinghamshire, October 9, 1253
Education: Educated at Lincoln and Oxford; master in theology, University of Paris (?), before 1215
Positions: Before 1209, Oxford University; 1214-21, chancellor, Oxford University; 1229-32, archdeacon of Leicester; 1235-53, bishop of Lincoln

Grosseteste played a leading role in the introduction of Latin translations of Greek and Arab philosophical and scientific works to European consciousness in the high Middle Ages. He wrote commentaries about Aristotle*, as well as independent works on physics, astronomy, and other scientific subjects. Philosophically, he blended Aristotelean and Neoplatonic ideas. He showed strong curiosity about natural phenomena and was intent on fitting both natural and supernatural things in rational schemes. He believed that natural phenomena could be best explained by mathematics, an idea based on the theory that the ultimate substance of which everything was made was light. Grosseteste distinguished, although incompletely, among the inductive, experimental, and mathematical approaches to the study of phenomena.

Biographies: A. C. Crombie, *Robert Grosseteste and the Origins of Experimental Science, 1100-1700*, 1953; D. A. Callus (Ed.), *Robert Grosseteste, Scholar and Bishop*, 1955; F. S. Stevenson, *Robert Grosseteste*, 1899; *DSB*, 5; *EB*, 10. ˇ

GRUHLE, HANS WALTHER
German Psychiatrist
Born: Lubben, Saxony, November 7, 1880
Died: Bonn, October 3, 1958
Highest Degree: M.D., University of Munich, 1905
Positions: 1912-34, University of Heidelberg; 1934-46, director of sanatoriums; 1946-52, Neurological Clinic, Bonn

Gruhle did research and wrote numerous articles and books about psychiatry, psychopathology, and schizophrenia (*Psychologie der Schizophrenie*, 1929; *Psychopathologie der Schizophrenie*, 1932), psychology of criminality (*Geistes-*

krankheiten und Strafrecht, 1927), and suicide (*Selbstmord*, 1940). He was a cofounder, with Wertheimer*, Köhler*, Koffka*, and Goldstein*, of *Psychologische Forschung* in 1921. In his *Verstehen und Einfühlen* (1953), he outlined a *verstehende*, or apprehending psychology, as a discipline concerned with inner experience, as well as a *verstehende* psychopathology.

Biographies: Lancet, 1958, *275*, 967-968; *Biog. Lex.*; *NDB*, 7; *PR*, 3.

GUILLAUME, PAUL

French Psychologist

Born: Chaumont, Haute Marne, June 26, 1878

Died: Paris, January 4, 1962

Highest Degree: *Agregé en philosophie*, Sorbonne, 1902; *Dr. des lettres*, Sorbonne, 1925

Positions, Honors: 1937-47, University of Paris; editor, *Journal de psychologie normale et pathologique*; president, Societé Française de Psychologie

Guillaume was a representative of the French school of *psychologie du comportement*, or behavior psychology. Guillaume stressed the similarity between psychology and physics and thought that the same methodology could be used in both disciplines (*Introduction à la psychologie*, 1942). In his *Manuel de psychologie* (1931) Guillaume broke with tradition in French textbook writing and presented psychology as a natural science, showing how psychology could solve real-life problems.

Guillaume worked in four areas of psychology: animal psychology (primate research), philosophical psychology, psychological theory, and child psychology. *La psychologie de la forme* (1937) was a very popular introduction to Gestalt psychology. Along with Guillaume's translation of Köhler's *Mentality of Apes*, it served to introduce Gestalt psychology in France. In 1936 Guillaume published a work on habit formation, *Formation des habitudes*. Guillaume's doctoral thesis, published in 1926 as *L'Imitation chez l'enfant*, presented a theory of imitation in children up to three years of age. This work resulted from Guillaume's study of his own two children and contains many terms that were not to become popular until much later, such as *behavioral feedback*, *infantile stimulation*, and *control of behavior*. In addition, the book was the beginning of Guillaume's influential work in psycholinguistics. He continued it in 1927 with two more books, *Les débuts de la phrase dans le langage de l'enfant* and *Le développement des éléments formels dans le langage de l'enfant*. He was particularly interested in the emergence of first sentences in a child's language and insisted that it was useless to apply adult grammatical categories to a developing child's speech.

Biographies: F. Bresson, *Psychol. franç.*, 1962, *7*, 178-179; B. Kaplan, In P. Guillaume, *Imitation in Children*, 1971, pp. xi-xvii; I. Meyerson, *J. psychol. norm. path.*, 1962, *59*, 1-13; H. Piéron, *Année psychol.*, 1962, *62*, 675-676; *PR*, 3.

GUTHRIE, EDWIN RAY

American Psychologist
Born: Lincoln, Nebraska, January 9, 1886
Died: Seattle, Washington, April 23, 1959
Highest Degree: Ph.D. in philosophy, University of Pennsylvania, 1912
Positions, Honors: 1914-56, University of Washington; since 1943, dean of Graduate School; LL.D., University of Nebraska, 1945; president, American Psychological Association, 1945; American Psychological Foundation Gold Medal, 1958

Guthrie worked in the fields of general psychology, social psychology, and the psychology of learning, but his most important contributions are in the psychology of learning. Trained in philosophy, Guthrie combined the associationist doctrine with instrumental conditioning to formulate a new theory of learning (*The Psychology of Learning*, 1935; rev. ed., 1952) that required only the contiguity of stimulus and response for learning to take place. "Stimuli acting at the time of a response tend on their reoccurrence to again evoke that response." The first significant theoretical paper introducing his ideas was "Conditioning as a principle of learning," published in 1930, which led to an attack by Pavlov* and a rebuttal by Guthrie, an exchange that placed Guthrie on the map.

Guthrie considered learning to be specific patterns of motor and glandular action called movements. When the learning situation remains ideal, only one trial is required for learning. Since, with each subsequent response, the stimulus situation is, however, slightly different, repetition may be necessary for learning to occur. Neither motivation nor reward are necessary conditions for learning but are part of the stimulus pattern. Guthrie did not resort to any processes intervening between stimulus and response to explain learning. Reward forms a new stimulus set and prevents the formation of other associations. Extinction is the inhibition of an old response by a subsequently learned one. *Cats in a Puzzle Box* (1946, with G. P. Horton) presents a specifically Guthrian notion, namely, that of *stereotypy*. Once a particular movement pattern is learned, the tendency is to repeat it exactly.

Guthrie did not establish a formal, but rather an informal, theoretical system. He deliberately avoided formalization, supporting his theoretical statements not by research findings but by illustrations, actual or anecdotal, from everyday life. Guthrie also established for himself a reputation in abnormal psychology when he published *The Psychology of Human Conflict* (1938), in which he favored Janet's* views over those of the psycholanalysts.

Biographies: *Amer. Psychologist*, 1958, *13*, 739-740; F. D. Sheffield, *Amer. J. Psychol.*, 1959, *72*, 642-650; *IESS*, 6; *PR*, 3.

H

HAECKEL, ERNST HEINRICH
German Biologist
Born: Potsdam, Brandenburg, February 16, 1834
Died: Jena, Thuringia, August 9, 1919
Highest Degree: M.D., University of Berlin, 1857
Positions: 1861-1909, professor of zoology and director of Zoological Institute, University of Jena

In 1866 Haeckel published a classic treatise of Darwinian biology, *Allgemeine Morphologie*, in which, among other things, he had formulated the principle that "ontogeny recapitulates phylogeny," or that during its developmental stages an organism repeats the evolutionary history of the species. G. Stanley Hall*, who pioneered in developmental psychology under the aegis of Charles Darwin*, based his cultural recapitulation theory on Haeckel's principle, substituting the evolution of human civilization for biological evolution. The cultural recapitulation theory was never proven, and Haeckel's principle has been found to be applicable only to certain aspects of morphology.

Biographies: W. Bölsche, *Haeckel: His Life and Work*, 1909; E. H. Haeckel, *The Confessions of Faith of a Man of Science*, 1903; J. Hemleben, *Ernst Haeckel in Selbstzeugnissen und Bilddokumenten*, 1964; W. May, *Ernst Haeckel: Versuch einer Chronik seines Lebens und Wirkens*, 1909; H. Schmidt, *Ernst Haeckel: Leben und Werke*, 1926; M. Verworn, *Z. allg. Physiol.*, 1921, *19*, 1-11; *Biog. Lex.*; *CE*, 6; *DSB*, 6; *EB*, 10; *EP*, 3; *NYT*, 1919, Aug. 10, 23:3.

HALL, GRANVILLE STANLEY

American Psychologist

Born: Ashfield, Massachusetts, February 1, 1844

Died: Worcester, Massachusetts, April 24, 1924

Highest Degree: Ph.D. in psychology, Harvard University, 1878, under William James*

Positions: 1882-88, Johns Hopkins University; 1889-1920, president and professor of psychology, Clark University; president, American Psychological Association, 1892 and 1924

Although Hall received the first Ph.D. in psychology to be conferred in the United States and did considerable doctoral and postdoctoral work in psychology, his fame rests more on his organizational activities than his research. In 1883, at Johns Hopkins University, Hall founded the second American psychological laboratory and in 1889 still another one at Clark University. Additional laboratories were founded elsewhere by those who had been Hall's students at Johns Hopkins. In 1887 Hall started publishing the *American Journal of Psychology*, first American psychological journal and first purely psychological journal in the English language. He also started the *Pedagogical Seminary* (now *Journal of Genetic Psychology*) in 1891 and the *Journal of Applied Psychology* in 1915 and published the *Journal of Religious Psychology* between 1904 and 1914. Most important was the founding of the American Psychological Association in 1892, an organization to which today more than one-half of the world's psychologists belong.

Hall was a pioneer of developmental psychology (he called it "genetic psychology") in the United States. Influenced by Charles Darwin's* evolutionary theory, Hall came to think of the development of the child as reflecting the evolutionary history of humankind. He introduced the use of the questionnaire to study "the contents of children's minds." Hall published his findings in his own *Pedagogical Seminary*, the second psychological journal to appear in the United States. Inspired by Hall, enthusiasm for child-study grew, and a child-study movement flourished for some years. Although it did not last, it established the notion of psychological development and the need for empirical work in child study. In a monumental two-volume work, *Adolescence*, published in 1904, Hall considered the later years of development. In it may be found Hall's cultural recapitulation theory, or the proposition that the child during its development repeats the evolution of civilization. Originally an idea of Rousseau's*, it found no empirical support in spite of Hall's having it bolstered with evolutionary biology taken from Darwin and Haeckel*. Toward the end of his life, Hall considered old age and pioneered in gerontology by publishing a volume on *Senescence* (1922).

Hall was also one of the first American psychologists to become interested in psychoanalysis. In 1909 he brought Freud* and Jung* to Clark University for a conference, in spite of the suspiciousness with which psychoanalysis was viewed. By doing this and by teaching a course in psychoanalysis himself, Hall introduced psychoanalysis in the United States. In his later years interest in the psychology of religion led him to publish a volume of *Jesus, the Christ, in the Light of Psychology* (1917). Hall also pioneered in educational psychology, first through his public lectures on education in 1880 and then by his child studies, by establishing a department of pedagogy at Clark University, and by providing an outlet for papers on educational psychology in his *Pedagogical Seminary*.

Biographies: W. H. Burnham, *J. Genet. Psychol.*, 1924, *31*, 105-107; W. H. Burnham, *Psychol. Rev.*, 1925, *32*, 89-102; I. H. Coriat, *Int. J. Psychoanal.*, 1924, *5*, 512-514; G. S. Hall, *Amer. J. Psychol.*, 1917, *28*, 296-300; G. S. Hall, *J. Genet. Psychol.*, 1899, *6*, 485-512; G. S. Hall, *J. Genet. Psychol.*, 1901, *8*, 92-143; G. S. Hall, *Life and Confessions of a Psychologist*, 1923; G. S. Hall, *Recreations of a Psychologist*, 1920; A. Meyer, *Amer. J. Psychiat.*, 1924-1925, *81*, 151-153; L. Pruett, *G. Stanley Hall: A Biography of a Mind*, 1926; D. Ross, *G. Stanley Hall: The Psychologist as Prophet*, 1972; E. C. Sanford, *Amer. J. Psychol.*, 1924, *35*, 313-321; E. D. Starbuck, *Psychol. Rev.*, 1925, *32*, 103-120; L. N. Wilson, *G. Stanley Hall: A Sketch*, 1914; L. N. Wilson, *Publ. Clark Univ. Libr.*, 1925, 7, 3-33; R. Zeligs, *J. Appl. Psychol.*, 1943, *27*, 83-87; *DAB*, 8; *DSB*, 6; *EB*, 11; *IESS*, 6; *NCAB*, 39; *NYT*, 1924, Apr. 25, 17:4.

HALL, MARSHALL

English Physiologist
Born: Basford, Nottinghamshire, February 18, 1790
Died: Brighton, Sussex, August 11, 1857
Highest Degree: M.D., University of Edinburgh, 1812
Positions: 1812-16, various medical appointments; 1817-26, private practice, Nottingham; 1826-50, private practice, London, some lecturing

Hall pioneered in the study of reflex action. He studied it during a period of twenty-five years, beginning in 1832. In an 1833 report he laid down the fundamentals of a theory of reflex action. Although others, such as Whytt*, Haller*, and Prochaska*, had also investigated the reflex, Hall showed it to be an essential function of the body, not just an isolated phenomenon. He made a distinction between voluntary and involuntary action, holding that reflexes are both involuntary and unconscious since the brain is not required to produce them. This stirred up considerable controversy, but for several decades Hall's convenient dichotomy of the conscious and the unconscious, voluntary and involuntary, was adhered to. Hall's work on reflex action found no recognition in England during his time, although foreign scientists thought him to be the most outstanding name in the field.

Biographies: R. Erez-Federbusch, *Marshall Hall 1790-1857: Physiologe und Praktiker*, 1963; J. H. S. Green, *Med. Hist.*, 1958, *2*, 120-133; W. Hale-White, *Great Doctors of the Nineteenth Century*, 1935; M. Hall, *Memoirs of Marshall Hall*, 1861; *Lancet*, 1850, *2*, 120-128; *Lancet*, 1857, *2*, 172-175; *DNB*, 8; *DSB*, 6.

HALLER, ALBRECHT VON
Swiss Anatomist, Physiologist, and Botanist
Born: Berne, October 16, 1708
Died: Berne, December 17, 1777
Highest Degree: Medical degree, University of Leiden, 1727
Positions: 1736-53, University of Göttingen

Haller, the father of experimental physiology of the modern era, established physiology as an independent science. His greatest work, *Elementa physiologiae corporis humani* (1757-66), remained the most important treatise on physiology for a century. Of importance to psychology are several of Haller's discoveries and demonstrations concerning the action of nerves and muscles. He showed that muscles shortened when stimulated and then returned to their original length. He labeled this property "irritability" (*vis insita*) and recognized it as essential in heart action and the action of the intestines. He thought of the nerves as tubes, however, and of vital spirits as a sort of watery juice flowing through them. Haller showed that body tissues are not of themselves capable of sensation, but that sensation depends on the presence of nerves. He introduced the notion of the adequate stimulus, or the normal and appropriate stimulus that a sense organ is designed to respond to. He showed that all nerves converge upon the brain and demonstrated the central role of the brain through experiments with lesions to the brain and the nerves. Haller also calculated, but did not measure, the velocity of the nerve impulse to be about one hundred fifty feet per second, which is within the range of modern measurements.

Biographies: R. Beer, *Der grosse Haller*, 1947; H. Chavannes, *Biographie de Albert de Haller*, 1845; E. Grünthal, *Albrecht von Haller, Johann Wolfgang von Goethe und ihre Nachkommen*, 1965; K. Guggisberg, *Bern. Z. Gesch. Heimatk.*, 1961, *1*, 1-12; A. Haller, *Albrecht von Hallers Leben*, 1954; J. C. Hemmeter, *Bull. Johns Hopkins Hosp.*, 1908, *19*, 65-74; S. d'Irsay, *Albrecht von Haller: Eine Studie zur Geistesgeschichte der Aufklärung*, 1930; L. S. King, In A. v. Haller, *First Lines of Physiology*, 1966, pp. ix-lxxii; O. Klotz, *Ann. Med. Hist.*, 1936, *8*, 10-26; H. Kronecker, *Haller redivivus*, 1902; F. Meier, *Beiträge zur Biographie Albrecht von Hallers*, 1915; A. Schierbeek, *Biol. Jb.*, 1956, 348-381; *ADB*, 10; *DSB*, 6; *EB*, 11; *EP*, 3; Hirsch, *Biog. Lex.*, 3, Suppl.; *NDB*, 7.

HALSTEAD, WARD CAMPBELL
American Psychologist
Born: Sciotoville, Ohio, December 31, 1908
Died: Chicago, Illinois, March 25, 1969
Highest Degree: Ph.D. in psychology, Northwestern University, 1935
Positions: 1936-69, University of Chicago

Halstead was internationally known for his work on the brain. The Halstead Laboratory of Medical Psychology at the University of Chicago was the first laboratory in the world to be devoted full-time to the study of higher brain activity in humans. In addition, Halstead established a graduate program in

biopsychology at Chicago. Concerned with the effect of brain lesions on behavior, Halstead developed, in 1950, a test battery of ten tests to diagnose brain damage by means of psychological tests. The battery (Halstead Battery of Neuropsychological Tests) is now in wide use, and its subtests have been incorporated by others in other similar tests. Also in 1950 Halstead, in collaboration with J. Katz, proposed the first formal theory of the biochemistry of learning. He was the first person to suggest that chemicals, namely, RNA and protein molecules, might be the place to look for the memory engram. Halstead wrote *Cerebellar Functions* (1935), *Medicine and the War* (1945, with W. H. Taliaferro), *Brain and Intelligence* (1947), and *Brain and Human Behavior* (1958, with J. Katz) and contributed chapters about brain mechanisms and behavior to numerous edited works.
Biographies: *NCAB*, 55.

HAMILTON, SIR WILLIAM
Scottish Philosopher
Born: Glasgow, March 8, 1788
Died: Edinburgh, May 6, 1856
Education: M.A., Oxford University, 1814
Positions: 1821-56, University of Edinburgh, until 1836, taught civil history, from 1836, taught philosophy

Hamilton not only edited the works of both Thomas Reid* and Dugald Stewart* of the Scottish school but in many respects derived his own philosophy from them. At the same time, his thinking was also considerably influenced by German transcendentalism. Hamilton acquired recognition by his 1829 essay *The Philosophy of the Unconditioned*, in which a mixture of Kant* and British empiricism predominates. What the mind knows is not objective reality but objective reality conditioned by the number and nature of the senses. Four hundred years after Bishop Nemesius had noted that one may not see at a glance more than a few objects, and in anticipation of twentieth-century findings about human information-handling capacity, Hamilton observed that "if you throw . . . marbles on the floor, you will find it difficult to view at once more than six . . . without confusion." Judgment is not entirely objective either, since it processes sensory data according to the rules of the mind. "To think is to condition." The ultimate reality (the unconditioned) is beyond the reach of philosophy. This latter Kantian notion Hamilton accepted, along with a faculty psychology of the Kantian variety.

Hamilton's most important contribution to psychology was his theory of memory and association. Its central concept is that of *redintegration*, the bringing back to consciousness, by a sense impression, of the entire situation of which it has been a part. The evocation of a whole rather than ideas in their associative sequence contrasted markedly with the notion of association of the British associationists and anticipated twentieth-century thinking.

Hamilton was primarily a philosopher, but because he was influenced by the more psychologically oriented Reid and Stewart and because he did discuss psychological topics, such as redintegration and the nature of consciousness (*Lectures on Metaphysics and Logic*, 1859), and was able to argue very competently the case of the Scottish school against British associationism, Hamilton had a measure of influence on the development of thought within the Scottish school of psychology. The Scottish school came to an end with Hamilton, but its philosophical ideas continued to live in the idealist movement.

Biographies: W. H. Monck, *Sir William Hamilton*, 1881; C. de Rémusat, *Rev. deux Mondes*, 1860, *26*, 133-160; J. H. Stirling, *Sir William Hamilton*, 1865; J. Veitch, *Hamilton*, 1905; *DNB*, 8; *DSB*, 6; *EP*, 3; *EUI*, 27.

HARLOW, HARRY F(REDERICK)

American Psychologist
Born: Fairfield, Iowa, October 31, 1905
Died: Tucson, Arizona, December 6, 1981
Highest Degree: Ph.D. in experimental psychology, Stanford University, 1930, under C. P. Stone*
Positions, Honors: 1930-74, founder and director Primate Laboratory, University of Wisconsin, 1956-74, director, Regional Primate Research Center, 1961-71, two terms as chairman, Psychology Department; 1939-40, Carnegie fellow in anthropology, Columbia University; 1950-52, chief, Human Resources Research, Department of the Army; 1974-81; professor emeritus, University of Wisconsin 1974-79, research professor, University of Arizona; president, American Psychological Association, 1958; editor, *Journal of Comparative and Physiological Psychology*, 1951-63; Warren Medal, 1956; American Psychological Association Distinguished Scientific Contribution Award, 1960; National Medal of Science, 1967; numerous other honors

The Wisconsin Primate Research Laboratory became known the world over because of the landmark research conducted there by Harlow on learning, motivation, the affectional systems, the effect of social isolation, and the treatment of the effects of isolation in rhesus monkeys.

Harlow's work on learning resulted in the development of the concept of learning set, or "learning how to learn"; the Wisconsin General Test Apparatus for studying problem solving; and the error-factor learning theory, which postulates that learning takes place as various tendencies that make for errors in learning are gradually eliminated. Harlow was also one of the first researchers to demonstrate that cognitive motives, such as exploration and curiosity, theretofore neglected by psychologists, were as important determiners of behavior as the deficiency motives, such as hunger.

By far the greatest renown was achieved by Harlow with his studies of the formation of the affectional bonds, especially between mother and offspring. He invented the surrogate-mother research technique, showing that contact comfort (skin contact and touch) was a variable more potent than feeding not only in establishing the affectional bond but in contributing materially to the emotional, social, mental, sexual, and physical well being of the monkey, both as infant and as adult. Contact with peers was shown by Harlow to be a substitute for maternal care, and he proposed experimentally tested techniques for treating monkeys whose behavior had suffered damage because of maternal deprivation. The comparative psychological studies of Harlow's on the nature of love was a pioneering effort in an area that had received little attention. They cast considerable light on human problems and made Harlow an influential figure in the area of psychopathology, human development, and childrearing.

Harlow wrote numerous journal articles and an introductory psychology text, *Psychology* (1971, with J. L. McGaugh and R. F. Thompson).

Biographies: American Psychological Association, *Amer. Psychologist*, 1960, *15*, 790-792; American Psychological Association, *Amer. Psychologist*, 1974, *29*, 48-50; R. R. Sears, *American Psychologist*, 1982, *37*, 1280-1281; *American Men and Women of Science*; *IESS*, 18; *Who's Who in America*.

HARTLEY, DAVID
English Philosopher
Born: Armley, Yorkshire, August 30, 1705
Died: Bath, Somersetshire, August 28, 1757
Highest Degree: M.A., Cambridge University, 1729
Positions: 1730-35, private practice of medicine, Newark, Bury, St. Edmunds; 1735-42, London; 1742-57, Bath

Although Hartley was less original than Locke*, Hobbes*, Hume*, or Berkeley*, his systematic presentation of the views of the British empiricists and associationists earned him the title of the founder of the British school of association psychology. His main work is *Observations on Man* (1749), in which, for the first time, the mind of the associationist doctrine is related to the body. Although Hartley's physiology was mostly theoretical, he consistently and consecutively stated his propositions in mental and physical terminology. One important statement that Hartley made was that often-repeated sensory vibrations left their impress as simple ideas, or conversely, that often-repeated sensory vibrations predisposed the brain to repeat similar but minute vibrations (*vibratiuncles*). Hartley subscribed to psychophysical parallelism in that he held that cerebral vibrations and the rise of ideas, while occurring simultaneously, were not the cause of each other. In line with Locke, Hartley said that at birth the mind is blank and that sensations arise from external impressions. Sensations, in turn, give rise to ideas. Simultaneous and successive contiguity is the main principle of association of sensations and ideas. Hartley consistently used the law of contiguity to explain all other mental phenomena. The fainter vibrations left in the wake of sensory vibrations are the basis of memory and imagination. One vibration, either sensory or its fainter trace in the brain, evokes another if they are associated. In this notion Hartley included motor acts, voluntary and involuntary, that could be evoked by ideas and vice versa.

Biographies: S. T. Coleridge, *Biographia literaria*, 1962; H. N. Fairchild, *Publ. Mod. Lang. Ass.*, 1947, (No. 2), 1010-1021; N. Moore, *Hibbert J.*, 1949, *48*, 73-79; *CE*, 6; *DNB*, 9; *DSB*, 6; *EB*, 11; *EP*, 3; *IESS*, 6.

HARTMANN, EDUARD VON

German Philosopher
Born: Berlin, February 23, 1842
Died: Berlin, June 5, 1906
Highest Degree: Ph.D. in philosophy, University of Rostock, 1867
Positions: No official positions

Hartmann evolved a metaphysics based on the notion of the unconscious (*Die Philosophie des Unbewussten*, 3 vols., 1869), which he considered to be the ground of all existence. Even the lowest organisms possess the unconscious, as indicated by the presence of reflexes and instincts that show purpose. Of the purely psychological processes, emotions have the deepest roots in the unconscious. The will, a part of the unconscious, is in constant strife with reason. The genius arises also from the unconscious. In fact, the conscious only reflects the powers of the unconscious. Although Ebbinghaus* wrote his doctoral dissertation about Hartmann's philosophy of the unconscious, Hartmann was not as influential in determining the course of development of the concept of the unconscious in psychology as were men such as Herbart*, James*, Janet*, Charcot*, and, above all, Sigmund Freud*.

Biographies: O. Braun, *Eduard von Hartmann*, 1909; D. N. K. Darnoi, *The Unconscious and Eduard von Hartmann*, 1967; A. Dorner, *Z. Phil. phil. Krit.*, 1906, *129*, 1-32; A. Drews, *Das Lebenswerk Eduard von Hartmanns*, 1907; W. Rauschenberger, *Eduard von Hartmann*, 1942; W. v. Schnehen, *Eduard von Hartmann*, 1929; *CE*, 6; *EP*, 3; *EUI*, 27; *NDB*, 7; *NYT*, 1906, June 7, 7:5.

HARVEY, WILLIAM

English Physician
Born: Folkeston, Kent, April 1, 1578
Died: London, June 3, 1657
Highest Degree: Doctor of medicine, University of Padua, 1602.
Positions: 1602-9, practiced medicine, London; 1609-29, St. Bartholomew's Hospital, London, physician extraordinary to James I, physician in ordinary to Charles I; 1636-46, practice of medicine, London and Oxford

Harvey's discovery of the circulation of the blood (*Exercitatio anatomica de motu cordis et sanguinis in animalibus*, 1628) was a turning point in the development of physiology and medicine, since much in these disciplines had been based on assumptions, mostly inherited from Galen*, about the blood. Harvey was more of an Aristotelean than Galenic physician, especially in subscribing to the view that the soul was not something separate or added to the body but was its form. To Harvey blood was practically identical with the soul or life, the body being merely an appendage to it. Harvey did not, however, accept Aristotle* unquestioningly but used him as a starting point for a radical departure from the traditional ways of thinking about human bodily functions. Very important also was his method of scientific observation of animal bodies, which later anatomists and physiologists sought to emulate.

More specifically psychological was Harvey's study of sensation and loco-motion (*De motu locali animalium*, begun in 1627 but left unfinished). Instead of viewing the brain as a distribution center of vital spirits that moved the muscles, Harvey held the correct view that the brain serves to process sensory information and to coordinate muscular movements, the muscles themselves having the power of sensation and contraction. The nerves are to convey messages to the brain; the brain is to make judgments. The brain is the Aristotelean *sensorium commune* that compares the different senses and unifies them. In anticipation of the concept of reflex action, Harvey recognized the difference between conscious sensations, mediated by the brain, and unconscious ones, shown by the direct response of individual bodily parts to stimulation, where the organism is not aware of the processes involved.

Biographies: J. Aubrey, In O. L. Dick (Ed.), *Brief Lives*, 1957, pp. 128-133; H. P. Bayon, *Ann. Sci.*, 1938, *3*, 59-82, 83-118, 435-456; H. P. Bayon, *Ann. Sci.*, 1939, *4*, 65-106, 329-389; L. Chauvois, *William Harvey: His Life and Times, His Discoveries, His Methods*, 1957; K. J. Franklin, *William Harvey, Englishman*, 1961; D. Goodman, In R. Harré (Ed.), *Early Seventeenth Century Scientists*, 1965, pp. 101-127; W. Herringham, *Circumstances in the Life and Times of William Harvey*, 1929; A. D. Keele, *William Harvey: The Man, the Physician and the Scientist*, 1965; G. Keynes, *The Life of William Harvey*, 1966; D. Power, *William Harvey*, 1897; T. Willis, In W. Harvey, *The Works of William Harvey, M.D.*, 1847, pp. xvii-lxxxvii; R. B. Wyatt, *William Harvey*, 1924; *DNB*, 9; *DSB*, 6; *EB*, 11; *EP*, 3.

HEAD, SIR HENRY
English Neurologist
Born: Stamford Hill, Lincolnshire, August 4, 1861
Died: Reading, Berkshire, October 8, 1940
Highest Degree: M.D., Cambridge University, 1892
Positions, Honors: Medical appointments in various hospitals, longest at London Hospital; two honorary degrees; several medals and prizes; knighted, 1927

Head's contributions are in the area of sensory physiology. In this work he collaborated with the psychologists W. R. R. Rivers* and F. C. Bartlett*. With the former he performed experiments (1905 and 1908) on cutaneous sensitivity by cutting two nerves in his own arm and observing the return of sensitivity. On the basis of this experiment Head theorized that three neural systems are involved in cutaneous sensitivity: deep sensitivity; *protopathic sensitivity*, a crude and strong system that is first to respond when a nerve regenerates; and *epicritic sensitivity*, a later and finer cutaneous discrimination. This and other experiments of Head's on the central nervous system, in which he traced the passage of sensory nerves through the spinal cord, brain stem, and thalamus to the cortex, were thought to present evidence for John Hughlings Jackson's* theory of the evolutionary levels of the nervous system. The results of Head's neurological work on the effects of lesions were published in 1920 in *Studies in Neurology*.

After 1910, Head became interested in aphasia. Work on aphasic cases produced during World War I led to the publication of *Aphasia and Kindred Disorders of Speech*, two volumes, in 1926. His view of aphasia struck between the classic view of it as a loss of images and the view that it involves more than just language functions. Head classified aphasias into the verbal, syntactical, nominal, and semantic. Jackson's theory of mental deterioration also led Head to formulate his theory of vigilance that is contained in this work. It is concerned with the manner in which hierarchically organized neural levels activate each other.

Biographies: R. Brain, *Brain*, 1961, *84*, 561-566; M. Critchley, in *The Black Hole and Other Essays*, 1964, pp. 98-107; K. W. Cross *et al.*, *Henry Head Century: Essays and Bibliography*, 1961; K. Kolle (Ed.), *Grosse Nervenärzte*, vol. 2, 1959, pp. 172-179; K. E. McBride, *Amer. J. Psychol.*, 1941, *54*, 444-446; C. S. Meyers, *Brit. J. Psychol.*, 1941, *32*, 5-14; *DNB*, Suppl. 4; *Obit. Not.*, 3.

HEALY, WILLIAM
American Psychiatrist
Born: Buckinghamshire, England, January 20, 1869
Died: Clearwater, Florida, March 15, 1963
Highest Degree: M.D., University of Chicago, 1900
Positions: 1900-1906, Northwestern University, medical appointments in various hospitals; 1906-7, postgraduate study, Vienna, Berlin, and London; 1909-17, director, Juvenile Psychopathic Institute, Chicago; 1917-47, director, Judge Baker Foundation (Judge Baker Guidance Center), Boston

In collaboration with his first wife, Grace Fernald, and later with his second wife, Augusta Bronner, both psychologists, Healy pioneered in the study of childhood delinquency. He organized and headed the first child-guidance clinic in Chicago in 1909, the Chicago Juvenile Psychopathic Institute (Institute of Juvenile Research since 1920). It began as a treatment center for delinquent children, later began to accept nondelinquent but emotionally disturbed children to be treated by a full-time staff of psychiatric and social workers. After Chicago Healy went to Boston's Judge Baker Clinic, where he conducted extensive research on delinquency. With Bronner, he wrote *New Light on Delinquency and Its Treatment* (1936) and *The Value of Treatment and What Happened Afterward* (1939). In his work with delinquent children Healy realized the need for performance tests to complement the more verbal types of intelligence-test tasks of the Stanford-Binet Intelligence Scale. The result was the Healy-Fernald series of twenty-three tests, put into use in 1911. Some of these tests were incorporated into later intelligence scales and are still in use today, such as the Healy Picture Completion Test and the Healy Puzzle. Healy wrote many articles and fourteen books. Of them, the most significant was *The Individual Delinquent*

(1915), in which Healy called for the application of psychology to broader things than just testing.

Biographies: G. E. Gardner, *J. Amer. Acad. Child Psychiat.*, 1972, *11*, 1-29; D. M. Levy, *Amer. J. Orthopsychiat.*, 1968, *38*, 799-804; H. Meltzer, *Psychol. Rep.*, 1967, *20*, 1028-1030; *EUI*, 27; *PR*, 3.

HECHT, SELIG
American Physiologist
Born: Glogau, Silesia, Germany, February 8, 1892
Died: New York, New York, September 18, 1947
Highest Degree: Ph.D. in physiology, Harvard University, 1917
Positions, Honors: 1917-25, Creighton University; 1926-47, Columbia University; recipient of the Frederick Ives Medal, Optical Society of America, 1941

Hecht was one of the principal contributors to modern vision theory. His special contribution lay in the study and theoretical formulation of photopigment processes in the retina. Hecht's theory (1929) proposed that the Bunsen-Roscoe law of photochemical reaction is the sum of two chemical processes, each of which is the other reversed: the decomposition of photopigments under light stimulation and their reconstitution in the dark. Of particular importance was the development by Hecht of an apparatus and method to test for vitamin A deficiency, vitamin A being one of the elements of the photochemical reactions in the retina. Hecht extended his theory to include color vision. It included an explanation of increasing visual acuity with increasing light intensity in terms of the two populations of retinal elements, the rods and the cones, and their varied thresholds. Hecht and his coworkers contributed many papers to the field of retinal photochemistry, many of which are classics, such as the 1942 paper by Hecht, Schlaer, and Pirenne in which the visual threshold was related to the amount of light quanta stimulating the receptors. Books written by Hecht include *The Retinal Processes Concerned with Visual Acuity and Color Vision* (1931) and *La bas chimique et structurale de la vision* (1938). He also wrote "The nature of the photoreceptor processes" for the *Handbook of General Experimental Psychology* (1934).

Biographies: C. H. Graham, *Amer. J. Psychol.*, 1948, *61*, 126-128; R. Kingslake, *J. Opt. Soc. Amer.*, 1942, *32*, 37-39; B. O'Brien, H. Grundfest, & E. Smith, *Science*, 1948, *107*, 105-106; M. H. Pirenne, *Nature*, 1948, 161, 673; *EJ*, 8; *NCAB*, 38; *NYT*, 1947, Sept. 19, 23:1; *PR*, 3; *Who Was Who in America*, 2.

HEGEL, GEORG WILHELM FRIEDRICH
German Philosopher
Born: Stuttgart, August 27, 1770
Died: Berlin, November 14, 1831
Highest Degree: Ph.D. in philosophy, University of Tübingen, 1790; certificate in theology, 1793

Positions: 1797-1800, University of Frankfurt; 1801-6, University of Jena; 1816-18, University of Heidelberg; 1818-31, University of Berlin

Hegel's *Die Phänomenologie des Geistes* (1807), one of his most important works, deals with the development of the human mind from consciousness to self-consciousness; then to reason, spirit, religion; and finally, to absolute knowledge. While working in the Kantian tradition, Hegel differed from Kant* in that he admitted the possibility of absolute knowledge.

Of his philosophical ideas, Hegel's dialectic has had the greatest influence on the social sciences, including psychology. In Hegelian dialectic, objects or concepts (*thesis*) have the tendency to develop contradictions (*antithesis*), which are resolved in a new form of the object or concept (*synthesis*). The synthesis serves as thesis for the next cycle and so on indefinitely. Dialectic processes occur in nature, human history, and human thought. The notion was extended by Marx* and Engel to include interaction between humans and the environment they create for themselves, including the social environment. By way of Marx and Lenin*, Hegelian dialectic became a cardinal principle of Soviet psychology, and it has played an important role in the thinking of individual psychologists, such as Piaget*.

Biographies: W. Dilthey, In *Gesammelte Schriften*, vol. 4, 1959, pp. 1-187; K. Fischer, *Hegels Leben, Werke und Lehre*, 1901; H. S. Harris, *Hegel's Development: Toward the Sunlight, 1770-1801*, 1972; K. Rosenkranz, *G. W. F. Hegels Leben*, 1844; *ADB*, 11; *EB*, 11; *EJ*, 8; *EP*, 3; *EUI*, 27; *IESS*, 6; *NDB*, 8.

HELLPACH, WILLY
German Psychologist
Born: Öls, Silesia, Germany, February 26, 1877
Died: Heidelberg, July 6, 1955
Highest Degree: Ph.D. in psychology, University of Leipzig, 1900, under W. Wundt*; M.D., University of Leipzig, 1903
Positions: 1906-22, Technische Hochschule, Karlsruhe; 1926-55, University of Heidelberg

Hellpach was active in psychology, medicine, education, and politics and as a columnist, often at the same time. In addition, he was a prolific writer. He became internationally known in 1911 upon the publication of his book *Geopsychische Erscheinungen*, in which he showed the effect of geography, climate, and other environmental conditions on behavior. His interest in this area continued in later years (*Mensch und Volk der Grosstadt*, 1939), as well as in related areas, such as industrial psychology (*Das Problem der Industriearbeit*, 1925). He was first in Germany to present academic lectures in industrial psychology, as well as in ethnopsychology and social psychology. In 1921 Hellpach founded the first German institute for research in social psychology, the Institut für Sozialpsychologie. After Wundt's death, Hellpach was the only representative of ethnopsychology in Germany. His most important work, *Einführung in Völkerpsychologie* (1937), is in this area. He wrote several additional related volumes, such as *Elementares Lehrbuch der Sozialpsychologie* (1933), *Deutsche Phy-siognomik* (1942), *Der deutsche Charakter* (1954), and *Kulturpsychologie* (1953). Hellpach distinguished between "people as a natural fact" from "people as a mental Gestalt" and "people as a creation of the will." To understand the motivational, organizational, and developmental aspects of ethnic groups they must be considered on all three levels. Social groups are best studied using sociological and social-psychological methods. Social institutions may replace specific motives in individuals: one acts according to the prescriptions of the society as they manifest themselves in its various institutions.

Biographies: W. Hellpach, *Wirken in Wirren*, 1948; H. v. Bracken & W. Witte, *Psychol. Beit.*, 1955, *2*; J. Rudert, *Psychol. Rundsch.*, 1955, *6*, 300-302; W. Witte, *Psychol. Beit.*, 1957, *3*, 3-20; *Biog. Lex.*; *NDB*, 8; *PR*, 3.

HELMHOLTZ, HERMANN LUDWIG FERDINAND VON
German Physicist and Physiologist
Born: Potsdam, Brandenburg, August 31, 1821
Died: Charlottenburg, Brandenburg, September 8, 1894
Highest Degree: M.D., Medico-Surgical Friedrich-Wilhelm Institute, Berlin, 1842
Positions: 1847-54, University of Königsberg; 1855-58, University of Bonn; 1858-70, University of Heidelberg; 1871-94, University of Berlin

Helmholtz is one of the great names in science. His genius encompassed theoretical physics, physiology, optics, vision, acoustics, and the psychology of the senses. Although he considered psychology to be related to philosophy, he made an exception of sensory psychology. Helmholtz's contribution to psychology is in this area and that of neurophysiology.

He was first to measure the speed of nerve conduction. His measurements meant that mental processes did not occur instantaneously but took finite time. Because Helmholtz had used muscular contraction to measure the rate of nerve conductivity (he invented the myograph for this purpose, an apparatus still used in the study of motor behavior), it also meant that motor acts could be used to measure the duration of mental events.

The excellence of presentation and the amount of original work on visual physiology, sensation, and perception in Helmholtz's classic *Handbuch der phy-siologischen Optik* (1856-66, reissued together in 1867; English translation, *Treatise on Physiological Optics*, 1925) were such that much of it is still valid today. In it may be found contributions such as his color vision theory, later named the Young-Helmholtz theory (Thomas Young*), and a theory of space perception. The basic features of the Young-Helmholtz theory remain undisputed today, the three-component theory having been basic to the development of color photography. With regard to space perception, Helmholtz's empiricist theory asserted that although each of the nerves pertaining to the various sense organs was characterized by a nerve energy specific to a sense, the sensations caused by them were meaningless until meaning was acquired through repeated associations. Perception of space was to Helmholtz the unconscious inference of relations from components whose meaning had been previously acquired. The doctrine of unconscious inference is still of more than just historic interest today.

Helmholtz also presented the first explanation of the additive and the subtractive color mixtures. There is a first recorded recognition of the role of motion parallax in depth perception in Helmholtz and many other original contributions to the physiology and psychology of vision. In the area of auditory perception Helmholtz clarified the meaning of timbre as the third major dimension of the acoustic stimulus by conducting experiments with tuning forks and resonators (the Helmholtz resonators) that he had invented. He used the idea of resonance in his theory of hearing to explain how the basilar membrane, by having hair cells of graduated length through its extent, responds selectively in accordance with the sound-wave frequency that stimulates it. Helmholtz's *Die Lehre von den Tonempfindungen* (1863), like his *Handbuch*, is another classic in the literature of the experimental psychology of sensation. In general, Helmholtz's research and his strong and successful arguments against the nativist and for the empiricist position (for instance, his demonstration that the geometric axioms are not innate ideas) gave a strong impetus to the emergence of experimental psychology.

Biographies: A. C. Crombie, *Sci. Amer.*, 1958, *198*(3), 94-102; H. Ebert, *Hermann von Helmholtz*, 1949; H. Gruber & V. Gruber, *Sci. Mon.*, 1956, *83*, 92-99; R. Kahl, In *Selected Writings of Hermann von Helmholtz*, 1971, pp. xii-xlv; L. C. Karpinski, *Sci. Mon.*, 1921, *13*, 24-32; K. Kolle (Ed.), *Grosse Nervenärzte*, vol. 2, 1959, pp. 67-77; L. Königsberger, *Hermann von Helmholtz*, 1906 (Reprinted 1956); J. C. Maxwell, *Nature*, 1877, *15*, 389-391; J. G. McKendrick, *Hermann Ludwig Ferdinand von Helmholtz*, 1899; W. Möller, *Naturwissenschaften*, 1923, *13*, 46-54; H. Morgenau, In H. L. F. v. Helmholtz, *On the Sensations of Tone*, 1954; W. Ostwald, *Grosse Männer*, 1910, pp. 256-310; A. W. Rücker, *Smithsonian Inst. Ann. Rep.*, 1894, 709-718; R. M. Warren & R. P. Warren, In *Helmholtz on Perception: Its Physiology and Development*, 1968, pp. 3-15; *ADB*, 51; *DSB*, 6; *EB*, 11; *EP*, 3; Hirsch, *Biog. Lex.*, 3, Suppl.; *IESS*, 6; *NDB*, 8; *NYT*, 1894, Sept. 9, 5:2.

HELSON, HARRY
American Psychologist
Born: Chelsea, Massachusetts, November 9, 1898
Died: Berkeley, California, October 13, 1977
Highest Degree: Ph.D. in psychology, Harvard University, 1924, under E. G. Boring*
Positions, Honors: 1924-25, Cornell University; 1925-26, University of Illinois; 1926-28, University of Kansas; 1928-49, Bryn Mawr College, 1933-49, chairman, Psychology Department; 1942-44, codirector, antiaircraft fire control laboratories, Foxboro Co., Massachusetts; 1949-51, chairman, Psychology

Department, Brooklyn College; 1951-61, University of Texas; 1952-54, director, Radiobiological Laboratory, University of Texas/U.S. Air Force; 1961-68, regents' professor, Kansas State University; 1967-68, distinguished professor, York University; 1968-71, University of Massachusetts; editorial work, *American Journal of Psychology* (1940-70), *Journal of Experimental Psychology* (1940-50), *Psychological Bulletin* (1959-64), *Psychological Review*, *Journal of General Psychology*; H. C. Warren Medal of Society of Experimental Psychologists, 1959; American Psychological Association Distinguished Scientific Contribution Award, 1962; I. H. Godlove Award, Inter-Societal Color Council, 1969

Helson's contributions are in the field of sensation and perception, especially color perception. He published more than 125 papers and books in this area. He leaned strongly toward Gestalt psychology and was one of the first American psychologists to present it to his colleagues, beginning with three monograph-size papers published in 1925 and 1926. Helson's work on color perception and lifted weights in the 1920s and 1930s led him not only to a realization of the relationship between the previously unrelated phenomena of color contrast, color induction, and color constancy but to the formulation of the concept of adaptation level, or the changeable psychological zero point with respect to which all stimuli of the same nature are judged as being either larger or smaller, stronger or weaker, and the like. A given adaptation level is determined by three kinds of stimuli: the stimuli being actually judged, background stimuli, and residual stimuli from past experience. The value of an adaptation level is calculated by taking the geometric (weighted logarithmic) mean of these stimuli. Helson considered the adaptation-level theory as an extension of the Gestalt theory and in the 1950s expanded it to include additional, more complex phenomena that involve judgment, such as social behavior. The basic postulate of the adaptation-level theory is that to predict a person's behavior, be it psychophysical judgment, decision making in social situations, aesthetic judgment, or emotional response, that person's current adaptation level must be taken into account. The adaptation-level theory is the closest that a psychologist has ever come to formulating a quantifiable explanatory principle of behavior that applied to a considerably broad spectrum of behavioral phenomena.

Books written or edited by Helson include *Theoretical Foundations of Psychology* (1951, editor), *Adaptation-Level Theory* (1964), and *Contemporary Approaches to Psychology* (1967, coeditor).

Biographies: *Amer. J. Psychol.*, 1962, *17*, 895-898; W. Bevan, *Amer. J. Psychol.*, 1979, *92*, 153-160; J. P. Guilford, *Amer. Psychologist*, 1979, *34*, 628-630; T. S. Krawiec (Ed.), *The Psychologists*, vol. 1, 1972; V. J. Nordby & C. S. Hall, *A Guide to Psychologists and Their Concepts*, 1974; *American Men and Women of Science*, 12th ed., Physical and Biological Sciences, vol. 1; *Contemporary Authors*, Permanent Series, vol. 1, 1975; *HPA*, 5; *NYT*, 1977, Oct. 21, D 13:4; *Who's Who in America*, 1976-1977.

HELVÉTIUS, CLAUDE ADRIEN
French Philosopher
Born: Paris, January 26, 1715
Died: Voré, December 26, 1771
Education: Collège Louis-le-Grand; graduated in 1738
Positions: No official positions

Helvétius was a French materialist who followed La Mettrie* and Condillac*. He considered human motivations hedonistically and may be viewed as an early dynamic psychologist. In his works *De l'esprit* (1758) and *De l'homme* (1773), Helvétius argued that all mental processes and capabilities may be reduced to sensations and that self-interest is the origin of all action and all effect because humans are guided by the desire to avoid pain and to seek pleasure.

Biographies: Y. Belaval, In C. A. Helvètius, *Oeuvres complétes*, vol. 1, 1969, pp. v-lxxx; I. Cumming, *Helvetius: His Life and Place in the History of Educational Thought*, 1955; I. L. Horowitz, *Claude Helvetius: Philosopher of Democracy and Enlightenment*, 1954; A. Keim, *Helvétius: Sa vie et son oeuvre, d'après ses ouvrages, des écrits divers et des documents inédits*, 1907 (Reprinted 1970); D. W. Smith, *Helvetius: A Study in Persecution*, 1965; *EP*, 3; *EUI*, 27.

HENMON, VIVIAN ALLEN CHARLES
American Psychologist
Born: Centralia, Wisconsin, November 27, 1877
Died: Wichita, Kansas, January 10, 1950
Highest Degree: Ph.D. in psychology, Columbia University, 1905, under J. McK. Cattell*
Positions, Honors: 1905-7, Columbia University; 1907-11, University of Colorado; 1911-26, University of Wisconsin; 1926, Yale University; 1927-39, University of Wisconsin; 1939, Civil Aeronautics Authority; 1940-48, University of Wisconsin, 1948, professor emeritus; honorary degree, Yale University, 1927

During his first period at the University of Wisconsin, Henmon taught in the School of Education. During the second period he was in the Psychology Department and became its first chairman. Henmon's interests were varied. He did research on teacher placement, language study, aptitude testing, and other topics in educational psychology. Most of his papers (beginning with his first publication on individual differences in reaction time) and books (*The Time Perception as a Measure of Differences in Sensation*, 1906; *Achievement Tests in the Modern Foreign Languages*, 1929; *The Measurement of Intelligence*, 1937), however, are concerned with individual differences. Henmon also constructed the Henmon-Nelson Test of Mental Ability (1931).

Biographies: H. F. Harlow, *Amer. J. Psychol.*, 1950, *63*, 462-463; *Science*, 1950, *111*, 348; *PR*, 3; *Who Was Who in America*, 3.

HENNING, HANS
German Psychologist
Born: Strasbourg, February 15, 1885
Died: 1946, Danzig (?)
Highest Degree: Ph.D., University of Strasbourg, 1910
Positions: 1914-22, University of Frankfurt; 1922-44(?), Technische Hochschule, Danzig

Henning is known for his research on smell. Until 1915 the classification of smells used was that of Linnaeus*, as modified by Zwaardemaker*. Although Henning kept most of the terms used by Linnaeus, he introduced a systematic conceptual change by placing all smells on the surfaces and edges of a prism (the Henning prism) whose six corners are the fragrant, putrid, ethereal, spicy, burned, and resinous smells (*Der Geruch*, 1916). The essential features of the smell prism were subsequently verified experimentally by others. Henning also attempted to fit an organic chemistry to his prism. Although logically consistent, it, like all other attempts of this nature made after Henning, showed too many exceptions to claim that the smell stimulus had been finally identified. In a similar vein Henning proposed a solution to the classification of the four basic tastes and how they relate to each other by placing them at the vertices of a tetrahedron and locating all intermediate tastes on its surfaces and edges. As in the case of smell, Henning tried to fit a chemistry to his taste tetrahedron, with similar results.
Biographies: PR, 3.

HENRI, VICTOR
French Psychologist and Chemist
Born: Marseille, June 6, 1872
Died: La Rochelle, Charente Maritime, 1940
Highest Degree: Ph.D. in psychology, University of Göttingen, 1897, under G. E. Müller*
Positions: 1919-30, professor of chemistry, University of Zurich; 1930-40, University of Liège

Henri was the collaborator and assistant of Alfred Binet*. With Binet and Beaunis* he was a cofounder of the first French journal of experimental psychology, *L'Année psychologique* (in 1895). In the 1890s he wrote, with Binet, several papers about individual differences and a book (*La fatigue intellectuelle*, 1898), but he also did some work in the area of psychophysics (*Revue générale des travaux recents de psychophysique*, 1899). At Göttingen, working with Georg Müller, he published *Über die Raumwahrnehmungen des Tastsinnes* (1898), a classic work about the error of localization and the tactual two-point threshold. Henri turned to chemistry, however, around the turn of the century, wrote a thesis in this area in 1903, proceeded to make important contributions to chemistry, and never returned to psychology.

Biographies: H. Piéron, In various, *Centenaire de Th. Ribot et jubilé de la psychologie scientifique française*, 1939, pp. 185-196; M. Reuchlin, *Histoire de la psychologie*, 1957.

HERACLITUS
Greek Philosopher
Born: Ephesus, ca. 540 B.C.
Died: Ephesus (?), ca. 475 B.C.
Education: Unknown
Positions: Of royal lineage, teacher of philosophy

A philosopher of the Ionian school, Heraclitus postulated change as the only reality (the proposition that one cannot step into the same river twice is his) and fire (energy?) as the basic principle or primary substance. He equated the soul with fire, did not give the soul any bodily localization, but did relate it to movement. Like most Greek philosophers, he thought of existence as constant motion or even strife: "Strife is the father of all things." He can therefore be considered a primitive evolutionist. Heraclitus thought knowledge to be derived from the senses, but he also believed that only the mind was able to understand the law of change.

Biographies: DSB, 6; EB, 11; EP, 3; HGP, 1.

HERBART, JOHANN FRIEDRICH
German Philosopher and Educator
Born: Oldenburg, Lower Saxony, May 4, 1776
Died: Göttingen, August 4, 1841
Highest Degree: Ph.D. in philosophy, University of Göttingen, 1804
Positions: 1802-9, University of Göttingen; 1809-32, University of Königsberg; 1833-41, University of Göttingen

Herbart's philosophy, pedagogy, and psychology form a related whole. Having evolved a system of ideas, Herbart also evolved a system of teaching these ideas. It was based on psychological considerations. His psychological views are found in his *Lehrbuch zur Psychologie* (1816) and particularly his *Psychologie als Wissenschaft neu gegründet auf Erfahrung, Metaphysik und Mathematik* (1824-25). Herbart's psychology was based upon observation, metaphysics, and mathematics. He specifically denied that it could be experimental. Neither was it analytic (he denied the existence of mental faculties) nor physiological. It was, however, scientific in that mental processes could be described in mathematical terms. For his mathematical formulations Herbart never supplied any empirical verification, however. His contribution was to view psychology as separate from both philosophy and physics and thus to present it as an independent scientific discipline.

Herbart's basic metaphysical tenet was that the universe consists of independent, unconscious elements, the *reals*. Despite his metaphysical bent, Herbart conceptualized the mind and psychology generally in mechanistic terms. Mental states are the result of interaction of ideas. Ideas are forces, however, and combine not in the passive fashion envisioned by the British associationists but dynamically and in a much more complicated manner. Ideas differ in quality and intensity. When ideas do not resist each other, they coalesce in the way postulated by the associationists. When ideas clash or contrast, they not only may fail to associate but one idea may expel another from consciousness. Inhibited ideas do not vanish, however, but remain as tendencies. The force of existing ideas Herbart called *apperceptive mass*, a term that was in vogue for some time after its introduction and for which Herbart is best known. When this force changes, a previously inhibited idea may return to consciousness. Herbart thus postulated the notion of a threshold of consciousness and the existence of conscious and unconscious mental processes. He was therefore in one of the several lines of development of thought that led to the modern notion of inhibition in learning and the dynamics of unconscious processes. The idea of the threshold and mathematical measurement led to Fechner* and psychophysics. In spite of himself, Herbart in this way contributed to the development of experimental psychology.

Herbart's theory of the apperceptive mass had the greatest influence in educational psychology, which he may be considered to have founded. Because new ideas that enter the mind have to contend with the existing apperceptive mass, or the individual's accumulated previous experience, for learning to take place in the easiest and most efficient way new ideas must be introduced so that they are related to what is already known. Herbart's reasoning eventually led educators to adopt teaching practices by which students were led from familiar to closely related but unfamiliar materials.

Biographies: W. Asmus, *J. F. Herbart: Eine pädagogische Biographie*, 1968-69; B. Bellerate, *J. F. Herbart*, 1964; O. Flügel, *Herbarts Lehren und Leben*, 1912; T. Fritzsch, *Johann Friedrich Herbarts Leben und Lehre*, 1921; W. Kinkel, *Johann Friedrich Herbart: Sein Leben und seine Philosophie dargestellt*, 1903; G. Weiss, *Johann Friedrich Herbart: Grundriss seines Lebens*, 1926; *CE*, 6; *DSB*, 6; *EB*, 11; *EP*, 3; *EUI*, 27; *NDB*, 8.

HERDER, JOHANN GOTTFRIED
German Philosopher, Critic, and Writer
Born: Mohrungen, East Prussia, August 25, 1744
Died: Weimar, Thuringia, December 18, 1803
Education: Theological degree, University of Königsberg, 1764; ordained, 1765
Positions: 1764-69, Cathedral school, Riga; later worked as preacher; had ecclesiastic appointments in Germany

In his major treatise *Ideen zur Philosophie der Geschichte der Menschheit* (1784-91), Herder suggested ideas that were later developed by other philosophers and psychologists. He held that body and mind are inseparable (providing, incidentally, a theoretical foundation for physiognomy), and that psychology was actually "physiology at every step." Nevertheless, all of his psychological writings are based on the metaphysical concept of *Kraft* (force), which he used in a manner not unlike Heraclitus's* use of fire. The idea emerged later in the vitalistic philosophies of Schopenhauer* and Bergson*.

Herder believed in the wholeness of human individuals and the inseparability of their psychological functions, opposing the notion of psychological faculties. He also held that human nature was active rather than passive (one has a soul only to the extent that one is active), for which he is held to be an early dynamic psychologist.

Herder was one of the originators of that specifically German product ethnopsychology (*Völkerpsychologie*), which was to reach its acme in Wundt's* multivolume opus. Herder believed that each nationality, even the smallest, develops its own spirit and laws. On this assumption, Herder attempted to write a history of the human psyche as it manifests itself in the different national groups and stages of historical development. His raw materials were the languages, literary monuments, and especially the folk songs of various ethnic groups, which Herder thought afforded an insight into and empathy with the spirit of these groups. Herder was also responsible for coining the terms *Naturvölker* and *Kulturvölker* and contrasting them by ascribing innate goodness to the former, in the manner of Rousseau*. The most developed *Kulturvölker* flourished only in the temperate zone, a statement of Herder's that became very well known and was repeated by many in the years to come.

Biographies: R. T. Clark, Jr., *Herder: His Life and Thought*, 1955; A. Gillies, *Herder*, 1945; R. Haym, *Herder nach seinem Leben und seinen Werken*, 1880-1885 (Reprinted 1954); *ADB*, 12; *CE*, 6; *EJ*, 8; *EP*, 3; *EUI*, 27; *Jewish*, 5; *NDB*, 8.

HERING, EWALD
German Physiologist
Born: Altgersdorf, Saxony, August 5, 1834
Died: Leipzig, January 26, 1918
Highest Degree: M.D., University of Leipzig, 1858
Positions: 1862-65, University of Leipzig; 1865-70, Josephs-Akademie, Vienna; 1970-95, University of Prague; 1895-1918, University of Leipzig

Hering began to practice medicine in 1860 but soon was devoting more time to science. The first ten years of his scientific career Hering spent studying space perception (*Beiträge zur Physiologie: Zur Lehre vom Ortsinn der Netzhaut*, 1861-64; *Die Lehre vom binokularen Sehen*, 1868). He defended nativism in space perception, arguing that each retinal point has a local sign for height, one for right-left and one for depth. In this he found himself opposing Helmholtz* who held to the empiricist position.

In the next decade, while working on vision, Hering opposed Helmholtz in his formulation of a color-vision theory (*Zur Lehre vom Lichtsinne*, 1872-74).

Instead of recognizing Helmholtz's three kinds of fibers, pigments, and basic colors, Hering proposed that there are three visual pigments that, depending on whether they are metabolically broken down or reconstituted, produce the six opponent pairs of color—black-white, blue-yellow, and red-green. Hering's theory is still alive in the opponent-process color-vision theory of Leo Hurvich and Dorothea Jameson, constituting a viable alternative to the Young*-Helmholtz* theory.

Hering made several additional contributions to the phenomenology of visual perception. Among them are the Hering illusion (1861) and the concept of memory color or color constancy (1905). For temperature sensations Hering proposed (in 1880) a theory similar to his color-vision theory. He suggested that warm and cold are a pair of opponent qualities, fluctuating about a physiological zero point and showing other phenomena similar to those of colors.

Hering's third contribution was his invention or modification of a large number of pieces of apparatus and materials for the study of color vision, such as Hering colored papers, Hering grays, Hering window, Hering binocular color mixer, and many others. The apparatus, used in many laboratories, did much to earn the "new psychology" the nickname of "brass-instrument psychology." In spite of the brass instruments, Hering was not an experimentalist like Wundt*. His experiments were mostly phenomenological and may be assigned to that psychological tradition to which belong Goethe*, Purkinje*, Dilthey*, and many of the Gestalt psychologists.

Biographies: S. Garten, *Arch. ges. Physiol.*, 1918, *170*, 501-522; F. B. Hofmann, *Münch. med. Wochenschr.*, 1918, *65*, 539-542; L. M. Hurvich, *Amer. Psychologist*, 1969, *24*, 497-514; A. v. Tschermak-Seysenegg, *Münch. med. Wochenschr.*, 1934, *81*, 1230-1233; *Biog. Lex.*; *DSB*, 6; Hirsch, *Biog. Lex.*, 3, Suppl.; *IESS*, 6; *NDB*, 8.

HEROPHILUS

Greek Anatomist
Born: Chalcedon, Bithynia, ca. 320 B.C.
Died: Place and date unknown
Education: Studied medicine with Chrysippus and Praxagoras of Cos
Positions: Taught and practiced medicine at Alexandria

Herophilus was one of the founders of anatomy. Together with Erasistratus*, his pupil, he founded the Alexandrian school of anatomy. His many discoveries and excellent knowledge of anatomy were in no small measure owing to the freedom he had to perform human dissections. Concerning the nervous system he knew that the nerves were different from the tendons and that they were sensitive to environmental stimulation. He also divided the nerves into sensory and motor kinds. Herophilus described and named the retina. He assigned a central role to the brain in the functioning of the nervous system and believed that the brain and not the heart (according to Aristotle*) was the seat of intel-

ligence. A notion of Herophilus's that was accepted by Erasistratus and enjoyed widespread acceptance throughout antiquity was that the ventricles of the brain were containers of the vital forces.
Biographies: *DSB*, 6.

HERRICK, CHARLES JUDSON
American Physiologist
Born: Minneapolis, Minnesota, October 6, 1868
Died: Grand Rapids, Michigan, January 29, 1960
Highest Degree: Ph.D. in physiology, Columbia University, 1900
Positions: 1893-1907, Denison University; 1907-37, University of Chicago; editor, *Journal of Comparative Neurology*, 1893-1948

Herrick contributed to the understanding of the histology of the nervous system. He studied the vertebrate brain for forty years, endeavoring to relate data from physiology, psychology, and psychiatry. His principal conclusion was that the brain of the lower animals is the basis of the brain structure of all higher animals. His doctoral thesis on cranial nerves was a major contribution to the establishment of the "American school" in neurology, which considered the structure of the nervous system in terms of its function. Herrick is therefore counted as one of the University of Chicago functionalists, along with Angell* and Carr*. Herrick wrote several volumes about neurology. Of them, important to psychology are *Neurological Foundations of Animal Behavior* (1924), *Brains of Rats and Men* (1926), *The Thinking Machine* (1929), and *The Evolution of Human Nature* (1956).
Biographies: G. W. Bartelmez, *Science*, 1960, *131*, 1654-1655; E. C. Crosby, *J. Comp. Neurol.*, 1960, *115*, 3-8; C. J. Herrick, *J. Comp. Neurol.*, 1954, *100*, 717-756; C. J. Herrick, In D. G. Ingle (Ed.), *A Dozen Doctors: Autobiographical Sketches*, 1963, pp. 25-40; *J. Comp. Neurol.*, 1932, *56*, 3-8; J. L. O'Leary & G. H. Bishop, *Arch. Neurol.* 1960, *3*, 725-731; *DSB*, 6; *NCAB*, 47; *NYT*, 1960, Jan. 23, 21:4.

HESS, WALTER RUDOLF
Swiss Physiologist
Born: Frauenfeld, Thurgau, March 17, 1881
Died: Locarno, Ticino, August 12, 1973
Highest Degree: M.D., University of Zurich, 1906
Positions, Honors: 1905-13, medical practice; 1913-17, assistant in physiology, Universities of Zurich and Bonn; 1917-51, professor of physiology, University of Zurich, since 1927, director of Physiological Institute, 1951, professor emeritus; several honorary doctorates; numerous other honors; Nobel Prize in medicine and physiology, 1949

Although the electrical excitability of the brain was demonstrated in the nineteenth century, lack of development of suitable technology held back the systematic exploration of the human brain through electrode stimulation until the

1930s. A pioneer in this area was Hess. Using cats as subjects, Hess explored particularly their thalamic and hypothalamic regions, being able to elicit behaviors ranging from sleep to rage. He called the latter "affective defense reaction," but it was dubbed "sham rage" by others, because at the time it was not believed that actual emotion could be produced by mere electrical stimulation. Hess's contribution lay in developing a method for preparing animals chronically so that the effects of electrical stimulation on their brains could be studied in freely moving subjects. Observing that electrical stimulation in the diencephalon produced behaviors such as attack, fearful withdrawal, eating, and drinking, Hess theorized that the entire area was a collection of related neural mechanisms that ensured the animal's survival. The Nobel Prize was awarded to Hess for developing the electrode-implantation technique and for discovering new information about brain functions. His psychologically significant books are *Beiträge zur Physiologie des Hirnstammes* (vol. 1, 1932; vol. 2, 1938); *Die funktionelle Organisation des vegetativen Nervensystems* (1948); *Das Zwischenhirn* (1949); *Psychophysiology* (1962); and *The Biology of the Mind* (1964).
Biographies: W. H. v. Wyss, *50 Jahre Psychophysiologie in Zürich: August Forel, Eugen Bleuler, Constantin v. Monakow, Walter Hess*, 1948; *The International Who's Who*; *NYT*, 1973, Aug. 18, 28:5.

HEYMANS, GERARDUS
Dutch Psychologist
Born: Ferrwerd, Holland, April 17, 1857
Died: Groningen, Holland, February 18, 1930
Highest Degree: Ph.D. in philosophy, University of Freiburg, 1890
Positions, Honors: 1890-1926, University of Groningen; president, Eighth International Congress of Psychology, 1926

A philosophically inclined psychologist, Heymans subscribed to a philosophy of psychic monism, according to which the universe consists of one substance, consciousness, of which each individual partakes. He established the first psychological laboratory in Holland at the University of Groningen in 1893 and did some empirical research in a variety of areas: individual differences, personality, dreams, geometric illusions, and inhibition. In the area of inhibition, the law that the threshold for one stimulus is raised in direct proportion to the intensity of another, inhibitory stimulus acting upon the organism at the same time bears his name. Heymans also wrote a volume about the psychology of women (1910), the use of the concept of energy in psychology (1921), and special psychology (1929).
Biographies: H. J. F. W. Brugmans, *Gerard Heymans*, 1942; H. J. F. W. Brugmans, [*Gerard Heymans: Professor of Philosophy and Psychology in the University of Groningen from 1890 to 1927*], 1948; G. Heymans, In R. Schmidt (Ed.), *Die Philosophie der Gegenwart in Selbstdarstellungen*, vol. 3, 1922, pp. 1-52; W. Peters, *Z. pädag. Psychol.*, 1929, *30*, 305-310; *EUI*, 27; *HPA*, 2; *PR*, 3.

HIPPOCRATES
Greek Physician
Born: Island of Cos, ca. 460 B.C.
Died: Larissa, Thessaly, ca. 370 B.C.
Education: Studied with father and Herodicus of Cnidus
Positions: Taught and practiced medicine

Hippocrates, the "father of medicine," exercised a tremendous influence on the development of medicine. He was first to separate medicine from religion, magic, and superstition, using biological facts and observation to explain disease. Thus he espoused the notion that imbalance in the four bodily humors—blood, phlegm, yellow bile, and black bile—was the cause of disease.

Hippocrates placed all of man's conscious life in the brain. He included here the emotions. Too much bile, he thought, caused overheating of the brain, which led to terror and fear (because the face is flushed); too much phlegm caused overcooling, leading to anxiety and grief. Hippocrates's doctrine of the humors was later applied by Galen* to explain differences in human temperament.

Hippocrates left behind a considerable number of writings, although not all of the Hippocratic writings may be attributed directly to him. A treatise that is of importance to psychology deals with epilepsy, entitled *On the Sacred Disease*. Hippocrates denied that this disease was any more sacred than other diseases, asserted that its origin was in the brain, but related it to humoral congestion. He strongly believed in the virtue of observation and in nature's way of curing diseases. As a founder of medicine, Hippocrates may be said to have propounded one of the basic assumptions on which modern psychology rests, namely, that the functioning of the human physical body can be understood.
Biographies: *DSB*, 6; *EB*, 11; *EP*, 4.

HITZIG, EDUARD
German Psychiatrist
Born: Berlin, February 6, 1838
Died: St. Blasien, Baden, August 21, 1907
Highest Degree: M.D., University of Berlin, 1862
Positions: 1875-79, University of Zurich; 1879-1903, University of Halle

Hitzig is known for the famous experiment, performed with Gustav Fritsch*, that established the electrical excitability of the brain tissue in 1870. The prevailing doctrine had been that the brain tissue was insensitive and unexcitable. Hitzig first observed that the electrical stimulation of a patient's cortex produced eye movements. He confirmed his observations in a rabbit and then proceeded to study the phenomenon systematically, using dogs. Applying electric current to the dog's brain, Fritsch and Hitzig also established that muscular contractions were controlled by certain areas of the brain only, as well as the location of some of the more specific motor centers.
Biographies: G. Anton, *Arch. Psychiat. Nervenkr.*, 1914, *54*, 1-7; H.-H. Eulner,

Wiss. Z. Martin-Luther-Univ., 1956-57, *6*, 709-712; H. Grundfest, *J. Hist. Med.*, 1963, *18*, 125-129; A. Stender, *Deutsch. med. J.*, 1968, *19*, 335-339; R. Wollenberg, *Arch. Psychiat. Nervenkr.*, 1908, *43*, iii-xv; *Biog. Lex.*; *DSB*, 6; *Enciclopedia Italiana*, 18; *NDB*, 9.

HOBBES, THOMAS
English Philosopher
Born: Westport near Bristol, April 5, 1588
Died: Devonshire, December 4, 1679
Education: B.A., Oxford University, 1608
Positions: Private tutor

Although Hobbes's fame rests on his social philosophy, he made significant contributions to psychological thought also. Hobbes is considered to be the first in the line of British empiricists. His psychological ideas are to be found mainly in his *Humaine Nature* (1650) and *Leviathan* (1651). The latter work deals with state and government, but it is based on what Hobbes considered to be a prerequisite to the understanding of state and government, the psychology of the individual. Hobbes's treatment of the relationship between the individual and society makes him the first social psychologist of the modern era.

The seemingly pessimistic Hobbesian view of humankind that sees people governed by selfishness, lust, greed, and aggression whenever reason or the restraints placed upon them by government do not control them is counterbalanced by the implication that, in spite of the sordid passions that govern human beings, they are constantly striving to control them through the exercise of reason or governmental restraints. But even the agreement among them to institute a government is guided by selfishness, however enlightened. Their motives are based on the expectations of pleasure or pain, the most important motive being fear. The Hobbesian doctrine that human behavior is guided by self-interest came to be known as "psychological hedonism." On it Hobbes bases human social behavior and social organization.

Hobbes rejected supernaturalism and conceived of mental functions in a mechanistic fashion. Mental processes to him were motions of brain atoms, aroused by motions in the external world. He used the concept of motion even where no motion was apparent: thinking, emotions, sensations, and consciousness itself. He had found a single, materialistic explanatory principle underlying all phenomena. Materialistic and monistic, Hobbes was also an empiricist in that he held that sensations lead to all simple ideas, and simple ideas combine to form complex ideas. Basically, all cognitions are transformed sensations. Memory and imagination are slowly decaying sensations. On this matter Hobbes opposed Descartes* and Descartes's philosophy of innate ideas. Sensations he held to inhere in the perceiver, not in the object, although they are caused by the objects. Sensations are motions of the brain.

Hobbes clearly stated the principle of association of ideas in terms of temporal sequences or "trains" of thought, but he did not develop it any further. Hobbes did mention "coherence" (that is, contiguity) as a factor in association, habit and desire as guides of attention, repetition as a factor in association, and he distinguished between free and controlled association of ideas. As to emotions, Hobbes stressed the motivational aspect of passions and desires, especially the desire for power. He mentioned the fact that passions may distort reason, distinguished between innate and acquired emotions, and even outlined a theory of humor and laughter. Hobbes did not have disciples or epigones, but many of the lines of thinking that he started were soon developed more fully by the British associationists and empiricists as well as by all of those who believed that human beings were part of the natural order, both physically and psychologically.

Biographies: J. Aubrey, In O. L. Dick (Ed.), *Brief Lives*, 1957, pp. 147-159; J. Bowle, *Hobbes and His Critics*, 1951; G. Davy, *Thomas Hobbes et J.-J. Rousseau*, 1953; T. Hobbes, Vita, In *Opera latine*, vol. 1, 1961, pp. 8-21; D. G. James, *Life of Reason: Hobbes, Locke, Bolingbroke*, 1949; J. Laird, *Hobbes*, 1934; R. S. Peters, *Hobbes*, 1967; G. C. Robertson, *Hobbes*, 1886; L. Stephen, *Hobbes*, 1961; A. E. Taylor, *Hobbes*, 1908 (Reprinted 1970); *DNB*, 9; *EB*, 11; *EP*, 4; *IESS*, 6.

HOBHOUSE, LEONARD TRELAWNEY

English Sociologist

Born: St. Ives, near Liskeard, Cornwall, September 8, 1864

Died: Alençon, Normandy, France, June 21, 1929

Education: Studied at Oxford University, 1883-87

Positions, Honors: 1890-97, tutor, Corpus Christi College, Oxford University; 1897-1907, editorial and newspaper work; 1907-29, taught sociology, University of London; D. Litt., Durham University, 1913; LL.D., St. Andrews University, 1919

Most of Hobhouse's writings were in philosophy and sociology. His contribution to psychology stems from his having written, in 1901, the book *Mind in Evolution*. The reason for Hobhouse's venturing into psychology as well as other fields was that he considered sociology to be not just a discipline among others but a conceptual framework that helped to explain all social life, as well as biology and philosophy. Hobhouse's book summarized and systematized the work of Lubbock*, Romanes*, C. L. Morgan*, and other early comparative psychologists; presented Hobhouses's own animal experiments, which were similar to those later performed by Köhler with apes; and served to found the science of phylogenetic psychology. Hobhouse traced the psychological development of animals by examining the evolution of instincts, habits, and higher processes from the simplest organisms to humans. He attempted to show that the human mind and body were the product of simultaneous evolution. *Mind in Evolution* was the first comprehensive treatment of such data and problems.

Biographies: E. Barker, *Proc. Brit. Acad.*, 1929, *14*, 536-554; J. A. Hobson & M. Ginsberg, *L. T. Hobhouse: His Life and Work*, 1931; P. Weiler, *Victorian Stud.*, 1972, *16*, 141-161; *DNB*, Suppl. 4; *EB*, 11; *EP*, 4; *IESS*. 6.

HÖFFDING, HARALD
Danish Philosopher
Born: Copenhagen, March 11, 1843
Died: Copenhagen, July 2, 1931
Highest Degree: Degree in theology, University of Copenhagen, 1865; Ph.D. in philosophy, University of Copenhagen, 1870
Positions: 1871-1915, University of Copenhagen

Although Höffding was a philosopher, his psychology was one "without soul," concerned with mental phenomena and their introspective investigation. He was a determinist and maintained the identity of the mental and the material. Mental elements (feeling, cognition, will) he regarded as abstractions rather than elements in the Wundtian (Wundt*) sense. Mental life, according to Höffding, has a passive and an active side. The active aspect is the synthesizing aspect. One form of its manifestation is the law of relativity, which states that the existence and qualities of a sensation depend on its relation to other sensations from its very beginning.

Höffding wrote the first psychology text in the Danish language in 1882 (English translation, *Outlines of Psychology*, 1892). It saw many editions and was translated into many other languages.

Biographies: D. H. Fuglsang, *Dansk Teologisk Tidsskrift*, 1943, *6*, 225-237; V. Hansen, *Nordisk Tidesskrift*, 1943, *19*, 169-173; H. Höffding, In R. Schmidt (Ed.), *Die Philosophie der Gegenwart in Selbstdarstellungen*, vol. 4, 1923, pp. 75-97; E. Rindom, *Harald Höffding: Bidrag til Biografi og Karakteristik*, 1913; E. Rubin *et al.*, [*Harald Höffding in Memoriam*], 1932; K. Sandelin (Ed.), [*Harald Höffding in Memoriam*], 1932; *EP*, 4; *HPA*, 2; *PR*, 3.

HOLLINGWORTH, HARRY LEVI
American Psychologist
Born: De Witt, Nebraska, May 26, 1880
Died: Montrose, New York, September 17, 1956
Highest Degree: Ph.D. in psychology, Columbia University, 1909, under J. McK. Cattell*
Positions, honors: 1909-46, Barnard College; LL.D., University of Nebraska; president, American Psychological Association, 1927; Hollingworth Psychological Laboratories opened at Barnard College in 1954

Hollingworth contributed to psychology principally as a teacher of psychology and as a writer. He wrote twenty-five books and seventy-five papers on a wide variety of psychological topics, plus thirty-six book reviews. Hollingworth's dissertation about the inaccuracy of movement, on the basis of which he rejected a one-to-one relationship between stimulus and response and stressed the importance of the context, was considered by Koffka* as one of the cornerstones of Gestalt psychology. Although Hollingworth also engaged in applied research and many of his papers and books bear on specific applied problems (*Vocational Psychology*, 1916; *Applied Psychology*, 1917, with A. T. Poffenberger; *Voca-*

tional Psychology and Character Analysis, 1928; *Educational Psychology*, 1933), his main interest was always systematic psychology (*Outlines of Experimental Psychology*, 1913: *The Psychology of Functional Neuroses*, 1920; *The Psychology of Thought*, 1926; *Psychology, Its Facts and Principles*, 1928; *Abnormal Psychology, 1930*).

Biographies: A. Poffenberger, *Amer. J. Psychol.*, 1957, *70*, 136-140; *NCAB*, 45; *NYT*, 1956, Sept. 18, 35:2; *PR*, 3; *Who Was Who in America*, 3.

HOLLINGWORTH, LETA STETTER
American Educator and Psychologist
Born: Near Chadron, Nebraska, May 25, 1886
Died: New York, New York, November 27, 1939
Highest Degree: Ph.D. in education, Columbia Teachers College, 1916
Positions, Honors: 1916-39, Columbia Teachers College; 1935-39, executive head, Speyer school; honorary degree, Columbia University, 1938

Hollingworth's earliest work was a pioneering one in the psychology of women. She published thirteen research papers demonstrating the falsity of various male-produced hypotheses, theories, and prejudices about women. She next turned to children, summarizing her research in *The Psychology of Subnormal Children* (1920) and *Special Talents and Defects* (1923). She realized that problem children suffer not only from lower intelligence but emotional problems as well, and that emotional problems play an even greater role in adolescence. Her research on the adolescent is summarized in *The Psychology of Adolescence* (1928), which was a standard text for a number of years.

The discovery of gifted children among maladjusted ones led to her interest in gifted children. They became her focus of interest for the rest of her life. Hollingworth published seventy-five articles, of which about forty-five were concerned with giftedness. A major discovery and concern of hers was that giftedness does not preclude maladjustment (*Gifted Children*, 1926). Hollingworth became a champion of the cause of the gifted, as well as of clinical psychology, in which area she especially tried to raise the standards of test administration and of test administrators.

Biographies: A. Gates, *Science*, 1940, *91*, 9-11; H. L. Hollingworth, *Leta Stetter Hollingworth: A Biography*, 1943; A. T. Poffenberger, *Amer. J. Psychol.*, 1940, *53*, 299-301; *Notable American Women, 1607-1950*, vol. 1, 1971; *PR*, 3; *Who Was Who in America*, 1.

HOLT, EDWIN BISSELL
American Psychologist
Born: Winchester, Massachusetts, August 21, 1873
Died: Tenants Harbor, Maine, January 25, 1946
Highest Degree: Ph.D. in psychology, Harvard University, 1901, under William James*

Positions: 1901-18, Harvard University; 1926-36, visiting professor of psychology, Princeton University

Holt advocated the study of behavior, but he is not counted formally among the behaviorists. The difference between him and Watson* was that Holt believed that one should study the "specific response relations" rather than muscular responses or reflexes. It was a more philosophically based and a more sophisticated view than Watson's (*The Concept of Consciousness*, 1914). The specific response relations were those between the organism's intents or purposes and the goals toward which action was directed. To Holt responses were wholes and they had a purpose. In his most important book, *Animal Drive and the Learning Process: An Essay Toward Radical Empiricism* (1931), Holt showed that learning and memory can be considered in physical and physiological terms. The book presents, among others, the reflex circle concept, on which theories of language development were later built.

Holt's book about the Freudian wish (*The Freudian Wish and Its Place in Ethics*, 1915) is an important link in the development of dynamic psychology. He saw the Freudian wish as a concept that provided psychology with a dynamic, since the wish as a specific response relation implied purpose and psychological causality. A *wish* is a course of action that the body is set to carry out. Holt, a determinist, saw the body as always executing behavioral acts that, impelled by the past, led to a future goal. Behavior thus always has a knowing, a meaning. Holt left a strong impress on Tolman* in the latter's formulation of purposive behaviorism.

Biographies: L. Carmichael, *Amer. J. Psychol.*, 1946, *59*, 478-480; D. Katz, *Science*, 1946, *103*, 612; H. S. Langfeld, *Psychol. Rev.*, 1946, *53*, 251-258; *EP*, 4; *IESS*, 6; *NYT*, 1946, Jan. 27, 42:5; *PR*, 3; *Who Was Who in America*, 3.

HORNBOSTEL, ERICH M. VON
German Psychologist
Born: Vienna, Austria, February 25, 1877
Died: England, June 13, 1935
Highest Degree: Ph.D. in psychology, University of Berlin, 1900, under C. Stumpf*
Positions: 1902-35, University of Berlin, 1902-6, director, Phonogram Archives of the Psychological Institute

A Gestalt psychologist, Hornbostel worked with Stumpf in establishing the Berlin Phonogram Archive of records of primitive music. Eventually, he took over the direction of the archive from Stumpf. During World War I Hornbostel worked with Max Wertheimer* on the detection of submarines by sound. In 1920 he published a paper that introduced the time-theory of sound localization. In a 1925 paper Hornbostel established himself as a major spokesman for the unity of senses, asserting that certain attributes, such as intensity, are common to all senses.

Biographies: *EJ*, 8; *EUI*, 28(1); *Jewish*, 5; *NDB*, 9; *PR*, 3.

HORNEY, KAREN
German-American Psychoanalyst
Born: Hamburg, Germany, September 16, 1885
Died: New York, New York, December 4, 1952
Highest Degree: M.D., University of Berlin, 1913
Positions: 1917-32, Psychoanalytical Institute, Berlin; 1932-34, Chicago Institute for Psychoanalysis; 1934-41, New School for Social Research, New York; 1941-52, dean, American Institute of Psychoanalysis, New York

A neo-Freudian, Horney accepted some of the tenets of classical psychoanalytical theory, such as unconscious motivation and strict determinism, and rejected others, such as the primacy of biological and instinctive (sexual) factors in personality development and interpersonal relations. Horney's views resemble those of Adler* in that she stressed the role of the child's feelings of insecurity. Basic anxiety, Horney's main concept, arises from anything that disrupts the child's security. The search for security and striving for superiority and the resulting conflict between attempted patterns of behavior may lead to the development of neurotic needs. Horney described ten such needs, divided into three groups: moving toward people, moving away from people, and moving against people.

Her view of the child-parent relationship allows for greater variability than in the classical psychoanalytical theory. The relationship does not always end in an Oedipus conflict but can be modified by a number of factors pertaining to the child's environment or current fears, drives, and conflicts. The cultural context of a behavior can be crucial in that it can define the behavior as neurotic in one case and as adaptive in another. Horney was influential through her writings, especially her books, which are written in a style a nonspecialist can understand. Among them are *The Neurotic Personality of Our Time* (1936), *New Ways in Psychoanalysis* (1939), *Self-Analysis* (1942), *Our Inner Conflicts* (1945), and *Neurosis and Human Growth* (1950).

Biographies: D. E. Cameron, *Amer. J. Psychoanal.*, 1954, *14*, 19-29; H. Kelman, In K. Horney, *Feminine Psychology*, 1967, pp. 7-31; N. Kelman, *Psychoanal. Rev.*, 1953, *40*, 191-193; R. McHenry (Ed.), *Famous American Women*, 1983; J. M. Natterson, In F. Alexander *et al.* (Eds.), *Psychoanalytic Pioneers*, 1966, pp. 450-456; C. P. Oberndorf, *Int. J. Psychoanal.*, 1953, *34*, 154-155; A. N. O'Connell, *Psychol. Women Quart.*, 1980, *5*(1), 81-93; *CE*, 7; *IESS*, 6; *NYT*, 1952, Dec. 5, 27:2.

HOVLAND, CARL IVER
American Psychologist
Born: Chicago, Illinois, June 12, 1912
Died: New Haven, Connecticut, April 16, 1961
Highest Degree: Ph.D. in psychology, Yale University, 1936
Positions, Honors: 1936-61, Yale University; 1942-45, psychological research,

Washington, D.C.; American Psychological Association Distinguished Contribution Award, 1957; Warren Medal, Society of Experimental Psychologists

Hovland's early research interests led to significant discoveries in the areas of retention, rote learning, and modes of resolution of motor conflicts. He was coauthor of two psychological classics: with Clark Hull* and others, *Mathematico-Deductive Theory of Rote Learning* (1940); and with John Dollard and others, *Frustration and Aggression* (1939). Later Hovland's interests shifted to social psychology, especially communication, attitude, and, later still, concept formation. His contributions in the field of social communication make him one of the outstanding social scientists of this century. Hovland's research on communication started during World War II when he was on a government assignment to study military morale. In this four-year study Hovland, in addition to conducting laboratory experiments, used groups of soldiers to test the effects of the different variables of communication using actual war-related issues. His *Experiments on Mass Communication* (1949) was the result of this work. After his return to Yale, Hovland and his former associates continued the systematic studies of factors affecting attitude change. *Communication and Persuasion* (1953), *Order of Presentation in Persuasion* (1957), *Personality and Persuadability* (1959), *Attitude Organization and Change* (1960), and *Social Judgment* (1961), which Hovland wrote with a number of other researchers in the Yale group, were the result of this period of Hovland's scientific activity. During the last decade of his life Hovland turned to thought processes, concept formation, and computer modeling of cognitive processes. His original and systematic studies advanced attitude research from mere demonstration of changes in attitude to the prediction of such attitude changes. His theorizing related this area of social psychology to the underlying fundamentals of the higher thought processes.

Biographies: *Amer. Psychologist*, 1958, *13*, 158-167; R. R. Sears, *Amer. J. Psychol.*, 1961, *74*, 637-639; W. R. Miles, In American Philosophical Society, *Year Book 1961*, 1962, pp. 121-125; *IESS*, 6; *Who Was Who in America*, 4.

HUARTE (Y NAVARRO), JUAN

Spanish Physician and Author

Born: Saint-Jean-Pied-Port, Navarre, between 1530 and 1535

Died: Probably at Baeza, Andalusia, 1592

Education: Studied medicine, University of Huesca

Positions: Practiced medicine, various places in Spain, between 1566 and 1592, in Baeza

Huarte may be considered to have written the first text of differential psychology. The text, *Examen de los ingenios para las scienzias* (1575), saw forty printings in Spanish and was translated into several other languages (English title: *The Tryal of Wits: Discovering the Great Differences of Wits Among Men and What Sort of Learning Suits Best with Each Genius*). Huarte believed that most people are engaged in activities for which they lack the necessary ability. He recommended that tests of ability be administered and vocational counseling be conducted to ensure the best match between a person and occupation. In considering the origin of individual differences in intelligence, Huarte listed the humors, climate, brain, and many other conditions as factors. In anticipation of the view that became generally accepted through Herder's* endorsement, Huarte asserted that intelligence and therefore the higher cultures could flourish only in the moderate climatic zones. Because he attributed individual differences to bodily build, among other things, Gall* and Lavater* looked upon him as a precursor of phrenology and physiognomy, respectively.

Biographies: K. Dieckhöffer, *Z. f. klin. Psychol. u. Psychother.*, 1978, *26*, 207-214; J. A. Paniagua A., In F. Pérez-Embid (Dir.), *Enciclopedia de la cultura española*, vol. 3, 1966; *EUI*, 28.

HULL, CLARK LEONARD

American Psychologist

Born: Near Akron, New York, May 24, 1884

Died: New Haven, Connecticut, May 10, 1952

Highest Degree: Ph.D. in psychology, University of Wisconsin, 1918, under V. A. C. Henmon*

Positions, Honors: 1916-27, University of Wisconsin; 1927-29, Harvard University; 1929-52, Yale University; president, American Psychological Association, 1936

Hull's early interests in psychology were varied. He wrote *The Evolution of Concepts* (1920), *Influence of Tobacco Smoking on Mental and Motor Efficiency* (1924), *Aptitude Testing* (1928), and *Hypnosis and Suggestibility* (1933). The 1933 book is now a classic. In the 1930s Hull became convinced that psychology could be an exact natural science and that behavior could be described in precise quantitative terms. He began research on conditioning, which he went about in a strictly systematic fashion, using the hypothetico-deductive method: logical statements clad in mathematical language were made and testable hypotheses were deduced, tested empirically, and incorporated into the existing body of knowledge or revised and tested again. Hull at first limited this approach to rote learning (*Mathematico-Deductive Theory of Rote Learning: A Study in Scientific Methodology*, 1940, coauthored with five others) but soon attempted to show that an objective, quantifiable general psychology was possible (*Principles of Behavior*, 1943). Hull modified his 1943 text eight years later (*Essentials of Behavior*, 1951) and extended it to *A Behavioral System* a year before his death.

Hull's system is highly quantified and elaborate, The early formulations of the theory stressed drive reduction as the main principle of learning. Later Hull began to emphasize drive stimulus reduction and secondary reinforcement. The reinforcement theme remained strong throughout his work. The theory proved to be very productive of research, although many of the more complicated postulates and corollaries were more programmatic than psychologically factual. Although his work was confined largely to learning, Hull's aim had always been to formulate a system of psychology in which all behaviors could be rigorously

predicted. Hull provided much of the intellectual stimulus to a group of colleagues at Yale's Institute for Human Relations (John Dollard, Neal Miller, Hobart Mowrer*, and Robert Sears, among others). During his stay at Yale, Hull also put his stamp on his students, so for a time one could speak of a Hullian school of psychology, at least in learning.
Biographies: C. I. Hovland, *Psychol. Rev.*, 1952, *59*, 347-350; K. W. Spence, *Amer. J. Psychol.*, 1952, *65*, 639-646; *Biog. Mem.*, 33; *HPA*, 4; *IESS*, 6; *NCAB*, 41; *NYT*, 1952, May 11, 92:3.

HUMBOLDT, WILHELM VON
German Philosopher
Born: Potsdam, Brandenburg, June 22, 1767
Died: Tegel, near Berlin, April 8, 1835
Education: Studied law, other areas, at the University of Frankfurt and University of Göttingen
Positions: No official positions; active in political life

Humboldt was one of the forerunners of social psychology. To designate the approach to social psychology that he was using, and that was typical of most later German social psychologists, Humboldt coined the term *Völkerpsychologie*, or ethnopsychology. His work was in the area of comparative linguistics, where his emphasis was on how to understand different peoples. He was first to make the explicit statement that language expresses the psychic reality of the speaker and that differences in languages parallel differences in their speakers. Humboldt asserted that the point where language originated historically was the point where nature and idea became connected. To him language was a uniquely human characteristic. The central concept in Humboldt's theory was the "inner form" of language, or the profoundly rooted subjective view of the world. The speaker of a language views the world through his language; it serves not only to reflect truth but to discover truth. Heyman Steinthal* in the nineteenth century and Benjamin Whorf and Edward Sapir* in the twentieth century developed very similar lines of thought. As a philosopher of history, Humboldt also influenced Wilhelm Dilthey* through his idea of historical experience, or the development of empathy and understanding through the study of history.
Biographies: M. Cowan, In *Humanist without Portfolio*, 1963, pp. 1-25; A. Dove, In T. Sebeck (Ed.), *Portraits of Linguists*, vol. 1, 1967, pp. 71-101; R. Haym, *Wilhelm von Humboldt: Lebensbild und Charakteristik*, 1856; *ADB*, 13, 37; *EP*, 4; *EUI*, 28(1).

HUME, DAVID
Scottish Philosopher
Born: Edinburgh, May 7, 1711
Died: Edinburgh, August 25, 1776
Education: Entered University of Edinburgh in 1723, no degree
Positions: Irregularly employed as tutor, librarian, in diplomatic service

Hume was one of the great English philosophers-empiricists and a representative of the school of associationism. He never occupied an academic post but gained fame as a philosophic writer. He may be considered Berkeley's* philosophical successor in that he carried Berkeley's idealistic position a step further toward its ultimate extreme. Of importance to psychology are Hume's *Treatise of Human Nature* (1739-40) and *An Enquiry Concerning Human Understanding* (1748), a revision of the first essay.

Hume tackled the question of cause and effect, which theretofore had been assumed to be a universal principle presenting no particular problem. He realized that although things may follow each other in a predictable sequence, the necessary connection between them cannot ever be observed. Yet although we never have a percept of a cause, we all believe that there is such a thing. Hume then set out to establish what there is in human nature that makes humans think in terms of cause and effect. In the *Treatise* Hume showed that some things that were previously thought of as belonging to the universe are in fact a function of human psychological makeup. All information is derived from experience. Sensing, feeling, and willing leave impressions as the first mental contents. When the sensory object is gone, impressions become ideas. The clear distinction between sense impressions and ideas was a major contribution of Hume to psychology. The main distinction between them is, according to Hume, in their degree of vividness, ideas being relatively faint.

When two objects occur together repeatedly, the appearance of one object later will evoke the idea of the missing object through association. This is the basis for the belief that the world continues even though there are no direct sense impressions at the moment. It is also the basis for the belief in a continuing self. Memory and imagination are only two ways in which ideas work. The principles that the association of ideas obeys are similarity, contiguity, and causality. Later Hume reduced causality to a special case of similarity and contiguity. The idea of causality arises because we may experience events together repeatedly. Thus causality is a mental habit that arises from experience and not an innate idea or law of thought. In fact, Hume explained all human experiences as habits. The soul was reduced by Hume to impressions and ideas. The mind became nothing but a congeries of sensations.

Hume was a most important link in the development of psychological thought from empiricism to modern learning theory by way of associationism. His other contribution to psychology was his "very curious discovery" that the idea of causality was an acquired habit of thought. Philosophers and psychologists of later generations, especially those concerned with the philosophy of science and the logic of scientific inquiry, have had to contend with it in one way or another. *Biographies*: A. H. Basson, *David Hume*, 1958; J. H. Burton, *Life and Correspondence of David Hume*, 2 vols., 1846-1850; J. Y. T. Greig, *David Hume*, 1931 (Reprinted 1970); F. H. Heinemann, *David Hume* . . . , 1940; D. Hume,

My own life, In T. H. Greem & T. H. Grose (Eds.), *The Philosophical Works of David Hume*, vol. 1, 1964, pp. xvii-xxiv; E. C. Mossner, *The Life of David Hume*, 1954 (Reprinted 1971); T. E. Ritchie, *Account of the Life and Writings of David Hume*, 1807; *DNB*, 28; *DSB*, 6; *EB*, 11; *EP*, 4; *IESS*, 6.

HUMPHREY, GEORGE
English Psychologist
Born: Boughton, Kent, July 17, 1889
Died: Cambridge, April 24, 1966
Highest Degree: Ph.D. in psychology, Harvard University, 1920
Positions: 1920-24, Wesleyan University; 1924-47, Queen's University, Kingston, Ontario; 1947-56, Oxford University, since 1948, director of Institute of Experimental Psychology; president, Canadian Psychological Association, 1942-44

Humphrey did not leave many experimental papers, but some are well known, for instance, one about inhibition. He did experimental work on conditioning, reinforcement, audiogenic seizures, and apparent motion, but his main effort was in the area of thinking. Humphrey at first tried to explain Freudian mechanisms and social psychological phenomena in terms of conditioning but then began to doubt the universality of application of conditioning principles and gravitated toward the Gestalt viewpoint. In his best-known book, *The Nature of Learning* (1933), Humphrey proposed that the organism is a system with a particular kind of organization, that the same learning principles underlie the different types of learning, and that learning means achieving homeostatic equilibrium between an organismic system and its environment. Humphrey took up the problem of thinking in additional works, such as *Directed Thinking* (1948). One-half of the book *Thinking: An Introduction to Experimental Psychology* (1951), written while Humphrey was the first occupant of a psychology chair at Oxford, is the first complete description in English of the work of the Würzburg school of imageless thought.
Biographies: M. Argyle & R. C. Oldfield, *Bull. Brit. Psychol. Soc.*, 1966, *19*(63), 35-37; F. C. Bartlett, *Amer. J. Psychol.*, 1966, *79*, 657-658; J. Blackburn, *Canad. J. Psychol.*, 1957, *11*, 141-150; O. L. Zangwill, *Quart. J. Exp. Psychol.*, 1966, *18*, 280; *PR*, 3.

HUNTER, WALTER SAMUEL
American Psychologist
Born: Decatur, Illinois, March 22, 1880
Died: Providence, Rhode Island, August 3, 1954
Highest Degree: Ph.D. in psychology, University of Chicago, 1912, under J.R. Angell*
Positions: 1912-16, University of Texas; 1916-25, University of Kansas; 1925-36, Clark University; 1936-54, Brown University; during both World Wars,

involved in army testing and related work, for which he received the President's Medal of Merit; president, American Psychological Association, 1931; editorial work, *Comparative Psychology Monographs, Psychological Index*, and *Psychological Abstracts*

Hunter was a behaviorist who investigated representational processes in animals. For this purpose he invented the delayed reaction test for animals: food was placed in one of several boxes in plain sight of the animal but with access allowed to the boxes only after a period of time. Phylogenetic differences in the toleration of delay become apparent in this test. Hunter did the delayed-reaction test work for his doctoral dissertation; it was published in 1913, establishing him immediately as an investigator of note. In 1920 Hunter invented the temporal maze, which requires double or triple alteration of responses. This device shows phylogenetic differences in animals in their ability to "count" to two or three. In the same year Hunter engaged in a polemic concerning behaviorism, penning several papers in the process. He suggested the use of the word *anthroponomy* as a synonym for behaviorism instead of *psychology*, to avoid its many mentalistic connotations. Hunter wrote many papers about animal behavior and other psychological subjects, as well as two introductory texts (*General Psychology*, 1919; *Human Behavior*, 1928).

Biographies: L. Carmichael, *Amer. J. Psychol.*, 1954, *67*, 732-734; J. McV. Hunt, *Psychol. Rev.*, 1956, *63*, 213-217; H. Schlosberg, *Science*, 1954, *120*, 441-442; *Biog. Mem.*, 31; *HPA*, 4; *IESS*, 7; *NCAB*, 42; *NYT*, 1954, Aug. 5, 23:6; *Who Was Who in America*, 3; *Yearb. Amer. Phil. Soc.*, 1954.

HUSSERL, EDMUND
German Philosopher
Born: Prossnitz, Moravia, April 8, 1859
Died: Freiburg-im-Breisgau, Baden-Württemberg, April 26, 1938
Highest Degree: Ph.D. in mathematics, University of Berlin, 1881
Positions: 1887-1901, University of Halle; 1901-16, University of Göttingen; 1916-28, University of Freiburg; editor, *Jahrbuch für Philosophie und phäno-menologische Forschung*, 1913-30

After studying philosophy under Franz Brentano* at the University of Vienna (1884-86), Husserl abandoned mathematics and turned to philosophy. Eventually, he brought about a radical change on the German philosophical scene by synthesizing in his phenomenology both the subjective and the objective viewpoints in philosophy. Since the philosophically oriented psychologist is constantly aware of the objective-subjective or inside-outside problem, Husserl's philosophy influenced psychologists, especially because he began to write at a time when dissatisfaction with one form of phenomenological research, introspection, was beginning to find resolution in Wertheimer's* Gestaltist phenomenology and Watson's* behaviorism (*Logische Untersuchungen*, 1900-1901; *Ideen zu einer reinen Phänomenologie und phänomenologische Philosophie*, 1913).

In psychology the term *phenomenology* was borrowed from Husserl. It means the description of immediate experience while keeping scientific biases at the lowest possible level. Husserl's phenomenology owes much to Brentano, such as his use of Brentano's intentionality concept, although with an altered content. According to Husserl, mind can intuit what is not part of mind itself. From the data within it consciousness synthesizes a meaningful universe. The objective universe is the ideal limit of the process of objectification. This transcendental productivity of consciousness works from inside out, instead of allowing objectivity to produce a view of the world from outside in, in a passive individual. Phenomenological observation of subjective experiences is the key to the understanding of being.

The phenomenological approach flourished in the Gestalt school of psychology. After the dominance period of the learning theories, Husserl experienced a revival in psychology, especially among the so-called third-force, or humanistic, psychologists.

Biographies: A. D. Osborn, *Edmund Husserl and His Logical Investigations*, 1949; *CE*, 7; *EP*, 4; *EUI*, 28(1); *IESS*, 7; *Jewish*, 5; *NYT*, 1938, Apr. 29, 21:2.

HUXLEY, THOMAS HENRY

English Biologist, Lecturer, Educator, and Essayist
Born: Ealing, Middlesex, May 4, 1825
Died: Eastbourne, Sussex, June 29, 1895
Highest Degree: M.D., Charing Cross Hospital, 1845
Positions, Honors: 1846-54, various medical appointments with the Royal Navy; 1854-92, taught natural sciences, Royal School of Mines, London; from 1870, numerous appointments on government commissions, boards; 1872-74, rector, University of Aberdeen; seven honorary degrees

To psychology Huxley's significance is in his advocacy and defense of Charles Darwin's* evolutionary theory. Immediately recognizing its value when it was published in 1859, he very ably defended it against the attack by Bishop Wilberforce at a famous meeting of the British Association for the Advancement of Science in Oxford a year later. The energetic defense of Darwin earned him the nickname "Darwin's bulldog." Through his writings and lectures Huxley continued to defend science and the evolutionary theory and to fight obscuritanism. Although he was an agnostic he asserted the certainty of determinism, albeit as an unprovable assumption necessary for science. The term *agnosticism* was coined by Huxley. To him it meant that the ultimate reality is unknowable and that speculation about it is useless. It also meant that one should not make statements and assert them to be true without being able to produce empirical evidence for them. His agnosticism hence rejected both materialistic and idealistic monism as unprovable, although Huxley accepted the use of materialistic language for scientific purposes. Huxley regarded animal and human bodies as mechanical systems. States of consciousness were real enough to him but only as effects of bodily processes. Although Huxley admitted that this was a definite epiphenomenalistic view of the body-mind relationship, he asserted that he actually knew nothing and could not hope to know anything.

Biographies: T. H. Huxley, Autobiography, In *Collected Essays*, vol. 1, 1970, pp. 1-17; A. Ashforth, *Thomas Henry Huxley*, 1969; H. C. Bibby, *Huxley, T.H.: Scientist, Humanist, and Educator*, 1959; H. C. Bibby, *Scientist Extraordinary: The Life and Scientific Works of Thomas Henry Huxley*, 1972; E. Clodd, *Thomas Henry Huxley*, 1905; L. Huxley, *Life and Letters of Thomas Henry Huxley*, 1903; W. Irvine, *Apes, Angels, and Victorians* . . . , 1955; W. Irvine, *Thomas Henry Huxley*, 1960; P. C. Mitchell, *Thomas Henry Huxley*, 1906; H. Peterson, *Huxley: Prophet of Science*; *DNB*, Suppl. 1; *DSB*, 6; *EP*, 4; *NYT*, 1895, June 30, 16:4.

HUYGENS, CHRISTIAN
Dutch Astronomer and Mathematician
Born: The Hague, April 14, 1629
Died: The Hague, June 8, 1695
Education: 1645-47, studied law and mathematics at the University of Leiden; 1647-49, studied law at Collegium Arausiacum, Breda
Positions: Supported by family until 1666; 1666-81, Académie Royale des Sciences, Paris; 1681-94, supported by income from family property

Huygens's main achievement was the formulation of the wave theory of light, but he contributed many other important new discoveries and inventions in the areas of astronomy, mathematics, mechanics, and optics. To psychology Huygens is important for two reasons: he invented the pendulum clock in 1656 and wrote, in 1657, the first systematic treatise on probability theory *Tractatus de ratiociniis in aleae ludo*). The treatise remained the only such work until the eighteenth century. Although Huygens was not very original, his work related all that was then known about probability and included a number of problems and exercises.

The pendulum clock allowed precise time measurements for the first time. This was important to astronomy, and problems concerning time measurement in astronomy led directly to the reaction time experiment in psychology in the nineteenth century (see Bessel*, Donders*, Wundt*).

Biographies: A. E. Bell, *Christian Huygens and the Development of Science in the Seventeenth Century*, 1950; D. E. Newbold, In D. W. Hutchings (Ed.), *Late Seventeenth Century Scientists*, 1969, pp. 107-131; Various, In C. Huygens, *Oeuvres complètes*, vol. 22, 1950, pp. 385-771; *ADB*, 13; *CE*, 7; *DSB*, 6; *EUI*, 28(1).

I

ITARD, JEAN (MARIE-GASPARD)
French Physician
Born: Oraison, Basses Alpes, April 24, 1775
Died: Paris, July 5, 1838
Education: Acquired medical knowledge through practice
Positions: 1800-1838, National Institute for Deaf-Mutes, Paris

Itard pioneered in the systematic study of mental deficiency when he undertook to train the "wild boy of Aveyron" (Victor) in 1801. The boy had been found in the woods. He was brought eventually to Itard to see if he could be civilized. The interest shown in the boy was owing to the then-current theory of the "noble savage" (Rousseau*) and the question of the relationship between humans and animals. Itard worked with Victor for five years, using testing techniques such as having him obtain food that was out of reach and delayed reaction, found useful by psychologists more than a century later. Influenced by Condillac*, Itard laid great stress on sensory training. Itard described his work and the progress made with Victor in two reports to the minister of the interior, dated 1801 and 1806. Basically, Itard established the methodology and principles of the reeducation of mental retardates that are in use today. They focus on the individual; are directed toward the development of the senses, the intellect, and affect; are adjusted to the developmental level of the individual; and involve the use of instructional aids.

His work with the wild boy of Aveyron led Itard to work with deaf-mutes. In 1807 and 1808 he reported on successful experiments in the training of deaf-mutes to communicate orally. In his *Traité des maladies de l'ouíe et de l'audition*

(1821), Itard made, for the first time, the differentiation between the diseases of the ear and hearing disorders. In addition to the two reports about the wild boy of Aveyron, this book is Itard's best-known work. In this and other works by Itard may be found the principles upon which rests today's oral education of the deaf-mutes.

Biographies: J. B. E. Bousquet, *Éloge historique de Itard*, 1839; M. L. Groff, *Psychol. clin.*, 1932, *20*, 246-256; H. H. Hunsicker, *Medical Record*, 1934, *140*, 682-684; L. Kanner, *Amer. J. Ment. Defic.*, 1960, *65*, 1-10; E. Morel, *Amer. Ann. Deaf*, 1853, *5*, 110-124; R. Shattuck, *The Forbidden Experiment: The Story of the Wild Boy of Aveyron*, 1980; R. M. Silberstein & H. Irwin, *J. Amer. Acad. Child Psychiat.*, 1962, *1*, 314-322; *EUI*, 28(2); Hirsch., *Biog. Lex.*, 3.

J

JACKSON, JOHN HUGHLINGS

English Neurologist
Born: Green Hammerton, Yorkshire, April 4, 1835
Died: London, October 7, 1911
Highest Degree: M.D., St. Andrews, 1860
Positions: From 1856, various hospital and medical appointments

Jackson was trained by Brown-Séquard* and took his scientific philosophy from Herbert Spencer*. He is known for his studies of epilepsy, aphasia, and paralysis. Jackson gave the classic descriptions of focal or hemiplegic epilepsy (*Jacksonian epilepsy*), relating cortical sites to movements in epilepsy. He identified sites of motor action, sensation, and language in the cortex and was first to demonstrate the use of the ophthalmoscope, invented by Helmholtz*, in the study of disorders of the nervous system.

Jackson conceived of a hierarchical relationship between nerve centers. Those that evolved later (higher centers) subserve more complex functions than those that evolved earlier (lower centers). Neurological disorders affect the higher nervous centers first and only then the lower centers (Jackson's law). *Dissolution* (Spencer's term), in contrast to evolution, characterizes nervous disease.

Because much of Jackson's work was advanced for his time, he laid the groundwork for future brain investigations. His doctrine of evolutionary levels in the brain and psychological functioning had a definite effect on physiological psychology, one of which was a deemphasis on exact localization of brain functions and a stress on evolutionary levels in the brain and the complexity of the functions involved.

Biographies: McD. Critchley, *Proc. Roy. Soc. Med.*, 1960, *53*, 613-618; *Lancet*, 1911, No. 2, 1103-1107; A. M. Lassek, *The Unique Legacy of Doctor Hughlings Jackson*, 1970; J. Taylor, In H. J. Jackson, *Neurological Fragments*, 1925, p. 1026; *DNB*, Suppl. 1; *DSB*, 7.

JAENSCH, ERICH RUDOLF
German Psychologist
Born: Breslau, Silesia, February 26, 1883
Died: Marburg, Hesse, January 12, 1940
Highest Degree: Ph.D. in psychology, University of Göttingen, 1908, under G. E. Müller*
Positions, Honors: 1908-10, University of Göttingen; 1913-40, University of Marburg; president, German Psychological Society, 1936-40

Jaensch's doctoral dissertation on visual perception already had a strong phenomenological component (*Zur Analyse der Gesichtswahrnehmungen*, 1909). Its topic was vision at short and long distances. Jaensch showed that visual acuity depends not only on the texture of the retina but also on additional, larger interacting systems. Jaensch discussed spatial vision in another monograph published two years later (*Über die Wahrnehmung des Raumes*, 1911). It concerned the phenomenology of empty space and the perception of size in space. Later, Jaensch contributed still another volume about perception, *Über den Aufbau der Wahrnehmungswelt* (1923). During his career Jaensch published 269 articles and monographs about perception, especially visual perception.

Jaensch is best known for his work on eidetic imagery. He published a book about this topic (*Die Eidetiker*, 1925; English translation, *Eidetic Imagery*, 1930) and some thirty articles. Jaensch distinguished two human types, the B-type (later called the integrate type) and the T-type (later called the distintegrate type). The former was characterized by good eidetic ability that was under voluntary control and was caused by a hyperactive thyroid gland; the latter, by afterimages not under voluntary control and caused by hypoactivity of the parathyroid. The descriptions of each type were later adjusted by Jaensch to suit the National-Socialist ideology (*Zur Eidetik und Integrationspsychologie*, 1941) and thus lost their value to science.

Biographies: G. H. Fischer, *Z. Psychol.*, 1940, *148*, 19-90; W. Wirth, *Arch. ges. Psychol.*, 1940, *106*, i-xl; F. Wyatt & H.-L. Teuber, *Psychol. Rev.*, 1944, *51*, 229-247; *CE*, 7; *IESS*, 8; *PR*, 3.

JAENSCH, WALTER
German Psychiatrist
Born: Breslau (now Wroclaw), Silesia, May 5, 1889
Died: Place and date unknown
Highest Degree: M.D., University of Marburg, 1919
Positions: 1918-21, University of Marburg; 1922-27, University of Frankfurt; 1928-?, University of Berlin

Walter Jaensch, brother of Erich Rudolf Jaensch*, collaborated with the latter in his pioneer work on eidetic imagery. As a result he published several papers in this area. Jaensch's main interest was, however, in the constitutional theory of personality. Most of his papers are in this area, as well as several books, such as *Grundzüge einer Physiologie und Klinik der psychophysischen Persönlichkeit* (1926) and *Klinische Rassenhygiene und Eugenik* (1934). In the latter and other works Jaensch attempted to relate skin capillary characteristics to personality types.
Biographies: PR, 3.

JAMES, WILLIAM
American Philosopher and Psychologist
Born: New York, New York, January 11, 1842
Died: Chocorua, New Hampshire, August 26, 1910
Highest Degree: M.D., Harvard University, 1868
Positions: 1872-1907, taught physiology, then psychology, followed by philosophy, Harvard University; president, American Psychological Association, 1894 and 1904

James is still considered by many to be America's foremost psychologist. James achieved this distinction without founding a school, without formulating a comprehensive psychological theory, without performing any notable experiments, and without having his students, of which he had very few, perform them. James's contributions were several; they were all significant and to a considerable extent continue to be significant.

Early in his career at Harvard James established a psychological laboratory to give demonstrations. It was in the same year, 1875, that Wundt* established his laboratory at Leipzig. Although James recognized the importance of experimentation, he was not an experimentalist by nature and did little experimental work of his own. The historic significance of the founding of the laboratory was great, however, in that it signaled the introduction of the ''new'' psychology in the United States.

In 1890 James published his *Principles of Psychology*. His influence on psychology and psychologists occurred mainly through his *Principles* as well as through his personal contacts and lectures. In one case the important factor was James's literary style, in the other his personality. The main distinction of James's book was not its originality (although many of James's ideas were original) or exhaustive treatment but a style of writing that even today brings James as an individual close to the reader. In 1892 an abridged textbook version of *Principles* appeared that was used as a university text for many years.

James's psychological views lack systematicity, which may be explained by his conviction that psychology in its incipient stage did not need definitive conclusions as much as it needed suggestions and inspiration for the future. The term *stream of consciousness* is of James's coinage. He contrasted this view of the nature of consciousness with that of Wundt and the structuralists who thought of it as consisting of discrete elements. James was thus supporting the new psychology in his book by presenting its findings, but he also criticized it by reinterpreting these findings in the light of his own view of the human psyche. James saw consciousness as continuous, personal, selective, constantly changing, and different from the objects of consciousness. Concerning association and memory, James held that they are physiological processes in the nervous system. What is associated is not ideas but physiological processes. Although granting that Hartley* had adequately described the process of association, James nevertheless did not think that it explained everything about the human mind and felt the need to assume the existence of inborn capacities of the mind to order reality. Habit was likewise treated by James as a phenomenon of the nervous system. Concerning emotion, James reversed the customary notion that emotion causes behavior. "We are afraid because we run" is a summary statement of what became known as the James-Lange theory of emotion, since Carl Lange* came to similar conclusions about the same time as did James. It is the only specific psychological theory of James that ever became famous. It produced much controversy and research. Although incomplete, the Jamesian theory in various modified forms is still current.

In the 1890s James thought and wrote in a more philosophical vein. Thanks to his writings that appeared in the next decade (*Pragmatism*, 1907; *The Meaning of Truth*, 1909), pragmatism as a philosophical theory became important, and James himself gained the distinction of being considered America's most outstanding philosopher. The doctrine of pragmatism, that beliefs are true because they work instead of the other way around, was germane to what later became known as the functionalist school of psychology in America, which stressed the adaptive functions of behavior. James himself stressed that the primary function of mind is the acquisition of knowledge. James's psychology of knowledge and its use made him a precursor of the functionalist school that flourished in America in the 1920s and 1930s. James sought to advance pragmatism as a solution to the recurring struggle between the rationalists and the empiricists. In the process of doing so, James labeled the monistic rationalists "tender-minded" and the pluralistic empiricists "tough-minded," terms that are a current coin of the psychological realm today. James himself advanced a monism that held the distinction between subject and object, between knowing and that which is known to be false. He proposed a radical empiricism to eliminate the subject-object dualism.

James wrote two additional books around the turn of the century, *Talks to Teachers* (1899) and *Varieties of Religious Experience* (1902). Both arose from his university lectures. The first reflects his pragmatic bent in that it is intended to bring psychology into the classroom by showing how psychology can be applied to everyday problems. The second book is a classic in the field of the psychology of religion. While showing that many religious experiences are correlated with psychopathology, James also asserted that mental stability was not a criterion of the value of religious experience.

Biographies: G. W. Allen, *William James: A Biography*, 1967; J. R. Angell, *Psychol. Rev.*, 1911, *18*, 78-82; B. P. Brennan, *William James*, 1968; E. Claparède, *Arch. psychol.*, 1910-1911, *10*, 96-105; E. C. Moore, *William James*, 1965; L. Morris, *William James: The Message of a Modern Mind*, 1950; *DAB*, 9; *DSB*, 7; *EB*, 12; *EP*, 4; *IESS*, 8; *NCAB*, 18, 31; *NYT*, 1910, Aug. 27, 7:5.

JANET, PIERRE
French Psychologist
Born: Paris, May 30, 1859
Died: Paris, February 24, 1947
Highest Degree: Docteur des lettres, University of Paris, 1889; M.D., University of Paris, 1893
Positions, Honors: 1890-94, La Salpêtrière Hospital, Paris; 1895-1920, Sorbonne; 1920-36, Collège de France; general secretary, Fourth International Congress of Psychology; honorary president, Eleventh International Congress of Psychology, 1937; three honorary doctorates

Janet was a systematic psychopathologist. He came to the attention of Charcot* through his interest in and report on the case of Léonie, a patient who could be hypnotized from a distance. Although Janet worked in Charcot's laboratory and Charcot was concerned with the neural bases of pathology, Janet thought of hysteria as a mental disorder. He developed a system of psychology and psychopathology that he called *psychologie de la conduite*. He attempted to systematize the existing knowledge about hysteria and to relate clinical and academic psychology to it. His major efforts in this direction were *L'État mental des hystériques* (1892; English translation, *Mental States of Hystericals*, 1893) and *The Major Symptoms of Hysteria* (1907; English translation 1924).

Janet saw hysteria as a disorder characterized by exaggerated suggestibility, faulty memory, and fixed ideas. Hysteric patients have a weakness. Fluctuations in psychic energy determine mental health and disease. "Lowered mental tension" means insufficient energy mobilized to cope with obstacles, leading to neurosis. Decrease in psychic energy was a central concept in Janet's explanations of mental disorders. To Janet a healthy personality was one that had a stable, integrated system of ideas and emotions, the cardinal property of mind being its ability to integrate. Hysterical personalities lack integration. In extreme cases a dissociation of the mind into conscious and unconscious portions occurs and multiple personalities may result. The hysteric experiences a narrowing of consciousness as unacceptable mental contents are driven out of it. These contents are converted into symbolic symptoms, however. This view bore considerable resemblance to that of Sigmund Freud's*, and a controversy arose between Janet and Freud concerning priority in the use of the concept of the unconscious.

Janet wrote fifteen additional books, some of which have been also translated into English (*Principles of Psychotherapy*, 1924; *Psychological Healing*, 1925), and many articles, a total of about ninety titles. Many of the articles appeared in *Journal de psychologie*, founded by Janet in collaboration with Georges Dumas* in 1904 and of which Janet was the editor until 1937.

Biographies: M. Culpin, *Nature*, 1947, *159*, 357-364; J. Delay, In K. Kolle (Ed.), *Grosse Nervenärzte*, vol. 3, 1953, pp. 77-85; H. F. Ellenberger, *Dialogue*, 1973, *12*, 254-287; H. Ey, In B. B. Wolman (Ed.), *Historical Roots of Contemporary Psychology*, 1968, pp. 177-195; E. R. Guthrie, *Psychol. Rev.*, 1948, *55*, 65-66; L. L. Havens, *J. Nerv. Ment. Dis.*, 1966, *143*, 383-398; R. Le Senne, *Notice sur la vie et les travaux de Pierre Janet*, 1953; I. Meyerson, *J. psychol. norm. path.*, 1946, *39*, 385-386; H. Pichon-Janet, *Évol. psychiat.*, 1950, (3), 345-355; W. S. Taylor, *Amer. J. Psychol.*, 1947, *60*, 637-645; R. M. Yerkes, *Yearb. Amer. Phil. Soc.*, 1947, 253-258; *CE*, 7; *EB*, 12; *IESS*, 8; *HPA*, 1; *PR*, 3.

JASTROW, JOSEPH

American Psychologist

Born: Warsaw, Poland, January 30, 1863

Died: Stockbridge, Massachusetts, January 8, 1944

Highest Degree: Ph.D. in psychology, Johns Hopkins University, 1886, under G. S. Hall*

Positions, Honors: 1888-1927, University of Wisconsin; 1927-33, New School for Social Research, New York City; president, American Psychological Association, 1900

Jastrow's was the first American doctorate taken specifically in psychology. His early work was in psychophysics. An important paper, written with C. S. Peirce* in 1884, anticipated the work of Fullerton* and Cattell* concerning the substitution of the probable error for the ordinary threshold measure and hence fixing the difference threshold at the point where discrimination is made 75 percent instead of 50 percent of the time. After this Jastrow published numerous papers on a variety of topics in general psychology, in line with his nonadherence to any school, eclectically borrowing the best from all of them. At Wisconsin Jastrow began publishing a series of "minor studies," a custom soon emulated by psychologists elsewhere. His own series numbered twenty-five studies. They resulted from his and his students' work in the experimental psychology laboratory that Jastrow established at Wisconsin in 1888.

Jastrow is best known as a popularizer of the "new" psychology. In 1895 he arranged an exhibit of psychology at the Chicago World's Fair, which aroused popular interest in psychology. He wrote a column, "Keeping Mentally Fit," which was syndicated in many newspapers, and gave daily broadcasts under the same name. He was skilled in presenting scientific psychology, both orally and in writing, in a way that appealed to the general public. Of his many books, such as *Fact and Fable in Psychology* (1900), *The Subconscious* (1906), *Psychology of Conviction* (1918), *Keeping Mentally Fit* (1928), *The House That Freud Built* (1932), and *The Betrayal of Intelligence* (1938), his *Fact and Fable* was the most popular. In this book and in its later rewritten version, *Wish and*

Wisdom (1935), Jastrow dealt with anomalous behavior and experience, referring them all to scientific psychological knowledge. The central theme of *Wish and Wisdom* was that wishing interferes with rationality and leads to propensities such as credulity and forcing facts to follow belief.

Biographies: V. A. C. Henmon, *Science*, 1944, *99*, 193; C. L. Hull, *Amer. J. Psychol.*, 1944, *57*, 581-585; W. B. Pillsbury, *Psychol. Rev.*, 1944, *51*, 261-265; *EUI*, 28(2); *HPA*, 1; *Jewish*, 6; *NCAB*, 11; *NYT*, 1944, Jan. 9, 43:1; *PR*, 3; *Who Was Who in America*, 2.

JENNINGS, HERBERT SPENCER

American Biologist
Born: Tonica, Illinois, April 8, 1868
Died: Santa Monica, California, April 14, 1947
Highest Degree: Ph.D. in zoology, Harvard University, 1896
Positions: 1897-98, Manhattan State College; 1898-1900, Dartmouth College; 1900-1903, University of Michigan; 1903-6, University of Pennsylvania; 1907-37, professor of experimental zoology, Johns Hopkins University, since 1910, director of zoological laboratory; president, American Zoological Society (1908), American Society of Naturalists (1910)

Jennings is noted for his work on the physiology of micro-organisms, genetics, and animal behavior. Jennings believed that the behavior of organisms on even the lowest level of the phylogenetic scale could not be explained entirely in mechanistic terms. He studied the behavior of protozoans and found it to be too adaptable to warrant the view that only simple chemical and physiological reactions were involved. In contrast to the view of Loeb* and others, Jennings proposed that modifiable behavior implies consciousness, because the function of consciousness is adaptation. Jennings objected to Loeb's explanation of animal behavior in terms of tropisms. He thought they were artifactual collections of certain selected behaviors only and that other significant behaviors had been omitted. Jennings insisted that "the organism responds as a whole, by a reaction involving all parts of the body." To study animal behavior Jennings proposed as a guiding principle the study of an animal's actions system, "the characteristic set of movements by which its behavior under all sorts of conditions is brought about." His important volume, *Behavior of the Lower Organisms* (1906), supported those who believed animal life meant consciousness. Jennings did not have an answer, though, to the question of whether continuity of psychological processes in the animal kingdom also meant continuity of subjective states. He left that answer to be worked out by the philosophers, being satisfied with providing experimental and other objective evidence for his statements concerning animal behavior. This attitude sets Jennings apart from comparative psychologists such as Romanes*.

Biographies: D. D. Jensen, In H. S. Jennings, *Behavior of the Lower Organisms*, 1962, pp. ix-xvii; T. C. Schneierla, *Amer. J. Psychol.*, 1947, *60*, 447-450; T. M. Sonnenborn, *Genetics*, 1948, *33*, 1-4; *DSB*, 7; *NCAB*, 47; *NYT*, 1947, Apr. 15, 25:1; *PR*, 3; *Who Was Who in America*, 2; *Yearb. Amer. Phil. Soc.*, 1947.

JOHNSON, SAMUEL

American Philosopher and Educator

Born: Guilford, Connecticut, October 14, 1696

Died: Stratford, Connecticut, June 6, 1772

Education: Graduated from College of New Haven (Yale University) in 1714

Positions, Honors: 1754-63, president, King's College (Columbia University); three honorary degrees

In the first textbook of philosophy published in America, *Elementa philosophica* (1752), Johnson considered psychological topics such as sensation, perception, emotions, and the will, as well as some anatomy and physiology of the nervous system. He made comments on the possibility of a genetic and comparative psychology. The treatise in general followed the British empiricists, Johnson having become a disciple of Berkeley* after the latter's visit to America, but contained an admixture of Christian theology and the notion of innate ideas: Johnson proved the existence of God by the existence of eternal truths in the mind, truths that did not depend on experience. The will Johnson held to be free, unlike his pupil Jonathan Edwards*, who believed that all decisions were made by God.

Biographies: In S. Johnson, *Samuel Johnson, President of King's College: His Career and Writings*, 4 vols., 1929, vol. 1, pp. 1-50; E. E. Beardsley, *Life and Correspondence of Samuel Johnson*, 1873; T. B. Chandler, *The Life of Samuel Johnson, D.D.*, 1805; M. J. C. Hodgart, *Samuel Johnson and His Times*, 1963; *DAB*, 10; *EP*, 4; *NCAB*, 6; *Who Was Who in America*, Historical vol.

JONES, (ALFRED) ERNEST

English Psychoanalyst

Born: Gowerton, Glamorganshire, Wales, January 1, 1879

Died: London, February 11, 1958

Highest Degree: M.D., University of London, 1903

Positions, Honors: 1903-8, various hospital appointments; 1908-13, University of Toronto; from 1913, consulting physician; president, International Psychoanalytic Association, 1920-24 and 1932-49, honorary president, 1949-58; honorary D.Sc., Yale University, 1954

Jones came into contact with Sigmund Freud* in 1907 and became his disciple and member of the inner, "secret" committee that was to guide the destiny of the psychoanalytic movement (and which he himself had suggested). He became the leader of the English-speaking psychoanalysts and, at the death of Freud, the recognized leader of psychoanalysis worldwide. Among his contributions are the introduction of psychoanalysis in England, the defense of psychoanalysis against attacks during its early days of existence, and his successful efforts at keeping the psychoanalytic movement from splitting up. Jones founded the *International Journal of Psychoanalysis* in 1920 (and was its editor until 1939) and the *London Psychoanalytic Society* (later the British Branch of the International Psychoanalytic Association). His writings about psychoanalysis were

collected in *Papers on Psychoanalysis*, and he published about fifty volumes of the *International Psychoanalytic Library*, a collection of standard works on psychoanalysis. Jones is best known, however, as the foremost biographer of Freud (*The Life and Works of Sigmund Freud*, 3 vols., 1953-57).
Biographies: V. Brome, *Ernest Jones*, 1983; *Brit. Med. J.*, 1958, *126*, 463-465; E. Glover, *Brit. J. Psychol.*, 1958, *49*, 177-191; E. Jones, *Free Associations: Memories of a Psychoanalyst*, 1959; D. W. Winnicatt, *Int. J. Psychoanal.*, 1958, *39*, 298-304; G. Zilboorg, *Psychoanal. Quart.*, 1954, *23*, 250-259; *IESS*, 8; *NYT*, 1958, Feb. 12, 29:1; *PR*, 3.

JOST, ADOLPH
German Psychologist
Born: Graz, Austria, August 22, 1874
Died: Ca. 1920, place unknown
Highest Degree: Ph.D. in psychology, University of Göttingen, 1896, under G. Müller*
Positions: Unknown

Jost worked with Georg Müller on human learning, using the method of right associates (*Treffermethode*), now known as the method of paired associates (in paired verbal items presented for learning, one item serves as the stimulus, the other as the response). The method was invented by Müller but published first by Jost. Jost's work on his doctoral dissertation led to the formulation of the so-called Jost's law: of two associations of equal strength, the older association will be strengthened more by repetition than the more recent one. It was Jost's explanation of why learning is improved if the repetitions are distributed in time.
Biographies: In A. Jost, Die Assoziationsfestigkeit in ihrer Abhängigkeit von der Verteilung der Wiederholungen, 1897 (Doctoral dissertation).

JUDD, CHARLES HUBBARD
American Psychologist
Born: Bareilly, India, February 23, 1873
Died: Santa Barbara, California, July 18, 1946
Highest Degree: Ph.D. in psychology, University of Leipzig, 1896, under W. Wundt*
Positions, Honors: 1896-98, Wesleyan University; 1898-1901, New York University; 1901-2, University of Cincinnati; 1902-9, Yale University; 1909-38, University of Chicago, 1920-25, chairman, Department of Psychology, also chairman, Department of Education; taught psychology, philosophy, and pedagogy at all of these institutions; president, American Psychological Association (1909), National Society of College Teachers in Education (1911, 1915); several honorary degrees

At Leipzig and Wesleyan Judd studied time and space perception and wrote several papers on these topics. He translated Wundt's *Grundriss der Psychologie* into English (1896). At Yale he studied visual perception, motor processes, and learning. His interest in applying psychology, especially in the field of education, arose soon after his obtaining his doctorate. Judd's first book, written while at Yale, was *Genetic Psychology for Teachers* (1903). He next wrote a general psychology text *(Psychology: General Introduction,* 1907) and some laboratory manuals. It was at Chicago that Judd turned educational psychologist. He studied reading, problems of high school education, and the number concept; formulated a social psychology for the educational setting; and published most of his books while at Chicago. Among them are *Psychology of High School Subjects* (1915), *Introduction to the Scientific Study of Education* (1918), *Silent Reading* (1923), *Psychological Analysis of the Fundamentals of Arithmetic* (1926), *Psychology of Social Institutions* (1926), *Psychology of Secondary Education* (1927), and *Educational Psychology* (1939). Judd insisted that instead of applying findings from general psychology to education, educational psychology should derive its own principles from data of educational research, which should be as rigorous as any psychological research. When rote learning and faculty psychology were still prevalent in education, Judd stressed the role of generalization in learning. *Biographies*: G. P. Buswell, *Amer. J. Psychol.*, 1947, *60*, 135-137; F. N. Freeman, *Psychol. Rev.*, 1947, *54*, 59-65; W. D. Reeve, *Math. Teacher*, 1946, *39*, 291-292; *American Men of Science*, 7th ed.; *HPA*, 2; *IESS*, 8; *NCAB*, 42; *NYT*, 1946, July 19, 19:1; *PR*, 3; *Who Was Who In America*, 2.

JUNG, CARL GUSTAV
Swiss Psychiatrist
Born: Kesswil, Thurgau, July 26, 1875
Died: Küsnacht, Zurich, June 6, 1961
Highest Degree: M.D., University of Basle, 1900
Positions, Honors: 1900-1909, University of Zurich Psychiatric Clinic; 1905-13, University of Zurich; 1913-33, private practice; 1933-42, Federal Polytechnical Institute, Zurich; four honorary degrees and many other honors

Jung's first publication in 1902 about the psychology and pathology of occult phenomena set the tone for much of his later work. His earliest work, however, was experimental. He introduced the method of measuring the emotional content that words have for a subject by the subject's associative reaction time, a method still in use. When the subject showed no knowledge of the significance of an emotion-arousing word, Jung attributed this to the existence of a complex or unconscious psychic contents having functional autonomy. After reading Sigmund Freud* Jung began to apply his ideas in treating his own patients (*The Psychology of Dementia Praecox*, 1907). He met Freud in 1907; in 1911 he became the first president of the International Psychoanalytic Society and heir apparent to Freud. He also began to have doubts about some aspects of Freud's theory. Although recognizing the importance of early sexual conflict situations, Jung did not place as much emphasis on sexual libido as did Freud. By 1914 Jung's views had grown sufficiently apart from those of Freud for him to sever his connections with Freud and the psychoanalytic movement. Jung began to call his own theory "analytic psychology."

The book *Psychological Types*, published in 1921, is the best known among the many that Jung has written. It introduced into common language the terms *extrovert* and *introvert*. The core of Jung's type theory of personality was that every psychological phenomenon implies the opposite of itself. Thus in addition to the opposition between extroversion and introversion, the psychological functions of thinking and feeling (the rational functions) are the opposites of sensation and intuition (the irrational functions). The dominance of one of them (the superior function) further determines the psychological type of an individual. The principle of opposites also implies that both manifest and latent tendencies need to be recognized and dealt with if one is to live in harmony with oneself. Jung gave up his university position to devote his time to the study of the unconscious and its manifestations. He traveled to make cross-cultural studies and studied the myths, religions, and symbols of many cultures and different historical eras. These studies included even the lore of alchemy. Out of Jung's inmense erudition emerged a complex view of man, which Jung presented in numerous volumes and monographs.

The Jungian individual consists of an ego (self-awareness), a persona (the expected social role played by him), the shadow (a concept not unlike the Freudian id), the animus (in a female) or the anima (in a male), the unconscious attitude pertaining to the opposite sex, the self (the soul, in some respects similar to Freud's superego), and the unconscious, consisting of a personal and a collective layer. The collective unconscious is a deposit of archetypes or fundamental modes of apprehension that are common to all humanity because of the universality of certain underlying experiences. The archetypes manifest themselves symbolically in myths, graphic representations, dreams, and the like. The process of attaining a healthy, creative personality, the process of individuation, involves the differentiation of as well as the compensatory balancing of the opposite facets of personality in relation to its central core, the self. Jungian analysis is based on this conception of a human being. Its purpose is to help the patient to achieve individuation, to become an integrated personality.

After the organization of the first Jungian training center in Zurich in 1948, additional training centers have been established in Europe and America. Jung's books have been translated into almost all European languages. There are seventeen volumes in the English edition of his collected works. They offer a view of the human being that although psychoanalytically based, is an alternative to that of Freud's. Jung's influence on psychological thinking about the dynamics of human behavior and humans as symbol-using beings has been far reaching.

Biographies: E. A. Bennet, *C. G. Jung*, 1961; J. Campbell, In *The Portable Jung*, 1971, vii-xlii; W. Douglas, *Amer. J. Psychol.*, 1961, *74*, 639-641; A. M. Dry, *Brit. J. Psychol.*, 1961, *52*, 311-315; F. Fordham, *An Introduction to Jung's Psychology*, 1959; H. Gottschalk, *C. G. Jung*, 1960; E. Harms, *Amer. J. Psychiat.*, 1962, *118*, 728-732; A. Jaffe, *From the Life and Work of C. G.*

Jung, 1971; C. G. Jung, *Memories, Dreams, Reflections*, 1973; S. T. Selesnick, In F. Alexander *et al.* (Eds.), *Psychoanalytic Pioneers*, 1966, pp. 63-77; A. Storr, *C. G. Jung*, 1973; G. Wehr, *Portrait of Jung*, 1971; *Biog. Lex.*; *DSB*, 7; *EB*, 13; *EP*, 4; *IESS*, 8; *NYT*, 1961, June 7, 1:2.

K

KAFKA, GUSTAV

German Psychologist

Born: Vienna, Austria, July 23, 1883

Died: Veitshochheim, near Würzburg, Bavaria, February 12, 1953

Highest Degree: Ph.D. in psychology, University of Leipzig, 1906, under W. Wundt*

Positions: 1905-16, University of Munich; during World War I, set up psychotechnical services for the Austro-Hungarian army (with Géza Révész*); 1923-35, Technische Hochschule, Dresden; 1947-52, University of Würzburg; president, German Psychological Society, 1951-53 (Kafka reestablished it after World War II)

Kafka's main interest was in philosophy, but eventually he began to relate philosophy and psychology, for instance, by introducing concepts of developmental psychology in philosophy (*Geschichtsphilosophie der Philosophiegeschichte*, 1933). His psychological investigations were in the areas of developmental, comparative, and ethnopsychology. His text of comparative psychology (*Handbuch der vergleichenden Psychologie*, 3 vols., 1922) encompassed all three areas. *Was sind Rassen?* (1949) likewise touched all three areas. Kafka wrote many papers, a good number of which show him as an incisive critic of fundamental concepts of psychology. His aim for psychology was to go beyond mere accumulation of facts, to reckon with the concept of soul, and to add to psychology the dimension of *Höhenpsychologie* that would deal with the human spirit and the human being as a whole, composed of body, soul, and spirit.

Biographies: P. Lersch, *Jb. Psychol. Psychother.*, 1953, *1*, 375-376; W. J. Revers, *Amer. J. Psychol.*, 1953, *66*, 642-644; G. Révész, *Acta psychologica*, 1953, *9*, 183-188; A. Wellek, *Psychol. Rundsch.*, 1953, *4*, 224-225; *EUI*, 28(2); *Jewish*, 6; *PR*, 3.

KANT, IMMANUEL

German Philosopher
Born: Königsberg, East Prussia, April 22, 1724
Died: Königsberg, East Prussia, February 12, 1804
Highest Degree: Ph.D. in philosophy, University of Königsberg, 1775
Positions: 1755-96, University of Königsberg

Kant, one of the greatest philosophers of all times, was orthodox in his approach to philosophy until he was aroused from his "dogmatic slumber" by the reading of Hume* and Hume's psychological analysis of causality. Although Kant's main works are related to psychology, his approach to the problems of philosophy was not psychological. Kant thought of psychology as an empirical study of the laws of mental functioning. His psychological views are contained in his *Anthropology* (first published in German in 1798). His significant contributions to psychology are contained, however, in his critical volumes, especially the *Critique of Pure Reason* (1781), which deals with the process of knowing, but also to a lesser extent in his *Critique of Judgment* (1790) and *Critique of Practical Reason* (1788), which treat of feeling and willing.

Kant, avoiding the extremes of both the rationalists, such as Descartes*, and of the empiricists, such as Locke*, combined the views of both schools in a new and more complex system. Although agreeing with the empiricists that objects are known through the senses and that the ultimate reality is unknowable, he argued that the mind brings to experience certain qualities of its own that order it. They are the twelve a priori categories of causality, unity, totality, and the like and the *a priori* intuitions of time and space. Although the mind has no substance, it is an active process that serves to convert raw sensory data into meaningful, ordered experiences. Kant named this process "apperception." Things in themselves cannot be known; we perceive the world only the way our mind makes us do it, that is, through the instrumentality of the innate mental categories. Kant thus accepted the notion of mental faculties—cognition, feeling, desire, understanding, judgment, and reason—and his treatment of them in his critique volumes sanctioned their acceptance and use by others.

Kant stated that since mental processes have no substance and have only the time dimension, it is impossible to measure them. For this reason Kant specifically denied the possibility of psychology as an experimental science. Because Kant was an extremely influential philosopher, this view of his delayed the emergence of psychology as an experimental science. On the other hand, his statement that mathematics is a source of scientific knowledge (because it is based on a priori axioms) and is basic to all science led those who were seeking an experimental psychological science to introduce mathematics in psychology at an early date.

Another direct and important influence of Kant's on psychology was through his insistence that experience, particularly in the form of perception, is a unitary act. Although the sensory elements of the associationists are there, the mind performs an integrative act that makes a coherent, meaningful experience out of them. This view undermined the associationists' position and contributed to the demise of associationism as a systematic school of thought.

Kant's stress on innate mental categories labels him as a nativist. By presenting time and space as innate intuitions, Kant gave support to nativist theories of space perception and was therefore the philosophical godfather of the forthcoming phenomenological and nativist schools of psychology, such as the Gestalt school. *Biographies*: E. F. Buchner, In *The Educational Theory of Immanuel Kant*, 1904, pp. 11-98; J. W. H. Stuckenberg, *The Life of Immanuel Kant*, 1882; K. Vorländer, *Immanuel Kant: Der Mann und das Werk*, 2 vols., 1924; *ADB*, 15; *CE*, 8; *DSB*, 7; *EB*, 13; *EP*, 4; *EUI*, 28(2); *IESS*, 8.

KARDINER, ABRAM

American Psychiatrist
Born: New York, New York, August 17, 1891
Died: Easton, Connecticut, July 20, 1981
Highest Degree: M.D., Cornell University, 1917
Positions: Since 1920, private practice of psychoanalysis; 1955-57, Columbia University

Before starting his psychoanalytical practice, Kardiner underwent a six-month analysis with Sigmund Freud* in Vienna. Ten years later (1930), he was a cofounder of the New York Psychoanalytical Institute, the first psychoanalytical training school in the United States. Kardiner became a leader in the "environmental" school of psychiatry, which stresses the interplay of the psyche and culture. In collaboration with cultural anthropologists, such as Ralph Linton*, Kardiner engaged in a series of cross-cultural studies. He emphasized the "basic character structure" that emerges as a result of mother-child interaction. As adults we impose our infantile experiences on our basic ways of thinking. Through our philosophies and theologies, these experiences determine the way we perceive the world. Kardiner showed that both the basic character of groups and of individuals within groups may be identified through ethnological observations.

Kardiner wrote *The Individual and His Society* (1939), *The Psychological Frontiers of Society* (1945, with R. Linton, C. Du Bois, and J. West), *The Mark of Oppression* (1951, with W. L. Ovesay), and *They Studied Man* (1961, with E. Preble).
Biographies: *Contemporary Authors*, v. 104; *EJ*, 10; *NYT*, July 22, 1981.

KATZ, DAVID
German Psychologist
Born: Kassel, Hessen, October 1, 1884
Died: Stockholm, Sweden, February 2, 1953
Highest Degree: Ph.D. in psychology, University of Göttingen, 1906, under G. Müller*
Positions, Honors: 1906-19, University of Göttingen; 1919-33, University of Rostock; 1937-53, University of Stockholm; president, Thirteenth International Congress of Psychology, 1951

Katz was the first prominent representative of experimental phenomenology in the twentieth century. Although he was a student of Georg Müller's and worked for some time in the latter's laboratory after obtaining his doctorate, his researches were largely phenomenological. They yielded facts that were added to the store used by the Gestalt psychologists to argue their case. Katz himself sympathized with the Gestalt movement.

Katz is best known for his study of the phenomenology of color. His important monograph on the modes of appearance of colors appeared in 1911 and was later published in book form as *Der Aufbau der Farbenwelt* (1930). Katz demonstrated that subjective colors can be described as surface colors (those pertaining to objects), volume colors (such as those of colored liquids), and film colors (like the colors in a spectroscope), and that one mode of appearance may change into another depending on viewing conditions.

Nativistic factors were stressed by Katz in his discussion of perceptual constancies. This phenomenon runs as the main theme through his many and varied researches (he published more than one hundred titles, twenty of them books and monographs). In 1925 Katz's phenomenological study of touch appeared (*Der Aufbau der Tastwelt*), similar in its conception to that of colors. Some of Katz's more significant books are *Gespräche mit Kindern* (1927), *Hunger und Appetit* (1932), and *Gestalt Psychology* (1950, first published in Swedish in 1942).

Biographies: R. Arnheim, *Amer. J. Psychol.*, 1953, *66*, 638-642; G. Ekman *et al.*, *Nordisk Psykologi*, 1953, *5*, 1-9; D. Katz, *Psychol. Beit.*, 1954, 1, 470-491; R. B. McLeod, *Psychol. Rev.*, 1954, *61*, 1-4; R. Meili, *Schweiz. Z. Psychol.*, 1953, *12*, 153-154; I. Meyerson, *J. psychol. norm. path.*, 1953, *46*, 379-381; T. H. Pear, *Brit. J. Psychol.*, 1953, *44*, 197-199; G. Révész, *Acta psychologica*, 1953, *9*, 97-98; *Biog. Lex.*; *EUI*, 28(2); *HPA*, 4; *IESS*, 8, 18; *Jewish*, 6; *PR*, 3.

KELLEY, TRUMAN LEE
American Psychologist
Born: Whitehall, Michigan, May 25, 1884
Died: Santa Barbara, California, May 2, 1961
Highest Degree: Ph.D. in psychology, Columbia University, 1914, under E. L. Thorndike*

Positions: 1914-17, University of Texas; 1917-20, Teachers College, Columbia University; 1920-31, Stanford University; 1931-50, Harvard University

Kelley, a statistician and psychometrician, disagreed with Spearman's* approach to factor analysis of mental abilities by proposing the existence of group factors in addition to a general and many specific factors, thus a multiple-factor theory (*Crossroads in the Mind of Man: A Study of Differential Mental Abilities*, 1928). He also disagreed with Thurstone* on a number of points: he held that it was important to incorporate the value of a mental function in an analysis before executing it, so that important (useful) factors may be obtained rather than accurate but perhaps inconsequential ones; he analyzed the total variance of a correlation matrix rather than just the communalities; and he favored orthogonal rotation rather than rotation to simple structure. Simultaneously with H. Hotelling, Kelley formulated the method of canonical correlation as well as his own form of the principal-axes solution in factor analysis (*Essential Traits of Mental Life*, 1935).

Kelley did much additional work in statistics, scaling and psychometrics, and individual differences in general. He was one of the authors of a widely used college entrance examination, the Stanford Achievement Test (1953). The books written by Kelley in these areas include *Educational Guidance* (1914), *Mental Aspects of Delinquency* (1917), *Statistical Method* (1923), *The Influence of Nurture upon Native Differences* (1926), *Interpretation of Educational Measurements* (1927), *Tests and Measurements in the Social Sciences* (1934, with A. C. Krey), *The Kelley Statistical Tables* (1938, 1948), and *Fundamentals of Statistics* (1947).

Biographies: *Brit. J. Stat. Psychol.*, 1962, *15*, 95-96; I. Flanagan, *Psychometrika*, 1961, *26*, 343-345; *IESS*, 8; *NCAB*, 49; *NYT*, 1961, May 3, 37:5; *PR*, 3; *Who Was Who in America*, 4.

KELLY, GEORGE ALEXANDER

American Psychologist
Born: Near Perth, Kansas, April 28, 1905
Died: Waltham, Massachusetts, March 6, 1967
Highest Degree: Ph.D. in psychology, State University of Iowa, 1931
Positions: 1931-44, Kansas State College; 1945-46, University of Maryland; 1946-65, Ohio State University, 1946-51 and 1963-65, director of clinical psychology; 1965-67, Brandeis University

Kelly developed a cognitive personality theory that he referred to as the "psychology of personal constructs." He published a two-volume work under that title in 1955. It was a theory of cognition applied to the psychology of personality. Kelly attributed most human behaviors to thinking, expectations, and other cognitions rather than motives or needs. Each person's behavior is guided by the way he interprets a situation, by the way he constructs his own theory of reality. An individual is therefore able to control his own life to a considerable degree. Kelly denied that it was necessary to consider motivation in a personality theory. The most important and the only element of personality is the personal construct or idea about the world that is based on self-evaluation and the evaluation of factors that most influence an individual's life, especially relationships to significant others. Kelly's theory has led to the development of a number of therapeutic techniques, such as the fixed-role therapy. Kelly himself developed a personality test, the Rep Test, to assess the client's problems. Hundreds of papers have been published with personal constructs as their theme, but Kelly himself published only about twenty. *Clinical Psychology and Personality* was published posthumously in 1969.

Biographies: B. Maher, In *Clinical Psychology and Personality: The Selected Papers of George Kelly*, 1969, pp. 1-3; G. G. Thompson, *J. Gen. Psychol.*, 1968, *79*, 19-24; *Who Was Who in America*, 4.

KENT, GRACE (HELEN)

American Psychologist
Born: Michigan City, Indiana, June 6, 1875
Died: Silver Spring, Maryland, September 18, 1973
Highest Degree: Ph.D. in psychology, George Washington University, 1911
Positions: 1906, Philadelphia Hospital for Insane; 1907-10, Kings Park State Hospital, New York; 1910, Government Hospital for Insane, Washington, D.C.; 1911-12, State Hospital, Warren, Pennsylvania; 1920-22, State Training School for Feeble-Minded, Clinton, South Carolina; 1922-26, Worcester State Hospital; 1928-46, Danvers State Hospital; 1947-48, visiting professor, University of Miami

Kent's name became well-known in connection with the publication of the Kent-Rosanoff Free Association Test in 1910. It was a psychiatric screening instrument that was one of the first to have objective scoring and objective norms. A patient's associative responses were compared with frequency tables prepared on a norm group of one thousand individuals. The test fell into disuse when it was realized that the associative response is also a function of the patient's socioeconomic status, age, education, and the like, not only of his psychopathology. Kent continued to work in the area of clinical psychometrics, producing additional instruments—the Kent-Shakow Formboards (1928), the Kent-Shakow Industrial Formboards (1928), the Kent Series of Emergency Scales for the quick and rough classification of psychiatric patients (*Series of Emergency Scales*, 1946)—and some twenty-five papers in this area. One of her last publications was *Mental Tests in Clinics for Children* (1950).

Biographies: D. Shakow, *J. Hist. Behav. Sci.*, 1974, *10*, 275-280; *American Men of Science*, 9th ed.; *PR*, 3.

KEPLER, JOHANNES

German Astronomer and Mathematician
Born: Weil der Stadt, Württemberg, December 27, 1571
Died: Regensburg, Bavaria, November 15, 1630

Highest Degree: M.S., University of Tübingen, 1591
Positions: 1594-97, University of Graz; 1597-1612, University of Prague, imperial mathematician

Kepler, the discoverer of the elliptic course of planetary motion, also founded modern optics through his experiments with telescopes, the refraction of light, and the properties of lenses. Of significance to psychology was his work on vision. In *Ad vitellionem paralipomena* . . . (1604), and later in *Dioptrice* (1611), he proposed a theory of vision that replaced the prevailing one according to which the lens of the eye was an organ of visual sensation. Kepler asserted correctly that the lens acts only as a lens, that it casts an inverted image on the retina, and that "sight is a sensation of the stimulation of the retina." He noted the existence of afterimages, theorized that light effects a chemical reaction in the retina, assumed that the retinal image had to be transmitted beyond the retina to the brain to be perceived, and correctly interpreted the function of the accommodation of the lens. Kepler also raised for the first time the question of why the world appears to be right side up when the retinal image is upside down.
Biographies: M. Caspar, *Johannes Kepler*, 1959; R. Harré, In R. Harré (Ed.), *Early Seventeenth Century Scientists*, 1965, pp. 81-100; J. Schmidt, *Johann Kepler: Sein Leben in Bildern und eigenen Berichten*, 1970; H. W. Turnbull, In J. R. Newman (Ed.), *The World of Mathematics*, vol. 1, 1956, pp. 75-168; *ADB*, 15, 27; *CE*, 8; *DSB*, 7; *EB*, 13; *EP*, 4; *EUI*, 28(2).

KIESOW, FEDERICO
German-Italian Psychologist
Born: Brüel near Schwerin, Mecklenburg, Germany, March 28, 1858
Died: Turin, Piedmont, December 9, 1940
Highest Degree: Ph.D. in philosophy, University of Leipzig, 1894, under W. Wundt*
Positions, Honors: 1895-1933, University of Turin; honorary LL.D., Wittenberg College

Before moving to Turin, Kiesow studied taste with Wundt. At Turin he established a psychological laboratory in 1895 and, in general, brought Wundtian experimental psychology to Turin. He worked there for four decades, studying touch and other sensations, psychophysics, geometric illusions, eidetic imagery, and other phenomena. Kiesow produced numerous publications and for many years was Italy's most prominent experimental psychologist.
Biographies: H. Misiak & V. M. Staudt, *Catholics in Psychology: A Historical Survey*, 1954; M. Ponzo, *Arch. ges. Psychol.*, 1941, *108*, 5-6; M. Ponzo, *Arch. psicol. neurol. psichiat.*, 1942, *3*, 3-25; M. Ponzo, *Psychol. Rev.*, 1941, *48*, 268-269; various, *Arch. ges. Psychol.*, 1928, *65*, 1-320; *CE*, 8; *HPA*, 1; *PR*, 3.

KINSEY, ALFRED CHARLES
American Biologist
Born: Hoboken, New Jersey, June 23, 1894
Died: Bloomington, Indiana, August 25, 1956

Highest Degree: Ph.D. in zoology, Harvard University, 1920
Positions: 1920-47, taught zoology, Indiana University; 1947-56, director, Institute for Sex Research, Indiana University

Kinsey's interest and research on human sexual behavior, which started in 1938, led to the establishment of the Institute for Sex Research at Indiana University. The results of 18,500 personal interviews concerning sexual behavior were published in *Sexual Behavior in the Human Male* in 1948 and in *Sexual Behavior in the Human Female* in 1953. They were the first large-scale empirical studies of sexual behavior. They presented quantified description of sexual behavior, showed an unexpected range of variation in such behavior, corrected misconceptions and upset many established opinions concerning human sexual behavior, and demonstrated that sexual behavior can be studied scientifically, objectively, and publicly.

Biographies: C. V. Christensen, *Kinsey: A Biography*, 1971; W. B. Pomeroy, *Psychol. Today*, 1972, 5(10), 33-40, 82; W. B. Pomeroy, *Dr. Kinsey and the Institute for Sex Research*, 1972; L. Rosenzweig & S. Rosenzweig, *J. Hist. Behav. Sci.*, 1969, 5, 173-191; *IESS*, 8; *NCAB*, H; *NYT*, 1956, Aug. 26, 1:3

KLAGES, LUDWIG
German-Swiss Psychologist
Born: Hanover, Germany, December 10, 1872
Died: Kilchberg, Zurich, Switzerland, July 29, 1956
Highest Degree: Ph.D. in chemistry, University of Munich, 1900
Positions: 1901-19, University of Munich; 1919-56, Seminar für Ausdruckskunde, Kilchberg, near Zurich

Klages contributed to the psychology of expressive movements, especially graphology. He founded the German Graphological Society in 1897, *Graphologische Monatshefte* (1897-1908), and in 1905 the Seminary for the Science of Expressions, which became the main German-language center of characterology. Klages wrote *Die Probleme der Graphologie* (1910) and *Einführung in die Psychologie der Handschrift* (1924), but it was *Handschrift und Charakter* (1916) that brought him fame. It saw twenty-four editions in forty years and, in the 1920s and 1930s, made Klages's name about as famous as that of Sigmund Freud*.

The term *characterology* (*Charakterkunde*) was coined by Julius Bahnsen in 1867, but Klages became the foremost representative of characterology. Philosophically, Klages was a neo-Romanticist and anti-intellectualist, stressing instincts and life forces. He was influenced by such men as Carl Gustav Carus, Johann Goethe*, Arthur Schopenhauer*, Theodor Lipps*, and Friedrich Nietzsche*. Klages held that humans differ from animals in their ability to represent sensations in images and by having acquired in their development a *Geist*, or spirit. The *Geist* and nature (life) are engaged in a combat within a person. A person's character is the relative balance between these forces. Klages assigned characterology the role of clarifying the relationship between spirit and nature. Nature should destroy spirit and help people return to their primitive, undifferentiated, natural state.

Klages's main thesis was that "the body is a manifestation of the soul, and the soul is the essence of the living body." The psychic aspect of a human being can be apprehended only in the totality of the besouled body, that is, expressive movements. Physiological psychology is useless in understanding personality. Expressive movements yield data that can be analyzed exactly, especially if they also yield a graphic record, such as a writing or a drawing. Although contributions to characterology were also made in other countries (Bain*, Janet*), characterology, as exemplified by Klages, has remained a typical German development, and it is in Germany that it has played an important role in both theoretical and applied psychology.

Biographies: R. Heiss, *Z. diagnost. Psychol.*, 1956, *4*, 215-217; H. Hönel (Ed.), Ludwig Klages, *Erforscher und Künder des Lebens*, 1947; H.-E. Schröder, *Psychol. Rundsch.*, 1957, *8*, 75-76; H.-E. Schröder, In E. Frauchiger *et al.* (Eds.), *Ludwig Klages, Sämtliche Werke*, vol. 1, 1966, vol. 2, 1972; C. Wandrey, *Ludwig Klages und seine Lebensphilosophie*, 1933; *Biog. Lex.*; *CE*, 8; *EP*, 4; *EUI*, 28(2); *PR*, 3.

KLEIN, MELANIE
German-English Psychoanalyst
Born: Budapest, Hungary, March 30, 1882
Died: London, England, September 22, 1960
Education: Studied art and history at the University of Vienna around 1900
Positions: 1921-26, child therapist, Psychoanalytical Institute, Berlin; 1926-60, British Psychoanalytical Society, London

Although Klein never received an academic degree, she became one of the two (with Anna Freud*) most prominent child psychoanalysts in the world. Klein's work with children led to the development of ideas that did not always match those of Sigmund Freud*. Klein placed the development of the superego in infancy, for instance, believing that the seeds of it are already to be found in the first and second years of life. She thought that fear and aggressive tendencies were also present at this age and held them to be more important in understanding deviant development than psychosexual development. As a substitute for free association, of which very young children are incapable, to uncover children's unconscious motivations, Klein developed the technique of play therapy, now used worldwide. Not hewing to the classical Freudian lines created controversy around Klein, eventually leading to the formation of her own group of analysts within the British Psychoanalytical Society, the "Kleinians."

Of Klein's books the more significant ones are *The Psychoanalysis of Children* (1932), *Contributions to Psychoanalysis, 1921-1945* (1948), and *Our Adult World and Other Essays* (1963).

Biographies: W. R. Bion *et al.*, *Int. J. Psychoanal.*, 1961, *42*, 4-7; A. Freud,

Psychoanal. Stud. Child, 1966, *21*, 7-14; W. Hoffer, *Int. J. Psychoanal.*, 1961, *42*, 1-3; S. Isaacs, *J. Child Psychol. Psychiat.*, 1961, *2*, 1-4; J. A. Lindon, In F. Alexander *et al.* (Eds.), *Psychoanalytic Pioneers*, 1966, pp. 360-372; T. F. Main, *Brit. J. Med. Psychol.*, 1961, *34*, 163-166; R. E. Money-Kryle, *Bull. Brit. Psychol. Soc.*, 1961, *43*, 29-30; *EJ*, 10; *IESS*, 8; *NYT*, 1960, Sept. 23, 29:2.

KLEMM, GUSTAV OTTO
German Psychologist
Born: Leipzig, March 8, 1884
Died: Leipzig, January 5, 1939
Highest Degree: Ph.D. in psychology, University of Leipzig, 1906, under W. Wundt*
Positions: 1906-39, University of Leipzig

Klemm did laboratory research and wrote papers on a variety of psychological subjects. He also engaged in consulting and applied work out of Felix Krüger's* Institute at Leipzig and was a member of the Leipzig school of *Ganzheitspsychologie* headed by Krüger. Klemm did editorial work for several journals and was active within the German Psychological Society. Of the fifty-four titles in his bibliography by far the best known is his *Geschichte der Psychologie*, written in 1911. It was translated into English (in 1912) and several other languages and became highly popular. No other history of psychology was written in the German language for several decades.

Biographies: F. Baumgarten, *Travail hum.*, 1940, *8*, 96-98; G. W. Hartmann, *Amer. J. Psychol.*, 1939, *52*, 308-309; F. Krueger, *Z. angew. Psychol.*, 1939, *56*, 253-346; W. Wirth, *Arch. ges. Psychol.*, 1939, *102*, vii-xii; *Z. pädag. Psychol.*, 1939, *40*, 57-59; *HPA*, 3; *PR*, 3.

KLUCKHOHN, CLYDE KAY MABEN
American Anthropologist
Born: Le Mars, Iowa, January 11, 1905
Died: Santa Fe, New Mexico, July 29, 1960
Highest Degree: Ph.D. in anthropology, Harvard University, 1936
Positions, Honors: 1935-60, Harvard University; president, American Anthropological Association, 1947; honorary L.H.D., University of New Mexico, 1949; Viking Fund Medal and Award, 1950

Kluckhohn spent most of his life as an ethnographer of the Navajo Indians. He wrote two books and a number of monographs and articles about the Navajo. In the Harvard Department of Social Relations, which he helped to organize, Kluckhohn shared not only departmental affiliation but also ideas with the psychologists who were part of it: Gordon Allport*, Hobart Mowrer*, Henry Murray, Robert Sears, and others. His interests were in culture (*Culture*, 1952, with A. L. Kroeber), the problem of values (Values and value-orientedness in the theory of action, in *Toward a General Theory of Action*, 1951), and the relationship between culture and personality. With H. A. Murray, Kluckhohn edited *Personality in Nature, Society, and Culture* (1948; 2nd ed., 1953), a popular source book about personality formation in which personality was defined by the editors as "the continuity of functional forms and forces manifested through sequences of organized regnant process and overt behaviors from birth to death." *Biographies*: G. P. Murdock, *Behav. Sci.*, 1961, *6*, 2-4; T. Parsons, *Amer. Sociol. Rev.*, 1960, *25*, 960-962; T. Parsons & E. Z. Vogt, *Amer. Anthropologist*, 1962, *64*, 140-418; *Biog. Mem.*, 37; *IESS*, 8; *NCAB*, H; *NYT*, 1960, July 30, 17:1; *Yearb. Amer. Phil. Soc.*, 1961.

KLÜVER, HEINRICH
German-American Psychologist
Born: Schleswig-Holstein, Germany, May 25, 1897
Died: Oak Lawn, Illinois, February 8, 1979
Highest Degree: Ph.D. in psychology, Stanford University, 1924
Positions, Honors: 1924-26, University of Minnesota; 1926-28, Social Science Research Council fellow; 1928-33, Behavior Research Foundation, Chicago; 1933-46, Otho S. A. Sprague Memorial Institute, Chicago; 1936-62, University of Chicago, 1963-79, professor emeritus; editorial work, *Journal of Psychology* (from 1935), *Journal of Comparative and Physiological Psychology*, and many others; honorary M.D., University of Basle (1965), University of Kiel (1971); honorary Ph.D., University of Hamburg, 1969; several awards (APA Psychological Foundation Gold Medal, 1965); other honors

Beginning in 1957 Klüver was Sewell L. Avery Distinguished Service professor of biological psychology, one of the many honors that came to him for his brilliant research in neuropsychology. He first conducted classic studies on the phenomenology of eidetic imagery (first ones in the English language) and the effects of mescal (first scientific investigation of this substance) and then devoted the rest of his life to work on neuroanatomical and psychological relationships, using monkeys of many different species. In 1936 Klüver established experimentally that the optical cortex was the monkey's primary visual area, without which it was able to perceive only degrees of light intensity. Following this, Klüver, with the assistance of the neurosurgeon Paul Bucy, performed temporal lobectomies in monkeys and found that the temporal lobe, too, was involved in visual perception by supplying seen objects with meaning. The syndrome of psychic blindness, aggressiveness, and hypersexuality following the ablation of regions in the anterior portion of the temporal lobe in the monkey, first described by Klüver and Bucy in 1938, became known as the Klüver-Bucy syndrome. Klüver also discovered the propensity of the white neural tissue to stain with porphyrin derivatives, which resulted in the now widely used copper phthalocyanin stain of microscopic preparations.

Klüver's most important book was the 1933 volume *Behavior Mechanisms in Monkeys*, which, among other topics, presents the classic statement of the problem of stimulus equivalence. In 1955 Klüver undertook the completion and publication of the unfinished book of his colleague Stephen Polyak*, *The Vertebrate Visual System*.

Biographies: APA Foundation, *Amer. Psychologist*, 1965, *20*, 1089-1090; W. A. Hunt, *Amer. J. Psychol.*, 1980, *93*, 159-161; S. Schulman, *Amer. Psychologist*, 1980, *35*, 380-382; *NYT*, 1979, Feb. 12, 13:6.

KOFFKA, KURT
German-American Psychologist
Born: Berlin, Germany, March 18, 1886
Died: Northampton, Massachusetts, November 22, 1941
Highest Degree: Ph.D. in psychology, University of Berlin, 1909, under C. Stumpf*
Positions: 1911-27, University of Giessen; 1927-41, Smith College

Koffka was one of the founders of the Gestalt school of psychology. Before 1910, when he came in contact with Max Wertheimer*, Koffka had studied imagery and thought with Stumpf. In 1910 Koffka and Wolfgang Köhler* served as subjects in a crucial experiment of Wertheimer's. A year later Wertheimer explained the significance of the experiment to Köhler and Koffka. They immediately accepted Wertheimer's ideas and became cofounders, with Wertheimer, of one of the major schools of psychology. These three, with Kurt Goldstein* and Hans Gruhle*, founded the organ of the school, *Psychologische Forschung*, in 1921.

During his years at Giessen, Koffka wrote *Die Grundlagen der psychischen Entwicklung* (1921; English translation, *The Growth of the Mind*, 1927). In this book Koffka applied Gestalt notions to the problems of developmental psychology. Although the Gestalt psychologists leaned in their theorizing more toward nativistic than empiricist explanations, Koffka stressed the interaction between innate capacities and environmental conditions, calling it the convergence theory of development (after William Stern*, who had formulated the idea originally). Koffka extended the convergence principle to all psychological events, holding that there was a convergence of inner and outer factors in all such events. Reflexes, instincts, and learning were discussed by Koffka in Gestalt terms. Like Köhler, Koffka stressed the insightful nature of learning, to the point of denying that trial and error was a meaningful explanation of learning except in situations that allow no other alternative.

Of the three founders of Gestalt psychology, Koffka was the most prolific writer. He was also a propagandizer of the Gestalt theory. Before going to the United States Koffka wrote a long series of papers about Gestalt psychology and an article for the *Psychological Bulletin* in 1922 to introduce Gestalt psychology to Americans, and he made several visits to the United States. He later wrote a comprehensive, ambitious, and difficult statement about Gestalt psychology, presenting it as a complete theory of behavior. The book *Principles of Gestalt Psychology* (1935) is the only such presentation extant and a classic of psychological literature.

Biographies: W. Eisen, *Brit. J. Psychol.*, 1942-1943, *33*, 69-76; J. Germain, *Psicotécnia*, 1945, *5*, 114-124; M. R. Harrower, *Amer. J. Psychol.*, 1942, *55*, 278-281; W. Köhler, *Psychol. Rev.*, 1942, *49*, 97-101; *EJ*, 10; *EP*, 4; *IESS*, 8; *NYT*, 1941, Nov. 23, 52:l; *PR*, 3.

KÖHLER, WOLFGANG
German-American Psychologist
Born: Revel, Estonia, January 21, 1887
Died: Enfield, New Hampshire, June 11, 1967
Highest Degree: Ph.D. in psychology, University of Berlin, 1909, under C. Stumpf*
Positions, Honors: 1910-13, University of Frankfurt; 1913-20, Anthropoid Station, Tenerife; 1920-21, University of Berlin; 1921-22, University of Göttingen; 1922-35, University of Berlin; 1935-55, Swarthmore College; president, American Psychological Association, 1959; American Psychological Association Distinguished Scientific Contribution Award, 1956

Köhler was one of the founders of the Gestalt school of psychology. Before 1910, when he came in contact with Max Wertheimer*, Köhler had done important work with Stumpf on the perception of tones. In 1910 Köhler and Kurt Koffka* served as subjects in a crucial experiment of Wertheimer's. A year later Wertheimer explained the significance of the experiment to Koffka and Köhler. They immediately accepted Wertheimer's ideas and became cofounders, with Wertheimer, of one of the major schools of psychology. The three of them, with Kurt Goldstein* and Hans Gruhle*, founded the organ of the school, *Psychologische Forschung*, in 1921. Köhler subsequently wrote several books presenting aspects of the Gestalt school of psychology: *Gestalt Psychology* (1929), *The Place of Value in a World of Facts* (1938), and *Dynamics in Psychology* (1940).

A major contribution of Köhler's was his work with chicks and chimpanzees in the Canary Islands during World War I. Köhler demonstrated the perception of and response to relationships (rather than absolute stimulus values) in chicks (later known as transposition) and insight learning (closure over psychological gaps) in chimpanzees. *Intelligenzprüfungen an Menschenaffen* (1917; English translation, *The Mentality of Apes*, 1924) was one outcome of his studies. They later led to much research and controversy over whether learning could be insightful or had to proceed by trial and error.

A second major contribution of Köhler's was the postulation of the principle of isomorphism. In a classic monograph, published in 1920 (*Die physischen Gestalten in Ruhe und im stationären Zustand*), Köhler first expanded Wertheimer's idea that to perceive actual and apparent movement as the same, brain processes in themselves must show properties of patterning or be *Gestalten* (configurations, structures). Köhler theorized that *Gestalten* exist not only mentally but physically. There is a correspondence in form between physical events in the brain, he said, and the subjective events caused by them. The postulation of electrical fields in the brain, topologically equivalent to percepts, led to a well-publicized exchange of opinion and neurological experiments. Although the existence of brain fields was never satisfactorily demonstrated, the field concept has been used and developed by individuals sympathetic to the Gestalt school (such as Kurt Lewin*) and others. A related line of inquiry that developed from the field theory concerned figural aftereffects, in which area a substantial literature has developed because of its theoretical importance to the question of how the brain works. The figural aftereffect phenomenon was first described and explained in terms of satiation of brain electrical fields in a paper written by Köhler and H. Wallach in 1944.

Biographies: *Amer. Psychologist*, 1957, *12*, 131-133; S. E. Asch, *Amer. J. Psychol.*, 1968, *81*, 110-119; R. Bergius, *Psychol. Forsch.*, 1967-68, *31*, i-v; C. W. Crannell, *J. Hist. Behav. Sci.*, 1970, *6*, 267-268; M. Henle, *Amer. Psychologist*, 1978, *33*, 939-944; M. Henle, *Yearb. Amer. Phil. Soc.*, 1968, 141ff.; H. Hörmann, *Psychol. Forsch.*, 1967-1968, *31*, xv-xvii; W. Metzger, *Psychol. Rundsch.*, 1968, *19*, 55; C. C. Pratt, In W. Köhler, *The Task of Gestalt Psychology*, 1969, pp. 3-29; H. L. Teuber, *Psychol. Forsch.*, 1967-1968, *31*, vi-xiv; *EB*, 13; *EP*, 4; *IESS*, 8; *Yearb. Amer. Phil. Soc.*, 1968.

KÖNIG, ARTHUR

German Physicist
Born: Krefeld, North Rhine-Westphalia, September 13, 1856
Died: Berlin, October 26, 1901
Highest Degree: Ph.D. in physics, University of Berlin, 1882
Positions: 1884-1901, University of Berlin

In the 1880s and 1890s König studied color vision. He measured changes in the Weber fraction for colors as a function of light intensity; established spectral mixtures (König's color triangle), showed brightness and light sensitivity to be a joint function of wavelength and intensity (a generalization that brought brightness and the Purkinje shift under the same heading), drew the first curves comparing color sensitivity of normal individuals and the color blind, defended the Young*-Helmholtz* theory of color vision, showed that total color blindness is blindness in the center of the retina, demonstrated that color confusion in red-blind and green-blind persons can be explained in terms of the Young-Helmholtz theory, and identified the role of the visual purple in retinal rod cells. König published the second edition of Helmholtz's *Physiological Optics* after Helmholtz's death, adding to it a 7,833-item bibliography on vision. He was a co-founder (in 1890) and editor, with Ebbinghaus*, of *Zeitschrift für Psychologie und Physiologie der Sinnesorgane*.

Biographies: H. Ebbinghaus & J. A. Barth, *Z. Psychol.*, 1902, 27, 145-147; T. W. Engelmann, In A. König, *Gesammelte Abhandlungen zur physiologischen Optik*, 1903, pp. v-viii; *Biog. Lex.*; *DSB*, 7.

KONORSKI, JERZY

Polish Physiologist
Born: Łódź, December 1, 1903
Died: Warsaw, September 14, 1973
Highest Degree: M.D., University of Warsaw, 1929
Positions: 1929-31, State Psychiatric Hospital, Pruszków; 1931-33, visiting scientist, Pavlov's Institute of Physiology, Leningrad; 1933-39, scientific worker, Nencki Institute of Experimental Biology, Warsaw; 1941-44, head, Physiology Department, Biological Station, Sukhumi, Georgia; 1945-55, University of Łódź and Nencki Institute of Experimental Biology (relocated to Łódź); 1955-68, head, Department of Neurophysiology, Nencki Institute of Experimental Biology, Warsaw

Konorski discovered early (1927) that the classical conditioning paradigm did not account for the formation of all behaviors. He began (with Stefan Miller) experiments on conditioned motor responses (which he called Type II conditioning), or instrumental learning. Konorski thought that the conditioning of voluntary behavior was different from Pavlov's* conditioned reflexes, although Pavlov denied that there was a difference. Konorski discovered and worked on operant conditioning before B. F. Skinner (*[Fundamental Principles of the Physiological Theory of Acquired Movements]*, 1933). He developed a difference of opinion with Skinner, though, on the nature of operant learning. Konorski also decided that Pavlov's neurophysiological theorizing on inhibition and excitation in relation to reflex formation was not correct and that Sherrington's* theory was more appropriate. The idea was presented in *Conditioned Reflexes and Neuron Organization* (1948). Konorski did considerable work with dogs and primates that contributed to the body of knowledge concerning the principles of operant conditioning. He also performed ablation experiments to study the functional organization of the brain and studied the effects of lesions on the human brain. His last book summarized his views on how the brain functions as it acquires habits (*Integrative Activity of the Brain*, 1967).

Biographies: O. H. Mowrer, *Amer. Psychologist*, 1976, *31*, 843-857; K. Zielinski, *Nauka Polska*, 1974, No. 1, 233-239; *HPA*, 6; *The International Who's Who*.

KORNILOV, KONSTANTIN NIKOLAEVICH

Russian Psychologist
Born: Tyumen, Siberia, March 9, 1879
Died: Moscow, July 10, 1957
Education: Graduated in philology from Moscow University in 1910
Positions, Honors: 1910-21, Moscow State University; 1921-51, Lenin Teachers College, Moscow; 1923-31, head, Institute of Psychology, Moscow; 1944-50, vice-president, USSR Academy of Pedagogical Sciences; editor, *Semya i Shkola* (1946-57), *Voprosy Psikhologii* (1955-57)

One of Kornilov's first investigations concerned the strength of reactions.

Noticing constant differences in the strength of handshakes, Kornilov measured both the reaction time and response strength with a "dynamoscope" of his own invention and identified four types of reactions. He also worked in the area of child psychology and education, publishing a number of works, such as *Ocherk psikhologii rebenka doshkol'nogo vozrasta* (1917).

When in the 1920s and early 1930s Bekhterev* campaigned against psychology and proposed the reduction of psychology to biology and sociology and the substitution of reflexology for psychology, Kornilov was the chief spokesman for psychology as an independent discipline. Kornilov also opposed, however, the Leipzig-trained Wundtian (Wundt*) G. I. Chelpanov because of his idealistic position. Kornilov proposed that a psychology based on dialectic materialism be established. He called it "reactology" and presented it in *Uchenie o reaktsiyakh cheloveka* (1922), in the paper "Psychology in the light of dialectic materialism" (in Murchison's* *Psychologies of 1930*), and in *Uchebnik psikhologii, izlozhennoĭ s tochki zreniya dialekticheskogo materializma* (1926), which went through five editions in as many years and was translated into several other languages. Although reactology postulated, as Karl Marx* had, that the nature of consciousness was determined by the conditions of social existence, it did not regard behavior only in terms of its mechanics but stressed the subjective aspects as well. The main features of reactology were the measurement of human reactions, emphasis on wholeness, and the economic determinants of behavior. Kornilov became the editor of the first purely psychological journal in Russian, *Psikhologiya* (founded in 1928). During the 1920s reactology, pedology, and psychotechnology flourished under Kornilov's leadership. In the early 1930s, however, Soviet political leaders decided that reactology did not reflect the dynamic, active nature of Marxism-Leninism and abolished it along with pedology and psychological testing. Kornilov lost his leadership but continued to be prominent in Soviet psychology. He shifted his interests back to educational and child psychology as well as the popularization of psychology. He penned several volumes in these areas: *Psikhologiya* (1938, with B. M. Teplov* and L. M. Shvarts), *Psikhologiya* (1946, a secondary school text), *Psikhologiya* (1948, with A. A. Smirnov and B. M. Teplov), and others.

Biographies: N. F. Dobrynin, *Vop. Psikhol.*, 1969, *15*(2), 183-185; G. Razran, *Science*, 1958, *128*, 74-75; *Bol'shaya Sovetskaya Entsiklopediya*; *PR*, 3.

KRAEPELIN, EMIL
German Psychiatrist
Born: Neustrelitz, Mecklenburg, February 15, 1856
Died: Munich, October 7, 1926
Highest Degree: M.D., University of Leipzig, 1878
Positions: 1879-82, University of Munich; 1882-86, University of Leipzig; 1886-90, University of Tartu; 1890-1904, University of Heidelberg; 1904-26, University of Munich

Although Kraepelin's field was medicine, his most revered teacher was Wundt*, who influenced his work in psychiatry. Kraepelin applied psychology to psychiatry by extending the use of the Wundtian association experiment to psychiatric problems (1895). He found that associations produced in states of fatigue or alcoholic intoxication resemble those of psychotic patients in that they are more superficial and determined by habit rather than meaning. At Tartu Kraepelin continued the work he had begun in 1883 in Wundt's laboratory on psychopharmacology. Kraepelin tested the effects of ethyl alcohol, morphine, and other substances on human behavior using Wundt's experimental procedures. For his work Kraepelin may be called the father of psychopharmacology.

Concerning the etiology of mental disorders, Kraepelin was instrumental in establishing the organic viewpoint that stressed the importance of brain pathology. It was first presented in his *Compendium der Psychiatrie* (1883). This work was a major contribution to the development of psychiatry and underlies the present-day classificatory system of mental disorders. Kraepelin presented a systematic classification of mental disorders, introducing terms such as *manic-depressive psychosis* and *paranoia* in their present meanings. Kraepelin believed that since mental disorders were basically organic, a clear division of disorders into categories was not only possible but that the course of development of each disorder was predictable, even if it could not be controlled. This led to the development of an interest in the accurate description and classification in psychopathology. Because of his contributions Kraepelin is also known as the father of modern psychiatry.

Biographies: F. J. Braceland, *Amer. J. Psychiat.*, 1957, *113*, 871-876; L. Brink & E. Jeliffe, *J. Nerv. Ment. Dis.*, 1933, *77*, 134-152, 274-282; O. Bumke, *Klin. Wochenschr.*, 1926, *5*, 1905-1908; R. Gaupp, *Emil Kraepelin*, 1939; H. W. Gruhle, *Nervenarzt*, 1956, *27*, 241-244; E. Harms, In E. Kraepelin, *Dementia Praecox and Paraphrenia*, 1971, pp. vii-xviii; L. L. Havens, *J. Nerv. Ment. Dis.*, 1965, *141*, 16-28; S. E. Jeliffe, *Arch. Neurol. Psychiat.*, 1932, *27*, 761-775; E. Kahn, *Amer. J. Psychiat.*, 1956, *113*, 289-294; E. Mapother, *J. Ment. Sci.*, 1927, *73*, 509-515; A. Meyer, *Amer. J. Psychiat.*, 1926-1927, *83*, 749-755; E. Trömner, *Deutsch. Z. Nervenheilk.*, 1927, *96*, 1-7; W. Weygandt, *Allg. Z. Psychiat.*, 1927, *85*, 443-458; W. Wirth, *Arch. ges. Psychol.*, 1927, *58*, i-xxxii; *Biog. Lex.*; *EB*, 13; *IESS*, 8.

KRECH, DAVID

American Psychologist

Born: Svenchanka, Belorussia (White Russia), March 27, 1909

Died: Berkeley, California, July 14, 1977

Highest Degree: Ph.D. in psychology, University of California at Berkeley, 1933, under E. C. Tolman*

Positions, Honors: 1933-37, research fellow, research assistant, research associate, University of Chicago; 1937-38, research associate, Swarthmore College; 1938-39, instructor, University of Colorado; 1939-42, political activity, government employment; 1942-45, U.S. Army; 1945-47, Swarthmore College; 1947-

71, University of California at Berkeley; 1949-50, visiting professor, University of Oslo, Norway; 1971, emeritus professor of psychology, University of California; American Psychological Association Distinguished Scientific Contribution Award, 1970; honorary doctorate, University of Oslo

Krech was brought to the United States in 1913. During his career as a psychologist Krech worked in the areas of animal learning, social psychology, and the neurophysiology of learning and memory. His work with Lashley* at the University of Chicago resulted in his proposing the noncontinuity hypothesis of problem solving (1938). Krech's wartime experience with practical problems of a social-psychological nature led him, after the war, to the field of social psychology. In addition to contributing journal articles, Krech published, with R. S. Crutchfield as coauthor, a very successful textbook in social psychology, *Theory and Problems of Social Psychology* (1948; revised as *Individual in Society*, 1962). He was involved in launching, in 1948, the "New Look" in psychology, originated by Jerome Bruner and Leo Postman, which stressed social psychological factors in perception. The term *New Look* was introduced by Krech. In this connection, Krech and Bruner published a joint volume, *Perception and Personality* (1950).

Krech made his most important contribution to psychology during the two decades 1950-70. He returned to animal studies, exploring the relationship between environmental factors and changes in the biochemistry and neuranatomy of the brain. Under the leadership of Krech, an interdisciplinary team whose principal members were E. L. Bennett and M. R. Rosenzweig, published some sixty papers in this area during the period. Their work produced solid chemical and anatomical proof of what learning theorists had postulated all along, namely, that the brain responds, in physically measurable ways, to environmental influences, whether they take the form of learning or sensory stimulation.

Krech also excelled as a teacher. The introductory psychology text, first published in 1958 with R. S. Crutchfield (*Elements of Psychology*), has been widely used and has seen two additional editions (1969 and 1974). Krech's publications number about 120.

Biographies: *Amer. Psychologist*, 1971, *26*, 81-86; M. R. Rosenzweig, *APA Monitor*, Sept./Oct., 1977, *8*, 13; *HPA*, 6; *IESS*, 18.

KRETSCHMER, ERNST
German Psychiatrist
Born: Wüstenrot, near Heilbronn, Baden-Württemberg, October 8, 1888
Died: Tübingen, Baden-Württemberg, February 8, 1964
Highest Degree: M.D., University of Munich, 1914
Positions, Honors: 1918-26, University of Tübingen; 1926-46, University of Marburg; 1946-64, University of Tübingen; honorary Ph.D., University of Bonn

Kretschmer made significant contributions to psychiatry and wrote several volumes about abnormal psychology, such as *Hysterie, Reflex und Instinkt* (1923), in which he proposed that hysteria originates in conscious mechanisms that later become automated and unconscious; *Die sensitive Beziehungswahn* (1918); and *Medizinische Psychologie* (1922).

Kretschmer is important to psychology for his contributions to the constitutional theory of personality. The modern constitutional theory begins with Kretschmer. As a result of his psychiatric practice Kretschmer decided that physique had a bearing on behavior, especially behavior in two major types of mental disorders, manic-depressive psychosis and schizophrenia. Kretschmer devised an objective method for classifying individuals according to type of physique and also related physique to normal behavior patterns. He established three basic body types: asthenic, athletic, and pyknic. A fourth category, dysplastic, included markedly deviant physiques. After measuring the physiques of two hundred sixty psychotic patients, Kretschmer concluded that there was a "clear biological affinity" between manic-depressive psychosis and the pyknic physique on the one hand and the asthenic and athletic body builds and schizophrenia on the other. Kretschmer assumed continuity between normal and abnormal behavior and therefore a relationship between physique and normal patterns of behavior, but he never demonstrated such a relationship. Later, William Sheldon* provided a much more sophisticated development of Kretschmer's ideas. Kretschmer's constitutional type theory is presented in his *Körperbau und Charakter* (1921).

Biographies: H.-J. Eysenck, *Brit. J. Psychol.*, 1964, *55*, 249-251; K. Hoehne, *Amer. J. Psychiat.*, 1964, *121*, 206-208; E. Kretschmer, *Gestalten und Gedanken*, 1963; *Rev. psychol. appl.*, 1953, *3*, 43-48; W. Schulte, *Z. Psychother. med. Psychol.*, 1965, *15*, 65-72; F. Steinwachs, *Psychol. Rundsch.*, 1964, *15*, 144-145; *Biog. Lex.*; *EB*, 13; *IESS*, 8; *NYT*, 1964, Feb. 10, 27:3.

KRIES, JOHANNES VON

German Physiologist

Born: Roggenhausen, West Prussia, October 6, 1853

Died: Freiburg-im-Breisgau, Baden-Württemberg, December 30, 1928

Highest Degree: M.D., University of Leipzig, 1876

Positions: 1876-77, University of Berlin; 1877-80, University of Leipzig; 1880-1924, University of Freiburg

Kries's main contributions to psychology were in the area of the physiology of vision. Among them the most notable was his "duplicity" theory of vision (1894) that associated the rodlike cells of the retina with brightness discrimination and vision at reduced levels of illumination and the cone-shaped cells with daylight and color vision. Kries measured difference thresholds for hue; studied additive color mixture, color blindness and color weakness; and identified and named protanopia, deuteronopia, deuteroanomalous trichromacy, and prontanomalous trichromacy. He clarified the nature of color blindness and thereby reconciled the Hering* and the Young*-Helmholtz* theories concerning this phenomenon. Kries wrote books about vision (*Die Gesichtsempfindungen und seine Analyse*, 1882) and sensory physiology (*Allegemeine Sinnesphysiologie*,

1923) and sections about vision in books edited or compiled by others. He was also one of the first editors of the *Zeitschrift für Psychologie*, of which he and Ebbinghaus* were the cofounders.

Biographies: E. v. Skramlik, *Z. Sinnesphysiol.*, 1929, *60*, 249-256; *Biog. Lex.*

KRIS, ERNST

Austrian-American Psychoanalyst
Born: Vienna, Austria, April 26, 1900
Died: New York, New York, February 27, 1957
Highest Degree: Ph.D. in art history, University of Vienna, 1922
Positions: Private practice of psychoanalysis; with BBC in England during World War II; coeditor, *Imago*, since 1933

Kris was one of several ego psychologists who extended the Freudian concept of ego to make it less dependent on the id. Kris held that both the id and the ego arise from a more primitive matrix. He thus conferred greater functional autonomy to the ego than is possible in Freudian theory. In comparison with Sigmund Freud*, Kris attributed more functions to the ego that do not arise from conflict: movement, perception, reality testing, and thinking. Kris's ego-regression theory develops Freud's idea of the nature of genius. Psychotics cannot control the eruptions from the unconscious, and because they do not elaborate on the contents of the unconscious, they do not communicate. A creative person who faces a problem may, on the other hand, regress to an earlier stage of development when the problem used to be less structured, restructure it, and formulate it in productive, communicable terms. By his emphasis on ego psychology, Kris contributed toward a rapprochement between psychoanalysis and general psychology.

In England during World War II Kris studied German radio propaganda and, on arriving in the United States, published his *German Radio Propaganda: Report on Home Broadcasts During the War* (with Hans Speier, 1944). Kris applied psychoanalytic concepts to the study of art (*Psychoanalytic Explorations in Art*, 1952) and children. He initiated the Child Study Center at Yale University Medical School and the Gifted Adolescent Research Project at New York Psychoanalytic Institute to study the dynamic factors underlying children's behavior. In a discussion with Leopold Bellak, Kris suggested that children may be expected to identify more readily with animals than with humans. Bellak (and S. S. Bellak) constructed the *Children's Apperception Test* (1949) on the basis of Kris's idea.

Biographies: H. Hartmann, *Psychoanal. Stud. Child*, 1957, *12*, 9-15; W. Hoffer, *Int. J. Psychoanal.*, 1957, *38*, 359-362; R. M. Loewenstein, *J. Amer. Psychoanal. Ass.*, 1957, *5*, 741-743; S. Ritvo, *Psychoanal. Quart.*, 1957, *26*, 248-250; S. Ritvo & L. B. Ritvo, In F. Alexander, S. Eisenstein, & M. Grotjahn (Eds.), *Psychoanalytic Pioneers*, 1966, pp. 484-500; *EJ*, 10; *IESS*, 8; *NYT*, 1957, Feb. 28, 27:3.

KRÜGER, FELIX (E.)

German Psychologist
Born: Posen, Posen, Germany, August 19, 1874
Died: Basel, Switzerland, February 25, 1948
Highest Degree: Ph.D. in psychology, University of Munich, 1897, under H. Cornelius and T. Lipps*
Positions: 1898-1900, University of Kiel; 1901-5, University of Leipzig; 1906-8, University of Buenos Aires; 1909-10, University of Leipzig; 1910-17, University of Halle; 1917-35, University of Leipzig

Krüger followed two great psychologists in their chairs: Ebbinghaus* at Halle and Wundt* at Leipzig. He established the Leipzig Gestalt school of psychology (as contrasted with the Berlin school of Wertheimer*, Köhler*, and Koffka*), also known as the school of *Ganzheitspsychologie*, or holistic psychology (*Über den Strukturbegriff in Psychologie*, 1923). The school was influenced by the Graz, or Austrian, school of psychology. Although accepting the idea of wholes, or *Gestalten*, as basic, it criticized the Berlin school for not including all psychological phenomena in its purview, such as emotions, feelings, and social and cultural phenomena. Krüger's goal was to study the totality of the person, which he later named "structure," in accord with Dilthey*. It included not only that which the phenomenologist studies but also all dispositional and determining tendencies that underlie mental events. In Germany holistic psychology became the leading school of psychology in the mid-twentieth century. Other works of Krüger's that present the ideas of holistic psychology are *Komplexqualitäten, Gestalten und Gefühle* (1926), *Das Wesen der Gefühle* (1928), *Ganzheit und Form* (1932), *Lehre von dem Ganzen* (1948), and *Zur Philosophie und Psychologie der Ganzheit* (1953).
Biographies: A. Wellek, *Die Widerherstellung der Seelenwissenschaft im Lebenswerk Felix Kruegers*, 1950; F. Wyatt & H.-L. Teuber, *Psychol. Rev.*, 1944, *51*, 229-247; *EP*, 4; *PR*, 3.

KÜLPE, OSWALD

German Psychologist
Born: Kandava, Latvia, August 3, 1862
Died: Munich, December 30, 1915
Highest Degree: Ph.D. in psychology, University of Leipzig, 1887, under W. Wundt*
Positions, Honors: 1887-94, University of Leipzig; 1894-1909, University of Würzburg; 1909-13, University of Bonn; 1913-15, University of Munich; honorary medical degree, 1907, University of Giessen

Külpe began to take issue with Wundtian psychology publicly in 1893 when in his *Grundriss der Psychologie* (English translation, *Outlines of Psychology*, 1895) he criticized the subtractive procedure used by Wundt to measure the duration of thought processes. Külpe was at first strictly Wundtian. He elaborated on Wundt's notion of attributes in his doctrine of attributes (quality, intensity, duration, plus extension for vision and touch). It added an element of nativism (he thought space could not be constituted from nonspatial attributes) to his basically empiricist orientation. He made no mention of thinking but counted a very large number (twelve thousand) of sensations. Külpe's reaction-time work in Wundt's laboratory, however, started him on a line of thought that eventually led away from Wundtian psychology toward the experimental study of thought, which Wundt held to be an impossibility. Külpe applied the method of "systematic experimental introspection" to the investigation of thinking. Subjects performed some cognitive task and then analyzed their own thought processes used in the task.

Although Külpe established psychological laboratories at Würzburg (1896) and Bonn, he himself did little experimental work. He headed a group of psychologists, however, who did. The most important of them were Ach*, K. Bühler*, Marbe*, and Watt*. They and their work came to be called the Würzburg school of imageless thought. The writings of the school began with a 1901 paper by A. Mayer and J. Orth. To Külpe there were cognitive contents and cognitive acts. The cognitive acts were states of awareness of the existence of rules, relations, and intention and could not be said to have a sensory content, representation, or image. It was imageless thought. Külpe's psychology included both content and function or act. In his own day Külpe and the Würzburg school made important new contributions to the study of thought. A broader additional effect that, through later psychologists, has continued to this day was the emphasis placed on the role of motivation, set, and the nature of the cognitive task on thinking, as well as the recognition that not only elements consciously present in mind could affect thinking but that unconscious determinants were at work also. The radical development of the latter proposition is to be found in Sigmund Freud*. Külpe's criticism of Wundt's elementism and his inclusion of both content and act in psychology, on the one hand, and his analysis of mental life that was still done in terms of elements, albeit nonsensory ones, on the other hand, placed him midway between structuralism and Gestalt psychology. The originator of the Gestalt theory, Max Wertheimer*, was a student of Külpe's.
Biographies: C. Bäumker, *Jb. Bayr. Königl, Akad. Wiss.*, 1916, 73-102; K. M. Dallenbach, *Amer. J. Psychol.*, 1951, *64*, 3; A. Fischer, *Z. pädag. Psychol.*, 1916, *17*, 96-99; K. Marbe, *Fortschr. Psychol. Anwend.*, 1914, *2*, 302-320; R. M. Ogden, *Amer. J. Psychol.*, 1951, *64*, 4-19; *EP*, 4; *EUI*, 28(2); *IESS*, 8.

L

LADD, GEORGE TRUMBULL

American Psychologist
Born: Painesville, Ohio, January 19, 1842
Died: New Haven, Connecticut, August 8, 1921
Highest Degree: Degree in divinity, Andover Theological Seminary, 1869
Positions: 1869-79, minister; 1879, professor of mental philosophy, Bowdoin College; 1881-1905, professor of mental philosophy, Yale University; president, American Psychological Association, 1893; three honorary degrees

Although influenced strongly by Lotze*, Ladd was a pioneer of the "new" psychology who emphasized the functional aspects of mind and its biological and adaptive significance. Ladd's influence was felt not through his theories or research (although he and E. Scripture* founded the Yale psychological laboratory in 1892) but in the textbooks he wrote. *Elements of Physiological Psychology* (1887) was a compendium of the "new," or Wundtian (Wundt*), psychology and represented the first survey of it in the English language. It remained one of the most important texts of the new psychology for some time and appeared in updated form in 1911 when R. S. Woodworth* revised it. A short edition of the *Elements* appeared in 1891 and then a larger *Psychology, Descriptive and Explanatory* (1894). Ladd's *Psychology* was another compendium of the new psychology, but it did not receive the acclaim of the 1887 text. It was, however, an important event in that Ladd's emphasis on the adaptive functions of mind was clearly evident, and the volume may thus be considered a cornerstone of the edifice of American functionalism that was to appear full fledged later.

In his conception of psychology Ladd had a place for an active self. Consciousness he viewed as the activity of the self. Inasmuch as he felt that he had to describe consciousness also in terms of Wundt's contents, his view was similar to that of Külpe's*. The function of the active self Ladd considered to be the solving of problems of adaptation. Consciousness to Ladd thus had a purpose. In 1894 Ladd published a *Primer of Psychology* and in 1895, *Philosophy of Mind*. Afterward he reverted to philosophy, so his influence in psychology lasted only the eight or so years of his writing of the textbooks. That activity was important enough for him to have merited the appelation "the Sully* of America."
Biographies: A. C. Armstrong, *Phil. Rev.*, 1921, *30*, 639-640; G. D. Hicks, *Nature*, 1921, *108*, 23-24; E. S. Mills, *George Trumbull Ladd: Pioneer American Psychologist*, 1969; C. E. Seashore, *Science*, 1921, *54*, 242; E. B. Titchener, *Amer. J. Psychol.*, 1921, *32*, 600-601; *DAB*, 10; *NCAB*, 33; *NYT*, 1921, Aug. 9, 9:5; *Who Was Who in America*, 1.

LADD-FRANKLIN, CHRISTINE

American Psychologist
Born: Windsor, Connecticut, December 1, 1847
Died: New York, New York, March 5, 1930
Highest Degree: Ph.D. in mathematics, Johns Hopkins University, 1926
Positions, Honors: 1904-9, Johns Hopkins University; 1910-30, Columbia University; two honorary degrees

Ladd-Franklin's interest in mathematics extended to the investigation of the *horpoter* (the locus of all points in the field of vision that fall on corresponding parts in the two retinas) in 1886, which led to the study of color vision. Her work between 1891 and 1892 in Georg Müller's* laboratory at Göttingen and in Helmholtz's* laboratory in Berlin led her to develop a new theory of color vision, for which she is best known. In a paper published in 1892 Ladd-Franklin developed Hering's* hypothesis that the red-green visual substance was a later evolutionary development than the blue-yellow substance. Her theory was that black-white vision was the most primitive form of color vision, that white became differentiated into blue-yellow vision, and that later still in the evolutionary history yellow differentiated into red-green vision. This differentiation she thought was represented in the decomposition products of a retinal color molecule. Red, green, and blue are fundamental colors. The simple colors are those that can be obtained by backtracking the steps of evolution, such as yellow. Other colors, such as purple, are complex colors. It was only a year before her death that Ladd-Franklin published a book about color vision, *Colour and Colour Theories* (1929).
Biographies: R. McHenry (Ed.), *Famous American Women*, 1983; R. S. Woodworth, *Science*, 1930, *71*, 307; *DAB*, 10; *NCAB*, 26; *Notable American Women 1607-1950*, vol. 2; *PR*, 3; *Who Was Who in America*, 1.

LADYGINA-KOTS, NADEZHDA NIKOLAYEVNA

Russian Psychologist

Born: Penza, Russia (now Russian SFSR), May 19, 1889

Died: Moscow, September 3, 1963

Highest Degree: Graduated from Women's Superior School, Moscow, 1916; doctor of biological sciences

Positions, Honors: 1913-45, Laboratory of Animal Psychology, Darwin Museum, Moscow; 1945-63, senior scientific worker, Institute of Philosophy, USSR Academy of Sciences, Moscow; Order of Lenin, 1955; honored scientist, 1960

Ladygina-Kots was a comparative psychologist who studied the adaptive behavior of primates. Much of her work was done at the Darwin Museum, where she established the Laboratory of Animal Psychology in 1913. She tested the cognitive abilities of chimpanzees, using the matching-to-sample method of her own invention, and habit formation in monkeys, using puzzle boxes. She performed many experiments and produced rich data on the use of tools by chimpanzees and on the comparative psychology of the preschool child and the ape in building and imitation. Her comparative study of the child and the ape showed qualitative differences in their mental development, for instance, that the chimpanzee "thinks" in terms of spatio-temporal connections and the child looks for causal relationships. Among the many monographs about the evolution of behavior written by Ladygina-Kots are [*An Investigation of the Cognitive Abilities of the Chimpanzee*](1923); [*Adaptive Motor Habits of the Macaque in Experimental Situations*](1928): [*The Young of the Chimpanzee and the Human Child*] (2 vols., 1935); and [*Activity Involving the Use of Tools and Construction in the Higher Apes (Chimpanzees)*](1959).

Biographies: J. Brožek & D. I. Slobin (Eds.), *Psychology in the USSR: An Historical Perspective*, 1972, p. 25; *Who Was Who in the USSR*, 1972.

LAMARCK, JEAN BAPTISTE PIERRE ANTOINE DE MONET

French Biologist

Born: Bazentin, Somme, August 1, 1744

Died: Paris, December 18, 1829

Education: Studied medicine, meteorology, botany, at the University of Paris

Positions: Various botanical appointments; from 1793, taught invertebrate zoology, University of Paris

In addition to making very significant contributions to the development of animal taxonomy, Lamarck is most often associated with the doctrine of the genetic transmission of acquired characteristics. In his *Philosophie zoologique* (1809), he proposed a theory of evolution whose main tenet was that the use and disuse of organs leads to their modification, and that these modifications are passed on to descendants (Lamarckian transmission). Lamarck was the first biologist of prominence to adopt the evolutionary point of view, even though his particular theory was soon proved to be wrong.

Lamarck was an important link in the development of evolutionary thought that reached its peak in Charles Darwin's* theory. For that reason alone he may be considered an important contributor to the development of scientific psychology. Although proven wrong repeatedly, the doctrine of Lamarckian transmission still haunts science, including psychology. The idea that behaviors acquired during one's lifetime may pass on to the offspring has appealed to many a psychologist, and individuals as prominent as William McDougall* have attempted to demonstrate it by animal rearing and breeding experiments.

Biographies: M. Barthelemy-Madaule, *Lamarck the Mythical Precursor*, 1982; M. Landrieu, *Lamarck: Le fondateur du transformisme*, 1909; A. S. Packard, *Lamarck: The Founder of Evolution*, 1901; E. Perrier, *Lamarck*, 1925; L. Roule, *Lamarck et l'interprétation de la nature*, 1927; *CE*, 8; *DSB*, 7; *EB*, 13; *EP*, 4.

LA METTRIE, JULIEN OFFRAY DE
French Philosopher
Born: St. Malo, Ille et Vilaine, December 25, 1709
Died: Berlin, Germany, November 11, 1751
Highest Degree: M.D., University of Reims, 1733
Positions: 1735-42, private practice, St. Malo; 1742-45, surgeon to the guards, Paris; 1748-51, court reader to Frederick the Great

La Mettrie lived but forty-one years. He nevertheless left his mark on the history of philosophy as well as psychology by pioneering in the materialistic conception of the human being. Although he started out as a theologian, a severe fever during a military campaign convinced him that mental life is nothing but the result of the mechanical action of the nervous system, that soul and thinking could not be distinguished from each other, and that the former was just as perishable as the latter—without a body, neither one had an existence. The volume *L'Homme machine* (1748) places La Mettrie at the beginning of the line of descent of behaviorism. La Mettrie extended Descartes's* view of animals as reflexive automata and applied it to humans. His physiology, however, was still speculative. He considered organisms to be mechanisms, made of matter that not only moved but had consciousness. To a person, La Mettrie asserted, the only reality is the body. A person's apparent uniqueness is only due to the complexity of that person's actions. His extreme views attracted attention but also led to persecution, making him a landmark that signified the increasing materialism of eighteenth-century science.

Biographies: R. Boissier, *La Mettrie: Médecin, pamphlétaire et philosophe*, 1931; P. Lamée, *Julien Offray de La Mettrie, médecin, philosophe: Sa vie, son oeuvre*, 1954; J. M. L. C. J. de Maître, *Un médecin philosophe: De La Mettrie*, 1919; L. Mendel, *La Mettrie: Arzt, Philosoph, und Schriftsteller*, 1965; J. E. Poritzky, *Julien Offray de LaMettrie: Sein Leben und seine Werke*, 1900 (Reprinted 1971); M. Tisserand, In *La Mettrie: Textes choisis*, 1954, pp. 7-46; G. F. Tuloup, *Un précurseur méconnu: Offray de La Mettrie, médecin-philosophe*, 1938; *DSB*, 7; *EP*, 4.

LANDIS, CARNEY
American Psychologist
Born: West Alexandria, Ohio, January 11, 1897
Died: New York, New York, March 5, 1962
Highest Degree: Ph.D. in psychology, University of Minnesota, 1924, under K. S. Lashley*
Positions: 1926-30, Wesleyan University; 1930-62, New York State Psychiatric Institute and Hospital, New York City, and Columbia University

Landis was mainly a laboratory research psychologist with a wide range of interests, of which the strongest was in psychopathology and psychosexual development (*Modern Society and Mental Disease*, 1938; *Sex in Development*, 1940; *Personality and Sexuality of the Physically Handicapped Woman*, 1942; *Varieties of Psychopathological Experience*, 1964). He introduced quantification in these areas of research. With W. A. Hunt, Landis penned a classic monograph about the startle response (*The Startle Pattern*, 1939). He also wrote a number of papers about the expression and physiology of emotion, personality inventories, psychosurgery, flicker fusion, and psychopharmacology.
Biographies: W. A. Hunt, *Amer. J. Psychol.*, 1962, *75*, 506-509; *NYT*, 1962, Mar. 6, 35:1; *PR*, 3; *Who Was Who in America*, 4.

LANGE, CARL GEORG
Danish Physiologist
Born: Vordingborg, Sjaelland, Denmark, December 4, 1834
Died: Copenhagen, May 29, 1900
Highest Degree: M.D., University of Copenhagen, 1859
Positions: 1859-75, various medical appointments in Denmark; 1869-72, lecturer, University of Copenhagen; 1875-1900, University Hospital, lecturer, later professor of pathological anatomy, University of Copenhagen

About the same time that James* offered his theory of emotion (1884), and independently of him, Lange conceived a very similar theory. In studying the circulatory system he came to the conclusion that emotion was the result of felt changes in the blood vessels and published his views in an 1885 paper. It appeared later in his *Om Sidsbevaegelser* (1885; German translation, *Uber Gemüthsbewegungen*, 1887). Lange's theory was not so broad as James's and stressed vascular rather than all visceral changes. James republished his own theory in his *Principles of Psychology* in 1890, taking Lange's contribution into account. The theory became known as the James-Lange theory of emotion. Lange also wrote *Bidrag til mydelsernes fysiologi* (1889; English translation, *Contribution to the Physiology of Sensual Pleasure*, 1889), a study of pleasurable emotions that, in accordance with his theory of emotion, were the effect of vasomotor activity occurring during an aesthetic experience.
Biographies: K. Faber, *Erindringer om C. Lange*, 1927; E. Gotfredsen, *Medecinens Historie*, 1964; V. Meisen, *Prominent Danish Scientists Through the Ages*, 1932; *DSB*, 8.

LANGE, LUDWIG

German Physical Scientist
Born: Giessen, Saxony, June 21, 1863
Died: Weissenhof near Weinsberg, Württemberg, July 12, 1936
Highest Degree: Ph.D., University of Leipzig, under W. Wundt*
Positions: University of Leipzig, 1885-87

Working in Wundt's laboratory, Lange established that some of the differences in reaction time between individuals were owing to the individuals' attending either to the stimulus (sensorial reaction) or to the response (muscular reaction). In the latter case the reaction time was shorter. This clarified the nature of the personal equation devised by astronomers to account for individual differences between them in the observation of stellar transits. Oswald Külpe* used Lange's finding to support his contention that the subject's predisposition affects his sensory and motor responses. Lange's work created interest in the role of attention in sensory and perceptual processes. Later, Lange was cited as a pioneer in the experimental investigation of the dynamics of attitude.

Lange contributed to psychology only during the two years he was Wundt's assistant. It was also during that time that he made his even more important contribution to mechanics, his main interest. (His doctoral thesis was about the evolution of the concept of movement.) Recurring manic-depressive episodes forced him to leave Wundt's laboratory and destroyed his career as a scientist.
Biographies: M. v. Laue, *Naturwissenschaften*, 1948, *35*(7), 193-196; *EUI*, 29.

LANGFELD, HERBERT SIDNEY

American Psychologist
Born: Philadelphia, Pennsylvania, July 24, 1879
Died: Princeton, New Jersey, February 25, 1958
Highest Degree: Ph.D. in psychology, University of Berlin, 1909, under C. Stumpf*
Positions, Honors: 1910-24, Harvard University; 1924-47, Princeton University, 1937-47, Psychology Department chairman; editorial work, *Psychological Monographs* (1931-33), *Psychological Review* (1934-47); president, American Psychological Association, 1930; secretary-general, International Congress of Psychology (1945-51), International Union of Scientific Psychology (1951-54); honorary doctorate, University of Montreal, 1954

Langfeld was the last American psychologist to study under the first generation of German psychologists. Unlike his teachers, Langfeld could not believe that consciousness could be separated for study in isolation. He subscribed to a motor theory of consciousness, which said that sensations, emotions, and thoughts are all bound to motor processes. In his best-known book, *The Aesthetic Attitude* (1920), Langfeld appealed to a related idea to explain the emotional tone of works of art. Drawing heavily on Lipps* and his theory of sympathy, Langfeld asserted that although an emotional feeling originates in the perceiver, it is immediately and unconsciously projected to the work or art, which then seems to possess that emotional quality. The origin of the perceiver's state of mind may be, Langfeld thought, incipient muscular movements.

Langfeld did experimental work on action, inhibition, vision, synesthesia, aesthetics, and emotional expression. He wrote *On the Psychophysiology of a Prolonged Fast* (1914), *Psychology for the Armed Services* (1945), and, with Floyd Allport, *An Elementary Laboratory Course in Psychology* (1916), which was widely used for some years. He was coeditor of *Psychology for the Fighting Man* (1943), *Foundations of Psychology* (1948), and the first four volumes of *History of Psychology in Autobiography*. With Edwin Boring* and H. P. Weld, Langfeld started the "BLW" series of psychological texts. He was much interested in the international aspects of psychology and contributed to creating a greater interest in and acceptance of American psychological work in Europe.
Biographies: F. C. Bartlett, *Amer. J. Psychol.*, 1958, *71*, 616-619; C. C. Pratt, *Psychol. Rev.*, 1958, *65*, 321-324; A. T. Welford, *Nature*, 1958, *181*, 1241; *NYT*, 1958, Feb. 26, 27:3; *PR*, 3; *Who Was Who in America*, 3.

LAPICQUE, LOUIS
French Physiologist
Born: Epinal, Vosges, August 1, 1866
Died: Paris, December 6, 1952
Highest Degree: M.D., 1895; Sc.D., Sorbonne, 1897
Positions, Honors: 1894-1936, Sorbonne; numerous medals, awards, other honors

Lapicque acquired distinction for his work in neurophysiology. Of importance to physiological psychology was his work on nervous excitability (*La machine nerveuse*, 1943; *L'Isochronisme neuromusculaire et l'excitabilité rhythmogène*, 1946; a number of papers), especially that on the *chronaxie* (the duration that an electric current, twice the intensity threshold value, required to produce stimulation), which he named (*La chronaxie*, 1925; *L'Excitabilité en fonction du temps*, 1926; *La chronaxie et ses applications physiologiques*, 1938; additional papers). The chronaxie allowed the direct measurement of the effects on the nervous system of drugs, anesthetics, and other agents, as well as the study of the progress of nerve degeneration or regeneration. In 1913 Lapicque predicted that the chronaxie of motor fibers would be in inverse ratio to the diameter. This was later confirmed through the use of electronic instruments.
Biographies: E. D. Adrian, *Nature*, 1953, *171*, 153; A.-M. Monnier, *J. psychol. norm. path.*, 1953, *46*, 373-378; J. F. Fulton, *J. Neurophysiol.*, 1953, *16*, 97-100; *DSB*, 8; *EUI*, 29.

LAPLACE, PIERRE SIMON DE
French Astronomer and Mathematician
Born: Beaumont-en-Auge, Calvados, March 28, 1749
Died: Paris, March 5, 1827
Education: Military school at Beaumont, University of Caen
Positions: 1767-87, École Militaire, Paris; 1787-1827, École Polytechnique

Laplace was one of the top men of science of eighteenth-century France. His major contribution to science was in astronomy. He was also a first-rate mathematician. Laplace is important in the history of psychology because he formulated the normal law of error (in 1786), although the bell-shaped distribution of errors was already known to de Moivre. Laplace must also be credited with the application of this law to errors in scientific observation in general rather than just to specific instances, such as gambling events and life expectancies. The importance of the concept of normal distribution to statistics, especially inferential (decision-making) statistics is crucial. It is also therefore of crucial importance to psychologists, who use statistics in their work daily.

Biographies: D. F. Arago, *Ann. Rep. Board Smithsonian Inst.*, 1874, 129-168; J. J. Fourier, *Éloge historique de M. le Ms. de Laplace*, 1929; R. Hahn, *Laplace as a Newtonian Scientist*, 1967; S. Lilley, *Nature*, 1949, *163*, 468-469; *DSB*, 15; *EB*, 13; *EP*, 4; *IESS*, 9.

LASHLEY, KARL SPENCER
American Psychologist
Born: Davis, West Virginia, June 7, 1890
Died: Poitiers, France, August 7, 1958
Highest Degree: Ph.D. in genetics, Johns Hopkins University, 1914
Positions, Honors: 1915-17, St. Elizabeth's Hospital, Washington, D.C.; 1917-18, University of Minnesota; 1918-20, U.S. Interdepartmental Social Hygiene Board; 1920-26, University of Minnesota; 1926-29, Behavior Research Fund; 1929-35, University of Chicago; 1935-55, Harvard University; 1942-55, Yerkes Laboratory of Primate Biology; 1955-58, emeritus professor; president, American Psychological Association, 1929; five honorary degrees; Warren Medal in psychology, 1937; Elliot Medal in zoology, 1943; Baly Medal in physiology, 1953

Lashley's contribution to psychology was his studies of the cerebral localization of functions using learning and discrimination as the behavioral measures of the effects of ablation. He was responsible for pushing the localization-nonlocalization pendulum once more in the direction of nonlocalization. Although Lashley was a student of Watson's* and a behaviorist, he seldom engaged in school-related polemics but dedicated his efforts to research in physiological psychology. Franz* had already indicated that functional localization in the brain was not as specific as had been thought, and Lashley did his postdoctoral work under Franz. They published together a paper about the effects of cerebral ablation on learning and memory in the rat. From there on, Lashley published a long series of papers dealing with the effects of extirpation of various sites in the rat's brain and of different amounts of brain tissue removed upon learning, memory, and discrimination. In doing so he introduced a new animal testing device that became known as the Lashley jumping stand. It has enjoyed wide use in the study of the rat's behavior. By 1929 Lashley was able to publish a book summarizing the results of his work (*Brain Mechanisms and Intelligence*).

Two of the principles uncovered were that the rate and accuracy of learning is proportionate to the amount of brain tissue available (law of mass action), but that it is independent of the particular tissue that is available (principle of equipotentiality). These findings were revolutionary in view of the then-current conception of the brain as a set of isolated neurons, reflex paths, and synaptic resistance, the nervous system often being compared to a telephone switchboard. Lashley did not completely deny localization but stated that it was less precise and more complex than imagined before and that equipotentiality held sometimes (in the case of complex acts) but not always (especially for simple problems). Nevertheless, an antiphysiological trend set in, because it seemed to many that there was little left for the physiological psychologist to study.

In addition to studying brain functioning and learning, Lashley studied other behavioral phenomena: color vision, instinctive behavior, and, as a ramification of his ablation studies, pattern vision. In the latter area, his seminal idea that pattern vision may be explained in terms of interference or standing waves in the brain found a new life some forty years after its formulation. Lashley published more than one hundred major papers.

Biographies: F. C. Bartlett, *Biog. Mem. Fellows Roy. Soc.*, 1959, 5, 107-118; L. Carmichael, *Science*, 1959, *129*, 1410-1412; D. O. Hebb, *Amer. J. Psychol.*, 1959, *72*, 142-150; *Biog. Mem.*, 35; *DSB*, 8; *EB*, 13; *IESS*, 9; *NCAB*, 44; *NYT*, 1958, Aug. 17, 86:2; *PR*, 3.

LAVATER, JOHANN CASPAR
Swiss Pastor, Writer, and Patriot
Born: Zurich, November 11, 1741
Died: Zurich, January 2, 1801
Education: Degree in theology, University of Zurich, 1786
Positions: 1787-1801, pastor, St. Peter's Church, Zurich

Lavater was the founder of physiognomics. His interest in mesmerism and physiognomics was rooted in his religious convictions. It was an attempt to demonstrate visibly the divine in humans and the interaction between mind and body. Lavater was part of an antirational movement that had strong religious and literary components, and the writing of *Von der Physiognomik* (1772) and the four volumes of *Physiognomische Fragmente zur Beförderung der Menschenkenntnis und Menschenliebe* (1775-78; English translation, *Essays on Physiognomy*, 1789-98) was prompted more by religious and metaphysical considerations than scientific curiosity. His *Essays* were translated into ten languages and won him an European reputation and the friendship of people such as Goethe*. Herder* collaborated with him on these volumes. Because Lavater's style was simple and readable and he related physiognomy and character in the description of well-known contemporary figures, his book was widely read and Lavater himself became the most publicized physiognomist in history. Lavater did not accept the assumption made by earlier physiognomists of a direct and simple correlation between animal and human physiognomy and character. His own physiognomy, in turn, may be seen appearing in a more sophisticated form in later German physiognomy, graphology, and characterology.

Biographies: G. Gesner, *Johann Caspar Lavaters Lebensbeschreibung*, 3 vols., 1802; O. Guinaudeau, *Études sur Johann Caspar Lavater*, 1924; C. Janensky, *Johann Caspar Lavater*, 1928; J. C. Lavater, *Unveränderte Fragmente aus dem Tagebuch eines Beobachters seiner Selbst*, 1978; M. Lavater-Slomann, *Genie des Herzens*, 1939; F. Muncker, *Johann Caspar Lavater*, 1883; A. Vömel, *Johann Caspar Lavater: Ein Lebensbild*, 1927; *EP*, 4.

LAVOISIER, ANTOINE LAURENT

French Chemist
Born: Paris, August 26, 1743
Died: Paris, May 8, 1794
Highest Degree: Lic. juri, College Mazarin, 1764
Positions: Various scientific positions with the French government

As a member of the commission charged by the king of France to examine the phenomenon of animal magnetism, Lavoisier wrote a report in 1784 about the results of the investigation, including the description of several experiments on the efficacy of hypnotism performed by Benjamin Franklin*. The conclusion of the commission was that "animal magnetism" had no reality and that the phenomena attributed to it could be explained entirely in terms of suggestion. Lavoisier's report was the first scientific study of hypnotic phenomena. It anticipated the keen interest in hypnosis elicited by French medical men and psychologists in the nineteenth century.

Biographies: W. R. Aykroyd, *Three Philosophers*, 1935; J. A. Cochrone, *Lavoisier*, 1931; M. Daumas, *Lavoisier: Théoricien et expérimentateur*, 1955; R. Dujarric de la Rivière & M. Chabrier, *La vie et l'oeuvre de Lavoisier d'après ses écrits*, 1959; S. J. Feench, *Torch and Crucible: The Life and Death of Antoine Lavoisier*, 1941; M. L. Foster, *Life of Lavoisier*, 1926; D. McKie, *Antoine Lavoisier: Scientist, Economist, Social Reformer*, 1952; L. Velluz, *Vie de Lavoisier*, 1966; M. Vergnaud, *Cah. int. sociol.*, 1954, *17*, 123-139; *CE*, 8; *DSB*, 8; *EB*, 13; *EUI*, 29.

LAZARUS, MORITZ

German Philosopher
Born: Filehne, Posen, September 15, 1824
Died: Merano, Italy, April 13, 1903
Education: Studied philosophy at the Braunschweiger Institut, 1844-46; later, philology, law, and history
Positions: 1860-66, University of Bern; 1867-73, Kriegsakademie, Berlin; 1873-97, University of Berlin

Lazarus was a Herbartian but with the distinction of being also a social psychologist. He was a pioneer in ethnopsychology in the mid–nineteenth century. He and Steinthal* used data from comparative linguistics and mythological research and applied to them ideas developed by Humboldt*, Herder*, Hegel*, and especially Herbart*. Both Lazarus and Steinthal expected ethnopsychology to use exact scientific methods to study social psychological phenomena on the assumption that the mental phenomena to be studied existed only in their objective manifestations, such as religious practices and language. Lazarus accepted Kant's* idea that the categorical imperative exists universally but that no universal concrete ethical rules exist. The feelings of a person or a group of persons become behavior; these behaviors are imitated by others and institutionalized and, in turn, determine the feelings of other individuals. The realized similarity in attitudes leads to a feeling of similarity and solidarity in general, hence to the formation of political entities, such as nations. Lazarus's ideas concerning the reality, autonomy, and influence of social groups influenced such thinkers as Durkheim*. In 1859 Lazarus and Steinthal founded the first journal of social psychology, the *Zeitschift für Völkerpsychologie, und Sprachwissenschaft*. In 1890 it was continued as the *Zeitschift des Vereins fur Volkskunde*. In 1862 the University of Bern created the first chair in ethnopsychology, and Lazarus was its first occupant. He wrote about a dozen books on ethnopsychological topics. *Biographies*: M. Lazarus, *Aus Meiner Jugend: Autobiographie*, 1913; N. R. Lazarus, *Ein deutscher Professor in der Schweiz*, 1910; A. Leicht, *Lazarus, der Begründer der Völkerpsychologie*, 1904; J. Lorenz, *Lazarus als Pädagog*, 1914; B. Munz, *Moritz Lazarus*, 1900; *EJ*, 10; *EUI*, 29; *Jewish*, 6.

LE BON, GUSTAVE
French Sociologist
Born: Nogent le Totrou, Eure et Loire, May 7, 1841
Died: Marne-la-Coquette, near Paris, December 13, 1931
Highest Degree: M.D., 1876
Positions: From 1884, in government service; writer; at University of Paris

In spite of his medical degree, Le Bon felt no calling for the practice of medicine. He turned, in succession, to hygiene and physiology, archeology and anthropology, and sociology and social psychology. In all of these and many other areas he wrote a large number of articles and books.

In social psychology Le Bon influenced not only that field but also the thinking of the general public through his writings about the psychology of crowds and nations. *La psychologie des foules* (1895), his best-known work, saw many editions and was soon translated into other languages. His thesis was that mental phenomena that are easily controlled in individuals—strong emotions, affects, excitement—propagate and contaminate other individuals in unorganized groups, such as crowds, people in traffic jams, and groups of juveniles and children. These mental phenomena are contagious because of a lowering of resistance that takes place in groups. People in unorganized groups become uncritical and lose their ability to judge. Even so, a crowd possesses psychological unity, a collective mind (the law of the mental unity of crowds). Le Bon also believed that an idea becomes an impulse to action only after it enters the unconscious. This principle applied to both individuals and groups, including whole peoples.

Le Bon believed in racial hierarchy. He placed the white race above the colored ones and the Teutons and Anglo-Saxons with their individuality and rationality above the Latins, who to him were overemotional and reflected mob psychology (he held the same view of women, children, and socialists). After World War I he revised his opinion of the Teutons, however. Presented in books such as *Les lois psychologiques de l'évolution des peuples* (1894), *La psychologie du socialisme* (1898), *La révolution française et la psychologie des révolutions* (1912), and *La psychologie des temps nouveaux* (1920), these views, although unsupported by research, found a wide readership because of Le Bon's facile style. He may be said to have continued and developed the sociological ideas of Tarde* and Durkheim* concerning the nature of unorganized groups, as well as the views of the German ethnopsychologists, such as Herder*.

Biographies: E. Picard, *Gustave Le Bon et son oeuvre*, 1909; *EUI*, 29; *IESS*, 9; *NYT*, 1931, Dec. 15, 27:3.

LEEUWENHOEK, ANTONI VAN
Dutch Microscopist
Born: Delft, October 24, 1632
Died: Delft, August 26, 1723
Education: Grammar school
Positions: Dutch civil service

Leeuwenhoek constructed the first simple microscope in 1671. He proceeded to investigate microscopic animals and the microscopic structure of animal and plant tissue. His studies of animal reproduction showing the presence of spermatozoans refuted the then-prevailing theory of spontaneous generation. Basically, Leeuwenhoek's invention furthered the development of the biological sciences, including physiology and thereby neurophysiology and physiological psychology.

Biographies: C. Dobell, *Antony van Leeuwenhoek and His "Little Animals,"* 1932; M. Rooseboom, *Bull. Brit. Soc. Hist. Sci.*, 1950, *1*(4), 79-85; A. Schierbeek, *Measuring the Invisible World*, 1959; *DSB*, 8; *EB*, 13.

LEHMAN, HARVEY CHRISTIAN
American Psychologist
Born: Allen County, Kansas, March 13, 1889
Died: Athens, Ohio, August 8, 1965
Highest Degree: Ph.D. in psychology, University of Chicago, 1925
Positions: 1916-23, Hibbing Junior College; 1923-27, University of Kansas; 1927-59, Ohio University, 1959, professor emeritus

Lehman contributed to developmental psychology, especially in two areas, child play and achievement in the middle years. In each area he published papers and a book: *The Psychology of Play Activities* (1927, with P. A. Witty) and *Age and Achievement* (1953). The latter was his most significant contribution. Lehman collected a vast amount of data on achievement in all areas of human endeavor and studied the relationship between achievement and age. He established the age at which one is most likely to be most creative in the sciences and the arts, make the most money, achieve championships in sports, become president of a professional or scientific organization, and the like. He also theorized about the causes of the variations in the age of maximum achievement as a function of the type of endeavor. Lehman's work was a pioneering effort, and no similar effort has been made since. He also published a number of papers treating the same question in more specific detail.

Biographies: *NCAB*, 52.

LEHMANN, ALFRED GEORG LUDWIG

Danish Psychologist

Born: Copenhagen, December 29, 1858

Died: Copenhagen, September 26, 1921

Highest Degree: Ph.D. in psychology, University of Copenhagen, 1884

Positions, Honors: 1886-1921, University of Copenhagen; Danish Scientific Society Gold Medal, 1889

After obtaining his doctorate, Lehmann worked for a year in Wilhelm Wundt's* laboratory at Leipzig. There he first studied brightness contrast and then worked out pulse and breathing curves and correlated them with psychological processes according to Wundt (the "method of expression"). This work was published in 1893, causing a considerable stir because of its supposed accurate demonstration of the relationship between physiological and psychological processes. The relationship between the physical and the psychological always focused Lehman's interest. He demonstrated the relationship between mental work and the amount of carbon dioxide in breath and postulated a particular form of energy, the P-energy, to account for mental life. He was unable to prove its existence, however.

Upon his return to Copenhagen, Lehmann started the first Danish psychological laboratory at the University (in 1886). It was officially recognized in 1903. *Die Hauptgesetze des menschlichen Gefühlslebens* (1892, a translation of the Danish original of the same year) was his best-known book, but he wrote several additional ones, both in Danish and German: *Die körperlichen Äusserungen psychischer Zustände* (3 vols., 1898-1905), *Lehrbuch der psychologischen Methodik* (1906), *Stofskifte ved sjaelelig virksomhed* (1918), *Om størst udbytte af legemligt og aandelight arbejde* (2 vols., 1919), and others. His *Aberglaube und Zauberei* (1898; a translation from the 1896 Danish original) may be considered the first text of anomalistic psychology, the scientific study of extraordinary phenomena of behavior and experience.

Biographies: A. Aall, *Scand. Sci. Rev.*, 1922, *1*, 7-13; R. H. Pederson, *Arch. ges. Psychol.*, 1921-1922, *42*, 283-294; *EUI*, 29.

LEIBNIZ, GOTTFRIED WILHELM VON

German Philosopher
Born: Leipzig, July 1, 1646
Died: Hanover, November 14, 1716
Education: Doctorate in law, University of Altdorf, 1666
Positions, Honors: 1667-72, in service of the elector of Mainz; 1673-1716, in service of the house of Brunswick, since 1676, at Hanover; president, Berlin Academy of Science, 1700

To the scientific world Leibniz is important as a mathematician, and his psychological view of reality left a mark in the history of psychology. Leibniz viewed reality as activity. Substance, according to Leibniz, is being. Substance may be simple or compound. Simple substance is called the monads. The monads are indestructible, uncreated, and immutable elements of all being; hence their essence is also activity. Although monads develop, they do not affect each other. The world is thus an infinite set of independent monads, which precludes causation. Causation is mere coincidences in time and space. The activity of the monads is akin to perception. Thus monadal development implies the clarification of perception, and substance shows degrees of consciousness. Even the unconscious is only relatively so, for it is potentially capable of being perceived, just as the totality of countless drops of water is heard as the splash of a wave (apperception), although no single drop of water makes a perceptible sound (*petites perceptions*).

Leibniz's emphasis on activity places him as the forerunner of all of the activity psychologies that came later, such as act psychology. The notion that mind is a unitary, albeit developing, entity is found in later psychologies, such as the Gestalt theory. Leibniz also stands at the beginning of the development of the idea of the unconscious that, through Herbart*, Fechner*, and Wundt*, reached its culmination in Sigmund Freud*. In the question of mind-body relationship, Leibniz's acausality helped strengthen the doctrine of psychophysical parallelism, to which a number of prominent psychologists later subscribed. In this view body and mind are in agreement not because of some external intervention of causal act but because they obey parallel laws.

Biographies: H. W. Carr, *Leibniz*, 1960; H. H. Holz, *Leibniz*, 1958; K. Huber, *Gottfried Wilhelm Leibniz, Bildnis eines deutschen Menschen*, 1951; K. Kanthack, *Leibniz: Ein Genius der Deutschen*, 1946; R. W. Meyer, *Leibniz and the Seventeenth Century Revolution*, 1952; K. Müller & G. Krönert, *Leben und Werk von Gottfried Wilhelm Leibniz*, 1969; R. L. Saw, *Leibniz*, 1954; H. Schmalenbach, *Leibniz*, 1921; G. Stieler, *Gottfried Wilhelm Leibniz: Ein Leben der Wissenschaft, Weisheit und Grösse*, 1950; W. Totok & C. Haase (Eds.), *Leibniz: Sein Leben, sein Wirken, seine Welt*, 1966; K. Zimmerman, *Gottfried Wilhelm Leibniz: Leben und Lehre eines weltumfassenden Geistes*, 1947; *ADB*, 18, 29; *DSB*, 8; *EB*, 13; *EP*, 4.

LENIN, VLADIMIR ILYICH
Russian Communist Leader and Philosopher
Born: Simbirsk (now Ulyanovsk), April 22, 1870
Died: Gorkii, Russian SSR, January 21, 1924
Education: Passed final examinations in law, University of St. Petersburg, 1891
Positions: No academic positions; chairman, Council of People's Commissars, 1917-24

Lenin developed the philosophical theory of dialectic materialism of Marx* and Engels, including the theory of reflection. The latter forms the basis of present-day Soviet psychology. It may be found in Lenin's *Materializm i empiriokrititsizm* (1909) and *Filozofskie tetradi* (1929-30). According to this theory, matter is primary. Mind, consciousness, the psyche, are secondary. Matter exists independently of consciousness; consciousness depends on matter. Consciousness is the highest product of matter organized in a special way. It represents the reflection, by the brain, of the objective, material world that exists outside the individual and independently of him. In *Materializm i empiriokrititsizm*, Lenin criticized Mach* and Avenarius* for viewing sensations as neutral elements, neither material nor mental, and for coming perilously close to Berkeley's* mentalism. According to Lenin sensations are the fundamental source of knowledge about the world. They are representations of objective reality rather than merely signals of that which inheres in the nerve fibers (as Johannes Müller* had it) or mere symbols of things (according to Helmholtz*). Reality inheres in cognition, and cognition and objective reference proceed from subjective sensation to action and through action to objective reality.
Biographic data: *DSB*, 8; *EB*, 13; *EP*, 4; *IESS*, 9.

LENNENBERG, ERIC HEINZ
American Psychologist
Born: Germany, September 19, 1921
Died: White Plains, New York, June 2, 1975
Highest Degree: Ph.D., Harvard University, 1958
Positions: 1956-58, resident, Russell Sage Foundation; 1958-67, Harvard University and Harvard Medical School; 1959-62, research associate, Massachusetts Institute of Technology; 1964-65, visiting professor, University of Zurich; 1967-68, University of Michigan; 1968-75, Cornell University; 1970-72, visiting professor, University of Rochester; 1971-72, staff scientist, Massachusetts Institute of Technology

Lennenberg's major achievement was his proposal, formulated in the late 1950s, that the acquisition and possession of language are to be explained mainly in terms of biological properties of the brain and the vocal apparatus. He summarized his work in *Biological Foundations of Language* (1967), a work whose considerable influence was enhanced by the swing of the nature-nurture pendulum in psychology toward the nature side at that time.

Biographies: American Men and Women of Science, 12th ed.; *NYT*, 1975, June 7, 30:1.

LEONT'EV, ALEKSEĬ NIKOLAEVICH

Russian Psychologist

Born: Moscow, February 5, 1903

Died: Moscow, January 22, 1979

Highest Degree: Graduated in social sciences, Moscow State University, 1924; doctor of science, 1940

Positions, Honors: 1924-31, Institute of Psychology, Academy of Communistic Education, Moscow; 1931-34, Ukranian Psychoneurological Academy, Khar'kov; 1934-63, Institute of Psychology, Moscow; 1963-79, Moscow State University, 1967-79, dean, faculty of psychology; recipient of the Lenin Prize, several other medals and honors; honorary degree from Sorbonne; president, eighteenth International Psychological Congress, 1966

In the 1920s Leont'ev studied the historical development and structure of thinking with Vygotskiĭ*. Both formed the school of "cultural and historical development of the mind," distinguished by the first application of the historical method to the study of mental processes. His work on memory, done from this point of view, was published in 1931 in his *Razvitie pamyati*. During the Khar'kov period the work of a group of young psychologists under Leont'ev's direction yielded the initial idea of the "unity of external action and internal mental activity." Leont'ev elaborated this idea upon his return to Moscow in a series of papers in which he considered the historical development of consciousness in humans, relating it to the nature of human activity. Further work with children on the development of mental processes as a function of activity yielded a large number of publications. From 1963 on Leont'ev changed to the study of the nature of mental processes themselves. *Deyatel'nost', soznanie, lichnost'* (1975) contains Leont'ev's elaboration of Vygotskiĭ's ideas in the form of the "theory of activity," which is the major theoretical orientation of Soviet psychology.

Leont'ev was instrumental in separating psychology from pedagogy, the establishment of departments and faculties (at Moscow State University) of psychology, and the recognition of psychology as an independent branch of science by the USSR Academy of Sciences. He was a leading figure in Soviet psychology for several decades and evolved into the most important theorist.

Leont'ev was the author of some two hundred scientific publications, sixty of which have been translated into other languages. A collection of his most significant works, *Problemy razvitiya psikhiki* (1959; 2nd ed., 1965; 3rd ed., 1972), has been translated into thirteen languages.

Biographies: H. L. Pick, *Amer. J. Psychol.*, 1979, *92*, 555-556; *Psychol. Today*, March 1971; *Vop. Psikhol.*, 1973, *19*(1), 176-178.

LESSING, GOTTHOLD EPHRAIM
German Writer and Critic
Born: Kamenz, Saxony, January 22, 1729
Died: Braunschweig, Lower Saxony, February 15, 1781
Highest Degree: *Candidat en médecine*, University of Leipzig, 1748; master's, University of Wittenberg, 1751
Positions: Self-employed

Lessing was unoriginal as a thinker, but he was very influential in spreading ideas. He advanced psychology by translating Huarte's* *Trial of Wits* from Spanish into German (1752) and by proposing, in his own *Die Erziehung des Menschengeschlechts* (1777), one form of the recapitulation theory: he described the development of personality as a recapitulation of the development of humankind. Rousseau* had already stated his cultural recapitulation theory. G. S. Hall* picked up this theme again in 1904, but it was soon and for the last time laid to rest since it failed to find any empirical support.

Biographies: G. Bauer & S. Bauer, *Gotthold Ephraim Lessing*, 1968; F. A. Brown, *Gotthold Ephraim Lessing*, 1971; E. H. Gombrich, *Proc. Brit. Acad.*, 1957, *43*, 133-156; K. S. Guthke & H. Schneider, *Gotthold Ephraim Lessing*, 1967; H. Leisegang, *Lessings Weltanschauung*, 1931; O. Mann, *Lessing: Sein und Leistung*, 1961; W. Ritzel, *Gotthold Ephraim Lessing*, 1966; E. Schmidt, *Lessing: Geschichte seines Lebens und seiner Schriften*, 2 vols., 1923; *ADB*, 19, 45; *EP*, 4.

LEUBA, JAMES HENRY
American Psychologist
Born: Neuchâtel, Switzerland, April 9, 1868
Died: Winter Park, Florida, December 8, 1946
Highest Degree: Ph.D. in psychology, Clark University, 1895, under G. S. Hall*
Positions: 1898-1933, professor of psychology, head of Psychology Department, Bryn Mawr College, after 1933, professor emeritus

The topic of Leuba's doctoral dissertation was the psychology of religion, a topic he pursued throughout his career in spite of criticism from the press and churchmen. His pioneer studies resulted in several books about the psychology of religion: *A Psychological Study of Religion: Its Origin, Nature, and Future* (1912; translated into French and Japanese), *The Belief in God and Immortality* (1916), *The Psychology of Religious Mysticism* (1925; translated into French and German), *God or Man? A Study of the Value of God to Man* (1933), and others. Leuba's other interests included perception, comparative psychology, and motivation. In the latter area he adhered to Pierre Janet* and William McDougall* rather than Sigmund Freud*, whom he did not respect.

Biographies: K. E. McBride, *Amer. J. Psychol.*, 1947, *60*, 645-646; *NYT*, 1946, Dec. 10, 31:2; *PR*, 3.

LÉVY-BRUHL, LUCIEN
French Anthropologist
Born: Paris, April 10, 1857
Died: Paris, March 13, 1939
Highest Degree: Docteur des lettres, University of Paris, 1884
Positions: 1895-1939, Sorbonne (University of Paris), Paris

Lévy-Bruhl's main concern was to demonstrate the essential differences between the thinking of the civilized and the primitive human being. He thought that the primitive had no conception of physical causality, that the primitive's thinking was magic, confusing the natural with the supernatural, lacking in logic and the ability to form abstractions. All categories of logic, he thought, are produced by the collective consciousness. Lévy-Bruhl wrote several books about the mind of the primitive, among them *How Natives Think* (1910), *Primitive Mentality* (1922), *The Soul of the Primitive* (1927), and *Primitives and the Supernatural* (1931). His contention that the primitive mind is prelogical, unable to think logically, has been disproved, and he himself in his later life conceded that his theories had been inadequate. In spite of that, his ideas influenced minds such as Jung's*. Jung repeatedly referred to Lévy-Bruhl, particularly his idea that the native, being unable to draw a clear line between himself and his environment, lives in a *participation mystique*; the notion of the *abaissement du niveau mental*, a "lowering of the mental level" during which abnormal states of mind and abnormal mental phenomena ensue; and the notion of *représentations collectives*, which became Jung's archetypes.
Biographies: J. Cazeneuve, *Lucien Lévy-Bruhl*, 1972; R. Lenoir, *Amer. J. Sociol.*, 1939, *44*, 980; H. Wallon, *Rev. phil.*, 1939, *5-6*, 254-257; *EJ*, 11; *EUI*, 30; *EP*, 4; *IESS*, 9; *Jewish*, 7; *PR*, 3.

LEWES, GEORGE HENRY
English Philosopher
Born: London, April 18, 1817
Died: London, November 28, 1878
Education: Various schools in London, Jersey, Brittany, and Greenwich
Positions: No academic or official appointments; writer and critic

Lewes's education was spotty, but he was gifted and engaged in a number of activities. He is known mainly for his efforts as a writer and critic. He stated more fully (*Problems of Life and Mind: The Study of Psychology*, 5 vols., 1873-79) than Charles Darwin* or Herbert Spencer* had done the significance of the evolutionary theory for psychology, namely, that humans, being part of nature, can be studied like any other animal by the scientific method. He added that since humans were also social beings, they must be studied in their interaction with the social environment, since all mental activity is the result of the interaction of an organism with its physical and social environment. While describing human nature in associationistic and empiricist terms, Lewes avoided materialism, subscribing to the double aspect theory of body-mind relationship. He was a determinist who included free will in his world picture by stating that although unpredictable events do occur, they occur subject to the existing laws of nature. Only choices that are compatible with physical laws can be made. To illustrate his position he used the analogy of the sailor who is free to move about the ship but cannot change the course of the ship.

Lewes also dabbled in physiology where he achieved minor standing by investigating the sensations of innervation (1878) and argued against the Bell-Magendie law, substituting for it the notion of the recurrent impulse to account for sensory and motor acts. In this area he wrote *Physiology of Common Life* (2 vols., 1858-1860), and *Studies in Animal Life* (1862).

Biographies: H. Green, *Contemp. Rev.*, 1878, *31*, 25-53; E. Hardwick, *Partisan Rev.*, 1955, *22*, 260-264; A. R. Kaminsky, *George Henry Lewes as Literary Critic*, 1968; A. T. Kitchel, *George Lewes and George Eliot: A Review of Records*, 1933; R. E. Ockenden, *Isis*, 1940, *32*, 70-86; A. Trollope, *Fortn. Rev.*, 1879, *31*, 15-24; *DNB*, 11; *EP*, 4; *NYT*, 1878, Dec. 2, 1:6.

LEWIN, KURT

German-American Psychologist
Born: Mogilno, Prussia, September 9, 1890
Died: Newtonville, Massachusetts, February 12, 1947
Highest Degree: Ph.D. in psychology, University of Berlin, 1914, under W. Köhler*
Positions: 1922-32, University of Berlin; 1932-35, Cornell University; 1935-44, Child Welfare Research Station, University of Iowa; 1944-47, director, Research Center for Group Dynamics, Massachusetts Institute of Technology

Lewin began to study the effects of motivation on psychological processes before 1917. At Berlin he became acquainted with the founders of the Gestalt school of psychology and is sometimes counted as a member of that school. Lewin's contribution was to add and emphasize the factor of motivation within the Gestalt framework, especially the Gestalt concept of the field. In 1917 his first publication on the strength of association as a function of motivation appeared. Before he went to the United States, Lewin's students had already conducted a series of studies of the dynamics of behavior, which made him well known.

Although Köhler applied the notion of fields and field forces to the physical and biological world to explain perception, Lewin applied these concepts to behavior in general. Each person lives in a psychological field, his life space, which is the totality of his psychological reality as it exists at a given moment. To understand a person's life space, it is unnecessary to include an account of that person's past history, since the field, as presently constituted, is the totality of his present psychological reality and determines his actions completely. Actions are caused by the person's wishes. Actions are paralleled by locomotion within the psychological life space. Since physical space and psychological space do not have a one-to-one relationship, Lewin postulated that psychological space is topological, that is, it has no metric but only relationships of order. To preserve the advantages of a metric space, such as the possibility of quantitative prediction of behavior from quantified desires and wishes, which Lewin represented as vectors, he suggested that life space was "hodological," or having differentiated paths.

The concept of field forces was explored experimentally by Lewin and his students in a variety of settings involving tension, such as the study by Bluma Zeigarnik of the influence of uncompleted acts upon their retention (the Zeigarnik effect); the effect of success and failure on the level of aspiration; reaction of children to frustration; the behavior of people in small groups; the effects of authoritarian, laissez-faire, and democratic leaderships; and others. The group dynamics field may be said to have been originated by Lewin. Group dynamics research and practical applications of the principles of group dynamics (T-groups, sensitivity training) originated with Lewin's work at the Massachusetts Institute of Technology. Conflict and conflict resolution was also analyzed by Lewin, and terms like *approach-avoidance conflict*, *leaving the field*, and others have become stock-in-trade terms in general psychology. Lewin thus contributed to the development of Gestalt psychology by including in it motivational factors, launched experimental dynamic psychology, and pioneered in experimental social psychology.

Lewin exercised his influence largely through his personality, charisma, and democratic leadership rather than his writings, which consisted mostly of articles and monographs and very few books. His first book was a collection of seven of his articles under the title *A Dynamic Theory of Personality* (1935). *Principles of Topological Psychology* (1936) is the standard presentation of Lewin's theory. The representation and measurement of psychological forces are described in *Contributions to Psychological Theory* (1938). Lewin's *Resolving Social Conflicts* (1948) was published posthumously.

Biographies: D. Cartwright, *Int. J. Opin. Attitude Res.*, 1947, *1*, 96-99; R. Likert, *Hum. Relat.*, 1947, *1*, 131-139; R. Lippitt, *Sociometry*, 1947, *10*, 87-97; A. J. Marrow, *The Practical Theorist: The Life and Work of Kurt Lewin*, 1969; E. C. Tolman, *Psychol. Rev.*, 1948, *55*, 1-4; *EJ*, 11; *EP*, 4; *IESS*, 9; *Jewish*, 7; *NYT*, 1947, Feb. 13, 23:5; *Who Was Who in America*, 2.

LIÉBEAULT, AMBROISE-AUGUSTE

French Hypnotist

Born: Favières, Meurthe-Moselle, September 16, 1823
Died: Favières, Meurthe-Moselle, February, 1904
Highest Degree: M.D., University of Strasbourg, 1850
Positions: 1850-64, private practice, Pont-Saint-Vincent: from 1864, private practice, Nancy

At first a country doctor, Liébeault began using hypnotism (in 1860) on those of his patients who agreed to it. He was successful in using hypnotic treatment, especially with a patient whom Hyppolite Bernheim*, a much better known physician, had failed to cure with orthodox treatment. This converted Bernheim to hypnotism, and he and Liébeault together founded a clinic at Nancy where both practiced hypnotic treatment. In 1866 Liébeault published his first book about hypnosis, *Du sommeil et des états analogues....* It was followed by *Ébauche de psychologie* (1873), *Étude sur le zoomagnétisme* (1883), *Thérapeutique suggestive* (1891), and a number of journal articles. Liébeault's and Bernheim's explanation of the hypnotic state disagreed with that of the famous Charcot* who also used hypnotic treatment at the La Salpêtrière hospital in Paris, and a rivalry between the two schools ensued, with the view of the Nancy school prevailing in the light of accumulating evidence.

Biographies: A. Forel, *J. Psychol. Neurol.*, 1904, *3*, 97-99; M. Goldsmith, *Franz Anton Mesmer: The History of an Idea*, 1934; *EUI*, 30; Hirsch, *Biog. Lex.*, 3.

LIKERT, RENSIS
American Psychologist
Born: Wyoming, August 5, 1903
Died: Ann Arbor, Michigan, September 3, 1981
Highest Degree: Ph.D. in social psychology, Columbia University, 1932, under G. Murphy*
Positions: 1930-35, New York University; 1935-36, Sarah Lawrence College; 1935-39, director of research, Life Insurance Agency Management Association; 1939-44, head, Division of Program Surveys, U.S. Department of Agriculture; 1944-46, director, Morale Division of U.S. Strategic Bombing Survey; 1946-70, University of Michigan, 1946-48, Director, Survey Research Center, 1948-70, director, Institute for Social Research; 1971, professor emeritus; 1971-81, chairman of board, Rensis Likert Associates

Likert's contributions to psychology were in the areas of social psychology and industrial organization. In methodology his name is associated with a method of measuring attitudes, a psychological scale that has become known as the "Likert scale." It is suitable for measuring the strength and dimensionality of attitudes toward the most diverse topics and has been used in countless studies after Likert introduced it in his dissertation work in 1932. He introduced the open-ended, intensive interviewing technique in survey studies called the "funnel technique." He developed the procedure for obtaining true probability samples from large populations for survey purposes and may be considered one of the chief creators of modern population survey methods.

Likert wrote on his early work in social psychology in *Public Opinion and the Individual* (1938, with G. Murphy) and *Morale and Agency Management* (4 vols., 1940-41, with J. M. Willits). Likert's theory of organization was instrumental in creating a new field, that of organizational psychology. The theory's main feature is Likert's attempt to integrate the social and the individual-psychological approaches in explaining how organizations function and how to optimize the individual's functioning in a hierarchical social structure (*New*

Patterns of Management, 1961; *The Human Organization*, 1967; *New Ways of Managing Conflict*, 1976, with J. G. Likert).

Likert preferred to do his research through research teams, of which he organized four (see *Positions*, above): in the Life Insurance Agency Management Association, Division of Program Surveys, Institute for Social Research, and Rensis Likert Associates. The earlier ones were important in the development of social psychology, because Likert assembled research staffs that counted many individuals who were to become important contributors to the field later. The Institute for Social Research in particular achieved reputation as a research center in the social sciences, both among academicians and government officials. Likert contributed chapters about industrial organization and related topics to numerous edited books and wrote more than sixty journal articles.

Biographies: S. E. Seashore & D. Katz, *Amer. Psychologist*, 1982, *37*, 851-853; *American Men and Women of Science*, Social and Behavioral Sciences, 12th ed.; *Contemporary Authors*, 93-96; *IESS*, 18; *NYT*, 1981, Sept. 4, 12:2; *Who's Who in America*, 1974.

LINDWORSKY, JOHANNES
German Psychologist
Born: Frankfurt am Main, January 21, 1875
Died: Essen, North Rhineland-Westphalia, September 9, 1939
Highest Degree: Ph.D. in psychology, University of Munich, 1915, under J. Fröbes*
Positions: 1920-28, University of Cologne; 1928-39, German University (University of Prague)

Lindworsky studied thinking and emotion and counted himself among the Würzburg psychologists of imageless thought. His main concern, however, was the will. In his first book, *Der Wille* (1919), Lindworsky presented a survey of the contemporary literature on the will as well as his own theory of the will, which was his most important contribution to psychology. According to his theory, motivation precedes willing. Motives are "everything which is represented to the mind as a value realizable through the voluntary act." All phenomena of volition are the voluntary direction of attention toward a complex of images. The will, not being a force but a switching mechanism, cannot be strengthened by repetition but by directing attention to motives. Will training occurs when an appreciation of values and motives is produced. In this context Lindworsky interpreted the spiritual exercises of Ignatius Loyola, thus establishing a link between the school of imageless thought and Thomistic psychology. Lindworsky was also a good experimenter, wrote an *Experimentelle Psychologie* (1921; English translation, 1931) and numerous articles on a wide variety of subjects, many of them in popular magazines; *Theoretische Psychologie* (1932; English translation, 1931); *Psychologie der Aszese* (1935; English translation, 1936); and other books.

Biographies: H. Misiak & V. Staudt, *Catholics in Psychology*, 1954, pp. 111-125; *PR*, 3.

LINNAEUS, CAROLUS

Swedish Botanist
Born: Råshult, Sweden, May 23, 1707
Died: Uppsala, Uppsala, Sweden, January 10, 1778
Highest Degree: M.D., University of Harderwijk, Holland, 1736
Positions: 1732-78, University of Uppsala

The name of Linnaeus, the founder of taxonomy in botany and zoology, is one of the famous names in biology. One direct contribution of Linnaeus to psychology was the classification of odors that he proposed in a 1752 paper. Linnaeus suggested the classification of odors into the aromatic, fragrant, ambrosiac, alliaceous, hircine, foul, and nauseous. With minor variations, this classification has been retained to this day through the work of investigators of smell such as Henning* and Zwaardemaker*.

In a more general way, the classificatory work of Linnaeus made classification and description in science, including psychology, important. The classificatory and phenomenological tradition in psychology continued through the work of individuals such as Goethe* in the eighteenth century, Purkinje* and Hering* in the nineteenth century, and the Gestalt psychologists in the twentieth century. Linnaeus opposed any idea of organic evolution. His taxonomic trees of plants and animals, however, stimulated thought along evolutionary lines. Systematic evolutionary thought began after Linnaeus, leading to Charles Darwin* and the evolutionary theory.

Biographies: W. Blunt, *The Compleat Naturalist: A Life of Linnaeus*, 1971; A. J. Boerman, *Taxon*, 1953, *2*, 145-156; T. Frängsmyr (Ed.), *Linnaeus: The Man and His Work*, 1983; T. M. Fries, *Linnaeus*, 1923; H. Goerke, *Linnaeus*, 1973; N. Gourlie, *The Prince of Botanists*, 1953; K. Hagberg, *Carl Linnaeus*, 1953; B. D. Jackson, *Linnaeus: The Story of His Life*, 1923; A. H. G. Uggla, *Linnaeus*, 1957; *DSB*, 8; *EB*, 14.

LINTON, RALPH

American Anthropologist
Born: Philadelphia, Pennsylvania, February 27, 1893
Died: New Haven, Connecticut, December 24, 1953
Highest Degree: Ph.D. in anthropology, Harvard University, 1925
Positions: 1928-37, University of Wisconsin; 1937-46, Columbia University; 1947-53, Yale University

Linton brought to bear psychological theories and findings on his study of culture. His most important theoretical work, *The Study of Man* (1936), is a synthesis of sociological, anthropological, and psychological theories about culture. The effect of culture upon personality is considered by him in *The Cultural Background of Personality* (1945). Although considering sociological, psychological, anthropological, and biological factors, Linton believed the primary determinant of personality to be sociological. The developing individual's personality is shaped by culture: culturally patterned behavior of other individuals

toward the child and those influences that derive from the individual's observations of, or instruction in, the patterns of behavior characteristic of his society. Although individuals tend to imitate the culture patterns of their society when confronted by a new situation, they try to adjust these patterns to their individual needs as the situation is repeated. Even so, throughout their lives culture continues shaping individuals' personalities by providing models for their specific responses.
Biographies: J. Gillin, *Amer. Anthropologist*, 1954, *56*, 274-281; A. Linton & C. Wagley, *Ralph Linton*, 1971; M. W. Smith, *Man*, 1954, *54*, April, Art. 78; *IESS*, 9; *NACB*, H; *NYT*, 1953, Dec. 25, 17:1; *Who Was Who in America*, 3.

LIPPS, THEODOR
German Psychologist
Born: Wallhalben, Rhineland-Palatinate, July 28, 1851
Died: Munich, October 17, 1914
Highest Degree: Ph.D. in philosophy, University of Bonn, 1874
Positions: 1877-90, University of Bonn, 1890-94, University of Breslau; 1894-1914, University of Munich

Although Lipps was a student of Wundt's* and stated that the subject matter of psychology was content, he may also be counted as belonging to the Austrian act school, particularly because of his emphasis on empathy, which is an act. Lipps postulated that consciousness is a function of the interaction of previous experiences, which are unconscious, and present experiences (apperception). Mind is the totality of these past experiences, and as such determines the way in which present stimulation is experienced, organized, and retained.

Lipps is best known for his empathy theory and aesthetics (*Raumaesthetik und geometrisch-optische Täuschungen*, 1897). According to this theory the perceiver perceives the nature of an object when he feels like that object or projects himself into the object. Lipps applied this theory both to aesthetics and the geometric illusions. A form is beautiful if it fulfills the function assigned it, as when the empathy felt for a column in a building that is too thin makes one feel the stress it experiences, creating thus a negative aesthetic impression. The vertical line in the vertical-horizontal illusion, for instance, is experienced as being longer because the upward direction of the vertical makes the observer feel like stretching up, and that feeling is projected into the vertical line.

In addition to *Raumaesthetik*, Lipps's *Grundtatsachen des Seelenlebens* (1883) was also well known. He produced several other books and many articles and monographs, although few of them are experimental, because Lipps was not an experimentalist.
Biographies: *Amer. J. Psychol.*, 1915, *26*, 160; G. Anschütz, *Arch. ges. Psychol.*, 1915, *34*, 1-13; E. v. Aster, *Z. Psychol.*, 1915, *70*, 429-433; *EP*, 4; *EUI*, 30.

LOCKE, JOHN
English Philosopher
Born: Wrington, near Bristol, August 29, 1632
Died: Oates, Essex, October 28, 1704
Education: M.A., Christ Church, Oxford University, 1658; B.M., 1675
Positions: 1667-75, in service of earl of Shaftesbury; later supported by studentship and inheritance; 1689-91, 1696-1700, government positions

Locke started the age of Enlightenment in England and France. He launched empiricism in England and thus laid the foundations of contemporary psychology. Locke's psychological views are in *An Essay Concerning Human Understanding*, first published in 1690. The essay is based on the proposition that understanding the way in which the human mind works is a prerequisite to understanding anything else. Psychology in Locke thus became propaedeutic to all other knowledge. Locke asserted with Aristotle* and Thomas Aquinas* that there are no innate ideas in the human mind; that the notion that there are such ideas comes from habit; that the mind is at first like blank paper or an empty cabinet that is gradually filled with ideas; and that these ideas are entirely the result of experience. Ideas are units of mind and arise from the working of the senses. The senses supply the simple, indivisible sensory ideas. Primary sensible qualities are solidity, form, substance, and motion. Colors, tastes, smells, and the like are secondary qualities since they do not inhere in the sensible objects themselves but produce sensations as modes of appearance of the primary qualities. To illustrate the nature of the secondary qualities, Locke used the famous example of the reversed sensations produced in a cold and a warm hand when both are placed in a basin of water at room temperature. In addition to sensory ideas there are also ideas that arise from reflection (such as perception and thinking), although the raw material that reflection works upon is supplied by the sense organs. Sensory ideas and those that come from reflection constitute the totality of mental activities. Simple ideas resulting from sensation and simple ideas resulting from reflection may combine to form complex ideas. Pain and pleasure are simple ideas. They occur simultaneously with the experience of sensations or reflection, and emotions are derived from the experience of pleasure and pain.

Locke coined the expression "association of ideas" but used it only to explain how wrong ideas become associated with each other, whereas the associationists that followed him used it to explain how any two ideas combine and therefore to explain the structure of mind itself. In the various aspects of Locke's treatment of mind—its analysis into the elements of ideas, the distinction between primary and secondary qualities, the careful and systematic use of introspection, denial of innateness of ideas, reflection as an inner sense, the association of ideas, and the referral of all mental life to experience—may be found the beginning of several trends and lines of thought that were to flourish in psychology in later centuries—associationism, structuralism, act psychology, and behaviorism—and through which Locke continues to exercise his influence even today.
Biographies: R. I. Aaron, *John Locke*, 1971; S. Alexander, *Locke*, 1970; H. R.

F. Bourne, *The Life of John Locke*, 2 vols., 1876 (Reprinted 1971); M. Cranston, *John Locke: A Biography*, 1957; K. Dewhurst, *John Locke*, 1963; P. King, *The Life and Letters of John Locke*, 2 vols., 1829; W. v. Leyden, In J. Locke, *Essays on the Law of Nature*, 1954, pp. 1-92; D. J. O'Connor, *John Locke*, 1952 (Reprinted 1967); *DNB*, 12; *DSB*, 8; *EB*, 14; *EP*, 4; *IESS*, 9.

LOEB, JACQUES

German-American Physiologist
Born: Mayen, Rhineland-Palatinate, Germany, April 7, 1859
Died: Hamilton, Bermuda, February 11, 1924
Highest Degree: M.D., University of Strasbourg, 1884
Positions: 1881-88, University of Würzburg; 1888-89, University of Strasbourg; 1889-91, Naples Biological Station; 1891-92, Bryn Mawr College; 1892-1902, University of Chicago; 1902-10, University of California at Berkeley; 1910-24, Rockefeller Institute for Medical Research, New York

Loeb headed the mechanistic school of animal psychology. In his theory of tropisms, presented in an 1890 paper, he proposed that tropisms exist not only in plants but also in animals, and that animal behavior is largely orienting movements determined by physical and chemical reactions in a field of force. Unlike Descartes*, however, Loeb attributed consciousness to animals having "associative memory," thus denying it only to animals on the lowest levels of the phylogenetic scale. His tropistic psychology fit in well with and supported the objective psychology of Watson*, under whose aegis behaviorism was beginning to emerge at the time Loeb was writing his books. In them he further expounded his mechanistic psychology: *The Mechanistic Conception of Life* (1912), *The Organism as a Whole* (1916), and *Forced Movements, Tropisms, and Animal Conduct* (1918). Earlier, Loeb had penned a text of comparative psychology stressing tropistic behavior on the basis of his observations of invertebrates (*Einleitung in die vergleichende Gehirnphysiologie und vergleichende Psychologie*, 1899). Toward the end of his career, Loeb founded, with W. J. V. Osterhout, the *Journal of General Physiology* (1918).

Biographies: R. L. Duffus, *Century Mag.*, 1924, July, *108*, 374-383; D. Fleming, In J. Loeb, *The Mechanistic Conception of Life*, 1954, pp. vii-xli; S. Flexner, *Science*, 1927, *66*, 333-337; A. E. Gussin, *J. Hist. Med.*, 1963, *18*, 321-336; *J. Gen. Physio.*, 1923-1924, *6*, unnumbered (after p. 347); P. A. Levene, *Science*, 1924, *59*, 427-428; W. J. V. Osterhout, *J. Gen. Physio.*, 1925-1928, *8*, ix-lix; D. E. Palmer, *J. Gen. Psychol.*, 1929, *2*, 97-114; N. Reingold, *Libr. Cong. Quart. J. Curr. Acq.*, 1962, *19*, 119-130; T. B. Robertson, *Sci. Prog.*, 1927, *21*, 114-129; M. Rothberg, *The Physiologist Jacques Loeb (1859-1924) and His Research Activities*, 1965; *Biog. Mem.*, 13; *DAB*, 11; *DSB*, 8; *EB*, 14; *EJ*, 11; *EP*, 4; *Jewish*, 7; *NCAB*, 11; *NYT*, 1924, Feb. 13, 19:3.

LOMBROSO, CESARE
Italian Psychiatrist and Anthropologist
Born: Verona, November 18, 1835
Died: Turin, October 19, 1909
Highest Degree: M.D., University of Pavia, 1858
Positions: 1862-71, University of Pavia; 1871-76, director, lunatic asylum at Pesaro; 1876-1909, University of Turin

Lombroso developed the positive school of criminology that, in contrast to the classical school that concentrated on the crime, concentrated on the criminal. Lombroso saw the criminal as an instance of physical degeneration and atavism. A criminal commits his criminal acts because he is a throwback to a more primitive state of development. Lombroso's was a theory of hereditary determinism. He believed that degeneration showed itself in certain physical characteristics, or stigmata, such as a narrow forehead, protruding ears, exaggerated facial bones, and the like, which permitted the identification of criminals (*L'Uomo delinquente*, 2 vols., 1876; *La Donna delinquente*, 1893). Although Lombroso's theory was discredited and Lombroso later gave up his biological theory and attempted to explain crime by reference to psychological and social factors, the notion of the criminal as a physically identifiable "type" persisted for a long time. Lombroso's emphasis on the criminal rather than the crime was emulated by many sociologists and criminologists.
Biographies: P. E. Bowers, *J. Delinq.*, 1919, *4*, 210-220; C. A. Ferrari, *Riv. psicol.*, 1906, *2*, 137-147; H. G. Kurella, *Cesare Lombroso: A Modern Man of Science*, 1911; A. Lacassagne, *Prof. sanit. morale*, 1964, *36*, 89-98; L. Lattes, *Scuola positiva*, 1959, *1*, 335-363; C. Legiardi-Laura, *Med. Life*, 1933, *40*, 354-390; G. L. Lombroso-Ferrero, *Cesare Lombroso*, 1921; M. E. Wolfgang, *J. Crim. Law Criminol.*, 1961, *52*, 361-391; *EJ*, 11; *EUI*, 30. Hirsch, *Biog. Lex.*, 3, Suppl.; *IESS*, 9; *Jewish*, 7; *NYT*, 1909, Oct. 20, 9:4; Pagel, *Biographisches Lexikon*.

LORGE, IRVING
American Psychologist
Born: New York, New York, April 19, 1905
Died: New York, New York, January 23, 1961
Highest Degree: Ph.D. in psychology, Columbia University, 1930
Positions: 1927-61, Columbia University, 1927-46, Teachers College, 1946-61, executive officer, Institute of Psychological Research

Lorge was an educational psychologist, known for his contributions to the measurement of intelligence (The Lorge-Thorndike Intelligence Tests, 1954-57; The Columbia Mental Maturity Scale, 1954, constructed with L. Blum and B. Burgmeister). He was one of the first to question the stability of the IQ and showed that proper schooling produced substantial increases in the IQ. Lorge's primary contribution was in the area of readability. He developed a readability scale in his capacity as a government consultant, improved army training of illiterates, and established the frequency of occurrence of different words in the general literature. These counts of semantic frequency (*The Teacher's Word Book of 30,000 Words*, 1944, with E. L. Thorndike*; and *Semantic Count of the 570 Commonest English Words*, 1949) have been used extensively by researchers in educational, learning, and other areas of research.

Biographies: *EJ*, 11; *NYT*, 1961, Jan. 24, 29:3; *PR*, 3; *Who Was Who in America*, 4.

LOTZE, RUDOLF HERMANN

German Philosopher
Born: Bautzen, Saxony, May 21, 1817
Died: Berlin, July 1, 1881
Highest Degree: M.D., University of Leipzig, 1838
Positions: 1839-44, appointments in medicine and in philosophy, University of Leipzig; 1844-81, University of Göttingen

Lotze's contributions to psychology were his book *Medizinische Psychologie oder Physiologie der Seele* (1852) and his theory of the local signs. His book was the first text of physiological psychology. Although it was heavily metaphysical, it was his empiricism that became part of the "new" psychology that arrived with Wundt*. Of the topics included in the book, Lotze's theory of space perception was his most important and influential contribution. Although he endowed the mind with the capacity to perceive space, the main point of the theory was that the mind produces spatial experience from nonspatial information, namely, intensity. A pattern of pressure intensities creates a local sign for touch. Eye movements create patterns of experienced intensity of these movements, which are the visual local signs. Local signs identify locations in two-dimensional space. They are joined into a perception of solid space through experience, as movements of the body piece together these local signs. When no actual movement occurs, there may be a tendency set up for movement, which takes the place of actual movement. The spatial relating of local signs obtained through experience is accomplished by the mind's ability to interpret movement in terms of space and thus to reestablish space from what was originally only a pattern of intensities. Lotze also held that with repetition local signs become unconscious, and visual space perception at least may be entirely non-experiential, a notion akin to that of unconscious inference advanced by Helmholtz*. In addition to writing *Medizinische Psychologie*, Lotz also wrote *Grundzüge der Psychologie* (1881) and, in general, was an enthusiastic supporter of psychology. Carl Stumpf* and Georg Elias Müller* were his students.

Biographies: R. H. Falckenberg, *Lotze*, vol. 1, 1906; A. Krohn, *Z. Phil. phil. Krit.*, 1882, *80*, 56-93; T. H. Lindsay, *Mind*, 1876, *1*, 363-382; E. Rhenisch, *Rev. phil.*, 1881, *12*, 321-336; F. Seibert, *Lotze als Anthropolog*, 1900; C. Stumpf, *Kant-Stud.*, 1917, *22*, 1-26; M. Wentscher, *Hermann Lotz*, vol. 1, 1913; *ADB*, 19, 52; *DSB*, 8; *EP*, 5; Hirsch, *Biog. Lex.*, 3, Suppl.; *IESS*, 9.

LUBBOCK, SIR JOHN (BARON AVEBURY)
English Amateur Scientist and Banker
Born: London, April 30, 1834
Died: Kinggate Castle, Kent, May 28, 1913
Education: Some private and public schooling, no university education
Positions: Banking; leisure-time naturalist

In addition to being a banker, Lubbock was a member of the Parliament; worked in anthropology, geology, and botany; popularized science (through his writings and the presentation of numerous lectures on all subjects); and was a prolific writer (some twenty-five books and more than one hundred articles). He pioneered in comparative psychology with his studies of insect behavior (*Ants, Wasps, and Bees*, 1882; *On the Senses, Instincts, and Intelligence in Animals*, 1888; *Intelligence of Animals, with Special Reference to Insects*, 1904). He investigated the social behavior as well as the sensory capacities and learning ability of insects. To observe ants in a controllable environment, he devised the ''Lubbock nest.'' Lubbock produced the first data on the longevity of ants, introduced the use of paint to identify individual animals, discovered the hearing organ in ants, used mazes and obstacles, tested the color vision of ants, bees, and *Daphnia*, and otherwise broke ground in the area of comparative psychology some time before C. L. Morgan* and E. L. Thorndike*.

Biographies: U. Grant-Duff, *The Lifework of Lord Avebury*, 1934; H. G. Hutchinson, *Life of Sir John Lubbock, Lord Avebury*, 2 vols., 1919; R. J. Pumphrey, *Science*, 1959, *129*, 1087-1092; *DNB*, Suppl. 2, 3; *DSB*, 8; *EUI*, 31; *IESS*, 9; *NYT*, 1913, May 29, 11:5.

LUDWIG, CARL FRIEDRICH WILHELM
German Physiologist
Born: Witzenhausen, Hesse, December 29, 1816
Died: Leipzig, Saxony, April 27, 1895
Highest Degree: M.D., University of Marburg, 1840, under Johannes Müller*
Positions, Honors: 1842-49, University of Marburg; 1849-55, University of Zürich; 1855-65, Academy for Military Surgeons, Vienna; 1865-95, University of Leipzig; numerous honorary titles, medals, awards

Ludwig was one of the founders of modern physiology in the latter half of the nineteenth century. His physiological institute at Leipzig became world famous. He performed brilliant experiments in physiology, attracting many students and visitors who later became famous themselves. He was one of four students of Johannes Müller (Ludwig, Du Bois-Reymond*, Brücke*, Helmholtz*) who in 1845 formed a pact to disprove vitalism. Ludwig did it by his study of the circulatory system. As early as 1846 he measured blood pressure continuously using his own invention, the kymograph (although the idea had been conceived earlier by Thomas Young*), and showed that blood circulation could be explained without resorting to the notion of any ''vital force.'' The kymograph itself became part of the standard equipment found in the early psychological laboratories.

Biographies: J. S. Burdon-Sanderson, *Smithsonian Inst. Ann. Rep.*, 1896, 365-370; W. P. Lombard, *Science*, 1916, *44*, 363-375; W. J. Meek, *The Gamma Alpha Record*, 1933, *23*(2), May, 31-43; H. Rein, *Klin. Wochenschr.*, 1936, *48*, 159; G. Rosen, *Bull. Hist. Med.*, 1936, *4*, 609-650; K. W. Rothschuh, *Deutsch. med. Wochenschr.*, 1953, *75*, 71-74; *ADB*, 52, 55; *DSB*, 8; *EUI*, 31; Hirsch, *Biog. Lex.*, 3, Suppl.; Pagel, *Biographisches Lexikon*.

LURIA, ALEKSANDR ROMANOVICH
Russian Psychologist
Born: Kazan, July 16, 1902
Died: Moscow, August 15, 1977
Highest Degree: Dr. of pedagogical sciences (psychology), Moscow University, 1936; Dr. of medical sciences, Moscow University, 1943
Positions, Honors: 1923-34, Institute of Psychology, Moscow University; founder and member, Center of Psychology, Ukrainian Psychoneurological Academy, and Department of Psychology, N. K. Krupskaya Academy of Communist Education; 1934-36, Moscow Medical Institute of Genetics; 1936-53, founder and member, Laboratory of Neuropsychology, Institute of Neurosurgery, USSR Academy of Medical Sciences, Moscow; 1953-59, Institute of Defectology, USSR Academy of Pedagogical Sciences; 1945-77, head, Department of Neuropsychology, Faculty of Psychological Sciences, Moscow State University; editorial work, *Voprosy Psikhologii*, *Neuropsychology*, *Cortex*, *Cognition*; vice-president, International Union of Psychological Sciences, 1969-72; honorary doctorates from the universities of Leicester (1968), Nijmegen (1969), Lublin (1973), Brussels (1975), and Tampere (1975); member of USSR and foreign academies of science; honorary member of foreign psychological associations, Order of Lenin; other orders and honors

Luria's early work was prompted by his interest in psychoanalysis and the desire to introduce objectivity in the study of affective processes. It led to the development of his "combined motor method" for relating affective states and motor behavior, a technique resembling lie detection (*The Nature of Human Conflicts*, 1932). From the beginning Luria was strongly influenced by L. S. Vygotskiĭ*, and he conducted a series of studies on the evolution of psychological processes and mental retardation. Luria and Vygotskiĭ next began the study of changes in mental functioning that occur in aphasia. Luria continued the work on brain organization, brain processes, and speech functions after Vygotskiĭ's death in 1934. It produced international fame for him. His early books in this area were *Traumatic Aphasia* (1947) and *The Restoration of Functions Following War-Caused Trauma of the Brain* (1948). Luria postulated that the higher cortical functions are carried out through the interaction among cortical areas that work in a more general way but become associated through concrete activity and language. Restoration of impaired brain functions may be achieved by finding the unimpaired links in the functional systems that may be substituted for the damaged ones. Luria's methods of restoring brain functions received widest recognition in the case of the Soviet physicist Landau, who had been declared dead four times after a car accident.

In the 1950s Luria made several important findings in the development of pathology of the control function of speech and in the 1960s and 1970s published a considerable number of papers and books that established what he considered to be a new branch of science, neuropsychology. They include *Higher Cortical Functions in Man* (1962), *The Human Brain and Psychological Processes* (1963), [*Neuropsychological Analysis of the Solution of Problems*](1966, with L. S. Tsvetkova), *The Frontal Cortex and the Regulation of Psychological Processes* (1970, editor, with E. D. Khomskaya), *An Introduction to Neuropsychology* (1973), *Psychophysiology of the Frontal Lobes* (1973, editor, with K. H. Pribram), *The Working Brain* (1973), *Basic Problems of Neurolinguistics* (1976), and *The Neuropsychology of Memory* (1976). Luria summarized his view of neuropsychology as follows: "[T]he higher psychological processes represent complex functional systems, social in their origin, mediated in their structure, and carried out by whole complexes of jointly working areas of the brain. . . . Each area of the brain, including the cortex, enters into functional systems in terms of its own particular role and makes its own specific contribution to the work of the whole functional system. Therefore, disturbance of any of the areas of the brain may lead to a loss of the entire functional system, but each disturbed center excludes a special factor from a given functional system." This view led to the development of a diagnostic system called "syndrome analysis." In a well-known book, *The Mind of a Mnemonist* (1968), Luria described how this method was applied to the study of the mental makeup of an individual with extraordinary memory. *A Man with a Shattered World* (1972) is a case history of a patient with a brain lesion and disturbed mental functioning where the syndrome-analysis method was likewise applied. Many of Luria's more than three hundred scientific works have been published in English and other languages.

Biographies: M. Cole, *Amer. Psychologist*, 1977, *32*, 969-971; M. Cole, *Amer. J. Psychol.*, 1978, *91*, 349-353; *Psychol. Today*, March 1971, 79-89; *Contemporary Authors*, 25-28; *HPA*, 6; *IESS*, 18; *NYT*, 1977, Aug. 17, IV, 19:4; *Prominent Personalities in the USSR*, 1968.

M

MACH, ERNST

Austrian Physicist

Born: Chirlitz-Turas, Moravia, February 18, 1838
Died: Vatterstetten, near Haar, Bavaria, February 19, 1916
Highest Degree: Ph.D. in physics, University of Vienna, 1860
Positions: 1864-67, University of Graz; 1867-95, University of Prague; 1895-1901, University of Vienna

Mach's contributions to psychology stem from his work as a philosopher of science as well as his purely psychological work. The latter included research on visual space perception and time perception and his experimental work on the perception of rotation (*Lehre von den Bewegungsempfindungen*, 1875), which was his most significant empirical contribution to psychology. His theory of the functioning of the semicircular canals is yet to be replaced by another.

At Prague Mach published his most important book, *Analyse der Empfindungen* (1886; English translation, *The Analysis of Sensations*, 1897). In this book, Mach set forth the principles of a positivist philosophy of science. With Hume*, Mach asserted that causality exists only as observed concomitant relationships, that all science is observational, and that the data of any science, including the "hard" sciences, are sensations. In echoing Berkeley*, Mach insisted that the physical world exists only in the form of sensations and that they are to be taken as they occur, meaning, for instance, that there were no such things as illusions. Among the immediate data of consciousness, that is, sensations, Mach included those of time and space, in contrast to Kant, who thought of time and space as innate reference systems with respect to which sensations were ordered, and

Wundt*, who thought in Kantian terms. Külpe*, however, was influenced by Mach and so, through him, was Gestalt psychology. Although Mach was a phenomenalist, the resemblance of his views to those of Berkeley made him appear an idealist, for which he was severely criticized by materialists such as Lenin*.

The scientific study of form perception begins with *The Analysis of Sensations*, for by making space a sensation that was correlated with the physical world, Mach made it amenable to scientific study. A form is recognized independently of other attributes, Mach said; hence there are form sensations. Mach also analyzed the physical form dimensions that determine the recognition of shape, such as rotation and reflections; made a contribution to the aesthetics of visual form; discovered the phenomenon known as Mach bands; and, in relation to the latter, made a mathematical analysis to demonstrate the origin of contour perception. Mach's seminal ideas concerning the nature of form were developed by the school of form qualities, a transitional stage between Mach and the Gestalt psychologists.

Biographies: M. H. Baege, *Die Naturphilosophie von Ernst Mach*, 1916; J. T. Blackmore, *Ernst Mach: His Life, Work, and Influence*, 1972; P. Carus, *Monist*, 1911, *21*, 19-42; H. K. F. Henning, *Ernst Mach als Philosoph, Physiker und Psycholog*, 1915; F. Herneck, *Phys. Bl.*, 1958, *14*, 385-390; A. Lampa, *Ernst Mach*, 1918; H.W. Pittenger, *Science*, 1965, *150*, 1120-1122; F. Ratliff, *Mach Bands*, 1965; A. Sommerfeld, *Jb. Bayr. königl. Akad. Wiss.*, 1917, 58-67; *DSB*, 8; *EB*, 14; *EP*, 5.

MAGENDIE, FRANÇOIS

French Physiologist
Born: Bordeaux, October 15, 1783
Died: Sannois, near Paris, October 17, 1855
Highest Degree: M.D., University of Paris, 1808
Positions: 1813-31, private teacher of physiology; 1831-55, Collège de France and Hôtel-Dieu hospital in Paris

In 1809 Magendie acquired a name by attacking in a paper Bichat's* doctrine of "vital properties." In the same year he conducted and reported an experiment on the effects of certain vegetable poisons (later known to have contained strychnine) on animals, for which Magendie has been called the father of experimental pharmacology. He is known, however, mostly for his discovery of the difference between sensory and motor nerves. Although Charles Bell* had described the distinction first (in 1811), Magendie did his work independently of Bell and stated the experimentally established distinction between the two kinds of nerves with greater clarity than Bell had done (*Expériences sur les fonctions des racines des nerfs quie naissent de la moelle épinière*, 1822). The principle that the posterior spinal roots are afferent or sensory and that the ventral roots are efferent or motor was eventually named the Bell-Magendie law but not until after a prolonged controversy over the question of priority between the two physiolo-

gists. The significance of this law is that it affirmed the possibility of an experimental approach to the study of feeling and acting. Magendie made several other important contributions to physiology that were unrelated to behavior and founded in 1821 the *Journal de physiologie experimentelle et pathologie*.
Biographies: L. Carmichael, *Psychol. Rev.*, 1926, *33*, 188-217; J. M. D. Olmsted, *François Magendie*, 1944; *DSB*, 9; *EB*, 14; *EUI*, 32; Hirsch, *Biog. Lex.*, 4; Pagel, *Biographisches Lexikon*.

MAIMONIDES (MOSES BEN MAIMON)
Jewish Philosopher
Born: Córdoba, Spain, 1135 or 1138
Died: Cairo, Egypt, 1204
Education: Schooled in law, philosophy, and science in Andalusia and Maghreb
Positions: Leader of Egyptian Jewry in Cairo; court physician to Saladin

Maimonides was attracted to Aristotelean philosophy (as taught by Alfarabi and Avicenna*), and his best-known work, *Guide of the Perplexed*, is an exposition of rabbinic theology in terms of Neoplatonic Aristoteleanism. He did not, however, invariably or fully accept Aristotle's* views.

In an untitled work of eight chapters written in 1168 as an introduction to a Talmudic treatise on ethics, *Ethics of the Fathers*, Maimonides presented a psychological view of the soul and its disorders. "Diseases of the soul" are due to following extremes rather than Aristotle's golden mean. Extremes in behavior are "moral imperfections." The brain, contrary to Aristotle, being the organ that enables one "to learn, remember, and understand things," is also the means to achieve moral healing. Instead of using magical or supernatural concepts, Maimonides speaks in medical terms and sees the morally inadequate person as learning to overcome neurotic tendencies. He also asserts that natural handicaps may be overcome by training and experience. As the physician must understand the body to heal it, those who would heal the soul are urged by Maimonides to understand the whole soul as well as its parts, to know "how to prevent it from becoming diseased, and how to maintain its health." Maimonides's position on disorders of the soul is similar to that taken by the twentieth-century American psychologist H. O. Mowrer*.

In addition to discussing the cure of souls, Maimonides took on other psychological topics, such as the nature of human faculties, motivation, reason, constitutional influences on behavior, and the role of the brain. Maimonides anticipated Spinoza* in stating that the geometric axioms are innate ideas (but not sin or virtue), in stressing the importance of the will, and in considering the soul's faculties as activities rather than independent "powers." His views on the soul qualify him as a forerunner of dynamic psychology. His view that the emotions are not a separate faculty but a state that accompanies motivation (appetitive faculty) has a very modern ring.
Biographies: I. Epstein (Ed.), *Moses Maimonides, 1135-1204*, 1935; F. M. Ibáñez, *International Record of Medicine and General Practice Clinics*, 1952, *165*, 221-228; *DSB*, 9; *EB*, 14.

MAINE DE BIRAN, MARIE FRANÇOIS PIERRE GONTHIER

French Philosopher
Born: Bergerac, Dordogne, November 29, 1766
Died: Paris, July 16, 1824
Education: Studied at the Collège at Périgeux
Positions: No official positions

As one of the idéologues, Maine de Biran was part of the idealistic reaction to the French eighteenth century materialism and mechanism. He was at first instrumental in spreading Lockian empiricism in France. He gradually discovered inadequacies in the Lockian view and added a metaphysical turn to his psychological thinking. In *Influences de l'habitude sur la faculté de penser* (1802), Maine de Biran argued that if the mind were only sensations, habituation would make one lose consciousness. It is the will, something besides mere sensations, that maintains a state of consciousness. In *Mémoire sur la décomposition de la pensée* (1804), Maine de Biran took issue with Descartes*. The subject of experience, so runs his argument, is not only the external but also the internal world. Statements about the latter can be made with a far greater degree of certainty because the inner experiences are the first experiences. It is certain from these experiences that the self is active. The first and fundamental certainty is the activity of the self, the efforts of the will, the *ego*, not the *cogito* of Descartes. Because the self as substance is not the same as self as subject, the methods of the physical sciences are inadequate to study the self as subject. All cognitive acts are basically activity and will. Although the self is at first not aware of its own existence, repeated experiences lead to a separation between the self and the nonself. The experience of resistance offered by the external world yields self-awareness as the will to respond to the environment is exercised. In his *Essai sur les fondements de la psychologie* (1812), Maine de Biran established the existence of a "hyperorganic" element in the psyche, an idea that was developed later in *Nouveaux essais d'anthropologie* (1823-24), where he described the development of the self through the stages of animal or sensory life, human life of will and freedom, and the spiritual life of transcended humanity.

In spite of his writing on psychological subjects (he also wrote *L'Apperception immédiate*, 1807; and *Rapports du physique et du moral*, 1814) Maine de Biran's influence on psychology in terms of the specifics of his philosophy was minimal, and his genetic approach to psychological questions was not emulated. His emphasis on activity and the will, however, left a legacy of a dynamic approach to psychology that has persisted in French psychology.

Biographies: V. Delbos, *Maine de Biran et son oeuvre philosophique*, 1931; A. Girard, *Le journal intime*, 1963; H. Gouhier, *Maine de Biran par lui-même*, 1970; P. P. Hallie, *Maine de Biran: Reformer of Empiricism*, 1959; R. Lacroze, *Maine de Biran*, 1970; P. Lemay, *Maine de Biran et la Société Médicale de Bergerac*, 1936; L. Lévy-Bruhl, *Open Court*, 1899, *13*, 458-464; A. de la Valette-Monbrun, *Maine de Biran*, 1914; D. Voutsinas, *La psychologie de Maine de Biran*, 1964; D. Voutsinas, *Rev. int. phil.*, 1966, *20*, 69-89; *EP*, 5.

MALEBRANCHE, NICOLAS DE
French Philosopher and Physicist
Born: Paris, August 8, 1638
Died: Paris, October 13, 1715
Education: Studied philosophy at Collège de la Marche, theology at Sorbonne
Positions: No official positions

Malebranche was a Cartesian philosopher who sought to complete Descartes's* philosophy with regard to body-mind interaction so that it would be compatible with Catholic theology and St. Augustine's* teachings. In Descartes's system, body and mind were completely separate; yet they interacted in the pineal gland. The problem created by Descartes of how the soul, an unextended substance, could influence the body, an extended substance, was solved by Malebranche by referring causation to God: if one event seems to cause another, it is because the first event gives the occasion for God to cause the second (*De la recherche de la vérité*, 1674-75). The soul mediates between God and the body, but its light comes mainly from the light of God. The bond to the body results in sense impressions, the bond to God in an insight into God's ideas. True cognition arises only from the latter bond; thus all sense impressions are deceitful and of practical use only. About the nature of the soul, one cannot have either ideas or knowledge in a strict sense; therefore there cannot be a strong science of the soul. Still, Malebranche valued inner knowledge above that of the sense impressions. Knowledge about other souls may be obtained on the assumption that all souls are the same. Although incomplete, inner knowledge of the working of the soul offers the possibility of having a science of mental life since introspection carries with it the seal of indubitable truth.

The soul has two kinds of faculties: understanding and will. Understanding is passive and includes sense impressions, imagination, and memory. The will manifests itself in attitudes, inclinations, and the "passions of the soul." Concerning psychophysical relationships, Malebranche held that to mental phenomena there correspond traces in the brain and that the brain is the nodal point in the mind-body relationship. The brain contains both mental and physical processes; hence it is possible to correlate the qualities of inner experience and physical quantities.

In addition to writing on philosophical psychology, Malebranche did research on light and vision, including color phenomena, and the psychological determinants of visual perception, such as the factors involved in the moon illusion.
Biographies: Y. M. André, *La vie du R. P. Malebranche*, 1886; P. Ducasse, *Malebranche: Sa vie, son oeuvre, avec un exposé de sa philosophie*, 1942; H. Gouhier, *La philosophie de Malebranche et son expérience religieuse*, 1948; M. Guérolt, *Malebranche*, 3 vols., 1955-59; L. Lévy-Bruhl, *Open Court*, 1898, *12*, 543-556; *EB*, 14; *EP*, 5.

MALINOWSKI, BRONISLAW KASPER
Polish-British Anthropologist
Born: Cracow, Poland, April 7, 1884
Died: New Haven, Connecticut, May 16, 1942

Highest Degree: Ph.D. in mathematics and physical sciences, University of Cracow, 1908; D.Sc. in anthropology, University of London, 1916

Positions, Honors: 1914-18, field work in anthropology in New Guinea and Melanesia; 1924-42, University of London; 1939-42, visiting professor of anthropology, Yale University; honorary D.Sc., Harvard University, 1936

Malinowski's work in anthropology focused on culture. He viewed culture as a system of collective habits that serves human needs. As humans seek satisfaction of their physiological drives, secondary drives arise that are also universal. The particular living conditions of a society give rise to motives derived from the secondary drives. All motives, however, rest basically on the physiological ones, and culture serves human needs. Malinowski found support for his views in psychology, especially in the ethnopsychology of Wundt*, with whom he studied between 1908 and 1910, and in the work of Clark Hull*, whose views also influenced him.

Malinowski acquired fame as a result of the thoroughness of his field work in the Trobriand Islands between 1914 and 1918. Of importance to psychology is his book *Sex and Repression in Savage Society* (1927), which reports his observations on the sex mores of the Trobrianders. These observations failed to support the supposed universality and innate nature of some of the phenomena basic to Sigmund Freud's* psychology, notably the Oedipus conflict. Malinowski's observations paved the way for cross-cultural and eventually experimental testing of the tenets of the psychoanalytical theory.

Biographies: C. Kluckhohn, *J. Amer. Folklore*, 1943, *56*, 208-219; M. F. A. Montagu, *Isis*, 1942, *34*, 146-150; G. P. Murdock, *Amer. Anthropologist*, 1943, *45*, 441-451; *IESS*, 9; *NYT*, 1942, May 17, 46:1.

MALTHUS, THOMAS ROBERT

English Economist and Demographer

Born: Dorking, Surrey, February 14, 1766

Died: St. Catherine's, near Bath, Somersetshire, December 23, 1834

Education: M.A., Cambridge University, 1791; took holy orders, 1797

Positions: 1805-34, professor of history and political economy, College of Haileybury

Malthus proposed the famous theory that although population increases on a geometric scale, food production increases on an arithmetic scale, and that for this reason humanity is destined to live in poverty (*An Essay on the Principle of Population*, 1798). Although "vice and misery," including contraception, war, famine, and disease, may keep check on population growth, the fact that there is an excess of population in relation to the amount of food available implies a struggle for survival. In general, Malthus viewed human society in biological terms. Charles Darwin*, Herbert Spencer*, and Alfred Wallace* read Malthus's *Essay* and were stimulated by it to begin thinking along evolutionary lines.

Biographies: J. Bonar, *Malthus and His Work*, 1924; J. M. Keynes, *Essays in Biography*, 1951; *CE*, 9; *DNB*, 12; *EB*, 14; *EP*, 5; *EUI*, 32; *IESS*, 9.

MARBE, KARL

German Psychologist
Born: Paris, France, August 31, 1869
Died: Würzburg, Germany, January 2, 1953
Highest Degree: Ph.D. in psychology, University of Bonn, 1893
Positions: 1895-1905, University of Würzburg; 1905-9, Academy of Social and Commercial Sciences (Akademie der Sozialwissenschaften), Frankfurt; 1909-34, University of Würzburg

Marbe first worked on classical problems in psychophysics and perception, as well as speech and language problems. He made the first distinction between popular and unusual associations in word-association tests and devised a soot-writing method for recording speech intonations. At Würzburg Marbe contributed to the development of the imageless-thought school through his work on judgment (*Experimentell-philosophische Untersuchungen über das Urteil, eine Einleitung in die Logik*, 1901). One of his important findings was that although the sensations and images produced by the stimulus being judged, such as a weight, were clearly present, the process whereby the judgment of "heavier" or "lighter" was arrived at could not be described by the subject. Marbe concluded that judgment is a logical and not a psychological concept. Later, he became disenchanted with Külpe's* "systematic experimental introspection," considered the then-current discussions about the concept of Gestalten unproductive, and turned to applied psychology. He started using aptitude tests in the various occupations and studied business psychology, accident proneness, and other related problems (*Fortschritte der Psychologie und ihre Anwendungen*, an applied psychological journal, was founded by Marbe in 1913). During his career Marbe published eighteen books and more than one hundred articles. An additional one hundred eighty books and papers were published by students and assistants who worked in his laboratory.
Biographies: K. Marbe, *Selbstbiographie...*, 1945; W. Peters, *Amer. J. Psychol.*, 1953, *66*, 645-647; *HPA*, 3.

MARIOTTE, EDMÉ

French Physicist
Born: Probably Chazeuil, Burgundy, ca. 1620
Died: Paris, May 12, 1684
Education: Self-taught
Positions: Prior of St. Martin-sous-Beaune, Dijon

Mariotte was one of the founders of experimental physics in France and an independent discoverer of Boyle's law. In 1668 (*Nouvelle discouverte touchant la veüe*) Mariotte discovered the blind spot in the retina, the site where the optic nerve enters it, and showed how it can be located by directing one's gaze in a certain way. He described the macula lutea and other parts of the eye. Mariotte also performed experiments to study the nature of light, color, and vision (*De la nature des couleurs*, 1681).

Biographies: L. Darmstaedter, *J. Chem. Educ.*, 1927, *4*, 320-322; *CE*, 9; *Chalmers*, 21; *DSB*, 9; *EUI*, 33; *Grande*, 23; *Nouvelle*, 33.

MARQUIS, DONALD G.

American Psychologist
Born: Two Harbors, Minnesota, June 22, 1908
Died: Cambridge, Massachusetts, February 17, 1973
Highest Degree: Ph.D. in psychology, Yale University, 1932
Positions, Honors: 1933-45, Yale University; 1945-57, University of Michigan; 1943-45, director, National Research Council Office of Psychological Personnel; 1947-50, chairman, Committee on Human Resources, Research and Development Board, U.S. Department of Defense; 1959-73, Massachusetts Institute of Technology; president, American Psychological Association, 1947

Until about 1940 Marquis did research and published in the area of conditioning and physiological psychology, especially the neurophysiology of vision. With E. R. Hilgard he wrote the widely used *Conditioning and Learning* (1940) text and with R. S. Woodworth*, *Psychology* (5th ed., 1947). Work on personnel problems during World War II oriented him toward applied and organizational psychology, especially the management of science and technology, social psychology of organizations, and group decision making. Marquis published a number of papers in these areas, two books—*Successful Industrial Innovations* (1969, with S. Meyers) and *Factors in the Transfer of Technology* (1969, with W. H. Gruber)—and was active on a number of committees and boards concerned with the problems of management of science and technology. An entrepreneur and organizer, Marquis was instrumental in organizing and expanding the activities of the Psychology Department at the University of Michigan after World War II. Because of his administrative and teaching ability his consulting advice was widely sought after by industries and institutions.

Biographies: R. R. Sears, *Amer. J. Psychol.*, 1973, *86*, 661-663; *American Men of Science*.

MARX, KARL HEINRICH

German Philosopher
Born: Trier, Rhineland-Palatinate, May 5, 1818
Died: London, England, March 14, 1883
Highest Degree: Ph.D. in philosophy and history, University of Jena, 1841
Positions: Various journalistic positions

Marx, the philosopher of history, greatest socialist thinker, and the ideological father of communism, influenced thinking in all of the behavioral sciences, including psychology. The fundamental assumptions of Marx's economic interpretation of history (*Misère de la philosophie*, 1847; and *Manifest der Kommunistischen Partei*, 1848) earn him a place in the history of psychology. One of his basic assumptions was that economic development is the primary determining factor of social development, and that it is social development that produces the development of ideas—political, philosophical, artistic, legal, and religious. Basically, consciousness is the product of the economic conditions of life: as they change, so does human thinking. Although ideas may also influence social and economic development, economic changes are primary. Although materialistic or selfish interests are important motivators, idealistic motives, such as altruism and patriotism, also play their part. Nevertheless, they themselves are a product of the material conditions of existence. The materialism of Marx and his coworker Friedrich Engels was later elaborated by Lenin*. Lenin's doctrine of reflection became the fundamental principle of Soviet psychology.

Biographies: I. Berlin, *Karl Marx: His Life and Environment*, 1963; J. D. Bernal, *Karl Marx and Science*, 1952; K. Korsch, *Karl Marx*, 1963; F. Mehring, *Karl Marx: The Story of His Life*, 1948; M. Rubel, *Karl Marx: Essai de biographie intellectuelle*, 1957; F. Tönnies, *Marx: Leben und Lehre*, 1921; *ADB*, 20; *DSB*, 15; *EB*, 14; *EP*, 5; *IESS*, 10; *Jewish*, 7; *NYT*, 1883, Mar. 17, 3:2.

MASLOW, ABRAHAM HAROLD
American Psychologist
Born: Brooklyn, New York, April 1, 1908
Died: Waltham, Massachusetts, June 8, 1970
Highest Degree: Ph.D. in psychology, University of Wisconsin, 1934, under H. Harlow*
Positions: 1934-35, University of Wisconsin; 1935-37, Teachers College, Columbia University; 1937-51, Brooklyn College; 1951-69, Brandeis University; president, American Psychological Association, 1968

Maslow was one of the moving forces behind what came to be called the "third force" in psychology, or humanistic psychology (in addition to behaviorism and psychoanalysis). It was not until the middle of his life that he began to produce writings that became the foundation stones of humanistic psychology. In his writings (*Abnormal Psychology*, 1941; *Motivation and Personality*, 1954; *Toward a Psychology of Being*, 1960; *Religion, Values, and Peak Experiences*, 1964) Maslow presented a holistic-dynamic theory that is based on a conception of the human being as healthy, normal, and having positive emotions and motives. There is a motivational hierarchy in which the higher motives are satisfied after the lower ones have been cared for. The lower motives are aroused by some deficiency (D-motives, such as hunger), the higher ones are to satisfy the higher needs of being (B-motives, such as self-actualization). Maslow makes *self-actualization*, a term coined by Jung*, a central theme of his psychology. The striving to realize the highest potential of the inner self, part of which is universal and part individual, leads to an integration of the various aspects of personality into a healthy, creatively functioning whole. For psychology to be more complete, it needs to study individuals who have come near the ideal of complete self-actualization.

Biographies: W. Bennis, *J. Creat. Behav.*, 1971, *5*, 7-18; *J. Hum. Psychol.*, 1970, *10*, 98-110; R. Lowrry, *A. H. Maslow: An Intellectual Portrait*, 1973; 11; *IESS*, 18.

MATSUMOTO, MATATARO

Japanese Psychologist

Born: Takasaki, Gumma, September 15, 1865

Died: Tokyo, December 24, 1943

Highest Degree: Ph.D. in psychology, Yale University, 1899, under E. W. Scripture*

Positions: 1900-1906, Tokyo Higher Normal School; 1900-1905, Tokyo Higher Female Normal School; 1901-6, University of Tokyo; 1907-16, University of Kyoto; 1910-15, Kyoto Municipal Higher School for Fine and Technical Arts; 1913-26, irregular member, University of Tokyo; 1920-29, Aeronautical Research Institute; 1929-43, Tokyo Bunrika University; 1929-43, Japan Women's University, Institute of Child Study; editor, *Japanese Journal of Psychology*; editorial work, *Journal of General Psychology*

Matsumoto was an assistant at Yale for three years and did work with Scripture in general experimental psychology. He was first to use the sound cage in the study of auditory perception. After obtaining the Ph.D. he worked for a year in the psychological laboratory at Leipzig. Upon his return to Japan, Matsumoto established a psychological laboratory at the University of Tokyo in 1903 and another at the University of Kyoto in 1908. In spite of his training Matsumoto gravitated toward experimental applied psychology. He may be credited with introducing experimental applied psychology in Japan, especially through his book *Psychocinematics* (1914), in which he described the objective study of purposive motor acts. His *Psychology of Intelligence* (1925) and *Psychology of Practical Life* (1926) were other works in applied psychology. In addition to being interested in applied psychology, Matsumoto was interested in art and wrote *Psychological Interpretation of Modern Japanese Paintings* (1915) and *Psychology of Aesthetic Appreciation of Pictorial Arts* (1926). He also wrote *Lectures in Experimental Psychology* (1914), *Outlines of Psychology* (1923), *Psychical Dispositions* (1929), and *Psychology of Childhood* (1930). Matsumoto contributed to the development of psychology in Japan through his writings and research as well as in training almost all of the senior psychologists in Japan.

Biographies: T. Watanabe, In [*A Collection of Psychological Theses*], 1959, pp. 18-35; *PR*, 3.

MAUDSLEY, HENRY

English Psychiatrist

Born: Rome, near Settle, Yorkshire, February 5, 1835

Died: Bushey Heath, Hertsfordshire, January 23, 1918

Highest Degree: M.D., University College, London, 1857
Positions, Honors: 1856-59, medical superintendent, Cheadle Royal; 1859-62, Manchester Royal Lunatic Hospital; 1864-74, West London Hospital; 1869-79, University College, London; editor, *Journal of Mental Science*, 1862-78; honorary LL.D.

In addition to making medical contributions to psychiatry, Maudsley conceived the idea and advanced some money for the London University Psychiatric Hospital, completed in 1915, that now bears his name. His *Physiology and Pathology of the Mind* (1867; third edition in two vols.: *The Physiology of Mind*, 1867; and *The Pathology of Mind*, 1879) was an influential book that formed the foundation of British medical psychology. In it Maudsley treated mental illness entirely on a physiological basis. At the same time he stressed the importance of considering those aspects of mind that are not accessible to introspection, that is, are unconscious, and believed that most behaviors are unconsciously motivated. Before Sigmund Freud*, he suggested that dreams might be used to reveal the specific effects of bodily organs on the mind. Some of the psychological wcrks that reflect Maudsley's viewpoint are *Body and Mind* (1870), *Responsibility in Mental Disease* (1874), *Body and Will* (1883), *Life in Mind and Conduct* (1902), and *Organic to Human, Psychological, and Sociological* (1917).

Biographies: A. J. Lewis, *J. Ment. Sci.*, 1951, 97, 259-277; P. Scott, *J. Crim. Law Criminol.*, 1956, 46, 753-769; *Biog. Lex.*; *EUI*, 33; *Grande*, 23; Hirsch, *Biog. Lex.*, 4; Pagel, *Biographisches Lexikon*.

MAXWELL, JAMES CLERK
Scottish Physicist
Born: Edinburgh, Scotland, November 13, 1831
Died: Cambridge, England, November 5, 1879
Highest Degree: Ph.D. in natural philosophy, Trinity College, Cambridge, 1854
Positions: 1856-60, Mariscal College, Aberdeen; 1860-65, King's College, London; 1871-79, Cambridge University

Maxwell, famous for his work in physics and electricity, contributed to psychology during his two postgraduate years at Trinity College. There he worked out, for the first time (1855), the quantitative laws of color mixture, recognizing that in such mixtures the intensity of light had to be taken into account and that therefore a color mixture diagram had to be a solid rather than a plane figure. He also developed a method, used ever since, for mixing colors using circles of colored paper (Maxwell discs) that were cut along a radius and could be superimposed on each other on a rotating disc showing sectors of varying width. Maxwell accepted Helmholtz's* three-color theory and computed from his color triangle (Maxwell triangle) the three excitation curves for the retina as well as those for a color-blind person. He wrote a number of significant papers about color and color vision, receiving for his work the Rumford Medal of the Royal Society. The Maxwellian view (through a hole smaller than the pupil) and the entoptical phenomenon called the Maxwell spot are also named after him.

Biographies: L. Campbell & W. Garnett, *The Life of James Clerk Maxwell*, 1970; R. T. Glazebrook, *James Clerk Maxwell and Modern Physics*, 1901; D. K. C. MacDonald, *Faraday, Maxwell, and Kelvin*, 1964; J. R. Newman, *Sci. Amer.*, 1955, *192*(6), 58-71; W. D. Niven, In *Scientific Papers of James Clerk Maxwell*, vol. 1, 1890, pp. ix-xxix; *DNB*, 13; *DSB*, 9; *EP*, 5.

McCOSH, JAMES
Scottish-American Philosopher
Born: Carskeoch, Ayrshire, Scotland, April 1, 1811
Died: Princeton, New Jersey, November 16, 1894
Education: Studied theology at the University of Edinburgh; licensed for ministry in 1834
Positions, Honors: 1852-68, Queen's College, Belfast; 1868-88, professor of history, philosophy, and psychology, College of New Jersey (Princeton College); 1870-92, president, Princeton College; honorary M.A., LL.D., D.D.

McCosh represented the Scottish school of philosophy (and psychology) in the United States. Both McCosh and Porter*, because of their position as professors of philosophy and psychology and presidents of Princeton and Yale, respectively, were the most prominent expositors of the Scottish view when the "new," or Wundtian, psychology was becoming known in the United States. They were also the last representatives of the Scottish school. McCosh wrote a work about motivation (*Psychology: The Cognitive Powers*, 1866), an exposition of the views of fifty philosophers of the Scottish school (*The Scottish Philosophy*, 1875), and a text about emotions (*The Emotions*, 1880) in which he adumbrated James's* theory of emotions.

Biographies: H. Calderwood, *United Presbyterian Mag.*, 1896, *13*, 454-457; A. A. Roback, *A History of American Psychology*, 1964; W. M. Sloane (Ed.), *The Life of James McCosh: A Record Chiefly Autobiographical*, 1896; *DAB*, 11; *EP*, 5; *NCAB*, 5; *NYT*, 1894, Nov. 17, 5:3.

McDOUGALL, WILLIAM
English-American Psychologist
Born: Oldham, Lancashire, England, June 22, 1871
Died: Durham, North Carolina, November 28, 1938
Highest Degree: M.D., St. Thomas Hospital, London, 1898
Positions: 1898-1904, Cambridge University; 1900-1906, University College, London; 1904-20, Oxford University; 1920-27, Harvard University; 1927-38, Duke University

Before beginning his work in psychology, McDougall had acquired a medical degree, with specialization in physiology and neurology, participated in the Cambridge University anthropological expedition to the Torres Straits, and studied with G. E. Müller at Göttingen. McDougall's initial work was in general experimental psychology. He studied vision, attention, memory, fatigue, emotions, and the effects of drugs. He formulated a drainage theory of inhibition.

He conducted psychological experiments at Oxford when Oxford had no psychology chair or even recognized experimental psychology and was thus instrumental in guiding British psychology in that direction. He was a cofounder of the British Psychological Society and the *British Journal of Psychology*. He wrote several psychology texts while at Oxford: *Physiological Psychology* (1905), *Introduction to Social Psychology* (1908), *Body and Mind* (1911), and *Psychology: The Study of Behaviour* (1912). Of them, the most influential was his *Social Psychology*. It was reprinted twenty-four times and continued to influence British psychology even after McDougall had moved to the United States. Although the book was a pioneer effort in a new branch of psychology, the theory of instincts that it contained proved to be a controversial issue. McDougall described human behavior in terms of a large number of instincts, each having a basic emotion at its core. Two or more instincts attaching themselves, through experience, to a single object, form sentiments. Most human behavior is motivated by sentiments and hence by emotions, not reason. Social behavior, too, although meeting and satisfying basic human needs, is driven mainly by sentiments.

McDougall's purposive psychology, or as he called it later (1923), hormic psychology, postulates goal seeking in all behavior. Instincts guide the organism toward goals. Cognition effects the guidance, which terminates when the goal is reached. Progression toward a goal is pleasant; being frustrated in such progress is unpleasant. Although hormic psychology never became a school, it tied in with the psychology of those learning theorists who recognized purpose (such as Tolman*) and with dynamic psychology in general.

McDougall's work during World War I on shell-shocked patients resulted in an *Outline of Abnormal Psychology*, published in 1926. It contained a discussion of mental disorders in terms of instincts, repression, and conflict, a discussion of hypnosis, and a criticism of psychoanalysis. He criticized the latter more amply and trenchantly in *Psychoanalysis and Social Psychology* (1935). Soon after going to the United States, McDougall made his systematic position known in his *Outline of Psychology* (1923). Many of his beliefs, however, made him less popular in the United States than in England because of the behavioristic aegis that the United States was entering under at the time. These beliefs included his instinct theory, the superiority of the Nordic race, the existence of a soul, and psychical research. In a famous experiment McDougall attempted to demonstrate the inheritance of acquired characters in white rats. His opposition to a mechanistic view of behavior brought McDougall into conflict with J. B. Watson*, with whom he carried on an extended and well-publicized polemic. McDougall's total published output was 24 books and 167 articles.

Biographies: D. K. Adams, *Psychol. Rev.*, 1939, *46*, 1-8; J. Drever & T. S. Good, *J. Ment. Sci.*, 1939, *85*, 615-618; J. W. Evans, *Int. J. Parapsychol.*, 1967, *9*(2), 69-85; J. C. Flugel, *Brit. J. Psychol.*, 1938-1939, *29*, 321-328; E. J. Garrett, In W. McDougall, *William McDougall: Explorer of the Mind*, Ed. R. v. Over & L. Oteri, 1967, pp. 1-33; L. S. Hearnshaw, *Bull. Brit. Psychol. Soc.*, 1962, *46*, 2-10; W. Line, *Amer. J. Psychiat.*, 1940, *97*, 633-649; H. G.

McCurdy, In B. B. Wolman (Ed.), *Historical Roots of Contemporary Psychology*, 1968, pp. 111-130; F. A. Pattie, *Amer. J. Psychol.*, 1939, *52*, 303-307; G. Révész, *Mensch Maatschappij*, 1939, *15*, 22-24; A. L. Robinson, *William McDougall, M.B., D.Sc., F.R.S.: A Bibliography, Together with a Brief Outline of His Life*, 1943; C. Spearman, *J. Pers.*, 1939, *7*, 175-183; K. Zener, *Science*, 1939, *89*, 191-192; *DAB*, 22; *DNB*, Suppl. 4, 5; *EP*, 5; *HPA*, 1; *IESS*, 9; *NYT*, 1938, Nov. 29, 23:1; *Obit. Not.*, 3.

McGEOCH, JOHN ALEXANDER
American Psychologist
Born: Argyle, New York, October 9, 1897
Died: Iowa City, Iowa, March 3, 1942
Highest Degree: Ph.D. in psychology, University of Chicago, under Harvey Carr*
Positions, Honors: 1920-28, Washington University; 1928-30, University of Arkansas; 1930-35, professor and head, Psychology Department, University of Missouri; 1935-39, Wesleyan University; 1939-42, professor and head, Psychology Department, State University of Iowa; editorial work, *Psychological Bulletin* (1931-42), *American Journal of Psychology*, *Journal of Psychology* (1935-1942); one honorary degree

McGeoch was a psychologist in the functionalist school who studied animal and human learning. He was first to formulate (in 1932) the basic ideas of forgetting in terms of interference, according to which an association becomes permanently stored after it is established and that forgetting is due to competition from associations that are already established or become established afterwards. Subsequent research on retroactive and proactive interference has lent support to the interference theory of forgetting. In a long series of experiments on the functioning of memory, McGeoch himself produced much new data on the conditions affecting it.

Another contribution of McGeoch's was his relating the different types of learning situations in terms of a hierarchy, from classical conditioning to problem solving, in which each higher type implies the presence of the lower ones. McGeoch's only book, *The Psychology of Human Learning*, appeared in the year of his death. Coauthored by A. L. Irion, the second edition of the book was published in 1952.
Biographies: M. E. Bunch, *Psychol. Rev.*, 1942, *49*, 293-297; C. C. Pratt, *Amer. J. Psychol.*, 1943, *56*, 134-136; *Psychol. Bull.*, 1942, *39*, 199; C. E. Seashore, *Science*, 1942, *95*, 293-294; *NYT*, 1942, Mar. 5, 23:2; *PR*, 3; *Who Was Who in America*, 2.

MEAD, GEORGE HERBERT
American Philosopher
Born: South Hadley, Massachusetts, February 27, 1863
Died: Chicago, Illinois, April 26, 1931

Education: Graduate work at Harvard University, 1887-88; studied psychology and philosophy in Europe, 1888-91

Positions: 1891-94, University of Michigan; 1894-1931, University of Chicago

Mead made a contribution to social psychology by way of his interpretation of the origin of the self. The self arises, according to Mead, from social interaction, and language plays a crucial part in its development. It is through language that a child, who at first has no innate self-consciousness, learns to play the role of other persons and experiences the social feedback from such role playing. As a result he learns to think of himself as an object, since others act toward him as an object, and he reacts in kind. Thus a notion of self can arise only in a social setting. In this way, also, more than one self can develop.

Mead influenced considerably the thinking of a number of prominent psychologists, such as Sullivan*, and psychological thinking in the area of personality. Mead and Dewey* knew each other, were both pragmatists, and went to Chicago from Michigan at the same time, and Dewey acknowledged his debt to Mead in the development of his own philosophy.

Biographies: J. Dewey, *J. Phil.*, 1931, *28*, 309-314; G. C. Lee, *Herbert Mead: Philosopher of the Social Individual*, 1945; H. C. A. Mead, In G. H. Mead, *The Philosophy of the Act*, 1938, pp. lxxv-lxxix; D. L. Miller, *George Herbert Mead: Self, Language and the World*, 1973; A. J. Reck, In G. H. Mead, *Selected Writings*, 1969, pp. xiii-lxii; D. Victoroff, *Mead: Sociologue et philosophe*, 1953; *DAB*, 21; *EP*, 5; *IESS*, 10.

MEINONG, ALEXIUS VON

Austrian Philosopher

Born: Lemberg (L'vov), Galicia, July 17, 1853

Died: Graz, Austria, November 27, 1920

Highest Degree: Ph.D. in philosophy, University of Vienna, 1878

Positions: 1878-82, University of Vienna; 1882-1920, University of Graz

Meinong was the leader of the Austrian school of psychology at the University of Graz. He was a philosopher but contributed to theoretical psychology, mainly in connection with the development of the school of form-quality. He established the first Austrian psychological laboratory at Graz in 1894 and was one of the editors of *Zeitschrift für Psychologie*. As a philosopher Meinong attained celebrity with his *Gegenstandstheorie*, or object theory, which, stemming as it did from Bretano's* philosophical psychology, had a psychological flavor. In this theory, as in Bretano's, mental states "intend" objects. They have two aspects, content and act, and may be classified into presentations, thought processes, emotions, and motives. The rest of the theory is concerned with different classes of mind-independent objects as a function of the type of mental act. In regard to the doctrine of form-quality, Meinong's ideas did not differ substantially from those of Ehrenfels*, who had formulated its basic propositions. Meinong introduced new terms for those used by Ehrenfels, however (*founding contents* for *Fundamente* and *founded contents* for *form-quality*). The founding and founded contents together were complexions, of which there were two kinds: real complexions, or perceptions, and ideal complexions, or concepts. Real complexions are determined primarily by stimulus characteristics, whereas ideal complexions depend on the productive process (*Produktionsvorgang*) that fuses sensory elements into unitary wholes, such as four straight lines of equal length into the unitary form of a square. Since Meinong was an important philosopher, his discussion of form-quality helped to establish the school of form-quality in psychology. Later, the Gestalt psychologists found much to criticize in Meinong's formulation.

Biographies: W. Frankl, *Arch. Gesch. Phil.*, 1922, *34*, 41-46; L. Hansel, *Wiener Arch. Phil. Psychol. Pädag.*, 1955, *5*, 224-239; E. Martinak, *Meinong als Mensch und als Lehrer*, 1925; A. Meinong, In R. Schmidt (Ed.), *Die Philosophie der Gegenwart in Selbstdarstellungen*, vol. 1, 1923, pp. 101-160; K. Radakovic et al. (Eds), *Meinong-Gedenkschrigt*, 1952; E. B. Titchener, *Amer. J. Psychol.*, 1921, *32*, 154; *CE*, 9; *EP*, 5; *EUI*, 34.

MEISSNER, GEORG
German Physiologist
Born: Hannover, November 19, 1829
Died: Göttigen, March 30, 1905
Highest Degree: M.D., University of Göttingen, 1852
Positions: 1855-58, University of Basel; 1858-60, University of Freiburg; 1860-1905, University of Göttigen

Meissner became known for his histological studies of the skin and the pressure receptors. He showed that the adequate stimulus for pressure receptors is not pressure itself but the deformation of the skin or changes in pressure pattern; also, that if pressure is uniform it is not perceived except around the edges of the uniform pressure area, that is, at a pressure-gradient contour. Meissner discovered touch receptors in hairless skin (palms and soles). They were named in his honor *Meissner corpuscles*. Meissner described his work on the skin in *Beiträge zur Anatomie und Physiologie der Haut* (1853). *Beiträge zur Physiologie des Sehorgans* (1854) reports on his work in physiological optics.

Biographies: H. Boruttau, *Med. Woche*, 1905, *18*, 139; O. Damreh, *Deutsch. med. Wochenschr.*, 1905, *31*, 758, 759; R. Du Bois-Reymond, *Berliner klin. Wochenschr.*, 1905, *42*, 487; O. Weiss, *Münch. med. Wochenschr.*, 1905, *52*, 1206; *EUI*, 34; Hirsch., *Biog. Lex.*, 4; Pagel, *Biographisches Lexikon*.

MENDEL, GREGOR JOHANN
Austrian Geneticist
Born: Heizendorf, Austria (now Hynčice, Czechoslovakia), July 22, 1822
Died: Brno, Moravia, January 6, 1884
Education: Studied philosophy at the University of Olmütz and physics and natural science at the University of Vienna

Positions: 1843, entered monastery; 1868, became abbot; 1849-68, high school teacher at Brno

In 1856 Mendel began his experiments with pea hybrids and in 1866 published the first paper describing the experiments and stating his theory of factorial inheritance. This paper started the science of genetics, even though at first it did not receive much attention, was forgotten, and the laws of genetic inheritance established by Mendel had to be rediscovered by De Vries* and others thirty-four years later. Because the capacity to behave is a matter of heredity—as are innate behaviors; physiological drives; fixed action patterns; and individual differences in temperament, intelligence, and other behavioral characteristics—Mendel's contribution was also of the greatest significance to psychology.

Biographies: A. Gustafsson, *Hereditas*, Lund, 1969, *62*, 239-258; H. Iltis, *Life of Mendel*, 1932 (Reprinted 1966); I. Krumbiegel, *Gregor Mendel und das Schicksal seiner Vererbungsgesetze*, 1967; C. Zirkle, *Isis*, 1951, *42*, 97-104; *CE*, 9; *DSB*, 9; EB, 15; Hirsch, *Biog. Lex.*, 4.

MERCIER, DESIRÉ FELICIEN FRANÇOIS JOSEPH

Belgian Philosopher
Born: Braine-l'Allend, November 21, 1851
Died: Brussels, January 23, 1926
Highest Degree: Ph.D. in philosophy and theology, University of Louvain, 1882
Positions: 1877-82, Malines Seminary; 1882-1926, University of Louvain

In response to the call of Pope Leo XIII to revive Christian philosophy, Mercier became a leader in the nineteenth-century revival of Thomistic philosophy (Neothomism), including neothomistic psychology. He wrote an account of psychology from the Thomistic point of view, *Psychologie* (1892), and another psychological text, *Les origins de la psychologie contemporaine* (1897), both of which appeared in several editions and were translated into other languages. At Louvain Mercier familiarized himself with the "new" psychology that was coming from Germany and established a psychological laboratory at that university in 1891. To organize it and direct its work, Mercier put a student of Wundt's*, Armand Thiéry, in charge of it. Although Mercier considered experimental psychology to be a natural science, separate from philosophy, and believed that rational psychology needed experimental psychology, he also believed that experimental psychology without rational psychology would become materialistic, mechanistic, and cease to be a separate science.

Biographies: L. De Raeymaeker, *Le cardinal Mercier et l'Institut Supérieur de Philosophie de Louvain*, 1952; J. A. Gade, *The Life of Cardinal Mercier*, 1934; A. Laveille, *A Life of Cardinal Mercier*, 1928; H. Misiak & V. Sexton, *Catholics in Psychology*, 1954, pp. 34-52; A. Simon, *Le Cardinal Mercier*, 1960; G. Verbeke, G. Nuttin, *et al.*, *Le Cardinal Mercier: Fondateur de Séminaire*, 1951; *CE*, 9; *EP*, 5; *EUI*, 34.

MERLEAU-PONTY, MAURICE

French Philosopher
Born: Rochefort, Charente Maritime, March 14, 1908
Died: Paris, May 3, 1961
Highest Degree: *Agrégé* in philosophy, École Normale Supérieure, Paris, 1931
Positions: 1945-48, University of Lyons; 1948-52, Sorbonne, (University of Paris); 1952-61, Collège de France

Merleau-Ponty was a philosopher and phenomenological psychologist, recognized for his originality and success in integrating philosophy and psychology. His psychologically most important works are *Structure du comportement* (1942; English translation, *The Structure of Behavior*, 1963) and *La phénoménologie de la perception* (1945; English translation, *Phenomenology of Perception*, 1962). In *The Structure of Behavior*, Merleau-Ponty proposed "to understand the relation between consciousness and nature." Although nature is subject to causality, consciousness is not, even when considered as behavior. The appropriate method for studying behavior is systematic phenomenology of perception, not the methods presently used by psychologists. In *Phenomenology of Perception* Merleau-Ponty derived a perceptual basis for his phenomenological philosophy. The essential human characteristic is the dynamic interaction between consciousness and nature. This interaction or dialectic is reflected in the perceptual process. Since perception "opens a window unto things," it is the starting point for the study of human beings. Although in fundamental agreement with the emphasis on wholes placed in Gestalt psychology, Merleau-Ponty thought that the doctrine of isomorphism was by its very nature in error.

Biographies: T. Langan, *Phil. Phenomenol. Res.*, 1962-63, *23*, 202-216; A. Robinet, *Merleau-Ponty: Sa vie, son oeuvre avec un exposé de sa philosophie*, 1962; J.-P. Sartre, *Temps mod.*, 1961, *184-185*, 304-376; *CE*, 9; *EP*, 5; *NYT*, 1961, May 5, 29:5.

MESMER, FRANZ ANTON

Austrian Physician
Born: Iznang, Baden-Württemberg, Germany, May 23, 1734
Died: Meersburg, Baden-Württemberg, March 5, 1815
Highest Degree: M.D., University of Vienna, 1766
Positions: Private practice, Vienna and Paris

Mesmer, at first a physician in Vienna, came under the influence of the occult teachings of Paracelsus*, believing that magnetism emanating from the stars affects human lives. His experiments on the effects of magnets on the human body led to the discovery that his passes made some people go into a trance. They also led him to the belief that the magnetism of iron and celestial bodies was similar to that possessed by living organisms. Mesmer therefore began to use the term *animal magnetism*, a term used by others before him. In 1766 he published a work about the postulated relationships (*De planetarum influxu*); and in 1779, an account of what later came to be called "mesmerism" (*Mémoire* *sur la découverte du magnétisme animal*). Although Mesmer never thought that he had any magical powers but, rather, that animal magnetism was a natural force, he was repeatedly accused of magic and charlatanism and was forced to change residence several times. In 1778 he moved to Paris to continue the cures of neurotic individuals begun in Vienna. His séances around the *baquet*, a chest filled with chemicals that had iron protrusions his patients held on to, became famous in Paris society, and Mesmer achieved many hypnotic cures. Eventually, he fell into disrepute because he maintained his belief in animal magnetism but could not explain it satisfactorily to the scientists who investigated him. Mesmerism continued to be practiced after Mesmer's death, and men like Elliotson* and Braid* began to explain it in scientific terms. Later, under the name of *hypnosis*, mesmerism became part of the psychiatrist's tools of trade.

Biographies: J. R. L. Delboeuf, *Magnétiseurs et médecins*, 1890; M. Goldsmith, *Franz Anton Mesmer*, 1934; C. Haensel, *Franz Anton Mesmer: Leben und Lehre*, 1940; R. Ince, *Franz Anton Mesmer: His Life and Teaching*, 1920; F. A. Mesmer, *Memoir of F. A. Mesmer, Doctor of Medicine, on His Discoverie: 1799*, 1957; G. Newbold, *Brit. J. Med. Hypno.*, 1949, *1*(2), 3-8; F. Schürer-Waldheim, *Franz Anton Mesmer*, 1930; R. Tischner, *Münch. Beit. Gesch. Lit. Naturwiss. Med.*, 1928, *1*(9/10), 541-714; J. Vinchon, *Mesmer et son secret*, 1936; D. M. Walmsley, *Anton Mesmer*, 1967; B. Winters, *J. Gen Psychol.*, 1950, *43*, 63-75; N. P. v. Wydenbruck, *Doctor Mesmer: An Historical Study*, 1947; S. Zweig, *Mental Healers: Franz Anton Mesmer, Mary Baker Eddy, Sigmund Freud*, 1932; *ADB*, 21, 29; *DSB*, 9; *EB*, 15; *EUI*, 34; *Grande*, 23; Hirsch, *Biog. Lex.*, 4; *IESS*, 10; *Nouvelle*, 35.

MESSER, AUGUST

German Psychologist

Born: Mainz, Rhineland-Palatinate, February 11, 1867

Died: Rostock, Pomerania, 1937

Highest Degree: Ph.D. in philosophy, University of Giessen, 1892

Positions: 1899-1933, University of Giessen

Messer was at first a philosopher who, impressed by Külpe's* approach to both philosophy and psychology, spent a semester studying thinking under Külpe's direction at Würzburg. Messer immediately published a book-size monograph (*Experimentellpsychologische Untersuchungen über das Denken*, 1906), consistent with the position of the Würzburg school; still another book in 1908 (*Empfindung und Denken*), and *Psychologie* in 1914. Messer developed a two-part psychology that Külpe himself was gravitating toward, namely, one in which the content of Leipzig and the acts of Würzburg both found a place. According to Messer, each kind of intentional experience—knowing, feeling, and willing (the proper subject matter for psychology)—involves activity that has a content. The contents of knowing are the sensations, images, time- and space-related contents, and the impressions or relational experiences. The acts of knowing are perception, memory, and imagination. The contents of feeling and willing are also sensations, and the acts of feeling are preferences and those of willing, desire and will.

Biographies: A. Messer, In R. Schmidt (Ed.), *Philosophie der Gegenwart in Selbstdarstellungen*, vol. 3, 1922, pp. 145-176; *EUI*, 34.

MEUMANN, ERNST

German Psychologist

Born: Uerdingen bei Wesel, North Rhine-Westphalia, August 29, 1862

Died: Hamburg, April 15, 1915

Highest Degree: Ph.D. in philosophy and theology, University of Tübingen, 1887

Positions: 1894-97, University of Leipzig; 1897-1905, University of Zurich; 1905-8, University of Königsberg; 1908-9, University of Münster; 1909-10, University of Halle; 1910-11, University of Leipzig; 1911-15, University of Hamburg

Meumann became a leader in experimental education and educational psychology in Germany, after having done general-experimental work under Wundt* and later independently. Among his researches are those on organic sensations, done in 1907 and 1909 (he differentiated the sensations of stomach repletion and emptiness, cardiac oppression, and suffocation, which have been discarded since); on time perception (1892 to 1896), for the study of which he invented an important piece of apparatus; on rhythm (1894); and on memory, types of attention, and aesthetics. In the area of educational psychology, Meumann started the *Zeitschrift für experimentelle Pädagogik* (1905), later renamed *Zeitschrift für padagogische Psychologie und Jugendkunde*; founded and edited the *Archiv für die gesamte Psychologie*; and wrote *Über Oekonomie und Technik des Lernens* (1903) and *Vorlesungen zur Einführung in die experimentelle Pädagogik und ihre psychologische Grundlagen* (1907-14), as well as a considerable number of papers.

Biographies: A. Fischer, *Z. pädag. Psychol.*, 1915, *16*, 214-227; F. Meumann, *Z. pädag. Psychol.*, 1915, *16*, 257, 262; G. Störring, *Amer. J. Psychol.*, 1923, *34*, 271-274; G. Störring, *Arch. ges. Psychol.*, 1915, *34*, i-xiv; *NYT*, 1915, July 5, 7:6.

MEYER, ADOLF

Swiss-American Psychiatrist

Born: Niederweningen, Zurich, Switzerland, September 13, 1866

Died: Baltimore, Maryland, March 17, 1950

Highest Degree: M.D., University of Zurich, 1892

Positions, Honors: 1892-93, University of Chicago; 1893-95, Illinois Eastern Hospital for the Insane, Kankakee; 1895-1902, Worcester Insane Hospital, Clark University; 1902-10, director, Pathological Institute, New York State Hospital Service; 1904-9, Cornell University; 1910-41, professor of psychiatry and director of Henry Phipps Psychiatric Clinic, Johns Hopkins University; president, American Psychiatric Association, 1927; several honorary degrees

Meyer was an outstanding psychiatrist of his time ("dean of American psychiatry"). He revolutionized methods of treatment while at the New York State Hospital Service Pathological Institute and developed that institute into a first-class training center for psychiatrists. Under his direction the Phipps Clinic at Johns Hopkins reached such levels of excellence that it became the foremost training center for English-speaking psychiatrists in the world.

Meyer made a substantial contribution to the promotion of the holistic view in psychopathology, in which both the organic and psychological factors are fused into a whole. Meyer's "psychobiology" is based on the assumptions that the behavior of a patient may be understood only if his total personality is understood and that the patient's behavior is determined by a variety of factors—biological, psychological, and sociological—that acting and interacting produce the patient's maladjustment. Neurotic maladjustments result from levels of aspiration that are too high and the inability to accept oneself as one is. Failure to achieve unrealistic goals results in feelings of inferiority and the use of defense mechanisms. In neuroses only a part of the total personality is involved, in contrast to psychotic decompensation that involves the entire person. Meyer viewed schizophrenia as the result of faulty habits, accumulated over a long period and often complicated by organic and hereditary factors. Psychobiological therapy is an attempt at integrating and synthesizing the different aspects of the patient's personality by analyzing the psychological, sociological, and biological factors involved, keeping close to the patient's complaint, and achieving a combination of treatment methods that both the psychiatrist and the patient find satisfactory. To understand the total patient, Meyer advised that the patient's developmental history be obtained. He introduced the psychiatric interview as a means of probing into the circumstances surrounding the patient's maladjustment and employed assistants to study the patient's home and to involve the significant persons in the patient's life in his treatment. This marked the beginning of psychiatric social work and the closing of the gap between psychiatry and the social sciences.

Meyer contributed a number of significant papers to the medical literature, suggested the term *mental hygiene*, and was instrumental in furthering the mental hygiene movement originated by Clifford Beers*. His *Collected Papers* were published after his death (1950-52), as was his *Psychobiology* (1957).

Biographies: C. M. Campbell, *Arch. Neurol. Psychiat.*, 1937, *37*, 715-731; L. W. Crafts, *Amer. J. Psychol.*, 1950, *63*, 620-622; F. G. Ebaugh, *Amer. J. Psychiat.*, 1950, *107*, 288-290; F. G. Ebaugh, *Amer. J. Psychiat.*, 1966, *123*, 334-336; F. G. Ebaugh, *Arch. Neurol. Psychiat.*, 1937, *37*, 732-741; *J. Nerv. Ment. Dis.*, 1951, *113*, 89-91; K. Kolle (Ed.), *Grosse Nervenärzte*, vol. 2, 1959, pp. 129-138; A. Lief, In A. Meyer, *The Common-sense Psychiatry of Dr. Adolf Meyer: Fifty-two Selected Papers*, 1948, pp. 17-24, 37-52, 77-86, 95-102, 145-

152, 227-232, 277-283, 335-341, 369-378, 449-456, 537-564; W. Muncie, *Ment. Hyg.*, 1950, *34*, 465-466; B. Sicherman, *Swiss Amer. Hist. Soc. Newsl.*, 1969, *5*, 2-14; J. C. Whitehorn, *Bull. Johns Hopkins Hosp.*, 1951, *89* (suppl.), 53-72; *EB*, 15; *IESS*, 10; *NCAB*, 38; *PR*, 3.

MEYER, MAX FREDERICK
German-American Psychologist
Born: Danzig, East Prussia, June 15, 1873
Died: Miami, Florida, March 14, 1967
Highest Degree: Ph.D. in psychology, University of Berlin, 1896, under C. Stumpf*
Positions: 1901-29, University of Missouri; 1929-30, Central Institute for the Deaf, St. Louis; 1932-40, University of Miami

On the subject of what psychology is and how it should be studied, Meyer expressed views that were very similar to those of the father of behaviorism, Watson*, and he expressed them before Watson (*The Fundamental Laws of Human Behavior*, 1911). His best-known work is *The Psychology of the Other One* (1921), whose point is that the task of psychology is the study of public data. Consciousness may be studied scientifically only if it is made public. Meyer's views never made the same impact as Watson's, however.

Meyer's contributions to empirical psychology were in the area of hearing and musical acoustics, where he published between the years 1899 and 1950. He proposed a hearing theory that was almost as well known as Helmholtz's*. Like Helmholtz's theory, it made pitch a function of frequency of sound waves but excluded the factor of resonance. The theory also explained the perception of loudness of complex sound waves. The analysis of such waves Meyer placed in the inner ear rather than in the brain.

Biographies: E. A. Esper, *J. Hist. Behav. Sci.*, 1966, *2*, 341-356; E. A. Esper, *J. Hist. Behav. Sci.*, 1967, *3*, 107-131; I. J. Hirsch, *Amer. J. Psychol.*, 1967, *80*, 644-645; *EUI*, 34; *PR*, 3.

MEYNERT, THEODOR HERMANN
German-Austrian Neurologist
Born: Dresden, Germany, June 15, 1833
Died: Vienna, Austria, May 31, 1892
Highest Degree: M.D., University of Vienna, 1865
Positions: 1866-92, University of Vienna

As a researcher Meynert contributed to the study of brain anatomy and brain functions. He wrote *Der Bau der Grosshirnrinde und seine örtlichen Verschiedenheiten* (1867-68) and several other books in this area. He described the association neuron and other brain structures, some of which have been named after him (Meynert's fasciculus. Meynert's commisure). As a practitioner Meynert advocated mental hospitals with minimal restraints. He is known as one of

Sigmund Freud's* teachers. His concept of *das primäre ich*, or bodily consciousness, bears some resemblance to Freud's id.

Biographies: G. Anton, In T. Kirchhoff (Ed.), *Deutsche Irrenärzte*, vol. 2, 1924, pp. 121-135; G. Anton, *Jb. Psychol. Neurol.*, 1930, *40*, 256-281; D. Stockert-Meynert, *Theodor Meynert und seine Zeit*, 1930; *ADB*, 52; *EUI*, 34; *Grande*, 23; Hirsch, *Biog. Lex.*, 4, Suppl.; Pagel, *Biographisches Lexikon*.

MICHOTTE, ALBERT EDWARD (BARON VAN DEN BERCK)
Belgian Psychologist
Born: Brussels, October 13, 1881
Died: Louvain, Belgium, June 2, 1965
Highest Degree: Ph.D. in philosophy, science, and physiology, University of Louvain, 1900, under D. J. Mercier*
Positions, Honors: 1905-14, 1918-56, University of Louvain; 1914-18, University of Utrecht (University of Louvain was burned down); president, Fifteenth International Congress of Psychology, 1957; three honorary degrees; made baron, 1954

During his lifetime Michotte was the most prominent Belgian psychologist. He was interested in perception from the outset. He studied psychology between 1905 and 1908 with Wundt* at Leipzig and Külpe* at Würzburg. He published his first monograph in the area of perception in 1905 (*Les signes régioneux*). Before World War I Michotte first studied volition using the systematic experimental introspection method of the Würzburg school but abandoned that approach when it proved to be inadequate. He then turned to the study of rhythm and movement and became interested in Gestalt psychology. Between 1918 and 1939 Michotte's laboratory produced research showing the development of motor and temporal Gestalten from a perceptual basis. In 1939, still inspired by Gestalt psychology, Michotte embarked on a study of the perception of physical causality. It attracted international attention.

In distinction from Jean Piaget* who relied on children's introspections as he studied the development of the notion of physical causality, Michotte designed a mechanical device that portrayed two objects in varying degrees of collision and asked subjects to describe the type of interaction that they perceived to exist between the two objects. By varying the velocity of approach, duration of contact, and other variables, Michotte was able to relate perceived causality to physical stimulus dimensions. He concluded that the perception of causality was like any other perception, a direct experience and not an interpretation of experience, because even knowing that no actual causal relation exists does not preclude the perception of causality when the stimulus constellation is right (*La perception de la causalité*, 1946).

Michotte was very active in international psychology. He organized and participated in the activities of international congresses, unions, and societies. At Louvain he organized the Institute of Psychology in 1944 and the Belgian Psychological Association in 1947.

Biographies: F. C. Bartlett, *Bull. Brit. Psychol. Soc.*, 1966, *19*, 35-37; H. Misiak & V. S. Sexton, *Catholics in Psychology*, 1954, pp. 98-110; J. R. Nuttin, *Amer. J. Psychol.*, 1966, *79*, 331-341; various, *Miscellanea Psychologica Albert Michotte*, 1947; *HPA*, 4; *PR*, 3.

MILES, WALTER R.
American Psychologist
Born: Silverleaf, North Dakota, March 29, 1885
Died: Sandy Spring, Maryland, May 15, 1978
Highest Degree: Ph.D. in psychology, Iowa State University, 1913, under Carl E. Seashore*
Positions, Honors: 1913-14, Wesleyan University; 1914-22, Carnegie Nutrition Laboratory, Boston; 1922-32, Stanford University; 1932-53, Yale University; 1954-57, University of Istanbul; 1957-65, Medical Research Laboratory, U.S. Naval Submarine Base, New London, Connecticut; president, American Psychological Association, 1932; Warren Medal, Society of Experimental Psychologists, 1949; Gold Medal, American Psychological Foundation, 1962; honorary Sc.D., Yale University, 1931, Earlham College, 1952; president, member of numerous organizations, boards, and committees

Most of Miles's approximately seventy publications fall into the categories of research on nutrition and the effects of alcohol, age and human ability, and vision. Their common theme is human response under handicap. At Stanford University, Miles, Lewis Terman*, Calvin Stone*, and E. K. Strong* conducted the first systematic, large-scale study of age and human performance, the Stanford Late Maturity Study. The finding that mature people do not necessarily show impaired performance changed the general idea that old age begins at forty and moved it closer to sixty. During World War II Miles was responsible for introducing the use of red goggles in the pilots' "ready rooms," so that they could engage in various activities and still be dark-adapted when the call came to scramble for a nighttime mission.
Biographies: *Amer. Psychologist*, 1962, *17*, 899-900; E. R. Hilgard, *Amer. J. Psychol.*, 1980, *93*, 565-568; N. E. Miller, *Amer. Psychologist*, 1980, *35*, 595-596; *HPA*, 5; *NCAB*, D; *NYT*, 1978, May 18, B 14; *Who's Who in America*.

MILL, JAMES
English Historian, Economist, and Philosopher
Born: Northwater Bridge, Angus, Scotland, April 6, 1773
Died: London, June 23, 1836
Education: Studied theology, philosophy, the classics, at University of Edinburgh from 1790; licensed as preacher in 1798
Positions: Editorial work, writing, with the East India Company, from 1819

Mill's greatest achievement was the writing of *The History of British India* (1818); in philosophy he subscribed to the ideas of the utilitarian Jeremy Bentham*. His historical, political, and economic works reflect the principles of utilitarianism and philosophical radicalism. Mill's psychology, which is contained in his 1829 volume *Analysis of the Phenomena of the Human Mind*, also served the cause of utilitarianism. The importance of this work to psychology lies in that in it Mill developed further the doctrine of associationism that began with Hartley*. According to Mill there are only two kinds of mental contents, sensations and ideas. The latter remain when the former are removed. Although sensation is primary, association occurs only among ideas. The association of two ideas, one of which is a word, gives the word its meaning (the associative theory of meaning). The association of ideas obeys one principle only, namely, contiguity, successive or simultaneous. The strength of an association is determined by its frequency and vividness. Association cements previous experiences together, so complex ideas contain all of the component simpler ideas, the most complex idea being that of "everything." Even though complex ideas may appear to be simple because the component ideas fuse together, analysis may still reveal their original structure. Mill's conception of association as a mechanical, noncreative, nonsynthesizing process marked the end of the logical development of a line of thinking—its culminating point and dead end at the same time.

Biographies: A. Bain, *James Mill: A Biography*, 1967; G. S. Bower, *Hartley and James Mill*, 1881; E. Halevy, *Encycl. Soc. Sci.*, 1933, *10*, 480-481; *DNB*, 13; *EB*, 15; *EP*, 5.

MILL, JOHN STUART

English Philosopher and Economist
Born: Pentonville (London), May 20, 1806
Died: Avignon, France, May 8, 1873
Education: Taught by father and self
Positions: East India Company

Mill, the eldest son of James Mill*, was a lesser figure of a psychologist than his father. He exercised a far greater influence as a philosopher, logician, and economist. Mill's psychological views may be found in *A System of Logic, Ratiocinative and Inductive* (1843), *Examination of Sir William Hamilton's Philosophy* (1865), and the notes written for the 1869 edition of his father's *Analysis of the Phenomena of the Human Mind*. Mill did not accept his father's notion of infinite compounding of associations. Instead, he suggested that the mind's activity produces, in combining simple elements, something new that is not present in the original components. The whole is different from the sum of its parts, which is what Wundt* said later and the Gestalt psychologists made into a cardinal proposition in their system. Mill himself called this notion "mental chemistry . . . in which . . . the simple ideas generate, rather than they compose, the complex ones." Mill's contribution, unlike his father's, was to demonstrate the need for empirical observation of the complex idea rather than assuming its identity with the sum of its parts. Mill thus called for the scientific study of associations. Like his father, Mill subscribed to the laws of similarity and contiguity in association; he added, however, intensity in his *Logic* but later replaced it with frequency and inseparability (in his *Examination*).

Mill also offered a theory of perception, which was not unlike that of Berkeley*. The mind is able to have expectations. Having had actual sensations sets up the expectation in the mind that these sensations would reoccur, that is, the idea of possible sensations. Thus there are "permanent possibilities of sensations." The perception of matter is but a belief in the permanent possibilities of sensations, which makes it a matter of association and therefore a "psychological theory of the belief in an external world." In his *Logic* Mill also proposed some basic postulates for ascertaining truth. They have become fundamental in scientific research, including psychological research, such as the logic underlying the use of control groups in experimentation.

Biographies: R. Borchard, *John Stuart Mill: The Man*, 1957; K. Britton, *John Stuart Mill*, 1953; W. L. Courtney, *The Life of J. S. Mill*, 1889; H. McCloskey, *John Stuart Mill: A Critical Study*, 1971; J. S. Mill, *Autobiography*, 1979; M. S. J. Packe, *The Life of John Stuart Mill*, 1954; B. Russell, *John Stuart Mill*, 1956; A. Ryan, *John Stuart Mill*, 1970; *Chalmers*, 22; *DNB*, 13; *DSB*, 9; *EB*, 15; *EP*, 5; *IESS*, 10; *NYT*, 1873, May 10, 6:4.

MIRA Y LÓPEZ, EMILIO
Spanish-Brazilian Psychiatrist
Born: Santiago, Cuba, October 24, 1896
Died: Petrópolis, Brazil, February 16, 1964
Highest Degree: M.D., Universidad Central de España, Madrid, 1923
Positions: 1919-39, director, Laboratory of Psychophysiology and Department of Psychology, Institute of Vocational Counseling, Barcelona, Spain; 1923-39, clinical psychiatrist, Barcelona; 1933-39, professor of psychiatry, University of Barcelona; 1936-39, director of Psychiatric Services, Spanish Republican Army; 1939-43, brief research, teaching, and lecturing appointments in France, England, United States, Cuba, Chile, and Argentina; 1943, director of psychiatric services, Santa Fé province, Argentina; 1944-47, director, Laboratory of Psychotechnology, Montevideo, Uruguay; 1947-64, Fundação Getúlio Vargas, Rio de Janeiro, Brazil; founder (1949) and editor of *Arquivos Brasileiros de Psicotécnica*; president, ninth International Congress of Psychology

Mira y López was a pioneer in psychology in Spain and Latin American countries. For three decades he epitomized psychology in the Spanish-speaking world. He was not only the first Spanish-speaking individual to become interested in and write about behaviorism and psychoanalysis, but he became familiar with and wrote and lectured on all schools of psychology and all of its fields. He was active and did pioneer work in applied psychology and psychotechnology (he introduced the term *psicotécnica* in Spanish) and in psychological organizations. He attended and presided over international meetings, founded the Brazilian institute of vocational counseling (Instituto de Seleção e Orientação Profissional) in 1947, founded the Associação Brasileira de Psicologia Aplicada in 1949, was a guest lecturer in several Latin American countries as well as in the United States, and wrote more than thirty books in practically every field of psychology. Among them are *Teoría y práctica del psicoanálisis* (1926), *Psicología jurídica* (1932), *Manual de psiquiatría* (1935), *Problemas psicológicos actuales* (1940), *Psicología evolutiva del niño y del adolescente* (1941), *Instantáneas psicológicas* (1943), *Cuatro gigantes del alma* (1947), *Manual de orientación profesional* (1947), *Cómo estudiar y cómo aprender* (1948), *Psicología experimental* (1955), and *Psicología de la vida moderna* (1963).

The single most important scientific contribution to psychology of Mira y López was the myokinetic psychodiagnostic test, first presented in 1939, published in book form in French in 1951 (*Le psychodiagnostique miocinetique*), and translated in several languages later (English translation, *M.K.P.: Myokinetic Diagnosis*, 1959). It has been used in South American countries, Mexico, and France. It is a culture-free personality test that is based on the motor theory of consciousness and involves the analysis of motor responses (copying).
Biographies: R. Ardila, *Rev. méx. psicol.*, 1969, *3*, 295-304 (Reprinted in R. Ardila, *Los pioneros de la psicología*, 1971); *PR*, 3.

MOEDE, WALTER
German Psychologist
Born: Sorau, Prussia (now Zary, Poland), September 3, 1888
Died: Berlin, May 30, 1958
Highest Degree: Ph.D. in psychology, University of Leipzig, 1911
Positions: 1921-51, Technische Hochschule, Berlin; 1951-58, Verwaltungsakademie, Berlin

Moede was a pioneer social psychologist who studied the effect of social variables in standard psychological experiments, such as threshold determination experiments. The study of the facilitating of inhibitory effects of other people on the performance of such tasks Moede dubbed "experimental mass psychology." He influenced Floyd Allport* but not many others, since his work (*Experimentelle Massenpsychologie*), published in 1920, was never translated. Later Moede worked in industrial psychology, publishing a number of books in this area: *Lehrbuch der Psychotechnik* (1930), *Konsum-Psychologie* (1933), *Arbeitstechnik* (1935), *Eignungsprüfung und Arbeitseinsatz* (1943), *Betriebliche Arbeitswissenschaft* (1954), and *Psychologie des Berufs und Wirtschaftslebens* (1958).
Biographies: M. Shorn, *Psychol. Rundsch.*, 1958, *9*, 307-309; *PR*, 3.

MOLYNEUX, WILLIAM
Irish Astronomer and Mathematician
Born: Dublin, April 17, 1656
Died: Dublin, October 11, 1698
Highest Degree: B.A., Trinity College, Dublin, 1675
Positions, Honors: 1695, University of Dublin; honorary LL.D., Trinity College

In *Dioptrica nova: A Treatise of Dioptricks* (1692), the first English work about optics, Molyneux provided the definitive answer to the question of how we see the world right side up when the retinal image is upside down, namely, that *up* and *down* are terms that refer to the gravitational pull and that vision takes no account of this since the mind does not look at the retinal image and its relation to the outside world. It was in this context that Molyneux directed his famous query in a letter to his friend John Locke* concerning the visual experiences of a hypothetical individual who, having been born blind, sees for the first time as an adult. Molyneux himself supplied the answer and Locke confirmed it by saying that such a person indeed would not be able to identify objects by sight alone. Molyneux was thus one of the first thinkers to suggest that meaning accrues to perception through experience.
Biographies: *DNB*, 13; *Grande*, 24; *Nouvelle*, 35.

MONTAIGNE
French Writer
Born: Château Montaigne, between Bordeaux and Périgueux, February 28, 1533
Died: Château Montaigne, September 12, 1592
Education: Collège de Guyenne at Bordeaux; studied law in Toulouse, 1546-50
Positions: 1557-70, *conseiller* at the *parlement* of Bordeaux

Montaigne originated a new literary form, the essay, by his best-known work *Essais* (1580). His essays are literary tests of ideas, of ideas in the process of welling up, before they freeze in systematic forms. Montaigne stated that he himself is the subject matter of his book, which thus becomes a document of intellectual, emotional, and physical self-disclosure. Moreover, Montaigne generalized his own psychological self-portrait because "every human contains the complete form of the human condition." By multiplying examples Montaigne stressed that aspect of this condition that manifests itself in the diversity and variability of human nature. He did not, however, relate it to any transcendental principles. All human mental functions are reduced to experience and explained in simple and natural terms. His observations of behavior are objective, even his self-observations, which he conducted as if looking at himself in a mirror. The generalized human that Montaigne saw in this mirror contrasts sharply with the view of humanity as the pinnacle of creation, a view held by both the Renaissance and medieval thinkers. He denied the uniqueness of humans and, in anticipation of Charles Darwin*, made them part of the natural order and considered them to be on a par with the animals. He showed the untrustworthiness of reason compared to experience but also demonstrated how easily the senses can be deceived and, in general, skeptically outlined the limitations of humanity.
Biographies: D. M. Frame, *Montaigne: A Biography*, 1965; *EB*, 15.

MONTESQUIEU, CHARLES LOUIS DE SECONDAT, BARON DE LA BRÈDE ET DE
French Philosopher
Born: Château La Brède, near Bordeaux, January 18, 1689
Died: Paris, February 10, 1755

Highest Degree: Studied law at the University of Bordeaux, admitted advocate, 1708
Positions: 1708-13, law practice, Paris; 1713, administrator of own estates; 1716-26, deputy president, *parlement* of Bordeaux

In books and essays like *The Persian Letters* (1721), *Considerations on the Causes of the Greatness of the Romans and Their Decline* (1734), and *The Spirit of the Laws* (1748), Montesquieu laid the foundations of the social and political sciences. In *The Spirit of the Laws*, his outstanding work, Montesquieu sought the laws of social institutions and social phenomena that would not be couched in religious, moral, or chance terms. He called upon climate, geography, economy, demography, and ethical and religious traditions as social facts, as well as psychological factors, to explain historical changes in government. He asserted that each type of government rests on a different psychological principle: republican government rests on civic virtue, monarchy on honor, and despotism on fear. Unlike Hobbes*, Montesquieu did not believe that self-interest is a sufficient cause for human institutions to come into being, since good government depends on education and example. Montesquieu's contribution was to seek a scientific approach to human behavior. This he did in a more specifically psychological monograph, *An Essay on the Causes That Can Affect the Spirits*, in which he presented a materialistic, physiological psychology.
Biographies: P. Barrière, *Montesquieu*, 1946; I. Berlin, *Proc. Brit. Acad.*, 1955, *41*, 267-296; J. Dedieu, *Montesquieu: L'Homme et l'oeuvre*, 1943; R. Shackleton, *Montesquieu: A Critical Biography*, 1961; A. Sorel, *Montesquieu*, 1888; *CE*, 9; *Chalmers*, 23; *DSB*, 9; *EB*, 15; *EP*, 5; *Grande*, 24; *IESS*, 10.

MONTESSORI, MARIA
Italian Educator
Born: Chiaravalle, near Ancona, August 31, 1870
Died: Noordwijk, Netherlands, May 6, 1952
Highest Degree: M.D., University of Rome, 1894
Positions: 1894-99, assistant physician at the Psychiatric Clinic, University of Rome; 1899-1901, directress, State Orthophrenic School, Rome; 1901-4, Scuola di Magistero Femminile, Rome; 1904-8, chair of anthropology, University of Rome; after 1906, La Case dei Bambini

Montessori, first woman in Italy to receive a medical degree, discovered that certain methods of teaching would enable the subnormal child to read and write like a normal child. She extended her method to normal slum children in the "children's houses" (Case dei Bambini). She described her work, begun with defective children in 1899, in the book *Metodo della pedagogica scientifica applicata all'educazione infantile nelle case dei bambini* (1909; English translation, *The Montessori Method*, 1912).

The main features of the Montessori method are to attract the child's attention to a task using certain specified educational materials, allowing the child freedom of movement, and gearing the task to be learned to the developmental level of the child. The Montessori school is a "prepared environment" in which the teachers keep themselves in the background, providing only minimal guidance and discipline, and the children themselves are entrusted with keeping things in their places. They acquire concepts through sensory-motor exercises and activities with Montessori's educational materials. From her observations Montessori derived certain generalizations concerning education and development: children go through certain "sensitive periods" during which they are particularly apt to learn certain things; they prefer to work with creative materials rather than play with toys; they are capable of extreme concentration if the situation is properly structured; they love orderliness, and under the conditions of a Montessori school, no punishment is needed to maintain discipline. Montessori's approach to education was in the tradition of Rousseau*, Pestalozzi*, and Fröbel*. Although developmental, it ran counter to Darwinism (Charles Darwin*) because of Montessori's emphasis on the importance of experience, behaviorism and its concept of learning as conditioning, fixed intelligence, and the psychoanalytic theory. Dewey's* progressive education eventually overshadowed the Montessori schools but not before her works had been translated in many languages and schools had been set up in several countries. In the United States a resurgence of interest in Montessori schools and the opening of many such schools occurred in the 1950s. Additional works by Montessori include *The Advanced Montessori Method* (1917-18), *The Secret of Childhood* (1936), *Education for a New World* (1946), *To Educate the Human Potential* (1948), and *The Absorbent Mind* (1949).

Biographies: R. J. Fynne, *Montessori and Her Inspirers*, 1924; A. Maccheroni, *A True Romance*, 1947; E. M. Standing, *Maria Montessori: Her Life and Work*, 1962; C. W. Valentine, *Nature*, 1952, *169*, 992-993; *CE*, 9; *EB*, 15; *EUI*, 36; *IESS*, 10; *NYT*, 1952, May 7, 27:1.

MORENO, JACOB L.
Rumanian-American Psychiatrist
Born: Bucharest, Rumania, May 6, 1889
Died: Beacon, New York, May 15, 1974
Highest Degree: M.D., University of Vienna, 1917
Positions, Honors: 1918, Mitterndorf State Hospital, near Vienna; 1918-1925, private practice, Vienna and Vöslau; from 1928, private practice, New York City; 1936-68, founder and director, Beacon Hill Sanitorium; 1951-66, adjunct professor of sociology, New York University; founder (1937) and editor, *International Journal of Sociometry*; founder (1947) and editor, *Group Psychotherapy and Psychodrama*; editor, *Group Psychiatry*; honorary degrees: University of Barcelona (1968), University of Vienna (1969); several citations, life memberships

Moreno's principal contribution to psychiatry and psychology was his introduction of a new therapeutic technique, the psychodrama. Before coming to the United States in 1925, Moreno had already established, between 1921 and 1925, the *Stegreiftheater*, or Spontaneity Theater, in Vienna, where actors acted in response to cues given by the audience. This evolved into psychodrama. In psychodrama the patient enacts, on a stage, a particular life situation or problem that relates to the present maladjustment. Other individuals are assigned the roles of other significant individuals in the patient's life (auxiliary egos). In acting out the situation, the patient reveals his personality structure, motivations, and conflicts. Cure comes about through catharsis and the acquisition of a greater spontaneity in meeting life's problems and in learning to deal with them in new ways. In psychodrama may be seen the beginning of the technique of group therapy. Moreno's activities in connection with psychodrama include work with children at the Plymouth Institute in Brooklyn, begun in 1928; the founding of several theaters for psychodrama, such as the Theater of Psychodrama at Beacon, New York, the publication of the *Impromptu Magazine* (since 1931); the founding of the Sociometric and Psychodramatic Institute (now the Moreno Institute); and serving as the president of the first seven international congresses on psychodrama.

Another contribution of Moreno's to psychology was his development of sociometry and the introduction of several sociometric techniques, including that of the sociogram (*Who Shall Survive?* 1934; rev. ed., 1953). Moreno himself conducted several sociometric studies in prisons and training schools. The sociogram is now a standard psychometric tool.

Books by Moreno include *Psychodrama* (vol. 1, 1946; 4th ed., 1972; vol. 2, 1959; vol. 3, 1969), *Group Psychotherapy* (1947), *Sociometry, Experimental Method and the Science of Society* (1951), *Sociometry and the Science of Man* (1956), *First Book of Group Psychotherapy* (1957), *The First Psychodramatic Family* (1964), and *Discovery of Spontaneous Man* (1965). He edited the *International Handbook of Group Psychotherapy* (1966) and *Psychodrama of Sigmund Freud* (1967).

Biographies: G. Bratescu, *Group Psychotherapy and Psychodrama*, 1975, *28*, 2-4; *EJ*, 12; *IESS*, 18; *NYT*, 1974, May 16, 44:4; *Who's Who in America*.

MORGAN, CLIFFORD THOMAS
American Psychologist
Born: Minnetola, New Jersey, July 21, 1915
Died: Austin, Texas, February 11, 1976
Highest Degree: Ph.D. in psychology, University of Rochester, 1939
Positions, Honors: 1939-43, Harvard University, Radcliffe College; 1943, technical aide, National Defense Research Committee, Department of Defense, Washington, D.C.; 1943-59, Johns Hopkins University, 1946-54, chairman of Psychology Department, 1951-53, chairman of biological sciences group; 1946-49, director, Systems Research Laboratory; 1950-59, consulting editor, McGraw-Hill Book Co.; 1959-62, University of Wisconsin; 1962-65, University of California, Santa Barbara; 1965-76, University of Texas; editorial work, *Journal of Comparative and Physiological Psychology* (1947-54), *Annual Review of Psychology* (1953-59), *Contemporary Psychology* (1955-60), *Psychological Abstracts* (1960-63), *Psychonomic Science* (1964-72), *Psychonomic Bulletin* (1964-76); director of publications, *Psychonomic Journals*, 1964-76; founder of *Psy-*

chonomic Science, *Psychonomic Monographs Supplements*, *Perception and Psychophysics*, *Behavior Research Methodology and Instrumentation*; president, Psychonomic Society, 1960

In the first phase of his career, Morgan did primarily experimental research with animals and humans, emphasizing the physiological bases of behavior. His best-known studies concern the discovery of audiogenic seizures in rats, hoarding of food in rats as a function of hunger and temperature, and the relation between pitch and sound intensity in human hearing. Morgan then turned to book writing, producing some well-known and widely used college texts. His *Physiological Psychology* first appeared in 1943 and was in its third edition in 1965. His *Introduction to Psychology* was first published in 1956 and was in its fifth edition in 1975, and *A Brief Introduction to Psychology* was published in 1974; both of these texts were widely used. Morgan also wrote *Applied Experimental Psychology* (1949, with A. Chapanis and W. R. Garner) and *How to Study* (1957, with J. Deese). In 1960 Morgan, with Stevens*, Spence*, and others, founded the Psychonomic Society and became its first president. The society was to be dedicated exclusively to psychological research and the dissemination of research results. Morgan continued to contribute to experimental psychology by starting several of the psychonomic journals and in his capacity as the director of publications of the society.

Biographies: E. Stellar & G. Lindzey, *Amer. J. Psychol.*, 1978, *91*, 343-348; *American Men and Women of Science*, 12th ed.; *NYT*, 1976, Feb. 17, 34:4; *Who's Who in America*.

MORGAN, CONWY LLOYD
English Psychologist and Biologist
Born: London, February 6, 1852
Died: Hastings, Sussex, March 6, 1936
Highest Degree: D.Sc., University of Bristol, 1910
Positions, Honors: 1878-83, lectureship in South Africa; 1884-1909, professor of zoology and geology, University College, Bristol, 1901, appointed professor of psychology and education, 1910-19, professor emeritus; 1919-36, lecturer, Clark University and Harvard University; honorary LL.D.

Morgan was one of the pioneers in comparative psychology. He performed the first psychological experiments on animals outside a laboratory and reported them in his early books, such as *Animal Life and Intelligence* (1890-91), *Introduction to Comparative Psychology* (1894), *Habit and Instinct* (1896), and *Animal Behavior* (1900). His best-known book is the *Introduction*. In it, to counteract the tendency that existed then of attributing reason, foresight, and other human mental functions to animals, Morgan stated a principle, to be applied in interpreting an animal's behavior: "In no case may we interpret an action as the outcome of the exercise of a higher psychical faculty, if it can be interpreted as the outcome of the exercise of one which stands lower in the psychological scale." As a form of the more general scientific law of parsimony, the principle came to be known as "Lloyd Morgan's canon" and served as a guideline in avoiding the anthropomorphization of animal behavior when it could be explained in terms of instinct or simple learned habits. Although Morgan believed that psychology's business was the study of the mind, and that in comparative psychology one should proceed by observing the behavior of animals, then drawing inferences about mental processes by analogy from one's own introspections, the very important difference between Morgan and Romanes*, who held identical views, and other Darwinians was that Morgan adhered to the canon of parsimonious interpretation of behavior.

Morgan's doctrine of emergent evolution (*Emergent Evolution*, 1923) stated that higher evolutionary stages emerged from lower ones by chance, whenever the necessary elements happened to come together in the necessary constellation. Consciousness, he thought, must have emerged by chance rather than by design. This view created considerable discussion among scientists from different fields.

Among Morgan's other books in comparative psychology and related areas may be mentioned *The Interpretation of Nature* (1905), *Instinct and Experience* (1912), *Life, Mind, and Spirit* (1926), *Mind at the Crossways* (1929), *The Animal Mind* (1930), and *The Emergency of Novelty* (1933).

Biographies: G. C. Grindley, *Brit. J. Psychol.*, 1936, 27, 103; *DNB*, Suppl. 5; *EUI*, 36; *HPA*, 2; *IESS*, 10; *Obit. Not.*, 2; *PR*, 3.

MORITZ, KARL PHILIPP

German Writer
Born: Hamel, Hanover, September 15, 1757
Died: Berlin, July 26, 1793
Education: Training for ministry (incomplete); self-instruction
Positions: 1789-93, professor of aesthetics and archeology, Academy of Arts, Berlin

Of the more than twenty volumes written by Moritz, the most important ones are his two autobiographic novels, *Anton Reiser* (4 vols., 1785-90) and *Andreas Hartknopf* (1786). *Anton Reiser* was the first psychological novel. It dealt with the inner life of a child and served to direct the attention of educators to the problems of the subjective life of children.

Moritz also established, in 1783, the first psychological journal, *Gnōthi sayton, oder, Magazin zur Erfahrungsseelenkunde*. The main type of content of the journal was case histories in child psychology, psycholinguistics, juvenile delinquency, problem children, and other applied subjects that suited Moritz's idea of psychology as a kind of physiology of the soul that would build up its theory by starting with cases, like medicine. The journal ceased publication under its original title with Moritz's death and was replaced by *Psychologisches Magazin*.

Biographies: C. Ziegler, *Moritz und sein psychologischer Roman*, 1913; *EB*, 15.

MOWRER, HOBART ORVAL

American Psychologist
Born: Unionville, Missouri, January 23, 1907
Died: Champaign, Illinois, June 22, 1982
Highest Degree: Ph.D. in psychology, Johns Hopkins University, 1932, under Knight Dunlap*
Positions, Honors: 1932-34, National Research Council Fellow, Northwestern University and Princeton University; 1934-36, Sterling Fellow, Yale University; 1936-40, Yale University, Institute of Human Relations; 1940-48, Harvard University; 1944-45, personality psychologist, Office of Strategic Services, Washington, D.C.; 1948-82, research professor, University of Illinois, Champaign; editor, *Harvard Educational Review*; honorary degree, Harvard University, 1946; president, American Psychological Association, 1953-54

Mowrer's importance to psychology is in his work on learning. His earliest significant contribution here was a 1938 paper, written with his wife, describing a successful enuresis treatment. It was a forerunner of what later became known as behavior therapy. Mowrer achieved prominence in the 1940s as one of the oustanding figures of "the age of learning theory." In a 1947 paper he described his two-factor learning theory: avoidance learning involved both Thorndikean reward learning and Pavlovian conditioning, or solution learning and sign learning. The theory was modified in 1956 to postulate only one type of learning, conditioning, but two types of reinforcement, one associated with the sudden onset of drive (punishment), the other with its termination (reward). This version was subsequently amended to include an explanation of secondary reinforcement. Mowrer's theory was based on a large amount of experimental work, both by himself and by others who were stimulated by his thinking. *Learning Theory and Behavior* (1960) and *Learning Theory and the Symbolic Processes* (1960) were also the result of his work in this area.

Mowrer's concern with psychoanalysis and psychotherapy paralleled his involvement in learning-theoretical research. At the Yale Institute of Human Relations, Mowrer, together with John Dollard, Neal Miller, and Robert Sears attempted to integrate psychoanalysis and learning theory, translating psychoanalytic concepts into learning-theoretical terms. Unlike the Freudian theory, this line of thinking was supported by experimental laboratory observations. *Learning Theory and Personality Dynamics* (1950) presents Mowrer's views on the subject.

Mowrer's own recurrent bouts with neurotic depression and his attempts to cope with it through psychoanalysis led to a view of neuroses that diverged from those of Freud.* His discovery that confessing one's misdeeds in a group led to relief that was not provided either by traditional psychology or the Protestant religion became one of the roots of the group-therapy movement of the 1960s (*Psychotherapy: Theory and Research*, 1953; *The New Group Therapy*, 1964). Concern with the relationship between psychology, religion, morality, and mental health marked the latter portion of Mowrer's career (*The Crisis in Psychiatry* *and Religion*, 1961; *Morality and Mental Health*, 1967). In addition to writing his books, Mowrer published more than two hundred articles and book chapters. *Biographies*: H. O. Mowrer, Abnormal reactions or actions? In J. Vernon (Ed.), *Introduction to Psychology: A Self-Selection Textbook*, 1966; *American Men and Women of Science*, 12th ed., Social and Behavioral Sciences, vol. 2; *HPA*, 6; *IESS*, 18; *Who's Who in America*.

MUENZINGER, KARL FRIEDRICH
American Psychologist
Born: Speyer, Rhineland-Palatinate, Germany, April 28, 1885
Died: Boulder, Colorado, November 23, 1958
Highest Degree: Ph.D. in psychology, University of Chicago, 1918
Positions: 1919-22, industrial psychologist, Lakeside Press; 1923-53, assistant professor to chairman, University of Colorado

At the University of Chicago Muenzinger engaged in research on learning, working with rats in spite of his allergy to them. His contributions stem from carefully executed experimental studies rather than from theory building. Muenzinger's theoretical outlook was close to Tolman's*. The work on vicarious trial and error was done mainly by Muenzinger, while Tolman provided the theory. Muenzinger's researches were published in some forty papers. He also wrote an introductory text in psychology (1942).
Biographies: D. Krech, *Amer. J. Psychol.*, 1959, *72*, 477-479; *PR*, 3.

MÜLLER, GEORG ELIAS
German Psychologist
Born: Grimma, Saxony, July 20, 1850
Died: Göttingen, Lower Saxony, December 23, 1934
Highest Degree: Ph.D. in philosophy, University of Göttingen, 1873
Positions: 1876-80, University of Göttingen; 1880, University of Czernowitz; 1881-1921, University of Göttingen

Müller's doctoral dissertation was the first empirical study of attention, and it was extensively cited by others, decades later. Müller next turned to psychophysics and presented some new ideas on psychophysical measurement in his 1876 *Habilitationsschrift*. In an article published the following year he proposed the new psychophysical method of constant stimuli. The Müller-Urban* weights, as they came to be known later, were to be used to find the ogive that best fits the data obtained by the method of constant stimuli and from which the difference threshold is determined. After Fechner's* death Müller became the leading psychophysicist. His laboratory at Göttingen, which he founded in 1881, was second only to Wundt's* laboratory at Leipzig.

The psychophysics of vision and memory were the two areas that Müller continued to work in for the rest of his life. *Zur Analyse der Unterschiedsempfindlichkeit* (1899) is a classic in psychophysics. Müller's theory of color vision is also well known. It incorporated Hering's* theory but with the difference that

Müller postulated a cortical gray from which all color sensations differ, rather than absence of vision when the black-white, red-green, and blue-yellow processes are in an equilibrium. Müller published four important papers about vision in the 1890s. The last summary of his views on psychophysics was his 1903 book, *Gesichtspunkte und Tatsachen der psychophysischen Methodik*. His interest in color and vision continued, and only four years before his death he completed the two volumes of *Über die Farbenempfindung: psychophysische Untersuchungen* (1930).

After Ebbinghaus* published his work on memory, Müller began studying learning. He worked out the "method of right associates," and his student Jost* developed a law concerning the strength of associations. While using Ebbinghaus's method of study, Müller added the introspective reports of the subjects and found that simple association by contiguity did not account for all that went on in learning, and that the learner's organizational activity, preparatory set (*Anlage*), and other internal processes affected learning. Müller's studies thus anticipated the findings of the Würzburg psychologists of the imageless thought school. On the technical side, Müller and Schumann* introduced the use of the memory drum in learning experiments, a device still in use today. Müller's experimental work on memory is brought together in the three volumes of *Zur Analyse der Gedächtnistätigkeit und des Vortstellungsverlaufes* (1911, 1913, 1917).

Müller was more clearly a pure psychologist than Wundt or Stumpf*, but he did not produce any systematic theoretical statement in book form. His Göttingen laboratory, like Wundt's laboratory at Leipzig, did become an institution producing many doctorates and individuals who were later to become well known. When psychology as an experimental science was getting started, Müller and his students exercised almost as great an influence as did Wundt.

Biographies: E. G. Boring, *Amer. J. Psychol.*, 1935, *47*, 344-348; E. Claparède, *Arch. psychol.*, 1935-36, *25*, 110-114; W. Hische, *Z. Psychol.*, 1935, *134*, 145-159; D. Katz, *Acta psychologica*, 1935, *1*, 234-240; D. Katz, *Psychol. Bull.*, 1935, *32*, 377-380; O. Kroh, *Z. Psychol.*, 1935, *134*, 150-190; O. Krohn, *Amer. J. Psychol.*, 1893, *5*, 282-284; J. Van Essen, *Ned. Tijdschr. Psychol.*, 1935, *3*, 48-58; *Biog. Lex.*; *Grande*, 24; *IESS*, 10; *PR*. 3.

MÜLLER, JOHANNES PETER
German Physiologist
Born: Koblenz, Rhineland-Palatinate, July 14, 1801
Died: Berlin, April 28, 1858
Highest Degree: Ph.D. in physiology, University of Bonn, 1822
Positions: 1824-33, University of Bonn; 1833-58, University of Berlin

Müller was the foremost physiologist of his day. He wrote a compendium of physiological knowledge, the *Handbuch der Physiologie des Menschen* (1833-40), which served as the primary reference text in physiology for some time. In it may be found not only a presentation of the state of knowledge of physiology of the time but also many of Müller's speculations, theories, research results, and conclusions. Müller shares with von Haller* the appellation "father of experimental physiology."

The fifth book of the *Handbuch* deals with the senses and contains the statement on the specificity of nerve energies. Although not entirely original with Müller, it was Müller who gave the principle a clear and precise formulation and made it known through his *Handbuch*. It states that we are not directly aware of objects themselves but of the quality of nerve activity that is triggered by the objects. There are five kinds of nerves, each conveying to the mind its own characteristic quality and not that of any other. The locus of specificity lies in the brain, however. Müller's doctrine led to later formulations such as the color vision theories of Helmholtz* and Hering*, all based on the notion of nerve-fiber specificity and the discovery of sensory spots in the skin. It was the most important law of physiology during the early nineteenth century. Philosophically, it stated that the nature of our knowledge was categorically tied to the nature of the bodily organs through which knowledge is acquired. It was an important contribution to physiological psychology. By placing the dimensions of experience in the nerves, that is, a material substrate, it furthered the removal of mind from the realm of metaphysics and into the realm of physical phenomena.

The sixth book of Müller's *Handbuch* deals with a variety of psychological subjects, such as memory, thought, temperament, and sleep. Müller discussed hearing at length and made some sound conjectures concerning the function of the middle and inner ear, as well as some erroneous ones. He described F. Aguilonius's concept of the horopter so well that it came to be known as Müller's circle. Earlier, Müller had written a text about the physiology of vision (*Zur vergleichenden Physiologie des Gesichtssinnes*, 1826) and one about perception *Über die phantastischen Gesitserscheinungen*, 1826). In all of his writings Müller's approach to physiology was that of a physiological psychologist, since he repeatedly referred to the mind to explain physiological functions. In some respects Müller was old-fashioned and believed in vital forces and the instantaneous transmission of nerve impulses, for instance, but he was also an inspiring teacher, and many physiologists and psychologists, who later acquired fame themselves, had studied with him.

Biographies: B. Chance, *Arch. Ophthalm.*, 1944, *32*, 395-402; E. Du Bois-Reymond, *Abh. preuss. Akad. Wiss.*, 1860, *4*, 25-190; U. Ebbeck, *Johannes Müller: Der grosse rheinische Physiologe*, 1951; W. Haberling, *Johannes Müller: Das Leben des rheinischen Naturforschers*, 1924; G. Koller, *Das Leben des Biologen Johannes Müller*, 1958; W. Stirling (Ed.), *Some Apostles of Physiology*, 1902; M. Stürzbecher, *Jb. Gesch. Mittel-Deutschlands*, 1972, *21*, 184-226; R. Virchow, *Johannes Müller: Eine Gedächtnisrede*, 1858; *ADB*, 22; *DSB*, 9; *Grande*, 24; Hirsch, *Biog. Lex.*, 4, Suppl.; *IESS*, 10; Pagel, *Biographisches Lexikon*.

MÜLLER-FREIENFELS, RICHARD

German Psychologist
Born: Bad Ems, Hessen, August 7, 1882
Died: Weilburg, Hessen, December 12, 1949
Highest Degree: Ph.D.; educated at Munich, Berlin, Geneva, Vienna, Tübingen, Paris, London, and Zurich
Positions: 1922-30, Kunstakademie, Berlin; 1930-33, Pädagogische Akademie, Stettin; 1933-45, Wirtschaftschochschule, Berlin; 1946-48, University of Berlin

Müller-Freienfels attempted to create an irrational-dynamic philosophical system (*Metaphysik des Irrationalen*, 1927) and to base his psychology, which he called *Lebenspsychologie*, or "life psychology," on it (*Lebenspsychologie*, 2 vols., 1916; *Grundzüge einer Lebenspsychologie*, 2 vols., 1924). Müller-Freienfels wrote a number of books, most of them in the area of social psychology and the psychology of personality. Some of them enjoyed considerable popularity and were reprinted several times: *Persönlichkeit und Lebensanschauung* (1919), *Psychologie der Religion* (2 vols. 1920), *Psychologie der Kunst* (2 vols., 1922), *Psychologie der deutschen Menschen* (1922), *Geheimnisse der Seele* (1927), *Hauptrichtungen der gegenwärtigen Psychologie* (1929), *Allgemeine Sozial- und Kulturpsychologie* (1930), *Gedächtnis- und Geistesschulung* (1933; 6th ed., 1966), *Menschenkenntnis und Menschenbehandlung* (1940; 4th ed., 1951).
Biographies: H. G. Böhme, *Richard Müller-Freienfels, 1882-1949, zum Gedächtnis*, 1950; *PR*, 3.

MÜLLER-LYER, FRANZ (CARL)

German Psychiatrist, Philosopher, Psychologist, and Sociologist
Born: Baden-Baden, Baden-Württemberg, February 5, 1857
Died: Munich, October 29, 1916
Highest Degree: M.D., University of Strasbourg, 1880
Positions: 1881-83, assistant director, psychiatric clinic, University of Strasbourg; after 1888, private practice, Munich

Between 1884 and 1888 Müller-Lyer studied psychology and sociology at the Universities of Berlin, Vienna, Paris, and London. He is best known for his sociological writings. He established a sociological and cultural philosophical system based on an analysis of the social causes of suffering. It had many adherents. In psychology Müller-Lyer wrote two monographs on psychophysics (*Physiologische Studien über Psychophysik*, 1886; *Psychophysische Untersuchungen*, 1889), but his name is firmly associated with a simple geometric illusion, first presented in 1889, rather than psychophysics or psychiatry. The Müller-Lyer illusion may be considered *the* geometric illusion since the largest number of studies by far have been done on it, and most theories of geometric illusions at least attempt to explain the Müller-Lyer illusion or take it to represent all other geometric illusions.
Biographies: G. Salomon, *Encycl. Soc. Sci.*, 1933, *11*, 83-84; *Biog. Lex.*

MÜNSTERBERG, HUGO
German-American Psychologist
Born: Danzig, East Prussia, June 1, 1863
Died: Cambridge, Massachusetts, December 16, 1916
Highest Degree: Ph.D. in psychology, University of Leipzig, 1885, under W. Wundt*; M.D., University of Heidelberg, 1887
Positions: 1887-92, University of Freiburg; 1892-95, 1897-1916, Harvard University; president, American Psychological Association, 1898

Although William James* started the first psychological laboratory in the United States at Harvard, he was temperamentally not an experimentalist and asked Münsterberg to take over the direction of the laboratory. Münsterberg at that time had attracted attention as an original experimenter (*Beiträge zur experimentellen Psychologie*, 1889-92). He directed the Harvard laboratory for a few years but began to be involved in other things and neglected it. These other things, however, were his major contribution to psychology, namely, the development of applied psychology in America. As his work as a researcher ended, his work in applying psychological principles to industrial, educational, legal, medical, clinical, and business problems began. When there was little application of psychological knowledge to practical affairs, Münsterberg wrote volumes such as *On the Witness Stand* (1908), *Psychology and the Teacher* (1909), *Psychotherapy* (1909), *Psychology and Industrial Efficiency* (1913), *Grundzüge der Psychotechnik* (1914), and *Psychology: General and Applied* (1914). Earlier, he had completed *Die Willenshandlung* (1888), an expanded version of his dissertation *Psychology and Life* (1899), and *Grundzüge der Psychologie* (1900), in which he set forth his philosophical theory of psychology, "voluntaristic idealism." Neither his philosophical nor his psychological theories (action theory) attracted much attention at the time. Neither did they leave much of an imprint on psychology.

Much of Münsterberg's applied psychology was armchair psychology, but he himself and his students did some empirical work also, such as producing some of the first efforts to validate aptitude tests. Münsterberg contacted business people with suggestions on how they might use psychology. In the area of psychotherapy, he was one of the early users of hypnotism. Although in the area of education his influence was not so strong because others were working in that field already, his book about the psychology of witness testimony was a landmark publication, and no other such book was written in the next twenty years. It included the suggestion that veracity and blood pressure might be related, a relationship that is now incorporated in the polygraph.

Advocacy of applied psychology, combined with his involvement in psychic research, made Münsterberg a public figure. He not only showed people outside of psychology how psychology can work for them but also convinced a small number of psychologists that applied psychology was a legitimate enterprise. This latter group has grown in size steadily ever since. Münsterberg's influence could have been greater had it not been for his vocal advocacy of things German and the beginning of World War I soon after the publication of his applied psychology texts. Animosity toward Germans even precluded the publication of an appreciation upon his death.

Biographies: M. Münsterberg, *Hugo Münsterberg: His Life and Work*, 1922; W. Stern, *J. Appl. Psychol.*, 1917, *1*, 186-188; J. H. Wigmore, *Ill. Law Rev.*, 1909, *3*, 399-445; *Biog. Lex.*; *DAB*, 13; *EJ*, 12; *IESS.* 10; *Jewish*, 8; *NCAB*, 13; *Who Was Who in America*, 1.

MURCHISON, CARL
American Psychologist
Born: Hickory, North Carolina, December 3, 1887
Died: Provincetown, Massachusetts, May 20, 1961
Highest Degree: Ph.D. in psychology, Johns Hopkins University, 1923, under K. Dunlap*
Positions, Honors: 1923-36, Clark University; 1936, manager, The Journal Press, Provincetown, Massachusetts; honorary degrees from Wake Forest College and the University of Athens

Murchison achieved distinction in psychology as the author, editor, and publisher of books, journals, and handbooks. First, upon G. S. Hall's* death in 1924, Murchison took over the editorship and management of *Pedagogical Seminary*. Under the name of The Clark University Press, Murchison founded, financed, edited, and managed *Genetic Psychology Monographs* (founded in 1925), *Journal of General Psychology* (1927), *Journal of Social Psychology* (1929), and *Journal of Psychology*. Upon leaving Clark University, he established The Journal Press, which continued to publish the same journals. Later, *Social Psychology Monographs* were added, and the name of *Pedagogical Seminary* was changed to *Journal of Genetic Psychology*. As he was leaving Clark, Murchison published, in 1935 and 1936, a well-known series of seven papers about the experimental measurement of a social hierarchy in the chicken.

Among Murchison's books are *American White Criminal Intelligence* (1924), *Criminal Intelligence* (1926), *Psychologies of 1925* (1926, editor), *The Case for and Against Psychical Belief* (1927, editor), *Social Psychology* (1929), and *Psychologies of 1930* (1930, editor). The topic of criminal intelligence was of particular interest to Murchison, and he published a considerable number of papers on this subject. In the 1930s he edited three handbooks: *The Foundations of Experimental Psychology* (1929), which was replaced by *A Handbook of General Experimental Psychology* (1934); *A Handbook of Child Psychology* (1931); and *A Handbook of Social Psychology* (1935). Murchison was also one of the five editors who prepared the first three volumes of *A History of Psychology in Autobiography* (vol. 1, 1930; vol. 2, 1932; vol. 3, 1936). Of lasting usefulness were also the two volumes of the *Psychological Register* (1928 and 1932), a Who's Who of the world of psychology.

Biographies: J. P. Nafe, *Amer. J. Psychol.*, 1961, *74*, 641-642; *NYT*, 1961, May 22, 31:2; *PR*, 3; *Who Was Who in America*, 4.

MURPHY, GARDNER

American Psychologist
Born: Chillicothe, Ohio, July 8, 1895
Died: Washington, D.C., March 19, 1979
Highest Degree: Ph.D. in psychology, Columbia University, 1923
Positions, Honors: 1921-40, Columbia University; 1940-52, City College of New York; 1952-67, director of research, Menninger Foundation, Topeka, Kansas; 1967-73, George Washington University; president, American Psychological Association, 1943-44; American Psychological Foundation Gold Medal, 1972; honorary doctorates, University of Hamburg (1976) and City University of New York

Gardner Murphy was one of the best-known psychologists during his lifetime. He became known through his writing, teaching, and involvement in parapsychology: he published twenty-five books and more than one hundred articles, taught and inspired many graduate students who later became prominent in psychology, and was one of the very few prominent psychologists who engaged in and defended parapsychological research.

Murphy's first major contribution was the writing of a history of psychology (*Historical Introduction to Modern Psychology*, 1929; 2nd ed., 1949; 3rd ed., 1972), which appeared the same year as Boring's* *History of Experimental Psychology* and enjoyed about the same success. Social psychology was Murphy's main concern during his Columbia years. His *Experimental Social Psychology* (1931; 2nd ed., 1937) received Columbia's Butler Medal. Murphy's work in social psychology led him into problems of personality and the publication of his most important book, *Personality: A Biosocial Approach to Origins and Structure* (1947), in which he presented his biosocial theory of personality. It was based on the concept of the field. Murphy held that the biological and the social are literally the same. This approach led to the integration and systematization of the lines of thought of many personality theorists and of virtually all areas of psychology. Murphy's theory was an example of an eclectic theory in the best sense. Concepts that Murphy particularly stressed and developed were *sensory and activity needs* (the organic need of the sense organs and the muscles to be stimulated), *canalization* (deepening of the channels for motivational energy by repeated acts that lead to the satisfaction of a motive), *perceptual learning* (learning to perceive), role, and situational determinants of behavior. Although the theory did not generate either much praise or criticism, it was accepted because it represented an approach to personality that very many psychologists were in fact using regardless of their professed theoretical preferences.

In the 1940s Murphy and his students produced a series of experiments on one aspect of perceptual learning, autism, or the effect of needs on perception. These experiments were influential in that they produced further research and became part of the foundation of the New Look in perception of the 1940s and 1950s that stressed emotional and motivational determinants.

Although he underplayed it, Murphy's interest in and support of parapsychology was lifelong. He bolstered parapsychology through his writings and research. His contribution was recognized through his election to the presidency of the Society for Psychical Research of London.

Biographies: *Amer. Psychologist*, 1973, *28*, 75-77; C. S. Hall & G. Lindzey, *Theories of Personality*, 1957, ch. 13; E. L. Hartley, *Amer. Psychologist*, 1980, *35*, 383-385; V. J. Nordby & C. S. Hall, *A Guide to Psychologists and Their Concepts*, 1974; G. R. Schmeidler, *J. Amer. Soc. Psychical Res.*, 1980, *74*, 1-14; *HPA*, 5; *IESS*, 18; *NYT*, 1979, Mar. 21, IV, 21:1.

MYERS, CHARLES SAMUEL

English Psychologist

Born: London, March 13, 1873

Died: Winsford, Somersetshire, October 12, 1946

Highest Degree: M.D., Cambridge University, 1901, Sc.D., 1909

Positions, Honors: 1904-22, Cambridge University; 1903-7, King's College, London; 1922-46, director, National Institute of Industrial Psychology, London; president, Seventh International Congress of Psychology, 1923; honorary Sc.D., University of Manchester; LL.D. University of Calcutta; Sc.D., University of Pennsylvania

Myers began his psychological career by participating, with Rivers* and McDougall*, in the Cambridge University anthropological expedition to the Torres Straits in 1898. He studied the sensory discrimination and reaction time of the natives. Upon his return to Cambridge, Myers became a cofounder, with Ward* and Rivers, of the *British Journal of Psychology* in 1904. Later, he was able to obtain funds for a psychology laboratory and opened one at Cambridge in 1913. As a director of the laboratory and lecturer in psychology at Cambridge, where many prominent British psychologists were trained, Myers was able to do much to change the emphasis in teaching psychology toward a more scientific approach. The experimental psychology text used in England in the 1910s and 1920s was *Textbook of Experimental Psychology* (1909) by Myers and Bartlett*. Myers also wrote *An Introduction to Experimental Psychology* soon after publishing the *Textbook* (1911).

As a result of his work during World War I on tests to select listeners for submarines, Myers became interested in applied psychology. He founded, with H. J. Welch, the National Institute of Industrial Psychology in 1921 and became the editor of *Occupational Psychology*, its organ. The several books that Myers wrote in the area of industrial psychology were also helpful in establishing a climate in Great Britain in which applied psychology was more readily accepted: *Mind and Work* (1920), *Industrial Psychology in Great Britain* (1926), *Ten Years of Industrial Psychology* (1923, with H. J. Welch), and *Psychology as Applied to Engineering* (1942).

Biographies: F. C. Bartlett, *Nature*, 1946, *158*, 657-658; C. Burt, *Occup. Psychol.*, 1947, *21*, 1-6; B. Edgell, *Brit. J. Psychol.*, 1947, *37*, 113-132; J. Germaine, *Rev. psicol. gen. aplic.*, 1947, *2*, 15-23; T. H. Pear, *Amer. J. Psychol.*, 1947, *60*, 289-296; T. H. Pear, *Brit. J. Psychol.*, 1947, *38*, 1-6; A. Rodger, *Bull. Brit. Psychol. Soc.*, 1971, *24*, 177-184; M. Viteles, *Psychol. Rev.*, 1947, *54*, 177-181; *DNB*, Suppl. 6; *EJ*, 12; *EUI*, 37; *Jewish*, 8; *Obit. Not.*, 5; *PR*, 3.

N

NAGEL, WILIBALD (A.)
German Physiologist
Born: Tübingen, Baden-Württemberg, June 19, 1870
Died: Rostock, Mecklenburg, January 14, 1911
Highest Degree: Ph.D., 1892; M.D., 1893
Positions: 1894-1902, University of Freiburg; 1902-8, University of Berlin; 1908-11, University of Rostock; physiological editor-in-chief, *Zeitschrift für Psychologie*

Nagel was primarily interested in vision (*Der Farbensinn der Tiere*, 1899; *Die Diagnose der praktisch wichtigen angeborenen Störungen des Farbensinns*, 1899), but he also worked on the chemical senses and on touch (*Die niederen Sinne der Insekten*, 1892). He published many papers in these areas in the *Zeitschrift für Psychologie*. Nagel was the editor of a *Handbuch der Physiologie* (1905-10), of which the third volume is about the psychophysiology of sensation. Other editorial work of Nagel's included his position on the Board of Editors of the third edition of Helmholtz's* *Handbook of Physiological Optics*. In connection with his work on color blindness, Nagel invented an anomaloscope (1898) that is used even now to measure the Rayleigh equation, named after John William Strutt, 3rd Baron of Rayleigh, for screening color blindness (red and green).
Biographies: *Biog. Lex.*; *Enciclopedia italiana*, 24; *EUI*, 37.

NEWTON, SIR ISAAC
English Scientist and Mathematician
Born: Woolsthorpe, Lincolnshire, December 25, 1642
Died: London, March 20, 1727

Highest Degree: B.A., Cambridge University, 1665

Positions, Honors: 1667-1703, Cambridge University; 1703-27, president, Royal Society; knighted, 1705

Newton, one of the greatest scientists of all times, contributed to psychology directly through his research and discoveries in the area of light as well as indirectly. Some time between 1665 and 1667, by breaking white light into chromatic components with a prism, recombining them into white light, and breaking it down again, Newton demonstrated the nature of white light and produced the first and entirely original theory of color. It explained why objects have different colors when illuminated by white light. Newton explained all colors as some combination of the spectral seven, described the nature of the complementarity of colors, described the color circle, formulated two laws of color mixture, and identified the whiteness of light with its intensity. Newton also knew that single objects are seen in binocular vision because of fusion of sensations from nerve fibers arising in corresponding points in the two eyes. He first described the nature of light in a paper presented to the Royal Society. All of his work on light and color was published in *Opticks*, which appeared in 1704.

In his principal work, *Philosophiae naturalis principia mathematica* (1687), Newton outlined the laws of the material universe that were to be accepted by the scientific world for the next two hundred years. The Newtonian view of the physical world had an immediate effect on the thinking of the British empiricists and associationists. The Newtonian particles found their correspondence in ideas as elements of thought. For Hume* the association of ideas played the same role in mental functioning as gravitation plays in the Newtonian universe. The New-tonian vibrations emerged as Hartley's* "vibratiuncles" of the brain, and the "mental chemistry" that both he and J. S. Mill* spoke about was a clear analog of Newton's finding that the seven primary colors, when combined, produce a completely new and different color, white. A more general and more important influence was exercised by Newton through his expectation that all phenomena of nature might be derived from the laws that he had formulated concerning the motion of bodies. Although the term *determinism* was not used until the nine-teenth century, Newton was the first to state clearly the propositions on which scientific determinism came to be based. Newton's "phenomena of nature" were eventually interpreted by some to include mental phenomena as well. In scientific psychology today, the hypothesis that all mental events and behaviors have a cause is accepted and must be accepted to proceed with psychology as a scientific enterprise.

Biographies: E. N. Andrade, *Isaac Newton*, 1950; H. D. Anthony, *Sir Isaac Newton*, 1960; D. Brewster, *Memoirs of the Life, Writings, and Discoveries of Sir Isaac Newton*, 2 vols., 1965; F. E. Manuel, *A Portrait of Isaac Newton*, 1968; L. T. Moore, *Isaac Newton: A Biography*, 1962; J. D. North, *Isaac Newton*, 1967; R. J. Westfall, *Never at Rest: A Biography of Isaac Newton* 1982; *Chalmers*, 23; *DNB*, 14; *DSB*, 10; *EB*, 16; *EP*, 5.

NIETZSCHE, FRIEDRICH WILHELM
German Philosopher
Born: Röcken, Saxony, October 15, 1844
Died: Weimar, Thuringia, August 25, 1900
Highest Degree: Ph.D. in classical philology, University of Leipzig, 1869
Positions: 1869-79, University of Basel

Nietzsche inspired many famous writers, poets, philosophers, and psychologists in Germany and France, although not in the English-speaking countries. Sigmund Freud* admired Nietzsche for his psychological insights, and in the instinct theory of Freud's may be found ideas very similar to those of Nietzsche. Nietzsche saw the principal human motives not in thought and reason but in instincts and drives. We try to hide our emotional nature (*ressentiment*, or repressed aggression) by inventing a system of rational motives and considering such motives as primary. The "real" human being is one with untamed drives, with consciousness and its acts in service to the drives. To see the real human being, the mask of rationality must be removed. Europeans deceive themselves in considering "facts of consciousness" as the first givens. The drives are unconscious, and the emphasis on consciousness leads one astray.

Nietzsche anticipated the emergence of a "third force" in psychology by voicing extreme criticism of the atomistic approach to the psyche shown by the experimental psychologists and by calling for a psychology "in the grand style" that would consider the psyche in its entirety. He was convinced that psychology should consider the will to power as the primary motive and all other motives as derivations from it.

Biographies: C. P. T. Andler, *Nietzsche: Sa vie et sa pensée*, 1934; L. Andreas-Salomé, *Friedrich Nietzsche in seinen Werken*, 1924; E. A. Bentley, *A Century of Hero Worship*, 1957; G. M. Brandes, *Friedrich Nietzsche*, 1914; E. Coplestone, *Friedrich Nietzsche: Philosopher of Culture*, 1942; A. Cresson, *Nietzsche: Sa vie, son oeuvre, avec un exposée de sa philosophie*, 1947; R. J. Hollingdale, *Nietzsche: The Man and His Philosophy*, 1965; W. Kaufmann, *Nietzsche: Philosopher, Psychologist, Antichrist*, 1968; W. Lange, *Nietzsche: Krankheit und Wirkung*, 1947; J. C. Lannoy, *Nietzsche: Ou l'histoire d'un égocentrisme athée*, 1952; H. Lefebvre, *Nietzsche*, 1939; *CE*, 10; *EB*, 16; *EP*, 5; *EUI*, 38; *Grande*, 24; *Jewish*, 8.

NISSEN, HENRY WIEGHORST
American Psychologist
Born: Chicago, Illinois, February 5, 1901
Died: Orange Park, Florida, April 27, 1958
Highest Degree: Ph.D. in psychology, Columbia University, 1929
Positions: 1929-56, research associate and professor of psychobiology, Yale University; 1939-58, associate director to director, Yerkes Laboratories of Primate Biology; 1956-58, professor of psychobiology, Emory University

Nissen, a comparative psychologist, was first to conduct experiments with chimpanzees in the late 1920s, continuing to work with this species throughout his career. He studied perception, learning, and the more complex behaviors in chimpanzees. In a well-known study (1951) Nissen and collaborators investigated the effect of tactual deprivation in a chimpanzee. He wrote a chapter about phylogenetic comparison for S. S. Steven's* *Handbook of Experimental Psychology* (1951). He wrote, himself or with others, some fifty papers, the majority of them about the behavior of chimpanzees.

Biographies: A. H. Riesen, *Amer. J. Psychol.*, 1958, *71*, 795-798; *Biog. Mem.*, 38; *NYT*, 1958, Apr. 30, 33:5; *PR*, 3; *Who Was Who in America*, 3.

O

OCKHAM, WILLIAM OF
English Schoolman
Born: Ockham, near London, ca. 1285
Died: Munich, Germany, 1349
Education: Degree of inceptor in theology, Oxford University, 1319
Positions: No academic or official positions

A Franciscan friar since an early age, Ockham was one of the most influential scholastic philosophers. He initiated the movement called "nominalism," which is of significance to psychology. In nominalism the problem of what constitutes a concept is resolved in a manner that is close to that of modern psychology. Ockham rejected Plato's* universals as a metaphysical idea, proposing instead that universal concepts should be made identical with the names given to classes of objects whose common features have been learned through experience with concrete, individual members of such classes. The abstract generalizations that may develop from such experience are entirely mental and do not exist outside the mind. The medieval realists and classical thinkers had assumed that to each mental concept there corresponded something real (or nonmental). Ockham thought of concepts as mental habits, and the seeds of British empiricism may be seen in Ockham's nominalism, his psychology a transition from the theologically oriented Thomistic psychology to one more open to experience, experiment, and natural causation.

Committed to both faith and reason, Ockham repeatedly invoked two maxims in his writings: God can bring about anything whose accomplishment does not involve a contradiction, and "what can be accounted for by fewer assumptions is explained in vain by more'' (or ''explanatory entities should not be multiplied beyond necessity''). The first maxim implies that any given case of dispute must be decided on the basis of empirical evidence. The second maxim is known as ''Ockham's Razor.'' It is one form of the principle of parsimony of modern science, according to which those explanations that are consistent with the fewest assumptions are to be preferred. Both Ockham's maxims imply an empiricist theory of knowledge. The first use of Ockham's canon in psychology occurred in the nineteenth century when Lloyd Morgan* applied it to the study of animal behavior.

Ockham drew a sharper distinction between faith and reason than did Thomas Aquinas*. Experience, he said, provided no evidence that the soul was immortal. Such evidence, however, came from faith. Concerning the soul's mental powers, Ockham held that the will, or the intellect, is not a faculty of the soul but the soul in the process of willing, thinking, and so on. In taking this dynamic view, Ockham differed from Thomas Aquinas and other faculty psychologists that followed Aquinas.

Biographies: M. G. Gottfried, *Wilhelm von Ockham,* 1949; C. Vasoli, *Guglielmo d'Occam*, 1953; *DNB*, 41; DSB, 10; *EB*, 16.

OGDEN, ROBERT MORRIS
American Psychologist
Born: Binghamton, New York, July 6, 1877
Died: Ithaca, New York, March 2, 1959
Highest Degree: Ph.D. in psychology, University of Würzburg, 1903, under O. Külpe*
Positions: 1903-5, University of Missouri; 1905-14, University of Tennessee; 1914-16, University of Kansas; 1916-45, Cornell University, until 1939, professor of education, until 1945, professor of psychology, 1923-45, dean, School of Arts and Sciences; president, Southern Society for Philosophy and Psychology, 1912-13; editorial work, *Psychological Bulletin* (1909-29), *American Journal of Psychology* (1926-58)

First, as an advocate of the imageless thought school of his teacher Külpe, Ogden published an introductory text (*An Introduction to General Psychology,* 1914) that was written from the point of view of that school. It was the only such text ever published. Soon after the Gestalt theory became known in Germany, however, Ogden asked Kurt Koffka* to write a paper for *Psychological Bulletin* explaining the theory to American readers. Ogden and Koffka's 1922 paper was instrumental in introducing Gestalt psychology in the United States. Ogden contributed to the dissemination of Gestalt ideas in America in other ways also, such as by translating Koffka's *The Growth of the Mind* in 1924 and by writing the first American Gestalt-oriented book, *Psychology and Education* (1926). Ogden also wrote the book *Hearing* (1924) and one entitled *The Psychology of Art* (1938). The contents of Ogden's approximately sixty scientific articles range from thinking and the Würzburg school to education, Gestalt psychology, and hearing.

Biographies: K. M. Dallenbach, *Amer. J. Psychol.*, 1959, *72*, 472-477; *EUI*, 39; *NCAB*, 43; *PR*, 3.

OLDS, JAMES
American Psychologist
Born: Chicago, Illinois, May 30, 1922
Died: Laguna Beach, California, August 21, 1976
Highest Degree: Ph.D. in psychology, Harvard University, 1952, under Richard Solomon
Positions, Honors: 1952-53, Harvard University; 1953-55, postdoctoral fellow, McGill University; 1955-57, research psychologist, University of California School of Medicine; 1957-69, University of Michigan; 1969-76, California Institute of Technology; Newcome-Cleveland Prize of the American Association for the Advancement of Science, 1956; Hoffheimer Prize of the American Psychiatric Association, 1958; Warren Medal of the Society of Experimental Psychologists, 1962; American Psychological Association Distinguished Scientific Contribution Award, 1967; Kittay International Award, Kittay Scientific Foundation, 1976

In 1953 Olds discovered, by accident, that rats would learn and do work when the reward was electrical stimulation in the septal area of the brain. Rats worked at much higher rates to obtain the reward of electrical stimulation than to obtain food. Olds eventually mapped a large number of these "pleasure centers" in the rat's brain, most of them concentrated in the limbic system. This discovery was published by Olds (with P. Milner) in 1954, the same year in which José Delgado published his discovery of aversive centers in the brain. All of this led to a very large amount of research on this aspect of motivated behavior. Although the technique and nature of stimulation were new, the discovery provided support for the old hedonistic theory of motivation and undermined those contemporary theories that saw motivation in the reduction of physiological drives. Olds himself performed a very large number of experiments. He studied, among other things, the effects of the intensity of stimulation and compared centrally administered electrical stimulation with ordinary reinforcers, finding that very intense stimulation of the pleasure centers could be aversive, that central stimulation could be more potent than food or sex, and that physiological drives and intracranial electrical stimulation potentiated each other. Olds wrote a book about motivation, *The Growth and Structure of Motivation* (1956) and some one hundred papers, most of them related to the electrical stimulation of the brain.

Biographies: *Amer. Psychologist*, 1967, *22*, 1135-1138; R. F. Thompson, *Amer. J. Psychol.*, 1979, *92*, 151-152; *NYT*, 1976, Aug. 24, 32:3

ORTH, JOHANNES
German Pathological Anatomist
Born: Wallmerod, Hessen-Nassau, January 14, 1847
Died: Berlin, January 13, 1923

Highest Degree: M.D., University of Berlin, 1871

Positions: 1873-78, Wirchow Institute, Berlin; 1878-1902, University of Göttingen; 1902-23, director and professor of pathology, Pathological Institute (Pathologisches Institut), Berlin

In 1901 Orth wrote a paper (with A. Mayer) about the qualitative nature of association that launched the writings from the Würzburg school of psychology. Orth stressed the importance of *Bewusstseinslagen*, or conscious attitudes, that, in addition to determining images and sensations, determine thinking. These conscious attitudes, according to Orth, are imageless feelings. *Gefühl und Bewusstseinslage* (1903) was another contribution of Orth's to the body of writings from the Würzburg school.

Biographies: K. Marbe, *Fortschr. psychol. Anwend.*, 1914, *2*, 302-320; *Biog. Lex.*; *EUI*, 40; Pagel, *Biographisches Lexikon*.

P

PARACELSUS (THEOPHRASTUS PHILIPPUS AUREOLUS
BOMBAST VON HOHENHEIM)
German Physician and Theosophist
Born: Near Einsiedeln, Schwytz, Switzerland, ca. 1493
Died: Salzburg, Austria, September 24, 1541
Education: Studied medicine at the University of Basel
Positions: 1526-29, University of Basel

Paracelsus did not believe that mental illness is caused by demoniacal possession, and he had other correct insights concerning mental disorders, such as the relationship between head injury and paralysis, cretinism and goiter (*The Diseases That Deprive Man of His Reason*, ca. 1567). He is also credited with the explicit recognition of the influence of unconscious motivation upon behavior. Although Paracelsus was a Neoplatonist, a mystic, and a cabbalist and believed in astrology and alchemy, he also believed that truth could be arrived at only through observation rather than reliance on authority. In this respect Paracelsus represents a stage of development of scientific thought intermediate between that of, for instance, Albert the Great (Albertus Magnus)* and Francis Bacon*. Because of his rejection of medical dogma (in stressing the use of minerals and metals rather than medicines derived from plants, he introduced chemistry in medicine), teaching medicine in German, and teaching the practice of medicine rather than theory and definitions, Paracelsus was expelled from the University of Basel.
Biographies: *DSB*, 10; *EP*, 6.

PARSONS, (SIR) JOHN HERBERT
English Ophthalmologist
Born: Bristol, September 3, 1868
Died: London, October 7, 1957
Highest Degree: M.B., St. Bartholomew's Hospital, London, 1892; D.Sc., University of London, 1904
Positions, Honors: Various medical appointments, private practice; president, Illuminating Engineering Society, 1921; honorary D.Sc., University of Bristol, 1925; honorary LL.D., Edinburgh University, 1927; three medals from ophthalmological societies; knighted, 1922; other honors

After considerable clinical and research work on the eye and eye diseases, in which he became a world expert, in 1913 Parsons turned to the psychology of vision. In 1915 he introduced the term *photopia* for daylight vision and *scotopia* for twilight vision. His *Introduction to the Study of Colour Vision* also appeared in that year. Later, in 1927, he wrote *An Introduction to the Theory of Perception*. Its main thesis was that perception can be studied only factually and materialistically using the method of physiological experimentation, and that introspection without biology is dangerous. Psychology outside of perception also attracted Parsons's interest, from the writing of *A Precis of Applied Psychology* in 1918 to *The Springs of Conduct* in 1950.
Biographies: Brit. Med. J., 1957, *50*, 945-946; *Biog. Lex.*; *DNB*, Suppl. 7; *EUI*, 42.

PASCAL, BLAISE
French Philosopher
Born: Clermont-Ferrand, Puy de Dôme, June 19, 1623
Died: Paris, August 19, 1662
Education: Educated by father
Positions: No official or academic positions

In response to the queries of a gentleman gambler, Pascal and Pierre de Fermat worked out (beginning in 1654) the answers as to why he was losing money in games of dice. From these beginnings, which included the famous Pascal triangle, probability calculus arose, of immense importance to science since it allowed predictions in the face of uncertainty. Because behavioral events are eminently uncertain, Pascal's work was of utmost importance to the development of psychology as a science, especially after subsequent elaboration of this work by men such as Christian Huygens*, Abraham de Moivre, Adolphe Quételet*, Karl Gauss*, and Francis Galton*.
Biographies: M. Bishop, *Pascal: The Life of Genius*, 1936; E. Boutroux, *Pascal*, 1924; L. Brunschvicg, *Blaise Pascal*, 1953; E. Cailliet, *Pascal: The Emergence of Genius*; J. Chevalier, *Blaise Pascal*, 1930; A. Cresson, *Pascal: Sa vie, son oeuvre, avec un exposé de sa philosophie*, 1947; E. Mortimer, *Blaise Pascal: The Life and Work of a Realist*; J. L. P. Segond, *La vie de Blaise Pascal*, 1929; *CE*, 10; *Chalmers*, 24; *DSB*, 10; *EB*, 17; *EP*, 6; *EUI*, 42; *Grande*, 26.

PATERSON, DONALD GILDERSLEEVE

American Psychologist
Born: Columbus, Ohio, January 18, 1892
Died: St. Paul, Minnesota, October 4, 1961
Highest Degree: M.A. in psychology, Ohio State University, 1916 under R. Pintner*
Positions: 1916-17, University of Kansas; 1917, psychologist, U.S. Army; 1918-21, Scott Company, consultant; 1921-60, University of Minnesota; editorial work, *Journal of Applied Psychology*, 1943-54

Paterson was an applied psychologist who developed vocational guidance techniques and became a leader in the field of student counseling (*Men, Women, and Jobs*, 1936, with J. Darley; *Student Guidance Techniques*, 1938, with G. Schneidler and E. Williamson). Paterson worked extensively in the field of intelligence and ability measurement. He produced, with R. Pintner, the Pintner-Paterson Scale of Performance Tests (1917), a nonlanguage intelligence test. Additional tests constructed by Paterson, with collaborators, were the Minnesota Mechanical Ability Test (1930), Minnesota Mechanical Assembly Test (1930), Minnesota Spatial Relations Test (1930), and Revised Minnesota Occupational Rating Scales (1953). Paterson did additional work in applied psychology, such as the study of legibility of type, which he published with M. Tinker (*How to Make Type Readable*, 1940). A bibliography of Paterson's publications contains more than three hundred items.
Biographies: *J. Appl. Psychol.*, 1961, *45*, 352; E. Williamson, *Personnel Guid. J.*, 1961, *40*, 235; *IESS*, 11; *PR*, 3; *Who Was Who In America*, 4.

PAVLOV, IVAN PETROVICH

Russian Physiologist
Born: Ryazan', Russia (near Moscow), September 26, 1849
Died: Leningrad, February 27, 1936
Highest Degree: M.D., University of St. Petersburg, 1883
Positions: 1890-1924, Military Medical Academy; 1924-36, director, Pavlov Institute of Physiology, Russian Academy of Science

Pavlov was fifty-five when he received the Nobel Prize for his work on the physiology of digestion. Before 1900 he had made the observation that dogs salivate not only when food is given them but also to other stimuli that accompany feeding. By 1901 he had given the name of "conditioned reflex" to the reflexive response to a stimulus that had previously not been able to elicit it but had acquired that power through association. Pavlov spent the next three decades studying conditioning.

Pavlov started with the basic form of conditioning in which an unconditioned (innately effective) stimulus was paired with a conditioned stimulus (bell, metronome, light flash) until the latter alone came to elicit the reflex (conditioned reflex) and its temporal variants (backward conditioning, trace conditioning). Then he progressed to the study of the extinction of the conditioned response with repeated presentation of the conditioned stimulus alone, *stimulus generalization* (response to other, similar stimuli), *discrimination learning* (response to only a determined value of the stimulus, but not to others), spontaneous recovery of the conditioned response after a period of extinction, higher-order conditioning, and other phenomena. Pavlov sought their explanation in terms of postulated excitatory and inhibitory processes in the nervous system and not in terms of any mental processes.

Although Pavlov did not perform any human conditioning experiments, he did make some theoretical statements concerning the organization of the more complex human behaviors that made it possible later to base the entire system of Soviet psychology on his teachings. Pavlov visualized both the unconditioned and the conditioned reflexes as effecting a connection between the organism and its environment. The nervous activity involved in forming the temporal (conditioned) connections he called higher nervous activity, to distinguish it from lower nervous system activity, which served to integrate the organism in Sherrington's* sense. Environmental stimuli significant to the organism's survival constituted the first signal system. A second signal system had developed in humans, Pavlov held, as a result of their practical experience. This system does not represent reality directly but rather through its data in the nervous system, which are then called thought or, in their physical manifestation, language. Rubinshteĭn* was instrumental in translating these Pavlovian premises into a new basis for Soviet psychology.

In studying discrimination learning, Pavlov observed that when forced to make very difficult or impossible discriminations, animals would begin to act in unusual or "neurotic" ways. This coincided with Sigmund Freud's* clinical observations that conflicts underlay all neuroses and thus opened a way for the experimental study of behavioral abnormalities. Between 1916 and 1936 Pavlov also studied types of the nervous system in terms of the innate relative predominance of the excitatory and inhibitory processes. He was prompted in this by the observed individual differences in his laboratory animals' behavior. Although Pavlov at first referred to different temperaments in his dogs and thought there were four such temperaments, he stopped referring to behavior after 1927 and from then on considered only the physiological properties of the nervous system. The fourfold classification of behaviors was continued, however, by Soviet psychologists, especially since Pavlov had at one time described them using the names of the Galenic temperaments. Present-day Soviet personality theory is based on Pavlov's classification of nervous systems, as elaborated by his own students who survived him. Pavlov wrote numerous papers, but only a few books, such as *Conditioned Reflexes* (English translation, 1927) and *Lectures on Conditioned Reflexes* (English translation of 3rd ed., 1928).

Pavlov had a pessimistic view of psychology and tried to avoid making any mentalistic, subjective, or "psychological" references with regard to conditioning. Because of his own insistence that his work was physiology and not psychology, his influence on Russian psychology became significant only after 1950 as the result of an official move to "pavlovianize" science. Nevertheless, conditioning as the simplest kind of learning was one of the cornerstones on which the school of behaviorism was built, and its study and application (as in the conditioning therapies) by Pavlov's own numerous coworkers and students, as well as psychologists throughout the world, has become a substantial portion of the psychological edifice.

Biographies: E. A. Asratyan, *I. P. Pavlov: His Life and Work*, 1953; B. P. Babkin, *Pavlov: A Biography*, 1949; H. Cuny, *Ivan Pavlov: The Man and His Theories*, 1965; A. V. Hill, *Science*, 1936, *83*, 351-353; M. Lapicque, *C. r. Acad. sci.*, 1936, *202*, 785-787; P. O. Makarov, *Conditional Refl.*, 1966, *1*, 288-292; H. Piéron, *Rev. Paris*, 1932, *6*, 359-376; M. J. Sereisky, *Character Pers.*, 1936, *4*, 344-348; H. K. Wells, *Ivan P. Pavlov: Toward a Scientific Psychology and Psychiatry*, 2 vols., 1956, 1960; *DSB*, 10; *EB*, 17; *EP*, 6; *IESS*, 11; *NYT*, 1936, Feb. 27, 19:1; *Obit. Not.*, 2; *Soviet Encyclopedia*.

PEARSON, KARL
English Mathematician
Born: London, March 27, 1857
Died: London, April 27, 1936
Education: Studied mathematics, engineering, and law, among other subjects, at King's College, Cambridge; graduated in 1879
Positions, Honors: 1884-1933, University College, London, since 1911, director, Department of Applied Statistics, and Sir Francis Galton Professor of Eugenics; founder (1901) and editor, (1902-36) *Biometrika*; editor, *The Annals of Eugenics*, 1925-36; honorary LL.D., University of St. Andrews; D.Sc., University of London; Darwin Medal of Royal Society, 1898

Pearson was one of the fathers of modern statistics. About 1890 he acquired an interest in heredity, eugenics, and biological problems in general and in the application of statistics to such problems. His aim was to verify Charles Darwin's* evolutionary theory. He developed a number of statistical treatments of biological data that are among the most widely used ones today. Pearson was a student, companion, and biographer of Sir Francis Galton* and with the latter's encouragement developed the mathematical formulation of the idea of correlation that Galton had conceived. The result was the now widely used Pearson product-moment correlation coefficient. Another statistic developed by Pearson was the chi square. Pearson's work found such broad application in other fields besides eugenics that students from all over the world came to Cambridge to study under him. To psychology the importance of the correlation coefficient and of the chi square statistic is such that much of psychological research work today would be unthinkable without them. They were first presented in a series of eighteen papers published between 1893 and 1912 under the title of *Mathematical Contributions to the Theory of Evolution*. Pearson shared with Hume* and Mach* their view of causality as concomitant variation (correlation). His views of the philosophy of science, presented in his early lectures, are to be found in the classic *Grammar of Science* (1892). Pearson published several other books and sets of statistical tables.

Biographies: B. H. Camp, *Amer. Stat. Ass. J.*, 1933, *28*, 395-491; J. B. S. Haldane, *Biometrika*, 1957, *44*, 303-313; R. Pearl, *Amer. Stat. Ass. J.*, 1936, *31*, 653-664; E. S. Pearson, *Karl Pearson: An Appreciation of Some Aspects of His Life and Work*, 1938; B. Semmel, *Brit. J. Sociol.*, 1958, *9*, 111-125; S. A. Stouffer, *Amer. Stat. Ass. J.*, 1958, *53*, 23-27; F. M. Urban, *Arch. ges. Psychol.*, 1936, *96*, 549-551; S. S. Wilks, *Sci. Mon.*, 1941, *53*, 249-253; *DNB*, Suppl. 5; *DSB*, 10; *EB*, 17; *EP*, 6; *IESS*, 11; *Obit. Not.*, 2.

PEIRCE, CHARLES SANTIAGO SANDERS
American Philosopher
Born: Cambridge, Massachusetts, September 10, 1839
Died: Milford, Pennsylvania, April 14, 1914
Highest Degree: A.M., Harvard University, 1860; Sc.B. in chemistry, Harvard University, 1863
Positions: 1879-84, lectured at Harvard, Johns Hopkins, and other universities

Peirce created pragmatism (1878) in American philosophy, although it remained for James* to develop and popularize it. Peirce used the term *pragmatism* for the first time in the English language in the article "How to Make Our Ideas Clear." The way to make an idea clear is to "consider what effects, that conceivably might have practical bearings we conceive the object of our conception to have. Then our conception of these effects is the whole of our conception of the object." Since the practical consequences of a concept can be experienced only through the senses, Peirce's pragmatism was a further development of empiricism; and since only that which is empirically observable can be measured, Peirce's definition of pragmatism anticipated the operational definition of Bridgman*. James and Peirce's conceptualizations of pragmatism did not coincide completely, with Peirce's view emphasizing the public nature of the criterion of "what works" and James's pragmatism being more subjective. Peirce considered that James's concept of pragmatism was that "the end of man is action," whereas Peirce's own doctrine was intended as a "theory of logical analysis." To distinguish his own definition of pragmatism from that of James's, Peirce called it "pragmaticism." It was, however, James's version that prevailed, and Peirce is now remembered more as an important developer of modern logic.

Biographies: J. Jastrow, *J. Phil.*, 1916, *13*, 723-726; T. S. Knight, *Charles Peirce*, 1965; E. Nagel, *Phil. Sci.*, 1940, *7*, 69-80; *CE*, 11; *DAB*, 14; *DSB*, 10; *EP*, 6; *EUI*, 42; *IESS*, 11; *NCAB*, 8; *NYT*, 1914, Apr. 22, 15:6; *Who Was Who in America*, 4.

PENFIELD, WILDER GRAVES
Canadian Neurosurgeon
Born: Spokane, Washington, January 26, 1891
Died: Montreal, Canada, April 5, 1976

Highest Degree: M.D., Johns Hopkins University, 1918
Positions, Honors: 1921-28, attending surgeon, Presbyterian Hospital, New York, and assistant professor of surgery, Columbia University; 1928-34, Royal Victoria Hospital, Montreal; 1928-60, McGill University; 1934-60, director, Montreal Neurological Institute, McGill University; president, Royal College of Physicians and Surgeons of Canada (1940-44), American Neurological Association (1951); fifteen medals, orders, and awards; numerous honorary doctorates

Penfield was a brain surgeon of world renown, especially for epileptic cases. The Montreal Neurological Institute, founded by Penfield, achieved worldwide fame both as a research center and a hospital. Penfield perfected the technique of electrical stimulation of the brain to pinpoint epileptic foci. He was interested in speech mechanisms and was able to produce disordered speech through electrical stimulation of the cortex, which led to formulations of theories concerning the nature of speech mechanisms. In 1931 Penfield, while stimulating electrically the brain of an epileptic patient preparatory to an operation, discovered accidentally that the stimulation of the temporal lobe would elicit long-term memories in the form of a vivid reexperiencing of past events. Penfield named this portion of the temporal lobe the "interpretive cortex." Although the phenomenon gave rise to theories of memory function, it has never been fully explained.

Penfield presented the results of his research and theorizing on the functioning of the brain in a number of volumes: *Epilepsy and Cerebral Localization* (1941, with T. C. Erickson); *The Cerebral Cortex of Man* (1950, with T. Rasmussen); *Epilepsy and Functional Anatomy of Human Brain* (1954, with H. Jasper); *The Excitable Cortex in Conscious Man* (1958); *Speech and Brain Mechanisms* (1959 with L. Roberts); and *The Mystery of the Mind* (1975).
Biographies: *The Canadian Who's Who*, 12th ed.; *Current Biography*, 1955, 1968; *The International Who's Who*, 38th ed; *NYT*, 1976, Apr. 6, 38:5.

PESTALOZZI, JOHANN HEINRICH
Swiss Educator
Born: Zurich, January 12, 1746
Died: Brugg, Aargau, February 17, 1827
Education: Studied law and theology
Positions: Organizer and teacher of experimental elementary schools

Pestalozzi is honored as a humanitarian who throughout his life was concerned with the fate of underprivileged and orphaned children. He was convinced that human society could be bettered through education and the perfection of human nature. He presented his views in fictional form, *Lingard und Gertrude* (1801; English translation, *How Gertrude Teaches Her Children*). His guiding principle was the development of human capabilities in accordance with nature. This was to be accomplished through activity, since activity is what is natural to the child. Activity should take the form of exercise. The first educator is the mother, then the school. The child's capacities need to be exercised in a sequential order. Pestalozzi's educational theory included physical, moral, and mental education.

332   PETER OF SPAIN

At the famous Yverdon boarding school that Pestalozzi established in 1805, he emphasized motor acts, such as singing, drawing, writing, and physical exercise, and activities such as collecting and model making. In moral development Pestalozzi thought the principal factor was the child's love for mother arising from the satisfaction of the child's needs by the mother. This love the child must transfer to family members, then to other people, and finally to all humanity. Important factors in moral development are the behavior of model adults and the practice of moral behavior. In mental education Pestalozzi stressed the accumulation of knowledge on the basis of sensory experience and the development of mental capacities. The principle of "sense impression" was the accurate relation of words and ideas to concrete objects and events so that thinking likewise may be accurate. Pestalozzi adjusted instruction to the difficulty level of the material and according to individual differences in ability. In developmental psychology Pestalozzi is credited with having published for the first time observations on a child (his own three-and-a-half-year-old son) in a scientific journal (1774).

Biographies: J. A. Green, *Life and Work of Pestalozzi*, 1913; R. d. Guims, *Pestalozzi: His Life and Work*, 1897; G. Gutek, *Pestalozzi and Education*, 1968; M. Heafford, *Pestalozzi: His Thought and Its Relevance Today*, 1967; G. E. Mueller, *Harvard Educational Review*, 1946, *16*, 141-159; P. G. Natorp, *Pestalozzi: Sein Leben und seine Ideen*, 1912; H. Otto, *Pestalozzi*, 1948; E. H. Reisner, *Encycl. Soc. Sci.*, 1934, *12*, 94-95; K. Silber, *Pestalozzi: The Man and His Work*, 1960; *ADB*, 25; *CE*, 11; *EP*, 6; *EUI*, 43; *Grande*, 26; *Nouvelle*, 39.

PETER OF SPAIN (PETRUS HISPANUS)
Spanish-Italian Philosopher, Physician, and Psychologist
Born: Lisbon, Portugal, between 1210 and 1220
Died: Rome, March 16, 1277
Education: Studied medicine, theology, and Aristotelean physics and metaphysics until 1245
Positions: 1246-50, University of Sienna; 1273, elected cardinal; 1276, crowned Pope John XXI

Like his contemporary Thomas Aquinas*, Peter of Spain wrote a commentary on Aristotle's* *De Anima*. Unlike Aquinas, he wrote an independent work called *De Anima* that was not a commentary but an original treatise on psychology, the first one to appear since antiquity. It was written some time between 1245 and 1250 and contained, among other topics of psychological interest, a history of psychology. He also wrote a very popular logic and a very popular medical textbook. In another health manual, *Commentaries on Isaac*, Peter of Spain, in speaking of medicines, compared the rational and experimental methods of gaining knowledge and gave six steps that are necessary to conduct an experiment on the efficacy of medicines. These steps implicitly show an understanding of the nature of the scientific experiment. Peter of Spain's contributions, however, stand in isolation, because the right climate for the development of science was not to arrive until some three hundred years later.

Biographies: E. John (Ed.), *The Popes*, 1964, p. 235; R. Stapper, *Papst Johannes XXI*, 1898; *CE*, 7; *EP*, 6.

PFLÜGER, EDUARD FRIEDRICH WILHELM
German Physiologist
Born: Hanau, Hesse, June 7, 1829
Died: Bonn, March, 16, 1910
Highest Degree: M.D., University of Giessen, 1851; Berlin, 1855
Positions: 1858-59, University of Berlin; 1859-1909, University of Bonn

Pflüger studied the effects of electrical stimulation on motor nerves and was the first to formulate the laws governing such effects. He also studied the functions of the spinal cord and, in this connection, became involved in a controversy with Lotze* and Marshall Hall* concerning the question of whether spinal reflexes were conscious or not. Pflüger held that they were conscious because they were purposeful and, being purposeful, they must be conscious (*Die sensorischen Funktionen des Rückenmarks der Wirbelthiere nebst einer neuen Lehre über die Leitungsgesetze der Reflexionen*, 1853). In 1868 Pflüger established *Pflügers Archiv für die gesamte Physiologie des Menschen und der Theire*, known simply as *Pflügers Archiv* and for many years an important forum for the works of both physiologists and psychologists who contributed significantly to the development of physiological psychology.

Biographies: H. Boruttau, *Deutsch. med. Wochenschr.*, 1910, *36*, 851-852; E. v. Cyon, *Arch. ges. Physiol.*, 1910, *132*, 1-19; I. P. Pavlov, In I. P. Pavlov, *Sämtliche Werke*, 2nd rev. ed., vol. 6, 1956, pp. 317-318; R. Rosemann, *Arch. ges. Physiol.*, 1929, *222*, 548-562; *DSB*, 10; *EUI*, 44; *Grande*, 26; Hirsch, *Biog. Lex.*, 4.

PFUNGST, OSKAR
German Psychologist
Born: Frankfurt am Main, April 21, 1874
Died: Berlin, August 14, 1932
Education: Studied humanities at the University of Munich and medicine and psychology at the University of Berlin
Positions, Honors: 1903-14, voluntary assistant to C. Stumpf* at the Psychological Institute, University of Berlin; 1914-18, Research and Training Institute for Police and War Dogs; 1918-21, Kaiser-Wilhelm-Institut für Neuro-Biologie; 1921-25, University of Frankfurt; 1925-32, lecturer in comparative biology and psychology, University of Berlin; honorary M.D., University of Frankfurt, 1924

Although Pfungst never earned an academic degree, his research work on animal psychology was good enough for him to be called to a number of academic positions, and his involvement in sensory physiology during his Berlin years (when he was a member of a small group of psychological and physiological researchers, the "Cortex") and the University of Frankfurt (where he was a collaborator of Kurt Goldstein's*) led to an honorary doctorate in medicine. Pfungst published little, only about fifteen titles, of which twelve were in comparative psychology. Of them, the book *Clever Hans: The Horse of Mr. von Osten* (1911; German original, 1907) earned him a name. It was not just an anecdotal description of how a circus horse solved problems (responding to very slight clues from his master) but a substantial contribution to comparative psychology. After World War I, Pfungst began to study animals experimentally and did work on the effects of isolation in monkeys, tonal memory in dogs, and the behavior of wolves, homing pigeons, and chimpanzees.

Biographies: R. Henneberg (Ed.), *Oskar Pfungst zum Gedächtnis*, 1933; *PR*, 3.

PIAGET, JEAN
Swiss Psychologist
Born: Neuchâtel, Neuchâtel, August 9, 1896
Died: Geneva, September 16, 1980
Highest Degree: Ph.D. in biology, University of Neuchâtel, 1918; studied psychology with T. Simon*, Sorbonne, University of Paris, 1919-21
Positions, Honors: 1921-33, Institut Jean-Jacques Rousseau, Geneva, 1921-25, director of studies, 1929-33, director of institute; 1925-29, professor of psychology, sociology, and philosophy of science, University of Neuchâtel; 1929-71, professor of child psychology and history of scientific thought, University of Geneva, 1940-70, chair of experimental psychology and director of Psychology Laboratory, 1971-80, honorary professor; 1929-67, director, International Bureau of Education; 1935-51, professor of psychology and sociology, University of Lausanne; 1952-63, professor of child psychology, Sorbonne (University of Paris); 1955-80, founder and director, International Center of Genetic Epistemology, Geneva; coeditor, *Archives de Psychologie*, *Revue Suisse de Psychologie*; more than thirty honorary degrees and awards from world universities; first European recipient of American Psychological Association Distinguished Scientific Contribution Award, 1969

Piaget was the most influential developmental theorist of the twentieth century. His early scientific work was on mollusks, but he began to research the development of thinking in 1920 and at his death had produced more than three hundred papers, book chapters, and introductions, as well as some thirty books on the subject, the largest collection of theory and observation on cognitive development to have come from the pen of a single individual. His writings have been translated into many languages.

Although Piaget is correctly described as a psychologist, his fundamental concern was epistemology. What distinguished him from the philosophers was his willingness to approach the question of what can be known and how empirically, by observing children and talking to them. Both the term and the area of *genetic epistemology* were his creations. From the philosophical point of view his most important contribution was to show that some of the concepts that were considered to exist a priori and to be simple and unitary, such as time and causality, were neither, requiring years of development and a transition through several intermediate stages of development before reaching the adult form.

According to Piaget, the basic properties of cognitive functioning are cognitive structures or concepts and cognitive functions or acts. The dynamic aspect of functions is adaptation in its two complementary aspects of assimilation and accommodation, the changes in the to-be-cognized objects brought about by existing cognitive structures in the individual, and changes in the individual's cognitive structures brought about by the incorporation of newly cognized objects, an incessant dialectic process. Intellectual development consists of a succession of qualitative changes (developmental stages) in intellectual structures (concepts). The main cause of these changes is the process of equilibration, the attainment of equilibrium between external intrusions and the activities of the individual. Additional causes of development are maturation, physical experience, logico-mathematical experience, and social transmission. On the nature-nurture issue Piaget occupied a position in the middle.

In cognitive development there is a progression from a state of egocentrism, characterized by the predominance of the assimilatory process, to a more balanced mixture of assimilation and accommodation. The mechanism whereby this shift is effected is action performed by the individual on the environment. Initially, intellectual operations are sensorimotor acts. They characterize the first two years of life. Between the ages of two and seven, the child acquires the ability to substitute symbols for motor acts. During this time, the *preoperational*, or *pre-logical, period of development*, the child is able to grasp concrete, rather than abstract, concepts; is egocentric; is unable to reverse logical operations; sees states rather than transformations; and centers his attention on some salient feature of an object, ignoring other aspects that may be more important. Between seven and eleven, the child acquires the rudiments of logical operations that, however, are first tied to concrete experiences (*the period of concrete operations*). In the *period of formal operations* (ages eleven to fifteen), further refinements of logical thinking take place, such as the ability to test hypotheses and to appreciate the difference between the actual and the merely possible: thinking becomes propositional.

In Piaget's view, thought is transformed action. Although he does not deny the reality of learning, it plays a relatively small role in intellectual development, which is basically the restructuring of the interrelationships among concepts. This restructuring will take place not because of motivational or reinforcement factors but because the combination of maturation and the child's actions will almost automatically bring it about. For this reason special training is by and large ineffective in bringing about an acceleration in the acquisition of basic concepts such as the conservation of mass, volume, number, and the development of notions of physical causality. Piaget himself was not particularly interested in applying his theory and findings to practical problems; yet he devised a number of simple, yet effective and face-valid tests for the presence of concepts in children. Piaget's method of child study emphasized heavily the analysis of the investigator's conversations with children, because it was Piaget's belief that a child's thought is reflected in the child's language. This method led to conclusions such as that the thinking of a young child resembles the thinking of a primitive tribesman more than it does the thinking of adults in the child's own society, and that the child's explanations of physical causality are characterized by magical ideas and by animism.

The aspects of cognitive development studied by Piaget are reflected in the titles of the many books that he wrote during a period of six decades: *Le langage et la pensée chez l'enfant* (1923), *Le jugement et le raisonnement chez l'enfant* (1924), *La répresentation du monde chez l'enfant* (1926), *La causalité physique chez l'enfant* (1927), *Le jugement moral chez l'enfant* (1932), *La naissance de l'intelligence chez l'enfant* (1936), *La construction du réel chez l'enfant* (1937), *La genèse du nombre chez l'enfant* (1941, with A. Szeminska), *Le développement des quantités chez l'enfant* (1941, with B. Inhelder), *Classes, relations et nombres*: *Essai sur les groupements de la logistique et sur la reversibilité de la pensée* (1942), *La formation du symbole chez l'enfant* (1946), *Le développement de la notion de temps chez l'enfant* (1946), *La psychologie de l'intelligence* (1947), *La géométrie spontanée de l'enfant* (1948, with B. Inhelder and A. Szeminska), *La réprésentation de l'espace chez l'enfant* (1948, with B. Inhelder), *Introduction à l'épistémologie génétique* (3 vols., 1950), *La genèse de l'idée de hasard chez l'enfant* (1951, with B. Inhelder), *La relation entre l'affectivité et l'intelligence dans le développement mental de l'enfant* (1954), *De la logique de l'enfant à la logique de l'adolescent* (1955, with B. Inhelder), *La genèse des structures logiques élémentaires, classifications et sériations* (1959, with B. Inhelder), *Les mécanisms perceptifs* (1961), *L'image mental chez l'enfant* (1966, with B. Inhelder), *Biologie et connaissance* (1967), *Le structuralisme* (1968), and *Mémoire et intelligence* (1968, with H. Sinclair-de Zwarts).

Piaget's ideas have generated a large body of research on the cognitive development of the child by his students, collaborators, and visiting researchers and other researchers elsewhere in the world. His research methods and interpretations have been criticized, but the basic soundness of his approach to the development of concepts cannot be disputed. His contributions are often compared to those of Sigmund Freud*, and during his lifetime he was counted among the greatest living psychologists.

Biographies: *Amer. Psychologist*, 1970, *25*, 65-79; V. J. Nordby & C. S. Hall, *A Guide to Psychologists and Their Concepts*, 1974; J. Piaget, In L. J. Pongratz *et al.* (Eds.), *Psychologie in Selbstdarstellungen*, vol. 2, 1979; *Psychol. Today*, May 1970; *Contemporary Authors*, vol. 21-24; *Current Biography*, 1958; *HPA* 4; *IESS*, 18; *NYT*, 1980, Sept. 17, A1:2; *Time*, Dec. 12, 1969, Sept. 29, 1980.

PIÉRON, HENRI
French Psychologist
Born: Paris, July 18, 1881
Died: Paris, November 6, 1964

Highest Degree: Doctorate in science, University of Paris, 1912

Positions, Honors: 1907-11, École Pratique des Hautes Études; 1911-23, Sorbonne (University of Paris); 1923-64, Collège de France; editor, *L'Année psychologique*, 1912-64; editorial work for many psychological journals; president, Eleventh International Congress of Psychology, 1937; numerous honors from world universities

After Binet's* death Piéron took over the direction of the psychological laboratory at Sorbonne in 1910. In 1920 he established the Institut de Psychologie at the University of Paris and remained its director until his retirement. During a large portion of his professional life, Piéron was considered the leading French psychologist.

Piéron was physiologically oriented, but he did not reduce psychology to physiology. His view was that both the response of the total organism (psychology) and its partial responses (physiology) had to be considered. Before Watson*, Piéron stated (in 1907, publication in 1908) that the subject matter of psychology was behavior. He was the originator of the French school of behaviorism, or *psychologie du comportement*.

Piéron was extremely versatile and productive. His list of publications contained some five hundred items, many of which were books, some of them influential. They ranged from experimental psychology, sensation, and physiological psychology to individual differences and applied psychology. Piéron did research in general, animal, and especially physiological psychology. The psychophysiology of the senses was his main concern for some fifty years (*Les sensibilités cutanées*, 3 vols., 1928-32; *La connaissance sensorielle et les problèmes de la vision*, 1936; *La sensation: Guide de vie*, 1945; *Les problèmes fondamentaux de la psychophysique dans la science actuelle*, 1951; *La vision en lumière intermittente*, 1961).

Piéron related psychology to physiology also by comparing and relating human and animal behaviors. He believed that the governing principles were the same in humans and animals (*De l'action à l'homme: Études de psychophysiologie comparée*, 1958). In the applied area, Piéron fostered psychotechnology all of his life. He founded the Institut National d'Études du Travail et d'Orientation Professionelle in 1928 and was its director. He was the editor of the seven-volume series *Traité de psychologie appliquée* and the author of its first volume, *La psychologie différentielle* (1949).

Biographies: A. Fessard, *Année psychol.*, 1951, *50*, vii-xiii; P. Fraisse, *Année psychol.*, 1965, *65*, 1-4; P. Fraisse, *Ann. Univ. Paris*, 1965, No. 2; Y. Galifret, *Psychol. franç.*, 1965, *10*, 113-118; G. Noizet, *Cah. psychol.*, 1965, *8*, 1-9; J. Piaget, *Amer. J. Psychol.*, 1966, *79*, 147-150; M. Reuchlin, *Travail hum.*, 1965, *28*(1-2), 1-2; M. Reuchlin, *J. psychol. norm. path.*, 1965, *62*, 139-144; *EUI*, 44; *HPA*, 4; *PR*, 3.

PILLSBURY, WALTER BOWERS
American Psychologist

Born: Burlington, Iowa, July 21, 1872

Died: Ann Arbor, Michigan, June 3, 1960

Highest Degree: Ph.D. in psychology, Cornell University, 1896, under E. B. Titchener*

Positions, Honors: 1897-1942, University of Michigan, since 1929, head of Psychology Department; editorial work, *American Journal of Psychology* (1897-1960), *Psychological Review* (1910-29), and *Journal of Social Psychology* (1930-60); president, American Psychological Association, 1910; honorary LL.D., University of Nebraska, 1933

Pillsbury established a psychological laboratory at the University of Michigan, did some research there at first, and then wrote his best-known book *L'Attention* (1906; English translation, 1908). It was successful, which set Pillsbury on to writing more books. He was an eclectic, and his textbooks (*The Essentials of Psychology*, 1911; *The Fundamentals of Psychology*, 1916) saw several editions. He wrote a well-known *History of Psychology* (1929), seven additional books, and sixty-nine articles.

Biographies: K. M. Dallenbach, *Amer. J. Psychol.*, 1961, *74*, 165-173; *HPA*, 2; *NCAB*, 15, 44; *PR*, 3; *Who Was Who in America*, 4.

PILZECKER, ALFONS
German Psychologist
Born: Militsch (Milicz), Silesia, January 24, 1865
Died: ca. 1920, place unknown
Highest Degree: Ph.D. in psychology, University of Göttingen, 1889, under G. E. Müller*; M.D., University of Heidelberg, 1903
Positions: 1886-89, 1891-1900, University of Göttingen

An assistant to and collaborator of Georg Müller's, Pilzecker produced only two publications in psychology. Both of them were important, however. His first publication was his dissertation about attention (*Die Lehre von der sinnlichen Aufmerksamkeit*, 1889). In 1900 he was coauthor, with G. Müller, of the book-length monograph (later published as a book) *Experimentelle Beiträge zur Lehre vom Gedächtniss*. It presents the method of right associates as a method in the study of learning and shows how reaction time varies with the strength of association. It also presents the first formulation of the consolidation theory of memory. The theory postulates that neural activity that ensues upon stimulation continues for some time and thereby fixates or consolidates memory in terms of physical changes in the nervous system. This theory was restated by D. O. Hebb in modern neurophysiological terms in 1949. Pilzecker and Müller also formulated the "drainage" hypothesis of association, according to which the strength of stimulus-response associations is like the pressure available at taps as a function of the number of taps open. After 1900 Pilzecker began the study of medicine and became lost to the field of psychology.

Biographies: A. Pilzecker, *Die Lehre von der sinnlichen Aufmerksamkeit*, 1889; A. Pilzecker, *Gallenuntersuchungen nach Phosophor- und Arsenvergiftungen*, 1903.

PINEL, PHILIPPE
French Psychiatrist
Born: Saint-André, Tarne et Garonne, April 20, 1745
Died: Paris, October 25, 1826
Highest Degree: M.D., University of Toulouse, 1773
Positions: 1792-95, Bicêtre hospital, Paris; after 1795, La Salpêtrière hospital, Paris

Pinel turned his attention to psychiatry when a friend lost his mind, ran away, and was killed by wolves. On being appointed superintendent of the insane asylum at Bicêtre, Pinel was appalled by the inhuman treatment of the insane and at once appealed to the Revolutionary Committee and was allowed to remove the chains from some of the patients as an experiment. Instead of the expected chaos, a much more orderly and peaceful asylum resulted.

Pinel instituted a humane, psychological management of the insane, removed them from dungeons into well-lit rooms, placed them under the care of physicians, abolished methods such as bleeding and purging, and allowed physical exercise. He repeated the reorganization of treatment at La Salpêtrière with the same excellent results.

Pinel believed that severe abnormalities of behavior were due to brain disorders rather than wickedness or demoniacal possession. These views and a plea for a more humane treatment of mental patients were published in his *Traité médico-philosophique sur l'aliénation mentale* (1801). As word of Pinel's success spread, other humanitarians followed his lead, such as William Tuke in England. Their success eventually revolutionized the treatment of the mentally ill in the Western world.

Biographies: K. M. Grange, *Bull. Hist. Med.*, 1961, *35*, 442-453; B. Mackler & E. Bernstein, *Psychol. Rep.*, 1966, *19*, 703-720; C. Pinel, *J. Psychol. Med. Ment. Pathol.*, 1860, *13*, 184-205; W. Riese, *J. Nerv. Ment. Dis.*, 1951, *114*, 313-323; W. Riese, *The Legacy of Philippe Pinel*, 1969; R. Semelaigne, *Philippe Pinel et son oeuvre au point de vue de la médecine mentale*, 1888; *DSB*, 10; *EUI*, 44; *Grande*, 26; Hirsch, *Biog. Lex.*, 4; *IESS*, 12; *Nouvelle*, 40.

PINTNER, RUDOLF
American Psychologist
Born: Lytham, Lancashire, England, November 16, 1884
Died: New York, New York, November 7, 1942
Highest Degree: Ph.D. in psychology, University of Leipzig, 1913, under W. Wundt*
Positions: 1912, University of Toledo; 1913-21, Ohio State University; 1921-42, Columbia University, Teachers College

While at Columbia Pintner and his former student Paterson* produced the Pintner-Paterson Scale of Performance Tests (*A Scale of Performance Tests*, 1917), an intelligence test intended for the deaf, the handicapped, and those whose native language is not English. It was the first major attempt to construct a series of performance tests with general norms. The scale consists of fifteen subtests, some of which have been used repeatedly by others to construct similar scales. One-half of the Army Beta test items, for instance, came from it.

The construction of the performance-test scale reflected one of Pintner's main concerns, the handicapped and especially the deaf child and the improvement of his education. Pintner's scientific interests lay in the field of mental measurement, and his activity therein promoted the scientific study of individual differences in the United States. Pintner constructed several other tests, such as the Pintner-Durost Elementary Test (1941), Pintner Intermediate Test (1942), Pintner Advanced Test (1942), Pintner Non-Language Test (1945), and the Pintner-Cunningham Primary Test (1946). In 1923 he wrote *Intelligence Testing: Methods and Results*, and in 1941, *The Psychology of the Physically Handicapped* (with R. Eisenson and M. Stenton).

Biographies: S. Arsenian, *In memoriam: Rudolf Pintner*, 1953; H. L. Hollingworth, *Amer. J. Psychol.*, 1943, *56*, 303-305; *In memoriam: Rudolf Pintner, November 16, 1884-November 7, 1942*, 1951; D. G. Paterson, *J. Consult. Psychol.*, 1943, *7*, 50-52; P. M. Symonds, *Teach. Coll. Rec.*, 1942, *44*, 204-211; *NYT*, 1942, Nov. 8, 51:3; *PR*, 3; *Who Was Who in America*, 2.

PLATEAU, JOSEPH ANTOINE FERDINAND
Belgian Physicist
Born: Brussels, October 14, 1801
Died: Ghent, September 15, 1883
Highest Degree: Doctorate in physics and mathematical sciences, University of Liège, 1829
Positions: 1830-35, Institut Gaggia, Brussels; 1835-72, University of Ghent; after becoming blind in 1843, continued research with the help of his son and son-in-law

Plateau introduced the psychophysical method of bisection in the 1850s by having painters paint a gray that was midway between a given white and a given black. He published the results in an 1872 article and proposed that instead of equal stimulus distances yielding equal sense distances (Fechner's* law), equal stimulus ratios yielded equal sense ratios (Stevens's* power law, published in 1953). Later Plateau agreed with Fechner since an equisection experiment with length (performed by Delboeuf*) did not yield a power function. Fechner was the greater authority in psychophysics then, but Plateau was right.

In his 1829 dissertation Plateau proposed the initial version of what came to be called the Talbot-Plateau law after H. F. Talbot used it in photometric matches. Plateau wrote again, discussing it and giving the principle specific formulation. The law deals with the time-intensity relationship of intermittent stimuli perceived as continuous.

Plateau also wrote a 266-page history of visual sensation in 1876. He had studied accidental colors and irradiation extensively himself. In 1830 he invented a stroboscope but did not publish its description until 1833, by which time another version of the stroboscope had been described by Faraday*. In 1850 Plateau described both the color sensations and the movement aftereffect obtained by looking at a rotating spiral (Plateau's spiral). Both the stroboscope and apparent movement played an important part later in the history of the Gestalt school of psychology.

Biographies: G. d. Montpellier, *Psychol. belg.*, 1971, *11*(2), 165-171; *DSB*, 11; *EUI*, 45; *Grande*, 26; *Nouvelle*, 40.

PLATO

Greek Philosopher
Born: Athens, 428 or 427 B.C.
Died: Athens, 348 or 347 B.C.
Education: Studied philosophy in Athens under Socrates between 408 and 400 B.C.
Positions: Ca. 387 B.C., established the Academy in Athens; taught philosophy there for forty years

Plato's views on psychology are entwined with his views on metaphysics, social theory, and related matters and are subordinate to those matters. He was a dualist both in that he recognized the body and the soul as two independent entities and in that he recognized a phenomenal but "unreal" world of the senses and physical processes and a "real" world of ideal forms, of which the former are only a shadow cast by the latter. Plato's philosophy has been influential throughout the centuries, and the habit of talking of a body and a soul and of positing a separate and distinct kind of existence for the soul may be attributed to Plato.

To Plato only the soul can know the ideal forms. When soul and body unite, body interferes with the soul and with its recall of the forms. When the soul does recall the forms, it is through an effort. Nevertheless, the only true knowledge comes when we recollect the permanent principles of the world. Plato called this process reminiscence. Reason, feeling, and appetite are three aspects of the soul. Reason is related to the immortal (rational) soul and resides in the brain; feeling and appetite belong to the mortal (irrational) soul and reside in the chest and the abdomen. All three are connected by the spinal cord. The immortal soul is also connected to the heart. In case of wrongdoing the heart is agitated and its agitation is carried to the rest of the body by the blood vessels, which Plato thought served the general purpose of transmitting sensations.

The essence of the soul is motion. The diverse psychological processes arise as a result of the motions of the soul, which in turn are caused by diverse external motions. Mind is an inner activity and acts on externally produced motions of the soul, as when the "fire of the eyes" meets the light of an object. Will, confidence, fear, pleasure, and other emotions, motives, and cognitions are also motions of the soul. Strong motion that conforms to nature is positive emotion; one that does not is unpleasant or painful emotion. Reason is the highest aspect of the soul. Knowledge is not given by the senses but acquired through them as reason organizes and makes sense out of that which is perceived. It reveals the ideal forms behind appearances. The second aspect of the soul has the properties of drive or will, the third that of emotion, desire, and bodily needs. The two are likened by Plato to two horses that the charioteer (reason) must guide to a goal, which he alone knows. The role of reason is to achieve harmony among the aspects of the soul, but reason must prevail nevertheless. Reason, spirit, and appetite are each like a drive themselves, drives for wisdom, for success, or for satisfaction. Reaching a goal brings about a state of pleasure. Thus on the level of reason, or of the immortal soul, the drive is to achieve union with the ideal form. Reaching that goal is pure love.

The irrational aspect of the human being was placed by Plato in the soul itself. Plato viewed much of human behavior as the result of a conflict between the rational and the irrational aspects. Although nothing was made of this side of Plato's philosophy for twenty-five hundred years, this view of the psyche is clearly present in Sigmund Freud's* conflict theory of neuroses and his personality theory.

Although Plato was a nativist, he recognized developmental influences and the role of education. Thus in his *Republic* he called for the early recognition of talent and training in accord with the child's native abilities. He recognized stages in cognitive development and the existence of critical periods and advocated the rhythmic rocking of infants to further harmonious body-mind relationship. Although he believed that abilities such as spatial perception and intelligence were innate, he also thought that interaction between a favorable environment and heredity allows the latter to manifest itself.

As to science and psychological science in general, Plato rendered both a service and a disservice. He was against experimentation and empirically derived or inductive knowledge. Plato was not against rational science, however, one derived deductively from a consideration of ideal forms. What psychology there was between his time and that of Thomas Aquinas* was deductive and introspective. Through Neoplatonism and St. Augustine*, Plato's thinking colored Christian thought until the thirteenth century when Aristotle began to dominate, but without displacing Plato.

Biographies: *DSB*, 11; *EP*, 6; *HGP*, 4; *IESS*, 12.

PLOTINUS
Roman Philosopher
Born: 205 A.D., birthplace unknown
Died: Rome, 270 A.D.
Education: Studied philosophy in Alexandria, 234-45 A.D., under Ammonius Saccas
Positions: 245-70 A.D., teacher of philosophy, Rome

Sworn to secrecy by his master, Plotinus did not write anything down until about 263 A.D. During the last six years of his life he produced the six *Enneads*. As the foremost Neoplatonist, Plotinus proclaimed the doctrine of overcoming the senses and the mortal self for the immortal soul to unite with the source of all, the ultimate good. This goal, he asserted, could be achieved while in the physical body. The dualism of Plato* was further accentuated by Plotinus, who placed the soul in the middle between the physical body as the prison of the soul and the spirit toward which the soul was to escape. His thinking concerning body-soul relationship predominated for the next one thousand years. Although Plato's soul resided in the body and was connected to it through internal organs, Plotinus's soul was only correlated with the body since it was immaterial. Plotinus held that although the soul knows about the experiences of the body, only the body actually has the experiences. The soul performs the functions of sensing, reflecting, and contemplating. In the latter activity the soul transcends the body to dwell on things eternal. Reflection involves awareness of both the object of reflection and the subject, hence self-awareness. In contemplation, the object-subject separation is absent; in its highest state contemplation is reunion with the ultimate. Plotinus attempted to contact Eastern philosophers, but he got only as far as Mesopotamia before being forced to return. The similarity between Plotinus and Indian religious philosophies is thus even more remarkable.

To demonstrate that a greater, ineffable reality lay beyond the sensory world, Plotinus resorted to phenomenological analysis of mental activity, which was open to introspection and could be understood. It is said by some that Plotinus was the first one to use the concept of the subconscious. By being a very skillful introspectionist, Plotinus helped to establish introspection as a method in psychology, next to be used as proficiently by St. Augustine*. Plotinus's introspection led him to raise many psychological questions that received an adequate answer only centuries later. His own answers were less provocative than the questions he raised. Plotinus's questions concerned the seat of emotions, suspension of consciousness by drugs, differences between actual and remembered sensations, the nature of love, the nature of beauty, and distance vision.
Biographies: DSB, 11; EP, 6.

POLYAK, STEPHAN
Yugoslav-American Anatomist
Born: Northern Croatia, Austria-Hungary, December 13, 1889
Died: Chicago, Illinois, March 9, 1955
Highest Degree: M.D., University of Odessa, 1916; M.D., University of Zagreb, 1920
Positions: 1920-28, University of Zagreb; 1921-28, various research appointments at European universities and University of Chicago; 1928-30, University of California at Los Angeles; 1930-55, University of Chicago

Polyak was a leading authority on the anatomy of the vertebrate visual system. He wrote three books on the subject. *The Main Afferent Fiber Systems of the Cerebral Cortex in Primates* (1932) considers normal and abnormal functions of the afferent somatosensory, auditory, and visual systems in the brains of monkeys. *The Retina* (1941) describes the anatomy and histology of the human and primate retina. *The Vertebrate Visual System* (1957), a monumental work of sixteen hundred pages, published posthumously, describes the origin, structure, and function of the visual system in vertebrates and humans.

Biographies: P. Bailey, *Anat. Rec.*, 1955, *122*, 648-649; H. Klüver, *J. Comp. Neurol.*, 1955, *103*, 1-9; *NYT*, 1955, Mar. 11, 25:2; *Who Was Who in America*, 3.

PONZO, MARIO
Italian Psychologist
Born: Milan, June 23, 1882
Died: Rome, January 9, 1960
Highest Degree: M.D., University of Turin, 1911; studied psychology under F. Kiesow* at the same time
Positions: 1905-31, University of Turin; 1931-58, University of Rome; president, Italian Society of Psychology, 1942-58

Ponzo did research in the area of psychophysics of touch and taste but turned to applied psychology after 1940 and pioneered in introducing applied psychology in Italy. He made contributions to aptitude testing and professional selection. His belief was that vocational guidance should be based on a consideration of personality characteristics and talent in addition to intelligence. Ponzo's bibliography numbers some 280 publications, most of them about the chemical senses, touch, temperature sensations, geometric illusions (the "Ponzo illusion" is named after him), and breathing as a psychophysical behavior (observations on changes in breathing as a function of mental activity).

Biographies: L. Canestrelli, *Amer. J. Psychol.*, 1960, *73*, 645-647; H. Misiak & V. M. Staudt, *Catholics in Psychology*, 1954; *PR*, 3; H. Misiak & V. M. Staudt, *Psychol. Bull.*, 1953, *50*, 347-361.

POPPELREUTER, WALTHER
German Psychologist
Born: Saarbrücken, Saarland, October 6, 1886
Died: 1939, place unknown
Highest Degree: Ph.D. in psychology, University of Königsberg, 1909; M.D., University of Munich, 1915
Positions: 1919-39, University of Bonn; editorial work, *Zeitschrift für Psychologie*, *Psychotechnische Zeitschrift*, *Zeitschrift für Menschenkunde*

After writing *Die psychischen Schädigungen durch Kopfschuss im Kriege 1914/17* (2 vols., 1917-18), the result of his experiences with brain injuries during the war, Poppelreuter turned to industrial psychology, producing a number of publications in this area: *Allgemeine methodische Richtlinien der praktisch-psychologischen Begutachtung* (1923), *Arbeitspsychologische Leitsätze für den Zeitnehmer* (1929), *Zeitstudie und Betriebsüberwachung im Arbeitsschaubild* (1929), and *Psychokritische Pädagogik* (1933). He later became an adherent of

national socialism, producing works such as *Hitler als politischer Psychologe*. During his Bonn period Poppelreuter founded and financed the Bonner Provinzialinstitut für klinische Psychologie, an institute of clinical psychology.
Biographies: F. Baumgarten, *Travail hum.*, 1940, *8*, 95-96; *PR*, 3.

PORTER, NOAH
American Philosopher
Born: Farmington, Connecticut, December 14, 1811
Died: New Haven, Connecticut, March 4, 1892
Highest Degree: Graduated from Yale University, 1831
Positions, Honors: 1847-92, professor of moral philosophy and metaphysics, Yale University, 1871-86, president; four honorary degrees

Porter and James McCosh* were the two best-known representatives of the Scottish school of psychology in the United States. They were also the last. Porter wrote on *The Human Intellect* (1868) and a psychology text, *Elements of Intellectual Science* (1871), which was an abridgment of the former.
Biographies: G. S. Merriam (Ed.), *Noah Porter: A Memorial by Friends*, 1893; A. R. Stokes, in *Memorials of Eminent Yale Men*, vol. 1, 1914, pp. 329-335; *DAB*, 15; *EP*, 6; *EUI*, 46; *Grande*, 27; *NCAB*, 1; *NYT*, 1892, Mar. 5, 4:6; *Who Was Who in America*, H.

PORTEUS, STANLEY DAVID
Australian-American Psychologist
Born: Box Hill, Victoria, Australia, April 24, 1883
Died: Honolulu, Hawaii, October 21, 1972
Education: High school graduate; studied at the University of Melbourne; D.Sc., University of Hawaii, 1932
Positions, Honors: 1912-15, Education Department, Melbourne; 1915-19, University of Melbourne; 1919-28, Vineland Training School (New Jersey); 1922-48, director, Psychological and Psychopathic Clinic, University of Hawaii, 1948, professor emeritus

Porteus's main interest was the effect of the environment on mental and cultural evolution. The first practicing psychologist in Australia, Porteus worked with the mentally retarded in Melbourne. He used the standard intelligence tests but decided that the children all lacked something that these tests did not measure, namely, planning ability. He therefore designed, in 1913, a test to measure this ability, the Porteus Maze Test (1913). It was a series of scaled pencil and paper mazes where the subject could plan his course before actually running the maze. The test is still in use, and research in relation to it has been described by Porteus in several publications (*Maze Tests and Mental Differences*, 1933; *The Maze Test and Psychosurgery*, 1948, with H. Peters; *The Maze Test and Intelligence*, 1950; *The Maze Test: Recent Advances*, 1955; *The Maze Test and Clinical Psychology*, 1959; *Porteus Maze Tests: 50 Years of Application*, 1965).

In 1929 Porteus went on an expedition to northwest Australia to study the

Australian aborigines. He had already published (with M. E. Babcock) *Temperament and Race* (1925). Upon his return he published two more books about culture and mental development (with D. M. Dewey) *Race and Social Differences in Performance Tests* (1930) and *The Psychology of a Primitive People* (1931). In 1934 he visited Africa on a similar mission and published *Primitive Intelligence and Environment* (1937).

Porteus produced more than one hundred publications. They include *Studies in Mental Deviations* (1922); *The Matrix of the Mind* (1929, with W. Jones); *The Practice of Clinical Psychology* (1941); *Mental Changes After Bifrontal Lobotomy* (1944, with R. D. Kepner), and a number of nonpsychological books. *Biographies*: S. D. Porteus, *A Psychologist of Sorts*, 1969.

PRESSEY, SIDNEY LEAVITT

American Psychologist
Born: Brooklyn, New York, December 28, 1888
Died: Columbus, Ohio, July 21, 1979
Highest Degree: Ph.D. in psychology, Harvard University, 1917, under R. M. Yerkes*
Positions, Honors: 1917-21, research assistant, Indiana University; 1921-59, Ohio State University; 1959-70, professor emeritus, Ohio State University, and visiting professor, University of Arizona; Honorary LL.D., Ohio State University

Pressey, an educational psychologist, introduced a number of innovative approaches to education. Of them, the most notable was the invention of the first teaching machine, exhibited at the 1925 meeting of the American Psychological Association. Pressey began to develop the machine for commercial use during the Depression. The financial crisis and the surplus of teachers forced its removal from the market, however. Pressey's machine had all the features of the type of teaching machine introduced by B. F. Skinner in the 1950s, which was enormously successful, but it was not based on learning-theoretical considerations, as Skinner's machine was.

Pressey's book *Life: A Psychological Survey* (written with J. E. Janney and R. G. Kuhlen) was one of the first life-span developmental psychology texts that, unlike earlier texts, stressed the adult years and social development. Pressey wrote more than one hundred papers and ten books, most of them about educational psychology. Among the books are *Research Adventures in University Teaching* (1927, with others), *Psychology and the New Education* (1933; rev. ed., 1944), *Educational Acceleration: Appraisal and Basic Problems* (1949), and *Psychological Development Through the Life Span* (1957, with R. G. Kuhlen). Some of the books were translated into other languages.
Biographies: HPA, 5.

PREYER, WILHELM THIERRY

German Physiologist
Born: Moss Side, near Manchester, England, July 4, 1841
Died: Wiesbaden, Hessen, July 15, 1897

Highest Degree: Ph.D. in physiology, University of Heidelberg, 1862; M.D., University of Bonn, 1866
Positions: 1865-67, University of Bonn; 1867-88, University of Jena; editor, *Zeitschrift für Psychologie*

As a physiologist Preyer did research on color vision and hearing. He invented the sound helmet for studying the localization of sound and wrote a number of papers about sensation and two texts, *Über die Grenzen der Tonwahrnehmung* (1876) and *Elemente der reinen Empfindungslehre* (1877). In the late 1870s he studied sleep (*Über die Ursache des Schlafes*, 1877), which led him to hypnosis. He translated Braid's* works into German (1882) and wrote two books on the subject, *Kataplexie und Hypnotismus* and *Der Hypnotismus* (1890). Hypnosis, in turn, led to an inquiry into the origins of psychological functions and thus the question of child development. *Die Seele des Kindes* (1882; English translation, *The Mind of the Child*, 1888-89, saw its ninth edition in 1923) turned out to be his most important work. It may be considered the first textbook of developmental psychology. It presented observations on the development of a child, arranged by topic (sensory, motor, intellectual development, and the like). The observations made by Preyer were not as rigorously controlled as those made later by others. Also, being a Darwinian (Charles Darwin*), he considered development to be merely a biological process. Nevertheless, Preyer's book provided the greatest single impetus to the development of modern ontogenetic psychology. It served as a textbook for a long time. Preyer also pioneered in the investigation of prenatal life in animals (*Specielle Physiologie des Embryo: Untersuchungen über die Lebenserscheinungen vor der Geburt*, 1885); wrote an additional developmental text, *Die geistige Entwicklung der ersten Kindheit* (1893); and wrote a volume about the psychology of writing (*Zur Psychologie des Schreibens*, 1895).
Biographies: C. Bühler, *Encycl. Soc. Sci.*, 1934, *12*, 349-350; *ADB*, 53; *DSB*, 11; *Biog Lex.*; *EUI*, 47; *Grande*, 27; Pagel, *Biographisches Lexikon*.

PRIESTLEY, JOSEPH

English Theologian and Chemist
Born: Fieldhead, Yorkshire, March 13, 1733
Died: Northumberland, Pennsylvania, February 6, 1804
Education: Studied for Presbyterian ministry
Positions, Honors: 1755-94, various positions as minister and tutor in languages and literature; honorary LL.D., University of Edinburgh, 1764

Priestley was a versatile man who published scientific studies about the chemistry of gases (he isolated oxygen but, favoring the phlogiston theory, failed to recognize it for what it was) and electricity, as well as papers and books about education, philosophy, history of science, religion, and political theory. ''An Essay on Government,'' published in 1768, contains a sentence seminal to Bentham's* famous principle of ''the greatest happiness of the greatest number.'' His *Examination of Scottish Philosophy* (1774) was his first psychological essay.

Priestley embraced associationism wholeheartedly and placed Hartley*, whom he had studied thoroughly, next to the Bible only. He published an abridged edition of Hartley's *Observations of Man*, to which he added three original essays of his own (*Hartley's Theory of the Human Mind* . . . , 1775). An important pioneering work in the history of science as it relates to psychology was his *History and Present State of the Discoveries Relating to Vision, Light, and Colours* (1772). Priestley also wrote about education, opposing innate ideas and embracing education based on the formation of associative bonds (*Miscellaneous Observations Relating to Education*, 1778). His religious unorthodoxy forced him to leave England and he went to the United States in 1794.

Biographies: J. G. Crowther, *Scientists of the Industrial Revolution* . . . , 1962; J. G. Gillam, *The Crucible*, 1954; A. Holt, *A Life of Joseph Priestley*, 1931; J. Lindsay (Ed.), *Autobiography of Joseph Priestley*, 1971; D. H. Peacock, *Joseph Priestley*, 1919; J. T. Rutt, *Life and Correspondence of Joseph Priestley*, 2 vols., 1831-1832; R. E. Schofield, *Ambix*, 1967, *14*, 1-15; T. E. Thorpe, *Joseph Priestley*, 1906; *Chalmers*, 25; *DNB*, 16; *DSB*, 11; *EB*, *18*; *EP*, 6; *Grande*, 27; *NCAB*, 6; *Nouvelle*, 41.

PRINCE, MORTON

American Psychiatrist

Born: Boston, Massachusetts, December 21, 1854

Died: Cambridge, Massachusetts, August 31, 1929

Highest Degree: M.D., Harvard University, 1879

Positions: 1880-1902, various nonacademic medical appointments; 1902-26, professor of diseases of the nervous system, Tufts University; 1926-29, professor of abnormal and dynamic psychology, Harvard University; president and founder, American Psychopathological Association; president, American Neurological Association; editorial work, *American Journal of Psychology*, 1906-29

One factor that turned Prince's interest from general practice to psychopathology was his wife's psychogenic symptoms. In the mid-1880s Prince began to specialize in nervous and mental disorders, especially in unconscious phenomena and multiple personalities, along the lines of Janet* (*The Nature of Mind and Human Automatism*, 1885). He came across the famous case of Miss Beauchamp who showed five personalities and described it in one of his two best-known books, *The Dissociation of a Personality* (1905). In it he also presented the concept of coconscious personalities. In a multiple personality one personality may function consciously and be the dominant one who sees, feels, and talks, while the other personality functions subconsciously and communicates indirectly, as through automatic writing. The coconscious personality is aware of the conscious personality, but the conscious personality knows nothing of the existence of the coconscious personality. The book was widely read. A year later Prince founded the *Journal of Abnormal Psychology*.

In 1910 Prince, with Ribot*, Janet, and Münsterberg*, contributed to a famous symposium on subconscious phenomena. In 1913 Prince published another widely read book, *The Unconscious*. It described the scientific method in psychopathology and distinguished clearly conscious and unconscious phenomena. It established Prince's reputation. Although recognizing the importance of motivational factors in psychopathology, Prince did not join the psychoanalytic movement and was opposed to its speculative and symbolic aspects, because they deviated from his ideal of scientific rigor and his goal of a marriage of clinical and academic psychology (*Clinical and Experimental Studies in Personality*, 1929). This goal Prince realized late in his life. Upon receiving his Harvard appointment and with money contributed by an anonymous donor, he established the Harvard Psychological Clinic in 1927. The donor had specified that the clinic should promote instruction and research in "abnormal and dynamic psychology." The term *dynamic psychology* appeared here for the first time in an official record and was incorporated in the psychology professor's (Prince's) title.

Biographies: M. Moore, *J. Nerv. Ment. Dis.*, 1938, *87*, 701-710; H. A. Murray, *J. Abn. Soc. Psychol.*, 1956, *52*, 291-295; A. A. Roback, *Amer. J. Orthopsychiat.*, 1940, *10*, 177-185; E. W. Taylor, *Arch. Neurol. Psychiat.*, 1929, *22*, 1031-1036; *Biog. Lex.*; *DAB*, 15; *EUI*, 47; *NCAB*, 25; *PR*, 3; *Who Was Who in America*, 1.

PROCHASKA, GEORGIUS
Czech Physiologist
Born: Blizkovice, Moravia, April 10, 1749
Died: Vienna, Austria, July 17, 1820
Highest Degree: M.D., University of Vienna, 1776
Positions: 1778-91, University of Prague; 1791-1819, University of Vienna

One of the earliest investigators of reflex action, Prochaska sectioned the spinal cord of frogs and observed their reaction to stimulation (*Comentatio de functionibus systematis nervosi*, 1784). He contended that although nervous energy was necessary for reflex action, reflex action also needed activation through the common sensorium, which exists in the brain and the spinal cord. Thus activated, reflex responses are automatic. The concept of a common sensorium, originated with Prochaska. It was an important concept in that it provided for a connection between stimulation and action without the intervention of the will. Prochaska did not assume that all action was automatic, however, allowing also for voluntary movements that were the result of the will. Prochaska's view of the reflex was an advance over Whytte's* and contributed to the development of the modern view of it.

Biographies: V. G. Kruta, *Epilepsia*, 1962, *3*, 446-456; M. Neuberger, *Das alte medizinische Wien in zeitgenössischen Schilderungen*, 1921; *ADB*, 26; *DSB*, 11; Hirsch, *Biog. Lex.*, 4.

PROTAGORAS
Greek Philosopher
Born: Abdera, Thrace, ca. 490 B.C.
Died: After 421 B.C., place unknown

Education: Self-educated
Positions: Professional Sophist

Protagoras, the most famous of the Greek Sophists, may be in one sense regarded as the first of a group of philosophers dedicated to teaching a "psychology of life adjustment" to the citizenry. None of Protagoras's works has survived. What is known about him and his philosophy comes largely from the Platonic dialogues *Protagoras* and *Theaetetus*.

In insisting that actual experience and not the hypothetically knowable is the basis of knowledge, Protagoras laid the groundwork for an empirical science of human nature. In experience the crucial fact is the relationship of object to the subject. To know an object, that object must affect the subject. Hence perception is an active process, and both the perceiver and the perceived are affected in the process of perception. It was this view that caused Protagoras to begin his work *Truth* with the famous declaration that "man is the measure of all things: of those that are that they are; of those that are not that they are not." This has been variously interpreted as expressing either the relativity of all perceptions to the individual, the relativity of all perceptions and judgments, or that reality is not larger than the sum of our experiences. It can also be interpreted as adumbrating the contemporary position of science, which states that although there is an objective, physical world, scientists deal with it in terms of a coded form that is the result of the information about the world being processed by a nervous system. On the other hand, this coded information is validated by the consensus of the scientists working in a given area. Protagoras's statement may be therefore seen reflected in pragmatism, positivism, and operationalism.
Biographies: M. Untersteiner, *The Sophists*, 1954; *EB*, 18; *HGP*, 3.

PURKINJE (or PURKYNE), JAN EVANGELISTA
Czech Physiologist
Born: Libochovice, Bohemia, December 17, 1787
Died: Prague, July 28, 1869
Highest Degree: M.D., University of Prague, 1818
Positions: 1818-23, University of Prague; 1823-50, University of Breslau; 1850-69, University of Prague

Purkinje pioneered in several areas: experimental physiology, microtechnique, neuranatomy, histology, embryology, pharmacology, and vision. He established the Physiological Institute at the University of Breslau in 1839, the first such institute. After him are named the large cells of the cerebellar cortex (Purkinje's cells), Purkinje's fibers (of the heart), and several other structures. In psychology his name is associated mainly with the Purkinje shift, or Purkinje phenomenon, the change in the visibility of blue and red in twilight: as illumination decreases, blue appears lighter while red begins to look black. Purkinje described this phenomenon in 1825, but it was not until the end of the nineteenth century that a neurophysiological explanation of it was provided.

Purkinje was first to observe the change in distance between the reflections of a flame in the anterior and posterior surfaces of the lens of the eye and the cornea as accommodation took place. The entoptically seen shadows of the retinal capillaries, which Purkinje first described, are called "Purkinje's figure." Purkinje also observed that visual acuity decreases toward the periphery and that color looks gray in extreme peripheral vision. He coined the term *indirect vision*. In addition, Purkinje described the phenomenology of a variety of other organismic states: vertigo, nystagmus, disturbances in sense organs, hearing (he discovered bone conduction in deaf-mutes), touch, sleep, and the effect of drugs (atropin, digitalis, camphor, and opium). Purkinje's phenomenological observations were bolstered by the use of the experimental method and a search for physiological explanations of the phenomena he observed. Unlike others who had observed disturbances of the sense organs and misperceptions before him, Purkinje saw these phenomena not as isolated curiosities but as instances of lawful events. He is one of the great figures in the phenomenological approach to sensation and perception, among whom are counted Goethe* and Hering*. Purkinje's main contributions to the phenomenology of vision are to be found in his *Beiträge zur Kenntnis des Sehens in subjektiver Hinsicht* (1818-19) and *Neue Beiträge zur Kenntnis des Sehens in subjektiver Hinsicht* (1825). His collected works occupy twelve volumes.

Biographies: W. J. Bishop, *British Medical Bulletin*, 1950, *7*, 99-100; O. Hykes, *Osiris*, 1936, *2*, 464-471; H. J. John, *Mem. Amer. Phil. Soc.*, 1959, No. 49; V. J. Kruta, *J. E. Purkyne (1787-1869): Physiologist* ..., 1969; V. J. Kruta (Ed.), *Jan Evangelista Purkyne, 1787-1869: Centenary Symposium*, 1971; V. J. Kruta & M. Teich, *Jan Evangelista Purkyne*, 1962; V. Robinson, *Sci. Mon.*, 1929, *29*, 217-229; E. Thomsen, *Skand. Arch. Physiol.*, 1918, *37*, 1-116; *ADB*, 26, 28; *DSB*, 11; *Grande*, 27; Hirsch, *Biog. Lex.*, 4, Suppl.

PUYSÉGUR, AMAND MARIE JACQUES DE CHASTENET, MARQUIS DE

French Artillery Officer
Born: Paris, 1751
Died: Buzancy, Aisne, 1825
Highest Degree: No academic degrees
Positions: Various positions as a military officer

Both Marquis de Puységur and his two younger brothers, Viscount Jacques Maxime de Chastenet de Puységur (1755-1848) and Antoine Hyacinthe, called the Count of Chastenet (1752-1809), distinguished themselves in the military life and were all enthusiastic disciples of Franz Anton Mesmer*. Count de Chastenet introduced mesmerism on the island of Hispaniola, where it contributed to Haiti's gaining its independence from the French.

In hypnotizing one of his first patients, Victor Race, Puységur discovered what he called the "perfect crisis," a hypnotic trance that, unlike the scenes of frenzy and fits that took place around Mesmer's *baquet*, was tranquil, with the subject becoming more lucid than in his normal state and being able to diagnose his own and others' illnesses and prescribe cures for them. A complete amnesia followed the experience, which did not, however, affect the cure suggested by Puységur during the trance. Moreover, under hypnosis Race felt free to talk to Puységur about his family problems. Puységur would suggest solutions, which Race carried out posthypnotically (posthypnotic suggestion). As Puységur's successful cures became known, he instituted mass treatments by having ropes hung from a large tree in the village square, to which patients would attach themselves to obtain the benefit of a magnetic cure. Working with Race, Puységur eventually decided that, contrary to Mesmer's belief, no magnetic fluids were involved in magnetic sleep and that the mesmerizer and his suggestions were the essential ingredients of the hypnotic phenomenon.

Puységur published four books and many articles about hypnotism in scientific journals. Hypnotism, however, was so named only much later by Braid*. Puységur's name was forgotten and then discovered in 1884 by Charles Richet*, who stated that although Mesmer had discovered the magnetic cure, Puységur was the true founder of magnetism and of equal status with Mesmer. Many of the discoveries in the field of hypnotism claimed by Richet's contemporaries had already been made by Puységur.

Biographies: H. F. Ellenberger, *The Discovery of the Unconscious*, 1970; *EUI*, 48.

PYTHAGORAS
Greek Philosopher
Born: Samos, ca. 560 B.C.
Died: Metapontum, ca. 480 B.C.
Education: Self-taught
Positions: Teacher of Philosophy

Before 529 B.C. Pythagoras traveled extensively and then settled in Crotona, Italy, where he founded a brotherhood for the moral reformation of society. The organization was widespread at first but disappeared about the middle of the fourth century B.C. Pythagoras himself apparently wrote nothing, and it is impossible to distinguish his teachings from those of his followers (the Pythagorean school) or the Orphic cult that developed from Pythagoras's mysticism.

Both scientific and religious elements are present in the Pythagorean school. Pythagoras believed in the transmigration of souls and held, like Plato* whom he influenced, that the soul was a pure, knowing entity that during its earthly existence was united with a corrupting and corruptible body that interfered with the soul's learning the truth. The philosophical core of Pythagoreanism was the idea that "all things are numbers." In the Pythagorean system numbers replaced the primordial elements of fire, water, air, and earth. The paired, opposite properties of numbers, like odd and even and limited and unlimited, led Pythagoras to consider the world also in terms of opposites: right and left, male and female, dark and light, and so on. He saw the universe as a harmony of opposites, however. On a more concrete level Pythagoras discovered that musical intervals could be expressed as arithmetic ratios of length of strings of musical instruments, and that the most pleasing chords were those of simple mathematical relations involving whole numbers. Pythagoras recommended music as an aid to the purification of the soul from the contaminating influences of the body. The insistence of the Pythagoreans that whole numbers are sacred and that particular numbers corresponded to particular realities still echoes in psychology (as well as in other disciplines) in the search for constants: psychophysics, learning, intelligence, and personality.

Biographies: C. J. de Vogel, *Pythagoras and Early Pythagoreanism*, 1966; *DSB*, 11; *EB*, 18; *HGP*, 1.

Q

QUÉTELET, (LAMBERT) ADOLPHE (JACQUES)

Belgian Mathematician, Astronomer, and Statistician
Born: Ghent, February 22, 1796
Died: Brussels, February 17, 1874
Education: Graduated from University of Ghent, 1814
Positions: 1814-28, University of Ghent; 1828-74, Royal Observatory, Brussels

In addition to having made important contributions to astronomy, Quételet was one of the fathers of modern statistics. The term *statistics* was coined by him. His main achievement was the application of probability theory and statistical computations to social and psychological data. He obtained a large number of chest measurements of Scottish and French soldiers. He observed that these measurements followed the same distribution as gaming events and other physical phenomena subject to laws of probability. Extending the work of Laplace* and Gauss* on human errors, Quételet applied the concept of normal distribution to human physical characteristics and other biological and social data and statistical organization to enterprises such as census taking.

The deviation of shots from the bullseye and of errors from the correct value Quételet generalized to biological phenomena, considering the distributions of values about their means as deviations by nature from a central ideal or the mean. He developed in his *Sur l'homme et le développement de ses facultés* (1835) the notion of the average individual (*l'homme moyen*), whose measurements are the measures of central tendency about which the measurements of all other individuals vary according to the normal probability distribution. Quételet also worked for international uniformity in statistics and organized the first international conference on statistics.

Biographies: E. H. Ackerknecht, *Bull. Hist. Med.*, 1952, *26*, 317-329; A. Collard, *Ciel, Terre*, 1929, *45*, 89-92, 127-145; S. Diamond, In A. Quételet, *A Treatise on Man and the Development of His Faculties*, 1969, pp. x-xii; C. Gini, *Giornale economico*, 1914, *48*, 1-24; J. Lottin, *Quételet: Statisticien et sociologue*, 1912; N. E. Mailly, *Smithsonian Inst. Ann. Rep.*, 1874, 169-183; N. E. Mailly, *Ann. Acad. Roy. Sci. Lettr. Beaux-Arts Belg.*, 1875, *41*, 109-297; N. Reichesberg, *Z. schweiz. Stat.*, 1896, *32*, 418-460; G. Sarton, *Isis*, 1935, *23*, 6-24; L. Wolowski, *J. Soc. stat.*, Paris, 1874, *15*, 118-126; *DSB*, 11; *Grande*, 27; Hirsch, *Biog. Lex.*, 4; *IESS*, 13; *NYT*, 1874, Mar. 4, 3:3; *Nouvelle*, 41.

R

RAMÓN Y CAJAL, SANTIAGO

Spanish Histologist

Born: Petilla de Aragón, Navarre, May 1, 1852

Died: Madrid, October 17, 1934

Highest Degree: M.D., University of Zaragoza, 1873

Positions, Honors: 1875-83, University of Zaragoza; 1883-87, University of Valencia; 1887-92, University of Barcelona; 1892-1922, University of Madrid; Nobel Prize in physiology and medicine (shared with Camillo Golgi*), 1906

Ramón y Cajal, often considered the greatest of all neuranatomists, studied and described all parts of the nervous system using the cell staining method newly developed by Golgi. He studied the microscopic structure of the nervous system, the neuroglial cells, and the degeneration and regeneration of neurons in great detail. His 1904 book *Textura del sistema nervioso del hombre y los vertebrados* contained 1,800 pages and 887 original illustrations, many of which are still being reproduced in textbooks. Ramón y Cajal identified the function of the neuronal synapse and of the dendrites, but his greatest achievement was the establishment of the neuron as the building block of the nervous system (1889). His formulation was of fundamental importance not only to neuranatomy but to physiological psychology.

Biographies: W. H. F. Addison, *Sci. Mon.*, 1930, *31*, 178-183; E. R. Ballester, *Santiago Ramón y Cajal*, 1967; D. F. Cannon, *Explorer of the Human Brain: The Life of Santiago Ramón y Cajal*, 1949; F. H. Garrison, *Bull. N.Y. Acad. Med.*, 1929, *5*, 483-508; W. C. Gibson, *Ann. Med. Hist.*, 1936, *8*, 385-394;

P. W. Lain Entralgo & A. A. Teulón, *Nuestro Cajal*, 1967; J. Lhermitte, *Arch. Neurobiol.*, 1934, *14*, 383-387; G. Marinesco, *Arch. Neurobiol.*, 1934, *14*, 873-878; S. Ramón y Cajal, *Recollections of My Life*, 1937; *DSB*, 11; *EB*, 18; *EUI*, 48; *Obit. Not.*, 1; Pagel, *Biographisches Lexikon.*

RANK, OTTO
Austrian Psychoanalyst
Born: Vienna, April 22, 1884
Died: New York, New York, October 31, 1939
Highest Degree: Ph.D. in German philology, University of Vienna, 1912
Positions: Private practice; editorial work, *Imago* and *Internationale Zeitschrift für Psychoanalyse*, 1912-24; founder and manager, Der Internationale Psychoanalytische Verlag, 1919-24

Rank joined the psychoanalytic movement in the 1900s. He showed ability in applying Freudian concepts to the interpretation of mythology, art, dreams, and literary works and was encouraged by Sigmund Freud* to take a nonmedical degree. Rank became a member of the inner committee of six that guided the psychoanalytic movement.

Rank's early works were *Der Künstler und andere Beiträge zur Psychoanalyse des dichterischen Schaffens* (1907; English translation of an expanded version, *Art and Artist*, 1932), in which Freud's dream theory was used to explain artistic creation, *Der Mythus von der Geburt des Helden* (1909), and *Das Inzest-Motiv in Dichtung und Sage* (1912). After writing, with Hanns Sachs*, *Die Bedeutung der Psychoanalyse für die Geisteswissenschaften* (1916), Rank published his most original contribution to psychoanalysis, *Das Trauma der Geburt* (1923), and began to interpret Freudian concepts in terms of birth trauma, the main points being that weaning causes anxiety because it represents separation from mother (as in birth), and that the male sexual urge represents the urge to return to the mother's womb. Rank's therapy consisted of helping the patient to reexperience the birth trauma. This reduced the duration of therapy to only weeks or months at most. Although Freud tried to reconcile Rank's interpretations with his own theory as well as with the views of those that Rank opposed, Rank became disturbed by the conflict and left Vienna in 1924, settling in the United States three years before his death. There he founded the Pennsylvania School of Social Work, in which his method of therapy was used. His last work was entitled *Will Therapy* (English translation, 1936), which is one of the names of Rankian analysis.

Biographies: F. H. Allen, *Amer. J. Orthopsychiat.*, 1940, *10*, 186-187; E. Jones, *Int. J. Psychoanal.*, 1940, *21*, 112-113; J. Jones, *Commentary*, Sept. 1960, 219-229; A. Nin, *J. Otto Rank Ass.*, 1967, *2*, 101-125; J. Taft, *Otto Rank*, 1958; *EJ*, 13; *IESS*, 13; *Jewish*, 9; *NYT*, 1939, Nov. 1, 23:1; *Who Was Who in America*, 4.

RAPAPORT, DAVID

Hungarian-American Psychologist
Born: Munkacs, Hungary, September 30, 1911
Died: Stockbridge, Massachusetts, December 14, 1960
Highest Degree: Ph.D. in psychology, Royal Hungarian University, 1938
Positions: 1938, Mount Sinai Hospital, New York; 1939, Osawatomie State
Hospital, Kansas; 1940-48, Menninger Clinic, Menninger Foundation; 1948-60,
Austen Riggs Center, Stockbridge, Massachusetts

Rapaport was a psychologist who made an attempt to make psychoanalysis
into a global behavioral theory that harmonized with general psychology. His
main concerns were thought processes and their development, organization, and
pathology. Rapaport believed that psychoanalysis cast the most light on thought
processes, but that it needed critical systematization. This he undertook to accomplish. There followed a series of books, reflecting his thinking and research:
Emotions and Memory (1942), *Diagnostic Psychological Testing* (1945, with
M. Gill and R. Schafer), *Organization and Pathology of Thought* (1951), and
"The structure of psychoanalytic theory: A systematizing attempt," in *Psychology: A Study of a Science* (vol. 3, 1959). In his psychology Rapaport attempted to incorporate and integrate ego psychology and social psychology and
preserve, at the same time, Sigmund Freud's* insights into the psychology of
the id. Through his writings and lectures on psychoanalysis Rapaport exerted
an influence in America that led clinicians away from IQ tests toward tests of
thinking and personality and brought about a better appreciation of psychoanalysis and ego psychology. His collected papers were published posthumously in
1967.

Biographies: M. M. Gill, In *The Collected Papers of David Rapaport*, 1967,
pp. 3-7; R. P. Knight, *Psychoanal. Quart.*, 1961, *30*, 262-264; *EJ*, 13; *IESS*,
13; *NYT*, 1960, Dec. 16, 38:3.

RAZRAN, GREGORY

American Psychologist
Born: Near Slutsk, Russia, June 4, 1901
Died: St. Petersburg Beach, Florida, August 31, 1973
Highest Degree: Ph.D. in psychology, Columbia University, 1933, under R. S.
Woodworth*
Positions: 1929-40, Columbia University; 1938-40, statistical consultant, Civil
Aeronautics Administration; 1941-44, consultant, Office of Strategic Services,
Department of Defense; 1940-72, instructor to professor of psychology, Queens
College, City University of New York, 1945-66, chairman, Department of
Psychology

Razran did extensive research and contributed more than fifty papers in the
area of classical conditioning. A series of ten of these papers is concerned with
the conditioned reflex as an index of meaning. Razran demonstrated in himself
how the strength of the salivary reflex varies with the degree of proficiency in

a language when words in different languages are used as the conditioned stimuli. Razran was also one of the very few individuals who, by way of review articles, kept American psychologists informed about developments in psychology in the Soviet Union. Two years before his death he brought together his knowledge of conditioning, learning, and Russian psychology in the book *Mind in Evolution* (1971), in which he attempted to integrate classical conditioning, instrumental conditioning, and sign learning within an evolutionary framework by relating the various types of learning to levels of evolutionary development.

Biographies: *American Men of Science*, 11th ed., Physical and Biological Sciences, vol. 5.

REICH, WILHELM
Austrian Psychoanalyst
Born: Dobrzcynica, Galicia, March 24, 1897
Died: Lewisburg, Pennsylvania, November 3, 1957
Highest Degree: M.D., University of Vienna, 1922
Positions: Private practice; founder of Sexpol-Verlag publishing house and of several journals of sex-economy and orgonomy

Initially, Reich was a close associate of Sigmund Freud's*. He began to stress the libidinal factors in personality and psychopathology very early. Theoretical and other differences led to a rejection of Reich by Freud and to his expulsion from the International Psychoanalytic Association in 1934.

Reich's most enduring contribution to psychoanalysis was his practice of psychoanalytic therapy (*Character Analysis*, 1949; translation of the 1933 German original). He developed the idea of character as an ego-defense mechanism. Character is profound and long-lasting changes in personality that serve as armor (character armor) against experiences considered dangerous, especially those arising from strong libidinal motives. It manifests itself as resistance to insight during therapy. To break down this resistance, Reich advocated a more active kind of therapy that involved the physical touching of the patient so that the patient's posture and expressive movements that represent the muscular counterpart of his attitude might be changed and his attitude (armoring) with it.

Beginning with a 1923 paper about genitality, Reich wrote (for instance, *Die Funktion des Orgasmus*, 1927) and did research on sex energy for the rest of his life. He held that sexual energy builds up in the body and requires release through orgasm that involves the whole body, pent-up sex energy leading to neurotic disorders. Reich came to equate sex energy with life energy, and named it "orgone," which he considered to be a hitherto unknown form of energy and himself as its discoverer. Reich's experiments with boxes that would concentrate orgone energy (orgone accumulators), radiation, and cancer cures (he established an orgone research center in Maine, which he called "Orgonon") led to problems with the Federal Drug Administration. Criticism and rejection accentuated Reich's own personality problems, leading to a persecution complex and some outlandish developments of the orgone theory. Reich's refusal to obey a court injunction against the use of orgone accumulators (which he claimed were being used for research and not in the practice of medicine) led to his imprisonment. He died in prison.

Biographies: M. Cattier, *The Life and Work of Wilhelm Reich*, 1971; I. Ollendorff Reich, *Wilhelm Reich*, 1969; *NYT*, 1957, Nov. 5, 31:4, Dec, 7, 20:6.

REID, THOMAS
Scottish Philosopher
Born: Strachan, Kincardine, April 26, 1710
Died: Glasgow, October 7, 1796
Education: Studied theology at Marischal College, Aberdeen; licensed for ministry, 1731
Positions: 1733-36, librarian, Marischal College; 1737, minister, New Machar; 1751, philosophy instructor, Aberdeen University; 1764-81, professor of moral philosophy, University of Glasgow

Reid came first in time among the philosophers who made up the so-called Scottish school. Reid and the Scottish school stood against associationism, especially Hume's* associationism, rejected references to physiology in any explanation of human behavior, and substituted for empiricist explanations of the perception of reality explanations that were in accord with Christian orthodoxy. The question of how the mind creates objects if the raw material available is only sensations Reid answered by reference to "common sense," or the agreement of all people through the ages, as evidenced in their actual conduct in real situations and the "structure and grammar of all languages." Common sense informs us that it is self-evident that physical objects exist. Reid added that although the senses provide sensations, a divinely implanted belief in the existence of objects to which the sensations correspond brings about the perception of the world as it is commonly experienced. The sensations "suggest" the physical objects.

Reid is also called a "faculty psychologist," mainly because of the contents of two books that he wrote, *Essays on the Active Powers of the Human Mind* (1788) and *Essays on the Intellectual Powers of Man* (1785). He listed twenty-four active powers of the mind and six intellectual powers, similar to those proposed by Wolff*. The phrenologist Gall* borrowed twenty-seven of these powers from Reid and Reid's disciple Stewart* and assigned them to twenty-seven brain areas. In addition, Reid's influence was felt later (nineteenth century) in France and in America, where pre-Jamesian psychology was largely of the Scottish variety. Reid's philosophy of common sense is expounded in his *Inquiry into the Human Mind on the Principles of Common Sense* (1764).

Biographies: A. C. Fraser, *Thomas Reid*, 1898; P. H. Mabire, *Philosophie de T. Reid . . .*, 1844; D. Stewart, In T. Reid, *Philosophical Works*, 8th ed., vol. 1, 1967, pp. 3-38; *CE*, 12; *Chalmers*, 26; *DNB*, 16; *EB*, 19; *EP*, 7; *EUI*, 50; *Grande*, 28; Hirsch, *Biog. Lex.*, 4; *Nouvelle*, 41.

RÉVÉSZ, GÉZA

Hungarian-Dutch Psychologist
Born: Siofek, Hungary, December 9, 1878
Died: Amsterdam, Netherlands, August 19, 1955
Highest Degree: Ph.D. in psychology, University of Göttingen, 1905, under
G. E. Müller*
Positions: 1908-14, University of Budapest; 1919-20, University of Groningen;
1921-22, University of Utrecht; 1923-55, University of Amsterdam; editor, *Nederlandsche Tijdschrift voor Psychologie*

With David Katz*, Révész performed some of the earliest experiments (1908)
on form discrimination in birds. Later, at Amsterdam, where Révész established
a psychological laboratory in 1939 and the Dutch Institute of Applied Psychology,
he cofounded with Katz the journal *Acta Psychologica* (in 1935).

Révész's early work was on the tonality attribute of sound (*Grundlegung der
Tonpsychologie*, 1912), to which he later added researches on genius and talent
(*Psychology of a Musical Prodigy*, 1925; *Talent und Genie*, 1951), the phenomenology of touch (*Die Formenwelt des Tastsinnes*, 1938), music (*Einführung
in die Musikpsychologie*, 1946), psychology of the blind (*The Psychology and
Art of the Blind*, 1950), vision, space perception, child, medical, educational,
social psychology, and language and thought. Révész's name became well known,
both because of his productivity (he wrote twenty books and more than one
hundred articles) and because he wrote in several languages.
Biographies: M. C. Bos & H. C. J. Duijker, *Acta psychologica*, 1950, *7*, 117-120; H. C. J. Duijker, *Acta psychologica*, 1955, *11*, 357-359; R. Meili, *Schweiz.
Z. Psychol.*, 1955, *14*, 316; H. Piéron, *Amer. J. Psychol.*, 1956, *69*, 139-141;
A. Wellek, *Psychol. Rundsch.*, 1956, *7*, 57-58; *EJ*, 14; *PR*, 3.

REYMERT, MARTIN LUTHER

Norwegian-American Psychologist
Born: Holmestrand, Norway, November 10, 1883
Died: Mooseheart, Illinois, June 2, 1953
Highest Degree: Ph.D. in psychology, Clark University, 1917
Positions: 1918-19, University of Iowa; 1919-20, Iowa Child Welfare Research
Station; 1920-25, State Agriculture College, Norway; 1925-30, head, Psychology
Department, Wittenberg College; 1930-53, director of research, Loyal Order of
the Moose

During his last five years (1920-25) in Norway Reymert worked on the standardization of Norwegian IQ tests. At Mooseheart he established a psychological
laboratory for child research, where he did educational counseling. In 1949 he
established another laboratory to study age-related changes in behavior, this time
in the aged, the Moosehaven Research Laboratory at Orange Park, Florida. Both
institutions were financed by the Loyal Order of the Moose, and Reymert became
its research director, supervising both laboratories. Reymert was a member of
several advisory and similar boards having charge of children's institutions. He

himself considered that his greatest contribution to psychology was the calling of two symposia on feeling and emotion, one at Wittenberg in 1928 and another in Mooseheart, Illinois, in 1948 (*Feelings and Emotion*, 1928 and 1950, both edited by Reymert).

Biographies: H. S. Langfeld, *Amer. J. Psychol.*, 1953, *66*, 649-650; *School & Soc.*, 1953, *77*, 383; *NCAB*, 42; *NYT*, 1953, June 4, 29:5; *PR*, 3; *Who Was Who in America*, 3.

RHINE, JOSEPH BANKS

American Parapsychologist

Born: Waterloo, Juniata County, Pennsylvania, September 29, 1895

Died: Hillsborough, North Carolina, February 20, 1980

Highest Degree: Ph.D. in botany, University of Chicago, 1925

Positions: 1925-26, University of West Virginia; 1926-27, Harvard University; 1927-65, Duke University, 1927-50, professor of psychology, 1935-65, director, Parapsychology Laboratory; 1966-80, executive director, Foundation for Research on the Nature of Man; founder and editor, *Journal of Parapsychology*, 1937-80

During his lifetime Rhine's name was the best-known name in parapsychology in the world. He adopted the term *parapsychology* from German and popularized its use through his work at the Parapsychology Laboratory. Early in his career Rhine abandoned efforts to work with mediums on the question of discarnate survival and concentrated on laboratory research into the question of mind-to-mind communication, or *telepathy*; the apprehension of remote objects and events without sensory means, referred to as *clairvoyance*; the foreseeing of future events without the use of direct information or inference, called *precognition*; and the direct effects of mind on matter, or *psychokinesis*. The term *extrasensory perception*, or *ESP*, to designate the first three phenomena was introduced by Rhine.

Although Rhine was a pioneer in the laboratory study of ESP, he was not the first to do experiments in parapsychology, nor was he the first to use cards in such experiments. The five-symbol deck of ESP cards was, however, introduced at Duke University, and it became a standard device in testing for ESP ability. Rhine's main contribution was the introduction of a standard scientific methodology in ESP and psychokinesis research, including the statistical evaluation of the results. Neither the method nor the statistical treatment differed from those current in orthodox psychological research. Rhine's model of parapsychological research became the model that other parapsychologists followed in their work.

Rhine wrote numerous research and discussion papers and several books. Among the latter are *Extrasensory Perception* (1934), *New Frontiers of the Mind* (1937), *Extrasensory Perception after 60 Years* (1940, with others), *The Reach of the Mind* (1947), *Parapsychology* (1957, with J. G. Pratt), *Parapsychology Today* (1968, editor, with B. Brier), *New World of the Mind* (1953), and *Progress in Parapsychology* (1971, editor).

Biographies: D. Brian, *The Enchanted Voyager*, 1982; *J. Parapsychology*, 1981, *45*, entire No. 1; T. S. Krawiec (Ed.), *The Psychologists*, vol. 3, 1978; B. Mackkenzie, *American Journal of Psychology*, 1981 *94*, 649-653; S. Mauskopf & M. McVaugh, *Amer. Psychologist*, 1981, *36*, 310-311; *IESS*, 18; *NYT*, 1980, Feb. 21, B 14:1.

RIBOT, THÉODULE ARMAND
French psychologist
Born: Guingamp, Côtes du Nord, December 18, 1839
Died: Paris, December 8, 1916
Highest Degree: Agrégé in philosophy, École Normale Supérieure, 1865
Positions: 1865-72, teacher at various *lycées*; 1872-85, clinical studies of mental abnormalities, city of Paris; 1885-89, taught experimental psychology, Sorbonne (University of Paris); 1889-96, Collège de France; founder (1876) and editor, *Revue philosophique*

Ribot had an interest in a wide variety of fields of psychology. He wrote a number of books that were well read by other French psychologists. These books introduced to them the ideas of evolution (*L'Hérédité psychologique*, 1873), the works of the German experimental psychologists (*La psychologie allemande contemporaine*, 1879), and the thinking of the English associationists (*La psychologie anglaise contemporaine*, 1870).

Although Ribot held the title of professor of experimental psychology at the Collège de France, he was not an experimentalist. His pattern of interest resembled more that of the French psychiatrist or physiologist who stressed medical psychology. His books about behavior disorders reflected that orientation (*Les maladies de la mémoire*, 1881; *Les maladies de la volonté*, 1883: *Les maladies de la personnalité*, 1885). Ribot was one of the first French psychologists to relate pathology to problem areas in general psychology. He helped thereby to fix the character of French psychology along these lines. He strived to separate psychology from philosophy, especially metaphysics; yet he considered physiology to be a clearly separate discipline also. He used psychopathology to arrive at insights concerning general behavioral principles. Abnormal behavior was to Ribot a form of disintegration of the normal, integrated personality. He considered affect and emotions to be the basis of mental life. He was a pioneer in introducing dynamic psychology in France. Between 1896 and 1914 he wrote several volumes on affective states, such as the *Essais sur les passions* (1907), *Problèmes de psychologie affective* (1910), and *La vie inconsciente et les mouvements* (1914). In his view, in pathological states one's experiences, habits, learned reactions, and the will retreat into the background while the emotional life emerges unveiled. The most recently learned behaviors are the first to disappear in mental disorders. Ribot stressed the analysis of abnormal behavior so much that he recommended to his students that they combine their psychological studies with the study of medicine.

In general, Ribot was very influential in France during his day and was well known in other countries, but he did not leave as deep an impression on psychology as did, for instance, Binet* and Janet*, even though his books were translated and read in other languages, including English.

Biographies: J. W. Baird, *Amer. J. Psychol.*, 1917, *28*, 312-313; G. Dumas, *Rev. phil.*, 1939, *138*, 5-16; L. de Foucauld, *Théodule Ribot: Sa vie, ses oeuvres*, 1885; S. Kraus, *Théodule Ribots Psychologie*, 1905; G. Lamarque, In G. Lamarque (Ed.), *Th. Ribot: Choix de textes et études de l'oeuvre*, 1913, pp. 11-45; G. Villa, *Rivista di filosofia*, 1917, *9*, 101-109; *Biog. Lex.*; *CE*, 12; *EP*, 7; *EUI*, 51; *Grande*, 28; *NYT*, 1916, Dec. 10, 21:1.

RICHET, CHARLES ROBERT

French Physiologist
Born: Paris, August 26, 1850
Died: Paris, December 4, 1935
Highest Degree: M.D., University of Paris, 1877, Ph.D. in physiology, 1878
Positions, Honors: 1877, Collège de France; 1877-1927, University of Paris; founder and first president, Institut Metapsychique International; Nobel Prize in physiology, 1913

Richet had manifold interests, within and outside of science. To French psychology he is important because of an 1875 article in which, as a physiologist, he made a positive evaluation of hypnotism and certified it to be a genuine phenomenon. A revival of interest in hypnotism followed, and in 1878 Charcot* was already demonstrating it. Throughout his career as a physiologist (he published a number of books and papers in this area, receiving the Nobel Prize for his work on hypersensitivity to foreign proteins) Richet was engaged in various psychological studies, publishing a number of volumes: *Les poisons de l'intelligence* (1877), *Recherches expérimentales et cliniques sur la sensibilité* (1877), *L'Homme et l'intelligence* (1884), *Essai de psychologie générale* (1887), *L'Homme stupide* (1919), *Le savant* (1923), *L'Homme impuissant* (1927), *L'Intelligence et l'homme* (1927). Richet was also the first major French researcher in parapsychology. He called psychic research *metapsychics*, a term that appears in the name of the institute he headed and the title of the book *Traité de metapsychique* (1923). This and another volume of Richet's about parapsychology were translated into English (*30 Years of Psychical Research*, 1923; *Our Sixth Sense*, 1929). Richet, a believer in paranormal phenomena, also coined the term *ectoplasm* to designate the mysterious substance that some mediums were alleged to exude.

Biographies: M. Juri, *Charles Richet, physiologiste*, 1965; O. Lodge, *Proc. Soc. Psychical Res.*, 1936, *44*, 1-4; A. Pettit (Ed.), *A Charles Richet*, 1926; C. Richet, *Souvenirs d'un physiologiste*, 1933; G. Roussy, *Bull. Acad. méd.*, 1945, *129*, 725-731; *Biog. Lex.*; *DSB*, 11; *EUI*, 51; *Grande*, 28; Pagel, *Biographisches Lexikon*; *PR*, 3.

RIGNANO, EUGENIO

Italian Philosopher
Born: Livorno, May 30, 1870
Died: Milan, February 9, 1930
Highest Degree: Degree in engineering, Polytechnical Institute, Turin, 1893
Positions: No academic positions; one of founders (1907) and editor (since 1915) of *Rivista di scienza* (later *Scientia*)

Rignano was a synthesizer (*Saggi di sintesi scientifica*, 1912). His philosophy included psychology and biology, and his studies ranged from those on metabolism and the behavior of lower organisms to psychic and social phenomena. The underlying theme of Rignano's many papers and books is that life is teleological. In his major psychological work, *Psicologia del raggionamento* (1920), Rignano maintained that thinking always contains an element of emotion. This element constructs thought out of items of sensory memory. Memory is the basis of all biological and mental phenomena. Reasoning is "a series of operations or experiences merely thought out simply," a concept similar to Mach's*. Life processes are finalistic as "nervous energy" in the form of memory is able to envision the future in terms of past experience and thus adapt the organism to future eventualities. Thus psychology and biology have a profound common basis. The developmental tendency is also found in moral life. The purpose of moral life is to satisfy the needs of all individuals and eventually to eliminate all conflict (*Il fine dell' uomo*, 1923). Among Rignano's other books of psychological significance are *Sur la transmissibilité des charactères acquis* (1906), *La memoria biologica* (1922), *Come funziona la nostra intelligenza* (1922), *Che cos'è la vita?* (1926), and *Problemi della psiche* (1928).
Biographies: V. D'Agostino, *Arch. ital. psicol.*, 1930, *8*(2), 127-128; A. Groppali, *Riv. int. fil. dir.*, 1930, *10A*, 603-605; G. Sarton, *Isis*, 1931, *15*, 158-162; *EP*, 7; *EUI*, 51; *PR*, 3.

RIVERS, (BARON) WILLIAM HALSE RIVERS

English Psychologist and Anthropologist
Born: Luton, Kent, March 12, 1864
Died: Cambridge, June 4, 1922
Highest Degree: M.D., St. Bartholomew's Hospital, London, 1886
Positions, Honors: 1893-1922, Cambridge University, 1897 appointed to first lectureship in experimental and physiological psychology, also first director, Cambridge psychological laboratory; 1914-18, psychologist, Royal Air Force; honorary degrees from St. Andrews University and Manchester University

Upon receiving his appointment at Cambridge, Rivers did some work on vision. He then participated (1898) with McDougall* and Myers* in the Cambridge anthropological expedition to the Torres Straits, did some of the first measurements of individual differences in nontechnological societies, and reported on the color vision, perception of geometric illusions, and other visual phenomena in the Torres Straits aborigines in 1901. Later, he visited southern

India (1902) and reported on the color vision on the inhabitants of that area in 1905. In 1908 he visited Melanesia. Rivers's anthropological observations were published in two books, *The Todas* (1906) and *History of Melanesian Society* (1914). Between expeditions Rivers collaborated with Henry Head* on a famous experiment (published in 1905 and 1908) on sensitivity changes during the regeneration of a cut nerve in the arm (Rivers's arm). In 1904 Rivers, Myers, and Ward* founded the *British Journal of Psychology*. During World War I and in connection with his work with the Royal Air Force, Rivers became interested in neurological problems. He was concerned with problems in medical psychology until his death. During this period Rivers also published the book *Instinct and the Unconscious* (1920), which was instrumental in providing a favorable reception of Sigmund Freud's* psychoanalytic theory in England.

Biographies: E. H. Ackerknecht, *Bull. Hist. Med.*, 1942, *11*, 478-481; F. C. Bartlett, *Amer. J. Psychol.*, 1923, *34*, 275-277; F. C. Bartlett, *Amer. J. Psychol.*, 1937, *50*, 97-110, esp. 102-107; A. A. Goldenweiser, *Encycl. Soc. Sci.*, 1934, *13*, 398-399; A. C. Haddon & F. C. Bartlett, *Man*, 1922, *22*, 97-104; H. Head, *Brit. Med. J.*, 1922, *1*, 977-978; *Biog. Lex.*; *EUI*, 51; *IESS*, 13.

ROBACK, ABRAHAM AARON

American Psychologist
Born: Poland, June 19, 1890
Died: Cambridge, Massachusetts, June 5, 1965
Highest Degree: Ph.D. in psychology, Harvard University, 1917
Positions: Brief academic appointments at University of Pittsburgh, Northeastern University, Harvard University, Massachusetts Institute of Technology, and Clark University; longer part-time appointments at Massachusetts Department of University Extension and Emerson College, Boston

Roback's contribution to psychology was primarily as a writer. He wrote some thirty books and a very large number of articles, although many of the articles were not about psychological subjects but Yiddish and Hebrew literature and folklore. *The Psychology of Character* (1927) was his book of most enduring value. Other significant books about psychology that Roback wrote were *Behaviorism and Psychology* (1923), *Behaviorism at Twenty-five* (1937), *History of American Psychology* (1952), and *History of Psychology and Psychiatry* (1961).

Biographies: G. W. Allport, *Amer. J. Psychol.*, 1965, *78*, 689-690; J. Berger, *The Destiny and Motivation of Dr. A. A. Roback: A Critical Essay*, 1957; *EJ*, 14; *PR*, 3.

ROBINSON, EDWARD STEVENS

American Psychologist
Born: Lebanon, Ohio, April 18, 1893
Died: New Haven, Connecticut, February 27, 1937
Highest Degree: Ph.D. in psychology, University of Chicago, 1920, under J. R. Angell*

Positions: 1920-21, Yale University; 1921-27, University of Chicago; 1927-37, Yale University; editorial work, *Psychological Bulletin* (1930-34), *Journal of Social Psychology* (1935-37), and *American Journal of Psychology* (1925-35)

Robinson was a Chicago functionalist. His initial work was on learning, particularly retroactive interference. The Skaggs-Robinson hypothesis (so named by McGeoch* to give credit also to E. B. Skaggs who had conceived of a similar idea earlier, in 1925) states that positive transfer of learning is greatest when the successively presented material is identical, that dissimilarity of materials also facilitates transfer, but that intermediate degrees of similarity produce the greatest interference. Robinson wrote two books applying the functionalist analysis to some concrete and practical problems: *Practical Psychology* (1926) and *The Behavior of a Museum Visitor* (1928). He then presented an overview, *Association Theory Today* (1931). In this work Robinson showed how all the associative laws could be dimensionalized and quantified. These laws, as formulated by Robinson, as well as Carr*, never caught on because they were too general and were replaced by more specific ones, defined in terms of specific learning situations. Later Robinson turned to social psychology, believing that the functionalist approach could be applied in this field also. He lectured on law and psychology in the Yale Law School and published a book reflecting this phase in his thinking, *Law and the Lawyers* (1935). *Man As Psychology Sees Him* (1932) and sixty-seven papers completed Robinson's bibliography when he died in an accident early in his life.

Biographies: J. R. Angell, *Psychol. Bull.*, 1937, *34*, 801-805; R. P. Angier, *Psychol. Rev.*, 1937, *44*, 267-273; H. A. Carr, *Amer. J. Psychol.*, 1937, *49*, 488-489; *DAB*, 22; *NCAB*, 28; *PR*, 3.

ROLANDO, LUIGI
Italian Anatomist
Born: Turin, Piemonte, July 20, 1773
Died: Turin, Piemonte, April 20, 1831
Highest Degree: M.D., University of Turin, 1793
Positions: 1807-14, University of Sassari; 1814-31, University of Turin

Rolando studied the anatomy and pathology of the brain. He published his findings on the localization of brain functions in 1809 (*Saggio sopra la vera struttura del cervello*) before Flourens*. Some of the functions he assigned the various portions of the brain were incorrect, however, and his experiments were inadequately described. Nevertheless, since he steered away from phrenology, did actual experiments on the brain, and used postmortem examinations, his work represents a definite advance in neurophysiology and neuroanatomy. Rolando localized the higher mental functions in the cerebral hemispheres. He attributed brain activity, however, to the movement of the fibers, thought that the white matter of the brain was more important than the gray matter, and localized sensation in the medulla rather than the cerebral cortex. Long before Gustav Fritsch* and Eduard Hitzig*, Rolando used the new discovery of his countryman Alessandro Volta, the electric pile, to stimulate brain tissue. Noticing that muscular contractions became more vigorous as he moved the electrodes closer to the cerebellum, he concluded, incorrectly, that the cerebellum was the source of nerve energy. The central fissure in each hemisphere of the brain as well as other brain structures have been named after Rolando.

Biographies: C. F. Bellingeri, *Mem. Accad. Sci. Torino*, 1934, *37*, 153-193; P. Capparoni, *Boll. Ist. stor. ital. arte sanit.*, 1926, No. 6; P. Capparoni, *Profili bio-bibliografici di medici e naturalisti celebri italiani dal sec. XVo al sec. XVIIIo*, 2 vols., 1925-28; C.-J.-F. Carron Des Villards, *Bull. Soc. anat.*, 1830, *5*, 195-205; E. Manni, *Exp. Neurol.*, 1973, *38*, 1-5; *DSB*, 11; *EUI*, 51; Hirsch, *Biog. Lex.*, 4.

ROMANES, GEORGE JOHN
English Biologist
Born: Kingston, Ontario, Canada, May 20, 1858
Died: Oxford, England, May 23, 1894
Highest Degree: M.A., Oxford University, 1873
Positions, Honors: 1886-90, University of Edinburgh; 1888-91, Fullerian Professor of Physiology, Royal Institute; LL.D., University of Aberdeen, 1882

In 1882, twenty-four years after the appearance of Charles Darwin's* *Origin of Species*, Romanes wrote what is often considered to be the first text of comparative psychology, *Animal Intelligence*. (Hermann Reimarus had written a book about animal instincts in the eighteenth century.) In writing this book Romanes's aim was to supply evidence for Darwin's theory by showing continuity between the mental processes of humans and animals, especially regarding the presence, to different degrees, of reason in animals. To Romanes comparative psychology meant the comparison of mental structures of organisms.

Romanes collected all available evidence on animals, from molluscs, through insects, to fishes and mammals, much of it supplied by pet owners, zoo keepers, and other individuals who dealt with animals. Romanes's contribution was to collect the material and to systematize it. The evidence was largely anecdotal, and Romanes did not avoid anthropomorphization by attributing, for instance, reason to animals where a simpler explanation in terms of instinct or habit would have been more appropriate. It was a direct result of Romanes's premise that psychology is the study of the mind, one's own mind, and that with animals (as well as with other people) inferences concerning mental processes based on analogy had to be made. Romanes's book was one of the stimuli for Lloyd Morgan* to state his canon concerning the interpretation of animal behavior. Romanes kept pursuing his original aim of proving Darwin's theory by writing *The Scientific Evidences of Organic Evolution* (1882), *Mental Evolution in Animals* (1883), and *Mental Evolution in Man* (1889), but his first book has been the most important one to comparative psychology.

Biographies: E. Romanes, *The Life and Letters of George John Romanes*, 5th ed., 1902; E. B. Titchener, *Phil. Rev.*, 1894, *3*, 766-767; *DNB*, 17; *DSB*, 11; *EP*, 7; *EUI*, 52; *Grande*, 28.

RORSCHACH, HERMANN
Swiss Psychiatrist
Born: Zurich, November 8, 1884
Died: Herisau, Appenzell-Ausser Rhoden, April 2, 1922
Highest Degree: M.D., University of Zurich, 1912
Positions: 1913, post in a mental hospital in Russia; 1912-22, positions in four mental hospitals in Switzerland; vice-president, Swiss Psychoanalytic Society, 1919

Rorschach's life and work are completely overshadowed by the personality test he invented. Stimulus materials that are subject to different interpretation had been used previously to study imagination. Rorschach constructed symmetric inkblots to study personality structure, especially unconscious motivation. The need to measure unconscious phenomena arose from the work of Sigmund Freud* and Carl Jung*. The rationale behind the test is that, given an unstructured stimulus, the subject is more likely to reveal concealed, problematic, traumatic, or subconscious contents of his mind when describing what he sees in an inkblot than when asked direct questions about such matters. The test hinges on the interpretation of what is said, and lengthy training is required for a diagnostician to become proficient in the use of the test, even though Rorschach provided detailed scoring norms. Rorschach used the test beginning in 1911 but did not publish the ten inkblots that are presently being used, along with a manual, until 1921 (*Psychodiagnostics: A Diagnostic Test Based on Perception*, English translation, 1942). The test as presently used was developed by others. Rorschach's inkblot test was the first in a series of projective tests that were to appear afterwards. Even though there is serious doubt that the test is valid, it is being widely used, especially by those who consider personality to be an organic whole rather than a collection of traits. The published literature on the Rorschach test is enormous, and the inkblot has become so well known, even among laymen, that it is often used to symbolize all of psychology.
Biographies: H. Ellenberger, *Bull. Menninger Clin.*, 1954, *18*, 173-219; M. Minkowski, *Schweiz. Arch. Neurol. Psychiat.*, 1922, *11*, 318-320; E. Oberholzer, *J. Project. Techn.*, 1968, *32*, 502-508; O. Rorschach, *Schweiz. Arch. Neurol. Psychiat.*, 1944, *53*, 1-11; *Biog. Lex.*; *IESS*, 13.

ROSANOFF, AARON JOSHUA
American Psychiatrist
Born: Pinsk, Russia, June 26, 1878
Died: Los Angeles, California, January 7, 1943
Highest Degree: M.D., Cornell University, 1900
Positions: 1901-22, State Hospital, King's Park, New York; 1917-19, Army Medical Corps; 1923-43, private practice; 1925-43, lecturer, University of Southern California; 1939-42, California State director of institutions

In 1910 Grace Kent* and Rosanoff designed a psychiatric screening instrument that was based on word associations. It consisted of one hundred common words that had been found to elicit similar associations in a group of one thousand subjects. The norms for the test were associative frequency tables for the various responses to each of the one hundred words. Schizophrenics were found, for instance, to give the less common responses. When it was discovered that word-association frequency depends not only on pathology but a host of other factors as well, the test fell into disuse. The Kent-Rosanoff list of associative frequency is still being used, however, in learning experiments and other research involving verbal materials (*Free Association Test*, 1927, with G. Kent).

Rosanoff's publications in the area of psychiatry included a wide range of topics: the relationship between heredity, constitution, and psychosis; degenerative brain diseases; war neuroses; organic psychoses; and others. Rosanoff subscribed to the idea that psychoses have a genetic and constitutional basis. He wrote several papers and monographs about the occurrence of mental disorders in twins. His theory of personality was based on this notion: mental disorders are hereditary patterns, and the origins of personality are seen in clinical types. Normal personality is an incomplete form of some clinical type; hence there are epileptoid, schizoid, and so on personalities, with no suggestion that the person is epileptic or otherwise mentally disturbed. Among Rosanoff's other contributions may be counted the publication of a *Manual of Psychiatry and Mental Hygiene* (1905), his work with World War I shell-shock cases that merited him a government citation, the organization of a private mental institution, and the planning of two mental hospitals, one in Los Angeles and one in San Francisco (the Langley Porter Clinic).

Biographies: J. Kasanin, *J. Nerv. Ment. Dis.*, 1943, *97*, 501-503; *NYT*, 1943, Jan. 8, 20:3; *PR*, 3.

ROSS, EDWARD ALSWORTH

American Sociologist

Born: Virden, Illinois, December 12, 1866

Died: Madison, Wisconsin, July 22, 1951

Highest Degree: Ph.D. in economics, Johns Hopkins University, 1891

Positions, Honors: 1891-95, taught economics briefly, Indiana University and Cornell University; 1895-1900, turned to sociology, Stanford University; 1900-1906, University of Nebraska; 1906-37, University of Wisconsin, from 1929, chairman, Department of Sociology and Anthropology; LL.D., Coe College, 1911

In 1908 Ross wrote a *Social Psychology*, the first text in social psychology written in English. It appeared just a few months before McDougall's* text but was different from his; it was a psychological sociology. Ross wrote much for popular presentation and thereby stimulated interest in social psychology.

Biographies: J. L. Gillin, *Amer. J. Soc. Phil.*, 1937, *42*, 534-542; J. O. Hetzler, *Amer. Sociol. Rev.*, 1951, *16*, 597-613; E. A. Ross, *Seventy Years of It*, 1936; J. Weinberg, *Edward Alsworth Ross and the Sociology of Progressivism*, 1972; *IESS*, 13; *NCAB*, 18; *NYT*, 1951, July 23, 17:5.

ROUSSEAU, JEAN-JACQUES
Swiss-French Moralist
Born: Geneva, Switzerland, June 28, 1712
Died: Ermenonville, Oise, France, July 2, 1778
Education: No formal education
Positions: No steady positions

As a philosopher and moralist Rousseau exercised great influence on Western thought. His influence on psychological thought was largely in the developmental and educational areas. His ideas there were so well accepted that the first radical deviation from the benevolent conception of the child that Rousseau had presented did not occur until the advent of psychoanalysis, and Rousseau's ideas may be seen even in some of Sigmund Freud's* theorizing. In the twentieth century G. S. Hall's* recapitulation theory, the "rosebud" theory in education, the "progressive" schools, Freud's instinct theory, and the early work of Jean Piaget* all reflected Rousseau's influence.

Rousseau's psychological ideas are contained mostly in his *Emile* (1762). Child study as a body of knowledge begins with *Emile*. In it, the following propositions may be found. Childhood is a natural event, important in and of itself. The child is born with an innate sense of right and wrong. Attempts by adults to "finish God's work" by prohibitions and restrictions corrupt the child. Children are not miniature adults. They are well adapted to their environment, and their mental life is appropriate to their needs. They will develop satisfactorily without much adult intervention, because nature itself has provided them with a built-in mechanism for healthy growth. Therefore education must follow children's spontaneous inclinations and be guided by their natural development. Knowledge is not poured into children by adults; rather, children find it by actively interacting with the environment. Children develop through a number of stages that follow each other in an invariant order. In this they recapitulate the stages of the cultural evolution of humanity. The first few years are the most influential ones in the child's development.

Biographies: W. H. Blanchard, *Rousseau and the Spirit of Revolt: A Psychological Study*, 1967; J. Borel, *Génie et folie de Jean-Jacques Rousseau*, 1966; J. H. Broome, *Rousseau: A Study of His Thought*, 1963; E. Cassirer, *The Question of Jean-Jacques Rousseau*, 1954; J. Charpentier, *Rousseau: The Child of Nature*, 1931; A. Cresson, *J.-J. Rousseau: Sa vie, son oeuvre, avec un exposé de sa philosophie*, 1940; L. G. Crocker, *Jean-Jacques Rousseau*, 2 vols., 1968-1973; L. Ducros, *Jean-Jacques Rousseau*, 3 vols., 1908-1918; B. Gagnebin, In J.-J. Rousseau, *Oeuvres complètes*, vol. 2, 1964, pp. 1961-1994; F. C. Green, *Jean-Jacques Rousseau: A Critical Study of His Life and Writings*, 1955; R. Grimsley, *J.-J. Rousseau: A Study in Self-awareness*, 1961; H. Höffding, *Jean-Jacques Rousseau and His Philosophy*, 1930 (Reprinted 1970); M. Josephson, *Jean-Jacques Rousseau*, 1932; F. Jost, *Jean-Jacques Rousseau suisse: Étude sur sa personnalité et sa pensée*, 2 vols., 1961; H. Moreley, *Rousseau and His Era*, 2 vols., 1923; D. Mornet, *Rousseau l'homme et l'oeuvre*, 1950; J.-J. Rousseau, *The Confessions of Jean-Jacques Rousseau*, 1959; *Chalmers*, 26; *EB*, 19; *EP*, 7; *IESS*, 13; *Jewish*, 9; *Nouvelle*, 42.

ROYCE, JOSIAH
American Philosopher
Born: Grass Valley, California, November 20, 1855
Died: Cambridge, Massachusetts, September 14, 1916
Highest Degree: Ph.D. in philosophy, Johns Hopkins University, 1878
Positions, Honors: 1878-82, University of California at Berkeley; 1882-1916, Harvard University; president, American Psychological Association (1901), American Philosophical Association, (1903); seven honorary degrees

Royce was a very versatile philosopher. In addition to contributing to philosophy, he contributed to literary criticism, social ethics, logic, mathematical logic, metaphysics, and psychology. He wrote some twenty books on these subjects. Philosophically, Royce was a monistic idealist. During his time he was the leader in American idealism. His idealism is reflected in the psychology text of which he was the author, *Outlines of Psychology: An Elementary Treatise with Some Practical Applications* (1903). In it consciousness is postulated to be the universal principle, and scientific laws are presented to be statistically established average behaviors. Royce wrote additional papers about psychological questions, for instance, extrasensory perception, moral training, imitation, and self-consciousness. Although, in line with his philosophy, he did not involve physiological considerations in his psychology, he was not averse to some of the practical aspects of mental activity—invention, consulting, mental disorders—and wrote about those subjects. Royce's seminars in logica were famous and were attended by individuals from different disciplines as he clarified the logic of their endeavors to them. William James* helped bring Royce to Harvard, and Royce was well known and influential among Harvard psychologists and psychology students.
Biographies: V. Buranelli, *Josiah Royce*, 1964; B. Kuklick, *Josiah Royce: An Intellectual Biography*, 1972; T. F. Powell, *Josiah Royce*, 1967; various, *J. Phil.*, 1956, *53*, 57-139; *DAB*, 16; *EB*, 19; *EP*, 7; *NCAB*, 25; *NYT*, 1916, Sept. 15, 11:3.

RUBIN, EDGAR JOHN
Danish Psychologist
Born: Copenhagen, September 6, 1886
Died: Copenhagen, May 3, 1951
Highest Degree: Ph.D. in psychology, University of Copenhagen, 1915
Positions, Honors: 1916-51, University of Copenhagen, since 1922, director, Psychological Laboratory; president, Tenth International Congress of Psychology, 1932

Rubin made a direct contribution to the raw material of which Gestalt psychology was made. His name is associated with the figure-ground phenomenon. Rubin started his research on this phenomenon in 1912. A first report on it was published in German in the proceedings of the Sixth Congress of Experimental Psychology, then in Danish (*Synslopevede figurer*, 1915), and again in German, but in a monograph form (*Visuell wahrgenommene Figuren*, 1921). Rubin analyzed visual perception in terms of its two basic components, figure and ground. *Figure* is that which one pays attention to, which has a "thingness" about it; *ground* is that formless, less conspicuous extent upon which the figure is seen. Rubin's phenomenological analysis of figure-ground relationships and his demonstrations, the phenomenologist's *experimenta crucis*, of the role of attention in the perception of ambiguous, figure-ground reversal pictures ("vase-profile", "finger-claw") made his work eminently suitable material for Gestalt-theoretical analysis. In a paper presented in the early 1930s, however, Rubin denied the need for the concept of attention and attempted to explain figure-ground phenomena solely in terms of the structural properties of the visual field. Following his lead, Gestalt psychologists dropped the term in their writings until about 1960. The figure-ground concept is now part of general psychology, with usually no reference made to Rubin. It is applicable not only to the visual sense modality but all other modalities as well.

In addition to his association with the figure-ground phenomenon, Rubin is also noted for the discovery, simultaneously with but independently of Goldscheider*, of paradoxical warmth: he reported that stimuli just below skin temperature produced a weak sensation of warmth when applied to "warm" receptors. Rubin also studied visually perceived movement (1927) and other perceptual phenomena. Until his death, he was Denmark's most distinguished psychologist. *Biographies*: D. Katz, *Psychol. Rev.*, 1951, *58*, 387-388; W. C. H. Prentice, *Amer. J. Psychol.*, 1951, *64*, 608-609; E. T. Rasmussen, *Bull. Ass. int. psychol. appl.*, 1961, *10*, 4-18; *PR*, 3.

RUBINSHTEĬN, SERGEĬ LEONIDOVICH
Russian Psychologist
Born: Odessa, Ukraine, June 6, 1889
Died: Moscow, January 11, 1960
Education: Graduated from Novorossiĭskiĭ University, Odessa, in 1913
Positions: 1919-30, University of Odessa; 1930-42, Gertsen Pedagogical Institute, Leningrad; 1942-50, Moscow State University; editor, *Voprosy Psikhologii*

During the years of World War II, Rubinshteĭn organized the Psychology Department at the University of Moscow and wrote a revised edition of his most significant work, *Osnovy obshcheĭ psikhologii* (1946; 1st ed., 1940). It was a text of general psychology based mostly on the work of Soviet psychologists and it received a government prize. Rubinshteĭn's thinking, as expressed in this book, was also reflected in his defense of psychology during the so-called Pavlovian sessions that took place in Moscow in 1950. In defending psychology from attacks by those who chided it for not using Pavlov's* teachings, Rubinshteĭn proposed a synthesis between dualism, as represented in psychology by the introspective approach to mind, and monism, as represented by behaviorism. He emphasized the unity of consciousness and behavior. Consciousness is not all internal, nor is behavior all external. They interpenetrate. Behavior reflects the inner world; objective reality is reflected in inner experience.

Phylogenetically, development is first determined by the laws of biology. Later, however, development is also determined by the laws of history and the laws of social development. The activities of humans transform their environment, and the environment, in turn, affects their development. It is a dialectic interaction. A further interactive system is seen in the relationship between the psyche and the nervous system and the psyche and the external world. Lenin's* doctrine of reflection was applied by Rubinshteĭn to Pavlov's view of the reflexes by adding the notion of refraction: not only does organic matter reflect the external world, but by its own nature, it changes or refracts the action of the external world. Hegel* and Lenin also appear in Rubinshteĭn's concept of *constitutive relationism*: things and phenomena are determined by their relation to the surrounding reality. Hence mental processes have several different structures that relate mental activity to the brain and others that relate the brain to external reality. Relations are prior to the elements related, hence meaning is prior to words. Mental activities are therefore to be studied in relation to internal physiological and biochemical processes, which are material in nature, and in relation to external social processes, which are also material. Rubinshteĭn's was a two-faced materialistic monism.

Rubinshteĭn continued to play the role of a major Soviet theoretical psychologist as he published additional works during the last years of his career: *Bytie i soznanie* (1957), *O myshlenii i putyakh ego razvitiya* (1958), and *Printsipy i puti razvitiya psikhologii* (1959).

Biographies: B. G. Anan'ev, *Vop. Psikhol.*, 1969, *15*(5), 126-129; T. R. Payne, *Stud. Sov. Thought*, 1963, *3*, 208-209; T. R. Payne, *Stud. Sov. Thought*, 1968, *8*, 144-156; *Vop. Psikhol.*, 1959, 5(3), 143-146; *Vop. Psikhol.*, 1960, 6(1), 4-6; *Great Soviet Encyclopedia*; *Who Was Who in the USSR*, 1972.

RUCKMICK, CHRISTIAN ALBAN

American Psychologist

Born: New York, New York, September 4, 1886

Died: Miami, Florida, 1961

Highest Degree: Ph.D. in psychology, Cornell University, 1913

Positions: 1913-21, University of Illinois; 1921-24, Wellesley College; 1924-39, State University of Iowa; 1939-42, sales manager, C. H. Stoelting Co.; 1942, chief civilian psychologist, U.S. Army Induction Station, Peoria, Illinois; 1943-46, various training positions; 1946-52, superintendent of education, Ministry of Education, Ethiopia; 1952-55, University of Miami

In psychological research Ruckmick produced some one hundred publications on a wide variety of subjects. A considerable portion of his papers were about audition, GSR and emotion, and rhythm. Ruckmick invented the *affectometer* and other scientific instruments, but his main work was in connection with psychological publications and editorial activities. Books written by Ruckmick include *The Brevity Book on Psychology* (1920), *German-English Dictionary of Psychological Terms* (1928), *The Mental Life* (1928), *The Emotional Responses of Children to the Motion Picture Situation* (1933, with W. S. Dysinger), and *Psychology of Feeling and Emotion* (1936).

Biographies: PR, 3; *Who Was Who in America*, 4.

RUSH, BENJAMIN

American Physician and Medical Educator
Born: Byberry, Pennsylvania, January 4, 1746
Died: Philadelphia, Pennsylvania, April 19, 1813
Highest Degree: M.D., University of Edinburgh, 1768
Positions: 1769-91, professor of chemistry, College of Philadelphia; 1791-97, professor of medicine, University of Pennsylvania; 1797-1813, Treasurer of National Mint

Rush was one of the pioneers in American medicine, a medical reformer and educator, deeply involved in social causes, including the establishment of the United States of America: he was one of the signers of the Declaration of Independence. Psychiatry was also one of his concerns and, following the lead of Philippe Pinel* in France and William Tuke in England, he advocated more humane treatment of the mentally ill, organized the first course in psychiatry in the United States, and wrote the first American medical treatise on psychiatry, *Medical Inquiries and Observations Upon the Diseases of the Mind* (1812). For these achievements he is called the father of American psychiatry. He was, however, dogmatic in his treatment of mental patients, a believer in the meliorating powers of tranquilization, which in medical patients he achieved through debilitating treatments (purges, bloodletting) and an immobilizing device of his own invention (the tranquilizer) in psychiatric patients. Although Rush represented an advance in comparison with the treatment accorded the mental patient before, he was also less progressive than Pinel.

Biographies: C. A. Binger, *Revolutionary Doctor: Benjamin Rush, 1746-1813*, 1966; D. J. D'Elia, *Proc. Amer. Phil. Soc.*, 1966, *110*, 227-234; N. G. Goodman, *Benjamin Rush: Physician and Citizen*, 1934; D. F. Hawke, *Benjamin Rush: Revolutionary Gadfly*, 1971; E. Kahn, *Confinia psychiat.*, 1967, *10*, 61-76; B. Mackler & K. Hamilton, *Psychol. Rep.*, 1967, *20*, 1287-1306; B. Rush, *The Autobiography of Benjamin Rush*, 1948; I. Veith, *Mod. Med.*, 1961, Feb. 20, 198-206, Mar. 6, 186-198, Mar. 20, 220-232; *Chalmers*, 26; *DAB*, 16; *DSB*, 11; *EB*, 19; *IESS*, 13; *NCAB*, 3.

RUSH, JAMES

American Physician and Psychologist
Born: Philadelphia, Pennsylvania, March 15, 1787
Died: Philadelphia, Pennsylvania, May 26, 1869
Highest Degree: M.D., University of Pennsylvania, 1809; postdoctoral training, University of Edinburgh
Positions: 1811-20s, private practice in medicine

James Rush, the son of Benjamin Rush*, studied at Edinburgh with the masters of the Scottish school but became dissatisfied with a psychology based on religion. After returning to America he embarked on a study of the human voice and in 1827 published a book that saw seven editions (*The Philosophy of the Human Voice*). Rush returned to psychology after 1857. In 1865 he published his most important work, the two-volume *Brief Outline of an Analysis of the Human Intellect....* In it Rush presented ideas that were not to reappear on the American psychological scene until the twentieth century. Rush claimed that he had held the views expressed in his book since the beginning of the century. The *Brief Outline* presents the viewpoint that mind is not only thinking and perceiving but also speaking and acting. Furthermore, "the mind has been and still is regarded as the working of a spiritual something in the brain, and therefore not to be investigated as a physical function of the senses and the brain conjoined. This appears to be the principal cause why the problem of the mind has not been fully solved, on the clear and assignable data of observation and experiment." Rush's view of philosophy and psychology was materialistic. He compared the brain to a mirror and thought to a reflection, the latter as material as the brain itself. In addition to advocating the study of the behavior of humans as the proper subject matter of psychology, Rush also endorsed the study of animal behavior. Objectivist Rush was ahead of the Zeitgeist, but he also managed to antagonize people by his manner of writing and the style of his criticism, so he was first ignored and then forgotten.

Biographies: A. A. Roback, *History of American Psychology*, 1964; *DAB*, 16; *NCAB*, 6.

S

SACHS, HANNS
Austrian Psychoanalyst
Born: Vienna, January 10, 1881
Died: Boston, Massachusetts, January 10, 1947
Highest Degree: Law degree from University of Vienna, 1904
Positions: 1918-20, private practice of psychoanalysis, Zurich; 1920-32, director, Psychoanalytical Institute, Berlin; 1932-47, training analyst, Boston, Massachusetts; and faculty member, Harvard Medical School

After reading Sigmund Freud's* works, Sachs joined his group in 1909 and became one of the ring-wearing members of Freud's inner group that was to guide the destiny of psychoanalysis. Sachs defended Freud constantly and, unlike other members of the inner group such as Jung*, Adler*, and Rank*, never defected. In Berlin Sachs became the first training analyst. He was a cofounder and editor of the psychoanalytic journal *Imago* (1912-38). When it was suppressed he reestablished it in America as *The American Imago*. Sachs's early works were concerned with the interpretation of dreams, but he later shifted to the application of psychoanalysis to literature and art. Of Sachs's seventy-eight publications, the most significant monographs are *The Significance of Psychoanalysis to the Mental Sciences* (1916, with O. Rank), *Notes About the Psychology of the Film* (1925) (he helped direct an early film about Freud), *The Creative Unconscious* (1942), and *Freud: Master and Friend* (1944).

Biographies: F. Deutsch, *Amer. Imago*. 1947, *4*(2), 3-11; M. Eitington, *Int. Z. Psychoanal.*, 1931, *17*, 158-159; E. Jones, *Int. J. Psychoanal.*, 1946, *27*, 168-169; R. M. Loewenstein, *Psychoanal. Quart.*, 1947, *16*, 151-156; F. Moellenhoff, In F. Alexander, S. Eisenstein, & M. Grotjahn (Eds.), *Psychoanalytic Pioneers*, 1966, 180-199; A. A. Roback, In H. Sachs, *Masks of Love and Life*, 1948, pp. 11-17; K. Spitteler, *Imago*, 1924, *10*, 443-447; *EJ*, 14; *NYT*, 1947, Jan. 11, 19:4.

SANFORD, EDMUND CLARK
American Psychologist
Born: Oakland, California, November 10, 1859
Died: Boston, Massachusetts, November 22, 1924
Highest Degree: Ph.D. in psychology, Johns Hopkins University, 1888, under G. S. Hall*
Positions, Honors: 1888-89, Johns Hopkins University; 1889-1924, Clark University; editorial work, *American Journal of Psychology*, 1888-1924; President, American Psychological Association, 1902; honorary degrees from Hobart College (1909), University of California (1912), and Clark University (1924)

After Sanford took his degree from Hall, he went with Hall from Johns Hopkins to Clark University, where he ran Hall's laboratory and published a series of twenty-two "minor" studies. He invented and built a vernier pendulum chronoscope that was used in reaction time work for some time. His most important contribution was the publication of a laboratory manual, which first came out in installments in the *American Journal of Psychology*, beginning in 1891, then in book form in 1898 (*Course in Experimental Psychology*). Although only Part 1 of the *Course* was ever published, Sanford's only book served as the standard laboratory manual for a long time. He published about thirty papers in psychology on a variety of subjects.
Biographies: W. H. Burnham, *J. Genet. Psychol.*, 1925, *32*, 2-7; E. B. Titchener, *Amer. J. Psychol.*, 1925, *36*, 157-170; L. N. Wilson (Ed.), *Clark Univ. Libr. Publ.*, 1925, No. 1; *DAB*, 16; *NCAB*, 12; *NYT*, 1924, Nov. 23, 7:1; *Who Was Who in America*, 1.

SANFORD, FILLMORE HARGRAVE
American Psychologist
Born: Chatham, Virginia, January 26, 1914
Died: Austin, Texas, August 5, 1967
Highest Degree: Ph.D. in psychology, Harvard University, 1941
Positions: 1941-42, Harvard University; 1943-45, U.S. Naval Reserve; 1946-47, University of Maryland; 1948-49, Haverford College; 1950-55, executive secretary, American Psychological Association; 1956, associate director of scientific studies, Joint Committee on Mental Illness and Health; 1957-64, University of Texas; 1965, New College, Sarasota, Florida, and Macalester College, St. Paul; 1966-67, University of Texas; editor, *Contemporary Psychology*, 1962-67

Sanford was the author of some twenty-five papers about language, mental health, and leadership and of the books *Psychology for Naval Leaders* (1949),

Authoritarianism and Leadership (1950), and *Psychology: A Scientific Study of Man* (1961; now entitled *Psychology: A Scientific Study of Human Behavior* and in its fourth edition). His main interest lay in the study of leadership and attitudes, in which area he conducted his most significant empirical studies. As the executive secretary of the American Psychological Association Sanford excelled as a fighter against quackery in the delivery of psychological services.

Biographies: A. Ellis, *Amer. Psychologist*, 1952, *7*, 129-131; *American Men of Science*, 10th ed.; *NYT*, 1967, Aug. 7, 29:5; *Who Was Who in America*, 4.

SAPIR, EDWARD
American Anthropologist and Linguist
Born: Lauenburg, Pomerania, January 26, 1884
Died: New Haven, Connecticut, February 4, 1939
Highest Degree: Ph.D. in anthropology, Columbia University, 1909
Positions: 1910-25, chief, Division of Anthropology, Canadian National Museum, Ottawa; 1925-27, University of Chicago; 1927-39, head, cultural anthropology section, Department of Social Sciences, Yale University; president, Linguistic Society of America and American Anthropological Association

In anthropology Sapir's name was known internationally, principally for his linguistic studies, such as of the American Indian languages (1906), which he turned to under the influence of Franz Boas*. Sapir's most important work in linguistics is his *Language* (1921). His ideas concerning the relationship between language and behavior appeared in a posthumous volume, *Selected Writings in Language, Culture, and Personality* (1949, edited by D. G. Mendelbaum).

Sapir pioneered in advocating a closer relationship between anthropology, sociology, and psychoanalysis and exercised considerable influence in this direction upon H. S. Sullivan*. He shared with Ralph Linton* the latter's view of culture as a sum total of the behavior patterns, attitudes, and values shared by members of a given society. He viewed personality as the result of an interaction between systems of ideas that pertain to the culture as a whole and those that arise when the individual transforms some of the cultural material to accommodate them to his particular physical and psychological needs.

Biographies: R. Benedict, *Amer. Anthropologist*, 1939, *41*, 465-477; F. Boas, *Int. J. Amer. Ling.*, 1939, *10*(1), 58-59; D. G. Mendelbaum, in *Selected Writings of Edward Sapir in Language, Culture, and Personality*, 1949, pp. v-xii; L. Spier, *Science*, 1939, *89*, 237; C. F. Voegelin, *Amer. Anthropologist*, 1942, *44*, 322-324; C. F. Voegelin, *Word Study*, 1952, *27*, 1-3; *DAB*, 22; *IESS*, 14; *Jewish*, 9; *NCAB*, 33; *NYT*, 1939, Feb. 5, 40:6; *PR*, 3; *Yearbook of the American Philosophical Society*, 1939.

SARTRE, JEAN-PAUL
French Philosopher and Playwright
Born: Paris, June 21, 1905
Died: Paris, April 15, 1980

Education: Graduate of École Normale Supérieure, 1929
Positions, Honors: Before World War II, schoolmaster in the provinces, later playwright and philosophical writer; Nobel Prize in literature, 1964 (refused); founder of monthly *Les temps modernes*, 1945

Sartre introduced into France the theories of phenomenology and existentialism of the German philosophers Edmund Husserl* and Martin Heidegger. Existential philosophy and the many fictional works and plays that turn on the existentialist theme achieved fame for him.

Of psychological interest are the early philosophical works of Sartre: *L'Imagination* (1936; *Imagination*, 1962), *Esquisse d'une théorie des émotions* (1939; English translation, *The Emotions: Outline of a Theory*, 1962), and *L'Imaginaire* (1940; English translation, *The Psychology of Imagination*, 1950). Sartre analyzed imagination phenomenologically. He saw emotions as a "certain way to apprehend the world." This way is to transform it when it becomes too difficult to deal with, as by changing it through fantasy or escaping from it by fainting.

The main tenets of his philosophy are found in his most important philosophical work, *Being and Nothingness* (*L'Être et le néant*, 1943). Its main concern is the meaning of existence, and Sartre found no reason why humans or the world should exist. Since there is no god, god cannot be the reason either. Consciousness is the main reality, and the awareness of freedom and choice are its main features. Since choice constantly forces decisions, attempts at escaping them are made. There is no way out, however, and such attempts only bring about anxiety and despair.

Being and Nothingness contains a long chapter on existential psychoanalysis. In existential psychoanalysis the patient's value system is disclosed by analyzing his behavior. Such an analysis should reveal the original choice that led to the present value system. This choice, when presented to the patient, is recognized by the patient. If the patient denies it, the analyst must work toward uncovering the original true choice and the reason for the patient's self-deception, or being in "bad faith." Sartre's most direct influence on psychology is through existential psychoanalysis.

Biographies: M. Cranston, *Sartre*, 1962; F. Jameson, *Sartre: The Origins of a Style*, 1961; P. Thody, *Jean-Paul Sartre*, 1960; *EB*, 19; *NYT*, Apr. 16, 1980.

SCHEERER, MARTIN
German-American Psychologist
Born: New York, New York, June 10, 1900
Died: Lawrence, Kansas, October 19, 1961
Highest Degree: Ph.D. in psychology, University of Hamburg, 1927
Positions: 1930-33, University of Hamburg; 1936-37, University of Louisville; 1937-40, Columbia University; 1940-41, Wells College; 1941-42, Brooklyn College; 1942-47, City College of New York; 1947-48, New School for Social Research; 1948-61 University of Kansas

Influenced by Gestalt theory, Scheerer wrote *Die Lehre von der Gestalt* in

1931. He wrote a few papers, and his major contribution was the development, with Kurt Goldstein* who was also influenced by the Gestalt theory, of several tests of concept formation that were incorporated in 1941 in a series of five diagnostic tests: Goldstein-Scheerer Cube Test, Weigl-Goldstein-Scheerer Color Form Sorting Test, Goldstein-Scheerer Stick Test, Gelb-Goldstein Sorting Test, and Goldstein-Scheerer Object Sorting Test.

Biographies: C. Scheerer, *Bull. Menninger Clin.*, 1966, *30*, 85-86; *NYT*, 1961, Oct. 20, 30:4.

SCHELLING, FRIEDRICH WILHELM JOSEPH VON
German Philosopher
Born: Leonberg, Baden-Württemberg, January 27, 1775
Died: Bad Ragaz, St. Gallen, Switzerland, August 20, 1854
Highest Degree: Master's in philosophy, University of Tübingen, 1792: Master's in theology, University of Tübingen, 1795; studied natural sciences and medicine at Leipzig, 1796-98
Positions: 1798-1803, University of Jena; 1803-6, University of Würzburg; 1806-27, in the service of the Bavarian state, Munich; 1827-41, University of Munich; 1841-45, University of Berlin

In his *Ideen zu einer Philosophie der Natur* (1797) and other writings, Schelling expressed the ideas that influenced some of the fundamental conceptualizations of the analytical psychology of C. G. Jung*. Schelling's philosophy of nature had a widespread influence among educated men, such as Johannes Müller* but also provoked violent reaction from those who subscribed to a monistic and materialistic view of nature, such as Helmholtz* and Du Bois-Reymond*. Schelling treated the problem of nature in terms of consciousness. His thesis was that the spiritual and the physical are only seemingly a pair of opposites. In reality they are two different manifestations of the absolute and specifically the manifestations of force: attraction is objective, repulsion is subjective. The spiritual is the invisible form of the absolute and also the principle of life in all nature, both of the macrocosm and the microcosm in individual beings. Duality and opposition is the general law of nature. The unconscious is the source of all ideas. It exists everywhere, and only the upper layers of the mental world exist on the conscious level. The myth is the concrete manifestation of the unconscious and semiconscious forces of the spiritual world.

Biographies: E. Bréhier, *Schelling*, 1912; K. Fischer, *Schellings Leben, Werke und Lehre*, 1897; H. J. Sandkühler, *Friedrich Wilhelm Joseph Schelling*, 1970; *ADB*, 31; *CE*, 12; *DSB*, 12; *EJ*, 14; *EUI*, 54; *Grande*, 29; *Nouvelle*, 43.

SCHILLER, JOHANN CHRISTOPHER FRIEDRICH
German Dramatist and Poet
Born: Marbach, Baden-Württemberg, November 10, 1759
Died: Weimar, Thuringia, May 9, 1805
Education: Studied medicine at Karlsakademie, Stuttgart, graduating in 1780

Positions: 1780-82, military surgeon; 1782-89, supported by admirers; 1790-1805, supported by various rulers of German states

Schiller, one of the greatest German poets, developed a typology of characters in his *Ueber naive und sentimentalische Dichtung* (1795-96). He recognized at least two major and opposing ways of viewing the world, or psychological functions (feeling/sensation and thinking), not only in the poet but in people in general. C. G. Jung* worked out Schiller's typology in his *Psychological Types*. More generally and philosophically Schiller's influence may be seen in Dewey*, Dilthey*, James*, Marx*, and Nietzsche*.

Biographies: K. Berger, *Schiller: Sein Leben und seine Werke*, 2 vols., 1905; E. Kuhnemann, *Schiller*, 2 vols., 1912; J. Minor, *Schiller: Sein Leben und seine Werke*, 1890; B. von Wiese, *Friedrich Schiller*, 1959; *ADB*, 31; *CE*, 12; *Chalmers*, 27; *EP*, 7; *EUI*, 54; *Grande*, 29; *Jewish*, 9; *Nouvelle*, 43.

SCHLOSBERG, HAROLD

American Psychologist
Born: Brooklyn, New York, January 3, 1904
Died: Providence, Rhode Island, August 5, 1964
Highest Degree: Ph.D. in psychology, Princeton University, 1928
Positions: 1928-64, Brown University; 1953-64, consultant to Surgeon General, U.S. Army

Schlosberg worked at first in the area of learning and conditioning and then made a major contribution in the area of emotion. In 1938 R. S. Woodworth* had developed a scale of emotions from judgments of posed photographs. Schlosberg used Woodworth's scale in 1941 and concluded that emotions vary along two bipolar dimensions: pleasantness-unpleasantness and attention-rejection. He then noticed that if these dimensions were placed at right angles to each other, photographs of posed emotions could be placed, according to their ratings, in an oval surface, with the bipolar axes dividing it into four quadrants (1952). In 1954 Schlosberg added a third dimension, intensity, making the surface of emotions into a cone, with sleep at its apex.

Woodworth wrote the first edition of his *Experimental Psychology* (1938) alone. He invited Schlosberg to be a coauthor of the 1954 edition. Their work became one of the great texts in American psychology, and for the next fifteen to twenty years most American psychologists were being exposed to it in some way. Schlosberg wrote about seventy papers on a variety of psychological subjects: conditioning, motivation, emotion, perception, play, laboratory experiments in an introductory psychology course, and others.

Biographies: J. W. Kling, *Psychol. Rep.*, 1965, *17*, 473-474; C. Pfaffman, *Amer. J. Psychol.*, 1965, *78*, 148-152; *IESS*, 18; *NYT*, 1964, Aug. 6, 29:5; *PR*, 3; *Who Was Who in America*, 4.

SCHNEIERLA, THEODORE C.
American Psychologist
Born: Bay City, Michigan, July 23, 1902
Died: New York, New York, August 20, 1968
Highest Degree: S.D., University of Michigan, 1928
Positions: 1927-46, New York University, 1945-58, adjunct professor; 1942-68, associate curator and curator, Department of Animal Behavior, American Museum of Natural History; 1947-68, adjunct professor, City University New York

Schneierla was the foremost representative of comparative psychology in America between 1930 and 1968. He was the chief opponent of Konrad Lorenz on theoretical questions. Schneierla stressed the impossibility of separating instinct from learning, urging the use of the terms *maturation* and *experience*, even though these too, he believed, could not be studied separately but were only conceptual conveniences. Schneierla's second basic idea was that of integrative levels of behavioral organization. These levels differentiate phylogenetic levels of animals in that qualitatively different behaviors may be observed under the same circumstances in two animal species. Schneierla's most significant contribution was his "biphasic A-W theory," which describes all existing behavior as well as the evolution and ontogeny of behavior in terms of approach and withdrawal with respect to points in the environment, weak stimulation from such points producing approach, strong stimulation producing withdrawal.

Schneierla's most important empirical observations were those on the behavior of the army ants, a subject that he began to work on early in his career (*Learning and Orientation in Ants*, 1928). With N. R. F. Maier, Schneierla wrote his most influential book, *Principles of Animal Psychology* (1935). A classic text of comparative psychology, it is still being used, and most contemporary comparative psychologists have been brought up on it. In 1938 Schneierla and L. C. Crafts published *Recent Experiments in Psychology*, and L. R. Aronson and others edited and published posthumously *Selected Writings of T. C. Schneierla* (1972).
Biographies: *NYT*, 1968, Aug. 21, 42:1.

SCHOPENHAUER, ARTHUR
German Philosopher
Born: Danzig, East Prussia, February 22, 1788
Died: Frankfurt am Main, September 20, 1860
Highest Degree: Ph.D. in philosophy, University of Berlin, 1813
Positions: 1820-22, University of Berlin

Schopenhauer contributed to psychology a color-vision theory and a philosophical viewpoint that influenced a considerable number of psychologists, such as William James*. An admirer of Goethe*, Schopenhauer emulated him in preparing a manuscript about vision and color (*Über das Sehen und die Farben*, 1816) and sending it to Goethe for approval. Before Hermann Helmholtz* and

Ewald Hering*, his theory and those of Johann Goethe and Thomas Young* were the only color-vision theories extant.

Philosophically, Schopenhauer was influenced mainly by Kant*, but he disdained Hegel*. In his principal philosophical work, *Die Welt als Wille und Vorstellung* (1819), Schopenhauer argued that a human being is more than is revealed to the senses, that it is more than just a phenomenal object. Humans are also aware that their actions are the result of their will. A person's activity can be explained ultimately as the manifestation of a force, and so can everything else in nature. The best analogy of this force is the will. Will thus becomes the most fundamental metaphysical truth. It also makes for determinism, since all human behavior is the expression of the will, and the will is fixed. Self-realization is the result of observing one's own actions, but since these actions are determined, so is one's self-concept. There is no freedom to be this or that: one is what one is because of one's own unalterable will. In humans, will reaches a conscious form. Conscious motives, however, do not explain all behavior. There are also unconscious motives, and secondary motives are sometimes invented to explain one's unacceptable behavior that has been actually caused by other motives. This view relates Schopenhauer to Sigmund Freud*, with whom unconscious motivation becomes a major tenet of psychoanalysis.

Biographies: A. Bossert, *Schopenhauer als Mensch und Philosoph*, 1904; F. C. Coplestone, *Arthur Schopenhauer: Philosopher of Pessimism*, 1947; W. Ebstein, *Arthur Schopenhauer: Seine wirklichen und vermeintlichen Krankheiten*, 1907; K. Fischer, *Schopenhauer's Leben, Werke und Lehre*, 1898; P. Gardiner, *Schopenhauer*, 1971; A. Hübscher, *Arthur Schopenhauer: Ein Lebensbild*, 1949; V. J. McGill, *Schopenhauer: Pessimist and Pagan*, 1931; K. A. Pfeiffer, *Schopenhauer*, 1925; H. Richert, *Schopenhauer: Seine Persönlichkeit, seine Lehre, seine Bedeutung*, 1920; W. Schneider, *Schopenhauer: Eine Biographie*, 1937; J. Volkelt, *Arthur Schopenhauer: Seine Persönlichkeit, seine Lehre, sein Glaube*, 1923; W. Wallace, *Life of Arthur Schopenhauer*, 1890; T. Whittaker, *Schopenhauer*, 1909; H. Zimmern, *Schopenhauer: His Life and Philosophy*, 1932; *EB*, 19; *EP*, 7.

SCHUMANN, FRIEDRICH
German Psychologist
Born: Hildsheim, Lower Saxony, June 16, 1863
Died: Frankfurt am Main, January 10, 1940
Highest Degree: Ph.D. in physics, University of Göttingen, 1885
Positions: 1885-94, University of Göttingen; 1894-1905, University of Berlin; 1905-10, University of Zurich; 1910-28, University of Frankfurt

In addition to studying physics, Schumann also studied psychology under G. E. Müller* at Göttingen. He conducted experiments and published with Müller studies on psychophysics, memory, sensory psychology, and perception. He constructed an apparatus for studying time perception and a tachistoscope and, in general, influenced Müller to become a real experimenter. With Müller,

Schumann was a cofounder of the Gesellschaft für experimentelle Psychologie and, when Ebbinghaus* died, took over the editorship of the *Zeitschrift für Psychologie*.

During the early 1900s Schumann conducted a large number of experiments that make him a direct precursor of the founders of the Gestalt school of psychology (Beiträge zur Analyse der Gesichtswahenehmungen, *Zeitschrift für Psychologie*, published between 1900 and 1904). The experiments were phenomenological but represented a definite advance over the speculations of the form-quality school. Always relating his results to the physical properties of the stimuli and to the factor of attention, Schumann arrived at a number of conclusions that later became basic Gestalt laws: attention may either join the parts of a figure into a whole or else emphasize a part so that the perception of the whole becomes secondary; incomplete figures tend to be perceived as complete; nearness, as well as equal distances among the components makes for the grouping of visual components into larger wholes; vertical symmetry favors perceptual connectedness; ambiguous figures tend to be seen as "good" figures; properties of figures, such as grouping and organization, have their origin in both central and stimulus factors. In spite of his contributions to Gestalt psychology, Schumann is not counted among its founders since he made no attempt to go beyond his empirical findings and fit them into a theoretical framework. *Biographies*: W. Metzger, *Z. Psychol.*, 1940, *148*, 1-18; *EUI*, 54; *PR*, 3.

SCOTT, WALTER DILL
American Psychologist
Born: Cooksville, Illinois, May 1, 1869
Died: Evanston, Illinois, September 23, 1955
Highest Degree: Ph.D. in psychology, University of Leipzig, 1900, under W. Wundt*
Positions, Honors: 1901-39, Northwestern University, until 1920, taught psychology, since 1920, president; 1912-21, president, The Scott Co., a personnel consulting firm; 1916-17, director of salesmanship research, Carnegie Institute of Technology; president, American Psychological Association, 1919; chairman, American Council on Education, 1927; two honorary degrees; other honors

Although Scott received his degree from Wundt, he developed into an industrial and business psychologist with an emphasis on motivation; his first book was *Die Psychologie der Triebe* (1900). He wrote a first text about the psychology of advertising (*Theory of Advertising*, 1903), followed by a series of other books about business and psychology: *Psychology of Public Speaking* (1907), *Psychology of Advertising* (1908), *Increasing Human Efficiency* (1911), *Influencing Men in Business* (1911), *The Psychology of Agreement and Suggestion* (1911), *Aids in Selecting Salesmen* (1916), *Psychology of Advertising in Theory and Practice* (1921), *Science and Common Sense in Working with Men* (1921), *Personnel Management* (1941). Scott was the author or coauthor of a number of other books. Between 1917 and 1919 he introduced the use of rating scales in the army, contributed to the production of the ten volumes of *Personnel Specifications*, and coauthored the two volumes of *The Personnel System of the U.S. Army* and *The Personnel Manual*. Scott was the director of the Committee on Classification of Personnel in the army, appointed by the secretary of war and consisting of ten psychologists. The committee prepared an army personnel classification system, for which service Scott received the Distinguished Service Medal.

Biographies: R. C. Clothier, *Science*, 1956, *123*, 408-409; L. W. Ferguson, *Heritage Indust. Psychol.*, 1963, No. 5, 53-66; J. Z. Jacobson, *Scott of Northwestern*, 1951; E. K. Strong, Jr., *Amer. J. Psychol.*, 1955, *68*, 682-683; *NCAB*, 42; *PR*, 3; *Who Was Who in America*, 3.

SCRIPTURE, EDWARD WHEELER
American Psychologist
Born: Mason, New Hampshire, May 21, 1864
Died: Henleaze, near Bristol, England, July 31, 1945
Highest Degree: Ph.D. in psychology, University of Leipzig, 1891, under W. Wundt*; M.D., University of Munich, 1906
Positions: 1891, Clark University; 1892-1903, Yale University; 1915-29, Columbia University Medical Center; 1929-33, University of Vienna; 1933-?, private practice, London

A year after receiving a doctorate from Wundt, Scripture became one of the cofounders of the American Psychological Association. At Yale he took over the direction of the psychological laboratory from G. T. Ladd* and, during the decade he was there, produced enough research to fill a yearly volume of articles (Scripture's complete bibliography contains 225 entries). He did much of the work himself, especially in the areas of reaction-time measurement and hearing. In the latter area he invented a device (the strobilion) that made the human voice visible. Also at Yale he wrote *The New Psychology* (1897). The "new psychology" was the scientific, experimental, physiological psychology of Helmholtz*, Fechner*, and Wundt*, and Scripture's label came into general use. Scripture's interest gradually turned from psychology to phonetics, speech, and speech defects. He left not only psychology but America to work in Europe, where he held a number of nonpsychological appointments, including the professorship of experimental phonetics at the University of Vienna for ten years. He wrote a number of papers and five books about phonetics and speech.

Biographies: M. F. Berry, *Amer. Speech & Hearing Ass.*, 1965, *7*, 8-9; E. G. Boring, *Amer. J. Psychol.*, 1965, *78*, 314-317; M. M. Sokal, In J. Brozek & L. J. Pongratz (Eds.), *Historiography of Modern Psychology*, 1980, 256-278; *Biog. Lex.*; *EUI*, 54; *HPA*, 3; *NCAB*, 10; *PR*, 3; *Who Was Who in America*, 4.

SEASHORE, CARL EMIL
American Psychologist
Born: Mörlunda, Sweden, January 28, 1866
Died: Lewiston, Idaho, October 16, 1949

Highest Degree: Ph.D. in psychology, Yale University, 1895, under E. W. Scripture*

Positions, Honors: 1897-1938, from assistant professor of philosophy to dean, Graduate College (from 1908), University of Iowa; president, American Psychological Association, 1911; three honorary degrees

At Iowa Seashore established a psychological laboratory and the second psychological clinic in the United States. He was also instrumental in promoting the Iowa Child Welfare Research Station. He was its general supervisor until his death. During his time the station issued some one thousand publications. Seashore wrote a number of general psychology texts, such as *Elementary Experiments in Psychology* (1908), *Psychology in Daily Life* (1918), *Introduction to Psychology* (1923), and *Pioneering in Psychology* (1923). He also contributed in the area of the psychology of speech and phonetics and in educational psychology. He was dean of the Graduate College at Iowa and helped to identify and measure special talent and scholastic aptitude. He produced the Iowa Placement Examinations, the Meier-Seashore Art Judgment Test (1930, with N. C. Meier), and the Seashore Measures of Musical Talents (rev. ed. 1939; preceded by his 1919 Psychology of Musical Talent). The Seashore Measures of Musical Talents is his best known and most widely used test. The recorded test consists of subtests measuring pitch, loudness, rhythm, time, and timbre discrimination, and tonal memory. Seashore also produced a complete, classic treatise on the psychology of music, *Psychology of Music* (1938), his lifelong interest. In this field Seashore's book finds few competitors even today.

Biographies: M. Metfessel, *Science*, 1950, *111*, 713-717; J. P. Porter, *Amer. J. Psychol.*, 1937, *50*, 218-228; D. Starch, *J. Educ. Psychol.*, 1950, *41*, 217-218; G. D. Stoddard, *Amer. J. Psychol.*, 1950, *63*, 456-462; J. Tiffin, *Psychol. Rev.*, 1950, *57*, 1-2; *Biog. Mem.*, 29; *HPA*, 1; *IESS*, 14; *NCAB*, A; *NYT*, 1949, Oct. 18, 27:2; *PR*, 3.

SECHENOV, IVAN MIKHAĬLOVICH

Russian Physiologist

Born: Teplyĭ Stan, Simbirsk, Russia, August 1, 1829

Died: Moscow, November 2, 1905

Highest Degree: M.D., Military-Medical Academy, St. Petersburg, 1860

Positions: 1860-70, Military-Medical Academy, St. Petersburg; 1870-76, University of Odessa; 1876-88, University of St. Petersburg; 1888-1901, University of Moscow (Moscow State University)

After obtaining his medical degree Sechenov studied at Berlin and Heidelberg, worked on the inhibition of reflexes by the cortex, and, as a result of this work, was soon attempting to show that all mental processes have a physiological basis, namely, that they are reflex activity, either innate or learned. Three years after receiving his doctorate, he wrote his most important work, *Refleksy golovnogo mozga* (1863; English translation, *Reflexes of the Brain*). He implied that learned reflexes arise through association, contiguity playing the most important role.

Sechenov considered thinking to be an inhibited reflex, or a reflex in which the motor-response portion was missing. In the second edition (1903) of his *Elements of Thought* (1878) he argued that the muscles are not only organs of activity but also organs of cognition. Muscular activity is thus the beginning of thought, and the muscle sense is Sechenov's solution to the philosopher's problem of objective reference. In general, he argued that mental life, being a function of the nervous system, is a physiological problem, that any mental activity expresses itself in some form of bodily activity, and that psychological problems ought to be studied by physiologists by studying the reflexes (*Who Must Investigate the Problem of Psychology and How*, 1873). Sechenov developed an objective psychology that was materialistic, reflexological, and associationistic and that stressed to the extreme the role of the environment in behavioral development.

Sechenov's views were very similar to those of Pavlov*, except that Pavlov demonstrated experimentally the truth of Sechenov's theoretical contentions. In the 1860s, though, Sechenov was ahead of everyone in physiological thinking in his assignment to the reflexes of a major role in cognitive processes. To the czarist autocratic regime he was too much of a materialist, and an attempt was made to suppress his book. His views were, however, accepted by the educated class.

Sechenov was the major figure in the rise of Russian physiology. He introduced, for instance, bioelectric research in Russia and founded a physiological laboratory in St. Petersburg. His views played an important role in the development of Pavlov's thinking, although Pavlov did not study under Sechenov and did not observe conditioning in dogs until the 1890s. Sechenov's influence outside of Russia during his lifetime was small. In the United States his works were not translated until the mid–twentieth century.

Biographies: N. Isschlondsky, *J. Nerv. Ment. Dis.*, 1958, *126*, 367-391; K. Koshtoyants, In I. M. Sechenov, *Selected Physiological and Psychological Works*, Moscow, n.d., pp. 7-27; I. M. Sechenov, *Autobiographical Notes*, 1965; M. G. Yaroshevsky, In B. B. Wolman (Ed.), *Historical Roots of Contemporary Psychology*, pp. 77-110; *DSB*, 12; *IESS*, 14; *Great Soviet Encyclopedia*.

SÉGUIN, EDOUARD

French-American Psychiatrist
Born: Clamecy, Nièvre, France, January 20, 1812
Died: Mt. Vernon, New York, October 28, 1880
Education: No university education: honorary M.D., University of the City of New York, 1861
Positions, 1846-50, head, Institution for the Training of the Feeble-Minded, Paris; 1850-80, School for Defectives, Randall's Island, New York

Séguin was a pioneer in the mental-retardation area. When Itard* was trying to improve the behavior of the wild boy of Aveyron, Séguin was his assistant. He continued Itard's efforts with mentally defective individuals. In 1839, a year after Itard's death, Séguin opened the first school for the feeble-minded in the world. Very soon other such schools opened in other countries using Séguin's method of training. Séguin based his training and educational method on physiological considerations, stressing especially the development of the sense organs. In his major work, *Traitement moral, hygiène et éducation des idiots* (1846), Séguin stated the main points of the training of the feeble-minded. Although such individuals cannot be brought to a level of normal intelligence, their existing capacities may be developed through the use of the "physiological method," or the stimulation of their senses and neuromuscular systems by the use of bright colors, repeated sounds, and muscular exercises requiring balance. Séguin went to the United States in 1848. He was one of the organizers of the School for Defectives at Randall's Island, New York, and for two decades worked on the improvement of training methods for mentally retarded children and for the establishment of special schools for them. In 1866 he published his second major work on the training of the feeble-minded, *Idiocy and Its Treatment by the Physiological Method.*

Biographies: C. L. Dana, *Ann. Med. Hist.*, 1924, *6*, 475-479; S. P. Davies, *Encycl. Soc. Sci.*, 1934, *13*, 647; H. Holman, *Seguin and His Physiological Method of Education*, 1914; L. Kanner, *Amer. J. Ment. Defic.*, 1960, *65*, 2-10; M. E. Talbot, *Amer. J. Ment. Defic.*, 1967-1968, *72*, 184-189; *EUI*, 54; Hirsch, *Biog. Lex.*; *NCAB*, 15; *NYT*, 1880, Oct. 29, 2:3; Pagel, *Biographisches Lexikon.*

SELYE, HANS
Austrian-Canadian Physiologist
Born: Vienna, January 26, 1907
Died: Montreal, October 16, 1982
Highest Degree: M.D., German University of Prague, 1929, Ph.D. in chemistry, 1931; D.Sc., McGill University, 1942
Positions, Honors: 1931-32, Johns Hopkins University; 1932-44, McGill University; 1945-82, professor and director, Institute of Experimental Medicine and Surgery, University of Montreal; founder, International Institute of Stress, Montreal, 1977; editorship of several journals; sixteen honorary degrees, numerous prizes, awards, medals, honorary memberships in scientific organizations, and honorary citizenships

For his research on stress, Selye became one of medicine's most honored individuals. He introduced the term *stress* from physics to describe the body's response to both physical and emotional stressors—cold, pain, anger, work pressures. He first presented the concept of stress and some of the evidence for it in 1936. Although it was a revolutionary idea at the time, he was able to gain acceptance for it by relating it to experimentally demonstrated changes in the endocrine system. Changes in the endocrine system, especially in the secretion of adrenal hormones, in response to stress determine the three stages of the general adaptation syndrome: the alarm reaction, the adaptive stage, and, if stress persists, the exhaustion stage. Arthritis, heart, and other "civilized" disease he attributed to the adaptive stage, during which stress leads to "overadaptation" and overproduction of adrenal hormones. Certain amounts of stress and certain kinds of stress, called "eustress" by Selye, are beneficial in that they help maintain the organism at a level of arousal and activity appropriate for its well-being.

Selye's work on stress was the most original contribution to psychosomatic medicine since its inception. It resulted in more than sixteen hundred technical medical articles and thirty-three books about the endocrine system, stress, and reaction to stress. Among them are a six-volume *Encyclopedia of Endocrinology* (1943-46), *Stress* (1950), *The Story of the Adaptation Syndrome* (1952), *The Stress of Life* (1956), *Hormones and Resistance* (1971), *Stress Without Distress* (1974; translated into a dozen languages), *Stress, Health and Disease* (1976), and *The Stress of My Life* (1977). Many of his books have been translated into several languages, and the work on stress is being carried on by many scientists throughout the world.

Biographies: *Psychology Today*, March 1978; *American Men and Women of Science*, Physical and Biological Sciences, 15th ed., vol. 6; *Contemporary Authors*, vol. 5-8 R; *Current Biography*, 1953; *NYT*, Oct. 22, 1982, B 10:5-6; *Who's Who in America*, 1982-83.

SELZ, OTTO
German Psychologist
Born: Munich, February 14, 1881
Died: Auschwitz, August 27, 1943
Education: Ph.D. in psychology, University of Munich, 1909, under T. Lipps*
Positions: 1912-23, University of Bonn; 1923-33, Handelshochschule, Mannheim, vice-chancellor since 1929; editorial work, *Archiv für die gesamte Psychologie* and *Psychotechnische Zeitschrift*

A member of the Würzburg school of psychology, Selz studied the organized thinking process (*Uber die Gesetze des geordneten Denkverlaufs*, 1913; *Zur Psychologie des produktiven Denkens und des Irrtums*, 1922; *Die Gesetze der produktiven und reproduktiven Geistestätigkeit*, 1924). In these books and some thirty papers and monographs about productive thinking, cognition, and Gestalt psychology, Selz stressed the notion that in thinking, active processing takes place in the mind, and he called for a psychology of thinking that would be concerned with processes rather than content. In opposition to the constellation theory of G. E. Müller*, Selz theorized that responses are specific to the structured complex of the task. He emphasized that thinking is influenced by the thinker's set of "anticipatory schema," a concept similar to that of *Aufgabe*, or task, as used in the Würzburg school.

Biographies: N. H. Fridja & A. D. de Groot (Eds.), *Otto Selz: His Contribution to Psychology*, 1981; H. B. Seebohm, "Otto Selz: Ein Beitrag zur Geschichte der Psychologie," Ph.D. dissertation, University of Heidelberg, 1970; *CE*, 13; *EJ*, 14; *PR*, 3.

SHAND, ALEXANDER FAULKNER
English Psychologist
Born: London, 1858
Died: London, January 6, 1936
Highest Degree: A.M., Cambridge University, 1881
Positions, Honors: Barrister-at-law, admitted to the bar, 1887; no academic
appointments; honorary LL.D., St. Andrews University

Shand wrote some fifteen papers about emotion, attention, will, and character,
as well as some papers in philosophy. His most important work was the book
The Foundation of Character. First published in 1914, it went through several
editions. Shand saw the foundation of character in the relation of sentiment to
emotion. He had earlier (1896) made the distinction between sentiment and
emotion. Emotions arise from and accompany motivated behavior but, with
repeated experience, may acquire functional autonomy. Sentiments are attitudinal
systems and include emotions and desires. Sentiments, emotions, and desires
are the first constituents of character. Shand's definition of sentiment acquired
currency almost immediately, and was being used by psychologists as well as
sociologists and philosophers. He was one of the founders of the British Psychological Society in 1901.
Biographies: B. Edgell, *Brit. J. Psychol.*, 1947, *37*, 113-132; L. S. Hearnshaw,
Bull. Brit. Psychol. Soc., 1962, *46*, 2-10; C. S. Myers, *Brit. J. Psychol.*, 1935-
1936, *26*, 323-324; G. F. Stout, *Proc. Brit. Acad.*, 1936, *22*, 401-407; *EUI*,
55; *PR*, 3.

SHELDON, WILLIAM HERBERT
American Psychologist
Born: Warwick, Rhode Island, November 19, 1898
Died: Cambridge, Massachusetts, September 16, 1977
Highest Degree: Ph.D. in psychology, University of Chicago, 1925; M.D.,
University of Chicago, 1933
Positions: 1923-24, instructor in psychology, University of Texas, Austin; 1924-
27, instructor, assistant professor of psychology, University of Chicago; 1927-
30, assistant professor of psychology, University of Wisconsin; 1934-36, trav-
eling fellow in psychiatry; 1936-38, professor of psychology, University of
Chicago; 1938-42, research associate in anthropology and lecturer in psychology,
Harvard University; 1946, director, Constitution Clinic, Presbyterian Hospital,
New York City; 1946-58, director, Constitution Clinic and Laboratory, College
of Physicians and Surgeons, Columbia University; 1951-70, clinical professor
of medicine, director of Constitution Clinic, University of Oregon Medical School,
1970, emeritus professor; 1951-77, director, Oregon follow-up studies in constitutional medicine; 1951-77, director of research, Biological Humanics Foundation, Cambridge, Massachusetts; 1956-77, research associate, University of
California, Institute of Human Development, Berkeley; 1961-77, attending chief
of research facility, Rockland State Hospital, Orangeburg, New York

Of the various attempts to link personality and body build, such as that of Kretschmer's*, Sheldon's constitutional psychology was most thoroughly grounded in empirical research. Most of Sheldon's professional life was dedicated to the identification and description of the dimensions of the human physique (*The Varieties of Human Physique*, 1940, with S. S. Stevens* and W. B. Tucker; *Atlas of Men*, 1954, with C. W. Dupertius and E. McDermott), the study of the relationship between physique and personality traits (*The Varieties of Temperament*, 1942, with S. S. Stevens), and the study of the relationship between physique and delinquency (*Varieties of Delinquent Youth*, 1949, with E. M. Hartl and E. McDermott) and physique and psychopathology.

Sheldon's description of body types (somatotypes) is based on careful measurements taken from the photographs of thousands of individuals. The three primary components of physique established by Sheldon were *endomorphy* (soft and rounded appearance), *mesomorphy* (athletic appearance), and *ectomorphy* (linear, thin, lightly muscled appearance), each measured in terms of several components. An individual's *somatotype* is the pattern of three digits, each varying between 1 and 7, that measure the degree of presence of the three primary components of physique. Thus unlike other constitutional psychologies, Sheldon's is based on continuous measurements.

Longtime observation and rating of individuals on a large number of behavior traits enabled Sheldon to identify three primary components of temperament, each of which correlated highly with one of the three primary components of physique: *viscerotonia* (sociability, love of food and people, joviality), *somatotonia* (love of physical activity, exhibiting masculine prowess), and *cerebrotonia* (desire for isolation, introversion). Sheldon theorized that the high correlation between physique and behavior could be attributed to the rewards that an individual of a particular physique may experience as a consequence of particular behaviors, as well as to culturally reinforced conformity to social expectations about what kind of behavior should be forthcoming from an individual of a given physique.

Sheldon's observations of mental patients over a period of years led to the description of mental disorders in terms of three primary dimensions: the affective, the paranoid, and the heboid. He found that endomorphy and mesomorphy correlated with the affective psychiatric component, mesomorphy alone with the paranoid component, and ectomorphy with the heboid (extreme withdrawal) component. Sheldon's eight-year study of delinquency led to parallel findings: mesomorphy was more broadly represented among delinquents than endomorphy, ectomorphs being a small minority. Studies of constitutional psychology performed by others have confirmed Sheldon's basic findings, although the level of correlation between physique and temperament has not been as high as that found by Sheldon.

In addition to the four volumes in the Human Constitution Series, Sheldon wrote two other books that have some bearing on psychology. His first book (*Psychology and the Promethean Will*, 1936) and his last one (*Prometheus*

Revisited, 1975) are essays about a humanistic substitute for religion, in which Sheldon proposed "to merge religion with a biologically grounded social psychiatry."

Biographies: C. S. Hall & G. Lindzey, *Theories of Personality*, 1957; *Contemporary Authors*, vol. 25/28, 1st rev.; *NYT*, 1977, Sept. 19, 38:6; *Who's Who in America*, 39th ed., vol. 2.

SHERRINGTON, SIR CHARLES SCOTT

English Neurophysiologist
Born: London, November 27, 1857
Died: Eastbourne, Sussex, March 4, 1952
Highest Degree: M.B., University of Cambridge, 1885
Positions, Honors: 1887-93, fellow, lecturer, St. Thomas Hospital, London; 1891-95, professor of pathology, University of London; 1895-1913, professor of physiology, University of Liverpool; 1913-35, professor of physiology, Oxford University; president, Royal Society, 1920-25; twenty-two honorary degrees; Nobel Prize in Medicine, 1932; knighted, 1922; many other honors

Sherrington was a pioneer and leading researcher in most areas of neurophysiology. Much of what is known today about neurophysiology may be traced to his work. The areas in which Sherrington did his most significant work were inhibition; the physiology of synapses; reflexes; activity of the cerebral cortex, especially the mapping of the motor area; functions of the inner ear; and reciprocal innervation (reflex behavior of antagonistic muscles and how this results in, for instance, upright posture without conscious participation). He coined terms such as *synapse, synaptic, perikaryion, proprioceptive, final common path, neurone pool, recruitment, occlusion*, and *subliminal fringe*. The present concept of the integrative and coordinating role that the nervous system plays in the economy of the organism was stressed by Sherrington (*The Integrative Action of the Nervous System*, 1906). He considered the reflex not in isolation but as part of a functioning whole in which it may be controlled by higher levels of neural functioning. *The Integrative Action of the Nervous System* was the most influential and stimulating volume in the history of physiology.

Sherrington supported psychology by permitting psychologists to work in his Liverpool laboratory as researchers as well as lecturers, by lending his prestige to it and by his work on sensory physiology (color vision, flicker fusion, tactual and muscular sensitivity—he demonstrated the presence of receptors in the muscles that, in turn, helped to explain the loss of coordination of motor acts in certain nervous disorders in terms of reduced feedback from the muscles).

Biographies: E. D. Adrian, R. Granit, & W. Penfield, *Nature*, 1952, *169*, 688-690; H. C. Cohen, *Sherrington: Physiologist, Philosopher and Poet*, 1958; R. S. Creed, *Brit. J. Psychol.*, 1953, *44*, 1-4; D. Denny-Brown, *Amer. J. Psychol.*, 1952, *65*, 474-477; A. R. Elridge & W. Penfield, *Arch. Neurol. Psychiat.*, 1935, *34*, 1299-1309; J. F. Fulton, *J. Neurophysiol.*, 1952, *15*, 167-190; R. Granit,

Charles Scott Sherrington: A Biography of the Neurophysiologist, 1967; J. B. Lyons, *Med. Hist.*, 1964, *8*, 122-136; W. Penfield, *Not. Rec. Roy. Soc. London*, 1962, *17*, 163-168; A. Tournay, *J. Psychol. norm. path.*, 1953, *46*, 1-11; *Biog. Lex.*; *DSB*, 12; *EB*, 20; *IESS*, 14; *NYT*, 1952, Mar. 6, 31:3.

SIDIS, BORIS
American Psychologist
Born: Kiev, Ukraine, October 12, 1867
Died: Portsmouth, New Hampshire, October 24, 1923
Highest Degree: Ph.D. in psychology, Harvard University, 1897, under Hugo Münsterberg*; M.D., Harvard University, 1908
Positions: 1896-1901, New York State Hospitals; 1901-4, New York Infirmary for Women and Children; 1904-9, private practice, Boston; 1909-23, Sidis Psychotherapeutic Institute, Portsmouth, New Hampshire; editorial work, *Archives of Neurology and Psychopathology* and *Journal of Abnormal and Social Psychology*

Sidis pioneered in the scientific study of unconsciously motivated behavior in the United States. He disagreed with Sigmund Freud*, emphasizing environmental and social factors in mental disorders. He showed that abnormal behavior involves the same mechanisms as normal behavior, except that the social pattern within which the behavior occurs is different. Sidis thought that the study of the unconscious was important also to sociology because humans are social insofar as they fear and are suggestible.

One of the adjuncts to therapy used by Sidis was the hypnoidal state. He described and named this state (halfway state between sleep and waking, characterized by suggestibility) in 1898 and later used it with patients to gain relief from tension and anxiety, a form of relaxation therapy. Sidis published a number of books, most of them about personality and abnormal behavior, such as *Multiple Personality* (1905, with S. P. Goodhart), *The Psychology of Laughter* (1913), *The Foundations of Normal and Abnormal Psychology* (1914), *Symptomatology, Psychognosis, and Diagnosis of Psychopathic Maladies* (1914), *The Causation and Treatment of Psychopathic Diseases* (1916), and *Nervous Ills, Their Cause and Cure* (1922).
Biographies: L. L. Bernard, *Encycl. Soc. Sci.*, 1934, *14*, 48-49; H. A. Bruce, *J. Abn. Psychol.*, 1923-24, *18*, 274-276; *DAB*, 17; *NCAB*, 24; *NYT*, 1923, Oct. 25, 19:6; *Who Was Who in America*, 1.

SIMON, THÉODORE
French Psychiatrist
Born: Dijon, Côte d'Or, July 10, 1873
Died: Paris, September 4, 1961
Highest Degree: M.D., University of Paris, 1900
Positions: 1899-1901, asylum at Perray-Vaucluse, Paris; 1901-4, Saint-Anne Hospital, Paris; 1904, Dury-les-Amiens and Saint-Anne hospitals, Paris; 1905-

20, Saint-You Hospital, Paris; 1920-30, Perray-Vaucluse colony; 1930-36, Henri-Rousselle Hospital

Simon always had an interest in philosophy and psychology. He initiated a collaboration with Alfred Binet* in 1899 when Binet learned of the ready availability to Simon of child subjects, his patients. Simon joined Binet in producing the world's first intelligence test, the Simon-Binet Test. He wrote with Binet some twenty-eight papers and a book (*Les enfants anormaux*, 1907). Simon failed to develop the Simon-Binet test after Binet's death, but his interest in psychology continued. He devised his own intelligence scale for children below the age of two and a group intelligence scale that was developed at Perray-Vaucluse and called the P.V. In 1912 Simon became president of the Societé Libre Pour L'Étude Psychologique de L'Enfant and editor of the Society's *Bulletin*. The name of the society was later changed to that of Societé Alfred Binet. Through it Simon sought to advance Binet's goal to understand human nature as well as to rectify the overuse and abuse of his intelligence test. Simon was also responsible for creating the first medico-psychological consultation for delinquent children brought before the courts.

Biographies: G. Avanzini, *Rev. belge psychol. pédag.*, 1968, *30*(122), 59-64; I. Rapaport, *Amer. J. Ment. Defic.*, 1962, *67*, 367-368; T. H. Wolf, *Alfred Binet*, 1973; T. H. Wolf, *Amer. Psychologist*, 1961, *16*, 245-248.

SMALL, WILLARD STANTON

American Psychologist

Born: North Truro, Massachusetts, August 24, 1870

Died: South Weymouth, Massachusetts, January 31, 1943

Highest Degree: Ph.D. in psychology, Clark University, 1900, under E. C. Sanford*

Positions: 1901-2, Michigan State Normal School; 1902-4, State Normal School, Los Angeles; 1904-23, various educational and school administrative positions; 1923-40, dean, College of Education, University of Maryland

In 1901 Small published a paper in which he described the study of the mental processes of the rat by means of a copy of the Hampton Court maze in England. Small's idea was that the behavior of the rat in the maze followed the principles of learning enumerated by E. L. Thorndike*. From then on both the maze technique and the albino rat were used more and more frequently until they became the standard technique and the preferred animal of the American student of animal learning. In Small's opinion the most significant aspect of his work with the rat in the maze was the possibility of translating thinking into motor and sensory terms.

Biographies: *American Men of Science*, 6th ed.; *NYT*, 1943, Feb. 2, 20:2; *PR*, 3; *Who Was Who in America*, 2.

SMITH, ADAM
Scottish Philosopher and Political Economist
Born: Kirkcaldy, Fife, baptized June 5, 1723
Died: Edinburgh, July 17, 1790
Highest Degree: M.A., Oxford University, 1740
Positions: 1751-63, Glasgow University

In *The Theory of Moral Sentiments* (1759) Smith presented a psychology of moral feeling and moral behavior. The basic explanatory concept used by Smith is sympathy: "Whatever is the passion which arises from any object in the person principally concerned, an analogous emotion springs up at the thought of his situation, in the breast of every attentive spectator." It is our conception of the cause of the situation and not the actual situation that we witness that arouses emotion. Sympathy is the major factor that accounts for the existence of social groups.

In his major work *The Wealth of Nations* (1776) Smith built his explanation of economic behavior on a psychological basis also: trade, commerce, exchange of goods, and the resulting institutions are explained in terms of human motives. The utilitarian principle ("the greatest happiness of the greatest number") was first formulated by Smith. It was taken over by Bentham*, who in turn influenced James Mill* and, through the latter, John Stuart Mill*.

Biographies: J. A. Farrer, *Adam Smith*, 1881; R. B. Haldane, *Life of Adam Smith*, 1887; F. W. Hirst, *Adam Smith*, 1904; J. Rae, *Life of Adam Smith*, 1965; D. Stewart, in A. Smith, *Collected Works*, vol. 10, 1971, pp. 2-98; *CE*, 13; *Chalmers*, 28; *DNB*, 18; *EB*, 20; *EP*, 7; *IESS*, 14.

SOCRATES
Greek Philosopher
Born: Ca. 470 B.C., place unknown
Died: Athens, Greece, ca. 399 B.C.
Education: Self-taught
Positions: Teacher of philosophy

Socrates devised a method of sharpening truth and exposing ignorance and falsehood in a dialogue. The Socratic method was designed to bring out the knowledge that resides in each person. Recognition of one's own ignorance results in self-knowledge. This method and its results stood in contrast to the method of the Sophists who insisted that truth was relative and that true knowledge could not be had, and also resulted in the addition of self-knowledge to the total of all knowledge. The Socratic injunction to "know thyself" was to be achieved by the use of introspection. Socrates was thus one of the first systematic users of introspection, a method used later by Plotinus*, St. Augustine*, and, much later, by the first scientific psychologists, such as Wundt* and Külpe*. One truth that Socrates discovered was that the soul is more important than the body, because it enables one to tell good from evil. Socrates was a dualist and was the first philosopher to identify the consciousness of one's existence with the soul. The psychological views of Socrates were recorded by Plato* in his dialogues. His contributions that go beyond the above cannot, however, be distinguished from those of Plato since Socrates himself never wrote anything down.

Biographies: *EP*, 7; *HGP*, 3.

SPALDING, DOUGLAS ALEXANDER
English Biologist
Born: Scotland, ca. 1840
Died: Dunkirk, France, October 31, 1877
Education: Studied law at the University of Aberdeen, qualified as barrister in London
Positions: No academic or research positions

Spalding was the first person to perform animal behavior experiments, thus establishing the experimental study of behavior as a valid method in psychology. He demonstrated how animal behavior could be studied by resorting to isolation and control of experience. His purpose was to study the relative importance of heredity and environment. In the process he established the basic experimental paradigm necessary to study the effects of each separately. He was first to study imprinting. He studied the releasers of instinctive behavior and developmental biology in general. Spalding was first to use the term *behavior* in its present-day psychological sense. He spurned anecdotes and mentalistic constructs, advocating an approach to the study of behavior that was very much like that of John Watson* and B. F. Skinner at a much later date but was very unpopular at the time.

Spalding wrote fourteen papers, most of them about instincts in animals. His very first publication, an 1872 paper about instinct, became so popular that it was reprinted twice in 1873 and its longer version three times that same year. This paper may be considered the first in the experimental study of animal behavior. Had Spalding lived longer he would be recognized as a founder of ethology.

Biographies: P. H. Gray, *J. Gen. Psychol.*, 1962, *67*, 299-307; J. B. S. Haldane, *Brit. J. Anim. Behav.*, 1954, *2*, 1; G. C. Robertson, *Mind*, 1878, *3*, 153-154.

SPEARMAN, CHARLES EDWARD
English Psychologist
Born: London, September 10, 1863
Died: London, September 17, 1945
Highest Degree: Ph.D. in psychology, University of Leipzig, 1904, under W. Wundt*
Positions: 1906-31, University College, London; president, British Psychological Society, 1923-26

Spearman had a late start in psychology, but he compensated for it by the thoroughness of his education (he spent several years in postdoctoral work with

Oswald Külpe* and G. E. Müller* and studying physiology) and the significance of his subsequent contributions. In 1904 he wrote two important papers, one about reliability measurements, the other about the structure of intelligence. By examining the intercorrelations of the scores on various intellectual tasks given schoolchildren he arrived at the conclusion that since most such measures were correlated, a general intelligence factor underlay all intellectual tasks (the *G* factor), while several different specific factors (*s* factors) were involved, each pertaining to its particular task. Spearman theorized that intelligence is made up of these two kinds of factors (the two-factor theory of intelligence).

Spearman contributed not only to the theory of intelligence but also to the extension of the use of correlation measures to infer structures and processes, as well as to the development of the notion of statistical factors. Factor analysis, however, was not developed until the 1930s, and Spearman used a technique known as the "tetrad equation," which he himself developed. Spearman summarized his work in a 1927 book *The Abilities of Man*, in which he also related the *G* and *s* factors to attention, conation, and similar psychological processes. He had always wanted to establish the fundamental laws of psychology. Seeing the scope of the concept of intelligence factors, Spearman wrote an article (in 1930) to show that the *G* concept represented a school to end all schools. The study of intelligence and the development of factor analysis have been closely related ever since, and the question of the structure of intelligence raised by Spearman has not been finally settled yet. Spearman's work in statistics yielded several well-known and widely used statistical measures, such as the Spearman rank-order correlation coefficient, the Spearman-Brown prophecy formula, and the correction for attenuation of the correlation coefficient. In addition to writing *The Abilities of Man*, Spearman wrote *The Nature of Intelligence and the Principles of Cognition* (1923), *Creative Mind* (1931), and *Psychology Down the Ages* (1937).

Biographies: P. B. Ballard, *Brit. J. Educ. Psychol.*, 1946, *16*, 1-4; C. Burt & C. S. Myers, *Psychol. Rev.*, 1946, *53*, 67-71; R. B. Cattell, *J. Pers.*, 1945-46, *14*, 85-92; J. C. Flugel, *Brit. J. Psychol.*, 1946, *37*, 1-6; R. Meili, *Arch. psychol.*, 1946, *31*, 283-286; H. Piéron, *Biotypologie*, 1947, *9*, 1-5; E. L. Thorndike, *Amer. J. Psychol.*, 1945, *58*, 558-560; *DNB*, Suppl. 5, 6; *IESS*, 15; *NYT*, 1945, Sept. 19, 25:5; *PR*, 3.

SPENCE, KENNETH WARTENBE
American Psychologist
Born: Chicago, Illinois, May 6, 1907
Died: Austin, Texas, January 12, 1967
Highest Degree: Ph.D. in psychology, Yale University, 1933, under R. M. Yerkes*
Positions, Honors: 1933-37, NRC fellow, Yerkes Laboratories of Primate Biology, Orange Park, Florida; 1937-38, University of Virginia; 1938-64, Uni-

versity of Iowa; 1964-67, University of Texas; American Psychological Association Distinguished Scientific Contribution Award, 1956; other medals and awards

A neobehavioristic theoretician and experimentalist, Spence first worked on discrimination learning, emphasizing stimulus discrimination and then concentrated on conditioning. He extended Hull's* learning theory and modified some of its postulates. Spence's learning theory was a two-factor theory, involving both classical and instrumental conditioning. In classical conditioning, excitatory potential, $_sE_R$, is increased by two prior intervening variables, habit and drive. Habit is an associative variable and is a function of reinforced trials. The pairing of the conditioned stimulus and the unconditioned stimulus is sufficient to produce an increase in excitatory potential. For instrumental conditioning the contiguity of stimulus and response is all that is necessary to increase habit strength. Here the amount of reinforcement may increase $_sE_R$ without increasing habit strength. Spence's theory differs from Hull's in that for Hull there was only one kind of learning, and habit was a function of reinforcement only. For Spence delay of reward works mainly by affecting the amount of incentive rather than being independent of incentive, as in Hull.

Throughout his career Spence was consistently and persistently engaged in the study of learning and conditioning phenomena, especially the dimensional analysis of conditioning. Spence, like Hull, attempted to formulate a general behavioral theory from the postulates of a learning theory (*Behavior Theory and Conditioning*, 1956). During his stay at Iowa, Spence exercised considerable influence on American psychology through the many (seventy-five) doctoral students who studied under him. The extensive experimental work on anxiety arose from the Iowa laboratory in testing Spence's concept of drive, especially in connection with the Manifest Anxiety Scale developed by Spence's student Janet Taylor. Spence was one of the founders of the Psychonomic Society in 1959.

Biographies: *Amer. Psychologist*, 1957, *12*, 125-128; H. H. Kendler, *Psychol. Rev.*, 1967, *74*, 335-341; H. H. Kendler & J. T. Spence, *Essays in Neobehaviorism: A Memorial Volume to Kenneth W. Spence*, 1971; *NYT*, 1967, Jan. 14, 31:14; *IESS*, 18; *Who Was Who in America*, 4.

SPENCER, HERBERT
English Philosopher
Born: Derby, Derbyshire, April 27, 1820
Died: Brighton, Sussex, December 8, 1903
Education: Self-educated
Positions: Worked as civil engineer, journalist, and writer

Spencer at first accepted the Lamarckian view of evolution and then developed his own, just before the appearance of Charles Darwin's* *Origin of Species*. He espoused Darwin's theory but, unlike Darwin, made the broadest possible generalization of it. Spencer's *Synthetic Philosophy* was an attempt to apply the idea of evolution to all human knowledge. The work appeared in ten volumes, between 1863 and 1893. The two volumes of *The Principles of Psychology*, first published in 1855, were revised several times.

According to Spencer, the course of evolution follows a movement from homogeneity to heterogeneity. As organic life increases in complexity, existence becomes increasingly marked by better adjustment of organisms to external conditions. With increasing complexity and specialization there arises consciousness and, later, increasing differentiation and complexity of consciousness. The constituents of consciousness are "feelings," or the most elementary units of consciousness, and relations between feelings. Emotions and sensations are primary feelings, memories and ideas of emotions and sensations are "ideal" feelings. They are fainter than the primary feelings; besides, although consciousness of sensory impressions is a continuous stream, consciousness of memories is easily disrupted. The feelings of relation are those of coexistence, sequence, and difference. Although the associationists thought of them as the result of association, Spencer made them exist before the formulation of associations. They played a role similar to that assigned them by the Würzburg school, and simplified the working out of associations that created a problem to James Mill*, John Stuart Mill*, and Alexander Bain*. Similarity, vividness, and repetition were the conditions stated by Spencer that furthered the formation of associations.

In Spencer's scheme psychology as a whole is part of biology, because psychology and physiological processes are correlated and behavior is a constant series of adjustments of the organism to the environment. The adjustment theme runs throughout Spencer's discussion. "The survival of the fittest" is a corollary of it and a phrase coined by Spencer. The function of intelligence is the adaptation of the organism to its environment. Intelligence increases in the course of evolution, representing increased flexibility in the use of the feelings of relation. This view of intelligence makes Spencer the forefather of the functionalist school of psychology that was to flourish later in America. Ontogenetically, the growth of intelligence shows itself in increasingly accurate adjustments to the environment and an increasing breadth and complexity of these adjustments. Association in Spencer's thinking becomes part of the evolutionary picture. Often repeated associations become part of the genetic material of the organism and are transmitted to offspring. The process is cumulative, more complex associations evolving from simple ones. Although the postulated transmission was Lamarckian and failed in its validation, Spencer, along with Darwin, by emphasizing the continuity from animals to humans not only in structure but also in psychic functions, was laying the foundation for comparative psychology. As part of his evolutionary psychology, Spencer also anticipated a most important concept in psychology by stating that pleasant associations tend to be repeated and transmitted, and unpleasant ones are abandoned. In a different form this principle later became known in learning theory as the "law of effect."

Biographies: L. L. Bernard, *Monist*, 1921, *31*, 1-35; D. Duncan, *The Life and Letters of Herbert Spencer*, 2 vols., 1908; S. Eisen, *Victorian Stud.*, 1968, *12*, 33-56; H. S. R. Elliot, *Herbert Spencer*, 1917; O. Gaupp, *Herbert Spencer*,

1900; J. D. Y. Peel, *Herbert Spencer: The Evolution of a Sociologist,* 1971; A. S. Pringle-Pattison, *Quart. Rev.,* 1904, *200,* 240-267; J. Royce, *Herbert Spencer,* 1904; H. Spencer, *An Autobiography,* 2 vols., 1904; J. A. Thomson, *Herbert Spencer,* 1906; *DNB,* Suppl. 1, Suppl. D; *DSB,* 12; *EB,* 21; *EP,* 7; *IESS,* 15; *NYT,* 1903, Dec. 9, 8:6.

SPINOZA, BENEDICTUS (or BARUCH) DE
Dutch Philosopher
Born: Amsterdam, November 24, 1632
Died: The Hague, February 20, 1677
Education: No university education
Positions: Lens grinder

To Spinoza psychology was a stepping-stone in the development of a system of ethics, which, in turn, was part of a great metaphysical system. Spinoza developed further the Cartesian system of philosophy and introduced changes and solutions to Cartesian difficulties. Like Descartes*, Spinoza based his metaphysics in the idea of God. Unlike Descartes's, Spinoza's philosophy was based on monistic parallelism, rather than a dualism and interactionism. The only substance is God. Human body and mind are only two aspects of the same reality, God. The modern version of Spinoza's double-aspect theory is the double-language theory, where the same event is described in one language by the subject in terms of his subjective experience and in another by an outside observer of the same event. Spinoza was also completely deterministic. Willing takes place when one thinks of the course of action that is to be followed. The illusion of free willing occurs when there is ignorance of antecedent causes. A corollary of this view is that both body and mind are subject to natural law. One can follow ethical dictates even in the face of complete determinism, because one can improve one's understanding of nature and act in accordance with it. Freedom is acting in the light of necessity.

Everything obeys the fundamental law of nature, which is self-preservation. This endeavor (*conatus*) to persist manifests itself as appetite on the bodily side and as desire on the mental side. Desire plus joy and grief are the primary emotions. When humans strive to achieve a greater understanding, active joy is the accompanying result. Freedom exists only when the emotions are active rather than passive. Freedom is relative: humans are free if they can think clearly, control their environment, and remain in an active state as long as possible. This is difficult because of the dominance of the passive emotions. Freedom is achieved as the causes of the passive emotions are understood.

Although Sigmund Freud* was not directly influenced by him, Spinoza, in his emphasis on striving and the acquisition of emotional freedom through the understanding of emotions, anticipated two cardinal points of psychoanalysis and, in general, qualifies as a forerunner of the dynamic view in psychology. The direct influence of Spinoza on psychology, however, has been slight.

Biographies: B. Alexander, *Spinoza,* 1923; L. Brunschvicg, *Spinoza et ses con-*

temporains, 1923; J. R. Carré, *Spinoza*, 1936; P. L. Couchoud, *Benedict de Spinoza*, 1924; A. Cresson, *Spinoza*, 1940; S. v. Dunin-Borkowski, *Spinoza*, 4 vols., 1933-1936; K. Fischer, *Spinoza's Leben, Werke und Lehre*, 1909; J. Freudenthal, *Die Lebensgeschichte Spinozas*, 1898; J. Freudenthal, *Spinoza: Leben und Lehre*, 1927; M. Gueroult, *Spinoza*, 1968; S. Hampshire, *Spinoza*, 1951; F. Mauthner, *Spinoza: Ein Umriss seines Lebens und Wirkens*, 1921; F. Pollock, *Spinoza: His Life and Philosophy*, 1899 (Reprinted 1936); L. Roth, *Spinoza*, 1929; A. Wolfson, *A Life of Reason*, 1932; *CE*, 13; *Chalmers*, 28; *EB*, 21; *EJ*, 15; *EP*, 7; *IESS*, 15, *Jewish*, 10.

SPITZ, RENE ARPAD

Hungarian-American Psychoanalyst
Born: Hungary, January 29, 1887
Died: Denver, Colorado, September 14, 1974
Highest Degree: M.D., Royal Hungarian University, 1910; M.D., University of Prague, 1932; M.D., New York University, 1940
Positions, Honors: 1933-38, Psychoanalytical Institute, Paris; 1940-43, adjunct psychiatrist, Mount Sinai Hospital, New York City; 1940-56, faculty member, New York Psychoanalytical Institute; 1947-50, visiting professor of psychiatry, City College of New York; 1955-56, visiting clinical professor of psychiatry, Lenox Hill Hospital, New York City; 1956-63, visiting clinical professor of psychiatry, University of Colorado, 1963, professor emeritus; vice-president, New York Psychoanalytical Society, 1950-52

After Sigmund Freud's* death Spitz became one of the foremost representatives of psychoanalysis in the United States. His research focused on the development of social relations in infancy and childhood. His most significant contribution to psychology was an extensive study, published in monographs and papers from 1945 onward, of the development of infants in orphanages of several countries, in which he found high death rates and a condition known as *marasmus*, or *hospitalism*: underdevelopment, apathy, and pining away of otherwise healthy infants in spite of adequate physical care. Although his interpretation (lack of love) of what is now known to be the result of understimulation and insufficient variety in stimulation has not been supported, the study was an important pioneer effort in the area of early experience that was to burgeon later.

Another important monographic study of Spitz's (1946) concerned the development of the smiling response in infants, in which he observed the appearance of indiscriminate smiling at moving faces and masks between the ages of two and six months and smiling at familiar faces only after that age. Spitz published some sixty papers and monographs about psychiatry and psychoanalysis, especially with regard to children. Among his books of importance to psychology are *No and Yes: On the Genesis of Human Communication* (1957), *A Genetic Field Theory of Ego Formation* (1959), and *The First Year of Life* (1965).
Biographies: *NYT*, 1974, Sept. 18, 44:2.

SPRANGER, EDUARD
German Psychologist, Philosopher, and Educator
Born: Berlin-Grosslichtenfelde, June 27, 1882
Died: Tübingen, Baden-Württemberg, September 17, 1963
Highest Degree: Ph.D. in philosophy, University of Berlin, 1909
Positions: 1911-20, University of Leipzig; 1920-36, University of Berlin; 1936-38, exchange professor, Japan; 1938-44, University of Berlin; 1946-63, University of Tübingen

Spranger was one of Dilthey's* most faithful students. In 1913 he published a book that became his best-known contribution to psychology. It was *Lebensformen*, translated into English as *Types of Men* (1928). It was an attempt to present a plan for a psychology based on understanding (*verstehende Psychologie*) and thus followed Dilthey in its basic approach. A developmental psychology volume published a decade later (*Psychologie des Jugendalters*, 1924) bore the same seal of *Verstehen*. Spranger named his psychology the psychology of structure (*Strukturpsychologie*) to contrast it with Wundt's* elementism.

In addition to recognizing the physical and mental realms, Spranger postulated a third one, that of the spirit, and asserted that a human being can be understood only within the framework of the spiritual. The spiritual realm is reflected in group norms, contents of the collective unconscious, and other manifestations of culture. The psychological realm can be understood only in relation to the spiritual. Specifically, Spranger postulated six types of people, or personality as it manifests itself within the six major areas of human activity, attitudes, and values: religion, science, social relations, aesthetics, economics, and politics. The predominance of one value may color the entire personality, and Spranger described the typical behaviors and attitudes of the six pure types.

Although Spranger's third mode of existence, the spiritual, is not accepted by most psychologists, that of the six realms of value has proved to be attractive. Soon after the publication of the English translation of Spranger's *Types of Men*, Gordon Allport* and P. E. Vernon constructed a value inventory (*Study of Values*, 1931) that has turned out to be a useful psychological instrument of considerable validity. More generally, Spranger, along with his teacher Dilthey, is counted among the forerunners of humanistic psychology.
Biographies: H. W. Bähr & H. Wenke, *Eduard Spranger: Sein Werk und sein Leben*, 1964; E. Croner-Kretschmer, *Eduard Spranger: Persönlichkeit und Werk*, 1933; A. Nickel, *Z. Psychoanal. Pädag.*, 1932, *6*, 333-340; *EP*, 8; *EUI*, 57.

SPURZHEIM, JOHANN KASPAR
Austrian Physiologist
Born: Near Trier, Rhineland-Palatinate, Germany, December 31, 1776
Died: Boston, Massachusetts, November 10, 1832
Highest Degree: M.D., University of Vienna, 1804, validated at University of Paris, 1821
Positions: 1804-13, Franz Joseph Gall's* companion and secretary

Franz Joseph Gall was the originator of the doctrine of phrenology. Spurzheim studied medicine under him and became his chief disciple in 1800 and later the chief propagandist for the doctrine. Spurzheim extended Gall's list of personality characteristics that could be localized on the cranium to thirty-seven. They were grouped into the affective and intellectual faculties, the former being in turn divided into propensities and sentiments, the latter into perceptive and reflective faculties. Spurzheim christened the new doctrine "phrenology."

Spurzheim traveled with Gall in Germany and France, settling with him in France. In 1813 he separated from Gall and traveled in France, England, and the United States (1813-32) to spread the doctrine. For this purpose he published a book in English, *The Physiognomic System of Gall and Spurzheim* (1815). He collaborated with Gall in preparing the first two volumes of one of the major statements of phrenology, the *Anatomie et physiologie du système nerveux en général* (1809). Spurzheim wrote additional volumes about phrenology, elaborating the details and revising the terminology: *Outlines of Phrenology* (1815), *Phrenology; or The Doctrine of the Mental Phenomena* (1815), *A View of the Elementary Principles of Education Founded on the Study of the Nature of Man* (1822), *A View of the Philosophical Principles of Phrenology* (1825), *Phrenology, in Connexion with the Study of Physiognomy* (1826), and others.

Biographies: N. Capen, *Reminiscences of Dr. Spurzheim and George Combe . . .*, 1881; A. Carmichael, *A Memoir of the Life and Philosophy of Spurzheim*, 1833; J. K. Spurzheim, *Phrenology in Connexion with the Study of Physiognomy*, 1833, pp. 9-168; A. Walsh, *J. Hist. Med.*, 1972, *27*, 187-205; *ADB*, 35; *DSB*, 12; *EUI*, 57; Hirsch, *Biog Lex.*, 5; *Nouvelle*, 44.

STARBUCK, EDWIN DILLER
American Psychologist
Born: Bridgeport, Indiana, February 20, 1866
Died: Rio del Mar, California, November 18, 1947
Highest Degree: Ph.D. in psychology, Clark University, 1897, under G. S. Hall*
Positions: 1897-1904, Stanford University; 1904-6, Earlham College; 1906-30, University of Iowa; 1930-43, University of Southern California; 1924-47, director, Institute of Character Research, Los Angeles

Starbuck's interests were in religion, philosophy, and education. He pioneered in the study of the psychology of religion both through research (such as the 1896 study of the phenomenon of religious conversion among young people) and writing (*The Psychology of Religion*, 1899). Starbuck was also first to offer university courses on character education, educational psychology, and tests and measurements. In these areas he wrote *Guide to Literature for Character Training* (2 vols., 1927, 1929), and *Moral Education in the Public Schools* (1904).

Biographies: H. Booth, *Edwin Diller Starbuck: Pioneer in the Psychology of Religion*, 1981; W. Long, *Res. News Univ. South. Calif. Grad. Sch.*, 1936, *2*(1) 1; *School & Soc.*, 1947, *66*, 413; *NCAB*, E; *NYT* 1947, Nov. 19, 17:4; *PR*, 3; *Who Was Who in America*, 2.

STEINTHAL, HEYMAN
German Philosopher and Linguist
Born: Gröbzig, Anhalt, May 16, 1823
Died: Berlin, March 14, 1899
Highest Degree: Ph.D. in philosophy, University of Berlin, 1850
Positions: 1850-59, University of Berlin; 1859-90, editor, *Zeitschrift für Völkerpsychologie und Sprachwissenschaft*

With his brother-in-law Moritz Lazarus*, Steinthal laid the foundation of ethnopsychology. The event that is often considered to have launched it was the founding, in 1859, of the journal *Zeitschrift für Völkerpsychologie und Sprachwissenschaft* by Steinthal and Lazarus. Materials on folklore, religion, myths, customs, and languages of different ethnic and national groups were presented there, the basic assumption being that such groups differ among themselves psychologically and hence perceive and react to reality in distinctive ways. Both Steinthal and Lazarus were linguists and disciples of Herbart*.

Steinthal produced many publications about the philosophy of language, mythology, ethics, logic, comparative religion, and psychology (for example, *Einleitung in die Psychologie und Sprachwissenschaft*, 1871). Often his ideas met opposition, especially the idea of a "group mind," by which he meant the integration of individual minds that, under given conditions, might function in a unitary fashion. Relevant to psychology is his work *Grammatik, Logik und Psychologie* (1855).

Biographies: T. Achelis, *Heyman Steinthal*, 1898; A. A. Roback, *Encycl. Soc. Sci.*, 1934, *14*, 384-385; *ADB*, 54; *EJ*, 15; *Jewish*, 10.

STEKEL, WILHELM
Austrian Psychoanalyst
Born: Bojan, Bucovinia, March 18, 1868
Died: London, England, June 21, 1940
Highest Degree: M.D., University of Vienna, 1897
Positions: 1898-1938, practiced medicine, Vienna; founder (1934) and editor, *Psychotherapeutische Praxis*

Stekel belonged to the original group of early Freudian psychoanalysts. Although he did not split off from this group to establish his own school, some of his interpretations of Sigmund Freud* differed enough from Freud's own views to draw Freud's criticism. Stekel was basically an eclectic interpreter of Freud. Some of his views were very similar to Adler's*. He emphasized the importance of life-style and life goals and held that for diagnostic purposes it was important to identify such goals and to distinguish between genuine and false goals, but that an explanation of the patient's childhood problems was not always necessary. Stekel called his approach "active analytic psychotherapy" to emphasize the active partnership role of the therapist in the therapeutic situation. In his symbolic interpretation of behavior, however, Stekel outdid Freud in seeing sex in its pure or sublimated form in almost everything. Stekel was a prolific but unsystematic and redundant writer who penned many a psychoanalytic volume. Among them are *Die Sprache des Traumes* (1910), *Der Wille zum Schlaf* (1916), *The Homosexual Neurosis* (1922), *Sex and Dreams* (1922), *Frigidity in Women in Relation to Their Love Life* (1926), *Impotence in the Male* (1927), *Sexual Aberrations* (1930), *Störungen des Trieb- und Affektlebens* (10 vols., 1932), *Fortschritte der Traumdeutung* (1935), *The Interpretation of Dreams* (1943), and *Compulsion and Doubt* (1949).

Biographies: E. A. Guthiel (Ed.), *The Autobiography of Wilhelm Stekel*, 1950; *Psychoanal. Rev.*, 1940, *27*, 506; W. Schindler, *Marriage and Hygiene*, 1948, *1*, 183-184; *EJ*, 15; *EUI*, 57; *Jewish*, 2; *NYT*, 1940, June 28, 19:3; *PR*, 3.

STERN, (LOUIS) WILLIAM
German Psychologist
Born: Berlin, April 29, 1871
Died: Durham, North Carolina, March 27, 1938
Highest Degree: Ph.D. in psychology, University of Berlin, 1893, under H. Ebbinghaus*
Positions, Honors: 1897-1916, University of Breslau; 1916-33, professor of psychology and director, Psychological Institute, University of Hamburg; 1933-38, Duke University; honorary degrees from Clark University (1909) and Wittenburg College (1928)

Stern was a versatile man. In 1898 he invented the Stern variator (Tonvariator), a device to produce tones of varying pitch. In a 1903 pamphlet he presented both the concept and the term of *applied psychology* as well as that of *psychotechnics*. He organized the Institut für angewandte Psychologie in Berlin in 1906 and a year later founded the journal *Zeitschrift für angewandte Psychologie*.

In the three-volume work *Person und Sache: System der philosophischen Weltanschauung* (1906), Stern presented a synthesis of laboratory psychology and "understanding psychology" advocated by Dilthey* and Spranger*, by focusing his attention on the total person (critical personalism). Every mental function is centered in a person, which is therefore the object of psychological study rather than the function. A person is a blend of the physical and the mental, of hereditary and environmental influences, and therefore can be adequately understood only by using both natural science methods and the cultural science approach. Stern's views of the person thus fit those of Bretano*, James*, and the contemporary humanistic psychologists. Stern's last statement on the psychology of personalism appeared in 1935 (*Allgemeine Psychologie auf personalistischen Grundlage*; English translation, *General Psychology from the Personalistic Standpoint*, 1938).

In the area of developmental psychology Stern published books (1907 and 1908) about observations made by him and his wife on their own three children. In 1914 he published *Psychologie der frühen Kindheit*, elaborating on a developmental theory proposed earlier in 1908, called the "convergence theory." According to this theory, convergence or collaboration of inner and outer conditions of development in the emergence of any ability takes place, although these conditions never interact in a simple or direct causal fashion.

The one contribution that Stern is mostly known for is the concept of the IQ. To estimate a child's intelligence on the basis of the Binet*-Simon* test independently of the absolute performance score and of his age, Stern proposed (in *Die psychologische Methoden der Intelligenzprüfung*, 1912) that the mental-age score obtained on this test be divided by the child's chronological age; and to avoid fractions, the ratio multiplied by one hundred. This measure, which Stern called the "mental quotient," was adapted by Terman* in his 1916 Stanford Revision of the Binet Scales.

Differential psychology was still another area in which Stern made a contribution. Starting his work before 1900, he published *Über Psychologie der individuellen Differenzen* in 1900. An expanded version of this book appeared in 1911 (*Die differenzielle Psychologie in ihren methodischen Grundlagen*). These works were followed by *Intelligenz der Kinder und Jugendlichen* (1920) and *Psychologie und Schülerauslese* (1920). Stern wrote a total of 139 articles and books.

Biographies: G. W. Allport, *Amer. J. Psychol.*, 1938, *51*, 770-774; A. Brand-Aruaban, *Koroth*, 1972, *5*, 808-813; E. Cassirer, *Acta psychologica*, 1940, *5*, 1-15; R. B. McLeod, *Psychol. Rev.*, 1938, *45*, 347-353; *CE*, 13; *EJ*, 15; *EP*, 8; *EUI*, 57; *IESS*, 15; *Jewish*, 10; *PR*, 3.

STEVENS, S. SMITH

American Psychologist
Born: Ogden, Utah, November 4, 1906
Died: Vail, Colorado, January 18, 1973
Highest Degree: Ph.D. in psychology, Harvard University, 1933, under E. G. Boring*
Positions, Honors: 1936-73, professor of psychophysics, Harvard University; H. C. Warren Medal, Society of Experimental Psychologists, 1943; American Psychological Association Distinguished Scientific Contribution Award, 1960; Rayleigh Gold Medal, British Acoustic Society, 1972

Stevens was the most prominent psychophysicist of the twentieth century. His early work was in audition, which eventually led him to formulate the power law of psychophysics. In 1934 Stevens devised a method for equating tones on one attribute when they differed on a second and was able to draw isophonic curves for pitch, loudness, volume, and density of sound, the latter a new tonal attribute discovered by Stevens. It was a first demonstration that the criterion for differentiating sensory attributes was not independent variability but independent constancy.

Additional contributions in the area of audition followed during the decade of the 1930s. In scaling the continua of pitch and loudness using equal sense distances rather than just noticeable differences, Stevens created a unit of sense distance for pitch, the mel, and one for loudness, the sone (1938). In 1936 he had already demonstrated that using the halving method, a true ratio scale for loudness could be constructed. He also studied auditory localization and in 1941 found evidence that the perception of pitch and loudness is quantal rather than continuous. With H. Davis, Stevens wrote a book bringing together his own work on audition and that of others (*Hearing*, 1938).

In his scaling work (*Theory of Scales*, 1941), Stevens abandoned the category scaling procedure used by Fechner* and others since him and developed some new ones, the direct scaling methods (magnitude estimation, ratio production, and others), and found that, when so scaled, most physical continua obeyed a psychophysical power law, $R = kS^n$, rather than the logarithmic law of Fechner's. Stevens argued that sensory continua are either qualitative (metathetic) or quantitative (prothetic), and that although the former may obey Fechner's law, most of them, being quantitative, obey the power law, equal stimulus ratios producing equal sense ratios. Much earlier, Plateau* had proposed a similar law, but he abandoned it in deference to Fechner. The power law was presented in the November 13, 1953, issue of *Science*, and has been subsequently bolstered by numerous research and theoretical papers. Stevens's work represented the most significant single attainment in psychophysics since Fechner.

A third area in which Stevens acquired distinction was that of philosophy of science. Not long after the appearance of Bridgman's* book *The Logic of Modern Physics*, Harvard psychologists were talking about operationism. It was through the writings of Stevens that American psychologists learned about operationism and began to apply operational definitions of psychological concepts.

Stevens wrote a total of more than one hundred and fifty articles. He edited the now classic *Handbook of Experimental Psychology* (1951) and was a coauthor of two books about somatotypes, *The Varieties of Human Physique* (1940, with W. H. Sheldon* and W. B. Tucker) and *The Varieties of Temperament* (1942, with W. H. Sheldon). He was also a cofounder of the Psychonomic Society in 1959 and the founder of the journal *Perception and Psychophysics* (1966).

Biographies: *Amer. Psychologist*, 1960, *15*, 794-797; *Biog. Mem.*, 47; *HPA*, 6; *NYT*, 1973, Jan. 20, 34:3.

STEWART, DUGALD
Scottish Philosopher
Born: Edinburgh, November 22, 1753
Died: Edinburgh, June 11, 1828
Education: Graduated from University of Edinburgh, 1769
Positions: 1772-1820, University of Edinburgh

Stewart, one of the three most prominent members of the Scottish school, was a disciple and follower of one of them, Thomas Reid*. He did not add anything new to Reid's common sense philosophy but was more influential than Reid as he interpreted and popularized Reid's philosophy. In Stewart's hands, Reid's faculty psychology became an easily absorbable doctrine, and Stewart was thus instrumental in spreading it among not only the philosophers but the laymen. Stewart's lectures at Edinburgh supplied the raw material for the psychological side of Gall's* and Spurzheim's* phrenology, the twenty-seven human faculties that Gall and Spurzheim related to prominences on the human head. Stewart's most important books were *Elements of Philosophy of the Human Mind* in three volumes (1792, 1814, 1827), and *The Philosophy of the Active Moral Powers of Man* (1828).

Biographies: *Fraser's Mag.*, 1839, *19*, 50-56; J. Veitch, In W. Hamilton (Ed.), *The Collected Works of Dugald Stewart*, vol. 10, 1858, pp. i-clxxvii; *DNB*, 18; *EB*, 21; *EP*, 8; *EUI*, 18(2); *Nouvelle*, 44.

STONE, CALVIN PERRY

American Psychologist
Born: Portland, Indiana, February 28, 1892
Died: Palo Alto, California, December 28, 1954
Highest Degree: Ph.D. in psychology, University of Minnesota, 1921, under K. S. Lashley*
Positions, Honors: 1921-22, University of Minnesota; 1922-54, Stanford University; editorial work, *Journal of Comparative and Physiological Psychology* (1947-50) and *Annual Review of Psychology* (1950-54); president, American Psychological Association, 1942; honorary D.Sc., Indiana University, 1954

Stone's main interest was comparative and physiological psychology. He did his early work on instincts in animals, later on animal learning, maturation, and the effects of electroconvulsive shock. In this area his major topic of research was the physiology of reproductive behavior. In 1923 he offered the first course on Freudian (Sigmund Freud*) psychology as part of the regular curriculum of an American university. Stone's publications consist of a fair number of research papers, chapters in edited books, and an edited volume of comparative psychology (1934) that saw three editions.

Biographies: C. R. Carpenter, *Science*, 1955, *121*, 658-659; H. E. Rosvold, *Amer. J. Psychol.*, 1955, *68*, 326-329; *NYT*, 1954, Dec. 30, 17:3; *PR*, 3; *Who Was Who in America*, 3.

STÖRRING, GUSTAV

German Psychologist and Philosopher
Born: Voerde, Westphalia, August 24, 1860
Died: Göttingen, December 1, 1946
Highest Degree: Ph.D. in philosophy, University of Halle, 1890; M.D.
Positions: 1902-11, University of Zurich; 1911-14, University of Strasbourg; 1914-?, University of Bonn

Störring wrote several books about emotion (*Zur lehre vom Einfluss der Gefühle auf die Vorstellung*, 1896; *Psychologie des menschlichen Gefühlslebens*, 1916; *Methoden der Psychologie des höheren Gefühlslebens*, 1938) and psychopathology (*Vorlesungen über Psychopathologie in ihrer Bedeutung für die normale Psychologie*, 1900; *Zur Psychologie und Klinik der Angstzustände*,

1934), as well as a general text (*Psychologie*, 1923). He emphasized the contributions of psychiatry and psychopathology to experimental psychology and, in turn, saw experimental psychology as the basis of both logic and epistemology. Störring wrote several experimental papers about emotion and thinking, as well as books and papers in philosophy.

Biographies: K. Hauss, *Psychol. Rundsch.*, 1961, *12*, 79-80; W. Wirth, *Arch. ges. Psychol.*, 1940, *107*, 384-391; *PR*, 3.

STOUFFER, SAMUEL ANDREW
American Sociologist
Born: Sac City, Iowa, June 6, 1900
Died: Cambridge, Massachusetts, August 24, 1960
Highest Degree: Ph.D. in sociology, University of Chicago, 1930
Positions, Honors: 1930-31, University of Chicago; 1931-35, University of Wisconsin; 1935-46, University of Chicago; 1946-60, Harvard University; president, American Sociological Society, 1952-53; honorary LL.D., 1939, Sc.D., 1948

Stouffer pioneered in large-scale quantitative research in sociology. His principal contributions lay in the correlational and descriptive analysis of survey data, as exemplified by the four volumes of *Studies in Social Psychology in World War II*. Stouffer was the senior author of the series *Measurement and Prediction* (1950). He stuck close to the data and ventured into theory only on a small-scale basis. One theoretical concept of considerable heuristic value that Stouffer stressed in *The American Soldier* was the concept of relative deprivation. He was influenced by quantitatively oriented psychologists such as Thurstone*, as well as by Pearson*, and Fisher*, and, in turn, influenced psychologists by setting an example in field research and through his contacts with them in the Laboratory of Social Relations that he established at Harvard University.

Biographies: *Publ. Opin. Quart.*, 1958, *22*, 81-82; P. M. Hauser, *Amer. J. Sociol.*, 1961, *66*, 364-365; M. W. Riley, *Soc. Forces*, 1961, *39*, 284; D. Young, *Amer. Sociol. Rev.*, 1961, *26*, 106-107; *IESS*, 15; *NYT*, 1960, Aug. 25, 29:1; *Who Was Who in America*, 4; *Yearb. Amer. Phil. Soc.*, 1961.

STOUT, GEORGE FREDERICK
English Psychologist
Born: South Shields, Durham, January 6, 1860
Died: Sydney, Australia, August 18, 1944
Highest Degree: A.M. in philosophy, Cambridge University, 1885
Positions: 1883-90, lecturer in moral science, Cambridge University; 1896-98, lecturer in comparative psychology, University of Aberdeen; 1898-1903, reader in mental philosophy, Oxford University; 1903-36, professor of metaphysic and logic, St. Andrews University; editor, *Mind*, 1891-1920

Stout's views on psychology were similar to those of Ward*, his teacher, but Stout was more popular than Ward, because he was easier to understand. He was influential because of his psychology texts: *Analytic Psychology* (1896, written for psychologists), *Manual of Psychology* (1899, written for students), *Groundwork of Psychology* (1903), and *Mind and Matter* (1931), but especially his *Manual*. Stout's position in the history of psychology rests mainly on his reputation as textbook writer.

Stout rejected associationism in favor of a psychology that was a form of act psychology, like Ward's. In his doctrine of conation Stout emphasized the individual's activity. He held that the objects of mental processes are mental entities (sensations) also. The processes are cognition and interest. Interest means conation or striving, plus feelings and attitudes. The goal object of striving may be immediate, or else such goal object may be only instrumental in attaining a superordinate goal. In this connection Stout discussed unconscious attitudes as factors that determine activity in addition to conation.

Stout was very influential, mainly because he provided the empirical psychologist with an explicit statement of the kind of simple body-mind relationship that he subscribed to but did not consciously try to formulate, as well as for his ability to assimilate, synthesize, and present the divergent viewpoints of the different schools of psychology as *the* psychology.

Biographies: C. D. Broad, *Mind*, 1945, *54*, 285-288; R. Knight, *Brit. J. Educ. Psychol.*, 1946, *16*, 53-56; C. A. Mace, *Brit. J. Psychol.*, 1946, *36*, 51-54; C. A. Mace, *Proc. Brit. Acad.*, 1945, *31*, 307-316; J. A. Passmore, *Austr. J. Psychol. Phil.*, 1944, *22*, 1-14; *CE*, 13; *DNB*, Suppl. 6; *EP*, 8; *IESS*, 15; *PR*, 3.

STRATTON, GEORGE MALCOLM
American Psychologist
Born: Oakland, California, September 26, 1865
Died: Berkeley, California, October 8, 1957
Highest Degree: Ph.D. in psychology, University of Leipzig, 1896, under W. Wundt*
Positions: 1896-1904, University of California at Berkeley; 1904-8, Johns Hopkins University; 1908-35, University of California; president, American Psychological Association, 1908

Stratton was part of the first crop of Wundtian experimentalists in America. With Wundt he performed experiments on pressure patterns on the skin and, on his arrival at the University of California, established there a psychological laboratory in 1899 and became its director. He is remembered mostly for having performed the first of the very few experiments on the effects of prolonged distortion of the visual field (1897). By wearing lenses that inverted the visual world for eighty-seven hours, distributed over eight days, Stratton answered a question that theretofore had been given only a priori answers. Although the world looked upside down at first and Stratton was greatly hampered in his behavior, adjustment quickly took place, and although the world did not look quite right side up even after eight days, his behavior adapted as if it were. Vision and kinesthesis had found a new basis on which to act in harmony.

In 1902 Stratton performed a classic experiment that settled empirically another theoretical question. By recording eye movements of subjects who were examining symmetric and asymmetric art objects, Stratton was able to establish that aesthetic experience could not arise from the presumed smooth and symmetric eye movements as the eyes explored symmetric and regular contours, because eye movements in response to even perfectly symmetric objects were jerky, did not follow the contours exactly, and were far from symmetrically distributed between the two halves of the symmetric object.

Stratton's reputation is based mainly on his work on the inversion of the retinal image. He believed that there was a point beyond which science could not go and that a higher reality existed beyond the senses. Although Stratton himself considered his contributions as a social psychologist the most important, his writings on the subject have elicited little attention from psychologists. They include the books *Experimental Psychology and Its Bearing Upon Culture* (1903), *Psychology of Religious Life* (1911), *Theophrastus and the Greek Physiological Psychology* (1917), *Anger: Its Religious and Moral Significance* (1923), *The Social Psychology of International Conduct* (1929), and a number of papers about social and political issues and their relation to human nature.

Biographies: O. Bridgman, *Amer. J. Psychol.*, 1958, *71*, 460-461; C. W. Brown, *Science*, 1958, *127*, 1432-1433; *Biog. Mem.*, 35; *EUI*, 57; *NCAB*, 13; *NYT*, 1957, Oct. 10, 33:4; *PR*, 3; *Who Was Who in America*, 3.

STRONG, EDWARD KELLOG, JR.

American Psychologist
Born: Syracuse, New York, August 18, 1884
Died: Menlo Park, California, December 4, 1963
Highest Degree: Ph.D. in psychology, Columbia University, 1911, under J. McK. Cattell*
Positions: 1914-17, George Peabody College for Teachers; 1917-19, army service; 1919-23, Carnegie Institute of Technology; 1923-49, Stanford University

Strong was prominent in vocational-interest measurement. An industrial psychologist, he developed an interest inventory, the Strong Vocational Interest Blank (*Vocational Interests of Men and Women*, 1943; *Vocational Interests 18 Years After College*, 1955). It has been revised and extended several times and is one of the most widely used interest inventories today. It compares the interest patterns of a person with the typical interest pattern for successful practitioners of many different occupations and is used mainly in vocational counseling. The Strong Vocational Interest Blank has been widely researched, and Strong himself wrote several research papers on it after the first appearance of the test. Strong's significance is measured by the thousands of young people who have been helped in their choice of a career through the use of the Strong Vocational Interest Blank.

Biographies: J. G. Darley, *J. Appl. Psychol.*, 1964, *48*, 74-75; *NCAB*, 51; *NYT*, 1963, Dec. 6, 35:2; *PR*, 3; *Who Was Who in America*, 4.

STUMPF, CARL
German Psychologist
Born: Wiesentheid, Bavaria, April 21, 1848
Died: Berlin, December 25, 1936
Highest Degree: Ph.D. in philosophy, University of Göttingen, 1868, under Rudolf Lotze*
Positions: 1870-73, University of Göttingen, 1873-79, University of Würzburg; 1879-84, University of Prague; 1884-89, University of Halle; 1889-94, University of Munich; 1894-1921, University of Berlin; joint president, International Congress of Psychology, 1896

Stumpf's most important work was on the psychology of music, but his first psychological book was about the origin of spatial perception, *Über den psychologischen Ursprung der Raumvorstellung* (1873). It set forth a theory of space perception that was related to that of his teacher Lotze. In 1875 Stumpf's early interest in music took a scientific form: he began to do experiments in the psychology of music and to write *Tonpsychologie*, his major contribution to psychology. Its first volume appeared in 1883, the second in 1890. In the second volume may be found the results of his important experimental investigation of tonal fusion. At Berlin University Stumpf's laboratory eventually expanded into an institute. He published extensively on audition and music and was active in many other psychological projects, including the founding of a Verein für Kinderpsychologie. He investigated a child musical prodigy and a mind-reading horse and established an archive of primitive music, Das phonographische Archiv, in 1900. The journal *Beiträge zur Akustik und Musikwissenschaft*, was founded by Stumpf in 1898.

Although Stumpf is remembered for his contributions in the narrower area of the psychology of tone and music, he also influenced the development of psychology systematically. As the incumbent of the most prestigious chair in psychology in Germany, Stumpf wrote two theoretical papers that placed the stamp of approval on the psychology of Brentano*, whose ideas Stumpf had accepted during his stay at the University of Würzburg. There was an impress of phenomenology on the Berlin laboratory, and Schumann*, Köhler*, and Koffka*, of Gestalt psychological fame were Stumpf's students.

Biographies: E. Becher, *Naturwissenschaften*, 1981, *6*, 265-277; J. v. Essen, *Ned. Tijdschr. Psychol.*, 1938, *6*, 131-142; W. Köhler, *Kant-Stud.*, 1928, *22*, unnumbered before p. 1; H. S. Langfeld, *Amer. J. Psychol.*, 1937, *49*, 316-320; K. Lewin, *Psychol. Rev.*, 1937, *44*, 189-194; M. Nadoleczny, *J. Speech Dis.*, 1938, *3*, 76-80; C. A. Ruckmick, *Psychol. Bull.*, 1937, *34*, 187-190; R. Schilling, In T. Sebeok (Ed.), *Portraits of Linguists*, vol. 1, 1969, pp. 563-574; M. Schneider, *Deutsche Musikkultur*, 1937, *2*, 44-47; G. Schünemann, *Arch. Musikforsch.*, 1937, *2*, 1-7; *EP*, 8; *IESS*, 15; *HPA*, 1.

SULLIVAN, HARRY STACK
American Psychiatrist
Born: Norwich, New York, February 21, 1892
Died: Paris, France, January 14, 1949

Highest Degree: M.D., Chicago College of Medicine and Surgery, 1917
Positions: 1922-23, St. Elizabeth's Hospital, Washington, D.C.; 1923-30, Shepard & Enoch Pratt Hospital, Towson, Maryland; 1923-31, University of Maryland; 1933-43, president, William Alanson White Foundation; 1936-44, director, Washington School of Psychiatry; editor, *Psychiatry*, 1938-49

Sullivan promoted a social-psychological theory that was based on his seven years' work with schizophrenics in Maryland. He began to formulate his theory in 1929, had it developed in the 1930s, but did not publish it in book form until 1947 (*Conceptions of Modern Psychiatry*). This was the only book he ever wrote. All others (*The Interpersonal Theory of Personality*, 1953; *The Psychiatric Interview*, 1954; *Clinical Studies in Psychiatry*, 1956; *The Fusion of Psychiatry and Social Sciences*, 1964) were published posthumously from his notes. The main influences on Sullivan's theory came from Sigmund Freud*, Adolph Meyer*, George Mead*, Edward Sapir*, and Ruth Benedict*, but it is otherwise an independent development within the group of sociopsychological theories of personality.

Sullivan's main tenet was that the concept of personality acquires meaning only in interpersonal relations. Personality is a hypothetical entity and can be observed only in interpersonal behavior. Personality processes include dynamisms, personifications, and cognitive processes. Dynamisms are the smallest units of recurrent behavior that can be used in studying behavior or habits. Most dynamisms develop to serve the basic needs, except the self-system, which develops as a result of anxiety that arises in interpersonal relations. To reduce anxiety the person takes protective or security measures, those that permit certain behaviors, or the good-me self, and those that forbid others, the bad-me self. They become the self-system. The self-system acquires autonomy and prevents objective evaluation of one's behavior. Personifications are self-images or images of others, formed in isolated instances of interaction but influencing attitudes toward people in subsequent transactions. Shared personifications are stereotypes. Cognitive processes are prototaxic, parataxic, or syntaxic. *Prototaxic experiences* are an unconnected stream of consciousness that characterizes the infant's world; *parataxic thinking* sees causal connections between events that are only contiguous in time, and *syntaxic thinking* involves the exchange of symbols whose meaning has been agreed upon by a group of people.

Sullivan's personality dynamics explains the handling of tensions by a person and the use of the three modes of thinking. In personality development Sullivan stressed definite stages, characterized by developing interpersonal relations (he rejected Freud's notion of the libido and subordinated biological factors to social relations) and a hierarchical transition to higher forms of cognitive activity. Thus during early infancy the oral experience of food intake is colored by the infant's evaluation of the mother as good, bad, or rejecting, and the latent period in Freud's system becomes a very important one in Sullivan's, because learning to behave appropriately in social situations or failure to do so is crucial to the person's future interpersonal relations.

Biographies: K. Chatelaine, *Harry Stack Sullivan: The Formative Years*, 1981; A. F. Emch, *Psychiatry*, 1949, *12*, 1; H. S. Perry, *Psychiatrist of America: The Life of Harry Stack Sullivan*, 1981; H. S. Perry, In H. S. Sullivan, *The Fusion of Psychiatry and Social Science*, 1964, pp. xiii-xlv et passim; H. S. Perry, In H. S. Sullivan, *Personal Psychopathology*, 1972, pp. ix-xxiii; C. Thompson, *Psychiatry*, 1949, *12*, 435-437; *CE*, 13; *IESS*, 15; *NYT*, 1949, Jan. 16, 68:5; *PR*, 3; *Who Was Who in America*, 4.

SULLY, JAMES
English Psychologist
Born: Bridgwater, Somersetshire, March 3, 1842
Died: London, November 1, 1923
Highest Degree: M.A., University of London
Positions: 1892-1912, Grote Professor of Mind and Logic, University of London

Sully acquired a name in the history of psychology not as a scientist or philosopher but as a writer of textbooks. After publishing books of more restricted scope, *Sensation and Intuition* (1874), *Pessimism* (1877), and *Illusions* (1881), he wrote *Outlines of Psychology* (1884), *Teacher's Handbook of Psychology* (1886), *The Human Mind* (1892), *Studies of Childhood* (1896), *Children's Ways* (1897), and *An Essay on Laughter* (1902). The *Outlines* and *Teacher's Handbook* were his most successful writing ventures, distinguished by lucidity and facility of style. They saw several editions and were used widely. Sully spread knowledge of psychological advances also among psychologists by writing about the achievements of German psychologists. He did this in the pages of *Mind*, beginning soon after the founding of that journal and continuing in this enterprise for some twenty years.

Biographies: B. Edgell, *Brit. J. Psychol.*, 1947, *37*, 113-132; G. Dawes Hicks, *J. Phil. Stud.*, 1928, *3*, 468-482; J. Sully, *My Life and Friends: A Psychologist's Memories*, 1918.

SWEDENBORG, EMANUEL
Swedish Scientist, Inventor, Philosopher, and Theologian
Born: Stockholm, January 29, 1688
Died: London, England, March 29, 1772
Highest Degree: Master's degree, University of Uppsala, 1709
Positions: 1716-45, assessor, Royal College of Mines

Swedenborg's psychological views are found in his three-volume treatise *Oeconomia regni animalis in transactiones divisa* (1740-41) and subsequent shorter works, first collected and published in 1846 and translated into English as *Psychological Transactions by Emanuel Swedenborg* (1920). They constitute only a fraction of the 20,000 handwritten pages he left behind. To Swedenborg consciousness has four functions: *anima*, which is the highest and of which we can have no direct knowledge; *mens rationalis*, or reason; *animus*, similar to Aristotle's* vegetative soul; and the sense organs. This functional division shows the influence of St. Augustine*. Influenced to some extent also by Locke* and Leibniz*, Swedenborg achieved a compromise between the *tabula rasa* and the innate idea positions.

At first only a covert mystic, Swedenborg made significant contributions to science and technology during the first half of his adult life. He spent several years studying the brain and is credited with being the first to place psychological functions in the cortex of the brain. In his later attempts to account for body-soul interaction, Swedenborg drew on his knowledge of physiology, which was good (*The Brain Considered Anatomically, Physiologically and Philosophically*, 2 vols., 1882-87; *Three Transactions on the Cerebrum*, 2 vols., 1938-40). To him, the soul was a separate entity, inherited from Adam through the semen of each individual's father. It is the life principle of the individual and possesses a store of wisdom from conception. There is no reason in the newborn child, though. This he acquires through experience. The *mens* thus becomes increasingly like the *anima*, and the *anima* reciprocates. The communication between reason and soul occurs through fibers and fluids, which Swedenborg attempted to explain in quasi-physiological terms in a manner reminiscent of Descartes*. Also, like Descartes, Swedenborg asserted that the body obeyed natural laws, which were mechanical. Unlike Descartes, to his physiology Swedenborg added mysticism instead of philosophy. In 1745 he experienced illumination that told him to abandon science and take up the interpretation of the Bible. Swedenborg acquired fame throughout Europe through his accounts of visits to the spirit world. The father of William James* was a Swedenborg enthusiast. James's own interest in psychic research was partly because of his father's influence.

Biographies: K. Akert & M. P. Hammond, *Med. Hist.*, 1962, *6*, 255-266; J. J. Hyde, *A Bibliography of Swedenborg*, 1906; I. Jonsson, *Emanuel Swedenborg*, 1971; S. Lindroth, In S. Koch (Ed.), *Swedish Men of Science, 1650-1950*, 1952, pp. 50-58; H. H. Maudsley, In *Body and Mind*, 1886, pp. 163-217; C. S. Sigstedt, *The Swedenborg Epic: The Life and Works of Emanuel Swedenborg*, 1952; H. D. Spoerl, *Psychol. Digest*, 1937, *2*, 70-75; E. Swift, *Swedenborg: The Man and His Works*, 1932; R. L. Tafel, *Documents Concerning the Life and Character of Swedenborg*, 3 vols., 1875-1877; S. Toksvig, *Emanuel Swedenborg: Scientist and Mystic*, 1948; G. Trobridge, *Emanuel Swedenborg: Life and Teaching*, 1944; *CE*, 13; *Chalmers*, 29; *DSB*, 13; *EB*, 21; *EP*, 8; *EUI*, 58; *Grande*, 13; *Nouvelle*, 44.

T

TAINE, HIPPOLYTE ADOLPHE

French Philosopher, Critic, and Historian
Born: Vouziers, Ardennes, April 21, 1828
Died: Paris, March 5, 1893
Highest Degree: Doctor of letters, University of Paris, 1853
Positions: 1864-84, École des Beaux-Arts, Paris

Taine was a convinced positivist. He believed that the scientific method should be applied not only in science but in sociology, psychology, the study of literature and art, philosophy, history, and even religion. He showed an interest in psychology very early, and his literary work is based on the theory of psychological determinism, stated in a two-volume work about psychology, *De l'intelligence* (1870). In it he rejected the concept of innate ideas and embraced empiricism.

In his literary criticism Taine stressed the examination of literary documents to achieve an understanding of the psychology of the author. The author's biographic data and personality characteristics, coupled with the ethnic, social, and political background, should produce an insight into the author's or artist's work. Taine's *De l'intelligence* helped prepare a favorable climate for the development of scientific psychology in the second half of the nineteenth century. A more limited and specific contribution of Taine's was a paper about the acquisition of language in a child, published in 1876. After the papers of Pestalozzi* and Tiedemann*, published a century earlier, Taine's was the third paper in developmental psychology published in a scientific journal.

Biographies: M. Barrès, *Taine: Sa vie et sa correspondance*, 4 vols., 1902-1907; A. Chevrillon, *Taine: Formation de sa pensée*, 1932; A. Cresson, *Hip-*

polyte Taine: Sa vie, son oeuvre, sa philosophie, 1951; V. Girdaud, *Essai sur Taine: Son oeuvre et son influence*, 1909; P. Lacombe, *Taine: Historien et sociologue*, 1909; M. Leroy, *Taine*, 1933; P. V. Rubow, *Hippolyte Taine*, 1930; *CE*, 13; *EP*, 8; *EUI*, 58; *Grande*, 30; *NYT*, 1893, Mar. 6, 5:1; *Nouvelle*, 44.

TARDE, GABRIEL
French Sociologist
Born: Sarlat, Dordogne, March 12, 1843
Died: Paris, May 13, 1904
Highest Degree: Law degree, University of Paris, 1869
Positions: 1900-1904, Collège de France

Tarde, distinguished as a philosopher, sociologist, and criminologist, pioneered in social psychology. His most important book, *The Laws of Imitation*, was published in 1890, and its English translation appeared in 1903, five years before McDougall's* *Introduction to Social Psychology*. Tarde's theory of imitation and his study of crowd psychology (*Opinion and the Crowd*, 1901) and of the psychology of economic behavior (*Economic Psychology*, 1902) make him one of the founders of social psychology. He saw imitation as the fashioner of all social interaction, although he estimated that only one person in a hundred would be inventive enough to serve as a model for imitation. Society, nevertheless, is a group of people who imitate each other. The psychological processes underlying social and historic progress are repetition, opposition, and adaptation. Since inventions differ in the degree to which they are imitated (repeated) and in the manner of imitation, opposition arises between different imitations as well as between tradition and innovation in a culture. This leads to a resolution or adaptation, which is an invention in its own right and subject to imitation. These Hegelian (Hegel*) dialectic cycles keep repeating themselves endlessly.

Biographies: T. N. Clark, In T. N. Clark (Ed.), *Gabriel Tarde on Communication and Social Influence: Selected Papers*, 1969, pp. 1-69; A. Espinas, *Notice sur la vie et les oeuvres de M. Gabriel de Tarde*, 1910; F. Giddings, In G. Tarde, *The Laws of Imitation*, 1903, pp. iii-vii; A. Lacassagne, *Arch. Anthrop. Crim.*, 1909, *24*, 895-906; M. S. Wilson, *J. Crim. Law Criminol.*, 1954, *45*, 3-11; *EUI*, 59; *Grande*, 30; *IESS*, 15.

TEPLOV, BORIS MIKHAĬLOVICH
Russian Psychologist
Born: Tula, October 21, 1896
Died: Moscow, September 28, 1965
Highest Degree: Doctor of pedagogical sciences, 1947
Positions, Honors: 1921-33, various Red Army research positions; 1929-1965, Institute of Psychology and Moscow State University; chief editor, *Voprosy Psikhologii*, 1958-65; several awards, prizes, other honors

After studying at Moscow University and graduating as an engineer from a military school of camouflage in 1921, Teplov did considerable work on camouflage, some of which was published in journals of military technology. He extended his work to problems of light and vision in architecture (*Tsvetovidenie dlya arkhitektorov*, 1938), did an original study of the psychology of the military leader during World War II (*Um i volya polkovodtsa*), and wrote a widely used psychology text for high schools that saw eight editions and was translated into fourteen languages. Teplov then shifted to the study of individual differences. In this area he wrote a volume about the psychology of musical abilities (*Psikhologiya muzikal'nykh sposobnosteĭ*, 1947) and one about individual differences in general (*Problemy individual'nykh razlichiĭ*, 1961). Immediately after the 1950 "Pavlovian sessions" in which scientists were urged to incorporate Pavlov's* teachings in their work, Teplov embarked on the most significant portion of his career, the study of the properties of the central nervous system. In contrast to other Russian psychologists, Teplov stressed the study of types of the nervous system, not of behavior types, his main thesis being that a distinction must be made between types of nervous system, which are innately determined, and types of behavior, which are alloys of innate temperament and experience, and that therefore prediction of behavior from a knowledge of type of nervous system alone is impossible, especially in humans in whom language plays a crucial modifying role. Teplov emphasized the study of the strength parameter of the nervous system and devised several methods for assessing this and other parameters postulated by Pavlov. Teplov's main publications in this area are *O ponyatiyakh slabosti i inertnosti nervnoĭ sistemy* (1955); *Ob izuchenii tipologicheskikh svoĭstv nervnoĭ sistemy i ikh psikhologicheskikh yavleniĭ* (1957); the four volumes of studies from his laboratory of which he was both an author and editor, *Tipologicheskie osobennosti vyssheĭ nervnoĭ deyatel'nosti cheloveka* (1959-65); and *Novye dannye po izucheniyu svoĭstv nervnoĭ sistemy cheloveka* (1963). *Biographies*: *Vop. Psikhol.*, 1965, *11*(6), 4-6.

TERMAN, LEWIS MADISON
American Psychologist
Born: Johnson County, Indiana, January 15, 1877
Died: Palo Alto, California, December 21, 1956
Highest Degree: Ph.D. in psychology, Clark University, 1905, under E. C. Sanford*
Positions, Honors: 1906-10, Los Angeles State Normal School; 1910-43, Stanford University, 1922-42, head, Psychology Department; president, American Psychological Association, 1923; four honorary degrees

Terman's major contribution to American psychology was his translation and adaptation to American circumstances of the Simon*-Binet* intelligence test in 1916 (*The Measurement of Intelligence*, 1916). One of Terman's changes was the introduction of Stern's* mental quotient to measure intelligence. Terman called it the "intelligence quotient," or IQ. Since Terman was at the time at Stanford University, the test became known as the "Stanford-Binet Intelligence Scale." In 1937 Terman and Maude Merrill published the first revision of the

Stanford-Binet, which had been ten years in preparation (*Measuring Intelligence*, 1937). The last revision of the test was published after Terman's death (*Stanford-Binet Intelligence Scale: Manual for the Third Revision*, 1960). For a long time the Stanford-Binet was the most widely used and researched individual intelligence test in English. During World War I Terman, with a group of other psychologists, participated in the construction of the first group intelligence test, the Army Alpha, and the nonverbal Army Beta. The Stanford Achievement Tests (with T. L. Kelley* and G. M. Ruch, 1923) and other psychometric instruments were the result of Terman's work.

Terman is also known for initiating a large-scale longitudinal study of the development of gifted children. Begun in 1921, the study encompassed an initial group of fifteen hundred California children with an IQ of 140 and above. The first report appeared in 1925. Terman continued the project until his death, and additional reports were prepared. Of the five volumes in the series, known as the Genetic Studies of Genius, the last one was published in 1959 (*The Gifted Group at Mid-Life*, with M. H. Oden). Terman found, among other things, that the gifted were taller, healthier, physically better developed, superior in leadership and social adaptability, dispelling the often held contrary notion.

Biographies: E. R. Hilgard, *Amer. J. Psychol.*, 1957, *70*, 472-479; W. B. Lewis, *Brit. J. Stat. Psychol.*, 1957, *10*, 65-68; R. R. Sears, *Science*, 1957, *125*, 978-979; *Biog. Mem.*, 33; *EUI*, 60; *HPA*, 2; *IESS*, 15; *NYT*, 1956, Dec. 23, 31:1; *Who Was Who in America*, 3; *Yearb. Amer. Phil. Soc.*, 1956.

TERTULLIAN (QUINTUS SEPTIMUS FLORENS TERTULLIANUS)
Christian Writer
Born: Carthage, ca. 155
Died: After 220, place unknown
Education: Studied Greek and Latin literature and law
Positions: After conversion to Christianity, became priest in the church of Carthage

Tertullian, one of the church fathers, defended the Christian faith in his writings between the years 195 and 220. He was violently opposed to science and Hellenic learning. He refuted Socrates*, Plato*, and Aristotle*, and his attitude is illustrated by the statement *credo quia absurdum est* ("I believe it because it is absurd").

Tertullian's importance to psychology is that he was the first to formulate a Christian doctrine concerning psychology, which is contained for the most part in his work *De anima*. The nature of the soul was Tertullian's main concern. The soul arises from the breath of God, but it is material: it is clear that states of the soul affect the body, and bodily conditions affect the soul. Besides, there is the revealed testimony of the Bible that souls suffer in hell, and that requires a material entity. The soul is extended substance, but it has no parts and is immortal. The senses are functions or powers of the soul, as is the mind. The seat of the soul is the heart. Tertullian insists on the veridicality of sensory perception, although he does so in the interest of theology and salvation. Thus

he resorts to naturalistic explanations to account for the appearance of bent oars in water, the apparent convergence of parallel lines with distance, and the like. Although the soul has free will, it is also influenced by environmental factors. In addition, Tertullian discusses sleep, dreams, and death.
Biographies: *EB*, 21.

TETENS, JOHANN NIKOLAS
German Philosopher
Born: Tetenbüll, Schleswig-Holstein, September 16, 1736
Died: Copenhagen, Denmark, August 15, 1807
Highest Degree: Master's degree, University of Rostock, 1759
Positions: 1763-76, Bützow Academy; 1776-89, University of Kiel; 1789-1807, finance official, city of Copenhagen

Tetens was the most prominent German philosopher of the era of Enlightenment and the only one to accept the empirical philosophy and psychology of Locke*, Hume*, and the associationists. He further emphasized the distinction made by Wolff* between rational and empirical psychology, but stressing the importance of the latter. His most important philosophical work, *Philosophische Veruche über die menschliche Natur* (1777; English translation, *Essays on Human Nature*, 1913), is also the most important one to psychology. In it Tetens asserted that a consideration of psychology must precede a consideration of metaphysics, and that the validity of the psychological considerations ultimately rests on the validity of empirical observations and experimentation. Although accepting association, Tetens pointed out that sensations and other mental contents are not simple building blocks that are put together without loss of identity. Rather, complex interactions are the rule, and even the simplest-appearing thinking process actually can be extremely complex. Throughout his book Tetens produced empirical evidence for his statements concerning the nature of sensations, perception (especially aftersensations and illusions), memory, thinking, habit formation, and development. Kant* was considerably influenced by Tetens's philosophy, especially by Tetens's attempts to state the principles governing the subjective a priori experiences and his threefold division of consciousness: feeling, will, and understanding.
Biographies: *ADB*, 37; *EP*, 8; *EUI*, 61.

TEUBER, HANS-LUKAS
American Psychologist
Born: Berlin, Germany, August 7, 1916
Died: Virgin Gorda, British Virgin Islands, January 4, 1977
Highest Degree: Ph.D. in psychology, Harvard University, 1947, under G. Allport*
Positions, Honors: 1946-47, research psychologist, Cabot Foundation, Cambridge, Mass.; 1947-61, Department of Neurology and Psychiatry, New York University Bellevue Medical Center and Graduate School of Arts and Sciences;

1961-77, professor, Massachusetts Institute of Technology, since 1964, founder and chairman, Department of Psychology, also director, psychophysiological laboratory; 1971-72, Eastman Professor, Oxford University; editorial work, *International Journal of Neuropsychology*, *Journal of Psychiatric Research*, *Experimental Brain Research Journal*; cofounder, of *Neuropsychologia*; Karl Spencer Lashley Award, American Philosophical Society, 1966; Apollo Achievement Award, NASA, 1969; Kenneth Craik Award, St. John's College, York University, 1971; James R. Killian, Jr., Faculty Achievement Award, Massachusetts Institute of Technology, 1977; honorary doctorate from Université Claude Bernard, Lyons, France, and Université de Génève, Switzerland

Teuber was an internationally known pioneer in the research of the relationship between brain anatomy, brain lesions, and behavior, especially perceptual behavior, such as vision with scotomata or blind areas and other perceptual distortions (spatial, haptic) following brain injury. His expertise as a consultant was widely sought, and Teuber was a member of numerous private and governmental panels and committees. He left about 160 publications, most of them in the area of brain injury and perception. Teuber's books include *Visual Field Defects After Penetrating Missile Wounds of the Brain* (1960, with W. S. Battersby and M. B. Bender), *Somatosensory Changes After Penetrating Brain Wounds in Man* (1960, written with J. Semmes, S. Weinstein, and L. Ghent), and a well-known chapter about perception in the *Handbook of Physiology* (1960) of the American Physiological Society.

Biographies: R. Held, *Neuropsychologia*, 1979, *17*, 117-118; H. Leibowitz & R. Held, *Psychol. Res.*, 1978, *40*, 1-3; H. Leibowitz & R. Held, *Amer. Psychologist*, 1979, *34*, 1107-1108; K. H. Pribram, *Amer. J. Psychol.* 1977, *90*, 705-707; W. Richards, *Vision Res.*, 1978, *18*, 357-364; *NYT*, 1977, Jan. 7, 19:4.

THALES
Greek Philosopher
Born: Miletus, ca. 624 B.C.
Died: Olympia, ca. 546 B.C.
Education: Unknown
Positions: Unknown

Of Thales' life nothing is known with certainty. He is called one of the Seven Wise Men of ancient Greece, credited with the introduction of geometry into Greece and feats such as predicting the solar eclipse of 585 B.C. and measuring the distance to inaccessible objects by means of triangulation.

Aristotle* stated that Thales was the founder of philosophy, and most of what is known about Thales comes from Aristotle because nothing of what was written by Thales himself remains. Thales was the first philosopher to suggest that there was one primordial substance that underlay all of the universe, namely, water. Water to Thales was both the origin and cause of the continuing existence of both organic and inorganic matter. His choice of water as the essential substance was probably due to the fact that water can be found both in the earth and in all living things, and also because it moved. Since motion, both of animate and inanimate objects, was a sign of life to the ancient Greeks, Thales considered the whole universe to be alive or besouled (having *psyche*). He referred to the behavior of the lodestone and of amber to illustrate his point with regard to inert matter.

Thales' main contribution is in his rejection of mythological explanations of universal origins and of life and the postulation of a natural, material cause. Humans were made of the same substance as all other units in the world and were totally part of the material world. Thales was the first in a long line of illustrious Greek thinkers to hold this enlightened position.

Biographies: D. R. Dicks, *Classical Quart.*, 1959, *53*, 294-309; *DSB*, 13; *EB*, 21; *HGP*, 1.

THEOPHRASTUS

Greek Philosopher
Born: Eresus, Lesbos, 371 to 370 B.C.
Died: Athens, 288 to 287 B.C.
Education: Studied in Athens under Aristotle*
Positions: Headed Aristotle's Lyceum for thirty-five years after Aristotle's departure from Athens

Theophrastus was a faithful disciple of Aristotle. He was even more naturalistically and empirically oriented than Aristotle. He wrote numerous treatises about a wide variety of subjects. For his work in botany he is considered the founder of that science. In his discussion of Aristotle's teachings, Theophrastus tried to minimize the Platonic elements. One important modification was his rejection of the search for final causes, stressed by Aristotle, and the emphasis on efficient causes in science. Also, unlike Aristotle, in his treatise *On the Senses*, Theophrastus placed intelligence in the brain. In that treatise of physiological psychology may be found detailed descriptions of sensations, perceptions, and affects. Theophrastus believed that under normal circumstances the senses inform us correctly about the nature of the material universe and that the material universe exists independently of our senses. He followed Aristotle in stating that external objects affect our senses, not directly or through emanations but through intervening media. Sensory qualities are not experienced until the activity of the sense organs affects the brain, a view that Aristotle held with regard to some of the sense modalities only.

Theophrastus is better known for a collection of thirty personality sketches, called *Characters*, in which he described the behavior of the typical flatterer, miser, and other types. Another volume of sketches of positive characters written by Theophrastus has been lost.

Biographies: *DSB*, 13; *EP*, 8.

THOMSON, SIR GODFREY HILTON

English Physical Scientist and Psychologist
Born: Carlisle, Cumberland, March 27, 1881
Died: Edinburgh, Scotland, February 9, 1955
Highest Degree: Ph.D. in physics and mathematics, University of Strasbourg, 1906; D.Sc. in psychology, Cambridge University, 1913
Positions, Honors: 1907-15, Armstrong College, Newcastle-upon-Tyne; 1920-25, King's College, Newcastle-upon-Tyne; 1925-55, University of Edinburgh; president, British Psychological Society, 1945-46; editorial work, *British Journal of Educational Psychology* and *British Journal of Psychology*; knighted, 1949

Thomson started his psychological work in psychophysics by analyzing the mathematical basis of threshold calculations. Later, he devised a test to select children who were to have free secondary education, the Northumberland Tests, now called the Moray House Tests, given every year in Britain to more than a million children. His last and most important contributions were in the area of factor analysis. Soon after Spearman* had presented his two-factor theory of intelligence, Thomson took issue with Spearman (1916, 1919) by pointing out that if there is one overlap among three or more variables (Spearman's *G*), there are additional, partial overlaps or group factors. Thomson was one of the men who developed the technique of factor analysis in the 1930s (*Factorial Analysis of Human Ability*, 1939). An important contribution to the field of psychological measurement was the book *The Essentials of Mental Measurement*, written first (1911) by William Brown* and then with Thomson in its second (1921) and third (1925) editions.

Biographies: A. C. Aitken, *Nature*, 1955, *175*, 620-621; C. Burt, *Brit. J. Stat. Psychol.*, 1955, *8*, 1-2; J. Drever, *Amer. J. Psychol.*, 1955, *68*, 494-496; W. Stephenson, *Brit. J. Psychol.*, 1955, *46*, 245-247; J. Sutherland, *Brit. J. Educ. Psychol.*, 1955, *25*, 65-66; L. L. Thurstone, *Psychometrika*, 1955, *20*, 171-172; *EUI*, 61; *HPA*, 4; *PR*, 3.

THORNDIKE, EDWARD LEE

American Psychologist
Born: Williamsburg, Massachusetts, August 31, 1874
Died: Montrose, New York, August 9, 1949
Highest Degree: Ph.D. in psychology, Columbia University, 1898, under J. McK. Cattell*
Positions: 1898-99, Western Reserve University; 1899-1940, Columbia University; president, American Psychological Association, 1912

Thorndike was the first psychologist to study animal behavior experimentally in a laboratory. He began using chicks at Harvard and then moved to Columbia and did his dissertation study on cats. The study was published in 1898 and became part of the classical literature of psychology. Thorndike observed the escape attempts, or trial and error learning, of cats in puzzle boxes and arrived at the first general principles governing such behavior. *The law of effect* stated that those movements that led to satisfaction would be stamped in, and that those that led to an unsatisfactory state of affairs would be stamped out. Thus from the random array of movements exhibited by the animal in the puzzle box, only those leading to escape would be learned. Later Thorndike discovered that noxious effects only suppressed behavior temporarily but did not actually stamp it out. *The law of exercise* stated that those associations that are practiced are stamped in and those that are not are extinguished. The law of effect was an empirically based restatement of what many philosophers and psychologists had previously said about the effects of pleasure and pain. The law of exercise restated how stimuli and responses become associated, hence hailed back directly to the associationistic doctrine. Although Thorndike's two laws in their original form are not accepted today, most learning theories incorporate them in some modified form.

Thorndike's interest later turned to human learning. In 1901 he and Woodworth* published a classic paper that demolished the doctrine of formal disciplines by showing that transfer of learning takes place only if the same general principles or identical elements are involved. In 1903 Thorndike published his *Educational Psychology* (the second edition consisted of three volumes: *The Original Nature of Man*, 1913; *The Psychology of Learning*, 1913; and *Individual Differences and Their Causes*, 1914) in which the learning principles Thorndike had discovered in his work with animals were applied to the human educational experience. Education led Thorndike to mental measurement. He became a leader in that field, publishing his *Introduction to the Theory of Mental and Social Measurements* in 1904 and later, with others, *The Measurement of Intelligence* (1927). The 1904 volume made statistical computations of test results available to the everyday user of such tests.

Additional efforts of Thorndike's included the construction of a scale to measure children's handwriting (1910) and a table of word-frequency counts in the English language (*The Teacher's Word Book of 30,000 Words*, 1944, with I. Lorge*), of considerable utility to researchers who use dictionary words in their work. Thorndike was prolific: he left a bibliography of more than four hundred fifty articles and books. Additional important books that Thorndike wrote were *The Elements of Psychology* (1905), *Animal Intelligence* (1911), *The Fundamentals of Learning* (1932), and *The Psychology of Wants, Interests, and Attitudes* (1935).

Biographies: A. I. Gates, *Psychol. Rev.*, 1949, *56*, 241-243; F. L. Goodenough, *Amer. J. Psychol.*, 1950, *63*, 291-301; G. Humphrey, *Brit. J. Psychol.*, 1949, *40*, 55-56; G. M. Joncich, *The Sane Positivist: A Biography of Edward L. Thorndike*, 1969; W. F. Russell, *Teach. Coll. Rec.*, 1949, *51*, 26-28; G. Thomson, *Nature*, 1949, *164*, 474; R. S. Woodworth, *Science*, 1950, *111*, 250-251; *Biog. Mem.*, 27; *HPA*, 3; *IESS*, 16; *NCAB*, 15; *NYT*, 1949, Aug. 10, 21:1; *PR*, 3; *Who Was Who in America*, 2; *Yearb. Amer. Phil. Soc.*, 1949.

THURSTONE, LOUIS LEON

American Psychologist
Born: Chicago, Illinois, May 29, 1887
Died: Chapel Hill, North Carolina, September 29, 1955
Highest Degree: Ph.D. in psychology, University of Chicago, 1917
Positions, Honors: 1917-24, Carnegie Institute of Technology; 1924-56, University of Chicago; 1952-55, University of North Carolina; president, American Psychological Association, 1933; first president of the Psychometric Society; honorary doctorate, University of Göteborg, 1954

Thurstone was the most eminent psychometrician of his time. Thurstone's main contributions are in the area of the application of statistics to psychological problems. In the United States the development of the technique of factor analysis is connected mainly with his name (*Vectors of the Mind*, 1935; *Factorial Studies of Intelligence*, 1941; *Multiple Factor Analysis*, 1947). Thurstone factor-analyzed intelligence tests and tests of perception. In the area of intelligence, his theory was that intelligence is made up of several primary mental abilities rather than a general and several specific factors. Spearman's* general factor he considered to be a second-order factor obtainable from a factor analysis of the first-order factors: verbal ability, number, spatial ability, perceptual ability, memory, reasoning, and word fluency. Thurstone's primary mental abilities (*Primary Mental Abilities*, 1938) have been used to construct intelligence tests that, unlike the general intelligence tests that yield a single score, yield a profile of the individual's performance on each of the ability tests.

The law of comparative judgments in psychophysics was a contribution that Thurstone himself considered to be his best. By introducing the concept of the discriminal dispersion, Thurstone produced a mathematical model that accounted for a set of comparative judgments made by a number of judges. Another contribution of Thurstone's was the construction of the earliest attitude scale. The scale was based on a modification of the psychophysical method of equal-appearing intervals. A series of statements on some subject are judged by a large number of judges. A person's score on the scale is the mean of scaled values of those items with which he agrees. The introduction of attitude scales did much to introduce quantification in social psychology (*Measurement of Attitudes*, 1929). Thurstone wrote 23 books and monographs, 165 articles, and 95 laboratory reports and constructed 47 tests.

Biographies: C. Burt, *Brit. J. Stat. Psychol.*, 1956, *9*, 104; J. Cardinet, *Rev. psychol. appl.*, 1955, *5*, 149-154; J. P. Guilford, *Psychometrika*, 1955, *20*, 263-265; H. Gulliksen, *Amer. Psychologist*, 1968, *23*, 786-802; P. Horst, *Science*, 1955, *122*, 1259-1260; D. Wolfle, *Amer. J. Psychol.*, 1956, *69*, 131-134; D. (Adkins) Wood, *Louis Leon Thurstone: Creative Thinker, Dedicated Teacher, Eminent Psychologist*, 1962; *Biog. Mem.*, 30; *HPA*, 4; *IESS*, 16; *NYT*, 1955, Oct. 1, 19:5; *Who Was Who in America*, 3; *Yearb. Amer. Phil. Soc.*, 1955.

TIEDEMANN, DIETRICH

German Philosopher
Born: Bremervörde, Lower Saxony, April 3, 1748
Died: Marburg, Hessen, May 24, 1803
Education: Studied at University of Göttingen
Positions: 1786-1803, University of Marburg

Tiedemann's observations on the development of the mental abilities of his own son, published in 1787 (*Beobachtungen über die Entwicklung der Seelenfähigkeit bei Kindern*), was the second (after Pestalozzi's*) instance of the publication of developmental observations of children in a scientific journal. Other instances did not occur until about a hundred years later. Tiedemann also published a *Handbuch der Psychologie* (1804), but his most important work was done in philosophy rather than psychology.

Biographies: ADB, 38; *Chalmers*, 29; *DSB*, 13; *EUI*, 61; *Grande*, 31.

TITCHENER, EDWARD BRADFORD

American Psychologist
Born: Chichester, Sussex, England, January 11, 1867
Died: Ithaca, New York, August 3, 1927
Highest Degree: Ph.D. in psychology, University of Leipzig, 1892, under W. Wundt*
Positions: 1892-1927, Cornell University; editor, *American Journal of Psychology*, 1895-1927

Titchener considered Wundt to be of utmost importance to psychology, and he spent his life expounding and systematizing the Wundtian point of view and producing laboratory research using Wundt's method of introspection. The school of structuralism was born at Cornell and had life in Titchener and the many doctoral students that he taught. In Titchener's view psychology's first task is to study structure before embarking on the study of function. Functionalism in his view was premature. Structuralism, however, died with Titchener, for he refused to change his thinking as psychology changed. He refused to consider applied psychology a valid enterprise and had no interest in studying animals, children, abnormalities of behavior, or individual differences. The organization of experimental psychologists that Titchener established in 1904, although intended to perpetuate Wundt's psychology, changed its name to Society of Experimental Psychologists after Titchener's death and used the introspective method only sparingly.

To Titchener psychology was the study of experience from the point of view of the experiencing individual. Mental processes are not to be confused with the material causes of these processes. In an experiment introspection consists of describing the conscious contents of experience. The tendency to describe the object instead is "stimulus error." Since psychology as a science depends on introspection as its method of observation, the avoidance of stimulus error is crucial. Mind is the totality of subjective experiences, past, present, conscious, and unconscious. It is correlated with the activity of the nervous system but is not caused by it (Wundt's psychophysical parallelism). Since nervous and mental processes parallel each other, the former may be used to explain the latter. Titchener, however, made no particular attempt to relate neurophysiology and experience. Neither did behavior play any particular role, because Titchener relegated it to biology, considering it irrelevant to the psychology of consciousness.

The building blocks of consciousness were the sensations, images, and affections. They were the ultimate irreducibles that went on to make up the perceptions (from sensations), ideas (from images), and emotions (from affections). Titchener characterized mental processes as having quality, intensity, duration, clearness, and extensity, the last three being Titchener's addition to Wundt's list of the dimensions of mental processes. The addition of clearness assigned attention a systematic place and eliminated some of the problems previously associated with its uncertain status.

Within the general framework of structuralism, Titchener provided one specific theory that became well known because it kept reappearing in different forms in the work of a number of psychologists and linguists. It is the *core-context theory of meaning*, according to which a new mental process (the core) acquires its meaning from the context of other mental processes within which it occurs. In its simplest form, the context may be just one other mental element, and, besides, a person does not have to be aware of the context to assign meaning (unconscious context).

Titchener wrote more than two hundred articles, eight books in psychology, and eleven translations of German psychological texts. His most important book is *Experimental Psychology*, four volumes (1901-5). The others are *Outline of Psychology* (1896), *Primer of Psychology* (1898), *Lectures on Elementary Psychology of Feeling and Attention* (1908), *Lectures on the Experimental Psychology of the Thought Processes* (1909), *A Textbook of Psychology* (1910), *Systematic Psychology: Prolegomena* (1929), and *A Beginner's Psychology* (1915).

Biographies: E. G. Boring, *Amer. J. Psychol.*, 1927, *38*, 489-506; K. M. Dallenbach, *Amer. J. Psychol.*, 1937, *50*, 489-506; R. B. Evans, *J. Hist. Behav. Sci.*, 1972, *8*, 168-180; C. S. Myers, *Brit. J. Psychol.*, 1927-1928, *18*, 460-463; H. C. Warren, *Science*, 1927, *66*, 208-209; *DAB*, 18; *EB*, 22; *IESS*, 16; *NCAB*, 22.

TOLMAN, EDWARD CHACE

American Psychologist

Born: West Newton, Massachusetts, April 14, 1886

Died: Berkeley, California, November 19, 1959

Highest Degree: Ph.D. in psychology, Harvard University, 1915, under E. B. Holt*

Positions, Honors: 1915-18, Northwestern University; 1918-54, University of California at Berkeley; president, American Psychological Association, 1937;

American Psychological Association Distinguished Scientific Contribution Award, 1957

Tolman brought to psychology a systematic theory of learning that stressed cognitive factors. Although basically behavioristic, the theory emphasizes significant units of behavior ("molar" behavior) rather than elementary reflexes ("molecular" behavior). Although Tolman was dissatisfied with the overly simple behavioristics of Watson*, he developed his systematic views on the basis of his studies of maze learning in rats. Tolman, however, was also influenced by Gestalt psychology, and his theory of purposive behaviorism is a blend of neobehaviorism and Gestalt notions. *Purposive Behavior in Animals and Men* (1932) was Tolman's great work. It contains a glossary of 123 terms, many of them neologisms, that Tolman used to describe his theory.

The rat in a maze, instead of learning stimulus-response chains, learns *sign Gestalten*, which are cognitive representations of what leads to what. A pattern of such Gestalten is a cognitive map. It enables the animal to run a learned maze even when the stimulus-response connections no longer obtain, for instance, when other responses must be employed to obtain food, such as swimming in a flooded maze. Rats (and humans) act for an end, that is, with a purpose. Tolman, true to an objective and behavioristic psychology, never discussed *purpose* in teleological terms but rather as a descriptive term applicable to what the rats were doing in the maze. Disturbance in an animal when a different reward is given, search for food when none is found, and the results of latent learning experiments were used by Tolman as evidence that cognitive expectations constituted the essence of learning, not conditioned responses. Expectations allow for the substitution of responses when necessary, which is what is observed in animal learning rather than strictly stereotyped sequences of behavior. Latent learning experiments led Tolman to the conclusion that a distinction must be made between learning as acquisition and learning as performance. For learning as acquisition no reward is necessary. To establish whether learning has actually occurred, performance of the learned task must be shown, for which reward is a prerequisite. Tolman called learning as acquisition an "intervening variable," a concept that he introduced in American psychology and one that has been universally accepted. Intervening variables he called "objective but unobservable variables" that could be defined in terms of observable antecedent conditions and observable response.

Biographies: *Amer. Psychologist*, 1958, *13*, 155-158; R. S. Crutchfield, *Amer. J. Psychol.*, 1961, *74*, 135-141; R. S. Crutchfield, D. Krech, & R. C. Tryon, *Science*, 1960, *131*, 714-716; G. W. H. Leytham, *Bull. Brit. Psychol. Soc.*, 1962, *49*, 21-28; *Biog. Mem.*, 37; *HPA*, 4; *IESS*, 16; *NCAB*, F; *NYT*, 1959, Nov. 21, 23:5; *PR*, 3; *Who Was Who in America*, 4.

TROLAND, LEONARD THOMPSON
American Psychologist
Born: Norwich, Connecticut, April 26, 1889
Died: Mount Wilson, California, May 27, 1932

Highest Degree: Ph.D. in psychology, Harvard University, 1915, under H. Münsterberg*, E. B. Holt*, and H. S. Langfeld*
Positions: 1916-32, Harvard University; president, Optical Society of America, 1922

Troland was a very versatile scientist. He made contributions to several fields besides psychology. He wrote several important papers about life and life processes, published a book about physics, was a coinventor of the Technicolor movie process, and wrote papers about philosophy and metaphysics. His psychological papers always began and ended with a philosophical discussion. In psychology Troland's most notable contributions were in the field of vision. His main interest there was to shape psychology after modern physics. Troland's vision research was formulated according to the "method of mathematical hypothesis," in which a process is first described by equations derived from a few simple mathematical premises. He published numerous papers in the field. In 1922 his book *The Present Status of Visual Science* appeared. He participated in the translation of Helmholtz's* *Handbook of Psychological Optics* and contributed a chapter about vision to Murchison's* *Handbook of General Experimental Psychology*. His presidency of the Optical Society of America and the posthumous naming of the unit of retinal illumination, *the troland*, after him were the honorific results of his work on vision. Troland also attempted to extend the "method of mathematical hypothesis" to the field of emotion (*Fundamentals of Human Motivation*, 1928), although there it never went past a programmatic statement. His theory was hedonistic, postulating three kinds of receptors, one receiving pleasant stimuli, one painful stimuli, and one neutral stimuli. Receptors of painful stimuli were assumed to lead, by retroflex action of the thalamus, to a reduction in the conductance of cortical synapses. "Retroflex action" was a process postulated by Troland to stamp responses in and out, depending on the nature of stimulation. Pleasure or pain, Troland said, is experienced as the rate of cortical conductance at the synapses changes. A person's general affective makeup is thus determined by the accumulated total effect of retroflexive processes. Troland also wrote a popular book about psychology, *The Mystery of Mind* (1925), and a three-volume *Principles of Psychophysiology* (1929-32).
Biographies: J. Alexander, *Science*, 1932, *76*, 255-257; J. G. Beebe-Center, *Amer. J. Psychol.*, 1932, *44*, 817-820; A. A. Roback, *Science*, 1932, *76*, 26-27; J. P. C. Southall, *J. Opt. Soc. Amer.*, 1932, *22*, 509-511; *DAB*, 18; *NYT*, 1932, May 28, 16:4; *Who Was Who in America*. 1.

TWITMYER, EDWIN BURKET
American Psychologist
Born: McElhattan, Pennsylvania, September 14, 1873
Died: Drexel Hill, Pennsylvania, March 3, 1943
Highest Degree: Ph.D. in psychology, University of Pennsylvania, 1902
Positions, Honors: 1897-1943, University of Pennsylvania; honorary LL.D., Lafayette College, 1933

Twitmyer's doctoral dissertation was about the knee jerk. To signal the striking of the hammer on the patellar tendon he rang a bell and thus discovered that eventually the ringing of the bell alone would cause the patellar reflex to occur. He reported his finding at the 1904 meeting of the American Psychological Association (Knee jerk without stimulation of the patellar tendon, *Psychological Bulletin*, 1905, *2*, 43ff.), but the significance of the first laboratory demonstration of the conditioned reflex was not then appreciated. Pavlov* published his findings with dogs the next year, persisted with his work, and having already won the Nobel Prize, commanded more attention than Twitmyer. Discouraged by the indifferent reception, Twitmyer switched to other work, mainly in the area of speech. In 1914 the University of Pennsylvania special speech clinic was established, the first of its kind in America, and Twitmyer became its first director. In 1932 he wrote with Y. S. Nathanson the book *Correction of Defective Speech.* In it he expressed the view that all disturbances of speech have a common etiology, namely, a disturbance in the rhythm of breathing. The latter, being partly habitual, could be cured using the learning methods.

Biographies: R. A. Brotemarkle, *J. Consult. Psychol.*, 1943, *7*, 200-201; K. G. Ecob, *Ment. Hyg.*, 1943, *27*, 331; S. W. Fernberger, *Psychol. Rev.*, 1943, *50*, 345-349; F. W. Irwin, *Amer. J. Psychol.*, 1943, *56*, 451-453; *NCAB*, 33; *NYT*, 1943, Mar. 4, 19:2; *PR*, 3; *Who Was Who in America*, 2.

TYLOR, SIR EDWARD BURNETT
English Anthropologist
Born: London, October 2, 1832
Died: Wellington, Somersetshire, January 2, 1917
Education: No university education; self-educated
Positions, Honors: 1883-88, Oxford University; 1888-96, University of Aberdeen; 1896-1909, Oxford University, occupying first chair of anthropology; president, Anthropological Society, 1891; knighted, 1912; honorary D.C.L., Oxford University, 1875

Tylor was a Darwinian anthropologist, known for his studies of mythology, magic, and primitive mentality and his pioneering work in developing anthropology as a science. In his work Tylor used psychological methods. His best-known work is *Primitive Culture* (1871). He emphasized that the psychological makeup of humans is basic to their behavior and that a psychological approach to anthropology is therefore the best approach. His main contribution to psychology was the doctrine that religion evolves from primitive mentality. Since primitives are animistic, endowing all things with life and motives, they worship those things that seem to be powerful and affect their lives. They consider the soul a separate entity that enters and leaves the body in sleep and dreams.

Biographies: R. R. Marett, *Tylor*, 1936; N. W. Thomas (Ed.), *Anthropological Essays Presented to Edward Burnett Tylor in Honor of His 75th Birthday*, 1907; *DNB*, Suppl. 2, 3; *EUI*, 65; *Grande*, 31; *IESS*, 16.

U

UEXKÜLL, (BARON) JAKOB JOHANN VON

German Biologist
Born: Kolbaste (now Mihkli), Estonia, September 8, 1864
Died: Capri, Italy, July 25, 1944
Education: Studied zoology at University of Tartu between 1885 and 1890, later at the University of Heidelberg
Positions: Naples Biological Station; 1925-44, director, Institut für Umweltforschung, Hamburg

Uexküll was one of the forerunners of ethology. He first attracted attention by publishing a paper in 1899, with T. Beer and A. Bethe*, in which they recommended that, in discussing animal behavior, all psychological terms, such as *sensation* and *memory*, be discarded and terms like *reception* and *resonance* be used instead. Independently of Jennings*, Uexküll arrived at views similar to his. He insisted that the observation of all behaviors must precede any attempt to explain specific behavior items in an animal species. Uexküll's major contribution was the concept of *Umwelt* (*Umwelt und Innenwelt der Tiere*, 1909; *Streifzüge durch die Umwelten von Tieren und Menschen*, 1934). He realized that only certain aspects of the animal's physical environment (*Merkwelt*, or the sum total of possible stimuli) have a significance for him. Only these stimuli (the releasers), either innately or through learning, release the animal's behaviors. The totality of such stimuli Uexküll named the animal's *Umwelt*. Each kind of animal lives in its special *Umwelt*. Internally, each animal has its *Innenwelt*, or an internal orienting mechanism that conditions the animal's response to the *Umwelt* in such a way as to produce and maintain some optimum adjustment to it. The relationship between the animal and the stimuli of the *Umwelt* is reciprocal. As the animal reacts to them, the reaction changes the sensory qualities of the stimuli, which elicits a new reaction on the part of the animal. The symbolic representation of this circular interaction Uexküll called the *Funktionskreis* ("functional circle"), which represents the perfectly matched worlds of releasers and the world of the animal's responses to them. Uexküll published a dozen major books in biology and animal behavior.

Biographies: F. Brock, *Arch. Gesch. Med.*, 1934, *27*, 193-212; R. Burkhardt & H. Erhard, *Geschichte der Zoologie*, 1921; *Festschrift für Jakob von Uexküll*, 1924; G. Uexküll, *Jakob von Uexküll: Seine Welt und seine Umwelt*, 1964; J. J. v. Uexküll, *Niegeschaute Welten*, 1957; *Biog. Lex.*; *DSB*, 15; *EP*, 8; *EUI*, 65.

URBAN, F(REDERICK) M(ARY)

Austrian Psychologist
Born: Brünn (Brno), Moravia, December 28, 1878
Died: Maisons-Lafitte, near Paris, France, May 4, 1964
Highest Degree: Ph.D. in philosophy, University of Vienna, 1902, under Friedrich Jodl; Ph.D. in psychology, University of Leipzig, 1903 (?)
Positions: 1904-5, Harvard University; 1905-14, University of Pennsylvania; 1914-17, Kungliga Vetenskapliga Akademien, Stockholm

Urban was a psychophysicist who contributed a book (*The Application of Statistical Methods to the Problem of Psychophysics*, 1908) and some fifteen papers to the area. He is known for having introduced (in 1909) a correction in the table of weights furnished by G. E. Müller* in 1903 for fitting the psychometric function to data obtained using the method of right and wrong cases. The table was named the "Table of Müller-Urban Weights." Urban also contributed the concept of the psychometric function, the phi-gamma function (1910), which is a curve obtained by plotting percentages of responses in the categories "less," "more," and "equal" against stimulus values when the method of constant stimuli is used in establishing the difference or absolute threshold. It is stated in terms of h, an index of the dispersion of response about the mean. The phi-gamma hypothesis states that data obtained with the constant stimuli method will fit the phi-gamma function.

Urban wrote his second doctoral dissertation about probability calculus. When circumstances forced him to remain in his home town between 1917 and 1948, unable to be active in psychology, he used his statistical knowledge in insurance work. He published a text about probability calculus and the theory of observation errors in 1923 (*Grundlagen der Wahrscheinlichkeitsrechnung und der Theorie der Beobachtungsfehler*).

Biographies: J. E. Ertle, R. C. Bushong, & W. A. Hillix, *J. Hist. Behav. Sci.*, 1977, *13*, 379-383; M. M. Sokal, *J. Hist. Behav. Sci.*, 1978, *14*, 170-172.

UZNADZE, DIMITRIĬ NIKOLAEVICH
Georgian Psychologist
Born: Georgia, Russia, January 1, 1887
Died: Tblisi, Georgia, October 12, 1950
Highest Degree: Ph.D., University of Leipzig, 1909
Positions: 1918-30, University of Tblisi; 1930-50, Pedagogical Institute, Tblisi

Uznadze, the most prominent Georgian psychologist, was a cofounder of the University of Tblisi in 1918. He established the Department of Psychology and an experimental psychology laboratory at that university. In 1941 he founded the Georgian Institute of Psychology as part of the Georgian Academy of Sciences. After his death it was named the Uznadze Institute of Psychology.

Uznadze's main contribution to psychology was his theory of set. Originally applied to perception to explain deviation in perception away from the physical stimulus characteristics under the influence of the perceiver's set established by previous experience, expectations, instructions, and the like, the theory was expanded by Uznadze to account for most behaviors. The theory continues to be developed by Uznadze's students and coworkers. The Georgian school of psychology is based on his theory.

Uznadze also worked in the area of child psychology, especially the development of thinking. He wrote several psychological texts in the Georgian language ([*Fundamentals of Experimental Psychology*], 1925; [*General Psychology*], 1940; [*Child Psychology*], 1947), including the first psychology text ever written in that language. He was also the author of a number of papers and monographs in German. Russian translations of his work in connection with the theory of set include *Eksperimental'nye osnovy psikhologii ustanovki* (1961) and *Psikhologicheskie issledovaniya* (1966).

Biographies: *PR*, 3.

V

VAIHINGER, HANS
German Philosopher
Born: Nehren, Württemberg, September 25, 1852
Died: Halle, Saxony-Anhalt, December 12, 1933
Highest Degree: Ph.D. in philosophy, University of Tübingen, 1874
Positions: 1877-84, University of Strasbourg; 1884-1906, University of Halle

Vaihinger's name is mentioned in histories of psychology because a book that he wrote, *Die Philosophie des Als Ob* (1911) influenced the development of Alfred Adler's* thinking. Vaihinger advanced the idea that although a person may be striving to achieve goals or to live by ideals that have no existence in reality, the mere striving for them and the pretense that they actually exist lends them some reality because they affect the person's attitudes and behavior. This idea may be seen in one of Adler's main conceptions, namely, that we create our own personalities.

Biographies: T. A. Castiglia, *Riv. int. fil. dir.*, 1934, *14*, 276-283; A. Kowalewski, *Jb. Schopenhauer-Ges.*, 1935-36, *22*, 3-21; *EP*, 8; *EUI*, 66.

VALENTINE, CHARLES WILFRID
English Psychologist
Born: Runcorn, Cheshire, August 16, 1879
Died: Birmingham, May 26, 1964
Highest Degree: Ph.D., St. Andrews University, 1913
Positions: 1914-19, University of Belfast; 1919-46, University of Birmingham

Valentine was the leader of British educational psychology during his lifetime,

but he worked in several additional areas as well. He founded the *British Journal of Educational Psychology* in 1931 and edited it for twenty-five years. His best-known educational text is *Psychology and Its Bearing on Education* (1950). He published additional volumes about the psychology of education, such as *The Reliability of Examinations* (1932), *The Psychology of Early Education* (1942), *Intelligence Tests for Young Children* (1945), *Intelligence Tests for Children* (1950), *Psychology and Its Bearing on Education* (1950), and *Parents and Children*. Valentine also penned an *Introduction to Experimental Psychology in Relation to Education* (1915; 2nd ed., *Introduction to Experimental Psychology*, 1926), *Dreams and the Unconscious* (1921), *The Human Factor in the Army* (1943), and *Psychology and Mental Health* (1948). In 1913 he wrote *The Experimental Psychology of Beauty*, presenting the results of his experimental work on the psychology of aesthetics. An enlarged version of the book appeared in 1919. It was at the time the only such book ever published, and it continued to be that until 1962 when Valentine published a final version of it.
Biographies: L. B. Birch, *Bull. Brit. Psychol. Soc.*, 1964, *17*, 47-50; T. H. Pear, *Brit. J. Psychol.*, 1964, *55*, 385-390; *EUI*, 66; *PR*, 3.

VERWORN, MAX
German Physiologist
Born: Berlin, November 4, 1863
Died: Bonn, November 23, 1921
Highest Degree: Ph.D. in zoology, University of Berlin, 1887; M.D., University of Jena, 1889
Positions: 1889-1901, University of Jena; 1901-10, University of Göttingen; 1910-21, University of Bonn

Founder of the well-known physiological journal *Zeitschrift für allgemeine Physiologie* (1902), Verworn wrote numerous papers and some ten volumes about physiology, most of them concerned with irritability, the response of living tissue to stimulation, and the problem of life. In his works Verworn did not limit himself to physiology as such but also stated the philosophical problems involved, such as the mind-body problem. His concern with philosophical and psychological issues is reflected in the titles of volumes such as *Die Entwicklung des menschlichen Geistes* (1910) and *Die Mechanik des Geistes* (1916). He even wrote about the psychology of art (*Zur Psychologie der primitiven Kunst*, 1908). In *Psychophysiologische Protisten-Studien* (1889) Verworn discarded dualism to embrace psychic monism. More importantly, the work marks the beginning of protopsychology, the study of the behavior of animals at the low end of the phylogenetic scale.
Biographies: F. W. Fröhlich, *Z. allg. Physiol.*, 1923, *20*, 185-192; *Biog. Lex.*; *DSB*, 14.

VESALIUS, ANDREAS
Flemish Anatomist
Born: Brussels, December 31, 1514
Died: Zakinthos, Greece, October 15, 1564
Education: University of Louvain, 1530-33; University of Paris, 1533-37; M.D.,
University of Padua, 1537
Positions: 1536-37, University of Louvain; 1537-43, University of Padua; 1543-
55, physician to emperor Charles V; 1555-64, physician to Philip II

Vesalius was the founder of modern anatomy. Beginning with Vesalius, anatomical knowledge will be gained from dissections carried out by scholars
trained in medicine. First in the *Tabulae anatomicae sex* (1538), and later in his
masterpiece *De humani corporis fabrica* (1543), Vesalius standardized the form
and meaning of anatomical terms and stated the necessity for the scientific method
in the study of anatomy. *De humani corporis fabrica* contained many new
discoveries and superb anatomical drawings, especially of the brain. Free of
Galenic ideas about medicine and anatomy, Vesalius denied that the ventricles
of the brain had any mental functions but that they mainly collected fluid. He
also denied that the mind could be split up into faculties. Finding that the brains
of the animals he had examined were all constructed on the same plan as the
brains of humans, Vesalius concluded that not only would it be fruitless to
attempt to establish how the brain remembers or thinks on the basis of anatomy
alone but that there was no basis for denying animals the same mental powers
that humans had. Vesalius's work was a milestone in achieving an understanding
of the physical basis of behavior and experience.
Biographies: H. W. Cushing, *A Bio-bibliography of Andreas Vesalius*, 1943;
C. D. O'Malley, *Andreas Vesalius of Brussels, 1514-1564*, 1964; *DSB*, 14;
EB, 22.

VIERORDT, KARL VON
German Physiologist
Born: Lahr, Württemberg, July 1, 1818
Died: Tübingen, Württemberg, November 22, 1884
Highest Degree: M.D., University of Heidelberg, 1841
Positions: 1849-84, University of Tübingen

In the area of psychophysics, Vierordt was first (in 1852) to use the method
of right and wrong cases (the method of constant stimuli) to establish sensory
thresholds. Fechner* was to develop this method later. In 1868 Vierordt published
a volume about the psychology of time (*Der Zeitsinn nach Versuchen*). In it he
introduced, among other things, the notion of the indifference point in time
estimation (0.75 seconds), where there is no constant error. Vierordt conducted
many additional researches on vision, hearing, and somesthesis. In 1869 he
measured the brightness of the solar spectrum. In the same and in the following
year he measured the two-point threshold, formulating the law that the two-point

threshold varies inversely with the mobility of the bodily part where it is measured (Vierordt's law).

Biographies: R. H. Major, *Ann. Med. Hist.*, 1938, *10*, 463-473; H. Vierordt, *Karl von Vierordt: Die Schall- und Tonstärke und das Schalleitungsvermögen der Körper*, 1885; C. v. Voit, *Sitzber. Bayer. Akad. Wiss.*, math.-phys. Kl., 1885, 180-185; *ADB*, 39; *EUI*, 68; Hirsch, *Biog. Lex.*, 5; Pagel, *Biographisches Lexikon*.

VIVES, JUAN LUIS
Spanish Philosopher
Born: Valencia, March 6, 1492
Died: Bruges, Belgium, May 6, 1540
Education: Graduated from University of Paris in 1512
Positions: 1519-23, University of Louvain; 1523-27, Oxford University

Vives, a Renaissance humanist, anticipated several later developments in psychology, but his work does not connect directly to the psychological work of Descartes*, and he stands alone as a forerunner of modern psychology that began with Descartes.

Vives wrote several works about education that went through many editions. In these works he advocated the education of women. His psychological volume is *De anima et vita libri tres* (1538). Among the points that Vives made are that psychology should be used in education; philosophical and psychological truths are to be discovered inductively rather than deductively, avoiding speculation; a knowledge of the essence of the soul is unimportant, but to know what the manifestations of the soul are is of great importance; knowledge is of any value only when it is used. Vives did not concern himself with the essence of mind but with how it works. A functionalist frame of mind is clearly evident in his *De anima*, 350 years before Spencer*, James*, and the functionalist school. Among the specific topics discussed in Vives's book are the association of ideas, memory and forgetting, emotions and passions, and intelligence. The emotions and passions are treated extensively by Vives. He stressed their manifold character, temporal variations, interaction with temperament and habit patterns, the coloring of perception by emotions, and their influence in creating for a person a special world, all his own.

Biographies: M. L. Bernabe M., In F. Pérez-Embid (Dir.), *Enciclopedia de la cultura española*, vol. 5, 1968; A. Bonilla y San Martín, *Luis Vives y la filosofía del renacimiento*, 3 vols., 1903; W. A. Daly, The Educational Psychology of Juan Luis Vives, 1924 (Doctoral dissertation, Catholic University of America); C. G. Noreña, *Juan Luis Vives*, 1970; F. Watson, *Psychol. Rev.*, 1915, *22*, 333-353; *DSB*, 14.

VOLKMANN, ALFRED WILHELM
German Physiologist
Born: Leipzig, Saxony, July 1, 1800
Died: Halle, Saxony-Anhalt, April 21, 1877

Highest Degree: Ph.D. in physiology, University of Leipzig, 1826
Positions: 1837-43, University of Tartu; 1843-73, University of Halle

Although Volkmann's first psychological publication was about animal magnetism (*Observatio biologica de magnetismo animali*, 1826), his major contributions were in the area of the physiology of vision. He wrote *Neue Beiträge zur Physiologie des Gesichtssinnes* (1836), the section about vision in Rudolph Wagner's *Handwörterbuch der Physiologie* (1844-46), and the volumes of *Physiologische Untersuchungen im Gebiete der Optik* (1863-64). Volkmann collaborated also with Fechner* in developing the psychophysical method of average error.

Biographies: *EUI*, 69; *Grande*, 31; Hirsch, *Biog. Lex.*, 5.

VOLTAIRE (pseud. of FRANÇOIS-MARIE AROUET)

French Author and Philosopher
Born: Paris, November 21, 1694
Died: Paris, May 30, 1778
Education: Attended the Jesuit school of Collège Louis-le-Grand, 1704-11
Positions: Dramatist and poet; 1744-47, 1751-53, court appointments

Voltaire, one of the greatest figures in French letters and thought, never wrote anything specifically psychological. In the classic *Lettres philosophiques* (1734), however, Voltaire, by espousing and presenting the Lockean point of view, performed the service of acquainting Europe, and especially France, with the Lockean doctrine. Voltaire admired Newton*, opposed Descartes*, and professed ignorance concerning the nature of the soul. He advocated empiricism, sensationism, and the scientific method but did not go to the extreme of atheism, as did French materialists such as La Mettrie*, whom he influenced.

Biographies: T. Besterman, *Voltaire*, 1969; G. Lanson, *Voltaire,* 1966; R. Naves, *Voltaire*, 1958; B. R. Redman, In *The Portable Voltaire*, 1949, pp. 1-47; *CE*, 14; *Chalmers*, 30; *EB*, 23; *EP*, 8; *EUI*, 69; *Grande*, 31; *IESS*, 16; *Jewish*, 10; *Nouvelle*, 46.

VON NEUMANN, JOHN

German-American Mathematician
Born: Budapest, Hungary, December 28, 1903
Died: Washington, D.C., February 8, 1957
Highest Degree: Ph.D. in mathematics, University of Budapest, 1926
Positions, Honors: 1927-29, University of Berlin; 1929-30, University of Hamburg; 1930-33, Princeton University; 1933-55, Institute for Advanced Study, Princeton University; 1955-57, Atomic Energy Commission; seven honorary degrees; Medal of Merit, 1946; Medal of Freedom, 1956; Enrico Fermi Award, 1956; president, American Mathematical Society, 1950-51; key adviser to a number of national scientific councils; editorial work, *Annals of Mathematics, Compositio Mathematica*

One of the foremost mathematicians of this century, von Neumann made many significant contributions to pure mathematics, the quantum theory, the theory of electronic computing devices, and the development of the first electronic computers (MANIAC, NORC). Both the quantum theory and electronic computers were crucial to the development of the hydrogen bomb, and von Neumann was involved in it. His fourth main contribution, the development of the theory of games, is of importance to the social and behavioral sciences. Von Neumann published the first paper about game theory in 1928. After coming to the United States, he began a collaboration with Oskar Morgenstern, a professor of economics at Princeton. The result was *Theory of Games and Economic Behavior*, published jointly by them in 1944. It initiated the modern period in the study of risky decision making.

The aim of von Neumann and Morgenstern was to demonstrate that "the typical problems of economic behavior become strictly identical with the mathematical notions of suitable games of strategy." It was one of the first applications of an elaborate mathematical treatment to the social sciences exclusively. Von Neumann believed that each science had its own specific logic, that the mathematical structure of the social sciences was different from that of the physical sciences, and that the mathematics applicable to the social sciences should be of a different kind. Von Neumann's 1928 paper contained the proof of the minimax theory, which states that in a two-person, zero-sum game (one in which one player's loss is the other's gain, and vice versa) with a finite number of strategies, there always exist optimal strategies for each player. Von Neumann and Morgenstern's 1944 book treated of n-person, non-zero sum games as well as of the theory of individual decision making in situations of risk. Game theory presents a model of economic and social behavior in any situation that is game-like—where there is a conflict of interests and where each participant has some control over some of the factors that determine the outcome, and the rest of the control is in the hands of others, including chance. The behavior of each participant varies according to the behavior strategies of the others and thus involves psychological factors. Game theory concerns the formulation of appropriate strategies that would maximize each player's utility (subjective value). In social psychology, game theory has been applied to behaviors such as voting, bargaining, and experimental games, such as the prisoner's dilemma games, which, if played repeatedly, becomes a problem in learning.

Biographies: *Amer. Math. Soc. Bull.*, 1958, *64* (3), pt. 2; O. Morgenstern, *Econ. J.*, 1958, *68*, 170-174; *Biog. Mem.*, 32; *DSB*, 14; *EJ*, 12; *IESS*, 16; *NCAB*, 46; *NYT*, 1957, Feb. 9, 19:1; *Who Was Who in America*, 3.

VYGOTSKIĬ, LEON SEMENOVICH
Russian Psychologist
Born: Gomel', White Russia, 1896
Died: Moscow, June 11, 1934
Education: Studied at First State University of Moscow between 1913 and 1917, under K. N. Kornilov*

Positions: Second State University, Moscow; Institute of Psychology, Moscow; editorial work, *Voprosy Defektologii*, *Pediatriya*, and *Voprosy Psikhologii*, *Pedologii i Psikhotekhniki*

Vygotskiĭ dealt with the development of consciousness in the course of evolution and in ontogeny. He considered the latter to be a qualitative change in the mind. Vygotskiĭ emphasized the role of education in psychological development, insisting that instruction must keep ahead of development. He conducted some of the first studies on concept formation in schoolchildren. He developed a test that bears his name, designed to test concept formation by having the subject group blocks according to different properties of the blocks. In his best-known work, *Mysl' i rech'* (1934; English translation, *Thought and Language*, 1962), Vygotskiĭ considered the determining factor of a child's psychological development to be social development, especially language development. During a child's mental development, mental functions not only grow but, in a complex system of interrelations, develop new mental functional systems. The main change-producing factor is speech. The meaning of a word changes as a child grows up, which, in turn, brings about changes in the child's mental structure.

Vygotskiĭ also conducted psychopathological studies. He was one of the first psychologists to investigate conceptualization in schizophrenia. One of his main findings was that for schizophrenics it is difficult, if not impossible, to use and understand metaphoric or figurative language. This finding forms the basis of a number of psychiatric diagnostic tests. Vygotskiĭ's work in pedology and defectology at the Institute of the Experimental Study of Mental Retardation in Moscow developed Soviet psychology in these areas and was used in applied situations of child care and training. Books written by Vygotskiĭ include *Pedagogicheskaya psikhologiya* (1926), *Pedologiya shkol'nogo vozrasta* (1928), *Etyudy po istorii povedeniya* (1930, with A. R. Luria*), *Pedologiya podrostka* (1931), and *Osnovy pedologii* (1934). A complete bibliography of Vygotskiĭ's works totals 186 items.

Biographies: A. N. Leont'ev, In L. S. Vygotskiĭ, *The Psychology of Art*, 1971, pp. v-xi; A. R. Luria, *J. Genet. Psychol.*, 1935, *46*, 224-225 (also *Character Pers.*, 1935, *3*, 238-240); *Vop. Psikhol.*, 1967, *13*(3), 179-184; *PR*, 3.

W

WALLACE, ALFRED RUSSEL
English Biologist
Born: Usk, Monmouthshire, January 8, 1823
Died: Broadstone, Dorsetshire, November 7, 1913
Education: Hertford Grammar School
Positions, Honors: 1848-62, land surveyor, architect, schoolteacher, traveling naturalist; honorary degrees, two medals

Wallace acquired fame for developing the evolutionary theory simultaneously with but independently of Charles Darwin*. He was stimulated by his reading of the *Essay on the Principle of Population* by Malthus*. He sent a manuscript of a paper on the topic of evolution to Darwin, who found that it contained ideas almost identical to his own. Darwin had Wallace's and his own paper presented jointly in 1858. A year later Darwin's *Origin of Species* appeared. Wallace later criticized Darwin's theory of sexual selection, and became, with Weissman, a leader in the neo-Darwinian movement.

Biographies: L. Eiseley, *Sci. Amer.*, 1959, *200*(2), 70-84; W. George, *Biologist Philosopher: A Study of the Life and Writings of Alfred Russel Wallace*, 1964; L. T. Hogben, *A. R. Wallace*, 1918; W. Irvine, *Apes, Angels, and Victorians*, 1955; A. R. Wallace, *My Life: A Record of Events and Opinions*, 1908 (Reprinted 1969); E. A. Williams, *Darwin's Moon: Alfred Russel Wallace*, 1966; *DNB*, Suppl. 2, 3; *DSB*, 14; *EP*, 8; *NYT*, 1913, Nov. 8, 13:5.

WALLON, HENRI PAUL HYACINTHE
French Psychologist
Born: Paris, March 15, 1879
Died: Paris, December 1, 1962

Highest Degree: *Agregé en philosophie*, École Normale Supérieure, 1902; *Dr. en médecine*, University of Paris, 1908; *Dr. des lettres*, 1925
Positions: 1920-27, University of Paris, Institute of Psychology; 1920-49, psychological laboratory, L'Institut d'Orientation Professionelle; 1927-37, Sorbonne (University of Paris); 1937-50, Collège de France, director of École Pratique des Hautes Études

Wallon's early papers and books were about psychopathology. He then turned to child psychology, founding a center for medical and educational consultation for children in 1921 and a laboratory for child study in 1927. Wallon was an adherent of dialectic materialism and of Pavlov's* teachings. He opposed Durkheim's* school with its sharp distinction between the individual and the social. To Wallon an individual becomes an individual only as a result of interaction with the social environment. A person's consciousness cannot be separated from that person's behavior. The natural and the individual presuppose the social, like lungs presuppose a breathable atmosphere. Society is a necessity and an organic reality to the individual. Society, contrary to psychoanalysis and existentialism, does not repress that which is natural and does not make one lonely and desperate. Society is the individual's natural habitat, and it grows more adequate to human nature in the course of history.

Behavioral acts and mind form a unity. To Wallon psychology is the study of people interacting with objects and other people. Therefore the child's psychological development is determined by the particular physical and social environment of the age the child is born into. Affective interaction between children and adults furthers the development of the clearly human qualities in the child. Emotional states are reflected in tonic, postural, and muscular states. These states, in conjunction with external conditions of the moment, determine the nature of the clonic response or action. External behavioral relationships between parent and child eventually become internalized by the child and serve as guides to action.

Wallon wrote the following books: *L'Enfant turbulent* (1925), *Psychologie pathologique* (1926), *Principes de psychologie appliquée* (1930), *Les origines du caractère chez l'enfant* (1934-49), *L'Evolution psychologique de l'enfant* (1941), *Les origines de la pensée chez l'enfant* (1945), *La psychologie scolaire* (1953), and others.
Biographies: L. I. Antsyferova, *Vop. Psikhol.*, 1969, *15*(2), 186-189; M. Bergeron, *Ann. méd.-psychol.*, 1963, *11*, 321-351; M. Bergeron, *Psychiat. enfant*, 1963, No. 2, 537-562; H. Gratiot-Alphandéry, *Psychol. franç.*, 1963, *8*, 77-79; R. Zazzo, *J. psychol. norm. path.*, 1963, *60*, 385-400; *EUI*, 69; *PR*, 3.

WARD, JAMES
English Psychologist
Born: Kingston upon Hull, Yorkshire, January 27, 1843
Died: Cambridge, March 4, 1925
Highest Degree: M.A. in philosophy, University of London, 1874

Positions: 1875-1925, fellow, lecturer, professor of mental philosophy, Cambridge University

Ward continued the philosophical psychology tradition of Bain*, but he was also influenced by Lotze*, Brentano*, and the evolutionary doctrine. Although Ward was in favor of experimentation and even attempted to establish a laboratory at Cambridge, he was temperamentally not an experimentalist. His emphasis on the subject-object relationship and the activity of the subject is act-psychological in nature. Ward's mature views of psychology are found in his *Psychological Principles* (1918), but even at the appearance of the book Ward's views were anachronistic since, by being entirely philosophical, he failed to give account of the many advances that empirical psychology had been making. Ward's fame rests chiefly on the article about psychology that he had prepared for the ninth edition (1886) of the *Encyclopedia Britannica* (rev. 11th ed., 1911), of which his *Psychological Principles* was an expanded version. The article was very influential and to generations of *Britannica* users represented *the* view of what psychology was.

Biographies: F. C. Bartlett, *Amer. J. Psychol.*, 1925, *36*, 449-453; W. E. Johnson, *Brit. J. Psychol.*, 1925-1926, *16*, 1-4; W. R. Sorley, *Mind*, 1925, *34*, 273-279; *DNB*, 1922-1930; *EB*, 23; *EP*, 8; *EUI*, 69; *IESS*, 16; *NYT*, 1925, Mar. 5, 19:6.

WARDEN, CARL JOHN

American Psychologist

Born: Hamilton, Missouri, March 18, 1890

Died: De Land, Florida, February 28, 1961

Highest Degree: Ph.D. in psychology, University of Chicago, 1922

Positions: 1923-24, University of Wisconsin; 1924-55, Columbia University; editorial work, *Journal of Genetic Psychology*, *Genetic Psychology Monographs*, and *Journal of Comparative Psychology*

Warden studied animal and human learning and animal drives. He introduced into use mazes that were simpler than the Hampton Court maze (first used by W. S. Small*), such as the U-maze (*Comparative Psychology*, 3 vols., 1935-40, with T. N. Jenkins and L. H. Warner*), and standardized the obstruction box, hence much used in animal laboratories (*Animal Motivation: Experimental Studies on the Albino Rat*, 1931). Warden wrote several additional texts in comparative psychology, *A Short Outline of Comparative Psychology* (1927), *Animal Drives* (1932), *The Evolution of Human Behavior* (1932), *Introduction to Comparative Psychology* (1934, with T. N. Jenkins and L. H. Warner), as well as an *Introduction to Psychology*.

Biographies: *NYT*, 1961, Mar. 1, 33:1; *PR*, 3.

WARNER, LUCIEN HYNES

American Psychologist

Born: Irvington, New York, September 9, 1900

Died: Las Vegas, Nevada, 1963

Highest Degree: Ph.D. in psychology, Columbia University, 1927
Positions: 1926-27, New York University; 1928-30, fellow, National Research Council; 1932-34, L'Oeil Qui Voie, Mont Pelerin, Switzerland; 1935-37, Duke University; 1938-41, Opinion Research Corporation, Princeton, New Jersey; 1942-43, Office of War Information; 1944-48, *Life* magazine; 1948-58, Claremont Graduate School; 1959-63, business consultant

Warner was a comparative psychologist. He wrote several of his early papers with C. J. Warden* as well as several chapters of *Animal Motivation* (1931, edited by Warden) and two books, *Introduction to Comparative Psychology* (1934, with T. N. Jenkins and C. J. Warden) and the three-volume *Comparative Psychology* (1935-40, with T. N. Jenkins and C. J. Warden). Warner wrote a number of papers about animal drives, learning, and discrimination. He contributed to the development of the method for training seeing-eye dogs.
Biographies: *PR*, 3.

WARREN, HOWARD CROSBY

American Psychologist
Born: Montclair, New Jersey, June 12, 1867
Died: New York, New York, January 4, 1934
Highest Degree: Ph.D. in psychology, Johns Hopkins University, 1917
Positions: 1890-1934, Princeton University; president, American Psychological Association, 1913

Warren was a first-generation American psychologist, Darwinian (Charles Darwin*), materialistic, deterministic, but inclined toward introspection, and an adherent of the double-aspect theory of mind-body relationship. At Princeton he directed the psychology laboratory between 1904 and 1934 and in 1920 was able to establish the Psychology Department, separate from that of philosophy, becoming its first chairman.

Warren contributed few experimental papers. Most of his papers were theoretical because his poor eyesight prevented him from engaging in experimental work. He had a particular interest in bibliography and lexicography, however, and made several important contributions in this area. He wrote a *Dictionary of Psychology* (1934), compiled the *Psychological Index* between 1894 and 1907 and again from 1910 to 1914, contributed to Baldwin's* *Dictionary of Philosophy and Psychology*, and was on the American Psychological Association Committee on Psychological Bibliography since 1900 and chairman for many years of the APA Standing Committee on Psychological and Philosophical Terminology. Warren also contributed through editorial work and management of several psychological journals. He established the *Journal of Experimental Psychology* in 1916, was editor and business manager of *Psychological Review* from 1901 to 1934, and was first editor of *Psychological Bulletin*, which he edited from 1904 to 1934. Eventually, Warren's Psychological Review Company owned the *Psychological Review*, *Psychological Index*, *Psychological Monographs*, *Psycho-*

logical Bulletin, and *Journal of Experimental Psychology*. In 1922 he sold all of them to the American Psychological Association.

Warren's views on psychology may be found in his *Human Psychology* (1919), of which he published a simplified version in 1930 under the title of *Elements of Human Psychology*. He also penned a *History of the Association Psychology* in 1921.

Biographies: *Train. Sch. Bull.*, 1934, *30*, 165; S. W. Fernberger, *Psychol. Bull.*, 1934, *31*, 1-4; H. S. Langfeld, *Amer. J. Psychol.*, 1934, *46*, 340-342; R. S. Woodworth, *Psychol. Rev.*, 1934, *41*, 105-107; *DAB*, 19; *HPA*, 1; *NCAB*, 25; *NYT*, 1934, Jan. 5, 21:3; *PR*, 3; *Who Was Who in America*, 1.

WASHBURN, MARGARET FLOY

American Psychologist

Born: New York, New York, July 25, 1871

Died: Poughkeepsie, New York, October 29, 1939

Highest Degree: Ph.D. in psychology, Cornell University, 1794, under E. B. Titchener*

Positions, Honors: 1894-1900, Wells College; 1900-1902, Cornell University; 1902-3, University of Cincinnati; 1903-39, Vassar College, since 1908, head of Psychology Department; editorial work, *American Journal of Psychology* (1903-39), *Journal of Animal Behavior* (1911-17), *Psychological Bulletin* (1909-15), *Psychological Review* (1916-30), *Journal of Comparative Psychology* (1921-35); president, American Psychological Association, 1921; many honors, including membership in the National Academy of Science (second woman so honored) and an honorary D.Sc. from Wittenberg College

Washburn's main interest was in animal psychology. *The Animal Mind*, first published in 1908 (subsequent editions in 1917, 1926, and 1936), served as the standard comparative psychology text for the next twenty-five years and was translated in other languages. In her only other book, *Movement and Mental Imagery* (1916), Washburn broke with the Titchenerian tradition and presented her motor theory of consciousness. It was an attempt to reconcile introspection and behaviorism. She stated that consciousness comes from a certain balance between excitation and inhibition in a motor discharge. If excitation is at too low or at too high a level, consciousness is lessened. Visual imagery also depends on the simultaneous excitation and inhibition of a motor pathway. The association of ideas she thought occurred when the motor response to a stimulus was blocked and a weakened response or "tentative movement" took place instead.

Washburn published more than two hundred articles and reviews, among which is a series of sixty-eight Minor Studies, published from Vassar College between 1905 and 1938.

Biographies: K. M. Dallenbach, *Amer. J. Psychol.*, 1940, *53*, 105; K. M. Dallenbach, *Science*, 1939, *90*, 555-557; E. S. Goodman, *Psychol. Women*

Quart., 1980, 5(1), 69-80; R. McHenry (Ed.), *Famous American Women*, 1983; W. B. Pillsbury, *Psychol. Rev.*, 1940, *47*, 99-109; *Biog. Mem.*, 25; *DAB*, 22; *HPA*, 2; *IESS*, 16; *NCAB*, 30; *NYT*, 1939, Oct. 30, 17:4; *Who Was Who in America*, 1.

WATSON, JOHN BROADUS

American Psychologist
Born: Greenville, South Carolina, January 9, 1878
Died: New York, New York, September 25, 1958
Highest Degree: Ph.D. in psychology, University of Chicago, 1903, under J. R. Angell*
Positions, Honors: 1903-8, University of Chicago; 1908-20, Johns Hopkins University; 1921-46, with private firms; president, American Psychological Association, 1915; honorary LL.D., Furman University, 1919

A 1913 article by Watson, "Psychology as a behaviorist views it," presented a view of psychology that totally departed from all views of the past and started a new school of psychology, behaviorism. In that article Watson declared that psychology was an objective, experimental branch of natural science whose goal was to predict and control behavior. Introspection as a method was not part of it. Consciousness and the various mental states were not to be referred to. The object of psychology, all psychology, was to study behavior. The study of soul and mental states was a difficult, irrelevant, and unreal task. The history of psychology up to that point proved it. Watson rejected both structuralism and functionalism.

Watson's article and subsequent writings had such an impact on American psychology that a new discipline emerged. Many of Watson's radical statements were later modified, neobehavioristic schools arose, and behaviorism in its original form ceased to exist. Nevertheless, American psychology today conforms to Watson's conceptualization: it still defines itself as the study of behavior and, while admitting introspection in moderation and mind as an inference from behavior, largely eschews philosophy and speculation about subjective states. The influence of behaviorism in Europe and elsewhere was considerably weaker.

Watson did research on animals at Chicago, but his most important work was done at Johns Hopkins. His 1914 book *Behavior: An Introduction to Comparative Psychology*, advocated the study of animal behavior without resorting to mentalistic concepts. There was no reference in it to conditioning. Watson learned about conditioning in that year and made it the topic of his presidential address to the American Psychological Association the next year. The concept of the conditioned reflex became crucial in behaviorism. In 1918 Watson began experimentation with children, a pioneering effort, and later wrote *Psychological Care of the Infant and Child* (1928). His fame was such that he became an instant expert on child care and rearing, and his advice was followed by numerous parents.

In his 1919 book *Psychology from the Standpoint of a Behaviorist*, Watson showed how the methods of animal study and the principles of behavior derived from them could be applied to humans. Conditioning was given a particularly prominent role to play. Watson's last psychological publication was *Behaviorism* (1925; rev. ed., 1930), a book intended for popular consumption.

Central to Watson's view of psychology was his S-R formulation of behavior. Behavior always involves a response of the organism to a stimulus, and the task of the psychologist is to predict from S to R. The responses are muscular contractions or glandular discharges, and the S-R units are simply reflexes. Reflexes are innate or conditioned, but there are no instincts in humans. Not only are there no instincts, there are no other abilities that are transmitted genetically. Most emotions are conditioned reflexes. Given only three innate emotional responses—fear, rage, and love—all other emotions are conditioned elaborations of them. Watson's classic experiment of 1920 on the conditioning of fear in little Albert demonstrated the point. Sensations were treated by Watson as discriminatory behavior. The learning of habits is the formation of conditioned responses. Even speech is acquired through conditioning, and thinking is subvocal speech. Personality is but the combination of habit systems in an individual.
Biographies: P. G. Gray, *Actes XIIe Cong. Int. Hist. Sci., 1968*, 1971, *12*, 31-33; B. F. Skinner, *Science*, 1959, *129*, 197-198; R. S. Woodworth, *Amer. J. Psychol.*, 1959, *72*, 301-310; *EB*, 23; *HPA*, 3; *IESS*, 16; *NCAB*, 48, A; *NYT*, 1958, Sept. 26, 27:1; *Who Was Who in America*, 2.

WATT, HENRY JACKSON
Scottish Psychologist
Born: Aberdeen, July 18, 1879
Died: Glasgow, October 25, 1925
Highest Degree: Ph.D. in psychology, University of Würzburg, 1904, under Oswald Külpe*
Positions: 1907-8, University of Liverpool; 1908-25, University of Glasgow

Watt was one of the prominent psychologists in the Würzburg school, engaged in the study of thinking along the lines of the leader of the Würzburg, or "imageless thought," school, Oswald Külpe (*Experimentelle Beiträge zu einer Theorie des Denkens*, 1904). Watt, in explaining the thinking process, emphasized the importance of the task (*Aufgabe*) given the thinker. The conscious task or purpose of the thought problem brings about eventually an unconscious set (*Einstellung*) in the thinker, and the thinking process occurs without the thinker's being aware of what determines the course of his thoughts. Watt wrote a number of papers about the subject in both German and English. After taking the position of lecturer at Glasgow, his interest in psychology shifted to sensory processes, especially the psychology of music. He published many papers in this area. His love of systematizing showed itself in his theoretical papers. He emphasized the differences between problems in physics, physiology, and psychology, and in his theory of sound he attempted to present a purely psychological theory. Books by Watt include *The Economy and Training of Memory* (1909), *The Psychology of Sound* (1917), *The Foundations of Music* (1919), *The Sensory Basis and Structure of Knowledge* (1925), and *The Common Sense of Dreams* (1929). *Biographies*: *EUI*, 69; *Who's Who*, 1925.

WEBER, ERNST HEINRICH
German Physiologist
Born: Wittenberg, Saxony, June 24, 1795
Died: Leipzig, January 26, 1878
Highest Degree: M.D., University of Wittenberg, 1815
Positions: 1817-78, University of Leipzig

Weber worked on the physiology of the internal organs, but he is best known for his work on touch, on which subject he wrote a book (*De pulsu, resorptione, auditu et tactu: annotationes anatomicae et physiologicae*, 1834) and a chapter in R. Wagner's *Handwörterbuch der Physiologie* (vol. 3, 1846). He made a major contribution there in determining two-point thresholds on the skin. Weber found that the size of the threshold varied according to the skin area stimulated, which he explained by the hypothesis of "sensory circles": for two points to be perceived as separate, the corresponding nerve fibers must be separated by at least one fiber that is not being stimulated. The idea of skin areas sending messages to the brain where discrimination took place anticipated Lotze's* theory of local signs.

Weber's other work was not as well known at the time, and his discovery of the just noticeable difference in sensation might also have passed unnoticed if Fechner*, who at the time was also at Leipzig, had not made it into a cornerstone of psychophysics. Weber performed experiments in another, little studied area, the physiology of the muscle sense, and asked the question what would be the smallest difference between two weights that would be just noticeably different. He found that the absolute size of this difference varied depending on the size of the weights compared, but that the difference bore a constant relationship to the weight($\Delta S/S = k$). Weber determined that the relationship held also for the discrimination of the length of lines and the pitch of tones: for an increment in a stimulus to be just noticeably different, it had to be a certain proportion of the stimulus. To each sense modality there corresponded a different proportion. Fechner took Weber's formulation, assumed the just noticeable difference to be infinitely divisible and directly related to differences in sensation, integrated Weber's fraction, and introduced the logarithmic law of psychophysics, which he called "Weber's law." That term is now reserved for the original Weber's fraction, and the logarithmic law bears Fechner's name.

Biographies: U. Bück-Rich, *Ernst Heinrich Weber und der Anfang einer Physiologie der Hautsinne*, 1970; P. M. Dawson, *Phi Beta Phi Quart.*, 1928, *25*, 86-116; G. T. Fechner, *Leipziger Tageblatt*, 1878, Jan. 30; C. Ludwig, *Rede zum Gedächtniss an Ernst Heinrich Weber*, 1878; *ADB*, 41; *CE*, 14; *DSB*, 14; Hirsch, *Biog. Lex.*, 5; *Grande*, 31; *IESS*, 16; Pagel, *Biographisches Lexikon*.

WEBER, MAX

German Sociologist
Born: Erfurt, Thuringia, April 21, 1864
Died: Munich, June 14, 1920
Highest Degree: Ph.D., University of Berlin, 1889
Positions: 1893-1919, University of Heidelberg; 1919-20, University of Munich

Weber's sociology of understanding is based on psychological understanding, the understanding of human motivation. Social science differs from natural science, according to Weber, in that the latter is concerned with antecedent causes whereas the former is concerned with the future—the why and wither of human behavior. To formulate his hypotheses the sociologist needs ideal types. *Ideal types* are concepts formulated by abstracting and combining elements of reality into mental constructs that have no counterpart in reality but help to analyze reality. Of his many works, Weber's *Die protestantische Ethik und der Geist des Kapitalismus* (1904-5) is the best known. In it Weber, using ideal types such as "seventeenth-century Calvinism," "twentieth-century capitalism," and "Protestant ethic," developed the thesis that when the relationship between the various world religions and economics is compared, a close relationship is found only between Calvinism and the development of capitalism. The asceticism of the Middle Ages turned into an asceticism of the "inner world": work, activity, and entrepreneurship became behaviors willed by God. Human drives, instead of being suppressed, are converted into work and the building of capital. Work thus becomes service to God and prosperity a visible manifestation of God's favor. Since Weber, it has become common to analyze Christian reform movements in terms of transformation or sublimation of human drives.

Biographies: R. Bendix, *Max Weber: An Intellectual Portrait*, 1962; C. Diehl, *Quart. J. Econ.*, 1924, *38*, 87-107; P. Honigsheim, *On Max Weber*, 1968; M. Weber, *Max Weber*, 1970; *EP*, 8; *IESS*, 16; *Jewish*, 10; *NYT*, 1920, June 17, 11:4.

WECHSLER, DAVID

American Psychologist
Born: Lespedi, Romania, January 12, 1896
Died: New York, New York, May 2, 1981
Highest Degree: Ph.D. in psychology, Columbia University, 1925, under R. S. Woodworth*
Positions, Honors: 1922-24, Bureau of Child Guidance, New York City; 1925-27, Psychological Corporation; 1927-32, private practice; 1932-67, chief psychologist, Bellevue Psychiatric Hospital, New York City; 1933-67, clinical professor, New York University, Medical College; honorary doctorate, Hebrew University, Jerusalem; Special Award, American Association for Mental Deficiency, 1972; Distinguished Professional Contribution Award, American Psychological Association, 1973

Beginning with the early 1930s, Wechsler dedicated most of his work to the development of intelligence tests that have become internationally known. They include the Bellevue-Wechsler I (1939); Bellevue-Wechsler II, or Army Wechsler (1942); Wechsler Intelligence Scale for Children (1949); Wechsler Adult Intelligence Scale (1955); Wechsler Preschool and Primary Scale of Intelligence (1967); Wechsler Intelligence Scale for Children—Revised (1974); and Wechsler Intelligence Scale for Adults—Revised (1981). The Wechsler Intelligence Scale for Children and the Wechsler Adult Intelligence Scale came to be used as widely as the Stanford-Binet Scale, the current version of Alfred Binet's* first intelligence test. The Binet test, those derived from it, and the Wechsler tests together have been given to and thus have affected the lives of the majority of Americans born in the twentieth century.

Wechsler introduced the Deviation Quotient, an IQ computed by considering the individual's mental ability in comparison with the average individual of his or her own age. Wechsler's definition of *intelligence* as "the global capacity to act purposefully, to think rationally, and to deal effectively with his environment" included the idea that intelligence is not a single capacity but a multifaceted aggregate. The Wechsler tests are based on ten or eleven verbal and performance subtests.

In addition to the tests, Wechsler published *The Range of Human Capacities* (1935; 2nd ed., 1971), *The Measurement of Adult Intelligence* (1939; 2nd ed., 1972), and some seventy papers.

Biographies: *Amer. Psychologist*, 1973, *29*, 44-47; A. J. Edwards, *J. Hist. Behav. Sci.*, 1982, *18*, 78-79; J. D. Matarazzo, *Amer. Psychologist*, 1981, *36*, 1542-1543; *IESS*, 18; *NYT*, 1981, May 3, 44:4.

WEISS, ALBERT PAUL

American Psychologist

Born: Steingrund, Silesia, September 15, 1879

Died: Columbus, Ohio, April 3, 1931

Highest Degree: Ph.D. in psychology, University of Missouri, 1916, under Max Meyer*

Positions: 1912-31, Ohio State University; editorial work, Journal of Genetic Psychology

Weiss was one of the early behaviorists who advocated both the abandonment of consciousness in psychology and the observation of behavior as its proper task. In *A Theoretical Basis of Human Behavior* (1925) Weiss asserted that all psychological phenomena could be reduced to physics, chemistry, social relations, or a combination of them. Consciousness, when analyzed behavioristically, vanishes into biology and social science. It is thus an objective phenomenon. It can be handled in biological and social terms, there being no need for mentalistic ones. Even so, there is no dichotomy between the biological and the social. Humans, in addition to the "handling" responses, developed in the course of evolution a system of signaling responses or language. This response system accounts fully for all of the human phenomena that have been traditionally attributed to nonphysical forces.

Weiss wrote only about twenty-five papers and two books, half of them theoretical and half experimental and applied, such as his *Psychological Principles of Automotive Driving* (1930).

Biographies: L. Bloomfield, *Language*, 1931, 7, 219-221; R. M. Elliott, *Amer. J. Psychol.*, 1931, *43*, 707-709; S. A. Renshaw, *J. Gen. Psychol.*, 1932, *6*, 3-7; *PR*, 3; *Who Was Who in America*, 1.

WELLS, FREDERICK LYMAN

American Psychologist
Born: Boston, Massachusetts, April 22, 1884
Died: Belmont, Massachusetts, June 2, 1964
Highest Degree: Ph.D. in psychology, Columbia University, 1906, under J. McK. Cattell*
Positions: 1907-21, McLean Hospital, Waverly, Massachusetts; 1921-38, Boston Psychopathic Hospital; 1932-50, Harvard Medical School, 1938-50, Department of Hygiene, Harvard University

Wells was a clinical psychologist under whose direction the first internship for psychologists in a mental hospital was established at the Boston Psychopathic Hospital in 1913. Wells's pioneering efforts in experimental psychopathology are documented in some of the approximately 150 psychological papers that he published. His writing of *Mental Adjustments* (1917) marks the beginning of the "adjustment" literature that deals with the relationship between psychopathology and everyday life. In 1927 Wells provided one of the first summary accounts of the practice of clinical psychology (*Mental Tests in Clinical Practice*). In it he criticized some of the common practices of the clinicians and was prophetic of the future development of clinical psychology. Wells was much interested in the use of psychological tests. Among his ventures in this field may be counted his revision of the Army Alpha Test, first prepared during World War I (*Modified Alpha Examination*, 1941).

Biographies: L. F. Shaffer, *Amer. J. Psychol.*, 1964, *77*, 679-682; *NCAB*, 51; *NYT*, 1964, June 6, 23:2; *PR*, 3; *Who Was Who in America*, 4.

WERNER, HEINZ

German-American Psychologist
Born: Vienna, Austria, February 11, 1890
Died: Worcester, Massachusetts, May 14, 1964
Highest Degree: Ph.D. in psychology, University of Vienna, 1914
Positions: 1916-17, University of Munich; 1917-21, Psychological Institute, Hamburg; 1921-33, University of Hamburg; 1933-36, University of Michigan; 1936, visiting professor, Harvard University; 1937-43, Wayne County Training School; 1943-47, Brooklyn College; 1947-60, Clark University, since 1949, chairman, Psychology Department

Werner's early monographs were about aesthetics and music. During his Wayne County period he studied feeblemindedness, publishing some thirty articles. His work proved influential in the field of mental retardation. Werner, however, acquired prominence in the field of developmental psychology. His most notable work in this field was *Einführung in die Entwicklungspsychologie* (1926) whose English version (*Comparative Psychology of Mental Development*, 1940) saw several editions and was translated into other languages.

Although ideas about development include values placed on the developmental process, Werner believed that there are certain absolute, abstract truths that can be stated about it, which he called the "orthogenetic principle": development proceeds from that which is global, undifferentiated, and unarticulated to that which is differentiated, articulated, and hierarchically integrated. Unlike many other developmental psychologists, Werner believed that development takes place along many different lines but not necessarily on the same level. Werner added to the developmental picture forms of functioning such as aesthetics, expressiveness, and other "irrational" forms of knowing the world. The developed person has "mobility of operation" by having at his disposal more modes of knowing than the child. This includes the ability not only to function at a more differentiated level but to move backward in one's developmental level and deal with to-be-cognized materials in an undifferentiated way. Werner believed that developmental psychology is a way of looking at all psychological phenomena and sought to encompass all behavioral phenomena in a comprehensive system.

In 1949 Werner and Seymour Wapner formulated the sensory-tonic field theory of perception. The theory attempted to remedy a shortcoming of existing perceptual theories by incorporating the motor aspect of perception. It postulated the dynamic equivalence of sensory and tonic (motor) events and therefore an interaction and substitutability between them. The theory assumed the existence of only one kind of energy in the organism, sensory-tonic, which manifested itself in various ways. Although the theory was only moderately productive of research, the demonstrations of the effects of motor events upon perception given by Werner and Wapner were impressive and led to further developments such as the rod-and-frame test, tilting-room and tilting-chair experiments, and the relationship between personality and styles of perception (field dependence and independence). Werner produced about seventy publications on perception while he was chairman of the Psychology Department at Clark University. During the four years between retirement and death, he published an additional twenty-five papers and a book (*Symbol Formation*, 1963, with B. Kaplan). After Werner's death the Institute of Human Development at Clark University was renamed the Heinz Werner Institute of Developmental Psychology.

Biographies: T. Iritani, *Psychologia*, 1965, *8*, 111-119; S. Wapner & B. Kaplan, *Amer. J. Psychol.*, 1964, *77*, 513-517; H. A. Witkin, *Child Devel.*, 1965, *36*, 307-328; *EJ*, 16; *EUI*, 70; *NYT*, 1964, May 16, 25:6; *PR*, 3; *Who Was Who in America*, 4.

WERTHEIMER, MAX

German Psychologist

Born: Prague, Austria-Hungary, April 15, 1880

Died: New Rochelle, New York, October 12, 1943

Highest Degree: Ph.D. in psychology, University of Würzburg, 1904, under O. Külpe*

Positions: 1912-16, University of Frankfurt; 1916-29, University of Berlin; 1929-32, University of Frankfurt; 1933-43, New School for Social Research

In 1910 Wertheimer made the discovery that if two identical visual stimuli are presented successively, then with appropriate exposure times for each and an appropriate interval between them, they will appear as one object moving from one place to another. The significance of Wertheimer's discovery was not that it was new, because the phenomenon as such had been known for a long time, but because Wertheimer related his insights and his subsequent experiment, with Koffka* and Köhler* as subjects, in a novel way to perception and to the experience of physical phenomena in general. He wrote a paper in 1912 that marked the beginning of a major school of psychology, the Gestalt school. Contrary to previous explanations of apparent movement, Wertheimer argued that it could not be explained entirely in terms of the properties of stimulation. The perceived movement was a new phenomenon, a whole, a Gestalt, not reducible to the elements that gave rise to it. It was the prior perception of the whole that determined how the parts would be perceived, not the other way around. Wertheimer performed additional experiments on apparent movement, drew upon the work of Schumann* and Rubin*, and eventually applied the new way of looking at apparent movement to all perception. To publish works emanating from the new school, Wertheimer, Koffka, Köhler, Goldstein*, and Gruhle* began publishing a new journal, *Psychologische Forschung*.

In 1923 Wertheimer published an important paper about the Gestalt principles of organization (proximity, similarity, closure, symmetry, regularity, good continuation), including the organization of the visual field into figure and ground, all subsumed under the general law of Prägnanz, or the tendency of experienced fields to become as articulated as possible. Underlying the law of *Prägnanz*, including the perception of apparent movement, Wertheimer thought, were brain processes that in essence correspond to the perceived phenomena. This idea became the principle of isomorphism, later elaborated upon by Köhler.

In time Wertheimer became increasingly more interested in the analysis of thinking. His thoughts extending the idea of Gestalten to creative thinking were published posthumously in *Productive Thinking* (1945). In it Wertheimer argued for the replacement of rote, associationistic kind of learning in schools by methods that encourage flexible thinking and insightful solution of problems.

Biographies: H. Kallen, *Soc. Res.*, 1948, *15*, 235-243; W. Köhler, *Psychol. Rev.*, 1944, *51*, 143-146; E. B. Newman, *Amer. J. Psychol.*, 1944, *57*, 428-435; *EJ*, 16; *IESS*, 16; *Jewish*, 10; *NYT*, 1943, Oct. 13, 23:5; *PR*, 3.

WHEATSTONE, SIR CHARLES

English Physicist
Born: Gloucester, Gloucestershire, February 1802
Died: Paris, France, October 19, 1875
Education: No university education
Positions, Honors: 1834-40, professor of experimental philosophy, King's College, London; honorary D.C.L. (1862), LL.D. (1864); knighted, 1868

Among Wheatstone's numerous discoveries and other achievements in physics, two were of importance to psychology. In 1833 he discovered that retinal disparity is converted by the nervous system into a single percept of three-dimensionality and that all that is needed for three-dimensional perception is a difference between the two retinal images. He demonstrated this by constructing what he called a "stereoscope" and publishing a description of it in 1838. Of the various types of stereoscopes, Wheatstone's prism stereoscope has proved to be the best. It has been used in psychological experiments on perception since Wheatstone's time.

In 1840 Wheatstone constructed a chronoscope to measure the velocity of cannonballs. It was used subsequently to measure reaction time in psychological laboratories.

Biographies: *DNB*, 20; *DSB*, 14; *EB*, 23; *EUI*, 70; *Grande*, 31; *NYT*, 1875, Oct. 21, 5:5.

WHEELER, RAYMOND HOLDER

American Psychologist
Born: Berlin, Massachusetts, March 9, 1892
Died: Wellesley, Massachusetts, August 24, 1961
Highest Degree: Ph.D. in psychology, Clark University, 1915
Positions: 1915-25, University of Oregon; 1925-47, University of Kansas; 1947-48, Erskine College; 1948-61, Babson Institute of Business Administration

Wheeler defended Gestalt psychology against criticism, but he also modified it considerably, presenting it under the name of organismic psychology (*The Science of Psychology*, 1929; 2nd ed., 1940; *The Laws of Human Nature*, 1932). Wheeler deviated from the original position of the Gestalt school so much that he belongs only on the periphery of that school.

Wheeler wrote several papers about synesthesia and systematic psychology and, with F. T. Perkins, the widely used educational psychology text *Principles of Mental Development* (1932). Although the book contained some challenging ideas concerning development, it ceased to be influential, overshadowed by others.

Biographies: *American Men of Science*, 9th ed., vol. 3, The Social and Behavioral Sciences; *PR*, 3.

WHIPPLE, GUY MONTROSE
American Psychologist
Born: Danvers, Massachusetts, June 12, 1876
Died: Clifton, Massachusetts, August 1, 1941
Highest Degree: Ph.D. in psychology, Cornell University, 1900, under E. B. Titchener*
Positions: 1898-1914, Cornell University; 1914-17, University of Illinois; 1917-19, Carnegie Institute of Technology; 1919-25, University of Michigan; 1915-41, secretary-treasurer, National Society for the Study of Education, and editor of its yearbooks; editorial work, *Journal of Applied Psychology* and *Journal of Educational Research*

Whipple started out as an experimentalist but soon switched to educational psychology. By 1910 the testing movement had advanced so much that Whipple was able to publish a discussion of fifty-four tests and give directions for their administration (*Manual of Mental and Physical Tests*, 1910). In the same year he became a cofounder of the *Journal of Educational Psychology*. In 1915, at Whipple's instigation, the American Psychological Association expressed official disapproval of the use of psychological tests by unqualified individuals.

Being mechanically minded and before he turned to educational psychology, Whipple designed and constructed several pieces of laboratory equipment. The best known of them was the Whipple tachistoscope. It was described in the second edition (1914-15) of his *Manual*. Whipple produced about fifty publications in psychology, many of them about educational psychology and several books about educational problems.
Biographies: E. C. Ruckmick, *Amer. J. Psychol.*, 1942, *55*, 132-134; *NCAB*, 31; *NYT*, 1941, Aug. 3, 35:4; *PR*, 3; *Who Was Who in America*, 1.

WHITE, WILLIAM ALANSON
American Psychiatrist
Born: Brooklyn, New York, January 24, 1870
Died: Washington, D.C., March 7, 1937
Highest Degree: M.D., Long Island College Hospital, 1891
Positions, Honors: 1892-1903, New York State Hospital at Binghamton; 1903-37, St. Elizabeth's Hospital, Washington, D.C., and professor of nervous and mental diseases, Georgetown University, George Washington University; president, American Psychiatric Association, 1924; the psychiatric research institutes, William Alanson White Foundation, and William Alanson White Institute have been named in White's honor

White spent most of his professional life at St. Elizabeth's Hospital, where he was appointed to the position of superintendent because of the views he held concerning mental illness. During his tenure the hospital became one of the best-known mental institutions in the world. White's foremost principle was that only humane and kind treatment is likely to produce improvement in the mentally ill. He was strongly in favor of treating criminals rather than punishing or executing them. While emphasizing social pathology, White also conceived of the psychobiological organism as a whole and, on this basis, coined the term *mental hygiene*. *Mental Hygiene of Childhood* (1919) presents the mental hygiene point of view within the psychoanalytic framework. White's other books were mainly about psychiatry and nervous diseases: *Outlines of Psychiatry* (1907), *Diseases of the Nervous System* (1915, with S. E. Jeliffe), *Essays on Psychopathology* (1925). In 1913 White founded *Psychoanalytic Review* (with S. E. Jeliffe) and, in general, was considered the leader of the Washington school of psychiatry, which included Karen Horney*, Erich Fromm*, Harry Stack Sullivan*, and Frieda Fromm-Reichmann.

Biographies: *Science*, 1937, *85*, 326; R. M. Chapman, *Psychiatry*, 1938, *1*, 1-5; S. E. Jeliffe, *Ment. Hyg.*, 1937, *21*, 291-293; S. E. Jeliffe, *Psychoanal. Rev.*, 1937, *24*, 210-216; N. D. C. Lewis, *Arch. Neurol. Psychiat.*, 1937, *38*, 608-611; N. D. C. Lewis, *Sociometry*, 1937, *1*, 255-258; W. A. White, *The Autobiography of a Purpose*, 1938; G. Zilboorg, *Psychoanal. Quart.*, 1937, *6*, 383-387; *DAB*, 22; *NCAB*, 38; *NYT*, 1937, Mar. 8, 19:3; *PR*, 3; *Who Was Who in America*, 1.

WHITEHEAD, ALFRED NORTH
English-American Philosopher
Born: Ramsgate, Kent, February 15, 1861
Died: Cambridge, Massachusetts, December 30, 1947
Highest Degree: D.Sc. in mathematics, Cambridge University, 1905
Positions, Honors: 1885-1911, Cambridge University; 1911-24, University of London; 1924-36, Harvard University; several honorary doctorates, medals, and prizes

Although Whitehead did not present his psychological views in any specifically psychological paper or book, he discussed psychological problems to a considerable extent. He was in agreement on some points with the Gestalt, psychoanalytic, and dynamic schools and in disagreement on others, so no school label can be attached to him.

Although to Whitehead psychology was the basis of his metaphysics, he did not say much about psychology that others had not said before, although he did so in different terms. Whitehead considered the experiencing subject mainly from the point of view of his affects and purposes. There is a close interrelation between the subject's body, himself, and the external world. Whitehead made the distinction between *perception in the mode of causal efficacy*, which is perception as it relates to the past or the future, and *perception in the mode of presentational immediacy*, which is related to the here and now. Whitehead criticized the stress placed on the latter mode and unrelated bits of sensory experience and failure to consider the former. He thus rejected the Humean (Hume*) analysis of sense perception and his theory of the association of ideas. Whitehead's concept of thinking is very similar to that of Dewey's* in that he viewed thinking functionally and assigned it a pragmatic role of practical relevance. Whitehead believed, however, that much of our experience is unconscious and that the original source of knowledge is intuition.

Biographies: C. D. Broad, *Mind*, 1948, *57*, 139-145; W. W. Hammerschmidt, *Scripta math.*, 1948, *14*, 17-23; T. G. Henderson, *Rev. int. phil.*, 1967, *21*, 358-371; *DSB*, 14; *DNB*, Suppl. 6; *EP*, 8; *IESS*, 16; *NCAB*, 37; *NYT*, 1947, Dec. 31, 15:1; *Who Was Who in America*, 2.

WHYTT, ROBERT
Scottish Physiologist
Born: Edinburgh, September 6, 1714
Died: Edinburgh, April 15, 1766
Highest Degree: M.D., University of Rheims, 1736; M.D., St. Andrews University, 1737
Positions: 1738-47, private practice of medicine; 1747-61, University of Edinburgh; 1761, first physician to king of Scotland

Whytt repeated and extended an experiment performed in 1730 by Stephen Hales in which the existence of reflexes was demonstrated. In doing so he coined the terms *stimulus* and *response* (*An Essay on the Vital and Other Involuntary Motions of Animals*, 1751). Whytt performed the first important experiments on the reflex, demonstrating that the central nervous system is essential but that even a portion of the spinal cord is sufficient to maintain a reflex. He was first to demonstrate that the pupillary response is a reflex to light (Whytt's reflex). Whytt also distinguished between voluntary and involuntary movements. He considered the reflex as involuntary but not quite unconscious, since it was a response by the "sentient principle" in the nervous system, which was part of the mind.

Biographies: C. W. Burr, *Med. Life*, 1929, *36*, 109-117; L. Carmichael, *Psychol. Rev.*, 1927, *34*, 287-304; J. D. Comrie, *Edinb. Med. J.*, 1925, *32*, 755-761; R. K. French, *Robert Whytt: The Soul and Medicine*, 1969; W. Seller, *Trans. Roy. Soc. Edinb.*, 1864, *23*, 99-132; *Chalmers*, 32; *DNB*, 21; *DSB*, 14; Hirsch, *Biog. Lex.*, 5.

WIENER, NORBERT
American Mathematician
Born: Columbia, Missouri, November 26, 1894
Died: Stockholm, Sweden, March 18, 1964
Highest Degree: Ph.D. in philosophy, Harvard University, 1913
Positions: 1919-60, Massachusetts Institute of Technology

The idea for a new discipline, cybernetics, grew out of Wiener's work in devising a system for the rapid direction of antiaircraft fire. The discipline was launched when Wiener published his book *Cybernetics* in 1948. He defined *cybernetics* as a discipline concerned with the comparative study of control mechanisms in the nervous system and high-speed computers.

Wiener's effect on psychology was twofold. One was in the form of a new type of model to pattern human behavior after—the human being as a computer. In *Cybernetics* Wiener considered the automation of pattern perception, how to translate in computer terms the perception of invariants, and broad topics such as psychopathology and social psychology. The proliferation of computer models of form perception has been one direct effect of Wiener's book. The second effect was the introduction of the use of information theory in psychology. The information theory was presented simultaneously and independently in 1948 by Wiener and Claude Shannon. It gave, for the first time, the opportunity to quantify something that was of definite psychological interest but had theretofore been unquantifiable, namely, information. Since information reduces uncertainty and learning may be considered a case of uncertainty reduction, information theory was relevant to learning. Since organization is about the same as redundancy, a cybernetic concept, and Gestalt psychologists talked about organization, their propositions could be tested quantitatively. Since any stimulus may be considered to contain information, the behavior of organisms could be treated as information-processing behavior and quantified in addition, because all information could be converted to bits and added, regardless of the original form of the stimulation.

Cybernetic model building and the application of the information theory to psychological problems began immediately. They brought into psychology many terms that are now common: *input, output, signal, signal-to-noise ratio, uncertainty, redundancy, bits* and *chunks of information, information processing, encoding,* and the like. Of psychological interest are two other volumes of Wiener's, *The Human Use of Human Beings* (1950) and *Cybernetics of the Nervous System* (1965).

Biographies: N. Wiener, *Ex-prodigy: My Childhood and Youth*, 1953; N. Wiener, *I am a Mathematician: The Later Life of a Prodigy*, 1968; *DSB*, 14; *EJ*, 16; *IESS*, 16; *Jewish*, 10; *NYT*, 1964, Mar. 19, 1:3; *Who Was Who in America*, 4.

WIRTH, WILHELM
German Psychologist
Born: Wundsiedel, Bavaria, July 26, 1876
Died: 1952, place unknown
Highest Degree: Ph.D. in psychology, University of Munich, 1897, under T. Lipps*
Positions: 1898-1941(?), University of Leipzig; editorial work, *Archiv für die gesamte Psychologie* (from 1905), *Vierteljahrsschrift für Psychologie und Medizin*, and *Psychological Abstracts* (from 1926)

Wirth did experimental work on geometric illusions, color contrast, perception, and psychophysics, searching for a fundamental principle of phenomenology. He wrote *Vorstellungs- und Gefühlskontrast* (1900), *Fortschritte auf dem Gebiete der Psychophysik der Licht- und Farbenempfindungen* (1905), *Die experimentelle Analyse der Bewusstseinsphänomene* (1908; contains a theory of geometric il-

lusions), *Psychophysik* (1912), and *Spezielle psychophysische Massmethoden* (1920).
Biographies: F. Krueger, *Arch. ges. Psychol.*, 1936, *96*, 273-276; *Biog. Lex.*; *EUI*, 70; *HPA*, 3; *PR*, 3.

WISSLER, CLARK
American Anthropologist
Born: Wayne County, Indiana, September 18, 1870
Died: New York, New York, August 25, 1947
Highest Degree: Ph.D. in psychology, Columbia University, 1901, under J. McK. Cattell*
Positions, Honors: 1897-99, Ohio State University; 1901-9, Columbia University; 1902-42, American Museum of Natural History; 1924-40, Yale University; honorary LL.D., Indiana University, 1929

Wissler worked at first in the laboratory of his teacher Cattell and undertook to evaluate the results of Cattell's attempts to measure the mental ability of students at Columbia and Barnard by measuring their reaction time, movement time, and other simple sensory and mental processes. Wissler, using the measure of correlation developed by Spearman* just a few years earlier, found very low or near-zero correlations between academic standing and the tests, although students' grades in their different courses showed good correlation. Wissler's findings, published in a 1901 monograph, had the effect of undermining both Cattell's approach to mental testing and testing in general, although only temporarily since a different approach, that of Binet's*, was soon to yield much better results.

Under the influence of Franz Boas*, Wissler turned from psychology to anthropology. He became an authority on North American Indians and wrote more than two hundred scientific and popular articles in anthropology. Wissler's output in psychology was only about fifteen papers.

Biographies: F. C. Cole, *Amer. Anthropologist*, 1952, *54*, 157-167; R. H. Lowie, *Amer. Anthropologist*, 1949, *51*, 527-528; D. G. Mendelbaum, *Science*, 1948, *107*, 338-339; G. P. Murdock, *Amer. Anthropologist*, 1948, *50*, 292-304; *IESS*, 16; *NCAB*, 33, E; *NYT*, 1947, Aug. 26, 23:1; *PR*, 3; *Who Was Who in America*, 2; *Yearb. Amer. Phil. Soc.*, 1947.

WITASEK, STEPHAN
Austrian Psychologist
Born: Graz, Steiermark, Austria, 1870
Died: Graz, Steiermark, Austria, 1915
Highest Degree: Ph.D. in philosophy, University of Graz, 1898, under A. Meinong*
Positions: 1900-1915, University of Graz

Witasek's main interest was aesthetics, in which area he published extensively. His approach combined philosophy with empirical psychology. Although his doctorate was in philosophy, his dissertation was about geometric illusions, and he proposed a theory to explain them. A member of the Austrian school of form-quality, Witasek continued the work of Christian von Ehrenfels*, Alexius von Meinong, and Hans Cornelius in the early years of this century. Some of his work was empirical and even experimental. Subscribing to a psychology that allowed room for both psychological acts and psychological contents, his systematic views focused on perception and the act of production (*Grundlinien der Psychologie*, 1908; *Psychologie der Raumwahrnehmung des Auges*, 1910). The psychological act of production results in simple or complex complexions. Complex complexions are determined both by the internal act of production and the physical properties of the stimulus object.

Biographies: A. Meinong, *Z. Psychol.*, 1915, *73*, 137-141; *EUI*, 70.

WITKIN, HERMAN A.

American Psychologist
Born: New York, New York, August 2, 1916
Died: New York, New York, July 8, 1979
Highest Degree: Ph.D. in psychology, New York University, 1939, from T. C. Schneierla*
Positions, Honors: 1939-40, Swarthmore College; 1940-51, Brooklyn College; 1952-70, State University of New York, Downstate Medical Center; 1971-79, Educational Testing Service, Princeton, N.J.; honorary D.S.Sc., Tilburg University, 1977

The name of Herman Witkin is one of the most significant ones in the area of the relationship between learning, cognitions, and personality. He studied these relationships experimentally and from the perspectives of social, personality, and developmental psychologies. Witkin pioneered in the study of cognitive styles when he noticed individual differences in the ways people perceive spatial relations; devised a method for studying individual differences in the perception of the upright, the rod-and-frame test; and related this method to others, such as the embedded figures test, which also showed differences in cognitive styles. Witkin's concept of *field-dependence* and *field-independence*, which is the ability to respond to an aspect of stimulation within a context, turned out to be a major cognitive style and led to a large amount of research by others and to Witkin's becoming one of the most often cited authors in the area of social and behavioral sciences. Witkin published more than fifty papers about the subject of cognitive style and wrote three books: *Personality Through Perception* (1954, with others), *Psychological Differentiation* (1962), and *Experimental Studies of Dreaming* (1967).

Biographies: S. Messick, *Amer. Psychologist*, 1980, *35*, 99-100; *Rev. psychol. appl.*, 1979, *29*, 327-335; *NYT*, 1979, July 11, 12:5.

WITMER, LIGHTNER
American Psychologist
Born: Philadelphia, Pennsylvania, June 28, 1867
Died: Philadelphia, Pennsylvania, July 19, 1956
Highest Degree: Ph.D. in psychology, University of Leipzig, 1892, under W. Wundt*
Positions, Honors: 1893-1937, University of Pennsylvania; 1896-98, Bryn Mawr College; 1903-5, Lehigh University; honorary Sc.D., 1937

Although Witmer established a psychological laboratory at Bryn Mawr College in 1896 and another at Lehigh University in 1903, he did not remain experimentalist for very long. At the University of Pennsylvania he founded the first psychological clinic. It started without much planning, and its first patients were children. In 1896, which is taken as the year in which the clinic was established, Witmer reported on its operation to the American Psychological Association. He described its functioning, philosophy, and uses. He employed the terms *psychological clinic*, *clinical psychology*, and *the clinical method*. In his clinic, the first service-oriented enterprise of this sort, Witmer used the talents of a multidisciplinary group: neurologists, physicians, social workers, and special education teachers. Through the clinic he opened up a new field of psychology and is considered to be the "father" of clinical psychology.

Other activities of Witmer in this field include the founding of the journals *Analytical Psychology* in 1902 and *The Psychological Clinic* in 1907. He edited the second journal until it ceased publication in 1935. He also founded a hospital school at the University of Pennsylvania in 1907. It was later named the Orthogenic School and was established to prepare personnel in education, medicine, and social work to train normal and retarded children. Witmer saw the school as training ground for a new profession, the psychological expert. The Witmer School, established in 1920, served as an educational institution for mentally retarded children. Among other test devices, the Witmer Cylinder Test and the Witmer Form Board were used in this school and elsewhere.

Biographies: R. A. Brotemarkle (Ed.), *Clinical Psychology: Studies in Honor of Lightner Witmer* ..., 1931; J. M. Gardner, *Amer. J. Ment. Defic.*, 1968, *72*, 719-720; D. Shakow, *Amer. J. Orthopsychiat.*, 1968, *38*, 804-809; S. H. Tulchin, *Amer. J. Orthopsychiat.*, 1957, *27*, 200-201; R. I. Watson, *Amer. J. Psychol.*, 1956, *69*, 680-682; *NYT*, 1956, July 21, 15:5; *PR*, 3; *Who Was Who in America*, 2; *Yearb. Amer. Phil. Soc.*, 1956.

WOLFF, BARON CHRISTIAN VON
German Philosopher
Born: Breslau, Silesia, January 24, 1679
Died: Halle, Saxony-Anhalt, April 9, 1754
Education: Graduated from Leipzig University, 1703
Positions: 1706-23, University of Halle; 1723-40, University of Marburg; 1740-54, University of Halle

Wolff was a prominent systematizer of philosophy and the foremost exponent of faculty psychology in the eighteenth century. He had considerable influence on other philosophers, such as Kant*, in the way they conceptualized philosophical problems. In psychology Wolff wrote two volumes, *Psychologia empirica* (1732) and *Psychologia rationalis* (1734). The subdivision of psychology into a rational and an empirical branch begins with Wolff. *Rational psychology* comes from metaphysics and from the experience of the soul's activities, and it depends more on reason than experience; *empirical psychology* is about the human being (soul-body) and depends more on experience than reason. Wolff held that rational psychology is superior to empirical psychology in that it gives clear and distinct ideas, in contrast to empirical psychology whose product is vague, obscure ideas and sensations.

The soul is one, but it has different powers or faculties: feeling, desire, and knowing, the latter consisting of perception, memory, understanding, and reason. The most important function of the soul is to represent the world. Since the soul is tied to the body, the location of the body and the nature of the sense organs determine the way in which the world is perceived. In his *Psychologia empirica* Wolff relied more on Descartes* and related the existence of the I to the fact of self-awareness. Consciousness is the first datum that we come across in our attempts to find a basis for psychology. Without consciousness it is impossible to find out anything about the activity of the soul. Still, not all activity is conscious. Ideas can exist with or without consciousness. There is consciousness when the soul is aware of its own activities, but there is no consciousness in sleep. Sensations are likewise either clear or obscure and therefore are either conscious or unconscious.

Biographies: M. Campo, *Christiano Wolff e il razionalismo precritico*, 2 vols., 1939; O. Nippold, In C. v. Wolff, *Jus gentium scientifica pertractatum*, 1934, pp. xi-lii (1749); E. Utilz, *Christian Wolff*, 1929; C. v. Wolff, *Eigene Lebensbeschreibung*, 1841; *ADB*, 44; *Chalmers*, 32; *EB*, 23; *EP*, 8; *EUI*, 70; *Grande*, 31; *Nouvelle*, 46.

WOODWORTH, ROBERT SESSIONS
American Psychologist
Born: Belchertown, Massachusetts, October 17, 1869
Died: New York, New York, July 4, 1962
Highest Degree: Ph.D. in psychology, Columbia University, 1899, under J. McK. Cattell*
Positions, Honors: 1899-1902, New York University; 1902-3, University of Liverpool; 1903-42, Columbia University, retired 1942, 1942-58, lecturer on dynamics of behavior; president, American Psychological Association, 1914; editorial work for several psychological journals, including *Archives of Psychology* (1906-48); five honorary degrees; American Psychological Foundation Gold Medal, 1956

One of Woodworth's early notable contributions was a piece of research (published with E. L. Thorndike* in 1901) about transfer of learning. It effectively dismantled the doctrine of formal disciplines, that is, that the learning of subjects such as Latin and mathematics would develop logical thinking that, in turn, would help in the study of other subjects. This was followed by some 220 papers and 10 major books. Of the books, the most important ones were a revision of Ladd's* *Physiological Psychology* in 1911, which became the standard text in the area; *Dynamic Psychology* (1918), a call for functional psychology and a treatise on the psychology of motivation; *Psychology* (1921), a very popular textbook that saw five editions and was far ahead of any other such text in sales; *Contemporary Schools of Psychology* (1931), a much used text; and *Experimental Psychology* (1938; rev. ed., 1954, with H. Schlosberg*), one of the classic texts in psychology on which generations of psychologists were brought up.

Woodworth called himself a dynamic psychologist. The term *dynamic psychology* was coined by him. He was one of the first psychologists to veer away from the stimulus-response psychology of Wundt* and Watson* toward a stimulus-organism-response psychology that took into account the contribution to the response that was made by the experiencing individual. Woodworth's *Dynamic Psychology* and subsequent papers emphasize the study of cause-effect relationships and the use of motor behavior, physiology, and introspection in such study, depending on which method best fits the situation. Within this functionalist framework Woodworth wanted to study the motives that determine specific behaviors (motivology). He showed that motives do not arise from instincts (as McDougall* said they did), but that behavioral mechanisms, once started, begin to act on their own accord ("the mechanism becomes the drive").

Woodworth did not formulate any special psychological theory or found any school of psychology. His contribution was in taking a position on issues in dispute and clarifying them in such a way that his view became the accepted view in psychology. Through his teaching, the *Archives of Psychology*, and his approach to experimentation, Woodworth conveyed the idea that experimental psychology was a solid, fact- and method-oriented scientific enterprise. That was his major contribution during the first twenty-five years of this century.

Biographies: E. Heidbreder, *Brit. J. Psychol.*, 1963, *54*, 199-200; G. Murphy, *Amer. Psychologist*, 1963, *18*, 131-133; A. T. Poffenberger, *Amer. J. Psychol.*, 1962, *75*, 677-689; G. H. Seward & J. P. Seward (Eds.), *Current Psychological Issues: Essays in Honor of Robert S. Woodworth*, 1958; L. F. Shaffer, *Amer. Psychologist*, 1956, *11*, 587-589; *Biog. Mem.*, 39; *EUI*, 70; *HPA*, 2; *IESS*, 16; *NCAB*, 48, A; *NYT*, 1962, July 5, 25:1; *PR*, 3; *Who Was Who in America*, 4; *Yearb. Amer. Phil. Soc.*, 1962.

WUNDT, WILHELM (MAXIMILIAN)

German Psychologist

Born: Neckarau, Baden, August 16, 1832
Died: Grossbathen near Leipzig, Saxony, August 31, 1920
Highest Degree: M.D., University of Heidelberg, 1856

Positions: 1857-74, University of Heidelberg; 1874-75, University of Zurich; 1875-1917, University of Leipzig

Wundt's interests began to shift to physiology even before he received his medical degree. His first teaching appointment at Heidelberg was in physiology. He began to publish in physiology in 1858. The *Beiträge zur Theorie der Sinneswahrenehmungen*, which was an outline of much that Wundt taught and published later, came out in installments between 1858 and 1862 and in one piece in 1862. In his work Wundt made the point that psychology, before tackling metaphysical problems, should start by trying to understand the simplest experiences, and that this should be done using the methods of physiology. In 1867 he began teaching the first formal academic course in psychology, called "Physiological Psychology." The lecture notes were published in 1873 and 1874 in Wundt's most important book, *Grundzüge der physiologischen Psychologie*, which appeared in several enlarged editions. Upon his arrival at the University of Leipzig, Wundt established there, in 1875, the first psychological laboratory in the world. The laboratory became a famous training center for psychologists and the hub of what was soon to be known as the "new" psychology.

Using highly trained observers who introspected and reported on their experiences when presented visual, auditory, and other kinds of stimuli, Wundt collected data on the functioning of the senses, published them in the first purely psychological journal, *Philosophische Studien* (founded by him in 1881), and summarized the results in the changing editions of his *Grundzüge*. Most of the experimental studies were on sensation and perception, reaction time, attention, feeling, and association. About one hundred experimental studies were published in *Philosophische Studien* during its publication, by Wundt and his students, among whom were to be found some of the most famous names in the history of modern psychology. Wundt's written production is close to the five hundred-item mark, with a total of some fifty-four thousand printed pages. Some of the outstanding volumes are *Vorlesungen über die Menschen- und Thierseele* (1863), *Grundriss der Psychologie* (1896), and *Einführung in die Psychologie* (1911). Not all of Wundt's written output was about experimental psychology. He wrote several volumes about philosophy and a ten-volume ethnopsychology (*Völkerpsychologie*, 1900-1920). Although he was opposed to any form of applied psychology, he accepted social psychology and used it to account for those psychic processes that were more complex than sensation or memory and that could not, in his view, be studied experimentally.

Wundt's fame is based principally on his having founded an experimental psychological science. His systematic views are of lesser importance and constitute largely a descriptive system. Wundt saw the investigation of the contents of the mind as psychology's main task. The notion of consciousness consisting of elements and the method of introspection directed toward eliciting the elements put the mark of elementism on Wundt's psychology. Experience is always complex, and introspection must be used to break it down into elementary components, which are the sensations and feelings. Pure sensations differ in quality and intensity, feelings differ in pleasantness-unpleasantness, tension-relaxation, and excitement-depression (the three-dimensional theory of feeling). Sensations and feelings in combination become ideas and percepts. The latter acquire meaning only as apperceived, that is, combined with past experience and giving rise to feeling. This is active association. Basically, Wundt accepted the ideas of the associationists as to how successive ideas become passively associated. He added the notion of fusion to account for the tighter association between simultaneously occurring ideas as well as the notion of creative synthesis to explain how parts, in combining, may produce something different from a mere sum of the parts. Thus Wundt was somewhat inconsistent in that, in asserting the changing, dynamic nature of consciousness, he affirmed that it was not only content but also process. However, he did not elaborate further on this aspect of his psychology.

Wundt's elementism and the method of introspection did not survive the death of his truest disciple, E. B. Titchener*. His own students went on to establish branches of applied psychology. His theory of feeling reappeared in a modified form in later theories of emotion, and the idea of creative synthesis was made into a cardinal tenet of the Gestalt school of psychology, although it arose partly in opposition to Wundt's elementism. Wundt's greatest contribution, however, was to show that psychology could be an experimental science. The experimental study of thinking, which Wundt thought could not be done, was begun by others in his lifetime. Today, there is no area of human behavior that has not been studied experimentally, and experimentation is one of the cornerstones of the psychological edifice.

Biographies: W. Wundt, *Erlebtes und Erkanntes*, 1920; G. Hicks, *Nature*, 1920, *106*, 83-85; A. Hoffman (Ed.), *Wilhelm Wundt: Eine Würdigung*, 1924; G. Humphrey, In B. B. Wolman (Ed.), *Historical Roots of Contemporary Psychology*, 1968, pp. 275-297; F. Kiesow, *Arch. ital. psicol.*, 1923, *2*, 203-213; F. Kiesow, *Arch. ital. psicol.*, 1932, *10*, iii-xxii; P. Petersen, *Wilhelm Wundt und seine Zeit*, 1925; E. B. Titchener, *Amer. J. Psychol.*, 1921, *32*, 161-178; various, *Psychol. Rev.*, 1921, *28*, 153-188; W. Wirth, *Arch. ges. Psychol.*, 1920, *40*, i-xiv; *CE*, 14; *DSB*, 14; *EB*, 23; *EP*, 8; *EUI*, 70; Hirsch, *Biog. Lex.*, 5; *NYT*, 1920, Sept. 2, 9:2.

Y

YERKES, ROBERT MEARNS

American Psychologist
Born: Breadysville, Pennsylvania, May 26, 1876
Died: New Haven, Connecticut, February 3, 1956
Highest Degree: Ph.D. in psychology, Harvard University, 1902
Positions: 1908-17, Harvard University; 1917-24, University of Minnesota; 1924-44, Yale University; president, American Psychological Association, 1917

Yerkes and Thorndike* pioneered in the experimental study of animal behavior. Yerkes was primarily a comparative psychologist, although he called himself by preference a "psychobiologist." He wrote his first research paper in 1899, and it was followed by many others. He took charge of comparative psychology at Harvard in 1902. From then on he was a leader in the field of comparative psychology, both in terms of the output of comparative studies on many species of animals, especially the primates, and his other activities related to the field. His name is associated with the operation of the first primate laboratory at Yale, the Yale Laboratories of Primate Biology, of which he was the director between 1929 and 1941, and later in Orange Park, Florida. The Orange Park laboratory was named the Yerkes Laboratories of Primate Biology (now the Yerkes Regional Primate Center of Emory University) when he retired in 1942.

Out of his work on animal behavior arose statements such as the *Yerkes-Dodson law*, which states that strong motivation interferes with learning a difficult discrimination problem but helps to learn a simple one. Yerkes developed animal-testing devices such as the use of monochromatic light to study their color vision and the multiple-choice method to test concept formation. Later Yerkes also became interested in human abilities, developing an intelligence scale in 1915, the *Point Scale*. During World War I Yerkes headed the group of psychologists whose task it was to measure the ability of army recruits so as to make decisions concerning their rejection or discharge, assignment to specific duties, or training. The group developed the Army Alpha and Army Beta tests, which, by the end of the war, had been given to 1,726,000 men. Yerkes, however, is remembered mainly as a comparative psychologist who wrote books such as *The Great Apes* (1929, with Ada Yerkes) and *Chimpanzees: A Laboratory Colony* (1943).

Biographies: L. Carmichael, *Psychol. Rev.*, 1957, *64*, 1-7; R. M. Elliott, *Amer. J. Psychol.*, 1956, *69*, 487-494; W. R. Miles, *Amer. Psychologist*, 1946, *1*, 175-178; *Biog. Mem.*, 38; *DSB*, 14; *IESS*, 16; *NCAB*, 43; *NYT*, 1956, Feb. 5, 86:1; *PR*, 3; *Who Was Who in America*, 3; *Yearb. Amer. Phil. Soc.*, 1956.

YOUNG, PAUL THOMAS

American Psychologist

Born: Los Angeles, May 26, 1892

Died: Los Angeles, June 15, 1978

Highest Degree: Ph.D. in psychology, Cornell University, 1918, under E. B. Titchener*

Positions, Honors: 1918-19, Cornell University; 1919-21, University of Minnesota; 1921-60, University of Illinois; 1960-78, professor emeritus; editorial work, *Journal of Social Psychology* and *Comparative Psychology Monographs*; honorary D. Sc., Occidental College, 1961; Distinguished Scientific Contribution Award, American Psychological Association, 1965

For most of his career Young studied pleasantness and unpleasantness feelings, food preferences, emotions, motives, and the hedonistic factor in behavior in general. His theoretical position was that "although affective arousals depend on sensory stimulation, they are integrated at a higher level according to a nonsensory principle. Positive and negative affective arousals are incompatible but they combine according to precise laws of algebraic summation ... there is a genuine distinction between cognitive and affective processes.... Affective arousals are both activating and regulating. They are basic factors in reinforcement and the organization of goal-oriented behavior ... two dimensions of energy mobilization are required to give an account of motivation and development: activation and the hedonic dimension. The distinction between cognitive and affective processes has an objective neurophysiological basis."

Young also invented the *pseudophone* (a device that reverses the direction of auditory stimulation to the two ears) and conducted a series of studies on auditory localization.

Young left behind about one hundred and twenty scientific publications, chapters in encyclopedias and edited books, and the following books: *Motivation of*

Behavior (1936), *Emotion in Man and Animal* (1943; 2nd ed., 1973), and *Motivation and Emotion* (1961).
Biographies: *Amer. Psychologist*, 1965, *20*, 1084-1088; L. I. O'Kelly, *Amer. J. Psychol.*, 1979, *92*, 551-553; P. T. Young, In T. S. Krawiec (Ed.), *The Psychologists*, vol. 1, 1972.

YOUNG, THOMAS
English Physicist
Born: Melverton, Sommersetshire, June 13, 1773
Died: London, May 10, 1829
Highest Degree: Doctor of physics, University of Göttingen, 1796; M.D., Cambridge University, 1808
Positions: 1799-1801, physician, London; 1801-3, Royal Institute; 1802-29, foreign secretary, the Royal Society

In addition to having made many contributions in physics, Young was also the founder of physiological optics. In 1793 he explained the phenomenon of accommodation, demonstrating experimentally that it was due to the changing curvature of the lens of the eye. In 1801 he described astigmatism and explained it in terms of irregularities of the cornea. In the same year Young also determined the extent of the visual field and described how acuity decreases toward the periphery of the field.

Young's most notable contribution to psychology was the formulation of a color-vision theory in 1802. He developed Newton's* laws of color mixture, presented some one hundred and thirty years earlier, and hypothesized that all colors could be produced if only the three principal ones—red, yellow, and blue—were mixed in the right proportion. Young assumed further that the retina was so constituted that, instead of an infinite number of different structures, each responding to its own color, only three kinds of structures were necessary. It was not until 1852 that Helmholtz* presented a full-fledged theory of color vision referring to Young's original formulation. It was named the ''Young-Helmholtz color-vision theory.'' Young's explanation of color vision also implied specificity of nerve-fiber action even before Charles Bell* in 1811 and Johannes Müller* in 1826 had stated the general principle of specific nerve energies and before Helmholtz's definition of the specificity of nerve fibers in 1852.
Biographies: F. Arago, In *Biographies of Distinguished Scientific Men*, 2nd ser., 1972, pp. 280-350; H. Gurney, *Memoir of the Life of Dr. Thomas Young, M.D.*, 1831; J. Herivel, *Endeavour*, 1973, *32*, 15-18; G. Peacock, *Life of Thomas Young*, 1855; H. B. Williams, *J. Opt. Soc. Amer.*, 1930, *20*, 35-50; A. Wood & F. Oldham, *Thomas Young: Natural Philosopher*, 1954; *DNB*, 21; *DSB*, 14; *Grande*, 31; Hirsch, *Biog. Lex.*, 5; *Nouvelle*, 46.

YULE, GEORGE UDNY
English Statistician
Born: Morham, near Haddington, East Lothian, Scotland, February 18, 1871
Died: Cambridge, June 26, 1951

Highest Degree: M.A., Cambridge University, 1913

Positions, Honors: 1893-99, University College, London; 1899-1912, City and Guilds of London Institute; 1902-9, University College, London; 1912-31, Cambridge University; president, Royal Statistical Society, 1924-26; recipient of a variety of honors

Yule laid the foundation of the theory of partial correlation and linear regression for n variables, and described association in a 2×2 contingency table. He made numerous other contributions to statistics that were not directly related to psychological research. His *Introduction to the Theory of Statistics* (1911) was a well-known text that by 1968 had seen fourteen editions. It was the first comprehensive statistical text.

Biographies: E. G. C., *Brit. J. Psychol.*, 1952, *43*, 1; *Isis*, 1952, *43*, 56; M. G. Kendall, *J. Roy. Stat. Soc.*, 1952, *115A*, 156-161; *DNB*, 21; *DSB*, 14; *IESS*, 16; *Obit. Not.*, 8; *PR*, 3.

Z

ZENER, KARL EDWARD
American Psychologist
Born: Indianapolis, Indiana, April 22, 1903
Died: Durham, North Carolina, September 27, 1964
Highest Degree: Ph.D., in psychology, Harvard University, 1926
Positions: 1927-28, Princeton University; 1928-64, Duke University, since 1961, chairman, Psychology Department; editorial work, *Journal of Psychology*, *Journal of Personality*, and *Character and Personality*

In the 1930s Zener directed the work of a Pavlovian (Pavlov*) conditioning laboratory at Duke and, finding inadequacies in some of the Pavlovian formulations, introduced some changes. Most of Zener's scientific papers, which were not very numerous, were about problems in conditioning. He also studied motivation in relation to learning and perception, but the work for which he is best known was the phenomenological analysis of perceptual experience. This subject occupied Zener for the last fifteen years of his life. He analyzed the perceptual process that intervenes between the object and the central processes in the cortex into six phases and considered this sequence of phases "as constituting an alternating and interlocking series of relatively isomorphic energy transformations and transmissions with interactions at the nodal regions of object surfaces, receptor mosaic, and successive synaptic relay regions." Although in general approving of J. J. Gibson's* approach to perception, Zener stressed the necessity to reexamine the experiential properties of the world instead of limiting oneself to an examination of the stimulus and the response alone. For this purpose he studied, both phenomenologically and using the eye movement recording technique, the experience and behavior of individuals as they looked at photographs and paintings in which the right and left sides or top and bottom were reversed. Zener's major theoretical statement may be found in a chapter that he wrote with Mercedes Gaffron about perceptual experience for *Psychology: A Study of a Science* (vol. 4, 1962).

Biographies: E. E. Jones, *J. Pers.*, 1964, *32*, 511-513; S. Koch, *J. Pers.*, 1969, *37*, 179-189; *American Men of Science*, vol. 4, The Physical and Biological Sciences, 1961; *PR*, 3; *NYT*, 1964, Sept. 28, 29:5.

ZIEHEN, THEODOR

German Psychiatrist
Born: Frankfurt am Main, November 12, 1862
Died: Wiesbaden, Hesse, December 29, 1950
Highest Degree: M.D., University of Berlin, 1885
Positions, Honors: 1886-1900, University of Jena; 1900-1903, University of Utrecht; 1903-4, University of Halle; 1904-12, University of Berlin; 1917-30, University of Halle; honorary Ph.D., University of Berlin, 1910

Ziehen had an interest in both psychiatry and philosophy, as a result of which he wrote some successful books in psychology. Although not contributing much that was original, he seldom used the ideas of others in their original form but modified them or disagreed with some aspect of them. This made him a successful textbook writer. His *Leitfaden der physiologischen Psychologie*, first published in 1891 had twelve editions. Other successful books in psychology written by Ziehen were *Die Grundlagen der Psychologie* (2 vols., 1915), *Die Beziehung der Lebenserscheinungen zum Bewusstsein* (1921), *Das Seelenleben der Jugendlichen* (1923), *Allgemeine Psychologie* (1923), and others. His books, monographs, and articles in psychology, psychiatry, and philosophy were numerous.

Ziehen's view was that each science takes as its own a segment of the experientially given without the need to trace back its origin epistemologically. The knowledge of the epistemological origins of its raw material is, however, necessary for the psychologist, because he must know what it is that is given for him. There is the difficulty of defining either that which is being experienced or to derive it from anything else. Ziehen called the mental givens "gignomena," in analogy to phenomena, and stressed the necessity of studying them to remain entirely within the realm of that which is immediately given (the principle of immanence), beyond mind-body dualism, but without becoming transcendental and thus losing the scientific ground of enquiry.

Biographies: W. Peters, *Kant-Stud.*, 1932, *37*, 237-240; *Biog. Lex.*; *EP*, 8; *EUI*, 70; *HPA*, 1; Pagel, *Biographisches Lexikon*; *PR*, 3.

ZILBOORG, GREGORY

American Psychoanalyst
Born: Kiev, Ukraine, December 25, 1890
Died: New York, New York, September 17, 1959

Highest Degree: M.D., Psychoneurological Institute, St. Petersburg, 1917; M.D., College of Physicians and Surgeons, Columbia University, 1926
Positions, Honors: 1926-31, Bloomingdale Hospital; 1929-30, Psychoanalytical Institute, Berlin; 1931-59, private practice, New York City; honorary D.Sc., National University, Ireland, 1954

Zilboorg published numerous articles about psychiatry and psychoanalysis in medical journals as well as some books of psychological interest: *Mind, Medicine, and Man* (1943), *Sigmund Freud* (1951), *The Psychology of the Criminal Act and Punishment* (1954), and *Freud and Religion* (1959). His best-known work, however, was *A History of Medical Psychology*, which he published with G. W. Henry in 1941.

In addition to psychoanalysis and medical history, Zilboorg was also prominent in the study of suicide. He helped organize the Committee for the Study of Suicide in 1936 and, as its research director, guided the study of thousands of suicidal patients in the large cities of America. A four-volume handbook was the result of this project.

Biographies: G. Fountain, *Psychoanal. Quart.*, 1960, *29*, 1-5; L. Ancona, *Arch. psicol. neurol. psichiat.*, 1959, *20*, 537-539; *CE*, 14; *EJ*, 16; *Jewish*, 10; *NCAB*, 43; *Who Was Who in America*, 3.

ZWAARDEMAKER, HENDRICK
Dutch Otolaryngologist
Born: Haarlem, May 10, 1857
Died: Utrecht, September 19, 1930
Highest Degree: M.D., University of Amsterdam, 1883
Positions: 1897-1927, University of Utrecht

Zwaardemaker did his most important work on smell. His *Die Physiologie des Geruchs* (1895) was a classic; it was the first scientific treatise on smell and remained the most significant one during the first half of the twentieth century, creating much interest and research on the subject. A revised version of it was published in French as *L'Odorat* (1925).

Zwaardemaker spent much of his professional life looking for the physical key that makes substances odorous, but he never succeeded in finding it. His successes include the invention of a device for the administration of measured amounts of odorous substances, the olfactometer; the design of the odor-proof room; measurement of olfactory thresholds; and the introduction of the unit of olfactory intensity, the *olfactie*. Zwaardemaker attempted to show that the same laws that hold for vision also hold for smell, namely, those of mixture, adaptation, and compensation. He classified odors using the seven odors of Linnaeus* plus two additional ones and introduced several subclasses of each. This classification prevailed until Henning* introduced his smell prism.

Zwaardemaker also did important work on hearing. He studied speech sounds, measured pitch thresholds, and formulated the law of presbyacusis and a theory of hearing.

Biographies: C. E. Benjamins, *Acta Otolaryng.*, 1931, *15*, 1-6; G. Grijns, *Arch. neerl. physiol.*, 1931, *16*, 1-5; A. K. M. Noyons, *Amer. J. Psychol.*, 1931, *43*, 525-526; *Biog. Lex.*; *EUI*, 70; *HPA*, 1; *PR*, 3.

Chronological Listing by Birth Date

For historical continuity, the names listed in the dictionary are arranged here in chronological order by birth date. Only last names are used, except where two individuals have the same last name, in which case they are further identified by their initials.

	BORN B.C.	DIED B.C.
Thales	ca. 624	ca. 546
Pythagoras	ca. 560	ca. 480
Heraclitus	ca. 540	ca. 475
Alcmaeon	ca. 500	?
Anaxagoras	ca. 500	ca. 428
Empedocles	ca. 490	ca. 430
Protagoras	ca. 490	ca. 421
Socrates	ca. 470	ca. 399
Democritus	ca. 470	ca. 370
Hippocrates	ca. 460	ca. 370
Plato	ca. 428	ca. 348
Aristotle	384	323
Theophrastus	ca. 371	ca. 288
Epicurus	341	270
Herophilus	ca. 320	?
Erasistratus	ca. 304	ca. 250

	BORN	DIED
	A.D.	A.D.
Galen	130	200
Tertullian	155	220
Plotinus	205	270
St. Augustine	Nov. 13, 354	Aug. 28, 430
Avicenna	980	1037
Averröes	1126	1198
Maimonides	1135 (or 1138)	1204
Grosseteste	1168	Oct. 9, 1253
Albertus Magnus	ca. 1200	Nov. 15, 1280
Peter of Spain	1210 to 1220	Mar. 16, 1277
Bacon, R.	1214	1292
Thomas Aquinas	ca. 1225	Mar. 7, 1274
Ockham	ca. 1285	1349
Copernicus	Feb. 19, 1473	May 24, 1543
Vives	Mar. 6, 1492	May 6, 1540
Paracelsus	ca. 1493	Sept. 24, 1541
Vesalius	Dec. 31, 1514	Oct. 15, 1564
Montaigne	Feb. 28, 1533	Sept. 12, 1592
Huarte	1530 to 1535	1592
Bacon, F.	Jan. 22, 1561	Apr. 9, 1626
Galilei	Feb. 15, 1564	Jan. 8, 1642
Kepler	Dec. 27, 1571	Nov. 15, 1630
Harvey	Apr. 1, 1578	June 3, 1657
Hobbes	Apr. 5, 1588	Dec. 4, 1679
Gassendi	Jan. 22, 1592	Oct. 24, 1655
Comenius	Mar. 28, 1592	Nov. 15, 1670
Descartes	Mar. 31, 1596	Feb. 11, 1650
Mariotte	ca. 1620	May 12, 1684
Pascal	June 19, 1623	Aug. 19, 1662
Geulincx	Jan. 1624	Nov. 1669
Huygens	Apr. 14, 1629	June 8, 1695
Locke	Aug. 29, 1632	Oct. 28, 1704
Leeuwenhoek	Oct. 24, 1632	Aug. 26, 1723
Spinoza	Nov. 24, 1632	Feb. 20, 1677
Malebranche	Aug. 8, 1638	Oct. 13, 1715
Newton	Dec. 25, 1642	Mar. 20, 1727
Leibniz	July 1, 1646	Nov. 14, 1716
Molyneux	Apr. 17, 1656	Oct. 11, 1698
Wolff	Jan. 24, 1679	Apr. 9, 1754
Berkeley	Mar. 12, 1685	Jan. 14, 1753
Swedenborg	Jan. 29, 1688	Mar. 29, 1772
Montesquieu	Jan. 18, 1689	Feb. 10, 1755

	BORN	DIED
	A.D.	A.D.
Voltaire	Nov. 21, 1694	May 30, 1778
Johnson	Oct. 14, 1696	June 6, 1772
Bernoulli	Feb. 8, 1700	Mar. 17, 1782
Edwards	Oct. 5, 1703	Mar. 22, 1758
Hartley	Aug. 30, 1705	Aug. 28, 1757
Franklin	Jan. 6, 1706	Apr. 17, 1790
Euler	Apr. 15, 1707	Sept. 7, 1783
Linnaeus	May 23, 1707	Jan. 10, 1778
Buffon	Sept. 7, 1707	Apr. 16, 1788
Haller	Oct. 16, 1708	Dec. 17, 1777
La Mettrie	Dec. 25, 1709	Nov. 11, 1751
Reid	Apr. 26, 1710	Oct. 7, 1796
Hume	May 7, 1711	Aug. 25, 1776
Rousseau	June 28, 1712	July 2, 1778
Diderot	Oct. 5, 1713	July 30, 1784
Whytt	Sept. 6, 1714	Apr. 15, 1766
Helvetius	Jan. 26, 1715	Dec. 26, 1771
Condillac	Sept. 30, 1715	Aug. 3, 1780
d'Alembert	Nov. 17, 1717	Oct. 29, 1783
Bonnet	Mar. 3, 1720	May 20, 1793
Smith	June 5, 1723	July 17, 1790
Kant	Apr. 22, 1724	Feb. 12, 1804
Lessing	Jan. 22, 1729	Feb. 15, 1781
Darwin, E.	Dec. 12, 1731	Apr. 18, 1802
Priestley	Mar. 13, 1733	Feb. 6, 1804
Mesmer	May 23, 1734	Mar. 5, 1815
Tetens	Sept. 16, 1736	Aug. 15, 1807
Galvani	Sept. 9, 1737	Dec. 4, 1798
Lavater	Nov. 11, 1741	Jan. 2, 1801
Lavoisier	Aug. 26, 1743	May 8, 1794
Condorcet	Sept. 17, 1743	Apr. 8, 1794
Lamarck	Aug. 1, 1744	Dec. 18, 1829
Herder	Aug. 25, 1744	Dec. 18, 1803
Pinel	Apr. 20, 1745	Oct. 25, 1826
Rush, B.	Jan. 4, 1746	Apr. 19, 1813
Pestalozzi	Jan. 12, 1746	Feb. 17, 1827
Bentham	Feb. 15, 1748	June 6, 1832
Tiedemann	Apr. 3, 1748	May 24, 1803
Laplace	Mar. 28, 1749	Mar. 5, 1827
Prochaska	Apr. 10, 1749	July 17, 1820
Goethe	Aug. 28, 1749	Mar. 22, 1832
Puységur	1751	1825

	BORN A.D.	DIED A.D.
Stewart	Nov. 22, 1753	June 11, 1828
Destutt de Tracy	July 20, 1754	Mar. 9, 1836
Cabanis	June 5, 1757	May 5, 1808
Moritz	Sept. 15, 1757	July 26, 1793
Gall	Mar. 9, 1758	Aug. 22, 1828
Schiller	Nov. 10, 1759	May 9, 1805
Fichte	May 19, 1762	Jan. 27, 1814
Malthus	Feb. 14, 1766	Dec. 23, 1834
Dalton	Sept. 6, 1766	July 27, 1844
Maine de Biran	Nov. 29, 1766	July 16, 1824
Humboldt	June 22, 1767	Apr. 8, 1835
Cuvier	Aug. 23, 1769	May 13, 1832
Hegel	Aug. 27, 1770	Nov. 14, 1831
Bichat	Nov. 11, 1771	July 22, 1802
Esquirol	Feb. 3, 1772	Dec. 13, 1840
Fourier	Apr. 7, 1772	Oct. 10, 1837
Coleridge	Oct. 21, 1772	July 25, 1834
Mill, J.	Apr. 6, 1773	June 23, 1836
Young, T.	June 13, 1773	May 10, 1829
Rolando	June 20, 1773	Apr. 20, 1831
Bell	Nov. 1774	Apr. 28, 1842
Schelling	Jan. 27, 1775	Aug. 20, 1854
Itard	Apr. 24, 1775	July 5, 1838
Gauss	Apr. 30, 1775	Feb. 23, 1855
Feuerbach	Nov. 14, 1775	May 29, 1833
Herbart	May 4, 1776	Aug. 4, 1841
Spurzheim	Dec. 31, 1776	Nov. 10, 1832
Brown, T.	Jan. 9, 1778	Apr. 2, 1820
Fröbel	Apr. 21, 1782	June 21, 1852
Magendie	Oct. 15, 1783	Oct. 17, 1855
Bessel	July 22, 1784	Mar. 17, 1846
Rush, J.	Mar. 15, 1787	May 26, 1869
Purkinje	Dec. 17, 1787	July 28, 1869
Schopenhauer	Feb. 22, 1788	Sept. 20, 1860
Hamilton	Mar. 8, 1788	May 6, 1856
Hall, M.	Feb. 18, 1790	Aug. 11, 1857
Faraday	Sept. 22, 1791	Aug. 25, 1867
Elliotson	Oct. 29, 1791	July 29, 1868
Cousin	Nov. 28, 1792	Jan. 13, 1867
Flourens	Apr. 1, 1794	Dec. 6, 1867
Braid	ca. 1795	Mar. 25, 1860
Weber, E. H.	June 24, 1795	Jan. 26, 1878

	BORN	DIED
	A.D.	A.D.
Quételet	Feb. 22, 1796	Feb. 17, 1874
Comte	Jan. 19, 1798	Sept. 5, 1857
Beneke	Feb. 17, 1798	Mar.-June 1854
Volkmann	July 1, 1800	Apr. 21, 1877
Fechner	Apr. 19, 1801	Nov. 18, 1887
Müller, J.	July 14, 1801	Apr. 28, 1858
Plateau	Oct. 14, 1801	Sept. 15, 1883
Wheatstone	Feb. 1802	Oct. 19, 1875
Dix	Apr. 4, 1802	July 17, 1887
Mill, J. S.	May 20, 1806	May 8, 1873
Agassiz	May 28, 1807	Dec. 14, 1873
Esdaile	Feb. 6, 1808	Jan. 10, 1859
Darwin, C.	Feb. 12, 1809	Apr. 19, 1882
McCosh	Apr. 1, 1811	Nov. 16, 1894
Porter	Dec. 14, 1811	Mar. 4, 1892
Séguin	Jan. 20, 1812	Oct. 28, 1880
Bernard	July 12, 1813	Feb. 10, 1878
Carpenter	Oct. 29, 1813	Nov. 19, 1885
Boole	Nov. 2, 1815	Dec. 8, 1864
Ludwig	Dec. 29, 1816	Apr. 27, 1895
Brown-Séquard	Apr. 8, 1817	Apr. 2, 1894
Lewes	Apr. 18, 1817	Nov. 28, 1878
Lotze	May 21, 1817	July 1, 1881
Marx	May 5, 1818	Mar. 14, 1883
Donders	May 27, 1818	Mar. 24, 1889
Bain	June 11, 1818	Sept. 18, 1903
Vierordt	July 1, 1818	Nov. 22, 1884
Du Bois-Reymond	Nov. 7, 1818	Dec. 26, 1896
Brücke	June 6, 1819	Jan. 7, 1892
Spencer	Apr. 27, 1820	Dec. 8, 1903
Helmholtz	Aug. 31, 1821	Sept. 8, 1894
Galton	Feb. 16, 1822	Jan. 17, 1911
Mendel	July 22, 1822	Jan. 6, 1884
Wallace	Jan. 8, 1823	Nov. 7, 1913
Steinthal	May 16, 1823	Mar. 14, 1899
Liébeault	Sept. 16, 1823	Feb. 1904
Fabre	Dec. 21, 1823	Oct. 11, 1915
Broca	June 28, 1824	July 9, 1880
Lazarus	Sept. 15, 1824	Apr. 13, 1903
Huxley	May 4, 1825	June 29, 1895
Charcot	Nov. 29, 1825	Aug. 16, 1893
Aubert	Nov. 1826	Feb. 12, 1892

	BORN	DIED
	A.D.	A.D.
Taine	Apr. 21, 1828	Mar. 5, 1893
Pflüger	June 7, 1829	Mar. 16, 1910
Sechenov	Aug. 1, 1829	Nov. 2, 1905
Meissner	Nov. 19, 1829	Mar. 30, 1905
Beaunis	1930	Jul. 11, 1921
Delboeuf	Sept. 30, 1831	Aug. 14, 1896
Maxwell	Nov. 13, 1831	Nov. 5, 1879
Wundt	Aug. 16, 1832	Aug. 31, 1920
Tylor	Oct. 2, 1832	Jan. 2, 1917
Meynert	June 15, 1833	May 31, 1892
Dilthey	Nov. 19, 1833	Oct. 3, 1911
Haeckel	Feb. 16, 1834	Aug. 9, 1919
Lubbock	Apr. 30, 1834	May 28, 1913
Hering	Aug. 5, 1834	Jan. 26, 1918
Goltz	Aug. 14, 1834	May 4, 1902
Lange, C.	Dec. 4, 1834	May 29, 1900
Maudsley	Feb. 5, 1835	Jan. 23, 1918
Jackson	Apr. 4, 1835	Oct. 7, 1911
Lombroso	Nov. 18, 1835	Oct. 19, 1909
Hitzig	Feb. 6, 1838	Aug. 21, 1907
Mach	Feb. 18, 1838	Feb. 19, 1916
Fritsch	Mar. 5, 1838	June 12, 1927
Brentano	June 16, 1838	Mar. 17, 1917
Peirce	Sept. 10, 1839	Apr. 14, 1914
Bernstein	Dec. 18, 1839	Feb. 6, 1917
Ribot	Dec. 18, 1839	Dec. 8, 1916
Spalding	ca. 1840	Oct. 31, 1877
Bowditch	Apr. 4, 1840	Mar. 13, 1911
Bernheim	Apr. 17, 1840	1919
Le Bon	May 7, 1841	Dec. 13, 1931
Preyer	July 4, 1841	July 15, 1897
James	Jan. 11, 1842	Aug. 26, 1910
Breuer	Jan. 15, 1842	June 20, 1925
Ladd	Jan. 19, 1842	Aug. 8, 1921
Hartmann	Feb. 23, 1842	June 5, 1906
Sully	Mar. 3, 1842	Nov. 1, 1923
Ward	Jan. 27, 1843	Mar. 4, 1925
Höffding	Mar. 11, 1843	July 2, 1931
Tarde	Mar. 12, 1843	May 13, 1904
Golgi	July 7, 1843	Jan. 21, 1926
Avenarius	Nov. 19, 1843	Aug. 18, 1896
Hall, G. S.	Feb. 1, 1844	Apr. 24, 1924

	BORN	DIED
	A.D.	A.D.
Nietzsche	Oct. 15, 1844	Aug. 25, 1900
Emmert	Dec. 1, 1844	Oct. 10, 1911
Exner	Apr. 5, 1846	Feb. 5, 1926
Orth	Jan. 14, 1847	Jan. 13, 1923
Flechsig	June 29, 1847	July 22, 1929
Ladd-Franklin	Dec. 1, 1847	Mar. 5, 1930
De Vries	Feb. 16, 1848	Mar. 21, 1935
Stumpf	Apr. 21, 1848	Dec. 25, 1936
Romanes	May 20, 1848	May 23, 1894
Forel	Sept. 1, 1848	July 27, 1931
Pavlov	Sept. 26, 1849	Feb. 27, 1936
Blix	Dec. 25, 1849	Feb. 14, 1904
Ebbinghaus	Jan. 24, 1850	Feb. 26, 1909
Müller, G. E.	July 20, 1850	Dec. 23, 1934
Richet	Aug. 26, 1850	Dec. 4, 1935
Erdmann	May 30, 1851	June 7, 1921
Lipps	July 28, 1851	Oct. 17, 1914
Mercier	Nov. 21, 1851	Jan. 23, 1926
Morgan, C. L.	Feb. 6, 1852	Mar. 6, 1936
Ramón y Cajal	May 1, 1852	Oct. 17, 1934
Féré	June 13, 1852	Apr. 22, 1907
Vaihinger	Sept. 25, 1852	Dec. 12, 1933
Frey	Nov. 16, 1852	Jan. 25, 1932
Meinong	July 17, 1853	Nov. 27, 1920
Kries	Oct. 6, 1853	Dec. 30, 1928
Flournoy	Aug. 15, 1854	Nov. 5, 1920
Prince	Dec. 21, 1854	Aug. 31, 1929
Ewald	Feb. 14, 1855	July 22, 1921
Royce	Nov. 20, 1855	Sept. 14, 1916
Burnham	Dec. 3, 1855	June 25, 1941
Kraepelin	Feb. 15, 1856	Oct. 7, 1926
Freud, S.	May 6, 1856	Sept. 23, 1939
König	Sept. 13, 1856	Oct. 26, 1901
Bekhterev	Jan. 20, 1857	Dec. 24, 1927
Müller-Lyer	Feb. 5, 1857	Oct. 29, 1916
Coué	Feb. 26, 1857	July 2, 1926
Pearson	Mar. 27, 1857	Apr. 27, 1936
Lévy-Bruhl	Apr. 10, 1857	Mar. 13, 1939
Heymans	Apr. 17, 1857	Feb. 18, 1930
Bleuler	Apr. 30, 1857	July 15, 1939
Zwaardemaker	May 10, 1857	Sept. 19, 1930
Donaldson	May 12, 1857	Jan. 23, 1938

	BORN A.D.	DIED A.D.
Angell, F.	July 8, 1857	Nov. 2, 1939
Binet	July 8, 1857	Oct. 18, 1911
Babinski	Nov. 17, 1857	Oct. 29, 1932
Sherrington	Nov. 27, 1857	Mar. 4, 1952
Shand	1858	Jan. 6, 1936
Kiesow	Mar. 28, 1858	Dec. 9, 1940
Durkheim	Apr. 15, 1858	Nov. 15, 1917
Romanes	May 20, 1858	May 23, 1894
Boas	July 9, 1858	Dec. 21, 1942
Goldscheider	Aug. 4, 1858	Apr. 10, 1925
Lehmann	Dec. 29, 1858	Sept. 26, 1921
Ellis	Feb. 2, 1859	July 8, 1939
Loeb	Apr. 7, 1859	Feb. 11, 1924
Husserl	Apr. 8, 1859	Apr. 26, 1938
Janet	May 30, 1859	Feb. 24, 1947
Ehrenfels	June 20, 1859	Sept. 8, 1932
Fullerton	Aug. 18, 1859	Mar. 23, 1925
Bergson	Oct. 18, 1859	Jan. 4, 1941
Dewey	Oct. 20, 1859	June 1, 1952
Sanford, E. C.	Nov. 10, 1859	Nov. 22, 1924
Stout	Jan. 6, 1860	Aug. 18, 1944
Cattell	May 25, 1860	Jan. 20, 1944
Bourdon	Aug. 5, 1860	July 11, 1943
Störring	Aug. 24, 1860	Dec. 1, 1946
Bryan	Nov. 1, 1860	Nov. 21, 1955
Baldwin	Jan. 12, 1861	Nov. 8, 1934
Whitehead	Feb. 15, 1861	Dec. 30, 1947
Head	Aug. 4, 1861	Oct. 8, 1940
Groos	Dec. 10, 1861	Mar. 27, 1946
Külpe	Aug. 3, 1862	Dec. 30, 1915
Meumann	Aug. 29, 1862	Apr. 15, 1915
Ziehen	Nov. 12, 1862	Dec. 29, 1950
Jastrow	Jan. 30, 1863	Jan. 8, 1944
Mead	Feb. 27, 1863	Apr. 26, 1931
Calkins	Mar. 30, 1863	Feb. 27, 1930
Münsterberg	June 1, 1863	Dec. 16, 1916
Schumann	June 16, 1863	Jan. 10, 1940
Lange, L.	June 21, 1863	July 12, 1936
Spearman	Sept. 10, 1863	Sept. 17, 1945
Delabarre	Sept. 25, 1863	Mar. 16, 1945
Verworn	Nov. 4, 1863	Nov. 23, 1921
Rivers	Mar. 12, 1864	June 4, 1922

	BORN A.D.	DIED A.D.
Weber, M.	Apr. 21, 1864	June 14, 1920
Scripture	May 21, 1864	July 31, 1945
Cooley	Aug. 17, 1864	May 8, 1929
Hobhouse	Sept. 8, 1864	June 21, 1929
Uexküll	Sept. 8, 1864	July 25, 1944
Pilzecker	Jan. 24, 1865	ca. 1920
Matsumoto	Sept. 15, 1865	Dec. 24, 1943
Stratton	Sept. 26, 1865	Oct. 8, 1957
Seashore	Jan. 28, 1866	Oct. 16, 1949
Starbuck	Feb. 20, 1866	Nov. 18, 1947
Croce	Feb. 25, 1866	Nov. 20, 1952
Dumas	Mar. 6, 1866	Feb. 13, 1946
Lapicque	Aug. 1, 1866	Dec. 6, 1952
Goddard	Aug. 14, 1866	June 18, 1957
Fröbes	Aug. 26, 1866	Mar. 24, 1947
Meyer, A.	Sept. 13, 1866	Mar. 17, 1950
Ross	Dec. 12, 1866	July 22, 1951
Titchener	Jan. 11, 1867	Aug. 3, 1927
Dessoir	Feb. 8, 1867	July 19, 1947
Messer	Feb. 11, 1867	1937
Warren	June 12, 1867	Jan. 4, 1934
Farrand	June 14, 1867	Nov. 8, 1939
Witmer	June 28, 1867	July 19, 1956
Sidis	Oct. 12, 1867	Oct. 24, 1923
Driesch	Oct. 28, 1867	Apr. 17, 1941
Stekel	Mar. 18, 1868	June 21, 1940
Jennings	Apr. 8, 1868	Apr. 14, 1947
Leuba	Apr. 9, 1868	Dec. 8, 1946
Parsons	Sept. 3, 1868	Oct. 7, 1957
Herrick	Oct. 6, 1868	Jan. 29, 1960
Healy	Jan. 20, 1869	Mar. 15, 1963
Scott	May 1, 1869	Sept. 23, 1955
Angell, J. R.	May 8, 1869	Mar. 4, 1949
Baird	May 21, 1869	Feb. 2, 1919
Marbe	Aug. 31, 1869	Jan. 2, 1953
Woodworth	Oct. 17, 1869	July 4, 1962
Witasek	1870	1915
White	Jan. 24, 1870	Mar. 7, 1937
Adler	Feb. 7, 1870	May 28, 1937
Lenin	Apr. 22, 1870	Jan. 21, 1924
Rignano	May 30, 1870	Feb. 9, 1930
Bentley	June 18, 1870	May 29, 1955

| | BORN | DIED |
	A.D.	A.D.
Nagel	June 19, 1870	Jan. 14, 1911
Small	Aug. 24, 1870	Jan. 31, 1943
Montessori	Aug. 31, 1870	May 6, 1952
Wissler	Sept. 18, 1870	Aug. 25, 1947
Yule	Feb. 18, 1871	June 26, 1951
Dodge	Feb. 20, 1871	Apr. 8, 1942
Stern	Apr. 29, 1871	Mar. 27, 1938
McDougall	June 22, 1871	Nov. 28, 1938
Decroly	July 23, 1871	Sept. 12, 1932
Washburn	July 25, 1871	Oct. 29, 1939
Cannon	Oct. 19, 1871	Oct. 1, 1945
Ach	Oct. 29, 1871	July 25, 1946
Coghill	Mar. 17, 1872	July 23, 1941
Bethe	Apr. 25, 1872	Oct. 19, 1954
Henri	June 6, 1872	1940
Pillsbury	July 21, 1872	June 3, 1960
Klages	Dec. 10, 1872	July 29, 1956
Judd	Feb. 23, 1873	July 18, 1946
Myers	Mar. 13, 1873	Oct. 12, 1946
Claparède	Mar. 24, 1873	Sept. 29, 1940
Drever	Apr. 8, 1873	Aug. 11, 1950
Carr	Apr. 30, 1873	June 21, 1954
Berger	May 21, 1873	June 1, 1941
Meyer, M. F.	June 15, 1873	Mar. 14, 1967
Simon	July 10, 1873	Sept. 4, 1961
Ferenczi	July 16, 1873	May 22, 1933
Holt	Aug. 21, 1873	Jan. 25, 1946
Twitmyer	Sept. 14, 1873	Mar. 3, 1943
Delacroix	Dec. 2, 1873	Dec. 3, 1937
Pfungst	Apr. 21, 1874	Aug. 14, 1932
Franz	May 27, 1874	Oct. 14, 1933
Krüger	Aug. 19, 1874	Feb. 25, 1948
Jost	Aug. 22, 1874	ca. 1920
Thorndike	Aug. 31, 1874	Aug. 9, 1949
Brill	Oct. 12, 1874	Mar. 2, 1948
Lindworsky	Jan. 21, 1875	Sept. 9, 1939
Kent	June 6, 1875	Sept. 18, 1973
Downey	July 13, 1875	Oct. 11, 1932
Jung	July 26, 1875	June 6, 1961
Dunlap	Nov. 21, 1875	Aug. 14, 1949
Beers	Mar. 30, 1876	July 9, 1943
Yerkes	May 26, 1876	Feb. 3, 1956

	BORN	DIED
	A.D.	A.D.
Whipple	June 12, 1876	Aug. 1, 1941
Gosset	June 13, 1876	Oct. 16, 1937
Wirth	July 26, 1876	1952
Southard	July 28, 1876	Feb. 8, 1920
Terman	Jan. 15, 1877	Dec. 21, 1956
Hornbostel	Feb. 25, 1877	June 13, 1935
Hellpach	Feb. 26, 1877	July 6, 1955
Abraham	May 3, 1877	Dec. 25, 1925
Ogden	July 6, 1877	Mar. 2, 1959
Henmon	Nov. 27, 1877	Jan. 10, 1950
Watson	Jan. 9, 1878	Sept. 25, 1958
Benussi	Jan. 17, 1878	1927
Gemelli	Jan. 18, 1878	July 15, 1959
Guillaume	June 26, 1878	Jan. 4, 1962
Rosanoff	June 26, 1878	Jan. 7, 1943
Dearborn	July 19, 1878	June 21, 1955
Goldstein	Nov. 6, 1878	Sept. 19, 1965
Révész	Dec. 9, 1878	Aug. 19, 1955
Urban	Dec. 28, 1878	May 4, 1964
Jones	Jan. 1, 1879	Feb. 11, 1958
Kornilov	Mar. 9, 1879	July 10, 1957
Wallon	Mar. 15, 1879	Dec. 1, 1962
Bühler, K.	May 27, 1879	Oct. 24, 1963
Watt	July 18, 1879	Oct. 25, 1925
Langfeld	July 24, 1879	Feb. 25, 1958
Brett	Aug. 5, 1879	Oct. 27, 1944
Valentine	Aug. 16, 1879	May 26, 1964
Weiss	Sept. 15, 1879	Apr. 3, 1931
Hunter	Mar. 22, 1880	Aug. 3, 1954
Wertheimer	Apr. 15, 1880	Oct. 12, 1943
Hollingworth, H. L.	May 26, 1880	Sept. 17, 1956
Gesell	June 21, 1880	May 29, 1961
Ames	Aug. 19, 1880	July 3, 1955
Bingham	Oct. 20, 1880	July 8, 1952
Gruhle	Nov. 7, 1880	Oct. 3, 1958
Sachs	Jan. 10, 1881	Jan. 10, 1947
Selz	Feb. 14, 1881	Aug. 27, 1943
Hess	Mar. 17, 1881	Aug. 12, 1973
Thomson	Mar. 27, 1881	Feb. 9, 1955
Binswanger	Apr. 13, 1881	Feb. 5, 1966
Piéron	July 18, 1881	Nov. 6, 1964
Michotte	Oct. 13, 1881	June 2, 1965

| | BORN | DIED |
	A.D.	A.D.
Brown, W.	Dec. 5, 1881	May 17, 1952
Assagioli	Feb. 27, 1882	Aug. 23, 1974
Klein	Mar. 30, 1882	Sept. 22, 1960
Bridgman	Apr. 22, 1882	Aug. 20, 1961
Ponzo	June 23, 1882	Jan. 9, 1960
Spranger	June 27, 1882	Sept. 17, 1963
Müller-Freienfels	Aug. 7, 1882	Dec. 12, 1949
Jaensch, E. R.	Feb. 26, 1883	Jan. 12, 1940
Burt	Mar. 3, 1883	Oct. 10, 1971
Porteus	Apr. 24, 1883	Oct. 21, 1972
Kafka	July 23, 1883	Feb. 12, 1953
Reymert	Nov. 10, 1883	June 2, 1953
Sapir	Jan. 26, 1884	Feb. 4, 1939
Klemm	Mar. 8, 1884	Jan. 5, 1939
Malinowski	Apr. 7, 1884	May 16, 1942
Rank	Apr. 22, 1884	Oct. 31, 1939
Wells	Apr. 22, 1884	June 2, 1964
Hull	May 24, 1884	May 10, 1952
Kelley	May 25, 1884	May 2, 1961
Blonskiĭ	May 26, 1884	Feb. 15, 1941
Flugel	June 13, 1884	Aug. 17, 1955
Strong	Aug. 18, 1884	Dec. 4, 1963
Katz	Oct. 1, 1884	Feb. 2, 1953
Rorschach	Nov. 8, 1884	Apr. 2, 1922
Pintner	Nov. 16, 1884	Nov. 7, 1942
Beritashvili	Dec. 29, 1884	Dec. 29, 1974
Henning	Feb. 15, 1885	1946
Miles	Mar. 29, 1885	May 15, 1978
Muenzinger	Apr. 28, 1885	Nov. 23, 1958
Horney	Sept. 16, 1885	Dec. 4, 1952
Guthrie	Jan. 9, 1886	Apr. 23, 1959
Bykov	Jan. 21, 1886	May 13, 1959
Koffka	Mar. 18, 1886	Nov. 22, 1941
Tolman	Apr. 14, 1886	Nov. 19, 1959
Hollingworth, L. S.	May 25, 1886	Nov. 27, 1939
Goodenough	Aug. 6, 1886	Apr. 4, 1959
Ruckmick	Sept. 4, 1886	1961
Rubin	Sept. 6, 1886	May 3, 1951
Poppelreuter	Oct. 6, 1886	1939
Bartlett	Oct. 20, 1886	Sept. 30, 1969
Boring	Oct. 23, 1886	July 1, 1968
Uznadze	Jan. 1, 1887	Oct. 12, 1950

	BORN A.D.	DIED A.D.
Köhler	Jan. 21, 1887	June 11, 1967
Spitz	Jan. 29, 1887	Sept. 14, 1974
Thurstone	May 29, 1887	Sept. 29, 1955
Fernberger	June 4, 1887	May 2, 1956
Benedict	June 5, 1887	Sept. 17, 1948
Dallenbach	Oct. 20, 1887	Dec. 24, 1971
Gelb	Nov. 18, 1887	Aug. 7, 1936
Murchison	Dec. 3, 1887	May 20, 1961
Elliott	End of 1887	May 1969
Dashiell	Apr. 30, 1888	May 3, 1975
Moede	Sept. 3, 1888	May 30, 1958
Kretschmer	Oct. 8, 1888	Feb. 8, 1964
Pressey	Dec. 28, 1888	July 21, 1979
Lehman	Mar. 13, 1889	Aug. 8, 1965
Hunter	Mar. 22, 1889	Aug. 3, 1954
Troland	Apr. 26, 1889	May 27, 1932
Doll	May 2, 1889	Oct. 22, 1968
Jaensch, W.	May 5, 1889	?
Moreno	May 6, 1889	May 15,1974
Ladygina-Kots	May 19, 1889	Sept. 3, 1963
Rubinshteïn	June 6, 1889	Jan. 11, 1960
Humphrey	July 17, 1889	Apr. 24, 1966
Polyak	Dec. 13, 1889	Mar. 9, 1955
Werner	Feb. 11, 1890	May 14, 1964
Fisher	Feb. 17, 1890	July 29, 1962
Warden	Mar. 18, 1890	Feb. 28, 1961
Lashley	June 7, 1890	Aug. 7, 1958
Roback	June 19, 1890	June 5, 1965
Allport, F.	Aug. 22, 1890	Oct. 15, 1978
Lewin	Sept. 9, 1890	Feb. 12, 1947
Zilboorg	Dec. 25, 1890	Sept. 17, 1959
Alexander	Jan. 22, 1891	Mar. 8, 1964
Penfield	Jan. 26, 1891	Apr. 5, 1976
Kardiner	Aug. 17, 1891	July 20, 1981
Paterson	Jan. 18, 1892	Oct. 4, 1961
Hecht	Feb. 8, 1892	Sept. 18, 1947
Sullivan	Feb. 21, 1892	Jan. 14, 1949
Stone	Feb. 28, 1892	Dec. 28, 1954
Wheeler	Mar. 9, 1892	Aug. 24, 1961
Crozier	May 24, 1892	Nov. 2, 1955
Young, P. T.	May 26, 1892	June 15, 1978
English	Oct. 1, 1892	July 20, 1961

	BORN A.D.	DIED A.D.
Gantt	Oct. 26, 1892	Feb. 26, 1980
Fearing	Nov. 24, 1892	Mar. 26, 1962
Linton	Feb. 27, 1893	Dec. 24, 1953
Robinson	Apr. 18, 1893	Feb. 27, 1937
Bühler, C.	Dec. 20, 1893	Feb. 3, 1974
Kinsey	June 23, 1894	Aug. 25, 1956
Wiener	Nov. 26, 1894	Mar. 18, 1964
Murphy	July 8, 1895	Mar. 19, 1979
Rhine	Sept. 29, 1895	Feb. 20, 1980
Freud, A.	Dec. 3, 1895	Oct. 8, 1982
Vygotskiĭ	1896	June 11, 1934
Wechsler	Jan. 12, 1896	May 2, 1981
Piaget	Aug. 9, 1896	Sept. 16, 1980
Teplov	Oct. 21, 1896	Sept. 28, 1965
Mira y López	Oct. 24, 1896	Feb. 16, 1964
Landis	Jan. 11, 1897	Mar. 5, 1962
Beebe-Center	Mar. 19, 1897	Dec. 6, 1958
Reich	Mar. 24, 1897	Nov. 3, 1957
Klüver	May 25, 1897	Feb. 8, 1979
McGeoch	Oct. 9, 1897	Mar. 3, 1942
Allport, G. W.	Nov. 11, 1897	Oct. 9, 1967
Fenichel	Dec. 2, 1897	Jan. 22, 1946
Anokhin	Jan. 26, 1898	Mar. 6, 1974
Carmichael	Nov. 9, 1898	Sept. 16, 1973
Helson	Nov. 9, 1898	Oct. 13, 1977
Sheldon	Nov. 19, 1898	Sept. 16, 1977
Békésy	Jun. 3, 1899	June 13, 1972
Fulton	Nov. 1, 1899	May 29, 1960
Fromm	Mar. 23, 1900	Mar. 18, 1980
Kris	Apr. 26, 1900	Feb. 27, 1957
Stouffer	June 6, 1900	Aug. 24, 1960
Scheerer	June 10, 1900	Oct. 19, 1961
Warner	Sept. 9, 1900	1963
Nissen	Feb. 5, 1901	Apr. 27, 1958
Razran	June 4, 1901	Aug. 31, 1973
Luria	July 16, 1902	Aug. 15, 1977
Schneierla	July 23, 1902	Aug. 20, 1968
Duncker	Feb. 2, 1903	Feb. 23, 1940
Leont'ev	Feb. 5, 1903	Jan. 22, 1979
Brunswik	Mar. 18, 1903	July 7, 1955
Zener	Apr. 22, 1903	Sept. 27, 1964
Likert	Aug. 5, 1903	Sept. 3, 1981

	BORN	DIED
	A.D.	A.D.
Konorski	Dec. 1, 1903	Sept. 14, 1973
Von Neumann	Dec. 28, 1903	Feb. 8, 1957
Schlosberg	Jan. 3, 1904	Aug. 5, 1964
Gibson	Jan. 27, 1904	Dec. 11, 1979
Kluckhohn	Jan. 11, 1905	July 29, 1960
Lorge	Apr. 19, 1905	Jan. 23, 1961
Kelly	Apr. 28, 1905	Mar. 6, 1967
Buros	June 14, 1905	Mar. 19, 1978
Sartre	June 21, 1905	Apr. 15, 1980
Dennis	Sept. 1, 1905	July 21, 1976
Harlow	Oct. 31, 1905	Dec. 6, 1981
Graham	Jan. 6, 1906	July 25, 1971
Cantril	June 16, 1906	May 29, 1969
Stevens	Nov. 4, 1906	Jan. 18, 1973
Mowrer	Jan. 23, 1907	June 22, 1982
Selye	Jan. 26, 1907	Oct. 16, 1982
Spence	May 6, 1907	Jan. 12, 1967
Anan'ev	Aug. 14, 1907	May 18, 1972
Merleau-Ponty	Mar. 14, 1908	May 3, 1961
Maslow	Apr. 1, 1908	June 8, 1970
Marquis	June 22, 1908	Feb. 17, 1973
Frenkel-Brunswik	Aug. 18, 1908	Mar. 31, 1958
Halstead	Dec. 31, 1908	Mar. 25, 1969
Krech	Mar. 27, 1909	July 14, 1977
Rapaport	Sept. 30, 1911	Dec. 14, 1960
Fitts	May 5, 1912	May 2, 1965
Hovland	June 12, 1912	Apr. 16, 1961
Sanford, F. H.	Jan. 26, 1914	Aug. 5, 1967
Morgan, C. T.	July 21, 1915	Feb. 11, 1976
Witkin	Aug. 2, 1916	July 8, 1979
Teuber	Aug. 7, 1916	Jan. 4, 1977
Lennenberg	Sept. 19, 1921	June 2, 1975
Olds	May 30, 1922	Aug. 21, 1976
Berlyne	Apr. 25, 1924	Nov. 2, 1976

Relative Eminence of Names in the History of Psychology

The ranking of objects, events, and people according to merit is an activity that goes back to antiquity. In modern times, scientific ranking was introduced by the psychologist James McKeen Cattell in the form of the "order of merit." The first ranking of living psychologists was done by him in 1903, although the names involved were not published until 1929.

Ranking is usually done by a panel of judges who arrange the objects to be judged in a series according to the degree of presence of the quality that is being judged. The ranks assigned to an object by the judges are then averaged.

Another way of measuring eminence, achievement, and so on is to use a rating scale. If the relative eminence of people is being measured, a score of three on a five-point scale would indicate an average level of eminence for a given person. This is how most of the names that appear in this dictionary were once evaluated by a panel of nine judges, headed by E. G. Boring and R. I. Watson.[1]

A major drawback of the rating method is that the range of scores that can be assigned an individual is limited and that these scores have a ceiling. For instance, the maximum score that could be assigned an individual under the rating system used by the panel headed by E. G. Boring and R. I. Watson was twenty-seven. Thus although Sigmund Freud, the all-time most eminent name in psychology, was rated twenty-seven, so were a number of individuals of much lesser stature whose names are familiar for the most part only to historians of psychology.

1. E. L. Annin, E. G. Boring, & R. I. Watson. Important psychologists, 1600-1967. *J. Hist. Behav. Sci.*, 1968, *4*, 303-315.

   With the ranking method the problem of ceiling does not arise. The individuals
listed in this dictionary were ranked as follows.[2] It was assumed that the amount
of space that an author of a history of psychology devotes to the discussion of
the contributions of an individual is directly proportional to the eminence that
the author attributes to that individual in comparison with all others discussed
in the text. Hence to measure an individual's eminence, as judged by the author,
all that needs to be done is to count the number of pages devoted to that individual
in that author's text. Sixteen representative histories of psychology published in
1950 or later were used. In a given text, the pages devoted to an individual were
counted and expressed as a percentage of the total number of text pages in the
book. For each name, the percentages were averaged across the sixteen texts
and used to assign ranks to all individuals so measured. Appendix B gives the
percentages and rankings and, for comparison, the ratings of the Boring-Watson
panel.
   Appendix B lists all names in the dictionary except eleven. These eleven are
recently deceased individuals who were not included in the ranking. Some of
the entries do not show ratings. No ratings are given for individuals who lived
before 1600 or died after 1967, because they were not included by the Boring-
Watson panel in the original pool of 1040 names to be rated.

	MEAN PERCENTAGE	RANK	RATING
Freud, S.	3.2343	1	27
Aristotle	3.1861	2	—
Wundt	2.4565	3	27
James	1.7644	4	27
Watson	1.4630	5	27
Plato	1.3745	6	—
Descartes	1.3476	7	27
Fechner	1.1247	8	27
Hume	1.0425	9	27
Locke	1.0322	10	27
Titchener	.9143	11	27
Kant	.8923	12	25
Helmholtz	.8692	13	27
Lewin	.8497	14	26
McDougall	.8418	15	27
Pavlov	.7934	16	27
Berkeley	.7889	17	25
Galton	.7736	18	27

2. L. Zusne & D. P. Dailey. History of psychology texts as measuring instruments of eminence in
   psychology. *Revista de Historia de la Psicología*, 1982, *3*(1), 7-42.

	MEAN PERCENTAGE	RANK	RATING
Jung	.7638	19	27
Augustine, St.	.7428	20	—
Darwin, C.	.6912	21	27
Herbart	.6649	22	27
Leibniz	.6138	23	26
Hull	.5946	24	27
Tolman	.5922	25	27
Reid	.5695	26	25
Adler	.5689	27	27
Aquinas, St. Thomas	.5653	28	—
Mill, J. S.	.5645	29	27
Hartley	.5617	30	24
Hall, G. S.	.5542	31	27
Ebbinghaus	.5501	32	27
Spinoza	.5459	33	24
Thorndike	.5345	34	27
Bain	.5000	35	26
Hobbes	.4846	36	24
Cattell	.4624	37	26
Wertheimer	.4358	38	27
Mill, J.	4246	39	27
Piaget	.4168	40	—
Brentano	.4030	41	27
Külpe	.4002	42	27
Plotinus	.3894	43	—
Lotze	.3890	44	25
Sechenov	.3755	45	26
Müller, J.	.3656	46	25
Spencer	.3645	47	27
Brown, T.	.3456	48	22
Weiss	.3392	49	22
Weber, E. H.	.3243	50	27
Köhler	.3074	51	27
Woodworth	.2838	52	27
Vygotskiĭ	.2812	53	20
Bacon, F.	.2659	54	23
Guthrie	.2468	55	26
Binet	.2453	56	27
Horney	.2374	57	23
Stumpf	.2362	58	27
Husserl	.2345	59	26
Protagoras	.2309	60	—

	MEAN PERCENTAGE	RANK	RATING
Empedocles	.2257	61	—
Wolff	.2241	62	25
Lashley	.2182	63	27
Lenin	.2106	64	—
Allport, G. W.	.2097	65	27
Angell, J. R.	.2048	66	27
Fromm	.1974	67	—
Socrates	.1917	68	—
Gall	.1910	69	24
Müller, G. E.	.1894	70	26
Dewey	.1881	71	27
Galen	.1748	72	—
Democritus	.1718	73	—
Beneke	.1716	74	17
Janet	.1715	75	27
Ward	.1699	76	24
Carr	.1598	77	23
Mach	.1570	78	25
Marx	.1487	79	16
Dilthey	.1486	80	22
Sullivan	.1417	81	23
Hippocrates	.1385	82	—
Condillac	.1345	83	25
Morgan, C. L.	.1336	84	25
Hering	.1335	85	27
La Mettrie	.1334	86	26
Bekhterev	.1304	87	27
Spearman	.1302	88	27
Bell	.1221	89	24
Cabanis	.1190	90	22
Newton	.1189	91	26
Flourens	.1183	92	24
Hamilton	.1175	93	21
Hegel	.1155	94	18
Koffka	.1131	95	27
Münsterberg	.1123	96	24
Tetens	.1121	97	11
Epicurus	.1115	98	—
Anaxagoras	.1104	99	—
Vives	.1076	100	—
Breuer	.1067	101	23
Kornilov	.1050	102	13

	MEAN PERCENTAGE	RANK	RATING
Avicenna	.1034	103	—
Romanes	.1007	104	25
Comte	.0995	105	25
Pythagoras	.0968	106	—
Heraclitus	.0967	107	—
Galilei	.0919	108	22
Mesmer	.0904	109	25
Maimonides	.0902	110	—
Ehrenfels	.0901	111	26
Ockham	.0890	112	—
Mead	.0881	113	19
Bühler, K.	.0874	114	26
Maine de Biran	.0868	115	24
Malebranche	.0851	116	21
Michotte	.0832	117	27
Katz	.0824	118	25
Rousseau	.0823	119	24
Pinel	.0818	120	25
Charcot	.0808	121	27
Sheldon	.0796	122	—
Bartlett	.0778	123	—
Bridgman	.0776	124	24
Sherrington	.0766	125	27
Lipps	.0759	126	23
Herophilus	.0756	127	—
Copernicus	.0744	128	—
Rubinshteĭn	.0739	129	12
Maslow	.0719	130	—
Stern	.0692	131	26
Lavater	.0687	132	10
Braid } Ladd }	.0679	133.5	21 21
Stout	.0672	135	26
Albertus Magnus, St.	.0656	136	—
Kraepelin	.0654	137	27
Thales	.0644	138	—
Schopenhauer	.0641	139	22
Nietzsche	.0640	140	20
Loeb	.0634	141	26
Theophrastus	.0633	142	—
Baldwin	.0627	143	25
Ribot	.0596	144	26

	MEAN PERCENTAGE	RANK	RATING
Bacon, R.	.0590	145	—
Burt	.0582	146	—
Krüger	.0577	147	20
Bessel	.0572	148	23
Holt	.0568	149.5	22
Myers			21
Alcmaeon	.0565	151	—
Stevens	.0559	152	—
Moritz	.0550	153	—
Yerkes	.0534	154	27
Kardiner	.0531	155	—
Bentham	.0525	156.5	22
Rubin			27
Moreno	.0523	158	—
Hovland	.0522	159	23
Stewart	.0520	160	23
Donders	.0518	161.5	19
Kepler			19
Montaigne	.0506	163.5	—
Erasistratus			—
Uznadze	.0500	165	—
Voltaire	.0496	166	19
Kretschmer	.0491	167.5	26
Scripture			23
Murphy	.0482	169	—
Magendie	.0479	170.5	25
Allport, F.			—
Klages	.0472	172	15
Broca	.0471	173	24
Watt	.0459	174	19
Bonnet	.0455	175	20
Lamarck	.0445	176	23
Bergson	.0444	177	22
Spurzheim	.0440	178	21
Haeckel	.0424	179	15
Meinong	.0421	180	24
Hobhouse	.0419	181	19
Rivers	.0414	182	19
Cannon	.0402	183	27
Ach	.0401	184	26
Gassendi	.0398	185	11
Rorschach	.0396	186	26

	MEAN PERCENTAGE	RANK	RATING
Haller	.0393	187	17
Franz	.0390	188	20
Krech	.0375	189	—
Bernheim	.0373	190	23
Helvétius	.0369	191	15
Thurstone	.0363	192	27
Bühler, C.	.0362	193	—
Sully	.0355	194	22
Pearson ⎫	.0353	195.5	27
Spranger ⎭			25
Marbe	.0352	197	24
Hall, M.	.0345	198	21
Hunter	.0344	199	25
Terman	.0342	200	27
Herder	.0341	201	11
Whytte	.0332	202	15
Ziehen	.0331	203	18
Tertullian	.0330	204	—
Harvey	.0329	205	20
Averroës ⎫	.0325	206.5	—
Beritashvili ⎭			—
Uexküll	.0323	208	19
Malthus	.0320	209	17
Paracelsus	.0311	210	—
Witmer	.0307	211	19
Fisher	.0298	212	20
Messer	.0294	213	18
Claparède	.0290	214	26
Rush, J.	.0281	215	—
Quételet	.0276	216	24
Merleau-Ponty	.0274	217	16
Ellis	.0270	218	23
Elliotson ⎫	.0260	219.5	22
Sartre ⎭			—
Hartmann	.0258	221	15
Liébeault	.0257	222	21
Goldstein	.0254	223	26
Avenarius ⎫	.0250	224.5	23
Jaensch, E. ⎭			25
Purkinje	.0248	226	24
Jastrow	.0244	227	22
Jackson	.0241	228	21

	MEAN PERCENTAGE	RANK	RATING
Boring	.0237	229.5	—
Bykov			—
Alexander	.0228	231.5	18
Duncker			18
Lewes	.0226	233	11
Galvani	.0223	234	20
Head	.0219	235	25
Smith	.0218	236	17
Ladd-Franklin	.0211	237	22
Cuvier	.0210	238	12
Bethe	.0203	239.5	16
Young, T.			23
Esdaile			20
Hess	.0202	242	—
Vesalius			—
Ladygina-Kots	.0200	244	—
Bleuler	.0197	245	25
Wiener	.0195	246	18
Gesell	.0193	247	25
Bernard	.0191	248.5	25
Werner			24
Cooley	.0189	250	13
Grosseteste	.0187	251	—
Esquirol	.0186	252	18
Goethe	.0182	253.5	25
Spence			25
Geulincx	.0180	255	11
Gemelli	.0175	256	22
Pascal	.0174	257	14
Destutt de Tracy	.0172	258	11
Frey	.0172	259	23
Le Bon	.0171	260	24
Luria	.0170	261	—
Matsumoto	.0169	262	11
Diderot			19
Piéron	.0167	264	27
Wallace			15
Hitzig	.0165	266	18
Fichte	.0162	267	16
Small	.0160	268	18
Meyer, A.	.0159	269	21
Kries	.0158	270	25

	MEAN PERCENTAGE	RANK	RATING
Steinthal	.0156	271.5	12
Helson			—
Fritsch	.0152	273	16
Taine	.0151	274	21
Lazarus	.0148	275	13
Goltz	.0147	276	12
Du Bois-Reymond	.0146	277	23
Malinowski	.0144	278	22
Peirce	.0139	279	19
Blonskiĭ	.0138	280	—
Thomson	.0135	281	23
Anokhin	.0134	282	—
Goddard	.0133	283	19
Bichat			17
Huxley	.0132	285	18
Peter of Spain			—
Brunswik	.0129	287.5	26
Schelling			15
Lange, C. G.	.0128	289	14
Bernstein	.0126	290	12
Binswanger	.0123	291	19
Leont'ev	.0122	292	—
Witasek	.0120	293	19
Huarte	.0118	294	—
Linnaeus	.0117	295	19
Rolando	.0116	296	15
Spalding	.0114	297	12
Maxwell	.0112	298	19
Washburn	.0111	299	23
Orth	.0108	300	13
Coghill	.0107	301	20
Hellpach	.0105	302.5	12
Itard			23
Ross	.0103	304	11
Healy	.0100	305.5	17
Mendel			21
Lindworsky	.0099	307.5	15
Rank			23
Jennings	.0097	309	25
Sanford, E. C.	.0095	310	20
Gibson	.0094	311	—
Flournoy	.0092	312	11

	MEAN PERCENTAGE	RANK	RATING
Séguin	.0091	313	18
Delboeuf	.0090	314	11
Hollingworth, H. L.	.0088	315	20
Scott	.0087	316	11
Meumann ⎫			23
Schumann ⎬	.0086	318	19
Strong ⎭			20
Darwin, E.	.0083	320	16
Prochaska	.0082	321	11
Swedenborg	.0080	322	11
Maudsley	.0079	323	16
Montessori	.0078	324	21
Dix	.0077	325	11
Beers ⎫	.0076	326.5	17
Meynert ⎭			12
Ponzo ⎫			15
Preyer ⎬	.0075	329	22
Tarde ⎭			24
Coué ⎫	.0074	331.5	18
Flechsig ⎭			13
Priestley	.0072	333	13
Teplov	.0070	334	—
d'Alembert	.0069	335	15
Durkheim	.0067	336	23
Drever ⎫			23
Edwards ⎬	.0066	338	11
Tylor ⎭			13
Laplace ⎫	.0065	340.5	17
Békésy ⎭			—
Benussi ⎫	.0064	342.5	20
Golgi ⎭			14
Calkins	.0063	344	20
Judd	.0062	345	22
Ramón y Cajal	.0060	346	25
Valentine	.0058	347	13
Dumas	.0057	348	21
Johnson ⎫	.0056	349.5	12
König ⎭			16
Leeuwenhoek	.0055	351	16
Moede ⎫	.0054	352.5	12
Prince ⎭			23

	MEAN PERCENTAGE	RANK	RATING
Kelly ⎱	.0053	354.5	17
Ruckmick ⎰			17
Dalton	.0052	356	23
McGeoch ⎱	.0051	357.5	20
Volkmann ⎰			12
Shand	.0050	359	15
Bryan	.0049	360	16
Seashore	.0048	361	24
Gauss ⎫			24
Kiesow ⎬	.0047	363	19
Rhine ⎭			—
Brücke ⎱	.0045	365.5	20
Penfield ⎰			—
Franklin ⎫			13
Jones ⎬	.0044	368	22
Berger ⎭			—
Ogden ⎱	.0043	370.5	20
Puységur ⎰			—
Stratton ⎱	.0042	372.5	22
Olds ⎰			—
Benedict ⎱	.0041	374.5	16
Bowditch ⎰			12
Brown, W. ⎱	.0040	376.5	11
Klüver ⎰			—
Dallenbach	.0039	378	—
Fröbes	.0038	379	16
Aubert ⎱	.0037	380.5	20
Brill ⎰			18
Dunlap	.0035	382	22
Klein ⎱	.0034	383.5	17
Wallon ⎰			12
Humboldt ⎫			17
Mercier ⎪			13
Meyer, M. F. ⎪			20
Molyneux ⎬	.0033	388	13
Pflüger ⎪			18
Selz ⎪			17
Zwaardemaker ⎭			23
Razran	.0032	392	—

	MEAN PERCENTAGE	RANK	RATING
Abraham			20
Bernoulli			11
Flugel			16
Gelb	.0031	396	15
Jost			16
Pilzecker			15
Tiedemann			11
Ames	.0030	400.5	16
Exner			18
Lavoisier			16
McCosh	.0029	403	13
Stekel			16
Buffon			13
Féré	.0028	406.5	18
Höffding			24
Vaihinger			11
Ludwig	.0027	409.5	14
Nagel			12
Pintner	.0027	411	18
Lange, L.			12
Mariotte	.0026	413	22
Yule			20
Carpenter			14
Condorcet	.0024	416	20
Lubbock			16
Lévy-Bruhl			23
Lombroso	.0023	419.5	20
Murchison			20
Whipple			20
Boas			19
Montesquieu	.0022	423	17
Berlyne			—
Guillaume	.0021	425.5	16
Hornbostel			16
Porter	.0019	427.5	11
Richet			17
Gruhle	.0018	429	12
Huygens			14
Rapaport	.0017	431	21
Dashiell			—

	MEAN PERCENTAGE	RANK	RATING
Ewald			17
Fröbel			13
Révész	.0016	435.5	23
Robinson			16
Simon			21
Vierordt			17
Beaunis			18
Bourdon			13
Fitts			16
Kris	.0015	442	11
Rush, B.			15
Wheatstone			14
Buros			—
Fabre	.0014	446	20
Pestalozzi	.0013	447	22
Verworn	.0012	448	14
Bingham			23
Delabarre			12
Langfeld	.0011	451	20
Störring			15
White			14
Burnham			13
Coleridge			11
Farrand			11
Forel	.0010	457	12
Goodenough			20
Lehmann			16
Wirth			14
Agassiz			13
Donaldson	.0009	462.5	15
Groos			16
Warren			23
Bentley			21
Brown-Séquard			14
Hecht	.0008	467	22
Urban			14
Wells			11

	MEAN PERCENTAGE	RANK	RATING
Angell, F.			16
Brett			18
Fourier			14
Kelley			21
Nissen			14
Schlosberg	.0007	475	20
Stoufer			13
Wheeler			19
Whitehead			14
Konorski			—
Schneierla			—
Herrick			16
Lessing			11
Porteus	.0006	482.5	—
Plateau			18
Comenius			15
Dessoir			18
Ferenczi			19
Henri	.0005	487.5	16
Pillsbury			21
Pressey			—
Blix			14
Euler			12
Fullerton			14
Fulton			14
Goldscheider			18
Heymans			17
Humphrey			17
Klemm			20
Linton			19
Reymert	.0004	499.5	14
Rosanoff			15
Royce			16
Sachs			13
Scheerer			14
Zilboorg			17
Halstead			—
Kent			—
Marquis			—

	MEAN PERCENTAGE	RANK	RATING
Decroly			11
Driesch			18
Fearing			12
Hollingworth, L. S.			12
Jaensch, W.			11
Kinsey			21
Kluckhohn			18
Müller-Freienfels			15
Roback	.0003	517.5	17
Sapir			19
Schiller			13
Warden			19
Warner			11
Anan'ev			—
Cantril			—
Carmichael			—
Gantt			—
Reich			—
Cousin			15
Croce			15
Dearborn			12
De Vries			16
Downey			14
Erdmann			12
Faraday			15
Frenkel-Brunswik			19
Henmon	.0002	535	11
Henning			20
Leuba			15
Meissner			11
Poppelreuter			16
Starbuck			12
Troland			21
Wissler			14
Morgan, C. T.			—

	MEAN PERCENTAGE	RANK	RATING
Baird			17
Beebe-Center			19
Boole			15
Crozier			18
Dodge			20
Fenichel			15
Parsons			13
Paterson			15
Pfungst	.0001	551.5	14
Rignano			15
Weber, M.			19
Zener			15
Dennis			—
Miles			—
Spitz			—
Witkin			—
Babinski			20
Delacroix			15
Emmert			17
English			14
Fernberger			18
Feuerbach			14
Gosset			13
Kafka			14
Landis			14
Lapicque			18
Lorge			14
Mira y López	.0000	570.5	13
Muenzinger			16
Müller-Lyer			19
Polyak			12
Sanford, F. H.			16
Sidis			17
Stone			16
Twitmyer			14
Teuber			—
Von Neumann			—
Young, P. T.			—

Nineteenth- and Twentieth-Century Contributors in Academic and Research Institutions, Geographically and Chronologically Arranged

Psychological science arose in European universities in the nineteenth century, and since then much of it has been made at the world's universities and scientific research institutes. Listing the contributors to psychology by institution affords an insight into the pattern of mutual influences among scientists working in close proximity, the relative importance of the institutions in the development of psychological science, and the pattern of historical change in their relative importance.

Institutions are listed by country, using the present name of the country regardless of the name that may have been used at the time of a contributor's affiliation with a given institution. Thus it is Czechoslovakia, for instance, rather than Moravia or Austria-Hungary. The countries and their political subdivisions are listed alphabetically, as are the institutions within each country, state, or region. Individuals within an institution are listed chronologically by the year in which they were first employed.

ARGENTINA

University of Buenos Aires	Krüger, 1906-8

AUSTRALIA

University of Adelaide	Fisher, 1957-62
University of Melbourne	Porteus, 1915-19

AUSTRIA

Academy for Military Surgeons, Vienna	Ludwig, 1855-65
Josephs-Akademie, Vienna	Hering, 1865-70

University of Graz   Mach, 1864-67
                                            Meinong, 1882-1920
                                            Ehrenfels, 1885-88
                                            Witasek, 1900-1915
                                            Benussi, 1902-14
University of Vienna   Prochaska, 1791-1819
                                            Brücke, 1849-91
                                            Meynert, 1866-92
                                            Breuer, 1867-71
                                            Exner, 1870-1926
                                            Brentano, 1874-94
                                            Meinong, 1878-82
                                            Ehrenfels, 1889-96
                                            Mach, 1895-1901
                                            Benussi, 1914-20
                                            Bühler, K., 1922-38
                                            Bühler, C., 1923-38
                                            Brunswik, 1927-35
                                            Frenkel-Brunswik, 1931-38

BELGIUM

Institut Gaggia, Brussels   Plateau, 1830-35
University of Brussels   Decroly, 1920-32
University of Ghent   Quételet, 1814-28
                                            Plateau, 1835-72
                                            Delboeuf, 1863-66
University of Liège   Delboeuf, 1866-96
                                            Henri, 1930-40
University of Louvain   Mercier, 1882-1926
                                            Michotte, 1905-14, 1918-56

BRAZIL

Fundação Getúlio Vargas, Rio de Janeiro   Mira y López, 1947-64

CANADA

Canada National Museum, Ottawa   Sapir, 1910-25
McGill University, Montreal   Penfield, 1928-60
                                            Selye, 1932-44
                                            Olds, 1953-55
Queen's University, Kingston   Humphrey, 1924-47
Royal Victoria Hospital, Montreal   Penfield, 1928-34
University of Montreal   Selye, 1945-82
University of Toronto   Baldwin, 1890-93
                                            Jones, 1908-13

York University, Toronto

CZECHOSLOVAKIA
University of Prague

DENMARK
University of Copenhagen

FRANCE
Bicêtre Hospital, Paris

Collège Chapatal
College de France

École de Beaux-Arts, Paris
École des Hautes Études Sociales
École Normale Supérieure

École Polytechnique

École Pratique des Hautes Études
Institut d'Orientation Professionelle, Paris
Museum of Natural History, Paris

National Institute of Deaf-mutes, Paris

Brett, 1908-44
Berlyne, 1962-76
Helson, 1967-68

Purkinje, 1818-23, 1850-69
Mach, 1867-95
Hering, 1870-95
Stumpf, 1879-84
Ehrenfels, 1896-1929
Lindworsky, 1928-39

Lange, C. G., 1869-1900
Höffding, 1871-1915

Pinel, 1795-1826
Féré, 1882-1907
Dumas, 1894-1902
Couvier, 1799-1832
Flourens, 1828-30, 1855-67
Magendie, 1831-55
Bernard, 1841-54, 1855-68
Richet, 1877
Brown-Séquard, 1878-94
Ribot, 1889-96
Tarde, 1900-1904
Bergson, 1900-1914
Janet, 1920-36
Piéron, 1923-64
Wallon, 1937-50
Merleau-Ponty, 1952-61
Taine, 1864-84
Baldwin, 1913-18
Cousin, 1835-40
Bergson, 1898-1900
Laplace, 1787-1827
Comte, 1832-42
Piéron, 1907-11
Wallon, 1920-49
Flourens, 1830-55
Bernard, 1868-78
Itard, 1800-1838

La Salpêtrière, Paris

Esquirol, 1811-23
Charcot, 1862-93
Janet, 1890-1894
Claparède, 1897-98

Psychoanalytical Institute, Paris — Spitz, 1933-38
University of Bordeaux — Durkheim, 1887-1902
University of Caen — Delacroix, 1903-9
University of Lille — Bourdon, 1889-90
University of Lyons — Merleau-Ponty, 1945-48
University of Montpelier — Delacroix, 1899-1903
University of Nancy — Bernheim, 1872-82

Beaunis, 1880-89

University of Paris (Sorbonne)

Lamarck, 1793-1829
Cabanis, 1795-99
Cousin, 1815-21, 1828-30
Esquirol, 1823-26
Flourens, 1828-30
Broca, 1853-80
Bernard, 1854
Charcot, 1860-62
Richet, 1877-1927
Ribot, 1885-89
Beaunis, 1889-94
Binet, 1894-1911
Lapicque, 1894-1936
Janet, 1895-1920
Lévy-Bruhl, 1895-1939
Dumas, 1897-1939
Bryan, 1900-1901
Durkheim, 1902-17
Delacroix, 1909-37
Piéron, 1911-23
Wallon, 1920-37
Guillaume, 1937-47
Merleau-Ponty, 1948-52
Piaget, 1952-63
Berlyne, 1968-69

University of Rennes — Bourdon, 1890-1930

GERMANY

Akademie der Kriegsärzte — Ludwig, 1855-65
Akademie der Sozialwissenschaften, Frankfurt — Gelb, 1912-15

Marbe, 1912-15

Berliner Polyklinik — Goldscheider, 1910-23

Handelshochschule, Mannheim
Institut für Umweltforschung, Hamburg
Kaiser-Wilhelm-Institut für Neuro-Biologie
Kriegsakademie, Berlin
Kunstakademie, Berlin

Moabit Hospital, Berlin

Pädagogische Akademie, Stettin
Pathologisches Institut, Berlin
Psychoanalytical Institute, Berlin

Psychoanalytical Institute, Frankfurt
Psychological Institute, Hamburg
Sanitorium Bellevue, Berlin
Technische Hochschule, Berlin
Technische Hochschule, Danzig
Technische Hochschule, Dresden

Technische Hochschule, Karlsruhe
University of Berlin

Selz, 1922-33
Uexküll, 1925-44
Pfungst, 1918-21
Lazarus, 1867-73
Du Bois-Reymond, 1848-54
Müller-Freienfels, 1922-30
Goldscheider, 1894-1906
Goldstein, 1929-33
Müller-Freienfels, 1930-33
Orth, 1902-23
Horney, 1917-32
Alexander, 1920-30
Sachs, 1920-32
Klein, 1921-26
Fenichel, 1924-33
Zilboorg, 1929-30
Fromm, 1929-32
Werner, 1917-21
Binswanger, 1910-56
Moede, 1921-51
Henning, 1922-44(?)
Bühler, K., 1918-22
Bühler, C., 1920-23
Kafka, 1923-35
Hellpach, 1906-22
Fichte, 1809-12
Hegel, 1818-31
Schopenhauer, 1820-22
Beneke, 1832-54
Müller, J., 1833-58
Schelling, 1841-45
Steinthal, 1850-59
Du Bois-Reymond, 1854-96
Pflüger, 1858-59
Dilthey, 1865-66, 1882-1911
Fritsch, 1867-1921
Bernstein, 1871
Helmholtz, 1871-94
Lazarus, 1873-97
Kries, 1876-77
Erdmann, 1876-78, 1909-21
Ebbinghaus, 1880-93
König, 1884-1901
Bryan, 1886-87

Dessoir, 1889-1933
Weber, M., 1893-94
Schumann, 1894-1905
Stumpf, 1894-1921
Hornbostel, 1902-35
Nagel, 1902-8
Pfungst, 1903-14, 1925-32
Ziehen, 1904-12
Ach, 1906
Bühler, K., 1906-7
Gelb, 1909-12
Wertheimer, 1916-29
Köhler, 1920-21, 1922-35
Spranger, 1920-36, 1938-44
Lewin, 1922-32
Von Neumann, 1927-29
Jaensch, W., 1928-?
Duncker, 1929-37
Müller-Freienfels, 1946-48

University of Bonn   Müller, J., 1824-33
                                 Helmholtz, 1855-58
                                 Pflüger, 1859-1909
                                 Preyer, 1865-67
                                 Lipps, 1877-90
                                 Erdmann, 1898-1909
                                 Bühler, K., 1909-13
                                 Külpe, 1909-13
                                 Verworn, 1910-21
                                 Selz, 1912-23
                                 Hess, 1913-17
                                 Störring, 1914-?
                                 Poppelreuter, 1919-39

University of Breslau   Purkinje, 1823-50
                                 Aubert, 1852-62
                                 Dilthey, 1870-81
                                 Erdmann, 1884-90
                                 Lipps, 1890-94
                                 Ebbinghaus, 1894-1905
                                 Stern, 1897-1916

University of Cologne   Driesch, 1920-21
                                 Lindworsky, 1920-28

University of Erlangen   Fichte, 1805-8
University of Frankfurt   Köhler, 1910-13
                                 Schumann, 1910-28

	Wertheimer, 1912-16, 1929-32
	Henning, 1914-22
	Bethe, 1915-37, 1945-52
	Goldstein, 1916-29
	Gelb, 1919-31
	Pfungst, 1921-25
	Jaensch, W., 1922-27
University of Freiburg	Meissner, 1858-60
	Kries, 1880-1924
	Münsterberg, 1887-92
	Weber, M., 1894-97
	Nagel, 1894-1902
	Husserl, 1916-28
University of Giessen	Groos, 1892-98, 1901-11
	Messer, 1899-1933
	Koffka, 1911-27
University of Göttingen	Herbart, 1802-9, 1833-41
	Gauss, 1807-55
	Beneke, 1824-27
	Lotze, 1844-81
	Meissner, 1860-1905
	Stumpf, 1870-73
	Müller, G., 1876-80, 1881-1921
	Orth, 1878-1902
	Schumann, 1885-94
	Pilzecker, 1886-89, 1891-1900
	Verworn, 1901-10
	Husserl, 1901-16
	Ach, 1902-4, 1922-?
	Katz, 1906-19
	Jaensch, E., 1908-10
	Köhler, 1921-22
University of Halle	Volkman, 1843-73
	Goltz, 1870-72
	Bernstein, 1872-1917
	De Vries, 1877
	Hitzig, 1879-1903
	Stumpf, 1884-89
	Vaihinger, 1884-1906
	Husserl, 1887-1901
	Erdmann, 1890-98

	Ziehen, 1903-4, 1917-30
	Ebbinghaus, 1905-8
	Meumann, 1909-10
	Krüger, 1910-17
	Gelb, 1931-33
University of Hamburg	Meumann, 1911-15
	Stern, 1916-33
	Werner, 1921-33
	Von Neumann, 1929-30
	Scheerer, 1930-33
University of Heidelberg	Hegel, 1816-18
	Wundt, 1857-74
	Helmholtz, 1858-70
	Bernstein, 1864-71
	Kraepelin, 1890-1904
	Weber, M., 1893-1919
	Driesch, 1909-20
	Gruhle, 1912-34
	Hellpach, 1926-55
University of Jena	Feuerbach, 1795-1802
	Schelling, 1798-1803
	Hegel, 1801-6
	Haeckel, 1861-1909
	Preyer, 1867-88
	Ziehen, 1886-1900
	Verworn, 1889-1901
	Berger, 1901-41
University of Kiel	Feuerbach, 1802-4
	Dilthey, 1868-70
	Erdmann, 1878-84
	Krüger, 1898-1900
	Bethe, 1911-15
University of Königsberg	Herbart, 1809-32
	Helmholtz, 1847-54
	Brücke, 1848-49
	Meumann, 1905-8
	Goldstein, 1907-15
	Ach, 1907-22
University of Landshut	Feuerbach, 1804-5
University of Leipzig	Weber, E. H., 1817-78
	Fechner, 1824-87
	Lotze, 1839-44
	Hering, 1862-65, 1895-1918
	Ludwig, 1865-95

Flechsig, 1872-1921
Wundt, 1875-1917
Avenarius, 1876
Kries, 1877-80
Kraepelin, 1882-86
Frey, 1882-98
Lange, L., 1885-87
Külpe, 1887-94
Meumann, 1894-97, 1910-11
Wirth, 1898-1941(?)
Krüger, 1901-5, 1909-10, 1917-35
Klemm, 1906-39
Spranger, 1911-20
Driesch, 1921-41

University of Marburg
Tiedemann, 1786-1803
Ludwig, 1842-49
Ach, 1904-6
Jaensch, E., 1913-40
Jaensch, W., 1918-21
Kretschmer, 1926-46

University of Munich
Schelling, 1827-41
Forel, 1873-79
Kraepelin, 1879-82, 1904-26
Stumpf, 1889-94
Lipps, 1894-1914
Klages, 1901-19
Kafka, 1909-16
Bühler, K., 1913-14
Külpe, 1913-15
Werner, 1916-17
Weber, M., 1919-20

University of Münster
Meumann, 1908-9

University of Rostock
Aubert, 1862-92
Nagel, 1908-11
Katz, 1919-33

University of Strasbourg
Beaunis, 1848(?)-60(?)
Bernheim, 1868-72
Goltz, 1872-1902
Vaihinger, 1877-84
Ewald, 1880-1921
Müller-Lyer, 1881-83
Loeb, 1888-89

	Bethe, 1896-1911
	Störring, 1911-14
University of Tübingen	Vierordt, 1849-84
	Groos, 1911-29
	Kretschmer, 1918-26, 1946-64
	Spranger, 1946-63
University of Würzburg	Schelling, 1803-6
	Brentano, 1866-74
	Stumpf, 1873-79
	Loeb, 1881-88
	Külpe, 1894-1909
	Marbe, 1895-1905, 1909-34
	Frey, 1898-1932
	Bryan, 1901-2
	Bühler, K., 1907-9
	Kafka, 1947-52
Verwaltungsakademie, Berlin	Moede, 1951-58
Wirchow-Institut, Berlin	Orth, 1873-78
	Goldscheider, 1906-10
Wirtschaftshochschule, Berlin	Müller-Freienfels, 1933-45

GREAT BRITAIN

England

Armstrong College, Newcastle-upon-Tyne	Thomson, 1907-15
Cambridge University	Maxwell, 1871-79
	Ward, 1875-1925
	Stout, 1883-96
	Whitehead, 1885-1911
	Rivers, 1893-1922
	McDougall, 1898-1904
	Myers, 1904-22
	Yule, 1912-31
	Burt, 1913-15
	Bartlett, 1922-52
	Fisher, 1943-57
City and Guilds of London Institute	Yule, 1899-1912
College of Haileybury	Malthus, 1805-34
King's College, London	Wheatstone, 1834-40
	Maxwell, 1860-65
	Myers, 1903-7
King's College, Newcastle-upon-Tyne	Thomson, 1920-25
	Brown, William, 1925-31

National Institute of Industrial Psychology	Myers, 1922-46
Oxford University	Tylor, 1883-88, 1896-1909
	Hobhouse, 1890-97
	Stout, 1898-1903
	McDougall, 1904-20
	Sherrington, 1913-35
	Brown, William, 1921-47
	Fulton, 1923-25
	Humphrey, 1947-56
	Gibson, 1955-56
	Teuber, 1971-72
Rothamsted Experimental Agricultural Station	Fisher, 1918-33
Royal Institute	Young, T., 1801-3
	Faraday, 1813-62
	Carpenter, 1844
	Romanes, 1888-91
Royal School of Mines	Huxley, 1854-92
Royal Society	Young, T., 1802-29
St. Thomas Hospital, London	Sherrington, 1887-93
University of Birmingham	Valentine, 1919-46
University College, Bristol	Morgan, C. L., 1884-1909
University College, London	Elliotson, 1817-37
	Carpenter, 1845-56
	Maudsley, 1869-79
	Pearson, 1884-1933
	Yule, 1893-99, 1902-9
	McDougall, 1900-1906
	Spearman, 1906-31
	Flugel, 1909-55
	Burt, 1931-50
	Fisher, 1933-43
University of Durham	Thomson, 1906-15, 1920-25
University of Liverpool	Sherrington, 1895-1913
	Woodworth, 1902-3
	Watt, 1907-8
	Burt, 1908-13
University of London	Carpenter, 1856-79
	Sherrington, 1891-95
	Sully, 1892-1912
	Hobhouse, 1907-29
	Whitehead, 1911-24
	Brown, William, 1914-21
	Burt, 1924-31
	Malinowski, 1924-42

Scotland

Marischal College, Aberdeen	Maxwell, 1856-60
St. Andrews University	Stout, 1903-36
University of Aberdeen	Bain, 1860-87
	Huxley, 1872-74
	Tylor, 1888-96
	Stout, 1896-98
	Driesch, 1906-9
	Berlyne, 1953-56
University of Edinburgh	Stewart, 1772-1820
	Brown, Thomas, 1810-20
	Hamilton, 1821-56
	Bell, 1836-42
	Romanes, 1886-90
	Drever, 1919-44
	Thomson, 1925-55
University of Glasgow	Watt, 1908-25

Ulster

Queen's College, Belfast	McCosh, 1852-68
University of Belfast	Valentine, 1914-19

HOLLAND

Ignatiuskolleg	Fröbes, 1904-25
University of Amsterdam	De Vries, 1871-75, 1878-1918
	Révész, 1923-55
	Goldstein, 1933-35
University of Groningen	Heymans, 1890-1926
	Révész, 1919-20
University of Tilburg	Witkin, 1977-79
University of Utrecht	Donders, 1852-89
	Zwaardemaker, 1897-1927
	Ziehen, 1900-1903
	Michotte, 1914-18
	Révész, 1921-22

HUNGARY

University of Budapest	Révész, 1908-14
	Ferenczi, 1919-33
	Békésy, 1932-46

IRELAND

Queen's College, Cork	Boole, 1849-64

ITALY

Catholic University, Milan	Gemelli, 1922-59
Naples Zoological Station	Loeb, 1889-91
	Driesch, 1891-1900
	Bethe, 1895-96
University of Padua	Benussi, 1920-27
University of Pavia	Lombroso, 1862-71
	Golgi, 1875-1926
University of Rome	Montessori, 1894-99, 1904-8
	Ponzo, 1931-58
University of Sassari	Rolando, 1807-14
University of Turin	Rolando, 1814-31
	Lombroso, 1876-1909
	Kiesow, 1895-1933
	Ponzo, 1905-31
	Gemelli, 1914-22

JAPAN

Aeronautical Research Institute	Matsumoto, 1920-29
Japan Women's University	Matsumoto, 1929-43
Tokyo Bunrika University	Matsumoto, 1929-43
University of Kyoto	Matsumoto, 1907-16
University of Tokyo	Matsumoto, 1901-6, 1913-16

LEBANON

American University of Beirut	Dennis, 1955-56, 1958-59, 1964-65, 1974-75

MEXICO

National University, Mexico City	Baldwin, 1909-13
	Fromm, 1951-61

NORWAY

University of Oslo	Bühler, C., 1938-40
	Krech, 1949-50

POLAND

Nencki Institute of Experimental Biology, Warsaw	Konorski, 1933-39, 1945-68

SPAIN

Institute of Vocational Counseling, Barcelona	Mira y López, 1919-39
University of Barcelona	Ramón y Cajal, 1887-92
	Mira y López, 1933-39

University of Madrid   Ramón y Cajal, 1892-1922
University of Valencia   Ramón y Cajal, 1883-87
University of Zaragoza   Ramón y Cajal, 1875-83

SWEDEN

Karolinska Institute, Stockholm   Békésy, 1946
Kungliga Vetenskapliga Akademien,   Urban, 1914-17
   Stockholm
University of Lund   Blix, 1899-1904
University of Stockholm   Katz, 1937-53
University of Uppsala   Blix, 1879-99

SWITZERLAND

Centre International d'Épistemologie   Piaget, 1955-80
   Génétique, Geneva
Federal Polytechnical Institute, Zurich   Jung, 1933-42
Institut Jean-Jacques Rousseau, Geneva   Piaget, 1921-33
University of Basel   Meissner, 1855-58
                                             Dilthey, 1867
                                             Nietzsche, 1869-79
                                             Groos, 1898-1901
University of Bern   Lazarus, 1860-66
                                             Emmert, 1870-1911
University of Geneva   Claparède, 1904-40
                                             Flournoy, 1908-20
                                             Piaget, 1929-71
University of Lausanne   Piaget, 1935-51
University of Neuchâtel   Agassiz, 1832-47
                                             Piaget, 1925-29
University of Zurich   Ludwig, 1849-55
                                             Wundt, 1874-75
                                             Hitzig, 1875-79
                                             Avenarius, 1877-96
                                             Forel, 1879-98
                                             Meumann, 1897-1905
                                             Frey, 1898-99
                                             Bleuler, 1898-1927
                                             Jung, 1900-1913
                                             Störring, 1902-11
                                             Abraham, 1905-8
                                             Schumann, 1905-10
                                             Hess, 1913-51
                                             Henri, 1919-30
                                             Lennenberg, 1964-65

TURKEY

University of Ankara	Brunswik, 1935-36
University of Istanbul	Miles, 1954-57

UNION OF SOVIET SOCIALIST REPUBLICS

Academy of Pedagogical Sciences, Moscow	Kornilov, 1944-50
All-Union Institute of Experimental Medicine	Bykov, 1921-32
	Anokhin, 1934-45
Biological Station, Sukhumi	Konorski, 1941-44
Brain Research Institute, Leningrad	Bekhterev, 1918-27
Darwin Museum, Moscow	Ladygina-Kots, 1913-45
Gertsen Pedagogical Institute, Leningrad	Bykov, 1921-32
	Rubinshteĭn, 1930-42
Gorkiĭ Medical Institute	Anokhin, 1926-30
Institute of Defectology, Moscow	Luria, 1953-59
Institute of Neurosurgery	Luria, 1936-53
Institute of Philosophy, Moscow	Ladygina-Kots, 1945-63
Institute of Physiology, Moscow	Anokhin, 1946-49
Institute of Psychology, Moscow	Blonskiĭ, 1917-41
	Kornilov, 1923-31
	Luria, 1923-34
	Leont'ev, 1924-31, 1934-63
	Teplov, 1929-65
Leningrad State University	Bykov, 1927-40
	Anan'ev, 1944-51, 1960-67
Lenin Teachers College, Moscow	Kornilov, 1921-51
Military Medical Academy, St. Petersburg	Sechenov, 1860-70
	Pavlov, 1890-1924
	Bekhterev, 1894-1913
Moscow Medical Institute of Genetics	Luria, 1934-36
Moscow State University	Sechenov, 1888-1901
	Kornilov, 1910-21
	Blonskiĭ, 1913-41
	Teplov, 1929-?
	Rubinshteĭn, 1942-50
	Luria, 1945-77
	Leont'ev, 1963-79
N. K. Krupskaya Academy of Communist Education	Luria, 1923-34
Novorossiysk University	Beritashvili, 1915-19
Pavlov Institute of Physiology, Leningrad	Pavlov, 1924-36
	Konorski, 1931-33
	Bykov, 1950-59
Pedagogical Institute, Tblisi	Uznadze, 1930-50

Physiological Research Institute, Georgian Academy of Sciences	Beritashvili, 1919-51
Postgraduate Medical Institute	Anokhin, 1936-49, 1953-55
Psychoneurological Institute, St. Petersburg	Bekhterev, 1913-18
Second Moscow State University	Blonskiĭ, 1917-33
Ukranian Psychoneurological Academy, Khar'kov	Luria, 1923-34
	Leont'ev, 1931-34
University of Chernovtsy (Czernowitz)	Müller, G., 1880
University of Kazan'	Bekhterev, 1885-94
	Bykov, 1911-15
University of Leningrad	Bykov, 1927-50
University of Odessa	Sechenov, 1870-76
	Rubinshteĭn, 1919-30
University of St. Petersburg	Sechenov, 1876-88
	Beritashvili, 1910-15
University of Tartu	Volkmann, 1837-43
	Kraepelin, 1886-90
University of Tblisi	Uznadze, 1918-30
	Beritashvili, 1919-61
Vishnevskiĭ Institute of Surgery	Anokhin, 1955-74

UNITED STATES OF AMERICA

Arizona

University of Arizona	Harlow, 1974-79

Arkansas

University of Arkansas	McGeoch, 1928-30

California

California Institute of Technology	Olds, 1969-76
Claremont Graduate School	Werner, 1948-58
Institute of Character Research, Los Angeles	Starbuck, 1924-47
Stanford University	Angell, F., 1892-1922
	Ross, 1895-1900
	Starbuck, 1897-1904
	Terman, 1910-43
	Kelley, 1920-31
	Miles, 1922-32
	Stone, 1922-54
	Strong, 1923-49
University of California, Berkeley	Royce, 1878-82
	Stratton, 1896-1904
	Dunlap, 1902-6

Loeb, 1902-10
Tolman, 1918-54
Brunswik, 1936-55
Frenkel-Brunswik, 1938-58
Krech, 1947-71
Gibson, 1954-55
Sheldon, 1956-77
Berlyne, 1957
University of California, Los Angeles Stratton, 1908-35
Franz, 1924-33
Polyak, 1928-30
Fearing, 1935-60
Dunlap, 1936-47
University of California, Santa Barbara Morgan, C. T., 1962-65
University of California School of Medicine Olds, 1955-57
University of Southern California, Los Angeles Rosanoff, 1925-43
Starbuck, 1930-43
Bühler, K., 1945-55
Bühler, C., 1950-58
Alexander, 1957-64

Colorado
University of Colorado Henmon, 1907-11
Ferrand, 1914-19
Muenzinger, 1923-53
Krech, 1938-39
Spitz, 1956-63

Connecticut
U.S. Naval Submarine Base, New London Miles, 1957-65
Wesleyan University Judd, 1896-98
Dodge, 1898-1924
Miles, 1913-14
Humphrey, 1920-24
Landis, 1926-30
McGeoch, 1935-39
Yale University Porter, 1847-92
Ladd, 1881-1905
Scripture, 1892-1903
Judd, 1902-9
Gesell, 1911-61
Elliott, 1915-18
Robinson, 1920-21, 1927-37
Angell, J. R., 1921-37
Dodge, 1924-36

Wissler, 1924-40
Yerkes, 1924-44
Henmon, 1926
Sapir, 1927-39
Hull, 1929-52
Nissen, 1929-56
Fulton, 1929-60
Miles, 1932-53
Marquis, 1933-45
Mowrer, 1934-40
Hovland, 1936-61
Malinowski, 1939-42
Linton, 1946-53
Fromm, 1949

District of Columbia
Department of Defense   Razran, 1941-44
                                         Warner, 1942-43
                                         Morgan, C. T., 1943
                                         Mowrer, 1944-45
                                         Marquis, 1947-50
Georgetown University   White, 1903-37
George Washington University   White, 1903-37
                                         Franz, 1907-24
                                         Murphy, 1967-73
National Research Council   Warner, 1928-30
                                         Marquis, 1943-45
St. Elizabeth's Hospital   White, 1903-37
                                         Lashley, 1915-17
                                         Sullivan, 1922-23
Washington School of Psychiatry   Sullivan, 1936-44

Florida
New College, Sarasota   Sanford, F. H., 1965
University of Florida   Dashiell, 1958-74
University of Miami   Meyer, M. F., 1932-40
                                         Kent, 1947-48
                                         Ruckmick, 1952-55
Yerkes Laboratories of Primate Biology   Spence, 1933-37
                                         Nissen, 1939-58

Georgia
Emory University   Nissen, 1956-58

Hawaii

University of Hawaii

Porteus, 1922-48
Békésy, 1966-72

Illinois

Behavior Research Foundation

Lashley, 1926-29
Klüver, 1928-33

Chicago Institute for Psychoanalysis

Horney, 1932-34
Alexander, 1932-56
Fromm, 1933-34

Devereux Foundation
Judge Baker Foundation
Juvenile Psychopathic Institute
Lake Forest College
Northwestern University

Doll, 1949-53
Healy, 1917-47
Healy, 1909-17
Baldwin, 1887-90
Healy, 1900-1906
Scott, 1901-39
Tolman, 1915-18
Fearing, 1928-35
Mowrer, 1932-34

University of Chicago

Meyer, A., 1892-93
Loeb, 1892-1902
Donaldson, 1892-1906
Dewey, 1894-1904
Angell, J. R., 1894-1921
Mead, 1894-1931
Watson, 1903-8
Herrick, 1907-37
Carr, 1908-38
Dearborn, 1909-12
Judd, 1909-38
Crozier, 1919-20
Robinson, 1921-27
Polyak, 1921-28, 1930-55
Sheldon, 1924-27, 1936-38
Thurstone, 1924-52
Sapir, 1925-27
Lashley, 1929-35
Alexander, 1930-32
Stouffer, 1930-31, 1935-46
Krech, 1933-37
Klüver, 1936-62
Halstead, 1936-69

University of Illinois

Baird, 1906-10
Bentley, 1912-29
Ruckmick, 1913-21
Whipple, 1914-17
Crozier, 1918-19
Young, P. T., 1921-60
Helson, 1925-26
Mowrer, 1948-82

Indiana

Earlham College
Indiana University

Starbuck, 1904-6
Bryan, 1884-86, 1887-1900,
   1902-37
Ross, 1891-95
Pressey, 1917-21
Kinsey, 1920-56

Iowa

Iowa Child Welfare Research Station
State University of Iowa

University of Iowa

Reymert, 1919-20
Ruckmick, 1924-39
McGeoch, 1939-42
Seashore, 1897-1937
Starbuck, 1906-30
Reymert, 1918-19
Lewin, 1935-44
Spence, 1938-64

Kansas

Kansas State College
Kansas State University

Menninger Foundation

University of Kansas

Kelly, 1931-44
Coghill, 1913-25
Helson, 1961-68
Rapaport, 1940-48
Murphy, 1952-67
Ogden, 1914-16
Paterson, 1916-17
Hunter, 1916-25
Lehman, H. C., 1923-27
Wheeler, 1925-47
Helson, 1926-28
Scheerer, 1948-61

Kentucky

University of Louisville

Scheerer, 1936-37
Gantt, 1974-80

Louisiana

Louisiana State University	Dennis, 1942-43
State Normal School	Small, 1902-4

Maine

Bowdoin College	Ladd, 1879-81

Maryland

Johns Hopkins University	Peirce, 1879-84
	Hall, G. S., 1882-88
	Donaldson, 1883-89
	Burnham, 1888-89
	Sanford, E. C., 1888-89
	Baldwin, 1903-9
	Baird, 1904-6
	Stratton, 1904-8
	Ladd-Franklin, 1904-9
	Dunlap, 1906-36
	Jennings, 1907-37
	Watson, 1908-20
	Meyer, A., 1910-41
	Gantt, 1929-67
	Selye, 1931-32
	Morgan, C. T., 1943-59
University of Maryland	Small, 1923-40
	Sullivan, 1923-31
	Kelly, 1945-46
	Sanford, F. H., 1946-47

Massachusetts

Babson Institute of Business Administration	Wheeler, 1948-61
Brandeis University	Maslow, 1951-69
	Kelly, 1965-67
Carnegie Nutrition Laboratory, Boston	Miles, 1914-22
Clark University	Boas, 1888-92
	Donaldson, 1889-92
	Hall, G. S., 1889-1920
	Sanford, E. C., 1889-1924
	Burnham, 1890-1926
	Scripture, 1891
	Meyer, A., 1895-1902
	Baird, 1910-19
	Fernberger, 1912-20

Ames, 1914-17
Boring, 1919-22
Morgan, C. L., 1919-36
Murchison, 1923-36
Hunter, 1925-36
Graham, 1932-36
Bühler, C., 1943
Werner, 1947-60

Harvard University

Agassiz, 1847-73
Brown-Séquard, 1864-67
Bowditch, 1871-93
James, 1872-1907
Peirce, 1879-84
Royce, 1882-1916
Münsterberg, 1892-95, 1897-
    1916
Delabarre, 1896
Franz, 1899-1900
Cannon, 1900-1942
Holt, 1901-18
Urban, 1904-5
Yerkes, 1908-17
Bridgman, 1908-54
Langfeld, 1910-24
Dearborn, 1912-47
Elliott, 1914-15
Troland, 1916-32
Allport, F., 1919-22
Morgan, C. L., 1919-36
McDougall, 1920-27
Boring, 1922-68
Beebe-Center, 1923-58
Whitehead, 1924-36
Allport, G. W., 1924-67
Crozier, 1925-55
Rhine, 1926-27
Prince, 1926-29
Hull, 1927-29
Kelley, 1931-50
Cantril, 1932-35
Sachs, 1932-47
Wells, 1932-50
Lashley, 1935-55

	Kluckhohn, 1935-60
	Werner, 1936
	Stevens, 1936-73
	Goldstein, 1938-40
	Sheldon, 1938-42
	Morgan, C. T., 1939-43
	Mowrer, 1940-48
	Sanford, F. H., 1941-42
	Stouffer, 1946-60
	Békésy, 1947-66
	Olds, 1952-53
	Lennenberg, 1958-67
Lesley College	Dearborn, 1947-53
Massachusetts Institute of Technology	Wiener, 1919-60
	Lewin, 1944-47
	Lennenberg, 1959-62, 1971-72
	Marquis, 1959-73
	Teuber, 1961-77
Smith College	Koffka, 1927-41
	Gibson, 1928-49
Tufts University	Prince, 1902-26
	Carmichael, 1938-52
	Goldstein, 1940-45
University of Massachusetts	Helson, 1968-71
Wellesley College	Calkins, 1891-1930
	English, 1916-27
	Ruckmick, 1921-24

Michigan

Michigan State Normal School	Small, 1901-2
Michigan State University	Fromm, 1957-61
University of Michigan	Dewey, 1884-94
	Mead, 1891-94
	Cooley, 1894-1929
	Pillsbury, 1897-1942
	Jennings, 1900-1903
	Whipple, 1919-25
	Werner, 1933-36
	Marquis, 1945-57
	Likert, 1946-70
	Olds, 1957-69
	Fitts, 1958-65
	Lennenberg, 1967-68

Minnesota

Macalester College, St. Paul	Sanford, F. H., 1965
Minneapolis Child Guidance Clinic	Goodenough, 1924-25
St. Catharine's College	Bühler, C., 1940-43
St. Thomas College	Bühler, K., 1940-45
Scholastica College	Bühler, K., 1939
University of Minnesota	Angell, J. R., 1893
	Dashiell, 1915-17
	Lashley, 1917-18, 1920-26
	Yerkes, 1917-24
	Young, P. T., 1918-21
	Elliott, 1919-56
	Stone, 1921-22
	Paterson, 1921-60
	Klüver, 1924-26
	Goodenough, 1925-59

Missouri

University of Missouri	Meyer, M. F., 1901-29
	Ogden, 1903-5
	McGeoch, 1930-35

Nebraska

Creighton University	Hecht, 1917-25
University of Nebraska	Ross, 1900-1906

New Hampshire

Dartmouth College	Jennings, 1898-1900
	Franz, 1901-4
	Bingham, 1910-15
	Ames, 1919-45
	Cantril, 1931-32

New Jersey

Institute of Advanced Studies in Behavioral Sciences	Gibson, 1958-59, 1963-64
Princeton University	McCosh, 1868-92
	Warren, 1890-1934
	Baldwin, 1893-1903
	Dashiell, 1914-15
	Langfeld, 1924-47
	Carmichael, 1925-27

	Holt, 1926-36
	Zener, 1927-28
	Von Neumann, 1930-55
	Mowrer, 1932-34
	Cantril, 1936-55
Rutgers University	Crozier, 1920-25
	Buros, 1932-65
Vineland Training School for the Feeble-minded	Goddard, 1906-17
	Doll, 1913-19, 1925-49
	Porteus, 1919-28

New York

American Institute of Psychoanalysis	Fromm, 1941-42
	Horney, 1941-52
American Museum of Natural History	Wissler, 1902-42
	Schneierla, 1942-68
Barnard College	Hollingworth, 1909-46
City College of New York	Schneierla, 1947-68
	Dennis, 1962-64
City University of New York, Brooklyn College	Maslow, 1937-51
	Witkin, 1940-51
	Scheerer, 1941-42
	Werner, 1943-47
	Helson, 1949-51
	Dennis, 1951-70
	Berlyne, 1952
City University of New York, City College	Murphy, 1940-52
	Scheerer, 1942-47
	Spitz, 1947-50
City University of New York, Queens College	Razran, 1940-72
Columbia University	Cattell, 1891-1917
	Farrand, 1893-1914
	Boas, 1896-1937
	Thorndike, 1899-1940
	Wissler, 1901-9
	Woodworth, 1903-58
	Fullerton, 1904-17
	Dewey, 1904-29
	Henmon, 1905-7
	Bingham, 1908-10
	Ladd-Franklin, 1910-30
	Brill, 1912
	Hollingworth, L. S., 1916-39

Kelley, 1917-20
Penfield, 1921-28
Murphy, 1921-40
Pintner, 1921-42
Benedict, 1922-48
Warden, 1924-55
Adler, 1926-29
Hecht, 1926-47
Lorge, 1927-61
Buros, 1929-30
Razran, 1929-40
Landis, 1930-62
Cantril, 1935-36
Maslow, 1935-37
Goldstein, 1936-40
Linton, 1937-46
Scheerer, 1937-40
Harlow, 1939-40
Fromm, 1940-41
Graham, 1945-71
Sheldon, 1946-58
Kardiner, 1955-57

Cornell University   Angell, F., 1891
                                    Ross, 1891-95
                                    Titchener, 1892-1927
                                    Whipple, 1898-1914
                                    Bentley, 1899-1912, 1929-38
                                    Washburn, 1900-1902
                                    Baird, 1903
                                    Meyer, A., 1904-9
                                    Ogden, 1916-45
                                    Dallenbach, 1916-48
                                    Young, P. T., 1918-19
                                    Farrand, 1921-37
                                    Helson, 1924-25
                                    Lewin, 1932-35
                                    Gibson, 1949-72
                                    Lennenberg, 1968-75
Educational Testing Service   Witkin, 1971-79
International Institute for Social Research   Fromm, 1934-39
Long Island College of Medicine   Adler, 1932-37
Manhattan State College   Jennings, 1897-98
New School for Social Research   Jastrow, 1927-33
                                    Wertheimer, 1933-43

	Horney, 1934-41
	Scheerer, 1947-48
New York Psychoanalytical Institute	Spitz, 1940-56
New York State Psychiatric Institute and Hospital	Landis, 1930-62
	Goldstein, 1936-40
New York University	Judd, 1898-1901
	Woodworth, 1899-1902
	Brill, 1912
	Warner, 1926-27
	Schneierla, 1927-58
	Likert, 1930-35
	Wechsler, 1933-67
	Teuber, 1947-61
	Moreno, 1951-66
	Fromm, 1962-65
Pathological Service, New York Hospital Service	Meyer, A., 1902-10
Pratt Institute	Carr, 1906-8
Rockefeller Institute for Medical Research	Loeb, 1910-24
Russell Sage Foundation	Lennenberg, 1956-58
Sarah Lawrence College	Likert, 1935-36
State University of New York City, Downstate Medical Center	Witkin, 1952-70
Syracuse University	Allport, F., 1924-56
University of Rochester	Lennenberg, 1970-72
Vassar College	Washburn, 1903-1939
Wells College	Washburn, 1894-1900
	Scheerer, 1940-41

North Carolina

Duke University	McDougall, 1927-38
	Rhine, 1927-50
	Zener, 1928-64
	Stern, 1933-38
	Warner, 1935-37
University of North Carolina	Dashiell, 1919-58
	Allport, F., 1922-24
	Thurstone, 1952-55
Wake Forest College	Dashiell, 1958-74

Ohio

Antioch College	English, 1927-30
Denison University	Herrick, 1893-1907
	Coghill, 1907-13
Oberlin College	Dashiell, 1917-19

Ohio State Bureau of Juvenile Research	Goddard, 1918-21
Ohio State University	Wissler, 1897-99
	Weiss, 1912-31
	Pintner, 1913-21
	Dallenbach, 1915-16
	Pressey, 1921-59
	Goddard, 1922-38
	Doll, 1923-25
	English, 1930-61
	Kelly, 1946-65
	Fitts, 1949-58
Ohio University	Lehman, 1927-59
Ohio Wesleyan University	Fearing, 1926-28
University of Cincinnati	Judd, 1901-2
	Washburn, 1902-3
University of Toledo	Pintner, 1912-13
Western Reserve University	Thorndike, 1898-99
Wittenberg College	Burnham, 1888-89
	Reymert, 1925-30

Oregon

Pacific University	Coghill, 1902-6
University of Oregon	Dallenbach, 1913-15
	Wheeler, 1915-25
	Sheldon, 1951-70
Willamette University	Coghill, 1906-7

Pennsylvania

Bryn Mawr College	Loeb, 1891-92
	Witmer, 1896-98
	Leuba, 1898-1933
	Helson, 1928-49
Carnegie Institute of Technology	Bingham, 1915-24
	Scott, 1916-17
	Whipple, 1917-19
	Thurstone, 1917-24
	Strong, 1919-23
Haverford College	Sanford, F. H., 1948-49
Lehigh University	Witmer, 1903-5
Pennsylvania State Teachers College	Goddard, 1899-1906
Swarthmore College	Köhler, 1935-55
	Krech, 1937-38, 1945-47
	Duncker, 1938-40
	Witkin, 1939-40
Temple University	Graham, 1930-31

University of Pennsylvania	Fullerton, 1883-1904
	Cattell, 1887-1891
	Witmer, 1893-1937
	Twitmyer, 1897-1943
	Jennings, 1903-6
	Urban, 1905-14
	Fernberger, 1920-56
	Graham, 1931-32
University of Pittsburgh	Dennis, 1945-51
Waynesburg College	Dashiell, 1913-14
Wistar Institute of Anatomy and Biology	Donaldson, 1906-30
	Coghill, 1925-35

Rhode Island

Brown University   Delabarre, 1892-96, 1897-
                                1932
                                Carmichael, 1927-38
                                Schlosberg, 1928-64
                                Graham, 1936-45
                                Hunter, 1936-54

South Carolina

Erskine College   Wheeler, 1947-48

Tennessee

George Peabody College for Teachers   Strong, 1914-17
University of Tennessee   Ogden, 1905-14
                                         Fitts, 1938-41

Texas

University of Texas   Hunter, 1912-16
                                Kelley, 1914-17
                                Sheldon, 1923-24
                                Dallenbach, 1948-58
                                Helson, 1951-61
                                Sanford, F. H., 1957-64,
                                1966-67
                                Spence, 1964-67
                                Morgan, C. T., 1965-76

Vermont

Bennington College   Fromm, 1941-50

Virginia
University of Virginia

Dennis, 1929-42
Spence, 1937-38

Washington
University of Washington

Guthrie, 1914-56
McGeoch, 1920-26

West Virginia
University of West Virginia

Rhine, 1925-26

Wisconsin
University of Wisconsin

Jastrow, 1888-1927
Dearborn, 1905-9
Ross, 1906-37
Henmon, 1911-26, 1927-39,
    1940-48
Doll, 1912-13
Hull, 1916-17
Warden, 1923-24
Sheldon, 1927-30
Linton, 1928-37
Harlow, 1930-74
Stouffer, 1931-35
Maslow, 1934-35
Morgan, C. T., 1959-62

Wyoming
University of Wyoming

Downey, 1905-32

URUGUAY
Laboratory of Psychotechnology, Montevideo

Mira y López, 1944-47

YUGOSLAVIA
University of Zagreb

Polyak, 1920-28

Index

Note: *Italic* page numbers indicate the location of the actual entries of the dictionary.

About the Author

Leonard Zusne is Professor of Psychology at the University of Tulsa. He is the author of *Visual Perception of Form* and *Anomalistic Psychology* and of numerous articles that have appeared in *American Psychologist, Journal of Experimental Psychology,* and other journals.